Strategies for Minority Languages:
Northern Ireland, the Republic of Ireland, and Scotland

Edited by

John M. Kirk and Dónall P. Ó Baoill

Cló Ollscoil na Banríona
2011

First published in 2011
Cló Ollscoil na Banríona
Queen's University Belfast
Belfast, BT7 1NN

Belfast Studies in Language, Culture and Politics
www.bslcp.com

The publication of this volume has been made possible through the financial support of Foras na Gaeilge and Colmcille.

British Library Cataloguing-in-Publication Data
A catalogue record for this book is available from the British Library.

ISBN 978 0 85389 977 8

The cover painting 'Sunset over Ailsa Craig', by Donald Smith, is reproduced with the kind permission of the artist and by courtesy of Scotland Art Portfolio.

Typeset by Nigel Craig and John Kirk in Granjon
Cover design by Colin Young
Printing by MPG Books, Bodmin, Cornwall/Kernow

Contents

Contributors

Dr Timothy Currie Armstrong is a researcher on the Soillse Project based at Sabhal Mòr Ostaig. He is a graduate of Sabhal Mòr Ostaig and the University of Aberdeen, where in 2009 he completed a PhD in Sociolinguistics.

Dòmhnall Caimbeul is the Chief Executive of MG Alba.

Prof. Robert Dunbar is Research Professor for the Soillse Project based at Sabhal Mòr Ostaig. He holds numerous public appointments including membership of Bòrd na Gàidhlig, MG Alba and the Committee of Experts for the *European Charter for Regional or Minority Languages*.

Andy Eagle runs the popular Scots Online website (www.scots-online.org). His monograph arising from the *Wir Ain Leed: An Introduction to Modern Scots* section of his website is to be published by Cló Ollscoil na Banríona in 2011.

Eilean Green is a director of MG Alba.

Dr John M. Kirk is a senior lecturer in English and Scottish Language at Queen's University Belfast. In addition to titles in the present series, he has recently edited (with J. Derrick McClure and Margaret Storrie) *A Land that Lies Westward: Language and Culture in Islay and Argyll* (John Donald, 2009) and (with Michael Brown and Andrew United Islands? The Languages of Resistance* and *The Cultures of Radicalism in Britain and Ireland* (for the new *Political Poetry and Song in the Age of Revolution* series to be published by Pickering & Chatto).

Dr Alasdair MacCaluim is a Gaelic officer at the Scottish Parliament. His book, *Reversing Language Shift: The Role and Social Identity of Scottish Gaelic Learners*, was published by Cló Ollscoil na Banríona in 2007.

Dr Gordon McCoy is a development officer with the ULTACH Trust and a former board member of Foras na Gaeilge. He is the author of numerous papers on the linguistic situation in Northern Ireland.

Seosamh Mac Donnacha is the Comhordaitheoir Acadúil (Academic Coordinator) with Acadamh na hOllscolaíochta Gaeilge, National University of Ireland, Galway. With Conchur Ó Giollagáin, he published the influential report *Staidéar Teangeolaíoch ar Úsáid na Gaeilge sa Ghaeltacht / Comprehensive Linguistic Study on the Use of Irish in the Gaeltacht* (Dublin: Oifig an tSoláthair, An Roinn Gnóthaí Pobail, Tuaithe agus Gaeltachta, 2007).

Ruairidh Mackay is Leasaiche Seirbheis Teicneòlas na Gàidhlig (Gaelic Technology Services Developer) in the Sgioba Ionnsachaidh agus Fiosrachaidh (Learning and Information Services Department) at the Oilthigh na Gaidhealtachd is nan Eilean (University of the Highlands and Islands), Inverness.

Prof. Kenneth MacKinnon is Honorary Research Professor of Language Policy and Planning at the University of Aberdeen and the director of SGRÙD Research. He is a board member of Bòrd na Gàidhlig and MG Alba.

Dr Michelle Macleod is a lecturer in Gaelic at the University of Aberdeen. With Moray Watson, she co-edited *The Edinburgh Companion to the Gaelic Language* (Edinburgh University Press, 2010).

Dr Wilson McLeod is a senior lecturer in Celtic and Scottish Studies at the University of Edinburgh. His most recent book (co-edited with Emma Dymock) is '*Chunnaic Mi Lainnir A' Bhùirn Ud': Essays on Gaelic Literature in the Twentieth Century and Beyond* (Dunedin Academic Press, 2011).

Aodán Mac Póilin is Director of the ULTACH Trust and a former board member of Foras na Gaeilge. He is the author of numerous papers on the linguistic situation in Northern Ireland.

Dr Janet Muller is Director of NGO POBAL. Her book, *Language and Conflict in Northern Ireland and Canada: A Silent War*, was published by Palgrave Macmillan in 2010.

Dr Gillian Munro (Dr Gillian Rothach) is a senior lecturer and Deputy Head of Studies at Sabhal Mòr Ostaig. She has recently co-edited (with Iain Mac an Tàilleir) *Coimhearsnachd na Gàidhlig an-Diugh / Gaelic Communities Today* and (with Richard A.V. Cox) *Cànan & Cultar / Language & Culture* (each Dunedin Academic Press, 2010).

Prof. Dónall Ó Baoill, a native Irish speaker from Co. Donegal, is Professor of Irish at Queen's University Belfast. His most recent books (co-edited by with John Kirk) are *Language and Economic Development* (Cló Ollscoil na Banríona, 2009) and *Sustaining Minority Language Communities* (Cló Ollscoil na Banríona, 2011).

Colm Ó Coisdealbha is Compliance Manager in the the Office of An Coimisinéir Teanga.

Pádraig Ó hAoláin is Chief Executive Officer of Údarás na Gaeltachta, the regional enterprise and language promotion agency for the Gaeltacht.

Brian Ó hEadhra is Gaelic Arts and Culture Officer for Bòrd na Gàidhlig and Creative Scotland (Alba Chruthachail). As a traditional musician, his latest album, *An t-Allt* (The Stream), was released in January 2011. His website is www.brianoheadhra.com.

Dr Helen Ó Murchú is Cathaoirleach/Uachtarán (Chair/President) of Comhdháil Náisiúnta na Gaeilge, one of the Irish language voluntary organisations funded by Foras na Gaeilge. Her most recent books are *More Facts about Irish* (Coiste na hÉireann den Bhiúró Eorpach do Theangacha Neamhfhorleathana, 2008), *Ceisteanna na Linne* (Foilseacháin Ábhair Spioradálta, 2008), *An Chríostaíocht le Sinsearacht* (Foilseacháin Ábhair Spioradálta, 2010), and *An tOideachas Caitliceach* (Foilseacháin Ábhair Spioradálta, 2011).

Dónall Ó Riagáin, who holds an honorary doctorate from Trinity College Carmarthen, where he is an honorary fellow, is one of the world's leading independent specialist consultants on language policy. He has edited *Language and Law in Northern Ireland* and *Voces Diversae: Minority Languages in Europe* for the present series and contributed to numerous of its other volumes.

Dr Christine Robinson is Director of Scottish Language Dictionaries and is a visiting lecturer at the University of the Highlands and Islands where she teaches Scots. She is President of the Scots Language Society and was a member of the Ministerial Advisory Group on Scots. Her recent publications include *Scottish Wildlife*, *Wha's like us?* and (with Eileen Finlayson) *Scottish Weather* (each Edinburgh: Black & White, 2008). *Scotspeak* (with Carol Ann Crawford) will be republished by the Luath Press in 2011.

Dr John Walsh is a lecturer in Irish in the School of Languages, Literatures and Cultures at the National University of Ireland, Galway. He spent 2009–10 as a Fulbright Irish Language Scholar at the University of California, Santa Cruz. His book, *Contests and Contexts: The Irish Language and Ireland's Socioeconomic Development*, was published by Peter Lang in 2011.

Acknowledgements

For financial support towards the publication of this volume, Cló Ollscoil na Banríona is most grateful to Foras na Gaeilge and Colmcille. We are indebted to Dr Ian Malcolm for his translation into English of John Walsh's paper. For their help with the production of this volume, we are yet again deeply obliged to Nigel Craig and Colin Young. Cló Ollscoil na Banríona also wishes to acknowledge the permission to reproduce the map of the University of the Highlands and Islands which it has received from Ruairidh Mackay, and also the permission to reproduce the logos of 14 public authorities in Scotland which it has received from Wilson McLeod.

This volume of papers arises from the *Tenth Language and Politics Symposium on the Gaeltacht and Scotstacht*, which was held from 20–21 September 2010, at Queen's University Belfast. As a project within the AHRC Centre for Irish and Scottish Studies, it has always been a pleasure to deal with Cairns Craig and Jon Cameron. For additional financial support, we are again grateful to Foras na Gaeilge and Colmcille. For invaluable help and encouragement at various planning stages, we are grateful to Deirdre Davitt, Maolcholaim Scott, Alasdair MacKinnon and Dónall Ó Riagáin.

During the symposium, for the use of translation equipment, we are highly indebted to Donegal Council Council and Seán Ó Daimhín; for translation services, we are grateful to Dónall Mac Ghill Choil and Maolcholaim Scott; and for practical assistance to Patrick Connolly and Michael Gillespie. Our biggest debt, as always, is to each other.

John Kirk   Dónall Ó Baoill
27 May 2011

Introduction: Strategies for Minority Languages

John M. Kirk and Dónall P. Ó Baoill

The 10th and, in the present series, final symposium on Language and Politics in the Gaeltacht and Scotstacht devoted much of its attention to the *Straitéis 20-Bliain Don Ghaeilge 2010–2030 / 20-Year Strategy for the Irish Language 2010-2030,*[1] a draft of which had been issued by the Department of Community, Rural and Gaeltacht Affairs, Dublin in December 2009, and for which responses had been invited by June 2010. The strategy has its immediate origins in the *Official Languages Act 2003*[2] and the *Ráiteas an Rialtais / Statement on the Irish Language 2006*[3] issued by the Republic of Ireland's Government in 2006. Much of its substance is informed by a report entitled *Analysis by Consultants for the 20-Year Strategy for the Irish Language,*[4] produced for the Department in 2009 by FIONTAR at Dublin City University, and with input from a particularly renowned international team of language planners. The Strategy has also been influenced by the *Staidéar Teangeolaíoch ar úsáid na Gaeilge sa Ghaeltacht / Comprehensive Linguistic Study on the Use of Irish in the Gaeltacht*[5] published in 2007. The main goal of the Strategy is simply to increase the numbers of speakers of Irish on a daily basis, both in the Gaeltacht and throughout the country. And the main challenge is how the aspirational target of 250,000 speakers is to be created. Although the importance of those earlier documents for the Strategy is discussed in several papers in this volume, there is considerable emphasis on bilingualism. Many papers are concerned about the absence of any explicit mechanisms whereby the goals will be successfully implemented.

Whereas the Strategy takes cognisance of developments for Welsh, it also invites systematic, even detailed, comparison with Scotland where a similar but different strategy for Gaelic is being implemented for increasing the number of Gaelic speakers, based on the Bòrd na Gàidhlig report *Ginealach Ùr na Gàidhlig / An Action Plan to Increase the Numbers of Gaelic Speakers*, issued in April 2010.[6]

Although the symposium occurred before the Official Strategy was released, in December 2010, the symposium nevertheless provided a forum for comprehensive and critical review, involving many of the key parties, constituencies and stakeholders concerned, including officials, commentators and practitioners from Scotland, now reflected in the present volume of papers.

The Strategy proposes to increase the daily users of Irish speakers outside the education system throughout Ireland from currently 72,148 to 250,000 within its twenty year remit. Within that present number, there are 34,000 speakers of Irish in the Gaeltacht, according to the *Staidéar Teangeolaíoch ar Úsáid na Gaeilge sa Ghaeltacht / Comprehensive Linguistic Study on the Use of Irish in the Gaeltacht*[7] published in 2007. This target of 250,000 speakers and the means for its attainment receive much critical attention in the papers below.

---

[1] www.pobail.ie/ie/AnGhaeilge/; www.pobail.ie/en/IrishLanguage/. The Strategy was approved by the Government on 30 November 2010, and launched by an Taoiseach on 21 December 2010.

[2] www.pobail.ie/en/IrishLanguage/OfficialLanguagesAct2003/

[3] www.pobail.ie/en/IrishLanguage/StatementontheIrishLanguage2006/

[4] www.pobail.ie/ie/AnGhaeilge/

[5] www.pobail.ie/ie/AnGhaeltacht/AnStaidearTeangeolaioch/

[6] www.gaidhlig.org.uk/Downloads/Ginealach%20Ur%20na%20Gaidhlig%20-%20B.pdf

[7] see footnote 5.

The Strategy places much emphasis on education as the means for doing so. But where will all the resources which will be needed come from and be paid for? Given its track record, where does education really fit in? What is being done for teacher training? How is 'school Irish' to become communicative skills for – and in – a bilingual Ireland? Is education expected to deliver the target on its own? And how are educational methods to differ from those in the past? Is a bilingual Ireland to be achieved only through school education and therefore cross-generationally? And what of the much-larger adult population, with its diversified needs? A great many people and institutions will need to feed the 20-Year Strategy – but there is little attention given to who these enablers or implementers or, as MacLeod discusses below, *animateurs* might be? As part of the process, the Irish language voluntary sector is being forced into reorganisation, but how will the merging of language organisations serve the 20-year plan? What are the implications for the stakeholders? How are they all to tie in with the bilingual strategy? Also, is a co-ordinating, overseeing group needed? How is the Údarás na Gaeilge envisaged? Who will do its work, and from where will the undoubtedly-needed expertise be drawn? What overlap will there be between Údarás na Gaeilge and Foras na Gaeilge? The papers below raise many such questions not at all addressed in the Strategy.

For its effectiveness, the Strategy has to depend on existing research. How is one to map notions of a bilingual Ireland on to this Strategy? What is the research evidence for doing so or for its likelihood of success? On what basis is the Strategy being driven or informed?

Throughout the Strategy, there is a fairly unqualified discourse about a 'bilingual Ireland'. The papers here seek to ask what it means to be 'bilingual' in Ireland, what the role of policy and education to this end is supposed to be, and what wider concepts and experience need to be considered for implementing the Strategy. In the context of the Strategy, what does it mean to be bilingual? If a truly bilingual Ireland is to be achieved, what are the key elements needed for bringing it about? The Strategy may be a springboard for bilingualism, but it is not a mission statement as there are many implications not spelled out, and many weak links. Is there a policy for bilingualism or indeed any general language policy which lies behind the Strategy, for, if so, what is that Policy? Who has it? If the policy is about bilingualism, how is it to differ from present arrangements and practices?

A huge issue is that of Irish in Northern Ireland, to which several papers are devoted below. How is the Strategy to affect Northern Ireland? In what ways can the envisaged bilingual society in the South be replicated in the North? The papers in this volume caution against bolting Northern Ireland on to the present Strategy, urging, instead, a separate Strategy for the North. However, *A Strategy for Indigenous or Regional Minority Languages* announced by the Department of Culture, Arts and Leisure as forthcoming since the *Northern Ireland (St Andrews Agreement) Act 2006*, has yet to materialise. Let us hope that it will learn from all the criticism of the present southern Strategy.

So, whereas some papers which follow find the Strategy to be the best for Irish that there has ever been, their enthusiastic endorsement is not without criticism or concern, as indicated by the foregoing comments and questions. We will now summarise each paper individually.

Irish

The first paper, by **Seosamh Mac Donnacha**, one of the authors of *Staidéar Teangeolaíoch ar Úsáid na Gaeilge sa Ghaeltacht / Comprehensive Linguistic Study on the Use of Irish in the Gaeltacht*, sets the 20-Year Strategy in its recent context. Mac Donnacha explains that the Strategy is first and foremost about capacity building – i.e. substantial increases in the numbers of people with a knowledge of Irish or who speak Irish daily, especially in the Gaeltacht – but that it is also an exercise in societal planning. Mac Donnacha usefully sets out the main points of the Strategy; but he is not uncritical, realising that its success will depend on the provision of measures needed to underpin and implement it – ultimately personnel, organisational support, and funding. For Mac Donnacha, there are four key issues which will crucially affect the early establishment phase of the strategy: the organisational capacity of the Strategy; the development of the human resource capacity; the sustainability of the planning process; and the development of the research capacity necessary to underpin the implementation and evaluation of the Strategy. About each of these, Mac Donnacha raises many key questions, to which answers are needed, and identifies many tasks and challenges, none of which will be easy to surmount. But 'let us hope,' he concludes, 'that those organisations and individuals charged with the implementation of the Strategy have the necessary vision, knowledge, expertise and experience to build on this aspect of the Strategy document in the early implementation phases, and by so doing create an 'enabling environment', that will enable other 'organisations, institutions and agencies at all levels and in all sectors to enhance their capacities' and to contribute to the development of a sustainable future for the Irish language'.

Pádraig Ó hAoláin sets a broader historical context for the 20-Year Strategy. He usefully summarises previous initiatives and reports since the inception of the Free State culminating in the present clarion call to save the Irish language. Whereas he regards the Strategy literally as the last opportunity for the survival of the Gaeltacht, he considers the Strategy to be 'integrated', 'interwoven', 'interdependent' and, above all, entirely 'fit-for-purpose' for its task of increasing the number of Irish speakers to 250,000 within twenty years. His confidence comes from the Strategy's incorporation of the FIONTAR Report which was advised by an international panel of renowned language-planners, and which proposes three essential pre-requisites for successful revitalisation: capacity (or ability) to use the language, opportunity to use the language, and a positive attitude towards the use of the language. However, Ó hAoláin inevitably has concerns, not least in the leadership and management of the Strategy, particularly with regard to its ownership by the Irish-language community, and sensibly cautions that a two-year setting-up period might be more appropriate. It is important that, from his position as the Chief Executive Officer of Údarás na Gaeltachta, Ó hAoláin feels able to champion the Strategy and optimistically issue a resounding call to everyone else to keep their faith and be supportive.

Colm Ó Coisdealbha provides a fascinating report on the work of the Office of an Coimisiméir Teanga in monitoring the 'language schemes' of public bodies which became a legal requirement under the *Official Languages Act 2003 / Acht na dTeangacha Oifigiúla 2003*. The Act is intended to ensure the provision of high quality public services in Irish, specifically:

> [...] to promote the use of Irish for official purposes in the state; to provide for the use of both official languages of the state in parliamentary proceedings, in acts of the Oireachtas, in the

administration of justice, in communicating with or providing services
to the public and in carrying out the work of public bodies. (Preamble,
Official Languages Act 2003)

Ó Coisdealbha's experience has shown him that, for successful implementation of a
language scheme (or plan), three key criteria are needed: appropriate staff resources in
Irish; range and standard of services in Irish; and continuous monitoring and adherence
to it. He argues that, whereas staff are often retrained to provide services in Irish,
recruitment of specialist language staff is 'the only practical and realistic approach'.
However, it would appear that there are simply not sufficient suitably qualified staff
to meet the demands, so that it is the very shortage of appropriately qualified staff
which present the biggest threat to the fulfilment of these language schemes. By
implication, it is a huge threat to the Strategy as well. With regard to the range of
services, Ó Coisdealbha has found considerable variation in practice, even among local
authorities supposedly providing similar services. He detects a vicious circle, for the
lack of service provision is often justified through the lack of demand, whereas the
public is often simply unaware what services in Irish are available. As for monitoring,
part of the statutory obligation, Ó Coisdealbha has found that public authorities have
woken up to what provisions can be measured, with the result that they have become
a lot more cautious about provision.

John Walsh picks up the Strategy's objective of creating a bilingual Ireland and
subjects the notion of bilingualism to some rather challenging scrutiny. After
diagnosing the considerable complexity within what is a unidirectional bilingual
situation, Walsh reviews the main reports and documents preceding the Strategy (listed
in the opening paragraph) with regard not simply to their treatment of bilingualism but
to the ideological underpinnings thereof. He diagnoses an ideology of the *cúpla focal*
('the few words') which has sustained symbolically the national belief of an Irish-
speaking nation but which he finds missing in the Strategy. He discusses a range of
views about the bilingual situation of the Gaeltacht as well as possible developments in
the future, including monolingual policies for Irish in the Gaeltacht. Finally, he
identifies the fundamental language-planning issue: interventionism, or protection, of
which the Strategy is a manifestation, so that Irish will survive as a community
language.

For **Dónall Ó Riagáin**, international consultant and language planner, the Strategy
deals mostly with acquisition planning (how people acquire the language) rather than
status planning (how people use the language). He feels the Strategy shouldn't be based
on a west-coast littoral notion of the Gaeltacht, but rather on speakers of the language
throughout Ireland, thereby encompassing other, smaller areas, and making it more of
a national issue, based on a nationwide community of speakers and learners. Ó Riagáin
commends the recommendations regarding education, but points out with some
concern that they will only be worthwhile if accepted by the Department of Education,
evidently not a foregone conclusion. Moreover, he poses various other concerns: the
status of the Strategy, its final authorship, its ownership by the various political parties,
the membership of the new authority, Údarás na Gaeilge, and its relationship with
Foras na Gaeilge, the abolition of An Comhairle um Oideachas Gaeltachta agus
Gaelscolaíochta, and monitoring. Ó Riagáin's verdict that the Strategy is 'deeply flawed'
and that 'the Irish people deserve better' contrasts strikingly with Ó hAoláin's
enthusiastic endorsement.

Helen Ó Murchú is deeply concerned about the Irish language voluntary sector,
for it is that sector which has the experience and expertise to implement the Strategy

but which receives very short shrift in the Strategy. At the same time, the 19 organisations which comprise the sector are being reorganised by their funder, Foras na Gaeilge, into one massive power-sharing partnership on the dubious administrative grounds of 'efficiency' and 'effectiveness', leading Ó Murchú to pose the question 'who own the language?' Much of her rather trenchant critique is directed at the increasingly fraught relationship between Foras na Gaeilge and these organisations. There would appear to be some major disconnection within the state at the very heart of this daring Strategy.

The next three papers deal with Northern Ireland. Although there is only one Irish language, **Janet Muller** shows how the present 20-Year Strategy is only a Strategy for the Republic of Ireland. In Northern Ireland, separate initiatives for strategic planning are needed, and Muller carefully sets out developments for Irish since the *Belfast / Good Friday Agreement 1998* and more recently the *Northern Ireland (St Andrews Agreement) Act 2006* showing how energetically-researched proposals for Irish language policy have been frustrated by successive unionist ministers. Part of the problem has been the refusal of the Northern Ireland Executive to treat Irish on its own merits by linking it with Scots, but so far no all-embracing strategy has emerged.

A working group to produce a comprehensive policy and strategic framework for the Irish language in Northern Ireland has been set up by NGO POBAL. As a member of that group, **Dónall Ó Baoill** sets out its terms of reference and a key list of issues in need of consideration if such a northern strategy is to pursue and achieve its objectives.

Aodán Mac Póilin continues the critique of the treatment of the 19 organisations in the core voluntary sector funded by Foras na Gaeilge and places considerable emphasis on the neglect of the different linguistic as well as administrative and political arrangements in Northern Ireland by the authorities in the South as well as all-Ireland authorities such as Foras na Gaeilge in its dealings with the North-South Ministerial Council. He argues that, although Northern Ireland has been written out of the present Strategy, it should not be bolted on as an afterthought, but rather a whole new policy/strategy should be devised from scratch. He identifies many contrasts and contradictions between the situation of Irish in the South and the North, which are systematically and valuably set out in an extensive appendix prepared by the ULTACH Trust in response to decisions by the North-South Ministerial Council which are adversely affecting the development of policy and strategy in the North.

Scottish Gaelic

In **Scotland**, very different approaches towards a strategy for **Gaelic** are being pursued. Following the *Gaelic Language (Scotland) Act 2005* and the establishment of the Bord na Gàidhlig, the Bord issued a five-year *National Plan for Gaelic* in 2007. In 2010, it issued a strategy to increase the number of Gaelic speakers: *Ginealach Ùr na Gàidhlig*. Public authorities are required to devise Gaelic Plans, each inevitably different and tailor-made to suit the body, but also proving, perhaps unexpectedly, a greater challenge than envisaged. Behind these aspirations is also the concept of bilingualism but, there too, exactly how that is to take shape and function remains to be worked out, not least because of a dearth of primary research.

Given that the creation of a (rather unqualified) bilingual country is a stated goal of the 20-Year Strategy in Ireland, **Robert Dunbar** presents an important typology of bilingualism based on the situations in Canada and Scotland, and which could readily transfer to Ireland. For Dunbar, there are three types of bilingualism: personal (a matter of capacity of ability to use the language), societal (a matter of the opportunities to use the language), and institutional (a matter of both capacity and opportunity, a question of prestige and instrumental value). Other factors such as balance and function lead to further subtypes. Moreover, there is the question of native-speakers and learners (L1 and L2), who after a certain point sometimes become indistinguishable. Dunbar shows convincingly that bilingualism with Gaelic in Scotland is heavily unbalanced, even in the traditional heartlands such as the Western Isles, where only a minority of speakers are now in Gaelic-medium education. Whereas allowances may be made for different individuals in different places or domains, and even allowing for whether people are speaking or writing, or are only passively bilingual (can only understand) or illiterate (cannot read or write) in Gaelic, Dunbar shows the dominance of English in all domains. It may come as some relief to read that neither the Bòrd's National Plan nor the Western Isles' Gaelic Plan has bilingualism as a goal, nor that the *Gaelic Language Scotland Act (2005)* confers any rights to use Gaelic or expect its use with regard to public bodies or with the private or voluntary sector. Rather, Dunbar comes to show that it may be institutional bilingualism which the present Gaelic Plans are beginning to foster, not least because the Bòrd's Guidance is nudging public bodies in that direction. Dunbar rightly cautions us all to be careful when discussing the notion and practices of bilingualism because of its immense scope for diverse or ambiguous interpretation.

It is about bilingualism and the notion of 'community' that **Gillian Munro** next raises a number of central and important issues. Whereas her arguments are based on a study of community attitudes to language and abilities, which she has written with her colleagues but which awaits publication, she also has her sights on the issues in need of addressing in the Gaelic Plan beyond 2012. She considers three areas in need of clarification: accuracy of mapping of Gaelic speakers and communities and greater understanding of the fast changing nature of the Gaelic language and associated culture; specification of what bilingualism means and of how it will be planned for; and the need to bring communities or networks of Gaelic speakers together with agencies to micro-plan language developments locally. She is particularly concerned in her paper with planning for language use in the traditional Gaelic heartlands. She acknowledges that Gaelic-speaking communities are changing – no longer are there traditional stable heartlands, and, in any case, many more Gaelic speakers are now living outside the heartland areas. Without inter-generational transfer, which is declining, Gaelic-medium education and adult education for Gaelic learners have proven insufficient to create Gaelic-speaking communities. So what Munro finds is 'linguistic fragmentation', with the nature of a Gaelic-speaking community in need of renewed definition. In that context, the meanings of bilingualism also need rethinking and refocusing. For her, research should precede the formulation of future policy and strategies of implementation. Finally, she advocates an expansion and intensification of the *Iomairt* initiative in communities, so that communities can be more intensively involved in creating their own local development plans, and in developing community initiatives similar to the *Mentrau Iaith* in Wales.

As various papers in this volume show, the notion of bilingualism is fraught with difficulties because of the diversity and variability of bilingual situations and levels of linguistic proficiency which it can encompass. **Timothy Currie Armstrong** also begins by raising some fundamental questions about bilingualism as a policy goal and about the linguistic norms and ideologies which lie behind language revitalisation. Language use has to be strengthened, Armstrong contends, but so also do relationships in the social interaction accompanying the change of language use. Armstrong reports on the

Carntogher Gaeltacht in Co. Londonderry where a deliberate effort is being made to re-create an Irish-speaking community within two generations, and where revival is being brought about through a carefully orchestrated community project. Central to its success is the cultivation of a shared ideology about the project's goals: revival and revitalisation, restoration and bilingualism. Armstrong's fieldwork has led him to uncover various tensions surrounding both the goal as well as the concept and practice of bilingualism, not least because the term is understood in so many different, sometimes contradictory, ways. For Armstrong, successful Gaelic-revitalisation projects are BBC Radio nan Gàidheal and Gaelic-medium primary education, because each establishes its own clear institutionally-determined linguistic norms. However, such norms are a lot less clearly defined when it comes to community revitalisation and the daily operation of bilingualism. For Armstrong, revitalisation also requires 'restoration'. Given current developments in Scotland as well as the goal of bilingualism in Ireland within twenty years, Armstrong raises some useful questions about the norms and ideologies which such a societal goal entails.

Dòmhnall Caimbeul and **Eilean Green** are looking forward to Gaelic's embracing of the fullest range of twenty-first century digital media. They survey the background to the creation of BBC ALBA. More than any other resource, they believe it has greater scope and power to research more people than any other media, including education. Intended as a national resource, BBC ALBA is already fulfilling its objectives by being watched by 10% of Scottish viewers whereas Gaelic speakers only make up 2% of the Scottish population. But they are mindful of the non-broadcast digital media, such as social network sites, which are growing year on year, and of which the content is becoming ever more diversified, but where, despite the predominance of English, Gaelic is taking grip – as evidenced by the BBC's *naidheachdan* website or Derek 'Pluto' Moireach's *gu Seachd le Pluto* website. It remains to be seen what form of the language will come to evolve as 'standard' or as a 'new standard' on Twitter or Facebook.

As already indicated, the *Gaelic Language (Scotland) Act 2005* requires public bodies to produce Gaelic Language Plans. **Alasdair MacCaluim** discusses the plan produced by the Scottish Parliamentary Corporate Body for its entire range of administrative services to the Parliament – quite different from the conduct of parliamentary business in the chamber which is sometimes performed in Gaelic, and which is covered under standing orders. In addition to the range of services provided, MacCaluim discusses the range of audiences being addressed, including the general non-Gaelic-speaking public, each of whom sees some Gaelic when visiting the Parliament, accessing its website, or reading its publicity.

The University of the Highlands and Islands is a further public body which has developed a Gaelic Language Plan, discussed in the next paper by **Ruairidh Mackay**. The University of the Highlands and Islands comprises 13 autonomous academic institutions for which the university acts as a corporate body to provide co-ordinating and support services as well as a range of executive and professional duties. Thus, Mackay's emphasis is not on any teaching through Gaelic, but rather he focuses on the use of translation software technology for aiding some of the Gaelic plan's objectives. Similar to the Scottish Parliament, the UHI Gaelic plan is concerned with signage, documentation, the entire nomenclature and vocabulary of administration, staffing issues and above all the university's website, and the intention is that, through use of translation technology, a more consistent and standardised approach to Gaelic will be delivered within these areas, throughout the partnership. Thus Mackay shows how Gaelic lies at the heart of the University of the Highlands and Islands.

Wilson McLeod addresses one specific aspect of the Gaelic plans which public bodies are required to implement: the use of Gaelic in their corporate logo. The purpose is, of course, to increase the language's visibility in all the very wide range of contexts in which, these days, a logo is used. He identifies four options: a Gaelic-only logo, a bilingual logo, with equal prominence to English and Gaelic, a bilingual logo with greater prominence to English, and an English-only logo. Each option is found among the 15 authorities so far to declare, and McLeod presents examples of each type. In this case study within the burgeoning field of linguistic landscapes, he finds the diversity of practice quite striking.

By using data from the 2001 Census as well as figures for those in Gaelic-medium education in 2009–10, **Kenneth MacKinnon** sets out the background to the present numbers and structure of the Gaelic-speaking population. To achieve growth in speaker numbers, he stresses the continuing importance of education and intra-generational transfer within the family and briefly sketches various options for growth achievement

The implementation of language strategies inevitably entails, within agencies and organisations, the deployment of staff charged with language development. A growing term for these development officers or culture workers or strategy enablers is *animateurs*. **Michelle Macleod** finds that, although those community language workers have a crucial role in strategy implementation, they have rarely been treated or studied as a group or sector, so that there is little known about what they do, why they do it, how they do it, how they have been trained for the job, what training or support they would like for the job, how successful they are or feel they are or are perceived to be, etc. etc. At the same time, Macleod recognises that these workers form a pivotal role between funders, strategists and the community, and that that relationship might be difficult as well as poorly understood by all those concerned. Macleod reports on a survey of 25 such enablers in Scotland during 2010. She addresses issues of training, communication, working conditions, support systems and assessment, concluding that, although the individuals are highly experienced and committed, the sector is disjointed and needs better co-ordination of best practice not only for those workers but for funders, too, who are criticised for insufficient awareness of these grass-root, interface employment needs.

A further paper on Gaelic is rather personal and anecdotal. **Brian Ó hEadhra**, a native of Dublin now living in Inverness, and a traditional musician, discusses his personal plans for learning Gaelic; the local and community plans in Inverness in the formulation of which he plays an important part; and the national plans, in which, as the first Gaelic Arts and Culture Officer for both Bòrd na Gàidhlig and Creative Scotland (Alba Chruthachail), he plays a pivotal role and has devised the first National Gaelic Arts Strategy.

In this section, the final paper is a personal look at Gaeldom and how there are striking cultural differences over behaviour and attitude on the part of Irish and Scottish speakers. For some time, **Gordon McCoy**, an anthropologist who is also a learner of Irish and Gaelic, presents some anecdotes which reveal fascinating contrasts between Ireland and Scotland – and indeed within each place as well. He begins with the historical chestnuts of the origins of each people and their language but quickly moves to the present day. Among the personal factors which he compares are religion (and also secularism), sectarianism, nationalism, temperament, dress sense, attitudes towards formality and business, and the confidence and tenor of discourse when Gaels talk about Gaeldom. Other factors include national *vs.* rural or urban *vs.* rural identities, names and signage, and aspects of folklore. Perhaps most striking are the contrasts he draws between attitudes towards learners by hard-nosed native speakers. In a light-hearted and often humorous paper, McCoy connects a great many details into one intermeshed, multi-disciplinary tapestry presenting quite different cultural perspectives from within Ireland and Scotland on each country's Gaeldom.

Scots

Although the present focus has largely been on strategies for Irish and Gaelic, the existence since 2009 of a Ministerial Advisory Group on Scots (MAGOS), its report to the Scottish Government in 2010, and the Government's response in 2011, all make it appropriate to include strategies for Scots at this time. From her privileged position as a member of MAGOS, **Christine Robinson** provides a background sketch about the membership and deliberations of the group. She then sets out the particular recommendations of the MAGOS Report under the following headings: 'education', 'broadcasting', 'publishing', 'creative writing', 'international contacts', 'raising awareness' and 'dialect'. Each recommendation is accompanied by the Culture Minister's response, all of which are positive and enthusiastic. Robinson's paper is a succinct and valuable summary of these important exchanges, from which let us hope much will be forthcoming during the new Government's lifetime. The appointment in May 2011 of a Junior Minister within the Department of Education and Lifelong Learning with responsibility for Scots for the first time is another major step forward.[8]

By contrast, **Andy Eagle** considers from first principles what a language strategy or strategic planning process might be and asks what lessons can be learnt from corporate strategy planning and commercial marketing. Eagle presents a robust challenge to the Government and to any language planners delegated with producing or implementing a strategy in due course. Eagle usefully compares Scots with other languages where language planning and comparable revitalisation measures have been undertaken in recent years: Catalonia, Friesland, Luxembourg and Norway. He also considers the stable diglossia of German-speaking Switzerland and the bidialectal education policies found in the Caribbean and the United States. Studies of each of these situations should certainly inform any strategy for Scots.

The volume concludes with the present authors' review of the entire ten-year series of language and politics symposia and related publications. **John Kirk** and **Dónall Ó Baoill** take stock and provide an assessment on the impact which the symposia and publications have had on the glotto-politics of Northern Ireland, the Republic of Ireland and Scotland and of the Gaeltacht and Scotstacht which stretch across these three jurisdictions. Much work remains to be done, however, and various options for the future are raised. The paper is accompanied by an exhaustive bibliography of publications generated by the present ten-year series.

---

[8] The encumbent, Dr Alasdair Allan, MSP, also has responsibility for Gaelic, and his official title is Minister for Learning and Skills.

The Role of Capacity Building in the Implementation of the *20-Year Strategy for the Irish Language*

Seosamh Mac Donnacha

Introduction

The publication of a *20-Year Strategy for the Irish language* is the end result of an improvised language planning process that started with the establishment of *Coimisiún na Gaeltachta* (Commission for the Gaeltacht) in 2000. The Commission published its report in 2002 and the recommendations contained therein set in motion a process that culminated with the publication by the Irish Government of a *20-Year Strategy for the Irish Language* in December 2010. Understandably reactions to the Strategy document have been mixed, but most commentators agree that it contains many good recommendations and that the very existence of a strategy is in itself important.

The Strategy document represents, in some aspects at least, a radical departure from existing approaches to language planning in Ireland – both in terms of the substance of the strategy and the approach to language planning inherent within it. However, a radical change of approach in any aspect of societal planning, language planning included, calls into question the issue of capacity building – how to ensure that the ability and capability exists within the responsible organisations and institutions to plan and implement new policies, measures and actions; to try out and evaluate new and untested approaches; and to sustain a planning process that is both different and far more complex than anything hitherto tried. 'Capability' in this context encompasses the resources, expertise and organisational structures required to underpin the new planning process and to implement its measures.

The purpose of this paper is to discuss the main capacity building measures that will be required to ensure that those organisations responsible for the implementation of the *20-Year Strategy for the Irish Language* shall have the capacity to do so.

Capacity Building: An Integrated Process.

At the *societal level* the aim of capacity building is to create an 'enabling environment', defined by the United Nations Development Program (UNDP, 2009: 11) as 'the broad social system within which people and organisations function … [including] all the rules, laws, policies, power relations and social norms that govern civic engagement'. This includes 'institutional and legal framework development, making legal and regulatory changes to enable organisations, institutions and agencies at all levels and in all sectors to enhance their capacities'. (The Urban Capacity Building Network [UCBN]: Undated)

Capacity building at the *organisational level* 'refers to the internal structure, policies and procedures that determine an organisation's effectiveness' (UNDP 2009:11) and includes 'the elaboration of management structures, processes and procedures, not only within organisations but also the management of relationships between the different organisations and sectors (public, private and community)'. (UCBN: Undated) McKinsey & Co. (2001), based on their review of capacity building in nonprofit organisations, broadened the scope of this definition to include the following seven elements:

Aspirations: An organisation's mission, vision, and overarching goals, which collectively articulate its common sense of purpose and direction.

Strategy: The coherent set of actions and programs aimed at fulfilling the organisation's overarching goals.

Organisational Skills: The sum of the organisation's capabilities, including such things (among others) as performance measurement, planning, resource management, and external relationship building.

Human Resources: The collective capabilities, experiences, potential and commitment of the organisation's board, management team, staff, and volunteers.

Systems and Infrastructure: The organisation's planning, decision making, knowledge management, and administrative systems, as well as the physical and technological assets that support the organisation.

Organisational Structure: The combination of governance, organisational design, interfunctional coordination, and individual job descriptions that shapes the organisation's legal and management structure.

Culture: The connective tissue that binds together the organisation, including shared values and practices, behavior norms, and most important, the organisation's orientation towards performance.

Capacity building at the *level of the individual* encompasses the investment we make and the activities we undertake to equip 'individuals with the understanding, skills and access to information, knowledge and training that enables them to perform effectively'. (UCBN: Undated)

It should be noted however that 'access to resources and experiences that can develop individual capacity are largely shaped by the organisational and environmental factors ... which in turn are influenced by the degree of capacity development in each individual'. (UNDP: 11) Thus, for a capacity building strategy to be effective, it must be an integrated process whose measures encompass activities at the level of society, at the organisational level and at the level of the individual.

Background to the 20-Year Strategy for the Irish Language

The *20-Year Strategy for the Irish language* is an important capacity building measure by the Irish Government in support of the Irish language. The strategy strives to provide an enabling environment, which will facilitate institutions, organisations and individuals engaged in language planning in Ireland to work towards a clearly defined set of objectives over the next twenty years, in a planned and coordinated way.

The process which produced the Strategy started in the late 1990s with a call by a community arts group, *Pléaráca Chonamara Teo.*, for the establishment of a taskforce that would 'develop an integrated strategy to ensure the continued survival of the Gaeltacht as a bilingual community in which Irish would remain the primary language' (Pléaráca '98:2). This led to the establishment of *Coimisiún na Gaeltachta* in 2000. The Commission's report, published in 2002, identified the need for 'a comprehensive linguistic survey' to provide the basis for the redrawing of Gaeltacht boundaries (*Coimisiún na Gaeltachta*, 2002: 10), and recommended that the Government formulate 'a State policy to revive Irish as a national language' (*ibid.:* 12) and develop and implement 'a National Plan for Irish containing clearly defined targets and illustrating the role of the Gaeltacht in the national effort' (*ibid.:* 12).

The implementation of these recommendations gradually evolved into the improvised process that led to the publication by the Government of the 20-Year Strategy for the Irish Language in December 2010. This process included the commissioning of two major sociolinguistic reports, the issuing of a statement by the Government in 2006 outlining current State policy towards the Irish language and the Gaeltacht, and the preparation of a report on the draft version of the Strategy by the Joint Parliamentary Committee on Tourism, Culture, Sport, Community, Equality and Gaeltacht Affairs. The process, as a whole, provided several opportunities for consultation with the public, through an online survey, public meetings and written submissions.

The Strategy document outlines the objective of Government policy, which is 'to increase on an incremental basis the use and knowledge of Irish as a community language [and to] ensure that as many citizens as possible are bilingual in both Irish and English' (p. 3). Within this context the strategy commits to increasing 'the number of families throughout the country who use Irish as the daily language of communication' and to providing 'linguistic support for the Gaeltacht as an Irish-speaking community and to recognise the issues which arise in areas where Irish is the household and community language' (*ibid.*).

Specifically the Government has committed to increasing over the 20-year life of the Strategy:

- the number of people with a knowledge of Irish from the current 1.66 million to 2 million;
- the number of daily speakers of Irish from the current level of approximately 83,000 to 250,000;
- the number of speakers who speak Irish on a daily basis in the Gaeltacht by 25%.

Capacity Building Measures Outlined in the Strategy Document

Section 3 of the Strategy document (p. 8) proposes a phased approach to its implementation, with the two initial phases, referred to in the document as the *Establishment Phase* and *Implementation Phase 1 – Laying the Foundations*, appearing to place an emphasis on the capacity building measures required to underpin the Strategy. It is stated that the *Establishment Phase* will be devoted to the setting up of the required organisational and operational structures, the allocation of the overall resources required, the agreement and establishment of the ongoing monitoring, evaluation and modification procedures, and the development of operational plans. *Implementation Phase 1* commits to the putting in place of long term measures for the supply of qualified teachers and other specialists, and the establishment of 'systems for their preparation'.

The Strategy document (p. 10) also sets out the key organisational structures that will be responsible for ensuring the effective implementation of the Strategy. At the Government level these will include:

- A Cabinet Committee on Irish and the Gaeltacht, chaired by *An Taoiseach*, which will maintain oversight of progress and report to the Government as necessary.
- A Senior Officials Group made up of high level officials from relevant Departments which will support the Cabinet Committee.

- A senior Minister in the Department of Community, Equality and Gaeltacht Affairs, which will have central responsibility for Irish language affairs.

The planning and implementation of the Strategy will be directed from a Strategy Unit within the Department of Community, Equality and Gaeltacht Affairs, which will have responsibility for:

- overseeing the strategic planning process;
- monitoring the development of resources;
- ensuring cross-departmental implementation of initiatives;
- providing expert advice;
- overseeing operational plans as developed by the implementation bodies;
- publishing updates and relevant documentation for public information.

This unit will be able to recruit seconded staff with expertise in public administration management, language planning and education as required and to commission evaluations and other specific services from existing public agencies or from the private sector.

It is anticipated that the main implementation agency with responsibility for delivering the Strategy shall be a new Irish Language and Gaeltacht Authority (*Údarás na Gaeilge agus na Gaeltachta*) that will function on a national basis, incorporating relevant functions currently performed by *Údarás na Gaeltachta*, and other State and nonGovernmental organisations, as appropriate.

It is stated that Foras na Gaeilge will continue to deliver on its statutory responsibilities in relation to Irish on an All-Ireland level. These include undertaking supportive projects and grant-aiding bodies and groups to support the language as appropriate, developing terminologies and dictionaries, supporting Irish-medium education and the teaching of Irish, and generally facilitating and encouraging the use of the language in public and private life.

The effectiveness of these capacity building measures will determine the ultimate success or otherwise of the strategy, as much as the substantive policies contained therein. This is on the grounds that good policies if badly thought-through or implemented are unlikely to lead to the desired results. Alternatively, even if the Strategy document contains policies that prove to be ineffective or erroneous these can be identified and modified as its implementation progresses through its various cycles of implementation, evaluation and modification. This is contingent, however, on the competence and effectiveness of the organisations implementing the strategy and on the robustness of the capacity building measures underpinning it.

Further Capacity Building Requirements of the Strategy

In essence, the argument I am promulgating in this paper is that the long term success or otherwise of the 20-Year Strategy for Irish will depend ultimately on the provision and effective implementation of the capacity building measures that are needed to underpin it. The strategy document, as discussed above outlines some of these capacity building measures. Important issues still remain to be considered, however, concerning those measures that are outlined in the Strategy document and in relation to other capacity building requirements that have not been alluded to. Space does not allow for detailed consideration of all of these issues here, therefore I will concentrate in the rest of this paper on the four issues which I consider the most pertinent to the *establishment phase* of the Strategy. These are issues relating to:

- the organisational capacity of the Strategy;
- the development of human resource capacity;
- the sustainability of the planning process;
- the development of the research capacity necessary to underpin the implementation and evaluation of the Strategy.

The Organisational Capacity Underpinning the Strategy

The Strategy document outlines the main organisational structures which will underpin the implementation of the Strategy. These include a cabinet subcommittee, a unit within the Department of Arts, Heritage and the Gaeltacht, and the establishment of a new *Údarás na Gaeilge agus na Gaeltachta*, which will subsume the existing *Údarás na Gaeltachta* and (at least) some of its existing functions. In order for these organisational structures to be effective, however, key capacity building issues need to be carefully considered and worked through in more detail, as part of the development of the operational plans within the *establishment phase* of the Strategy.

The capacity building requirements of the strategy unit to be established within the Department of Arts, Heritage and the Gaeltacht have yet to be considered in any detail. Decisions made in relation to the following questions will have a significant influence on the capacity of this unit to work effectively:

> Will the strategy unit have detailed terms of reference, a work programme with clearly defined targets and objectives and access to the necessary resources to carry out its work?

Will resources be provided to the strategy unit to allow it to recruit and develop the expertise necessary to lead language planning initiatives in each of the Strategy's eight 'areas for action': education; the Gaeltacht; family transmission of the language; administration, services and the community; media and technology; dictionaries; legislation and status planning; and economic life?

Will the unit develop lingua-demographic targets for individual county and urban areas, with a view to identifying where the major gains in the number of daily speakers of Irish are expected to accrue over the twenty year lifespan of the Strategy; and develop a nationwide network of agencies to lead the language planning initiatives designed to achieve such targets?

Will the unit have the necessary expertise to lead the planning, resource allocation and evaluative functions of the unit?

The capacity building requirements of *Údarás na Gaeilge agus na Gaeltachta* will be defined by the as yet unpublished legislation under which it will operate. However, as language planning has not been a significant function of the existing Gaeltacht authority, a key element in the establishment of the new body should be the requirement to conduct a skills audit, with a view to identifying the level and range of language planning expertise that will be required by it.

The role of *Foras na Gaeilge* in the 20-Year Strategy remains ambiguous. While, the Strategy states that *An Foras* will continue to deliver on its statutory responsibilities, it is not clear if there is an intention to align the activities of *An Foras* with those of other organisations engaged in the implementation of the Strategy – or what structural arrangements will to be put in place to facilitate this.

Similarly, the role to be played by the nonprofit Irish language sector in the implementation of the strategy is unclear. This sector has made a major contribution to the development Irish language policy, both historically and in more recent times. The Strategy document (p. 25) refers to these organisations, in rather paternalistic terms, stating that 'a radical re-organisation' of these language organisations will be undertaken with a view to providing 'comprehensive language support services on an area basis'. However, it is not entirely clear what is meant by this, or if these organisations are to have any role other than the delivery of services. Significantly, no indication is given that these organisations might have a significant role to play in the planning and evaluation of the Strategy, or that they are to have a say in how resources are allocated. Neither is any mention made of an intention to invest in developing the expertise of these organisations with a view to increasing their ability to deliver on specific aspects of the strategy.

These are issues which relate to 'the elaboration of management structures, processes and procedures, not only within organisations but also the management of relationships between the different organisations and sectors (public, private and community)'. (UCBN: Undated) How these issues will be decided by the promoters of the 20-Year Strategy will have a major influence on its organisational capacity – on the ability of individual organisations to deliver within their own areas of expertise and responsibility, and on the ability of the overall network of organisations to function in a mutually rewarding and synergetic manner towards the achievement of the targets set out in the Strategy.

The Development of Human Resource Capacity

Very little attention has been given in the Strategy document to the development of expertise in the various disciplines of language planning, which will be necessary to underpin the implementation and evaluation of the Strategy for the 20-year period and beyond. The exception, of course, is the promise of increased provision for the training of teachers. This, while necessary, is not a sufficient human resource strategy to underpin the effective implementation of the Strategy as a whole, given the broad scope of its eight 'areas for action'.

Each of the organisations and institutions referred to above will be required to recruit, on an ongoing basis, a significant number of individuals with appropriate expertise, education and training, in the various disciplines of language planning appropriate to their work. They will require not only teachers, but education planners, linguists, sociolinguists, psycholinguists, language planners, community workers, youth workers, parenting advisors, and people with language planning expertise relevant to the areas of economics, education, local planning, community development, management, tourism, culture, arts and entertainment – to name but a few of the areas of expertise that are necessary to underpin the effective implementation of the Strategy, and which are currently in very short supply in Ireland, and in some cases currently non-existent.

In addition, these organisations will need to attract and recruit individuals who have the intellectual ability and professional expertise necessary to contribute to the organisational capacity requirements identified by McKinsey & Co. (2002). That is to say, professionals who can contribute to organisational aspirations and strategies; who have the organisational skills necessary to effectively manage an organisations resources and relationships; who know how to develop organisational systems and infrastructures; and who know how to establish the shared values, practices and norms that will orientate an organisation towards achieving its goals and the Strategy's goals.

Employment in other similar areas of societal planning – for example, teaching, social work, rural and town planning, nursing and other health professionals – generally requires a minimum of an honors level third level degree. Given the complexity and the social nature of the language planning pro, which the 20-Year Strategy represents, it is reasonable to assume that a similar level of training and education, or its equivalent, would be required by the professionals who are expected to implement it. Indeed, this has been one of the failings of language planning in Ireland in the last century. Little emphasis has been placed on the professional or academic training of those working in the sector, with the result that progress has depended on the work of 'gifted amateurs' rather than having a sound basis in a coterie of appropriately trained professionals who have an in-depth understanding of the discipline of language planning and of the specialist area in which they are working.

Thus, a key requirement of the *establishment phase* of the Strategy is the establishment of an education and training programme that seeks (a) to ensure an ongoing supply of qualified professionals to work on the delivery of the strategy and in related areas and (b) to underpin the professional development of those already working in the sector. In other words, a strategy to equip 'individuals with the understanding, skills and access to information, knowledge and training that [will enable] them to perform effectively'. (UCBN: Undated)

The Sustainability of the Planning Process

A key issue which will impact on the effective implementation of the strategy will be the sustainability of the planning process which underpins it. It is not unusual to find, particularly within official language planning organisations that have not been historically exposed to a planning culture and to robust planning procedures, that a 'planning process' is perceived to be those activities that lead up to the 'publication of the plan' and that the 'process' itself ends at this stage, either because the personnel involved have moved on, or the process 'runs out of steam' or because those who have promoted the process have lost confidence in it. As a result much of the analysis and thinking underpinning the objectives and measures contained in the published strategy, and which binds those measures and objectives into something resembling an integrated whole, tends to be overlooked or forgotten. The result of such an outcome tends to be at best, the implementation of some of the measures of the strategy (more than likely those measures which are the easiest to implement [and] at the lowest cost), or at worst the gradual 'forgetting' of the strategy to be replaced by an embarrassed and perhaps defensive silence in the space which represents the State's leadership of the language planning process. Indeed, several previous efforts at a more formalised approach to language planning in Ireland have led to similar outcomes, the most recent of these being Bord na Gaeilge's development of an *Action Plan for Irish* in the 1980s.

Thus, the promoters of the Strategy must ensure that the analytical, evaluative, consultative, and leadership processes that have underpinned the development of the Strategy to date continue to underpin its implementation and evaluation. Or, to paraphrase McKinsey & Co. (2002), they must maintain the 'organisational skills: ... including such things (among others) as performance measurement, planning, resource management, and external relationship building … [and the] planning, decision making, knowledge management, and administrative systems' that underpinned the planning process that produced the Strategy.

In this context it is imperative that they clarify for all stakeholders how the planning process underpinning the implementation of the Strategy going forward will operate. This clarification should include:

- Providing an outline of the process and identifying the main stakeholders and how their participation in, and engagement with, the planning and implementation process will be facilitated.
- How the multi-annual cycles of implementation, evaluation and modification will be managed.
- Identifying the main performance indicators that shall apply to the primary measures of the Strategy.
- Identifying who shall be responsible for developing operational plans for the functional aspects of the Strategy, including the 'areas of action' referred to in the Strategy document.
- Identifying who shall be responsible for developing operational plans for the regional and local aspects of the Strategy.
- Identifying the range and level of resources that will be provided for both the planning process and the implementation of its measures, and the criteria by which these resources will be allocated.

The Research Capacity Necessary to Underpin the Implementation and Evaluation of the Strategy.

The Strategy document acknowledges the importance of research and much of the document is underpinned by research carried out by Fiontar and Acadamh na hOllscolaíochta Gaeilge, amongst others. However, it makes no reference to developing the States research capacity in the area of language planning going forward, or to the need for an ongoing research programme that will be in line with the needs of the Strategy.

It is not difficult to extrapolate, in a general sense, what some of the Strategy's research requirements will be. These will accrue from the Strategy's need for evaluative measures; from its emphasis on the need to adapt international best practice in the implementation of its measures; from the need for action research covering a range of its measures; from the need for ongoing empirical research into patterns of language usage, competence and attitudes, and from the need for further research on the sociolinguistic dynamics that drive language shift and change.

Without such a research capacity in place, it is difficult to see how the implementation of the Strategy as a whole or of its individual measures can be adequately evaluated on an ongoing basis. In addition, it will be difficult to identify best practice approaches through study of the implementation of our own measures or through the study of international experience. Without an adequate in-house research capacity in the main organisations implementing the Strategy, the translation of research findings into better working models will be piecemeal and ineffective, with the serious possibility that the Strategy will fail because the praxis on which it is based remains stagnant.

While some of this research capacity already exists, it is by no means sufficient. This is especially so since the closure of *Institiúid Teangeolaíochta Éireann* (the Irish

Linguistics Institute) in 2004. Therefore, the implementation of the *establishment phase* of the Strategy should include consideration of an investment programme for the development of existing language planning research capacity in third level institutions; the establishment of a linguistics research institute to fill the void left by Institiúid Teangeolaíochta Éireann; and investment in in-house research capacity within the organisations responsible for the overall planning, evaluation and implementation of the Strategy.

Conclusion

Presumably, some of these issues will be considered in detail by the Strategy's promoters as part of the development of operational plans for the *establishment phase* of the Strategy. However, it should be noted that capacity building can be difficult to institute as an integral part of societal planning processes. This is true in the area of language planning as it is for other areas of societal planning. The reasons for this are complex and include the following.

Projects and programs that produce short term tangible results are easier to plan and implement and will have outputs that are easier to predict than capacity building measures that require a significant resource input at the planning stage and whose outcomes will be medium to long term, and are often intangible. Thus, investment in front line activity which is perceived to provide tangible results is generally given preference over investment in the development of effective managerial, administrative and planning structures, the outcome of which is often intangible and difficult to predict and measure.

In addition, capacity building is often resource intensive, particularly in the short term, with lead in and implementation times being considerable – for example, the lead in and implementation time for a new degree programme in language planning would be in the region of 4-6 years. With, possibly another ten years required before a critical mass of graduates would accrue with sufficient influence to make a significant impact on the level and quality of language planning expertise available to the language planning process.

Capacity building is often hindered by a lack of lack of vision, knowledge, training, expertise or experience, amongst the leadership of the various stakeholder bodies. This can lead to important aspects of the capacity building process, for example, research, planning, and evaluation activities, being perceived or belittled as 'time wasting' or 'vacillation'. This often presents itself in the form of funding mechanisms that focus on the need for short term tangible results and underestimate both the need for, and the level of funding required for, effective capacity building measures.

For these reasons most societal planning processes tend to emphasise projects, programs and schemes that produce tangible results in the short term and are reactive to the need to be seen to be 'doing something'. In drafting the 20-Year Strategy for the Irish Language, its promoters have recognised the need for capacity building measures and have indicated clearly that some capacity building should precede the actual implementation of the Strategy. Let us hope that those organisations and individuals charged with the implementation of the Strategy have the necessary vision, knowledge, expertise and experience to build on this aspect of the Strategy document in the early implementation phases, and by so doing create an 'enabling environment', that will enable other 'organisations, institutions and agencies at all levels and in all sectors to enhance their capacities' and to contribute to the development of a sustainable future for the Irish language.

References

20-Year Strategy for the Irish Language: 2010–2030. Dublin: Department of Community, Rural and Gaeltacht Affairs.

Coimisiún na Gaeltachta. 2002. *Tuarascáil*. Baile Átha Cliath. An Roinn Gnóthaí Pobail, Tuaithe agus Gaeltachta.

FIONTAR. 2009. *20-Year Strategy for the Irish Language: Prepared for the Department of Community, Rural and Gaeltacht Affairs*. Dublin: Dublin City University.

McKinsey & Co. 2001. *Effective Capacity Building in Nonprofit Organisations*. Washington: Venture Philanthropy Partners.

Ó Giollagáin, C., Mac Donnacha, S., Ní Shéaghdha, A. and F. Ní Chualáin. 2007. *Staidéar Teangeolaíoch ar Úsáid na Gaeilge sa Ghaeltacht / Comprehensive Linguistic Study of the Use of Irish in the Gaeltacht*. Dublin. The Department of Community, Rural and Gaeltacht Affairs.

Pléaráca Chonamara Teo. 1998. Eagarfhocal. *Pléaráca '98*.

United Nations Development Programme (UNDP). 2009. *Capacity Building: A UNDP Primer*. New York: United Nations Development Programme.

Urban Capacity Building Network (UCBN). www.gdrc.org/uem/capacity-define.html. Retrieved 20 April 2011.

Straitéis 20-Bliain don Ghaeilge: Promhadh ár gCreidimh

Pádraig Ó hAoláin

Cúlra

Ó foilsíodh an *Dréacht-Straitéis 20-Bliain don Ghaeilge* i mí na Samhna 2009 is iomaí uair ráite é ag cinnirí Gaeltachta agus Gaeilge araon gurb é seo *'seans deireanach na Gaeltachta'*. Ar ndóigh, is iomaí uair cheana a tuaradh a bás, is iomaí tuairisc agus tuarascáil a d'fhógair go raibh sí ar an dé deiridh agus is iomaí sin údar adúirt go raibh sí ar an leabhar ag an bhfiach dubh nó ráitis dá leithéid.

Mar shampla, dúirt Máirtín Ó Cadhain, atá aitheanta mar dhuine de na scríbhneoirí cruthaitheacha ba mhó ariamh i stair na Gaeilge, sa léacht stairiúil sin 'Páipéir Bhána agus Páipéir Bhreaca' a thug sé uaidh ag oscailte oifigiúil Chumann Merriman sa bhliain 1968:

> is deacair do dhuine a dhícheall a dhéanamh i dteanga arb é a chosúlacht
> go mbeidh sí básaithe roimhe féin, má fhaigheann sé cúpla bliain eile.

Mar adúirt mé cheana, tá cinnirí na Gaeilge agus na Gaeltachta araon ar aon tuairim gurb í an *Straitéis 20-Bliain don Ghaeilge* seans deireanach na Gaeltachta teacht slán mar theanga phobail. Sé an rud a chiallaíonn sé sin, de réir treocht na teanga faoi láthair, nach mbeidh iarsma ar bith den Ghaeltacht mar phobal teanga fós ann ag deireadh na tréimhse 20-bliain seo romhainn mura gcuirfear i bhfeidhm í. Ar an dtaobh eile den scéal bhí údar misnigh agus dóchais ann do phobal na Gaeltachta agus na Gaeilge trí chéile nuair a foilsíodh an Dréacht-Straitéis agus bhí trí ní ábharthacha ar chuir daoine eolacha an-mheáchan orthu:

(i)   gur sheas an Rialtas le Clár Páirtnéireachta don Rialtas i mí na Nollag 2006 'go mbeadh plean straitéiseach 20-bliain ina threoirphlean cuimsitheach d'fhorbairt úsáid na Gaeilge i ngach ceantar uirbeach agus tuaithe'.

   Bhí sé suntasach gur cuireadh a leithéid de gheallúint faoin nGaeilge i gClár an Rialtais agus gur coinníodh geallúint dá leithéid faoin nGaeilge!

(ii) gur eascair an Dréacht-Straitéis ó Choiste ComhAireachta faoi chathaoirleacht an Taoisigh – cé go raibh sí á stiúradh ag an Roinn Gnóthaí Pobail, Tuaithe agus Gaeltachta (mar a bhí) – agus thug sé sin meáchan, seasamh agus inchreidteacht bhreise di; agus

(iii) gur dhearbhaigh an té a thiomáin an próiseas ó gheallúint go Straitéis, An tIar-Aire, Éamon Ó Cuív, ar ócáidí éagsúla poiblí ina dhiaidh sin go raibh an Coiste ComhAireachta tiomanta do bhrú chun cinn na Straitéise go leibhéal an Rialtais ach go dtiocfadh sí tríd an bpróiseas comhairliúcháin mar chéad chéim ar aghaidh chuig Tithe an Oireachtais. Dhearbhaigh sé, lena chois sin, nach mbainfí cumhachtaí ná feidhmeanna ar bith d'Údarás na Gaeltachta de thoradh an phróisis seo ach go dtabharfaí feidhm don Údarás maidir le cur chun cinn na Gaeilge ar bhonn náisiúnta.

Ba shuntasach iad na geallúintí sin ag teacht tar éis bliana nuair a bhí na meáin ag tuairimíocht go rialta faoi rún na Roinne Airgeadais feidhm a thabhairt do mholadh de chuid ghrúpa comhairleoirí, a nglaotar go coitianta orthu *An Bord Snip Nua,* deireadh a chur le hÚdarás na Gaeltachta agus a feidhmeanna a dháileadh ar ghníomhaireachtaí eile.

Staid Reatha

Cén chaoi a sheasann sí anois mar sin deich mí tar éis a foilsithe? Tá sí sa riocht a mheabhraíonn dom an freagra a thug an Ciarraíoch ar an té a d'fhiafraigh de 'cén airde atá Cnoc Bhréanainn? (an cnoc is airde i gCiarraí). Tá 'brathann sé ar cé go híseal agus a thosaíonn tú ag dreapadóireacht'.

Tá an chuma ar chúrsaí go gcaithfimid roinnt mhaith spoir sléibhe a chur dínn fós i rith 2010 – agus fiú isteach go maith in 2011 – sula gcuirfear tús leis an dreapadóireacht dáiríre ar an *Straitéis 20-Bliain don Ghaeilge.*

Fágann sé sin gur tráth tuairimíochta atá ann maidir leis an amscála a bhainfidh lena cur i bhfeidhm. Lena chois sin is tráth tuairimíochta é maidir leis an leagan amach a bheidh ar an Straitéis féin sula gcuirfear os comhair an Rialtais í.

Tá cúis shimplí faoi nach bhfuil mórán tuairimíochta déanta fúithi go poiblí, mar atá, gurb é an toradh a bhí ar an bpróiseas comhairliúcháin a thionscain an Comhchoiste Oireachtais ná straitéis mhéadaithe a chur ar fáil don Aire a bhfuil neart moltaí breise inti nach raibh sa bhuncháipéis. Ní hionann í agus na leasuithe simplí a raibh súil ag an Iar-Aire Éamon Ó Cuív leo! Agus tá líon nach beag moltaí de chuid Fhoireann Fiontar DCU nár glacadh leo an chéad uair tagtha ar ais isteach sa cháipéis leasuithe seo. Seans nár glacadh leo an chéad uair de bhrí go raibh geallshealbhoirí áirithe míshásta leo.

Cinneadh Aireachta

Ceist a éiríonn mar sin – céard a dhéanfaidh an tAire Gnóthaí Pobail, Comhionannais agus Gaeltachta, Pat Carey T.D. anois? Glacadh leis na moltaí breise scun scan mar gur eascair siad ó phróiseas comhairliúcháin? Scagadh a dhéanamh orthu agus na cinn is dílse atá ag luí leis an mbun-straitéis a roghnú? agus, b'fhéidir, dá bharr sin, olc a chur ar chomhaltaí an Chomhchoiste agus deis a thabhairt do chuid acu féachaint le barrthuisle polaitíochta a bhaint as lá is faide anonn nuair a thiocfaidh an Straitéis os comhair Thithe an Oireachtais dá mbeannú! Tharlódh sé fiú go mb'fhéidir go mothóidh an tAire gur cheart dó filleadh ar athphlé a dhéanamh ar mholtaí áirithe leis na Ranna Rialtais lena bhaineann siad mar nár aontaigh siad leo i gcéaduair. Cá bhfios! Ní thig linn mórán seachas tuairimíocht a dhéanamh.

Ábhair Imní agus Dearbhuithe Áirithe

Is tráth é seo do phobal na Gaeilge lena misneach a choinneáil, tréith, ar ndóigh, a bhfuil siad cleachtaithe uirthi le fada. Tá údair níos mó ná riamh ag pobal na Gaeilge le haghaidh ghníomh creidimh! Tá an Rialtas ag iomrascáil leis an ngéarchéim eacnamaíochta is measa dár fhulaing an stát ariamh cheana. Tá Clár Athbhreithnithe Caipitil foilsithe ag an Roinn Airgeadais a léiríonn go bhfuil an chuma ar an scéal go mbainfear na putóga caipitil as an Roinn Gnóthaí Pobail, Comhionannais agus Gaeltachta agus as Údarás na Gaeltachta araon *má* bhunófar Buiséad 2011 ar na figiúirí caipitil don tréimhse 2011–15 a d'fhoilsigh An Roinn Airgeadais i mí Iúil seo caite.

Céard atá i ndán don Údarás, mar sin, mar cheann de phríomhfheithiclí an Rialtais leis an Straitéis 20-Bliain a chur i bhfeidhm? Tá sé ráite go poiblí roinnt uaireanta ag an Aire le déanaí go bhfuil todhchaí an Údaráis agus na Gaeltachta fite fuaite leis an Straitéis 20-Bliain – go bhfuil siad araon suite taobh istigh den Straitéis.

An mbeidh na hacmhainní cuí ar fáil leis an Straitéis a chur i bhfeidhm? Beidh acmhainní ar fáil. Deireann an tAire go mbeidh. De réir na Straitéise féin tá cúrsaí maoinithe nó na hacmhainní foriomlán le leithroinnt i rith na chéad bhliana. Promhadh creidimh atá sa phróiseas seo.

Tástálacha Éagsúla Creidimh

Léiríomar ariamh i gcónaí go raibh de chumas ionainn mar phobal Gaeilge ár muinín a chur sa 'Tuarascáil Shaineolach' is déanaí a thabharfadh aghaidh ar shlánú na Gaeilge agus neamhaird a thabhairt ar na tuartha tubaisteacha agus ar an easpa chur i bhfeidhm roimhe seo nó stairiúil.

Is fiú spléachadh a thabhairt ar roinnt de na tuarascálacha nó staidéir sin is mó a d'ardaigh ár gcroíthe agus a thástáil ár gcuid creidimh.

Féach an taithí atá againn sa réimse seo:

- **Coimisiún na Gaeltachta 1926:** Cuireadh tuarascáil chuimsitheach ar fáil. Níor cuireadh na moltaí i bhfeidhm, áfach, mar bhí géarchéim eacnamaíochta ann ag an am agus bhí ró-chostas ag baint leis na moltaí a chur i bhfeidhm.

- **1965: An Coimisiún um Athbheochan na Gaeilge:** Leag an Rialtas an Tuarascáil dheiridh faoi bhráid gach Tí den Oireachtas i mí Eanáir 1965. Chlúdaigh an tuarascáil agus na moltaí réimse leathan earnálacha. Siad na téarmaí tagartha a thug an Rialtas do Choimisiún um Athbheochan na Gaeilge nuair a bunaíodh é in 1958 ná:

  > Ag féachaint don chéim atá sroichte faoi láthair leis an iarracht chun an Ghaeilge a athbheochan, breithniú a dhéanamh agus comhairle a thabhairt faoi na bearta ba cheart don phobal agus don stát a dhéanamh anois d'fhonn go rachfar ar aghaidh níos tapúla chun an chuspóra sin.

Sé an cuspóir a bhí ann dul ar aghaidh níos tapúla leis an obair – tá ábhar machnaimh sa mhéid sin.

Labhair an tUachtarán, Éamon de Valera, leo ag cruinniú tionscnaimh na gcomhaltaí ar an 24ú Meán Fómhair 1958 agus i measc rudaí eile dúirt sé: 'Tuigeann sibh a riachtanaí atá sé go slánófaí an Ghaeilge agus go slánófaí *gan rómhoill í*. Tá a lán daoine nach bhfuil sásta leis an dul chun cinn. San obair seo, Athbheochan na Gaeilge, tá an pobal i gceist agus tá an Stát i gceist. Is féidir leis an Stát méid áirithe a dhéanamh. … ach is é an pobal sa deireadh a shlánóidh an Ghaeilge.'

Is í an Ghaeltacht príomhthaca nádúrtha na teanga, agus is ar an taca sin, thar rud ar bith eile, b'fhéidir a bhraithfidh an toradh a bheidh ar na hiarrachtaí chun an teanga a shlánú.

- **Comhairle na Gaeilge (1969–74):** Is ar éigean go raibh an dúch tirim ar thuarascáil mholtaí An Choimisiún um Athbheochan na Gaeilge i 1965 nuair a cheap an Rialtas Comhairle na Gaeilge ceithre bliana ina dhiaidh sin **chun cabhrú leis an mbeartas i leith na Gaeilge a athbhreithniú** agus chun comhairle a thabhairt i dtaobh a curtha chun cinn feasta.

  Tuigeadh don Chomhairle ón tús go mba cuid thábhachtach dá gcuid oibre é ionad na Gaeilge sa chóras oideachais a mheas. D'fhoilsigh An Chomhairle moltaí faoi réimse leathan earnálacha, gnéithe den chóras oideachais go háirithe, idir 1969 agus 1971–2. Nótáil go raibh Caibidil 1 de léirmheas substaintiúil ginearálta ar an nGaeilge sa chóras oideachais réidh ag an gComhairle in Earrach na bliana 1973 nuair a chinn an Rialtas nach mbeadh sé riachtanach do dhaltaí feasta pas sa Ghaeilge a fháil chun bheith i dteideal na scrúduithe Ardteistiméireachta.

  Chomh fada agus is léir dom níor cuireadh i bhfeidhm ach moladh sonrach amháin de chuid na Comhairle, sin bunú Bhord na Gaeilge, cé go mb'fhéidir gur ghlac an Bord féin cuid acu ar bord ina dhiaidh sin.

  Choinníomar ár gcreideamh slán ach cuireadh dianthástáil ar ár gcuid misnigh go tráthrialta.

  I 1990 foilsíodh *The Death of the Irish Language: A Qualified Obituary* le Reg Hindley. D'fhógair Hindley go raibh uasmhéid 10,000 cainteoir laethúil dúchais fágtha. *'I do not suggest this (figure) dogmatically but feel it safe to set this upper limit'*. Ar ndóigh, thuigeamar go léir go raibh sé mícheart, bhíothas amhrasach faoina mhodheolaíocht agus d'éirigh linn déileáil leis an droch-phoiblíocht.

  Go gairid ina dhiaidh sin i 1990 foilsíodh (nó sceitheadh!) *Tuarascáil ar Staid Láithreach na Gaeilge le Breandán Ó hEithir*, craoltóir agus údar mór le rá de bhunadh Árann. Iontas na n-iontas, sé an figiúr céanna 10,000 cainteoir laethúil Gaeilge a bhí ag an Árannach agus a bhí ag Reg Hindley! Ba dheacra dul ag sáraíocht le Breandán Ó hEithir ná le Reg Hindley mar gheall ar a sheasamh agus a stádas go náisiúnta agus i measc cainteoirí Gaeilge i gcoitinne. Dá ainneoin sin bhí amhras mór faoina mhodheolaíocht seisean freisin (nár míníodh i gceart ariamh) agus is beag airde a tugadh ar an tuarascáil. Ní gan dóchas a bhí Breandán, áfach, agus thug an méid seo a leanas údar áirithe misnigh go phobal na Gaeilge:

  > Tá sé thar am go dtuigeadh daoine atá i bhfabhar na hathbheochana/na Gaeilge nach mairfidh an teanga gan iarracht phearsanta de shaghas éigin uathu féin. Cé nach bhfuil ach 10,000 nó mar sin cainteoir dúchais fanta …ní hionann sin agus á rá nach féidir a staid a fheabhsú. Chuige sin, áfach, is gá na seanmhodhanna oibre a athrú agus tréan-iarracht pobal na Gaeilge a spreagadh agus a chur ag obair gach slí is féidir.

- **Coimisiún na Gaeltachta (2002):** Mhaigh Coiste an Choimisiúin ina réamhrá gur thug bunú an Choimisiún ag an Rialtas in 2000 léas dóchais do phobal agus do chairde na Gaeltachta 'a bhfuil imní orthu le fada an

lá go bhfuil an Ghaeltacht (féin) ag feo agus ag éalú os comhair a súil'.
Luaigh siad chomh maith cé go raibh bunú an Chéad Choimisiún
Gaeltachta i 1925 ar an gcéad bheart suntasach a rinne Rialtas an
tSaorstáit nua ar son na Gaeltachta, agus nár feidhmíodh moltaí an
Choimisiúin sin ná níor cuireadh na hacmhainní cuí ar fáil leis sin a
dhéanamh. Mhol an Coimisiún i measc réimse leathan moltaí
substaintiúla eile go n-ullmhófaí agus go bhfeidhmeofaí Plean Náisiúnta
don Ghaeilge ina mbeadh spriocanna cinnte sainithe agus a léireodh ról
phobal na Gaeltachta san iarracht. Sé an Coimisiún seo a spreag an tAire
lena leithéid seo a chur i gClár an Rialtais in 2006.

- **2007: Staidéar Cuimsitheach Teangeolaíochta ar Úsáid na Gaeilge sa
  Ghaeltacht:** Staidéar saineolach cuimsitheach a léiríonn an staid
  fhírinneach maidir le húsáid na Gaeilge sa Ghaeltacht. Siad
  tuismitheoirí na *Straitéise 20-Bliain don Ghaeilge* moladh an Choimisiún
  Plean Teanga a ullmhú agus torthaí agus tátail an Staidéir saineolach
  seo. Léiríonn an Staidéar gur timpeall 34,000 cainteoir laethúil Gaeilge
  atá sa Ghaeltacht ach sé an pátrún aistrithe tobann teanga is mó a
  dhúisigh na polaiteoirí agus atá mar ábhar imní ag cách.

Ceisteanna

Ceist mhór – an bhfuil an straitéis in oiriúint don dúshlán a bhaineann leis an sprioc
uaillmhianach de 250,000 cainteoir laethúil Gaeilge a bhaint amach? Sílim gur féidir
linn a rá go bhfuil, i gceachtar den dá dhréacht-straitéis, soláthar dóthanach moltaí
agus meicníochtaí sna doiciméid a fhreagraíonn do na príomhriachtanais agus a
líonann na príomhbhearnaí a aithníodh ó thaobh an stáit de.

Easnaimh

Siad an dá easnamh mhóra a fheicim fós ann, atá bunúsach agus criticiúil, ná an
struchtúr pleanála teanga ag leibhéal an phobail agus páirtíocht an phobail féin. Faoi
mar a mheabhraigh an tUachtarán Éamon de Valera do chruinniú tionscnaimh an
Choimisiún um Athbheochan na Gaeilge i 1958 – *'tá an pobal agus an stát i gceist san
obair seo, agus sé an pobal sa deireadh a shlánóidh an Ghaeilge'.*
Ní léir dom ag an bpointe seo go bhfuil dóthain machnaimh déanta ar na tionscnaimh
is gá a úsáid chun gluaiseacht phobail a eagrú chun gnímh san obair dhúshlánach seo.
Molann comhairleoirí Fiontar DCU go gcaithfí bliain thosaigh na straitéise i mbun
ullmhúcháin. Mholfainn féin go láidir go gcaithfí *dhá bhliain* i mbun réamhphleanála
agus i rith na tréimhse sin go n-eagrófaí feachtas fócasaithe feasachta ar aidhmeanna
agus cur chuige na Straitéise dírithe ar an bpobal ar fud na Gaeltachta agus ina bhfuil
páirtíocht ag geallshealbhóirí stáit agus pobail araon.

Focal Scoir

Mar achoimre, sí an staid ina bhfuil cúrsaí faoi láthair ná:
- go bhfuil cinneadh le déanamh ag an Aire Gnóthaí Pobail,
  Comhionannais agus Gaeltachta faoi Dhréacht-Straitéis agus moltaí
  Chomhchoiste an Oireachtais;

- go mbeidh an Straitéis le beannú ag an gCoiste ComhAireachta agus ag an Rialtas am éigin idir seo agus Márta 2011;
- go mbeidh an Straitéis le leagan os comhair gach Tí den Oireachtas chun tacaíocht traspháirtí a fháil tharla go mbeidh sí á feidhmiú thar thréimhse 20-bliain;
- go bhfuil soláthar airgid le socrú ag leibhéal Aireachta agus Rialtais do réamhchéimeanna cur i bhfeidhm na Straitéise;
- go bhfuil leasuithe reachtaíochta chun athstruchtúrú a dhéanamh ar Údarás na Gaeltachta le hullmhú agus le seoladh trí Thithe an Oireachtais – (ar ndóigh, d'fhéadfaí é seo a dhéanamh comhthreomhar le réamhchéimeanna eile den *Straitéis*. Is próiseas mall é go hiondúil reachtaíocht a leasú);
- go bhfuil clár oibre agus leagan amach an Údaráis mar ghníomhaireacht náisiúnta le socrú;
- tá Clár Athbhreithnithe Caipitil an Rialtais foilsithe ó mhí Iúil 2010 agus buiséad 2011 le hullmhú i rith an dá mhí seo romhainn.

Tá sé deimhnithe dúinn go bhfuil an *Straitéis* a bheag nó a mhór ag teacht leis an amscála a bhí leagtha amach di. Tugadh le fios dúinn gur figiúirí táscacha atá sa Chlár Athbhreithnithe Caipitil agus tá athdheimhnithe dúinn go bhfuil an tÚdarás agus An Ghaeltacht i gcroílár na Straitéise. Coinnígí bhur gcreideamh agus bhur misneach!

The *20-Year Irish Language Strategy*: Testing the Faith of Irish Speaker

Pádraig Ó hAoláin

Background

Since the publication of the *Draft 20-Year Strategy for the Irish Language 2010–2030*[1] in November 2009 both Gaeltacht and Irish-language movement spokespersons nationally have been of one mind that '*this is the last chance for the Gaeltacht*'. The revelation in the *Comprehensive Linguistic Study of the use of Irish in the Gaeltacht (2007)*[2] that the number of habitual speakers of Irish in the Gaeltacht was as low as approximately 34,000 people dispersed throughout the Gaeltacht, and the evidence of substantial erosion among the primary schoolgoing and teenage age-groups, was a clarion-call to action which was responded to positively and with alacrity by the then Minister for Community, Rural and Gaeltacht Affairs, Éamon Ó Cuív. The Minister established a Forum (Fóram na Gaeilge) representative of the main state and voluntary Irish-language organisations to advise him in relation to the next step. Out of that process, with much hands-on involvement by the Minister, emerged the proposal to initiate a tendering process for the formulation of a comprehensive national language plan with due regard for the special needs of the Gaeltacht. There were still doubters in the camp for whom the downward graph of the Gaeltacht language statistics was forebodingly pessimistic, but the Minister's strong commitment, both personal and political, was compellingly persuasive for addressing the issue with vigour, clear-sightedness and almost disconcerting optimism.

Of course, the demise of the language had often before been the basis of dire prognostications, and numerous reports, studies, commentators and authors have at various times announced that '*she was on her last legs*', or words to that effect. For example, Máirtín Ó Cadhain, generally recognised as one of the most outstanding creative writers of Irish of all time, stated in a powerful public lecture given at the Merriman Association Winter School in 1968: 'it is difficult for a person to do their best in a language which to all intents and purposes seems as if it will be dead before him, if he gets a few more years'.[3] Máirtín Ó Cadhain died two years later in 1970.

However, at this juncture in time there is a consensus that the scientific linguistic evidence of rapid language change now available is incontrovertible. Practitioners in the field in both the Gaeltacht and Irish language movement nationally are generally agreed that the *20-Year Strategy for the Irish language 2010–2030* will provide the last opportunity for the Gaeltacht to survive as a distinctive language community. That means in effect that, based on current patterns of language change, no vestige of the Gaeltacht as a living language community, other than isolated pockets of habitual speakers, will remain 20 years hence if this strategy is not implemented.

On the publication of the *Comprehensive Linguistic Study* there was a realisation at the political level that it would be naïve or irresponsible to ignore the evidence on the ground, so that continuing as we were was not an option. The messages from community groups that filtrated through the post-publication consultation process throughout the Gaeltacht communities of that Study in 2007 and 2008 were clear calls

[1] *Draft 20-Year Strategy for the Irish Language / Dréacht-Straitéis 20-Bliain do Ghaeilge*: Department of Community, Equality and Gaeltacht Affairs, 2009.

[2] *Comprehensive Linguistic Study of the Use of Irish in the Gaeltacht*. Acadamh na hOllscolaíochta Gaeilge, National Institute for Regional and Spatial Planning, NUI Maynooth, and the Department of Community, Rural and Gaeltacht Affairs, 2007.

[3] Ó Cadhain, Máirtín, *Páipéir Bhána agus Páipéir Bhreaca*, Dublin: An Clóchomhar Ita, 1969.

for action from community representatives. The political omens for action were better than at any other juncture in the history of action-plans for the Gaeltacht and for the Irish-language in general. Certain important factors gave the Draft 20-Year Strategy significant weight when it was published in November 2009. Firstly, building on the Government's 13-point *Statement on the Irish Language* of 2006,[4] the Government delivered on a commitment given in the Programme for Government 2007–2012[5] 'that a comprehensive 20-Year Strategic Plan would form a comprehensive pilot scheme for the development of the use of Irish in every urban and rural area' which arose from a recommendation made in the Coimisiún na Gaeltachta (The Gaeltacht Commission) report in 2002.[6] It was noteworthy that the Draft 20-Year Strategy was directed by a Ministerial Sub-Committee chaired by An Taoiseach albeit the compilation of the strategy was navigated through the preparatory stages by the Department of Rural, Community and Gaeltacht Affairs with expert linguistic support from the DCU Fiontar Team – that gave added weighting to the document. In addition, the now former Minister for Community, Rural and Gaeltacht Affairs, Éamon Ó Cuív, who navigated the process from commitment to compilation, confirmed publicly on subsequent occasions that the Cabinet Sub-Committee was committed to pressing ahead with the Draft Strategy to government level for approval and hence for the approval of both Houses of the Oireachtas (Dáil and Senate) as soon as it would proceed through the consultative process involving the Joint Committee on Tourism, Culture, Sport, Community, Equality and Gaeltacht Affairs (with all-party representation) as a first step.

Arising from concerns about the reference in the Draft Strategy to *Údarás na Gaeilge* as the name of the proposed restructured *Údarás na Gaeltachta* and that this in itself intimated that its enterprise function would be diluted, the then Minister also confirmed publicly on a number of occasions that not only would no powers or functions be taken from Údarás na Gaeltachta (as stated in the Draft Strategy) but that the restructuring of An tÚdarás would include a broadening of its language function to include a national Irish language dimension, presumably leaving the existing body, Foras na Gaeilge, to cater for all cross-border Irish-language functions. Those commitments were additionally significant and reassuring following a year of media speculation throughout 2009–10 about the persuasive evidence pointing to the intention of the Department of Finance, on foot of a recommendation by group of consultants headed by an economist, Colm McCarthy, known colloquially as *An Bord Snip Nua*[7] (The New Scissors Board), to dismantle Údarás na Gaeltachta and disperse its responsibilities among other agencies.

Tests of Faith

The Irish-speaking community has demonstrated time and time again its capacity to put its trust in the latest available expert report or strategy to address the issue of saving the language. It has learned to disregard the naysayers and the prognosticators of doom and gloom – and even the lack of implementation of these same reports or studies in the past has not dented their courage or faith. Some of the most significant milestones that tested the faith of Irish speakers and lifted their spirits in equal measure extended from the 1920s through to the present day.

---

[4] *Statement on the Irish Language / Ráiteas i leith na Gaeilge*, Government Publications, 2006.

[5] *Programme for Government 2007–2012*, Government Publications, 2007.

[6] *Coimisiún na Gaeltachta* (The Gaeltacht Commission). Department of Rural, Community and Gaeltacht Affairs, 2002.

[7] Report of the Special Group on Public Service Numbers and Expenditure Programmes, chaired by UCD Economist Mr Colm McCarthy, Department of Finance, July 2009.

The First Gaeltacht Commission, 1926, was a comprehensive report with a wide range of recommendations prepared within four years of the foundation of the new Irish Free State. However, the recommendations were not implemented as there was an economic recession at the time, and it was felt there was a prohibitive cost to implementation. *The Commission for the Revival of Irish*[8] was established in 1958 and completed in 1965. The Government laid the final report before both Houses of the Oireachtas (Dáil and Senate) in 1965. The report and recommendations were extensive and comprehensive. It is salutary to be reminded of the terms of reference which the Government gave to this Commission: 'Looking at the stage reached by the efforts to revive the Irish Language to consider and advice regarding the actions/measures which the community and the state should now take *for the purpose of proceeding more expeditiously* towards that objective'. Note that the objective was to proceed at a faster pace towards the objective of reviving the Irish language!

The then President, Éamon de Valera, addressed the inaugural meeting of the Commission on the 24 September 1958 and stated, amongst other things: 'You understand how necessary it is to save the Irish language and to do that as a matter of urgency. There are many people who are unhappy with the progress made. In this work, that of the Restoration of Irish, both the State and the People are involved. The State can do so much…but it is the people who will save the language in the final analysis. The Gaeltacht is the main natural support (base) of the language, and on the support-base, above all else, perhaps, will depend on the results of the efforts to save the language'. Comhairle na Gaeilge[9] (The Irish Language Advisory Group) sat for five years, 1969–74. The ink had scarcely dried on the Report and Recommendations of the Commission for the Restoration of Irish presented to the Houses of the Oireachtas (Parliament) in 1965 when four years later the Government appointed Comhairle na Gaeilge (The Irish Language Advisory Group) 'to assist in the review of policy in respect of the Irish language and to advise on its promotion in the future'. (In fact it was intended initially that Comhairle na Gaeilge would focus mainly on the issue of Irish in Education but the Government was persuaded to broaden its brief). The Comhairle published a wide range of reports and recommendations, including a broad range of education proposals, between the five years 1969–72. Chapter 1 of a major review of the place of Irish in the education system was just completed in 1973 when to the consternation of the Comhairle the government decided that it would no longer be necessary for pupils to achieve a pass in Irish in order to achieve a pass in the Leaving Certificate examination. In the event, only one recommendation by Comhairle na Gaeilge was implemented – the establishment of Bord na Gaeilge – though some others may have been absorbed and implemented later by that Board in due course. The Irish-speaking community kept faith, though their resolve was sorely tested!

The Death of the Irish Language – A Qualified Obituary[10] by Reg Hindley was published in 1990. He trumpeted that there were only 10,000 habitual speakers of Irish left in the Gaeltacht, stating 'I do not suggest this dogmatically but I feel it is safe to set this upper limit'. Of course, we all knew anecdotally that he was wrong, his methodology was questionable, and we handled the negative publicity fallout stoically! Only later did we realise, after mature consideration, that although his statistics and methodology were questionable, Hindley's assessment of the language issues and the factors impacting on the process of language change were linguistically sound.

---

[8] *The Commission for the Revival of Irish / An Coimisiún um Athbheochan na Gaeilge*, 1965, Foilseacháin an Rialtais/Government Publications, Dublin.

[9] *Comhairle na Gaeilge / The Irish Language Advisory Group*, Government Publications, Dublin, 1974.

[10] Reg Hindley, *The Death of the Irish Language: A Qualified Obituary*. London: Routledge, 1990.

We soon got a second jolt from a most unexpected source. That same year, 1990, Breandán Ó hEithir, renowned Irish-language broadcaster, writer and native Irish speaker from the Aran Islands was commissioned by Bord na Gaeilge to prepare a report on *'The Current State of Irish'*.[11] The Breandán Ó hEithir report gave the equivalent figure as Reg Hindley's study for the number of habitual speakers of Irish i.e. 10,000. The Ó hEithir report was leaked to the media rather than published by Bord na Gaeilge, which in effect disowned it.

However, even at the stark figure of 10,000 habitual Irish speakers Breandán Ó hEithir did not personally throw in the towel: 'Even though there are only about 10,000 native Irish speakers remaining ... that does not necessarily say that their situation cannot be improved. To that end, however, it is necessary to change the old ways of doing things and to make a herculean effort to incentivise/encourage/galvanise the Irish-speaking community and to set them working to this end in every possible way'.

After two such sobering reports and their accompanying stark statistics in 1990 Irish speakers and community leaders were getting rather accomplished at handling dire prognostications and moving on in anticipation of the next report or study!

The Gaeltacht Commission was established by the Government in 2002 to address the serious linguistic situation in the Gaeltacht. The Commission declared in its prefatory remarks that the establishment of the commission by the Government in 2002 gave a ray of hope to the community and friends of the Gaeltacht 'who are concerned for a considerable period of time that the Gaeltacht itself is withering away and disappearing before their eyes'. Their report and recommendations gave the basis for that ray of hope. They mentioned *en passant* that the establishment of the first Gaeltacht Commission in 1925 was the first major measure taken by the Government of the new Free State on behalf of the language but that the recommendations of that Commission were not implemented and that the necessary resources were not provided for that purpose.

The Commission's Report and Recommendations included a recommendation to prepare and implement a National Language Plan for Irish which would include specific targets and would set out the role of the people of the Gaeltacht in such a plan. It was this recommendation which prompted the then Minister for Community, Rural and Gaeltacht Affairs, Éamon Ó Cuív, T.D., to include a 20-Year Strategy for Irish in the Programme for Government in 2007–12. The Commission also recommended the commissioning of a Comprehensive Linguistic Survey of the use of Irish in the Gaeltacht. So, while the Commission made a total of 16 major recommendations in its report and may have felt that its report had fallen on deaf ears, it was the source of the two most powerful proposals that emerged as the basis for engendering a sense of faith and confidence in Irish language speakers.

The Government approved the funding and commissioning of the *Comprehensive Linguistic Study on the Use of Irish in the Gaeltacht* in 2007. This is a comprehensive linguistic study which shows the up-to-date numbers and geographical spread of Irish language usage throughout the Gaeltacht. The overall number of approximately 34,000 habitual speakers and the rapid process of language change identified in the study galvanised the Minister into action. Although a recommendation for a National Irish Language Plan had been accepted for inclusion by the Minister in the Programme for Government 2007–12, arising from the 2002 Coimisiún na Gaeltachta Report, this *Comprehensive Linguistic Study* was effectively the clarion call which galvanised the Minister and the government into action. The then Minister, Éamon Ó Cuív, grasped the initiative and set the process in train.

---

[11] Breandán Ó hEithir. A Report on the Current State of Irish. 1990. Commissioned by Bord na Gaeilge (now Foras na Gaeilge). Unpublished.

While the Comprehensive Linguistic Study shows the number of habitual speakers in the Gaeltacht as approximately 34,000, it was the stark evidence regarding the future viability of the Gaeltacht as an Irish-speaking community and the evidence of the rapid rate of language change, particularly among young schoolgoing children and teenagers, which awakened the politicians to action and which generated a serious level of concern among language speakers in general and practitioners in the field.

Present Situation

How does the Draft Strategy stand now coming into the last months of 2010 almost a year after its publication? It is in that state which reminds one of the response of the Kerryman when asked 'what height is Brandon Mountain?' (the highest mountain in Kerry) and he responded 'it depends on how low down you start climbing'?

It appears to me that we have to navigate a number of foothills yet before we face the real climb of the 20-Year Irish Language Strategy. On completion of the process of consultation with the heads of the most relevant departments of State regarding the expanded Draft Strategy the Minister will present it to the Cabinet Sub-Committee chaired by *An Taoiseach* (Prime Minister) and then it will be submitted to Government prior to Christmas 2010 or early in 2011. The final completed Strategy will then be launched publicly, its implementation will be set in train and will become the touchstone for Irish language revitalisation and promotional activity for the next twenty years.

Concerns and Assurances

This is a time for the people of the Gaeltacht and the Irish language community in general to keep their faith, a quality with which they are well-endowed as it has been forged in the furnace of large numbers of government and non-government reports since the foundation of the State. They have greater need than ever for that faith! While the Strategy seems set fair to emerge from the safe harbour of Ministerial and Cabinet Sub-Committee consideration in the near future storm clouds and breakers are already buffeting the mothership on the open seas. The Government is contending with the greatest economic crisis which has ever confronted the Irish State. I believe both the Department and Údarás na Gaeltachta will successfully navigate the budgetary constraints and be in a position to deliver on the Strategy on the basis of the incremental approach mapped out by the specialist advisers. The Department of Community, Equality and Gaeltacht Affairs and Údarás na Gaeltachta will be the two main vehicles charged with implementing the 20-Year Strategy. The Minister for Community, Equality and Gaeltacht Affairs has stated publicly a number of times – including to the Board of Údarás na Gaeltachta itself in July 2010 – that the future of both the Gaeltacht and of An tÚdarás are interwoven with the 20-Year Strategy. We are assured by the Minister that resources be available to implement the Strategy. I firmly believe that there is strong support for Údarás na Gaeltachta around the Cabinet table and while changes to its Board structure and statutory brief are proposed I am confident that a strong and refocused agency with a comprehensive range of economic, social and language functions will emerge from that process. Will Údarás na Gaeltachta retain its job-creation and enterprise promotion function? Our faith will be tested severely but I believe it will be recognised that a restructured Údarás na Gaeltachta without a strong enterprise function would be a shell deprived of a core element underpinning it. Co-ordination rather than amalgamation will achieve added value for the exchequer!

Questions Arising

A major question that arises – is the Draft Strategy fit for purpose as set out? Is it appropriately structured and geared for the achievement of the ambitious target of 250,000 habitual speakers of Irish by the end of the 20-year timescale? Is the elaborate linguistic scaffolding comprising the organisational and operational structures capable of engaging the Irish-speaking community and ensuring their engagement? I think we can say with reasonable confidence that the stratagem crafted by the linguistic specialists is fit for purpose and that adequate measures and mechanisms are included that respond to the core requirements and address the deficits of provision recognised by the authors of the Strategy, on certain conditions.

The Government already set out its Irish language vision and objectives in the *Statement on the Irish Language 2006*. The DCU Fiontar Team of specialists proposed a range of Primary and Secondary measures all interwoven expertly with the three essential pre-requisites for energetic revitalisation i.e. *capacity*, *opportunity* and *attitude*. The Strategy is underpinned by a rich base of experience, understanding and success which has been gleaned, not only from the national experience but also from 'the energetic language revitalisation efforts of many regions and countries across Europe and the world'.[12]

The Strategy has mined from that international research and thinking about language maintenance and revival a series of measures which the authors are confident can energise Irish language learning and use. The scaffolding they construct to achieve the ambitious political target of 250,000 habitual speakers of Irish within the 20-year timescale is a 'systemic approach, incorporating the relationships between language processes and their surrounding political, economic, social and educational environment as well as the links between various facets of language protection and promotion'. Extrapolating from a large body of evidence they concluded that language maintenance is enhanced when the conjunction of three processes is supportive: the *ability* (or capacity) to use the language; *opportunities* to use it; and *attitudes* towards its use. The strategy is organised around increasing linguistic capacity, creating and rewarding opportunities for use of Irish and fostering positive attitudes towards its use. The various measures are organised in clusters and designed to reinforce the interconnectedness of the overall policy plan with the aim of producing a coherent and ultimately self-sustaining long-term strategy. It is an integrated Strategy and cannot be cherry-picked on à la carte basis. All the elements are interwoven and interdependent.

However, the scaffolding needs to be constructed for the *implementation* of the Strategy. The apparatus of state administration in the Gaeltacht must be re-oriented towards this purpose and the three-pronged structure of *capacity*, *opportunity* and *attitude* embedded across the system.

Two main outstanding requirements or clarifications which I see – and which are fundamental and critical – are the basis and structure for the language planning process at local level, and the mechanism for community mobilisation, particularly in the Gaeltacht. The Irish-speaking community must take ownership of the process and engage proactively with it in all of the domains where language is spoken in their social networks. This requires leadership and management. The commitment and engagement of all stakeholders is crucial.

As President Éamon de Valera reminded the inaugural meeting of the Commission for the Revival of the Irish Language in 1958: '*both the State and the community are*

---

[12] *20-Year Strategy for the Irish Language* prepared for the Department of Community, Rural and Gaeltacht Affairs by Fiontar Dublin City University, February 2009.

involved in this work, and it is the community which in the final analysis will save the language'.[13] At this juncture it is not clear to me that sufficient thought has been given to the methods and initiatives required to mobilise a people's movement to become proactive in this challenging work. The Fiontar DCU Team recommended that an establishment year be spent gearing up at the start of the Strategy – the communication of the goals and content of the Strategy, setting up the required organisational and operational structures, allocation of the overall resources, and agreeing and establishing the ongoing monitoring, evaluation and modification procedure. Operational plans will be requested and received from all implementing public agencies and key priority measures will be established.

I do not believe it possible to achieve all this in a one-year establishment phase. We need to measure twice and cut once for this 20-year project. I strongly recommend a two-year preparatory period and that during that time, as well as the activities as set out in the establishment phase, a resources audit be done among all the implementing stakeholders, both state and voluntary; an intensive awareness campaign be organised involving all the state stakeholders and organised community groups throughout the Gaeltacht focussing on the aims of the Strategy, the methodology to be adopted and the role of local organised community groups in mobilising their communities. Amending legislation for both Údarás na Gaeltachta and An Chomhairle um Oideachas Gaeltachta agus Gaelscolaíochta (COGG) – the advisory body for Gaeltacht and Irish-medium schools – should be enacted, the tendering process for the National Centre of Excellence for Teaching Irish should be completed and all the preliminary work completed on the initiatives recommended for curricular development and teacher training. A large number of these establishment-phase initiatives can, in my view, be implemented without incurring any substantial additional resources.

Conclusion

The present state of Irish as a community and family language in the Gaeltacht is a matter of widespread concern among all those who view the language as the most unique aspect of our cultural heritage and of our cultural distinctiveness. Do the people of Ireland – or of the Gaeltacht for whom the language is part of what they are – have any realisation that a core aspect of our 'cultural heritage … is crumbling while we look on? Are we willing to shoulder the blame for having stood by and done nothing?'[14] The message needs to be carried to every family and community in the Gaeltacht, to Irish language speakers nationwide, and to that large population of people who have repeatedly shown in surveys that they are positively disposed towards the language, that everyone should be concerned because the loss of the Gaeltacht would not only be Ireland's loss but a loss to the world. The flipside of that coin is that saving and revitalising the language can and must be everyone's business through their active participation in the 20-Year Strategy for Irish. The State must provide access to every sector to participate so that *capacity*, *opportunity* and *attitude* become the familiar slogans of all who are mobilised into this movement. The 20-Year Strategy is our last great opportunity to halt the erosion and turn the tide. Is it fit for purpose? I believe it is. we?

---

[13] The Commission for the Revival of Irish/An Coimisiún um Athbheochan na Gaeilge. Final Report. 1965: Preface xi. Government Publications, Dublin.
[14] David Crystal. *Language Death*. Cambridge: Cambridge University Press, 2004.

Cur i Bhfeidhm/Géilliúlacht: Ceachtanna Foghlamtha ó Iniúchadh Scéimeanna Teanga

Colm Ó Coisdealbha

Tugadh isteach Acht na dTeangacha Oifigiúla le linn na bliana 2003, Acht a bhfuil de chuspóir aici an Ghaeilge a chur chun cinn chun críocha oifigiúil sa Stát. Déileálann an tAcht le réimsí áirithe den saol phoiblí, na dualgais atá leagtha ar eagraíochtaí stáit agus na cearta teanga atá bronnta ar an bpobal.

Sa gcuir i láthair seo, níl i gceist agam díriú go mion ar fhorálacha an Achta, ach ina ionad sin léargas áirithe a thabhairt ar na ceachtanna atá foghlamtha ón iniúchadh a bhíonn á dhéanamh againn ar chur i bhfeidhm an Achta i gcomhlachtaí poiblí ar fud an Stáit.

Thosaigh mise i mbun oibre le Oifig an Choimisinéara Teanga i bhfómhar na bliana 2008 agus feidhmíonn mar Bhainisteoir Géilliúlachta na heagraíochta. Is é an príomhchúram atá leagtha orm ná monatóireacht a dhéanamh ar an mbealach go bhfuil comhlachtaí poiblí nó eagraíochtaí stáit ag cur an Achta i bhfeidhm. Ní miste a luaigh gur oifig bheag atá againn le 6 baill foirne i láthair na huaire agus an Coimisinéir Teanga. Feidhmíonn an Oifig mar sheirbhís ombudsman maidir le gearáin i dtaobh seirbhís nó go deimhin easpa seirbhís a bheith ar fáil trí Ghaeilge. Nuair a smaoinítear go bhfuil isteach agus amach le 700 comhlacht poiblí ag teacht faoi scáth an Acht tuigtear an dúshlán atá ós ár gcomhair.

Baineann an chuid is mó de mo chuid oibre le faireachán a dhéanamh ar scéimeanna teanga agus is ar an taithí atá faighte againn sa réimse sin atáim chun díriú inniu, go háirithe na ceachtanna atá fogthlamtha againn ón bpróisis sin.

Mar chomhthéacs is ceart a rá gur uirlis atá sna scéimeanna teanga ina n-aontaíonn eagraíochtaí stáit na seirbhísí atá i gceist acu a sholáthar trí Ghaeilge. Ar ndóigh tá bunús reachtúil le geallltanais a dhaingnítear in aon scéim teanga agus tá dualgas dlíthiúil ar eagraíochtaí stáit an méid atá geallta a chur i bhfeidhm.

Nuair a tosaíodh ar an bpróisis iniúchta b'ábhar iontais do dhaoine áirithe é go ndéanfaí cur i bhfeidhm na ngealltanais sin a iniúchadh. 'Lip Service' a thugtar ar sin nó i bhfocail eile geallltanais gan bunús. Mar a dúirt oifigeach ó Roinn stáit amháin linn 'We never thought anyone would ask'. Nó mar a dúirt oifigeach eile linn 'These were dreams we had'. Tugann sé seo léargas ar an gcur chuige agus an dearcadh a bhí ag roinnt eagraíochtaí stáit i leith an phróisis seo. An príomh phointe anseo ná go bhfuil tábhacht mhór le iniúchadh lena chinntiú go gcuirtear i bhfeidhm geallltanais scéime. Samhlaím go mbeidh an méid céanna fíor leis an *Straitéis 20-Bliain don Ghaeilge* .

Ar mhaithe le soiléireacht is é an tAire Gnóthaí Pobail Comhionannais agus Gaeltachta a aontaíonn na scéimeanna teanga leis na eagraíochtaí stáit agus ní bhíonn aon bhaint ag Oifig an Choimisinéara Teanga leis an bpróisis sin. Is gnó dúinne áfach faireachán a dhéanamh ar an mbealach go gcuirtear na scéimeanna teanga mar aon le gnéithe eile den Acht i bhfeidhm.

Aontaíodh na chéad scéimeanna teanga le linn na bliana 2005 agus bhí an méid a bhí geallta iontu le bheith bainte amach le linn tréimhse trí bliana. Dá réir tugadh faoi na chéad iniúchtaí críochnúla le linn na bliana 2008 agus ó shin ar aghaidh. Cé go próisis í seo atá fós ag éabhlú is dóigh liom go bhfuil ceachtanna áirithe ag teacht chun cinn maidir leis an gcur chuige ginearálta agus go deimhin ag leibhéal na heagraíochta.

Ag díriú ar an dtimpeallacht go n-aontaítear scéimeanna teanga tá sé soiléir go dteastaíonn trí phríomh-thréith má táthar le scéim teanga a chur i bhfeidhm go sásúil, siad sin:

- Acmhainní cuí a bheith ar fáil
- Raon agus Caighdeán na seirbhísí atáthar le chur ar fáil a bheith soiléir agus socraithe ar bhonn náisiúnta nó earnála
- Monatóireacht leanúnach a bheith déanta

Acmhainní Cuí a Bheith ar Fáil

Ceann de na dúshláin is mó a bhaineann le feabhas a chur ar raon agus caighdeán na seirbhísí a sholáthraíonn eagraíochtaí stáit ná dóthain acmhainní a bheith ar fáil chuige sin. Gan soláthar ceart a bheith déanta d'acmhainn airgeadais ach níos dúshlánaigh fós d'acmhainn daonna is deacair d'eagraíochtaí aonaracha feabhas a chur ar raon agus caighdeán na seirbhísí atá le cur ar fáil trí Ghaeilge.

Feictear gur féidir dul chun cinn suntasach a dhéanamh chomh fada agus a bhaineann sé le bunábhar nó áiseanna ar nós foirmeacha iarratais, bileoga eolais, láithreáin gréasáin agus go deimhin córais ar-líne ach dóthain acmhainní airgeadais a bheith ar fáil chun an méid sin a bhaint amach. Nuair a smaoinítear go mbíonn na gealltanais a bhíonn tugtha i scéim teanga le baint amach thar tréimhse trí bliana is féidir an méid seo a bhaint amach go céimiúil.

Is ceist i bhfad níos anróití dóthain daoine le Gaeilge a bheith ar fáil d'eagraíocht chun cur lena gcumas seirbhís phearsanta trí Ghaeilge a chur ar fáil. Téann sé seo áfach go dtí croí lár an tairiscint seirbhíse trí Ghaeilge. Is beag an mhaith córais a bheith bunaithe a éascaíonn don chustaiméara a gcuid gnó a dhéanamh trí Ghaeilge nuair nach ann don fhoireann chun an tseirbhís sin a sheachadadh.

I bhformhór mór na scéimeanna teanga aithnítear an riachtanas go mbeadh foireann le Gaeilge ar fáil chun seirbhísí trí Ghaeilge a thairiscint. Aithnítear freisin go mbíonn an t-eagraíocht ag teacht ó phointe lag maidir le dóthain foirne le Gaeilge a bheith ar fáil dóibh. Minic go maith sonraítear trí bhealach ina dtiocfar i ngleic leis an easnamh foireann le Gaeilge, siad sin:

a. Breisoiliúint nó uas-scilliú
b. Sannadh foirne
c. Gníomh earcaíochta.

Tá sé tugtha faoi deara againn agus muid i mbun iniúchóireacht gur nós le eagraíochtaí san earnáil phoiblí béim a leagann ar chúrsaí oiliúna mar réiteach ar an easpa foireann le Gaeilge. Tá éascaíocht áirithe ag baint leis seo agus go deimhin is minic na deiseanna oiliúna seo a bheith ar fáil don fhoireann beag beann ar aon scéim teanga a bheith aontaithe.

Ag tógáil san áireamh an infheistiú ama is gá chun líofacht teanga a bhaint amach is deacair a fheiceáil cén chaoi go n-éireoidh le oiliúint inti féin, a fheabhas agus a bhíonn sí, leigheas a fháil ar an easnamh foirne le Gaeilge atá aitheanta sa earnáil phoiblí. Cinnte tacaíonn oiliúint le feasacht teanga a mhéadú ach is mór idir sin agus cumas a thabhairt do dhaoine a gcuid gnó gairmiúil a dhéanamh le lánéifeacht sa teanga sin.

Tá an Coimisinéir Teanga ar an dtaifead poiblí cheana féin ag nochtadh an tuairim gur gá tabhairt faoi ghníomh cothromacain earcaíochta chun leigheas a fháil ar an easpa foirne le Gaeilge atá fud fad an earnáil phoiblí. Is léir gurb é seo an bealach is stuama agus is réalaí le go bhfreagrófaí don easnamh atá ann i láthair na huaire.

Ar ndóigh is ceist níos goilliúnaigh í seo le linn cúlú eacnamaíochta agus an cosc ginearálta atá cúrsaí earcaíochta sa tseirbhís phoiblí san am i láthair. Ag an am céanna mura ndíreofar ar an gcroí cheist seo ar bhealach dírithe agus straitéiseach is deacair a fheiceáil cén chaoi go dtiocfaidh feabhas ar chumas an earnáil phoiblí dóthain daoine le Gaeilge a bheith ar fáil chun seirbhísí trí Ghaeilge a sholáthar.

Má ghlacaimid leis go dteastaíonn daoine le Gaeilge a bheith ar fáil chun seirbhís trí Ghaeilge a sholáthar, cén chaoi gur féidir le húsáideoirí nó custaiméirí a bheith muiníneach as rialtacht, as caighdeán ná as cinnteacht na seirbhíse a chuirtear ar fáil trí Ghaeilge nuair a admhaíonn eagraíochtaí nach bhfuil an foireann sin ar fáil dóibh?

Go deimhin is fánach dúinn a bheith ag trácht, fós ar aon nós, ar thairiscint gníomhach óna heagraíochtaí stáit nuair gur léir nach bhfuil ar chumas cuid mhór acu a leithéid a sholáthar ar aon bhealach bríomhar.

Tá sé mar cheann de chuspóirí an *Dréacht Straitéis 20-Bliain don Ghaeilge* go gcuirfí Acht na dTeangacha Oifigiúla i bhfeidhm go hiomlán. Tá sé ráite ann freisin go bhforbrófar cearta an phobail an Ghaeilge a úsáid agus iad ag plé leis an Stát agus le dreamanna eile agus go ndéanfaí socruithe cuí chun an méid seo a bhaint amach.

Is léir dúinne agus muid i mbun iniúchadh ar scéimeanna teanga gurbh í an constaic is mó a bhaineann leis an gcuspóir seo a bhaint amach ná dóthain foirne leis an cumas cuí teanga a bheith ar fáil.

Tá an méid seo aitheanta ag an gComhchoiste Oireachtais agus é molta acu go nglacfaí 'Gníomh cothromúcháin earcaíochta san Earnáil Phoiblí'. Moladh í seo a thagann leis an méid atá ráite cheana féin ag an gCoimisinéir Teanga.

Ag díriú ar an dara tréith a bhaineann le toradh éifeachtach a bheith ar scéim teanga, tá sé tábhachtach go mbeadh.

Raon agus Caighdeán na Seirbhísí

Raon agus Caighdeán na seirbhísí atáthar le chur ar fáil soiléir agus socraithe ar bhonn náisiúnta nó earnála. I láthair na huaire tá 102 scéim teanga aontaithe ag an Aire le comhlachtaí poiblí. Baineann 32 acu sin le Údaráis Áitiúla, 14 le Ranna Rialtais, 9 gcinn le Institiúid Oideachais tríú leibhéal, 9 gcinn le Coistí Gairmoideachais agus an chuid eile le réimse leathan eagraíochtaí Stáit. Aontaítear gach scéim teanga go haonarach le gach eagraíocht stáit agus ní mór cloí leis an gcreat atá leagtha amach sa Treoirleabhar atá buanaithe sa reachtaíocht agus an scéim teanga á aontú.

Is léir áfach agus muid i mbun iniúchadh ar scéimeanna teanga go mbíonn éagsúlacht mhór ag baint le gealltanais a bhíonn tugtha ag na heagraíochtaí atá ag soláthar seirbhísí don phobal fiú iad sin a bhíonn ag feidhmiú san earnáil chéanna. Is mór mar shampla an difríocht atá idir na gealltanais atá tugtha i scéim teanga Chomhairle Contae na Gaillimhe le hais ceann Chiarraí, Dhún na nGall agus Phort Láirge. Mar sin féin is údaráis áitiúla iad uile a sholáthraíonn na sórt céanna seirbhísí don phobal agus a fhreastalaíonn ar phobail le riachtanais aitheanta teanga.

Is amhlaidh an cás i measc údaráis áitiúla a fhreastalaíonn ar cheantair taobh amuigh den Ghaeltacht nó go deimhin i measc Ollscoileanna agus Institiúidí tríú leibhéal a bhfuil scéimeanna teanga aontaithe acu.

De bharr an easpa caighdeánú seo is deacair don duine aonair a bheith eolach ní áirím muiníneach maidir leis raon agus caighdeán na seirbhíse is féidir a bheith ag súil leis agus é nó í i mbun teagmhála le cuid éigin den stát.

Ceann de na hargóintí is mó a fhaigheann muid ó eagraíochtaí stáit ná an easpa éileamh a bhíonn ar sheirbhísí trí Ghaeilge. Is iomaí sin cúis a d'fhéadfadh a bheith leis an easpa éileamh seo ach go cinnte is féidir a rá nuair nach eol don phobal cén seirbhís ná caighdeán seirbhíse atá ar fáil dóibh gur lú an seans go lorgófar a leithéid de sheirbhís. Is cinnte freisin ar ndóigh go mbíonn an droch thaithí a bhíonn ag daoine a lorgaíonn seirbhís trí Ghaeilge ón stát mar spreagadh gan tabhairt faoi a leithéid a éileamh ar bhonn rialta

Ba mhór an chabhair do éifeacht scéimeanna teanga dá bhféadfadh an pobal a bheith eolach ar na seirbhísí is féidir leo a bheith ag súil leis i nGaeilge agus muiníneach as caighdeán na seirbhísí sin agus iad i mbun gnó leis an earnáil stáit.

Á chur seo i gcomhthéacs don *Straitéis 20-Bliain don Ghaeilge*, is léir go gcaithfidh an méid atáthar a thairiscint a bheith soiléir don phobal agus gan é a bheith léirithe mar thairiscint teibí.

Monatóireacht Leanúnach

Tá sé rí-shoiléir dúinn go dtacaíonn próisis éifeachtach monatóireacht, go hinmheánach agus go seachtrach, le spriocanna a bhaint amach. Gan a leithéid tá an baol ann go gcaillfí an fócas atá de dhíth chun go dtabharfaí faoi forfheidhmiú éifeachtach scéime. Tá tábhacht faoi leith leis sco nuair nach cuid lárnach de chultúr nó go deimhin feidhmiú na heagraíochta an méid atáthar ag iarraidh a bhaint amach ó thaobh cúrsaí teanga de.

Is pointe í seo atá aitheanta ag an gComhchoiste Oireachtais agus é molta acu go mbeadh córas monatóireachta agus measúnaithe bunaithe do chur i bhfeidhm na *Straitéise 20-Bliain don Ghaeilge*.

Ceann de na tréithe is tábhachtaí a bhaineann le scéimeanna teanga ná go bhfuil bunús reachtúil leo agus go bhfeidhmíonn siad mar chonradh dlíthiúil. Athraíonn sé seo an dinimic ó bheith ina thoilmhian go bheith ina dhualgas reachtúil.

Is léir dúinn óna hiniúchtaí a dhéanaimid go bhfuil tábhacht ar leith leis an bhfoclaíocht a úsáidtear agus gealltanais reachtúla á dtabhairt ag eagraíochtaí stáit i scéim teanga. Seachas aon ní eile tá sé tábhachtach nach mbeadh aon doiléireacht maidir leis na gealltanais a thugann an t-eagraíocht. Go simplí ba chóir go mbeifí in ann aon ghealltanas a thugtar a thomhais.

Mar atá ráite go minic 'What gets measured gets done'

Is teachtaireacht í seo atá ag dul i bhfeidhm ar eagraíochtaí stáit agus tuigtear dóibh go ndéanfar iniúchadh ar chomhlíonadh na ngealltanais a bhíonn tugtha. Ciallaíonn sin go bhfuil comhlachtaí stáit níos cúramaí faoina gealltanas atá siad sásta a thabhairt maidir leis na sórt seirbhísí a chuirfidh siad ar fáil do phobal na Gaeilge. Tá an chosúlacht air go bhfuil a rian seo le feiceáil sa dara babhta scéimeanna atá aontaithe le gairid agus comhdhlúthú á dhéanamh ar an méid a bhí aontaithe sna chéad scéimeanna.

Ag leibhéal na heagraíochta bíonn sé soiléir dúinn i gcónaí go n-éascaíonn dea-nósmhaireachtaí agus dea-chleachtais le cur i bhfeidhm éifeachtach a dhéanamh ar scéimeanna teanga.

Tá na tréithe seo uile inmhianaithe agus fiú riachtanach ag leibhéal na heagraíochta:

- Pleanáil agus anailís a bheith déanta ag an gcomhlacht poiblí ar a cumas gealltanais reachtúla a sheachadadh.
- Cúram a bheith déanta den chostas agus riachtanais acmhainní daonna a bhaineann le forfheidhmiú na scéime
- Úinéireacht glactha ag ardbhainistíocht an chomhlachta phoiblí ar an scéim teanga agus cultúr a chruthú a thacaíonn le seachadadh seirbhísí trí Ghaeilge.

- Plean agus struchtúir feiliúnach forfheidhmithe agus tuairiscithe agus córas monatóireachta feiliúnach a bheith forbartha lena chinntiú go ndéantar beart de réir briathar.

Mar chlabhsúr is ceart a rá go bhfuil dul chun cinn á dhéanamh san earnáil phoiblí maidir le cúrsaí Gaeilge. Níl aon cheist ach bhfuil an Ghaeilge níos feiceálaí anois ná mar a bhí riamh san earnáil phoiblí. Is cinnte go bhfuil teacht ar níos mó ábhar agus áiseanna ar nós foirmeacha iarratais agus láithreáin gréasáin.

Is í an chroí cheist anois ná cén chaoi go dtabharfar faoin easnamh foirne le Gaeilge sa earnáil phoiblí a réiteach, ceist nach mór freagra a fháil uirthi agus an *Straitéis 20-Bliain don Ghaeilge* á chur i bhfeidhm.

Ar deireadh cuirim i gcuimhne daoibh an méid a bhí le rá ag an gCoimisinéir Teanga faoin straitéis 20-bliain agus é ag seoladh an Tuarascáil Bhliantúil:

> Nuair a aontófar an Straitéis, tá sé riachtanach go gcuirfear tús éifeachtach agus gasta lena cur i bhfeidhm iomlán. Mura raibh seo le tarlú, agus go rabhthas le caitheamh léi mar a tharla le hiliomad tuarascálacha inmholta roimhe seo, b'fhearr dá gcaithfí i leataobh anois í ar mhaithe le tuilleadh soiniciúlachta a sheachaint. Beart de réir briathra a theastaíonn in áit focail mhilse.

Ensuring Implementation/Compliance: Lessons Learned from Auditing Language Schemes

Colm Ó Coisdealbha

The *Official Languages Act (2003)* was enacted with the aim of promoting the use of the Irish language for official purposes in the State. The Act deals with various aspects of the service, the responsibilities placed on public bodies, and the language rights bestowed on the public.

In this paper, I do not intend to dwell in detail on the various provisions of the Act; instead, I wish to provide an insight into the lessons that have been learnt from the audit process that is carried out to ensure compliance with the Act.

I began my role as compliance manager with the Office of an Coimisinéir Teanga in the Autumn of 2008. My primary responsibility is to monitor the compliance by public bodies with the Act. It is worth mentioning that the office is relatively small with six members of staff and an Coimisinéir Teanga. The office also acts as an ombudsman dealing with complaints in relation to services or indeed the lack of services through Irish. When one considers that approximately 700 public bodies are covered by the Act, one understands the challenge we face.

A significant part of my work relates to monitoring the implementation of language schemes and, accordingly, I intend to reflect on the lessons that we have learnt from that process.

To give this its proper context, it should be mentioned that language schemes form a legal instrument that sets out the commitments given by public bodies in relation to the delivery of services in Irish. Once a scheme has been agreed by the Minister, the public body is legally obliged to implement the commitments.

Initially, some people in the public service were greatly surprised that the implementation of these commitments would be audited. We refer to this as 'Lip Service' or in other words 'commitments without relevance'. As one official from a Government department remarked 'We never thought anyone would ask'. Or indeed as another official said to us 'These were dreams we had'. I believe that these comments provide an insight into the approach adopted by certain organisations in relation to this whole process. I imagine the same approach may be adopted in relation to the 20-Year Strategy.

To be clear, it is the Minister for Community, Equality and Gaeltacht who agrees the language scheme with the public bodies, and the Office of an Coimisinéir Teanga plays no part in this process. However we have responsibility for monitoring the way language schemes and other provisions of the Act are implemented.

The first language schemes were agreed during 2005 and the commitments were to be delivered over a three year period. As a result the first complete audits were conducted during 2008 and thereafter. Although this process is still evolving I believe that certain lessons can be learnt in relation to the approach at both a macro and a micro level.

Having considered the environment in which language schemes operate, I believe that the successful implementation of a language scheme depends on three key criteria being met. They are:

- Appropriate resources are available;
- Range and standard of services that the State wishes to provide in Irish are unambiguous and specified on a national basis or by sector;
- Continuous monitoring programme is adhered to.

The Provision of Appropriate Resources.

One of the greatest challenges that relates to improving the range and quality of services through Irish is the provision of proper resources. Without the provision of proper financial resources and, more challengingly, *human resources*, it is impossible for individual organisations to improve the range and quality of services to be provided through Irish.

More often than not we can see that significant improvements can be made in relation to the provision of basic materials and facilities such as application forms, information leaflets, websites and indeed on-line services once proper financial resources are made available. These services and expertise can be sourced from the private sector if need be. Once you consider that the commitments in a language scheme are to be delivered over a three year period, the associated cost can be borne in a planned manner.

Unfortunately, having sufficient staff with the necessary competency in Irish to provide personal service through Irish is a much more vexing question. This however goes to the heart of being able to deliver the service offering in Irish. It serves no purposes to have systems in place that facilitate the customer who wishes to do their business in Irish if there isn't sufficient staff to deliver those services.

Almost all language schemes recognise the requirement to have sufficient staff with competency in Irish. More often than not three methods are indentified to tackle this requirement

    a. Upskilling
    b. Staff deployment
    c. Recruitment.

We have noticed from the audit process that generally public bodies resort to training as their preferred choice to address this issue. This approach is easy to administer and tends to be already in place whether or not a language scheme is in existence.

When one considers the time investment that is required to achieve language proficiency it is difficult to see how training in itself, no matter how well it is structured, can address the issue of insufficient staff with Irish being available in the public sector. Obviously training has its merits especially to create general awareness of the language, but a significant chasm exists between this and the ability to conduct their business in Irish in a professional manner.

An Coimisinéir Teanga is already on record that he is of the opinion that recruitment is the only practical and realistic approach to deal with the issue of having insufficient staff with Irish in the public sector.

This is a much more sensitive issue in the current economic climate with a moratorium on recruitment in the public sector. At the same time, if this central question is not addressed in a clear and strategic manner it is difficult to see how the public sector can acquire the necessary staff to provide services through Irish.

If we accept the argument that you need people proficient in Irish in order to deliver services through Irish, how can service users or customers be confident as to the frequency, the standard and the quality of the service that is offered to them through Irish when organisations admit that suitably qualified staff with the necessary language competency are simply not available to them ?

Indeed it may be foolhardy, at this point in time at least, to promote a proactive offer when most public bodies are not in a position to provide such a service.

The *Draft 20-Year Strategy for the Irish Language 2010–2030* states that the *Official Languages Act (2003)* must be implemented in full. It also states that a person's right to use the Irish language when interacting with the State must be implemented and that arrangements must be put in place to ensure this.

It is obvious to us that, as a result of auditing the implementation of language schemes, the greatest obstacle to achieving this goal is the absence of sufficient number of staff with the appropriate language competency.

This difficulty has been recognised by the Oireachtas Subcommittee who have recommended that a recruitment strategy must be implemented in the public service to address this issue. This recommendation is very much in line with the approach of an Coimisinéir Teanga.

I now wish to turn to the second key characteristic necessary for the successful implementation of a language scheme.

Range and Standard of Services

The range and standard of services in Irish that the State wishes public bodies to provide should be unambiguous and a on a national basis or by sector. Currently 102 language schemes have been agreed by the Minister with public bodies. 32 of these relate to local authorities, 14 to Government departments, 9 to Third Level Institutions, 9 to Vocation Education Committees with the other schemes covering a wide range of organisations. Each scheme is agreed individually with each public body and they must adhere to the framework set out in the Guidebook which is part of the legislation.

As we conduct audit of language schemes it is very clear that a great deal of variation exists as to the various statutory commitments that have been given even as regards to bodies providing services within the same sector. There is for example a great deal of variation between the commitments outlined in the scheme agreed by Galway County Council versus those agreed by Kerry, Donegal and Waterford County Councils. However these are all local authorities providing similar or identical services to communities with the same language requirements.

The same can be said of other local authorities serving non-Gaeltacht communities or universities and other third level institutions that have agreed language schemes.

Due to this lack of commonality, it is difficult for the individual who wishes to access the service to be aware of, let alone have confidence in, the range and standard of services available from the public sector.

Lack of demand for services in Irish is the main argument put forward by many public bodies for the reluctance to properly deal with the provision of services through Irish. Although many reasons can be put forward for this lack of demand, I believe it is fair to say that, if the public is unaware of the services that are being provided or the quality they can expect, it lessens the chance that they will request those services in Irish. Indeed I believe that the poor service that people have become accustomed to for many years when requesting services through Irish has ensured that customers are less likely to demand such services in the future.

The effectiveness of a language scheme would be greatly assisted by the public knowing exactly what services they can expect in Irish from the various public bodies and having confidence in the availability of those services.

When considered in the context of the *20-Year Strategy for the Irish Language* it is obvious that it must be clear to the public what exactly is on offer and not presented as an intangible offering.

Continuous Monitoring

It is abundantly clear to us that an effective monitoring process, both internal and external, ensures that objectives are met. Without such a system there is a considerable risk that necessary focus required to ensure the effective implementation of a scheme is lost. This is all the more necessary when you are trying to achieve something that is not embedded in the organisation's culture or scope of operation.

This point has also been acknowledged by the Oireachtas subcommittee who have recommended that a monitoring and assessment process should be established for the implementation of the 20-Year Strategy.

One of the most important characteristics of a language scheme is its statutory effect: it operates as a legal contract. This status changes the dynamic of the commitments from being desirable to a statutory requirement.

One of the most obvious but important lessons that can be gained from the audit of language schemes is the actual words that are used by public bodies when giving statutory commitments. Statutory commitments must be clear and measurable. As is often said, 'What gets measured gets done.'

This is a message that is being realised by public bodies as we conduct our audits. Without such audits it is unlikely that the commitments would receive the same level of focus. However it is also noticeable that public bodies are becoming ever more careful in the commitments that they are providing in relation to the provision of services in Irish. This trait is visible in the second set of schemes recently agreed by public bodies with a consolidation of the commitments made in the first scheme

At the organisation level, it is clear that the application of best practices facilitate the effective implementation of language schemes. The following practices are desirable and necessary at the organisational level:

- Public bodies must plan for and analyse their ability to deliver statutory commitments
- Proper account be made for both the financial and human resources required to implement the scheme
- The public body's senior management accept ownership of the language scheme and create a culture that support the delivery of services in Irish
- An appropriate implementation plan, reporting structure and monitoring process is developed

In conclusion, it is fair to say that progress is being made in the public sector in relation to the delivery of services through Irish. Without a doubt Irish is much more visible in the public service today than has ever been the case. Also material and facilities such as application forms and websites are much more readily accessible.

However the central question remains, how to address to lack of personnel with Irish in the public service, a question that must be addressed with the implementation of the 20-Year Strategy.

Finally I would like to remind you of what an Coimisinéir Teanga had to say about the 20-Year Strategy whilst launching the Annual Report:

> When the Strategy is agreed, it is essential that its full implementation is commenced efficiently and speedily. If this were not to happen, as has been the fate of many well-intentioned reports in the past, it would be better that it be abandoned now to avoid more cynicism. Action not lip service is what is required.

Dátheangachas, Idé-eolaíocht agus an *Straitéis 20-Bliain don Ghaeilge*

John Walsh

Réamhrá

Cuirim romham san aiste seo cuid den díospóireacht maidir leis an dátheangachas Béarla-Gaeilge agus an *Straitéis 20-Bliain don Ghaeilge* a scrúdú, féachaint cad iad na hargóintí atá á ndéanamh faoin gceist seo i gcáipéisí beartais agus sa dioscúrsa poiblí faoi láthair (deireadh 2010). Ina dhiaidh sin, ba mhaith liom cíoradh a dhéanamh ar an mbonn idé-eolaíochta agus fealsúnach atá faoin idirghabháil a mholtar chun an Ghaeilge a threisiú mar theanga phobail agus teaghlaigh.

Tosóidh mé, mar sin, le roinnt fíricí a bhaineann le hábhar, faoi mar a fheicimse iad:

- Tá cainteoirí uile na Gaeilge, bídís sa Ghaeltacht nó lasmuigh di, dátheangach. Tá raon an-leathan cumais i gceist: ó chainteoirí dúchais arb í an Ghaeilge a bpríomhtheanga go cinnte go daoine a bhfuil an dá theanga ar a dtoil go cothrom acu go cainteoirí dúchais Béarla a bhfuil ardchumas Gaeilge acu go cainteoirí Béarla a bhfuil cumas feidhmeach i nGaeilge acu. Tá coincheap an chainteora Gaeilge an-chasta.
- Tá an Béarla agus an Ghaeilge ag maireachtáil taobh le taobh sa Ghaeltacht le fada an lá agus tá pobal na Gaeilge, sa chiall is leithne agus is fairsinge den fhocal sin (dlúthphobal Gaeltachta, gréasáin agus cainteoirí ócáideacha), i ngleic leis an dátheangachas mar fhíric de chuid an tsaoil laethúil.
- Léiríonn an fhianaise theangeolaíoch agus shochtheangeolaíoch go gcruthaíonn a leithéid de staid dhátheangach dúshláin mhóra do sheachadadh na Gaeilge traidisiúnta mar theanga phobail agus mar theanga teaghlaigh sa Ghaeltacht agus lasmuigh di.
- Tá idé-eolaíochtaí casta agus contrártha, go minic, i leith na Gaeilge agus an Bhéarla i measc phobal na Gaeilge.
- Straitéis don Ghaeilge ar fud stát na hÉireann, agus ní don Ghaeltacht amháin, atá á hullmhú faoi láthair. (deireadh 2010)

Is sa chomhthéacs sin, dar liom, is ceart dúinn an dátheangachas agus an *Straitéis 20-Bliain don Ghaeilge* a phlé. Is ceart chomh maith céanna ár gcúlraí pearsanta teanga agus ár n-idé-eolaíochtaí pearsanta i leith na Gaeilge a dhearbhú agus a aithint agus sinn ag plé na gceisteanna seo, cuid den 'prior ideological clarification' ar thagair Joshua Fishman dó (1991: 395, 397). Imríonn na nithe sin tionchar láidir ar ár gcuid oibre mar scoláirí atá gafa go pearsanta agus go gairmiúil le 'cúis' na Gaeilge. Faoi mar atá scríofa faoin gCorsaic: 'there are no neutral forms of endangered language advocacy' (Jaffe, 2008: 73). Mar sin, táimse ag labhairt libh inniu mar dhuine a chaith sealanna fada i nGaeltacht na Mumhan mar dhéagóir ag foghlaim na Gaeilge agus a dhein an cinneadh coinsiasach (nó idé-eolaíoch) an Ghaeilge a roghnú mar cheann de phríomhtheangacha a shaoil ina dhiaidh sin cé go mairim lasmuigh den Ghaeltacht. Gan an Ghaeltacht ní bheinn ag labhairt libh inniu ach aithním chomh maith céanna go bhfuil go leor cainteoirí cumasacha Gaeilge eile ann nach bhfuil luí láidir acu le ceantar Gaeltachta ar leith faoi mar atá agamsa. Den 72,148 cainteoir laethúil lasmuigh den chóras oideachais, tá níos mó ná dhá oiread ag maireachtáil lasmuigh den

Ghaeltacht ná mar a mhaireann laistigh di, cé nach ionann dlús na gcainteoirí in aon chor. Ní chuimsíonn an figiúr sin na cainteoirí cumasacha eile nach n-úsáideann an Ghaeilge chomh minic sin, ar chúiseanna éagsúla. Aithním chomh maith céanna go bhfuil a thuilleadh cainteoirí fós ann a bhfuil Gaeilge an-neamhthraidisiúnta ar fad á cleachtadh acu, go rialta nó go neamhrialta, agus glacaim leis gur cuid den chonstráid leathan, theibí sin, 'pobal na Gaeilge' iad. Mar sin, is mar theanga náisiúnta agus mhionlaithe araon a fhéachaimse ar an nGaeilge.

An réaltacht shochtheangeolaíoch

Ní feiniméan nua é an dátheangachas i gcás na Gaeilge, cé gur cinnte gur cuireadh dlús leis le caoga bliain anuas de bharr na mórathruithe deimeagrafacha agus sóisialta a thit amach sa Ghaeltacht agus sa tír trí chéile. Faoi mar a léiríonn Liam Mac Mathúna, tá fianaise den teagmháil teangacha idir an Ghaeilge agus an Béarla ar fáil sa litríocht chomh fada siar leis an dialann *Imeacht na nIarlaí* le Tadhg Ó Cianáin; nó sa dán suntasach *Beir mo beanocht go Dún Dalck* a chuirtear i mbéal fir ghnó darbh ainm Richard Weston agus a cumadh i Lováin i 1607/8; anuas go dtí an débhríochas cruthaitheach ba bhonn le saothair dála *Pairlement Chloinne Tomáis* sa 17ú haois agus *Stair Éamuinn Uí Chléire* a chum Seán Ó Neachtain san 18ú haois, tráth dá raibh an dátheangachas coitianta i mBaile Átha Cliath; agus anuas go dtí na hamhráin mhacarónacha i gCúige Laighean agus Uladh san 18/9ú haois. An bhuntéis atá ag Mac Mathúna ná go raibh feidhmeanna sóisialta agus/nó polaitiúla ag an gcódmheascadh Gaeilge-Béarla sa litríocht agus go minic gur scáthán é ar chleachtas nó ar idé-eolaíocht teanga an phobail ina raibh an Ghaeilge in úsáid go gníomhach nó ina raibh tuiscint fhulangach ag cuid den phobal uirthi. Ní go dtí gur tháinig ann d'idé-eolaíocht na hathbheochana ag tús an 20ú haois agus don fhlosc íonghlanta a ghabh léi a cuireadh deireadh obann leis an nglacadh a bhí leis an mBéarla i nGaeilge na litríochta. Ba chosc sealadach é sin, dar ndóigh, agus tá scríbhneoirí éagsúla ag léiriú réaltacht na sochtheangeolaíochta in Éirinn ina saothair le daichead éigin bliain anuas (Mac Mathúna, 2007: 266; feic chomh maith Nic Eoin, 2005).

Tá taighde á dhéanamh agam le tamall faoin mBreac-Ghaeltacht – téarma agus coincheap de chuid an tSaorstáit – a thagraíonn do na ceantair bhreaca sin, a raibh idir Ghaeilge agus Bhéarla á labhairt iontu, a aithníodh go hoifigiúil ó 1926 go 1956 nuair a cuireadh deireadh le 'Breac-Ghaeltacht' mar choincheap. Léiríonn na foinsí atá á scrúdú agam – idir fhoinsí béaloidis agus chuntais chomhaimseartha eile – a chasta agus a bhí staid shochtheangeolaíoch na gceantar sin ag an am. Tá ainmfhocal breá teibí ag Niall Ó Dónaill ar a leithéid sin de staid, 'brice', agus is cruinn an cur síos é ar an mBreac-Ghaeltacht agus, go deimhin ar Ghaeltacht an lae inniu. Mar is eol dúinn, mhol an *Staidéar Cuimsitheach Teangeolaíoch ar Úsáid na Gaeilge sa Ghaeltacht* (SCT feasta) go rangófaí gach ceantar Gaeltachta de réir neart na Gaeilge ann agus go n-aithneofaí trí shaghas Gaeltachta go reachtúil: A, B agus C. Tá níos mó ná macalla den Bhreac-Ghaeltacht ansin. Aitheantas cuí is ea é sin, dar liom, go bhfuil an-éagsúlacht shochtheangeolaíoch sa Ghaeltacht anois.

Tá tréith chomónta ag na pobail Ghaeilge sin go léir, bídís ina bpobail dhlútha Ghaeilge i gCorca Dhuibhne nó ar an gCeathrú Rua, ina ngréasáin ghníomhacha i gCúil Aodha nó sa Rinn, nó ina ngréasáin níos scáinte i ndeisceart Bhaile Átha Cliath nó i gContae Chill Dara: táid ar fad i ngleic leis an mBéarla ar bhonn laethúil agus táid go léir dátheangach toisc go dtiteann ualach an dátheangachais i gcónaí ar chainteoir na mionteanga, 'an dátheangachas aontreoch', mar a tugadh air le déanaí. Fillfidh mé ar an dátheangachas aontreoch ar ball.

An Dátheangachas agus Cáipéisí Beartais

Sa rannóg seo, pléifidh mé na cáipéisí beartais a bhfuil baint acu leis an Straitéis, féachaint cén idé-eolaíocht i leith an dátheangachais a léirítear iontu. Sula dtosóidh mé an cur síos sin, ba mhaith liom a dhearbhú go bhfuil dearcadh dearfach agam féin i leith na Straitéise, nó ar a laghad i leith na dréacht-cháipéise a foilsíodh i 2009. Creidim gurb í an togra beartais is tábhachtaí agus is uileghabhálaí i réimse na Gaeilge le nach mór caoga bliain, cé go bhfuil imní orm go gcuirfidh an ghéarchéim eacnamaíoch de dhroim seoil í. Tá laigí ar ar foilsíodh go dtí seo go cinnte, ach i dtéarmaí ginearálta is dóigh liom gur aimsíodh cothromaíocht mhaith idir riachtanais na Gaeltachta agus na coda eile den tír.

Beidh idir cháipéisí a bhfuil baint ghabhlánach acu leis an Straitéis agus chroícháipéisí na Straitéise féin faoi chaibidil agam san aiste seo. Ní hionann an stádas atá ag na cáipéisí seo: cáipéisí rialtais is ea cuid acu, cáipéisí comhairleacha, a ullmhaíodh ar iarratas ón Roinn Gnóthaí Pobail, Tuaithe agus Gaeltachta (mar a bhí) atá i gcuid eile agus tá cáipéis amháin ann ina dtugtar tuairimí an aosa pholaitiúil i leith na Straitéise. Seo a leanas na foinsí a scrúdófar:

- Ráiteas an Rialtais i leith na Gaeilge (2006)
- An Staidéar Cuimsitheach Teangeolaíoch ar Úsáid na Gaeilge sa Ghaeltacht (2007)
- Tuarascáil FIONTAR (2009)
- An Dréacht-Straitéis féin (2009)
- Tuarascáil an Chomhchoiste Oireachtais um Ghnóthaí Gaeltachta (2010).

Den chuid is mó, tá meon dearfach i leith an dátheangachais le brath ar na cáipéisí rialtais a bhaineann leis an Straitéis 20-Bliain, ach níl an tacaíocht chéanna le brath ar chuid de na cáipéisí comhairleacha.

Ráiteas an Rialtais
Luaitear an dátheangachas i *Ráiteas an Rialtais*, cáipéis a leag síos bunchloch na Straitéise reatha. Léirítear dearcadh dearfach i leith an dátheangachais, cé nach sainmhínítear é, ach dearbhaítear chomh maith go dtabharfar tacaíocht don Ghaeltacht 'mar phobal labhartha Gaeilge':

> Is í aidhm pholasaí an rialtais i leith na Gaeilge ná úsáid agus eolas ar an nGaeilge a mhéadú mar theanga phobail ar bhonn céimiúil.
> Is aidhm ar leith de chuid an Rialtais í a chinntiú go bhfuil an oiread saoránach gus is féidir dátheangach i nGaeilge agus i mBéarla.
> Is í aidhm pholasaí an Rialtais freisin an Ghaeltacht a neartú mar phobal labhartha Gaeilge agus chomh maith leis sin, líon na dteaghlach, atá ina gcónaí laistigh den Stát a bhfuil an Ghaeilge mar theanga laethúil chumarsáide acu, a mhéadú. (Rialtas na hÉireann, 2006: 7)

Faoi mar a deineadh sa *Pháipéar Bán um Athbheochan na Gaeilge* a foilsíodh i 1965, leagtar béim ar thábhacht an Bhéarla d'Éirinn chomh maith:

> Aithníonn an Rialtas an buntáiste mór freisin dá gcuid saoránach líofacht Béarla a bheith acu, an teanga is mó úsáide i ngnóthaí

idirnáisiúnta. Geallann an Rialtas go gcinnteoidh siad go gcoinneofar an buntáiste seo trí shochaí dhátheangach a fhorbairt ina mbeidh an oiread daoine agus is féidir in ann Gaeilge agus Béarla a úsáid chomh héasca lena chéile. (Rialtas na hÉireann, 2006: 9)

An Staidéar Cuimsitheach Teangeolaíoch

Ní luaitear an téarma 'dátheangachas' ach go hannamh san SCT ná ní phléitear an coincheap go mion. Féadfar a thuiscint ó roinnt den taighde agus ó na moltaí, áfach, gur tacaíocht don aonteangachas Gaeilge atá á mholadh, ar a laghad sa chuid sin den Ghaeltacht a dtabharfaí 'catagóir A' uirthi dá nglacfaí leis an athrangú a mholtar:

> Dá bhrí sin, má táthar le dlús na gcainteoirí Gaeilge sna limistéir Ghaeltachta a chaomhnú agus, ar an mbealach sin, cosaint a thabhairt don teanga mar phríomhtheanga theaghlaigh agus phobail sna limistéir atá i gceist, caithfear na gluaiseachtaí déimeagrafacha seo a bhainistiú go cúramach le go mbainfear an tairbhe shóisialta agus eacnamaíoch is fearr astu, gan dochar a dhéanamh do staid na Gaeilge mar theanga theaghlaigh agus phobail. (Ó Giollagáin *et al*., 2007: 499-500)
>
> Is léir, mar sin, gurb é an cuspóir is cóir a bheith leis an bpleanáil teanga i limistéir Chatagóir A ná *dlús na gcainteoirí Gaeilge a chosaint iontu* agus tacaíocht a chur ar fáil a dhéanfaidh buanú ar úsáid na Gaeilge mar theanga theaghlaigh agus phobail iontu. Beidh cuspóir eile i gceist leis an bpleanáil teanga i limistéir Chatagóirí B agus C, .i. na gréasáin aitheantais agus institiúideacha Gaeilge iontu a bhuanú agus a neartú. Ar ndóigh, agus an obair seo á déanamh, is é an príomhchuspóir a bheidh leis i ndeireadh an lae an chéad ghlúin eile agus na glúine tuismitheoirí óga Gaeltachta ina dhiaidh sin a spreagadh agus a chumasú *lena gclann a thógáil le Gaeilge*. (Ó Giollagáin *et al.*, 2007: 514, liomsa an bhéim)

Fillfidh mé ar théama seo an aonteangachais Ghaeilge thíos.

Tuarascáil FIONTAR

Dearcadh an-dearfach i leith an dátheangachais a léirítear i dtuarascáil FIONTAR, tuarascáil a bunaíodh ar thuairimí saineolaithe idirnáisiúnta ar an mbeartas teanga, ar iarratas ón Roinn Gnóthaí Pobail, Tuaithe agus Gaeltachta. Luaitear buntáistí an Bhéarla arís chomh maith:

> Tá an t-ádh ar Éirinn go bhfuil an Béarla, ceann de na foirmeacha cumarsáide is forleithne ar domhan, mar an teanga oifigiúil eile aici ... Tá deis d'inniúlacht dátheangach ar fud an daonra ach eolas níos leithne ar an nGaeilge agus a húsáid ar bhonn níos leithne a spreagadh. Is ionchas tábhachtach é sin a thacódh leis na leasanna is leithne ó thaobh na hÉireann, idir leasanna sóisialta, oideachasúla, teicneolaíochta agus leasanna eacnamaíocha. Níl tacaíocht fhorasach de dhíth ar an mBéarla agus bhí neart fianaise riamh ann ar ardéirim an Éireannaigh ó thaobh úsáid na teanga sin. Tá tuairisc fhorleathan ar fáil faoi oilteacht in dhá theanga, go háirithe sa dátheangachas ardoilte a fhorbraítear go luath sa saol, gurb iomaí tairbhe a thagann aisti don leanbh, idir thairbhe

chognaíoch agus tairbhe ó thaobh dearcaidh de. Is é atá i gceist, dá réir sin, le hardleibhéil d'eolas gníomhach ar an nGaeilge a chur leis an mBéarla ná plean don dátheangachas ar fud dhaonra na hÉireann agus acmhainní agus tairbhí intleachtúla, socheacnamaíocha agus cultúrtha don duine aonair agus ar deireadh thiar don tsochaí ar fad.

Ainneoin gur ar an nGaeilge a dhírítear an Straitéis áirithe seo agus an polasaí foriomlán ar comhpháirt de í, de bharr ról uathúil na Gaeilge agus an ghátair ina bhfuil sí, ba chóir breathnú ar an Straitéis mar ní atá comhlántach i leith pleanála teanga níos leithne chun acmhainní cumarsáide mhuintir na hÉireann a fhorbairt i saol ilteangach domhanda. D'fhéadfadh an dátheangachas Gaeilge-Béarla a bheith ina ardán táirgiúil ó thaobh teangacha breise a shealbhú, a bheith ina infheistíocht i gcaipiteal daonna a chuid saoránach, d'fhéadfadh sé tacú le comhtháthú sóisialta agus le dlúthpháirtíocht i measc na muintire agus dálaí a chur ar fáil do shochaí atá saibhir ó thaobh cultúir de agus sochaí a tharraingíonn níos fearr le chéile. (FIONTAR, 2009: 10)

Tá tuarascáil FIONTAR lomlán de thagairtí do bhuntáistí an dátheangachais, mar shampla an ceann seo sa rannóg faoin oideachas:

Moltar go ndéanfaí faisnéis a tháirgeadh d'earnálacha éagsúla daoine gairmiúla scoile amhail teiripeoirí urlabhra, treoirchomhairleoirí, comhairleoirí gairme agus daoine eile chun *buntáistí an dátheangachais a chur chun cinn*, go háirithe an buntáiste a bhaineann le foghlaim na Gaeilge. (FIONTAR, 2009: 24, liomsa an bhéim)

Is beag tagairt don Ghaeltacht a dhéanann tuarascáil FIONTAR toisc, a deir siad, go raibh an SCT ar fáil don rialtas cheana.

Dréacht-Straitéis an Rialtais
Arís eile, dearcadh dearfach i leith an dátheangachais a léirítear sa Dréacht-Straitéis a d'fhoilsigh an rialtas i 2009. Athdhearbhaítear na bunphrionsabail i leith an dátheangachais a bhí i *Ráiteas an Rialtais* 2006. Athdhearbhaítear chomh maith céanna aidhm an rialtais i leith na Gaeltachta: soláthrófar tacaíocht teanga don Ghaeltacht 'mar phobal labhartha Gaeilge'. Mar sin féin, nuair a luaitear an Ghaeltacht ina dhiaidh sin sa cháipéis, glactar leis go mbeidh tuismitheoirí ag iarraidh an Ghaeilge agus an Béarla *araon* a thabhairt dá gclann. Ní dhéantar tagairt do pháistí a bheith á dtógáil le Gaeilge *mar phríomhtheanga* ná *mar aonteanga*. Mar sampla, tá an méid seo scríofa sa rannóg faoin gcóras oideachais:

Cuirfear ábhair eolais agus acmhainní ar fáil do chatagóirí éagsúla de ghairmeacha scoile mar theiripigh cainte, comhairleoirí gairme, comhairleoirí slite beatha agus daoine eile a chuirfidh chun cinn *na buntáistí a bhaineann leis an dátheangachas* (go háirithe foghlaim na Gaeilge). (An Roinn Gnóthaí Pobail, Tuaithe agus Gaeltachta, 2009: 22, liomsa an bhéim)

Sa rannóg 'An Teaghlach ag cur na Teanga ar Aghaidh: Idirghabháil go luath', tá scríofa:

Teastaíonn treoir agus comhairle ó theaghlaigh ina labhraíonn na tuismitheoirí Gaeilge faoina gcuid leanaí a thógáil *agus iad cothrom ó thaobh an dá theanga* go háirithe mura labhraíonn ach tuismitheoir amháin an teanga.

Baineann na hidirghabhálacha atá molta sa réimse seo roinnt le spreagadh agus tacaíocht a thabhairt do thuismitheoirí *a gcuid a leanaí a thógáil leis an dátheangachas* agus roinnt le heolas fíriceach a chur ar fáil agus cur le feasacht faoi na buntáistí nádúrtha a bhaineann leis an leanbh a bheith ábalta níos mó ná teanga amháin a labhairt. (An Roinn Gnóthaí Pobail, Tuaithe agus Gaeltachta, 2009: 30, liomsa an bhéim)

Maidir le tíortha dátheangacha eile, scríobhtar: 'Tá go leor taithí i ndlínsí eile lena n-áirítear sa Bhreatain Bheag agus i dTír na mBascach maidir le tacaíocht do thuismitheoirí a bhíonn ag tógáil clainne *le dhá theanga*' (31). Agus faoi thionscnaimh phleanála teanga lasmuigh den Ghaeltacht, deirtear go dtabharfar: '[c]omhairle ... do thuismitheoirí nua ar mian leo a gcuid leanaí *a thógáil leis an dátheangachas*' (35, liomsa an bhéim sa dá chás).

Tuarascáil an Chomhchoiste Oireachtais
As measc na gcáipéisí beartais go léir, is í Tuarascáil an Chomhchoiste Oireachtais um Ghnóthaí Turasóireachta, Cultúir, Spóirt, Pobail, Comhionannais agus Gaeltachta is diúltaí i leith an dátheangachais. Bunaíodh an Tuarascáil seo ar thréimhse fhada chomhairliúcháin leis an bpobal agus ar chruinnithe poiblí idir polaiteoirí agus ionadaithe thar ceann na n-eagraíochtaí Gaeilge agus Gaeltachta:

Is léir ón bpróiseas comhairliúcháin go bhfuil imní ar phobal na Gaeltachta maidir le himpleachtaí polasaithe dátheangachais i gcás na Gaeltachta agus a hinmharthanacht mar phobal labhairt (sic) na Gaeilge. Tá sé léirithe ag an Staidéar Cuimsitheach nach maireann mionteanga i sochaí dátheangach (sic). Is gá mionteanga a shealbhú ar dtús, agus a úsáid mar phríomhtheanga má táthar chun í a chaomhnú.
Glactar leis go bhfuil ról dearfach ag an dátheangachas mar mhodh cumarsáide na bpobal seo laistigh de theaghlaigh áirithe. Ach i neart aighneachtaí a cuireadh os comhair an Choiste moladh nár chóir go mbeadh ról ag an dátheangachas i saol poiblí na Gaeltachta. Aithníonn an Coiste tábhacht an dátheangachais a chur chun cinn ar fud na hÉireann ach aontaíonn an Coiste leis an tuairim mhéaite a léiríodh sna haighneachtaí; ní shíleann an Coiste gur cheart an dátheangachas a úsáid mar mhodh cumarsáide poiblí laistigh den Ghaeltacht ...
Moladh 22: Dearbhú a chur sa Straitéis nach mbainfidh polasaí dátheangachais leis an nGaeltacht agus nach gcuirfear i bhfeidhm sa Ghaeltacht é. (An Comhchoiste um Ghnóthaí Turasóireachta srl., 2010: 21, béim sa bhunleagan)

Tá sé thar a bheith radacach a éileamh go gcuirfí deireadh leis 'an dátheangachas i saol poiblí na Gaeltachta' nó a mhaíomh nár cheart 'an dátheangachas a úsáid mar mhodh cumarsáide poiblí laistigh den Ghaeltacht'. Go deimhin féin, d'áiteoinn gur éileamh doshroichte agus dodhéanta é, i bhfianaise a bhrice agus atá an Ghaeltacht go teangeolaíoch anois. Bhíos féin i láthair ag an gcruinniú poiblí a reáchtáil an

Comhchoiste Oireachtais in Indreabhán i mí Feabhra 2010. Is cinnte gur chuir go leor in iúl – faoi mar a chuir an SCT rompu – go raibh páistí Gaeltachta ar cainteoirí dúchais iad thíos go mór leis na socruithe reatha i scoileanna na Gaeltachta. Tá go leor fianaise ar fáil gur amhlaidh atá. Ní cuimhin liom gur iarr aon ghrúpa pobail go ndéanfaí beart chomh radacach leis an mBéarla a ruaigeadh ón nGaeltacht, áfach. Go deimhin féin, is dóigh liom gur míléamh é an t-éileamh sin ar imní roinnt eagras Gaeltachta faoi úsáid an dá theanga i gcóras oideachais na Gaeltachta agus faoi chleachtas teanga príobháideach. Mar sin féin, tá gnéithe eile den ráiteas thuas a bhfuil macalla díobh i gcuid den dioscúrsa poiblí faoin dátheangachas. Pléifidh mé cuid den dioscúrsa sin anois.

An dátheangachas agus an dioscúrsa poiblí

Sa rannóg seo ba mhaith liom cuid den dioscúrsa poiblí mar gheall ar an dátheangachas a scrúdú, féachaint cén léiriú a thugtar ann ar idé-eolaíochtaí teanga. Ní fhéadfadh caint ghearr mar seo cothrom na Féinne a thabhairt don ualach mór alt agus páipéar taighde a foilsíodh faoin ábhar seo le dornán blianta anuas. Ní chuirim romham anseo ach blaiseadh beag den díospóireacht faoin nGaeilge sa Ghaeltacht agus sa chuid eile den tír a chur os bhur gcomhair, cuid di a tharla sular cuireadh tús le hullmhú na Straitéise agus cuid eile a tharla ina dhiaidh sin.

Náisiúnta

Tá léiriú suimiúil ar nádúr an dátheangachais lasmuigh den Ghaeltacht agus den idé-eolaíocht ina leith le fáil in Acht na dTeangacha Oifigiúla, dlí a bhfuil sé d'aidhm aige cur de réir a chéile le soláthar seirbhísí poiblí i nGaeilge. Seirbhísí poiblí ar ardchaighdeán Gaeilge do chainteoirí líofa Gaeilge a theastaigh ó na heagraíochtaí (cuid díobh sa Ghaeltacht) a chuaigh i mbun feachtais ar son an Achta (feic mar shampla, Comhdháil Náisiúnta na Gaeilge, 1998). Go deimhin, léiríonn foclaíocht na reachtaíochta féin gurb í úsáid fhoirmeálta na Gaeilge i réimsí áirithe den saol poiblí atá i gceist:

> Acht chun úsáid na Gaeilge a chur chun cinn chun críoch oifigiúil sa stát; chun socrú a dhéanamh maidir le dhá theanga oifigiúla an stáit a úsáid in imeachtaí parlaiminte, in achtanna an Oireachtais, i riaradh an cheartais, le linn cumarsáid a dhéanamh leis an bpobal nó seirbhísí a sholáthar don phobal agus le linn obair comhlachtaí poiblí a dhéanamh. (Réamhrá, Acht na dTeangacha Oifigiúla)

Is trí mheán na scéime teanga – plean inmheánach Gaeilge a aontaíonn comhlacht poiblí – a chuirfear an chuid is tábhachtaí de na seirbhísí Gaeilge ar fáil. Tá cuid de na scéimeanna, go háirithe iadsan a bhaineann le ceantar Gaeltachta, an-láidir agus déantar gealltanais shuntasacha iontu maidir le soláthar seirbhísí i nGaeilge. I gcás comhlachtaí poiblí eile, bhí an tairseach Gaeilge chomh híseal sin sular tháinig ann don Acht nach bhféadfaí a bheith ag súil le forálacha láidre iontu. Feictear dom, áfach, go bhfuil coimhlint bhunúsach idé-eolaíochta idir aidhmeanna na scéimeanna is laige agus aidhmeanna na reachtaíochta féin. Tá na scéimeanna sin lomlán de thagairtí don fheiniméan a dtabharfainnse 'idé-eolaíocht an chúpla focal' air. Idé-eolaíocht teanga an-fhorleathan agus an-láidir is ea í seo in Éirinn i measc an dreama sin a mhaíonn go bhfuil Gaeilge éigin acu – tuairim is 1.6 milliún duine – cé nár deineadh taighde mar is ceart ar an idé-eolaíocht sin fós. Mar sin, tá na scéimeanna laga breac le gealltanais go n-úsáidfear cúpla focal Gaeilge, nó na bunbheannachtaí simplí, nó Gaeilge shimplí leis an bpobal nó go gcruthófar 'atmaisféar' dátheangach, nó blaiseadh den dátheangachas ag cruinnithe poiblí na n-údarás áitiúil agus mar sin de. Sna scéimeanna sin, cuirtear béim láidir ar ranganna Gaeilge d'fhoireann na gcomhlachtaí poiblí chun go mbeidh ar a gcumas seirbhís Ghaeilge a sholáthar, bunaithe ar an tuiscint – dar liom – gur leor beagán oiliúna chun daoine a bhfuil an cúpla focal acu cheana a thabhairt go dtí an leibhéal cuí (tuiscint an-earráideach faoi mar a léiríonn an taithí i dtíortha dátheangacha eile dúinn; feic an plé in Walsh and McLeod, 2008: 30). Is fada idir cuid de na gealltanais theoranta sin agus seirbhísí i nGaeilge a sholáthar do chainteoirí líofa. Ní raibh sé i gceist ag an reachtaíocht riamh go ndéanfaí institiúidiú ar an gcúpla focal ach sin a tharla i go leor de na scéimeanna luatha, pleananna reachtúla a dhaingnigh an tAire Gnóthaí Pobail, Tuaithe agus Gaeltachta. Toisc nach cainteoirí líofa Gaeilge i gcónaí iad na hoifigigh a ullmhaíonn na scéimeanna, d'fhéadfaí a bheith ag súil leis an idé-eolaíocht sin iontu. Mar sin féin, is coimhlint bhunúsach idé-eolaíochta í seo i gcroílár Acht na dTeangacha Oifigiúla agus d'áiteoinn gur bac ar fheidhmiú éifeachtach an Achta í. Is furasta do chainteoirí gníomhacha, líofa Gaeilge caitheamh anuas ar lucht an chúpla focal, ach is idé-eolaíocht an-tábhachtach í sin a chomhlíonann feidhm shiombalach do go leor Éireannach. Cháin an sochtheangeolaí Pádraig Ó Riagáin an tAcht toisc nár aithníodh ann an tacaíocht bhog chultúrtha a thugann muintir na hÉireann don Ghaeilge (2008: 55). Níor chuige sin an tAcht, ach má táthar chun freastal ar gach cuid de phobal na Gaeilge – dá scaipthe agus dá ilghnéithí é, lucht lagchumais agus dea-mhéine chomh maith le cainteoirí ócáideacha agus gníomhacha – ba mhaith an mhaise don Straitéis aitheantas éigin a thabhairt don idé-eolaíocht fhulangach, fhorleathan sin chomh maith (feic chomh maith Walsh, 2011: 39-53).

Gaeltacht

Tá díospóireacht bhríomhar faoin dátheangachas sa Ghaeltacht ar siúl le tamall i measc scoláirí Gaeilge. Ní lia duine ná tuairim agus tá éagsúlacht dearcaí ann. Táim féin páirteach sa díospóireacht seo, mar Ghaeilgeoir ar cás leis dán na teanga agus mar léachtóir agus taighdeoir sa réimse seo. Mo dhála féin, tá na scoláirí eile gafa go pearsanta le cás na Gaeilge, ach tá difríocht béime i gceist. Tá daoine áirithe den tuairim gur cheart spás a dhearbhú don Ghaeilge ach gur gá feidhm agus ról an Bhéarla sa Ghaeltacht a aithint chomh maith. Creideann scoláirí eile go gcaithfear an dátheangachas a shrianadh sa Ghaeltacht ar an mbonn nach mairfidh mionteanga i gcomhthéacs dátheangach, más mórtheanga í an teanga eile. Fite fuaite leis seo, cuireann roinnt údar breis béime (nó an bhéim go léir) ar an nGaeltacht agus tá scoláirí eile den tuairim gurbh fhearr an Ghaeltacht a chíoradh i gcomhthéacs náisiúnta.

Ar na scoláirí sin a bhfuil ról an Bhéarla sa Ghaeltacht pléite acu tá Máire Ní Neachtain. Dar léi, ní féidir neamhshuim a dhéanamh den cheist sin:

> Tá na ceantair atá ar imeall na gcatagóirí [SCT] go mór faoi bhrú agus caithfear cuidiú leo teacht ar straitéisí a chinnteoidh go gcoinneoidh an Ghaeilge a bhfuil aici ar a laghad ar bith, den spás poiblí. Ní tharlóidh sé sin gan tuiscint ar fheidhm agus ar fheidhmiú an Bhéarla sna pobail ... Tá muintir na Gaeltachta ag roinnt an spáis chéanna thíreolaíoch lena gcomharsana ... ach níl na comharsana chomh haonchineálach agus a bhíodh! Daoine a bhfuil an Ghaeilge agus an Béarla acu is ea roinnt mhaith de phobal na Gaeltachta fós: caithfear an córas tacaíochta a

cheadóidh don Ghaeilge a bheith in uachtar a dheimhniú ar bhealach struchtúrtha córasach. Tá tuiscint ar fheidhmiú an Bhéarla sa Ghaeltacht ar cheann de na bealaí a ndéanfar sin. (Ní Neachtain, 2009: 14-5)

Tá an cheist chéanna tarraingthe anuas ag an teangeolaí Éireannach Jim McCloskey. Tá McCloskey ar dhuine de na scoláirí sin a phléann an Ghaeilge mar mhionteanga i gcomhthéacs náisiúnta agus, go deimhin, idirnáisiúnta. In ainneoin go n-aithníonn sé go bhfuil an Ghaeltacht go mór faoi bhrú agus gur cás leis an meath sin, tá McCloskey den tuairim go bhfuil athneartú na Gaeilge ar cheann de na feachtais athneartaithe teanga is rathúla ar domhan. Ní hionann an teanga a athneartófar agus Gaeilge thraidisiúnta na Gaeltachta, áfach:

> Of course, what is 'maintained' or 'revived' in this process, is very different indeed from the language which was the original focus of revivalist efforts and you may very well not much like the mongrels and hybrids that you bring into being along the way.
> But in this context, as in most, purism is surely misplaced. For you probably cannot 'revive' a seriously weakened language without in the very process transforming it in deep and unexpected ways. (McCloskey, 2008: 88)

In aiste faoin mbeartas teanga, scrúdaigh Tadhg Ó hIfearnáin an mhíréir, dar leis, idir idé-eolaíocht oifigiúil an stáit i leith na Gaeltachta agus idé-eolaíocht an phobail i nGaeltacht Mhúscraí i gCorcaigh. Dar leis, tá coimhlint bhunúsach idé-eolaíochta idir an t-aonteangachas Gaeilge agus an dátheangachas i gceist le Scéim Labhairt na Gaeilge, an scéim faoin n-íoctar deontas le tuismitheoirí páistí Gaeltachta a bhfuil Gaeilge ar a dtoil acu:

> Socraíodh ó 1926 i leith gur cheart an Ghaeltacht (nó an chuid di ar bronnadh an teideal *fíor-Ghaeltacht* uirthi an t-am sin) a riaradh i nGaeilge amháin agus gur cheart don scolaíocht a bheith sa Ghaeilge amháin chun an teanga a chur ina neart arís. Is í an idé-eolaíocht a bhí taobh thiar den bheartas sin go raibh muintir na Gaeltachta le cothú *mar phobal aonteangach Gaeilge* seachas mar phobal dátheangach a mbeadh máistreacht acu ar an nGaeilge agus ar an mBéarla araon. B'fhéidir gur tuigeadh go mbeadh an dátheangachas mar thoradh ar an mbeartas sin, ach ní hin í an sprioc a fógraíodh, agus tá meon an aonteangachais in inneach na hidé-eolaíochta oifigiúla stáit sa cheantar. Tugadh scéimeanna éagsúla deontas isteach de réir a chéile chun na daoine a ghríosú chun glacadh leis an mbeartas aonteangach sin. (Ó hIfearnáin, 2006: 16–7, béim sa bhunleagan)

Leanann Ó hIfearnáin air le staidéar faoi Scéim Labhairt na Gaeilge a léiríonn 'an [chodarsnacht] idir idé-eolaíocht an stáit, ina gcuirtear béim ar an gcleachtas aonteangach Gaeilge, agus idé-eolaíocht teanga an phobail urlabhra, a shantaíonn an dátheangachas' (17). Ní luaitear an Béarla ar fhoirmeacha na scéime, ná ní chuirtear aon cheist faoi chumas Béarla na bpáistí:

Ní iarrtar a dhath faoi chumas Béarla an pháiste – rud atá tábhachtach don chuid is mó de na tuismitheoirí a bhfuil insealbhú an dá theanga uathu dá gcuid páistí. Is amhlaidh a bhíonn go leor tuismitheoirí, go háirithe an dream is láidre Gaeilge, níos buartha faoi Bhéarla a gcuid páistí ná faoina gcumas sa Ghaeilge ... agus cuireann róbhéim na n-údarás ar an nGaeilge amháin as dóibh go dtí an pointe go gceapann cuid acu gur cheart Béarla a labhairt lena bpáistí ar an ábhar nach gcuireann na húdaráis suim ann agus nach bhfaighidh siad ar scoil é. (2006: 18)

In aiste eile dá chuid a bunaíodh ar an taighde céanna, léiríonn Ó hIfearnáin go raibh mionlach suntasach de na tuismitheoirí ar chainteoirí Gaeilge iad amhrasach faoi chleachtas aonteangach Gaeilge sa bhaile agus faoi bheartas an stáit gur i nGaeilge amháin a reáchtáilfí córas oideachais na Gaeltachta. Nuair a shealbhaigh a gcuid páistí an Béarla ní b'fhearr ná an Ghaeilge, tháinig aithreachas orthu nár labhair siad ní ba mhó Gaeilge sa bhaile, ach ní dóigh le Ó hIfearnáin go bhfuil a gcleachtas teanga ag athrú dá thoradh sin (2007: 520–1). Go deimhin, a scríobhann sé, cé go bhféadfaí a áiteamh gurbh fhearr beartas aonteangach Gaeilge i réimsí áirithe, ní cosúil gurb é sin an mhian atá ag go leor de mhuintir na Gaeltachta:

> It can be argued, of course, that to become a bilingual in a society where English is so dominant requires a strong monolingual Irish policy at home and at school, but .... this is not the understanding that a substantial part of the Irish-speaking population of the Gaeltacht have, as they seek to bring up their children to speak Irish and to be bilingual. (2007: 512)

Tugann scoláirí eile tacaíocht láidir do bheartas aonteangach Gaeilge mar seo sa Ghaeltacht. Luadh cheana go leagann an SCT an-bhéim ar a thábhachtaí agus atá sé dlús cainteoirí Gaeilge a chosaint chun go dtiocfaidh an Ghaeilge slán mar theanga phobail. In alt faoin dréacht-Straitéis a scríobh príomhúdar an SCT, Conchúr Ó Giollagáin, i gcomhar leis an teangeolaí Brian Ó Curnáin – 'Drastic steps needed to save native-spoken Irish' – lochtaítear an dréacht as suáilcí an dátheangachais a cheiliúradh agus tugtar foláireamh nach chun leas na Gaeilge é an dátheangachas 'aontreoch' (*unidirectional bilingualism*) a chleachtaítear in Éirinn ('bilingualism of native Irish speakers, monolingualism of native English speakers'):

> The draft includes many references to the positive aspects of bilingualism inside and outside the Gaeltacht. However, this appraisal of bilingual practice does not address the clear evidence, demonstrated both nationally and internationally, of a correlation between social bilingualism in minority language contexts and the erosion of minority languages. Minority-language speakers are bilingual because their acquisition of the majority language is compulsory and unidirectional. This is because majority-language speakers only acquire bilingual competence as a matter of choice.
>
> It is clear that a bilingual capacity is a positive personal asset. On the other hand, the promotion of bilingualism will erode the social use of Irish in the minority Gaeltacht community. Bilingual social practice is inherently problematic and disadvantageous for the minority language. (Ó Giollagáin and Ó Curnáin, 2009)

Cáintear an dréacht-Straitéis chomh maith as gan idirdhealú soiléir go leor a dhéanamh idir foghlaimeoirí agus cainteoirí dúchais agus moltar breis béime a leagan ar Scéim Labhairt na Gaeilge mar uirlis chun an Ghaeilge a threisiú i measc an aosa óig, an aoisghrúpa is tábhachtaí ach is laige ó thaobh úsáid na Gaeilge. In aiste eile, áitíonn Ó Giollagáin nach dtugtar dóthain airde ar chineál agus ar phráinn na géarchéime teanga sa Ghaeltacht agus molann sé gan béim a leagan ar shuáilcí an dátheangachais:

> Fearacht curaclam amháin bunscoile a bheith á fheidhmiú i scoileanna an Stáit beag beann ar a stádas mar scoil Ghaeltachta, mar Ghaelscoil nó mar ghnáthbhunscoil náisiúnta, is beag leas a dhéanann an cur chuige ginearálta a leagann béim ar shuáilcí an dátheangachais i gcás mionteangaithe óga Gaeilge atá ag coraíocht le brúnna an aistrithe teanga ina bpobail (Ó Giollagáin, 2009: 178).

I bpáipéar eile, úsáideann Ó Giollagáin na téarmaí bitheolaíochta 'non-viable/entropic' mar chur síos ar dhioscúrsa a thugann aird ar chleachtas sochaíoch dátheangach ina ndéantar díobháil don mhionteanga (2010: 13). Chun dul i ngleic leis an staid sin, molann sé 'postponed bilingualism' do chainteoirí dúchais mionteanga, coincheap a áitíonn gur cheart moill a chur ar shealbhú na mórtheanga. Is gá luath-aonteangachas a chothú sa mhionteanga ('early minority monolingualism') chun go sealbhófaí go hiomlán agus go cruinn í. Ní mhínítear, áfach, conas a chuirfí a leithéid de choincheap i bhfeidhm sa Ghaeltacht (2010: 20). In alt faoin ábhar céanna, diúltaíonn Ó Curnáin don Bhéarla agus molann go ndéanfaí 'tearmann Gaeilge. Pobal iomlán Gaelach' den Ghaeltacht (2009: 137). Cé go gcuireann na scoláirí seo go leor fianaise inár láthair gur gá beartas mar sin chun mionteanga a thabhairt slán mar theanga dhúchais, d'fhéadfadh sé go mbeadh deacrachtaí praiticiúla agus eiticiúla le moladh dá leithéid sa saol luaineach, síorathraitheach ina mairimid. Ní fheicim conas a d'fhéadfaí beartas an tearmainn aonteangaigh Ghaelaigh a chosaint ná a fheidhmiú i ndaonlathas. Dhéanfadh cur chuige dá leithéid spior spear de réaltacht shochtheangeolaíoch na Gaeltachta a bhfuil an dátheangachas fite fuaite inti agus i bhfianaise thaighde Uí Ifearnáin ar tagraíodh dó thuas, ní cosúil go mbeadh glacadh ag pobal na Gaeltachta leis.

Tá sé scríofa san SCT gur dócha nach mairfidh an Ghaeilge mar theanga phobail sa chuid is láidre den Ghaeltacht (Catagóir A) ach idir cúig bliana déag agus fiche bliain eile mura gcuirfear an patrún úsáide reatha ar mhalairt treo ('without a major change to language-use patterns' atá ar lch. 27 den achoimre Bhéarla). Cé go bhfuil amhras orm faoin bhfoclaíocht Bhéarla – is geall le réabhlóid teangeolaíoch an aidhm a leagtar síos – tá sé de bhua ag an SCT go ndéanann sé go leor moltaí faon idirghabháil is gá, dar leis na húdair, chun dul i ngleic le géarchéim teanga na Gaeltachta. Tá dealramh le cuid de na moltaí sin, dar liom ach is gá iad a phlé go mion agus go hoscailte féachaint conas a d'fhéadfaí iad a fheidhmiú. Ní fheictear dom gur tharla an plé sin go dtí seo.

Eitic na hidirghabhála?

Mar sin, tá ceist bhunúsach maidir leis an nGaeltacht atá fite fuaite le ceist an dátheangachais agus d'áiteoinn gurb í sin an cheist is cigiltí agus is bunúsaí ar fad do dhaoine ar cás leo mionteangacha na cruinne: cad iad na bearta beachta idirghabhála ar son phobal na mionteanga (pobal dlúth geografach cainteoirí atá i gceist agam anseo) atá cuí, réadúil, inghlactha agus infheidhmithe i ndaonlathas liobrálach? Cén costas sóisialta atá ag roinnt leis na bearta idirghabhála agus an ceart don phobal an costas sin a sheasamh ar mhaithe leis an mionteanga? Cén ról atá ag an mórtheanga sna pobail seo agus cad iad na himpleachtaí atá aige sin do chosaint na mionteanga? Seo an réimse is íogaire agus is casta den phleanáil teanga, faoi mar a áitíonn McCloskey:

> The conflicts and complicities that define the process [meathlú na mionteanga] work themselves out in the kitchen and in the bedroom, in the school playground rather than the school classroom – in private, familial, and domestic spaces defined by solidarity, where official and external agencies have virtually no influence ... It is very difficult indeed (and it is probably immoral) for government or movements to design and implement policies which will reach into such private spaces. But those private spaces, and the freedoms inherent in them, are where the conflict is worked out. It is therefore not surprising, I think, that it has proven so difficult to arrest the decline of Irish in Gaeltacht communities. (McCloskey, 2008: 83; feic chomh maith tráchtaireacht chontrártha Uí Ghiollagáin, 2009: 181–2)

Ar eagla na míthuisceana, ní dearcadh *laissez-faire*, ná dearcadh nualiobrálach, ná dearcadh liobraíoch atá á mholadh agamsa i leith na Gaeltachta agus na Gaeilge. Creidimse go láidir – dála na scoláirí eile ar tagraíodh dóibh san aiste seo – gur cheart an Ghaeltacht a chosaint chun go dtiocfaidh an Ghaeilge slán mar theanga phobail. D'áiteoinn go láidir, áfach, gur gá dúinn díospóireacht mhacánta agus oscailte a dhéanamh faoi na modhanna idirghabhála atáthar á moladh chun staid na Gaeilge sa Ghaeltacht a láidriú. Dar liom gur cheart an fhealsúnacht pholaitiúil atá ag treorú na hiarrachta a chíoradh chomh maith. An bhfuil leagan den liobrálachas i gceist, an liobrálachas sóisialta mar shampla, nó leagan éigin den phoblaíochas nó den daonlathas rannpháirteach? Cad faoin éiceolaíocht a chuireann béim ar chosaint na ngnéithe aiceanta sin atá leochaileach, lag agus i mbaol a mbasctha (ach a gcuirtear an t-údarásaíochas ina leith uaireanta?) Ceisteanna iad sin nach féidir a chíoradh go mion in aiste ghearr mar seo ach a bhfuil tábhacht mhór leo mar sin féin.

Mholfainn chomh maith go n-aithneofaí nádúr dátheangach na Gaeltachta, go stairiúil agus go comhaimseartha, agus go ndéanfaí machnamh agus taighde ar ról an Bhéarla sna pobail sin chomh maith céanna le straitéisí a cheapadh chun an Ghaeilge a chosaint. Ní i bhfolús a mhaireann an Ghaeltacht, faoin mar a aithnítear i gcroícháipéisí na Straitéise, agus caithfear na gréasáin eile Ghaeilge ar fud na tíre a chur san áireamh agus an bhaint atá nó nach bhfuil acu leis an nGaeltacht a mheá. Creidim gur cheart an cheist seo a chíoradh ar bhonn náisiúnta, seachas i gcomhthéacs na Gaeltachta amháin. Cuid thábhachtach den phobal leathan sin is ea gréasán na Gaeilge i dTuaisceart Éireann, nach bhfuair aon aitheantas oifigiúil sa Straitéis ach gur dlúthchuid den cheist é mar sin féin. Dar ndóigh, ní fhéadfadh stát na hÉireann straitéis a cheapadh do Thuaisceart Éireann ach léiríonn an t-easnamh a thábhachtaí is atá sé go gcuirfí straitéis chomhthreomhar i bhfeidhm ó thuaidh a mbeadh gnéithe comónta le Straitéis na Poblachta aici. Is ceart dúinn glacadh leis na fíricí gur eintiteas dátheangach (más ar éigean féin é go poiblí in áiteanna) í an Ghaeltacht, gur pobal dátheangach é pobal na Gaeilge go léir, go bhfuil patrún casta úsáide Gaeilge agus Béarla ar siúl ann agus go bhfuil 'creidimh' an-chasta i réim i leith an dá theanga (Ó hIfearnáin, 2006: 9, bunaithe ar Spolsky, 2004). Tá an ráiteas seo á dhéanamh agam ní le háiteamh go bhfuil gach idirghabháil ar son mionteanga mí-eiticiúil, frithliobrálach ná in aisce ach chun aird a tharraingt ar íogaireacht na pleanála teanga mar choincheap agus ar an teorainn atá le hidirghabháil sheachtrach i réimsí príobháideacha úsáide teanga. Thiocfainn le Ó hIfearnáin (2006: 26; 2008: 127) gur fearr cur chuige an bheartais teanga, mar a thuigeann an scoláire Bernard Spolsky é (2004, 2009), ná cur chuige na pleanála teanga chun nádúr na ceiste seo a thuiscint.

Tagairtí

An Comhchoiste um Ghnóthaí Turasóireachta, Cultúir, Spóirt, Pobail, Comhionannais agus Gaeltachta. *An Tríú Tuarascáil: an Straitéis 20-Bliain don Ghaeilge 2010–2030.* Baile Átha Cliath: Tithe an Oireachtais. Ar fáil ag: www.oireachtas.ie/documents/committees30thdail/j-artssportstcrga/reports_2009/20100728.pdf (léite 1 Samhain 2010).

An Roinn Gnóthaí Pobail, Tuaithe agus Gaeltachta. 2009. *Straitéis 20-Bliain don Ghaeilge, 2010–2030: Dréacht.* Ar fáil ag: www.pobail.ie/ie/AnGhaeilge/ (léite 1 Samhain 2010).

Comhdháil Náisiúnta na Gaeilge. 1998. *Plécháipéis maidir le hAcht Teanga / Towards a Language Act: A Discussion Document.* Baile Átha Cliath: Comhdháil Náisiúnta na Gaeilge.

FIONTAR. 2009. *Straitéis 20-Bliain don Ghaeilge: Arna Hullmhú don Roinn Gnóthaí Pobail, Tuaithe agus Gaeltachta.* Baile Átha Cliath: FIONTAR, DCU [ar líne]. Ar fáil ag: www.pobail.ie/ie/AnGhaeilge/file,10102,ie.pdf (léite 1 Samhain 2010).

Fishman, J.A. 1991. *Reversing Language Shift: Theoretical and Empirical Foundations of Assistance to Threatened Languages.* Clevedon: Multilingual Matters.

Jaffe, A., 2008. 'Discourses of endangerment: Contexts and consequences of essentializing discourses'. In eds. Duchêne, A. and M. Heller. *Discourses of Endangerment: Ideology and Interest in the Defence of Languages.* London: Continuum. 57–75.

Mac Mathúna, L. 2007. *Béarla sa Ghaeilge – Cabhair Choigríche: An Códmheascadh Gaeilge/Béarla i Litríocht na Gaeilge 1600–1900.* Baile Átha Cliath: An Clóchomhar.

McCloskey, J. 2008. 'Irish as a World Language'. In ed. Ó Conchubhair, B. *Why Irish? Irish Language and Literature in Academia.* Gaillimh: Arlen House, 71–90.

Ní Neachtain, M. 2009. 'An Spás Poiblí a Dheimhniú don Ghaeilge i Bpobail Ghaeltachta'. In ed. Ó Catháin, B. *Léachtaí Cholm Cille xxxix: Sochtheangeolaíocht na Gaeilge.* Maigh Nuad: An Sagart, 6–15.

Nic Eoin, M. 2005. *Trén bhFearann Breac: An Díláithriú Cultúir i Litríocht na Gaeilge.* Baile Átha Cliath: Cois Life.

Ó Curnáin, B. 2009. 'Mionteangú na Gaeilge'. In ed. Ó Catháin, B. *Léachtaí Cholm Cille xxxix: Sochtheangeolaíocht na Gaeilge.* Maigh Nuad: An Sagart, 90–153.

Ó Giollagáin, C. 2009. 'Torthaí an *Staidéir Chuimsithigh Theangeolaíoch ar Úsáid na Gaeilge sa Ghaeltacht*: impleachtaí don phobal agus don stát'. In ed. Ó Catháin, B. *Léachtaí Cholm Cille xxxix: Sochtheangeolaíocht na Gaeilge.* Maigh Nuad: An Sagart, 154–87.

Ó Giollagáin, C. and Ó Curnáin, B. 2009. 'Drastic Steps Needed to Save Native-spoken Irish'. *The Irish Times*, 29 Nollaig.

Ó Giollagáin, C. 2010. 'The Eclipse of the First Language Minority Speaker: Deficiencies in Ethnolinguistic Acquisition and its Evasive Discourse'. In eds. Glyn Lewis, H. and N. Ostler. *Reversing Language Shift: How to Re-awaken a Language Tradition (Proceedings of the Fourteenth FEL Conference)*. Bath: FEL, 11–22.

Ó Giollagáin, C., Mac Donnacha, S., Ní Chualáin, F., Ni Shéaghdha, A. and M. O'Brien. 2007. *Staidéar Cuimsitheach Teangeolaíoch ar Úsáid na Gaeilge sa Ghaeltacht*. Baile Átha Cliath: Oifig an tSoláthair.

Ó hIfearnáin, T. 2006. *Beartas Teanga*. Baile Átha Cliath: Coiscéim.

Ó hIfearnáin, T. 2007. 'Raising Children to be Bilingual in the Gaeltacht: Language Preference and Practice. *International Journal of Bilingual Education and Bilingualism* 10.4): 510–28.

Ó Ifearnáin, T. 2008. 'Endangering Language Vitality through Institutional Development: Authority, Ideology, and Official Standard Irish in the Gaeltacht'. In eds. King, K.A., Schilling-Estes, N., Fogle, L., Lou, J.J., and B. Soukup. *Sustaining Linguistic Diversity: Endangered and Minority Languages and Language Varieties*. Washington DC: Georgetown University Press, 113–28.

Ó Riagain, P. 2008. 'Irish-language Policy 1922–2007: Balancing Maintenance and Revival'. In eds. Nic Phaidin, C. and S. Ó Cearnaigh. *A New View of the Irish Language*. Baile Átha Cliath: Cois Life, 55–65.

Rialtas na hÉireann, 2006. *Ráiteas i leith na Gaeilge 2006 / Statement on the Irish Language 2006*. Baile Átha Cliath: Oifig an tSoláthair.

Spolsky, B. 2004. *Language Policy*. Cambridge: Cambridge University Press.

Spolsky, B. 2009. *Language Management*. Cambridge: Cambridge University Press.

Walsh, J. and W. McLeod. 2008. 'An overcoat wrapped around an invisible man? Language Legislation and Language Revitalisation in Ireland and Scotland'. *Language Policy* 7: 21–46.

Walsh, J. 2011. *Contests and Contexts: The Irish language and Ireland's Socio-economic Development*. Oxford: Peter Lang.

Bilingualism, Ideology and the 20-Year Strategy for Irish

John Walsh

Introduction

In this paper, I examine part of the debate on English-Irish bilingualism and the 20-Year Strategy for Irish, to see what arguments are being made about this issue in policy documents and the public discourse at present (end 2010). After that, I would like to scrutinise the ideological and philosophical basis of the intervention which is being recommended to strengthen Irish as a community and family language.

I shall start, therefore, with several relevant facts, as I see them:

- All Irish speakers, in the Gaeltacht and outside, are bilingual. The ability range is wide: from native speakers with Irish as their primary language to people who have equal facility in both, to native English speakers who have a high level of Irish, to English speakers who have a working level of Irish. The concept of the Irish speaker is very complicated.
- English and Irish have co-existed side-by-side in the Gaeltacht for a long time and the Irish language community, in the widest possible sense of the word (Gaeltacht community, networks and occasional speakers) is engaged with bilingualism as part of daily reality.
- Linguistic and sociolinguistic evidence shows that such a bilingual state creates major difficulties for the transmission of traditional Irish as a community and family language within the Gaeltacht and without.
- The ideology is often complex and contradictory when it comes to Irish and English in an Irish speaking community.
- What is being prepared at the moment (end 2010) is a Strategy for Irish for the whole State and not just for the Gaeltacht.

It is in that context, I believe, bilingualism and the 20-Year Strategy for Irish should be discussed. It is also right to state and acknowledge our personal language backgrounds and our personal ideologies regarding Irish, part of what Joshua Fishman (1991: 395, 397) referred to as 'prior ideological clarification'. Those matters strongly influence our work as scholars who are tied both personally and professionally to the Irish 'cause'. As written in the case of Corsica: 'there are no neutral forms of endangered language advocacy' (Jaffe, 2008: 73). Therefore, I am speaking to you today as one who spent long spells in the Munster Gaeltacht as a teenager learning the language and who made the conscious decision (or ideology) to choose Irish as one of his primary languages thereafter, even though I live outside the Gaeltacht. Without the Gaeltacht, I would not be speaking to you today but I also well recognise that there are many competent Irish speakers who do not have strong links with any Gaeltacht area. Of the 72,148 outside the education system who speak Irish daily, more than twice as many live outside the Gaeltacht as inside, although the density is not the same. That figure does not include the other competent speakers who do not use the language as frequently for various reasons. I also recognise that there are yet other speakers who use very non-traditional Irish, regularly and irregularly, and I accept them as part of that broad, abstract construct – 'pobal na Gaeilge'. Therefore, I look upon Irish as a national and minority language at the same time.

The Sociolinguistic Reality

Bilingualism is not new in the case of Irish, although it is certain that it has become more prevalent in the past 50 years because of major demographic and social changes in both the Gaeltacht and the country. As Liam Mac Mathúna demonstrates, there is evidence of linguistic contact between Irish and English in literature as far back as Tadhg Ó Cianáin in the diary *Imeacht na nIarlaí*; or in the notable poem *Beir mo beanocht go dún Dalck,* attributed to a businessman by the name of Richard Weston and composed in Louvain in 1607/8; up to the creative ambiguity behind works such as *Pairlement Chloinne Tomáis* in the seventeeth century and *Stair Éamuinn Uí Chléire* composed by Seán Ó Neachtain in the eighteenth century, a time when bilingualism was common in Dublin; and on to the macaronic songs of Leinster and Ulster in the eighteenth/nineteenth centuries. Mac Mathúna's basic argument is that social and/or political factors were at work in the Irish-English code-mixing in literature and that it often mirrors language practice or ideology in communities where Irish was actively used or passively understood. Only with the revival ideology and the associated excitement of purification of the early twentieth century did acceptance of English in Irish language literature come to an abrupt end. It was a temporary ban, of course, and various writers have illustrated the sociolinguistic reality in Ireland for some 40 years (Mac Mathúna, 2007: 266; see also Nic Eoin, 2005).

For a while I have been researching the *Breac-Ghaeltacht* (semi-Gaeltacht) – a Free State term and concept – which refers to those areas where both Irish and English were spoken and officially recognised from 1926 to 1956, when the Breac-Ghaeltacht concept ended. Sources I have examined – both oral and other contemporary sources – show how complicated the sociolinguistic position of those areas was at the time. Niall Ó Dónaill's dictionary contains a fine abstract noun for such a state: *brice* ('speckledness'). It is an accurate description of the Breac-Ghaeltacht and, indeed, the Gaeltacht today. As we know, the *Staidéar Cuimsitheach Teangeolaíoch ar Úsáid na Gaeilge sa Ghaeltacht / Comprehensive Linguistic Study of the use of Irish in the Gaeltacht* (CLS hereafter) recommended that every Gaeltacht area should be ranked according to the strength of Irish, and that three types of Gaeltacht should be recognised: A, B and C. That carries more than an echo of the Breac-Gaeltacht. It is proper recognition, I believe, of the wide sociolinguistic variety in the Gaeltacht now.

Irish-language communities have a common trait, be they concentrated communities in Corca Dhuibhne or An Cheathrú Rua, active networks in Cúil Aodha or An Rinn, or the sparser networks of Dublin or Co Kildare: each competes with English on a daily basis, and each is bilingual because the burden of bilingualism always falls on the minority language speaker; each develops 'unidirectional bilingualism', as it was recently described, a topic to which I shall return later.

Bilingualism and Policy Documents

In this section, I shall discuss policy documents relating to the Strategy, to see what ideology is revealed in relation to bilingualism. Before starting, I would like to state that I have a positive view of the Strategy, or at least in terms of the draft document published in 2009. I believe that it is the most important and most comprehensive proposal in the Irish language sector for 50 years, although I am concerned that the economic crisis might sweep it to the side. What has been published up to now has weaknesses for sure, but in general terms I think that a good balance between the needs of the Gaeltacht and the rest of the country has been found.

Both documents which are relevant to the Strategy and key-documents of the Strategy itself will be discussed in this paper. These documents do not have the same status: some of them are government documents, others are consultation documents prepared at the request of the Department of Community, Rural and Gaeltacht Affairs (as was) and one document sheds light on political views of the Strategy. These sources will be examined:

- Government Statement on Irish (2006)
- Comprehensive Linguistic Study of the use of Irish in the Gaeltacht (2007)
- FIONTAR Report (2009)
- The Draft Strategy itself (2009)
- Report of the Oireachtas Joint-Committee on Gaeltacht Affairs (2010).

In the main, the government documents relating to the 20-Year Strategy have a positive view of bilingualism, but the same support is not seen in some of the advisory documents (All extracts below are in the original version. Where they have been translated, that is noted).

Government Statement (Ráiteas an Rialtais)

Bilingualism is mentioned in the *Government Statement (Ráiteas an Rialtais)*, a document which laid the foundation of the current Strategy. It shows a positive, although undefined, view of bilingualism and declares that the Gaeltacht will be supported as 'an Irish-speaking community':

> The objective of Government policy in relation to Irish is to increase on an incremental basis the use and knowledge of Irish as a community language.
> Specifically, the Government aim is to ensure that as many citizens as possible are bilingual in both Irish and English.
> The aim of Government policy is also to strengthen the Gaeltacht as an Irish–speaking community and to increase the number of families living within the state who use Irish as the daily language of communication. (Government of Ireland, 2006: 6)

As was the case in the *White Paper on the Revival of Irish*, published in 1965, the importance of English to Ireland was also stressed:

> The Government also recognises the tremendous advantage to its citizens of fluency in English, the most widely used language in international affairs. The Government commits to ensuring that this advantage is retained through the development of a bilingual society, where as many people as possible can use Irish and English with equal ease and facility (Government of Ireland, 2006: 8).

The Comprehensive Linguistic Study (CLS)

The term 'bilingualism' is only rarely mentioned in the CLS, and the concept is not discussed in detail (Ó Giollagáin *et al.*, 2007a). It can be understood from some of the research and recommendations, however, that support for Irish monolingualism is being proposed, at least in that part of the Gaeltacht which would achieve 'category A' if the suggested re-categorisation were accepted:

> Accordingly, if the density of Irish speakers in Gaeltacht areas is to be preserved and, thus, the language protected as the primary language of family and community in the relevant areas, these demographic movements must be managed carefully, so as to provide the maximum socio-economic benefit while not damaging the position of Irish as a family and community language. (Ó Giollagáin *et al.*, 2007: 499–500, translation)
>
> It is therefore clear that the correct aim of language planning in Category A areas should be *protecting the density of Irish speakers* and making support available to preserve the use of Irish as a family and community language within them. A different objective applies in Category B and C areas, i.e. the preservation and strengthening of recognised and institutional Irish language networks.
>
> Of course, in doing so, the ultimate objective will be to inspire the next generation, and following generations of young Gaeltacht parents, *to raise their children through Irish*. (Ó Giollagáin *et al.*, 2007b: 514, translation, my emphasis)

I return to the theme of Irish monolingualism below.

The FIONTAR Report

Highly positive views on bilingualism are shown in the FIONTAR Report, informed by expert international opinions on language planning and conducted at the request of the Department of Community, Rural and Gaeltacht Affairs. The advantages of English are also mentioned:

> Ireland is fortunate to have English, one of the world's most widespread forms of communication, as its other official language. Encouraging the strengthening of Irish in light of the established domestic role of English involves a policy of bilingualism since most Irish people's communicative needs are met by English. Encouraging a wider knowledge and use of Irish offers the potential of bilingual competence throughout the population, which is an important prospect supportive of Ireland's widest social, educational, technological and economic interests. English does not require institutional support and historical evidence of the Irish genius in its use is ample. It has been well documented that two-language proficiency, especially highly skilled bilingualism developed at an early stage, stimulates many cognitive and attitudinal benefits in children. Adding high levels of active knowledge of Irish to English therefore, involves a plan for bilingualism throughout the Irish population offering intellectual, socio-economic and cultural resources and benefits for individuals and ultimately the whole of society.

Although the present Strategy and the overall policy of which it is a component focus on Irish because of the language's unique role and urgent needs, the Strategy should be seen as complementary to wider language planning for the development of the communication resources of the Irish people in a multilingual and globalising world. Irish-English bilingualism can also be a productive platform for the acquisition of additional languages, constitute an investment in the human capital of its citizens, support social cohesion and solidarity among its people and provide conditions for a culturally rich and more harmonious society. (FIONTAR, 2009: 10)

The FIONTAR report contains many references to the advantages of bilingualism, including this one in the section on education:

It is recommended that information be produced for various categories of school professionals such as speech therapists, guidance counsellors, careers advisers and others, *to promote the benefits of bilingualism* and especially of Irish language learning. (FIONTAR, 2009: 23, my emphasis)

The FIONTAR report makes few references to the Gaeltacht because, it points out, the government already had access to the CLS.

The Government Draft Strategy

Once again, the government's 2009 Draft Strategy took a positive view of bilingualism. The basic principles of bilingualism as outlined in the 2006 *Government Statement* are re-affirmed. Also reaffirmed is the government's objective for the Gaeltacht: linguistic support will be provided to the Gaeltacht 'as an Irish-speaking community'. That said, when the Gaeltacht is mentioned later in the document it is accepted that parents will want their children to have Irish and English. There is no mention of children being raised with Irish as *primary language* or *only language*. For example, this appears in the section on the education system:

Information and resource materials will be produced for various categories of school professionals such as speech therapists, guidance counsellors, careers advisers and others *promoting the benefits of bilingualism* (and especially of Irish language learning) (Department of Community, Rural and Gaeltacht Affairs, 2009: 22, my emphasis).

In the section 'Family Transmission of the Language: Early Intervention', it states:

Families where parents speak Irish need advice and guidance on how to raise their children *as balanced bilinguals*, especially if only one parent speaks the language ...
Therefore, the proposed interventions in this area are partly about encouraging and supporting parents *to raise their children bilingually*, and partly about providing factual information and raising awareness of the inherent advantages to the child's development of speaking more than one language. (Department of Community, Rural and Gaeltacht Affairs, 2009: 30, my emphasis)

As for other bilingual countries: 'There is considerable experience in other jurisdictions, including Wales and the Basque Country, in supporting families raising children with two languages' (31). Meanwhile, language planning initiatives outside the Gaeltacht will provide 'advice ... to new parents who wish to *raise their children bilingually*' (34, my emphasis in both cases).

The Oireachtas Joint Committee Report

Of all the policy documents, the Report of the Oireachtas Joint Committee for Tourism, Culture, Sport, Community, Equality and Gaeltacht Affairs is the most dismissive of bilingualism. This report was based on a lengthy public consultation process and meetings between politicians and representatives of Irish language and Gaeltacht organisations:

> It is obvious from the consultation process that the Gaeltacht community is fearful of the implications of bi-lingualism (sic) policies for the future of the Gaeltacht and its continuity as an Irish speaking community.
> It is clear from the Staidéar Teanga that minority languages do not survive in a bi-lingual society as it is necessary for the minority language to be the first language acquired by the child and to be used as her or his first language if it is to remain as her or his first language into adulthood. It is also necessary for the minority language to be continually supported and strengthened if it is to remain a vibrant spoken language.
> It is accepted that bi-lingualism has a positive role to play within some Gaeltacht households where English and Irish are equally used as the means of communication. However, in the various submissions made to the Committee, the argument is convincingly stressed that bi-lingualism should not be promoted as the means of communication in Gaeltacht communities, outside of these households. While fully recognising the importance of bi-lingualism as mentioned above and the importance of promoting bi-lingualism throughout Ireland, the Committee fully agrees with these submissions and does not believe that bi-lingualism is appropriate as the means of public communication within Gaeltacht communities.
> **Recommendation 22: Confirm that a policy of bi-lingualism will not apply to the Gaeltacht or be implemented therein by default.**
> (Oireachtas Joint Committee on Tourism, Culture, Sport, Community and Gaeltacht Affairs, 2010: 17, emphasis in original).

It is very radical to propose restricting 'bilingualism as a means of public communication within Gaeltacht communities'. Indeed, I would argue that it is an unachievable and impossible demand, given the linguistically speckled nature of the Gaeltacht today. I was personally present at the public meeting organised by the Joint Committee in Indreabhán in January 2010. Many made the point – as did the CLS before them – that Irish-speaking children were greatly disadvantaged by current arrangements in education in the Gaeltacht. Much of the evidence supports this but I don't recall any group going so far as to suggest restricting English in public life in the Gaeltacht. Indeed, I suspect that such a demand is a misreading of the legitimate fears of several Gaeltacht organisations about the use of both languages in the educational system of the Gaeltacht and private language practice. Even so, other aspects of the above statement have their echoes in part of the public discourse on bilingualism. I shall discuss that discourse now.

Bilingualism and the Public Discourse

In this section I would like to examine part of the public discourse in relation to bilingualism, so that we might see what insight is offered in terms of language ideology. A brief talk such as this cannot fairly take into account the many research papers published on this issue in recent years. I only hope to give a flavour of the debate about Irish in the Gaeltacht and the rest of the country, some of which took place before the preparation of the Strategy and some of which took place afterwards.

National
An interesting perspective on the nature of bilingualism outside the Gaeltacht and the related ideology is to be found in the *Official Languages Act*, legislation with the aim of gradually increasing the delivery of public services through Irish. The organisations who campaigned for the Act (some of them in the Gaeltacht) wanted high-quality public services through Irish for fluent speakers (see, for example, Comhdháil Náisiúnta na Gaeilge, 1988). Indeed, the wording of the legislation itself demonstrates that formal use of Irish in particular aspects of public life is the issue:

> An Act to promote the use of Irish for official purposes in the state; to provide for the use of both official languages of the state in parliamentary proceedings, in acts of the Oireachtas, in the administration of justice, in communicating with or providing services to the public and in carrying out the work of public bodies. (Preamble, *Official Languages Act*)

The most important elements of the Irish language services will be made available through the language scheme – an internal plan for Irish agreed by a public body. Some of the schemes, particularly those for Gaeltacht areas, are very strong and make significant promises in relation to the provision of services in Irish. In the case of other public bodies, the Irish language threshold was so low before introduction of the Act that no strong provisions can be expected. It seems to me, however, that there is a basic ideological conflict between the aims of the weakest schemes and the legislation itself. Those schemes are full of references to what I would call the 'ideology of the cúpla focal' ('the few words'). This language ideology is very widespread and strong in Ireland among that group who claim they have some Irish – around 1.6 million people – although that ideology has not yet been properly researched. Therefore, the weak schemes are dotted with promises that a few words of Irish will be used, or the simple greetings, or simple Irish to create a bilingual 'atmosphere', or a smattering of bilingualism at local authority public meetings and so on. In those schemes, there is a strong emphasis on Irish classes for public body staff so that they will be able to provide an Irish language service, based on the understanding – I presume – that a little training is enough to bring those with a few words already up to the appropriate level (a very mistaken understanding, as the experience in other bilingual countries tells us; see the discussion in Walsh and McLeod, 2008: 30). There is a huge gap between some of those limited promises and providing services in Irish to fluent speakers. The legislation never intended to institutionalise the 'cúpla focal' but that is what happened in many of the early schemes, statutory plans confirmed by the Minister of Community, Rural and Gaeltacht Affairs. Because the officers who prepare the schemes are not always fluent Irish speakers, that ideology could be expected. Even so, this is a fundamental ideological conflict at the heart of the *Official Languages Act* and I would argue that it is an obstacle to effective operation of the Act. It is easy for active, fluent Irish speakers to look down on those with the 'cúpla focal', but it is an important ideology which fulfils a symbolic purpose for many Irish people. The sociolinguist Pádraig Ó Riagáin criticised the Act because it did not recognise the soft cultural support the people of Ireland give to Irish (2008: 55). The Act was not designed to do so, but if Irish speakers are to be supported – however scattered and multi-faceted, from weak but well-intentioned speakers to occasional and active speakers – it would have served the Strategy well to give some recognition to that passive, widespread ideology as well (see also Walsh, 2011: 39-53).

Gaeltacht
There has been a lively debate among scholars about bilingualism in the Gaeltacht for some time. Everyone has their own opinion, and there is a range of views. I am part of this debate, as an Irish speaker concerned about the future of the language and as a lecturer and researcher in this field. Like me, the other scholars are personally tied to the case of Irish, but there is a difference in emphasis. Some people believe that a public space should be confirmed for Irish but that it is also essential to recognise the use and role of English in the Gaeltacht. Other scholars believe that bilingualism must be restrained in the Gaeltacht on the basis that a minority language will not survive in a bilingual context, if the other language is a major language. Interwoven with this, several authors place additional emphasis (or the entire emphasis) on the Gaeltacht and other scholars believe that the Gaeltacht should be handled in a national context.

Among those scholars who have discussed the role of English in the Gaeltacht is Máire Ní Neachtain. According to her, the question cannot be ignored:

> Those areas on the edge of the categories [CLS] are especially under pressure and must be helped to find strategies which will ensure that Irish will keep at least what it has of the public space. This will not happen without understanding of the use and operation of English in the communities ... The people of the Gaeltacht are sharing the same geographical space with their neighbours ... but the neighbours are not as homogeneous as they used to be! Many people in the Gaeltacht still have Irish and English; the support system which will give Irish an advantage must be confirmed in a structured systematic way. An understanding of how English functions in the Gaeltacht is one of the ways in which that will be done (Ní Neachtain, 2009: 14–5, translation).

The same question has been raised by the Irish linguist Jim McCloskey. McCloskey is one of those scholars who discusses Irish as a minority language in a national and, indeed, international context. Although he recognises that the Gaeltacht is under great pressure and expresses concern at the decline, McCloskey believes nonetheless that the revitalisation of Irish is one of the most successful language revitalisation campaigns in the world. However, the language which will be revived will not be the same thing as traditional Gaeltacht Irish:

Of course, what is 'maintained' or 'revived' in this process, is very different indeed from the language which was the original focus of revivalist efforts and you may very well not much like the mongrels and hybrids that you bring into being along the way.

But in this context, as in most, purism is surely misplaced. For you probably cannot 'revive' a seriously weakened language without in the very process transforming it in deep and unexpected ways (McCloskey, 2008: 88).

In a paper about language policy, Tadhg Ó hIfearnáin examined what he sees as the dissonance between official state ideology towards the Gaeltacht and community ideology in the Múscraí Gaeltacht in Cork. According to him, there is a fundamental ideological struggle between Irish monolingualism and bilingualism in relation to Scéim Labhairt na Gaeilge (the Irish Speaking Scheme), the scheme whereby parents whose children in the Gaeltacht speak Irish are paid a grant.

It was decided from 1926 onwards that the Gaeltacht (or the portion named the *fíor-Ghaeltacht* (true-Gaeltacht) at that time) be administered in Irish alone and that education should be only in Irish in order to strengthen the language again. The ideology behind that policy was that the people of the Gaeltacht be cultivated *as a monolingual Irish community* instead of a bilingual community with equal mastery of Irish and English. Perhaps it was understood that bilingualism would be the result of that policy, but that was not the declared aim, and the mindset of monolingualism is woven into the official state ideology of the area. Various grant schemes were introduced over time to persuade people to accept that monolingual policy (Ó hIfearnáin, 2006: 16–7, translation, emphasis in original).

Ó hIfearnáin continues with a study of Scéim Labhairt na Gaeilge which illustrates 'the [contrast] between state ideology, which puts emphasis on monolingual Irish practice, and the language ideology of the speaking community, which desires bilingualism' (17). English is not mentioned on the scheme's forms, and no question is asked about children's ability in English:

Nothing is asked about the child's ability in English – something which is important to most parents who want their children to pick up both languages. Therefore, many parents, especially the group with the strongest Irish, are more concerned about their children's English than their Irish ... and the over-emphasis of the authorities on Irish alone irritates them to the point that some think they should speak English with their children because the authorities are disinterested and they will not get it [English] at school (2006: 18, translation).

In another paper based on the same research, Ó hIfearnáin shows that a substantial minority of Irish-speaking parents were dubious about monolingual Irish use at home and state policy that the education system of the Gaeltacht should be conducted in Irish alone. When their children acquired English better than Irish they began to regret that they had not spoken more Irish at home, but Ó hIfearnáin does not believe their language practice is changing as a result (2007: 520–1). Indeed, he writes, even though it can be argued that a monolingual Irish policy is better in particular spheres, it does not appear that that is the wish of many in the Gaeltacht:

> It can be argued, of course, that to become a bilingual in a society where English is so dominant requires a strong monolingual Irish policy at home and at school, but ... this is not the understanding that a substantial part of the Irish-speaking population of the Gaeltacht have, as they seek to bring up their children to speak Irish and to be bilingual (2007: 512).

Other scholars strongly support such a monolingual policy in the Gaeltacht. It has already been mentioned that the CLS places strong emphasis on the importance of protecting the density of Irish speakers so that Irish will survive as a community language. In an article about the Draft Strategy written by CLS main author Conchúr Ó Giollagáin, in collaboration with the linguist Brian Ó Curnáin – 'Drastic steps needed to save native-spoken Irish' – the draft is faulted for celebrating the virtues of bilingualism and a warning is given that 'unidirectional' bilingualism practised in Ireland ('bilingualism of native Irish speakers, monolingualism of native English speakers') does not benefit Irish:

> The draft includes many references to the positive aspects of bilingualism inside and outside the Gaeltacht. However, this appraisal of bilingual practice does not address the clear evidence, demonstrated both nationally and internationally, of a correlation between social bilingualism in minority language contexts and the erosion of minority languages. Minority-language speakers are bilingual because their acquisition of the majority language is compulsory and unidirectional. This is because majority-language speakers only acquire bilingual competence as a matter of choice.
> It is clear that a bilingual capacity is a positive personal asset. On the other hand, the promotion of bilingualism will erode the social use of Irish in the minority Gaeltacht community. Bilingual social practice is inherently problematic and disadvantageous for the minority language (Ó Giollagáin and Ó Curnáin, 2009).

The Draft Strategy is also criticised for not making a clear distinction between learners and native speakers and greater emphasis on the Scéim Labhairt na Gaeilge is recommended as an instrument to strengthen Irish among the young, the most important but weakest age-group in terms of Irish use. In another essay, Ó Giollagáin argues that not enough attention is being paid to the nature or the urgency of the language crisis in the Gaeltacht, and he suggests putting less emphasis on the benefits of bilingualism:

> Similar to operating a single primary school curriculum in State schools regardless of whether it is a Gaeltacht school, a Gaelscoil or a standard national primary school, the general approach which emphasises the benefits of bilingualism in the case of a minority language does little to benefit young Irish speakers who are struggling with the pressures of language shift in their communities (Ó Giollagáin, 2009: 178, translation).

In another paper, Ó Giollagáin uses the biological terms 'non-viable/entropic' to describe a discourse which highlights societal bilingual practice damaging to the minority language (2010: 13). To counter this he suggests 'postponed bilingualism' for minority native speakers, a concept which holds that majority-language acquisition should be delayed. It is essential to cultivate early monolingualism in the minority language ('early minority monolingualism') so that it is acquired completely and accurately. Not explained, however, is how such a concept could be operated in the Gaeltacht (2010: 20). In an article on the same subject, Ó Curnáin rejects English and suggests that the Gaeltacht be made into 'an Irish language sanctuary. A completely Gaelic community' (2009: 137, translation). Although these scholars provide us with plenty of evidence that such a policy is needed to preserve a minority language as a native language, there could be practical and ethical difficulties with this recommendation in our volatile and ever-changing world. I do not see how the policy of a monolingual Gaelic sanctuary could be defended or operated in a democracy. Such an approach would make a mockery of the sociolinguistic reality of the Gaeltacht, where bilingualism is ingrained, and based on the evidence of Ó hIfearnáin's research, referred to above, it is unlikely the people of the Gaeltacht would accept it.

It is stated in the CLS that Irish will only survive as a community language in the strongest part of the Gaeltacht (Category A) for another 15 or 20 years unless the current usage pattern is changed ('without a major change to language-use patterns', on p.27 of the English summary). Although I am dubious about the English wording – the stated aim is equivalent to a linguistic revolution – a virtue of the CLS is that it makes many recommendations about necessary interventions. Some of those recommendations are worthwhile, I believe, but they should be discussed openly and in detail to tease out how they could be implemented. I do not believe that such a discussion has taken place as yet.

The Ethics of Intervention?

So, there is a basic question regarding the Gaeltacht which is interwoven with bilingualism and I would contend that it is the most delicate and fundamental question of all for those concerned about the minority languages of the world: what are the precise intervention measures on behalf of the minority-language community (I am referring to a dense geographic community of speakers) that are appropriate, realistic, acceptable and viable in a liberal democracy? What social cost accompanies the intervention policies and is it right for the community to pay that cost for the good of the minority language? What is the role of the majority language in these communities and what are the implications of that for the protection of the minority language? This is the most sensitive and the most complex field in language planning, according to McCloskey:

> The conflicts and complicities that define the process [the decline of the minority language] work themselves out in the kitchen and in the bedroom, in the school playground rather than the school classroom – in private, familial, and domestic spaces defined by solidarity, where official and external agencies have virtually no influence … It is very difficult indeed (and it is probably immoral) for government or movements to design and implement policies which will reach into such private spaces. But those private spaces, and the freedoms inherent in

them, are where the conflict is worked out. It is therefore not surprising, I think, that it has proven so difficult to arrest the decline of Irish in Gaeltacht communities (McCloskey, 2008: 83; see also the contrasting commentary of Ó Giollagáin, 2009: 181–2).

For fear of being misunderstood, I am not proposing a *laissez-faire*, neo-liberal or libertarian outlook in regard to the Gaeltacht and Irish. In tandem with the other scholars referred to in this essay, I believe that the Gaeltacht should be protected so that Irish will survive as a community language. I would argue strongly, however, that we must have an honest and open debate about the intervention methods being suggested to strengthen the state of the Gaeltacht. The political philosophy underpinning the effort should be scrutinised as well. Is it a version of liberalism, social liberalism for example, or some variety of populism or participative democracy? What about an ecological approach, which puts emphasis on the protection of those natural elements which are fragile, weak and in danger of extinction (but is sometimes accused of authoritarianism?) They are questions which cannot be examined closely in a short essay such as this but are nevertheless of great importance.

I would also suggest that the bilingual nature of the Gaeltacht be recognised, historically and contemporarily. The role of English in those communities should be considered and studied, as should the creation of strategies to protect Irish. The Gaeltacht does not exist in a vacuum, as recognised in the key documents of the Strategy, and the other Irish language networks throughout the country must be included and the connection they have, or do not have, with the Gaeltacht considered. I believe that this question should be explored at national level, and not just in the context of the Gaeltacht. An important part of this broad community is the Irish language network in Northern Ireland, which received no official recognition in the Strategy but is an inherent part of the question. Of course, the Irish state could not be expected to design a strategy for Northern Ireland but the gap reveals how important it is that a parallel programme with aspects common to the Strategy of the Republic should be implemented in the north. We have to accept the facts that the Gaeltacht is a bilingual entity (if barely so in the public realm in places), that all of the Irish-language community is bilingual, that a complicated usage-pattern of Irish and English exists and that 'beliefs' about the two languages are very complex (Ó hIfearnáin, 2006: 9, based on Spolsky, 2004). In making this statement, I do not intend to claim that every intervention on behalf of a minority language is unethical, illiberal or futile but rather to highlight the sensitivity of language planning as a concept and the limits of outside intervention in private aspects of language use. I would agree with Ó hIfearnáin (2006: 26; 2008: 127) that the language policy approach, as proposed by the scholar Bernard Spolsky (2004, 2009), is better than the language planning approach in understanding the nature of the question.

References

Comhdháil Náisiúnta na Gaeilge. 1998. *Pléchaipéis maidir le hAcht Teanga / Towards a Language Act: A Discussion Document*. Dublin: Comhdháil Náisiúnta na Gaeilge.
Department of Community, Rural and Gaeltacht Affairs. 2009. *Straitéis 20-Bliain don Ghaeilge, 2010–2030: Dréacht / 20-Year Strategy for the Irish Language: Draft*. Available at: www.pobail.ie/ie/AnGhaeilge/. (last accessed 1 November 2010)

FIONTAR, 2009. *0-Year Strategy for the Irish Language*. Prepared for the Department of Community, Rural and Gaeltacht Affairs. Dublin: FIONTAR, DCU. Available at: www.pobail.ie/en/IrishLanguage/Strategy/ FIONTAR%20report.pdf. (last accessed 1 November 2010)

Fishman, J.A. 1991. *Reversing Language Shift: Theoretical and Empirical Foundations of Assistance to Threatened Languages*. Clevedon: Multilingual Matters. Government of Ireland, 2006. *Ráiteas i leith na Gaeilge 2006 / Statement on the Irish Language 2006*. Dublin: Stationery Office.

Jaffe, A. 2008. 'Discourses of endangerment: Contexts and consequences of essentializing discourses'. In eds. Duchêne, A. and M. Heller. *Discourses of Endangerment: Ideology and Interest in the Defence of Languages*. London: Continuum. 57–75.

Mac Mathúna, L. 2007. *Béarla sa Ghaeilge – Cabhair Choigríche: An Códmheascadh Gaeilge/Béarla i Litríocht na Gaeilge 1600–1900*. Dublin: An Clóchomhar.

McCloskey, J. 2008. 'Irish as a World Language'. In ed. Ó Conchubhair, B. *Why Irish? Irish Language and Literature in Academia*. Galway: Arlen House. 71–90.

Ní Neachtain, M. 2009. 'An spás poiblí a dheimhniú don Ghaeilge i bpobail Ghaeltachta'. In ed. Ó Catháin, B. *Léachtaí Cholm Cille xxxix: Sochtheangeolaíocht na Gaeilge*. Maynooth: An Sagart. 6–15.

Nic Eoin, M. 2005. *Trén bhFearann Breac: An Díláithriú Cultúir i Litríocht na Gaeilge*. Dublin: Cois Life.

Oireachtas Joint Committee on Tourism, Culture, Sport, Community and Gaeltacht Affairs. 2010. The Third Report: *The 20-Year Strategy for the Irish Language 2010–2030*. Dublin: Houses of the Oireachtas. Available at: www.oireachtas.ie/documents/committees30thdail/j-artssportstcrga/reports_2009/20100728.pdf, (last accessed 1 November 2010)

Ó Curnáin, B. 2009. 'Mionteangú na Gaeilge'. In ed. Ó Catháin, B. *Léachtaí Cholm Cille xxxix: Sochtheangeolaíocht na Gaeilge*. Maynooth: An Sagart. 90–153.

Ó Giollagáin, C. 2009. 'Torthaí an *Staidéir chuimsithigh theangeolaíoch ar úsáid na Gaeilge sa Ghaeltacht*: impleachtaí don phobal agus don stát'. In ed. Ó Catháin, B. *Léachtaí Cholm Cille xxxix: Sochtheangeolaíocht na Gaeilge*. Maynooth: An Sagart, 154–87.

Ó Giollagáin, C. and B. Ó Curnáin. 2009. 'Drastic Steps Needed to Save Native-spoken Irish'. *The Irish Times*. 29 December.

Ó Giollagáin, C. 2010. 'The Eclipse of the First Language Minority Speaker: Deficiencies in Ethnolinguistic Acquisition and its Evasive Discourse'. In eds. Glyn Lewis, H. and N. Ostler. *Reversing Language Shift: How to Re-awaken a Language Tradition (Proceedings of the Fourteenth FEL Conference)*. Bath: FEL, 11–22.

Ó Giollagáin, C., Mac Donnacha, S., Ní Chualáin, F., Ni Shéaghdha, A. and M. O'Brien. 2007a. *Comprehensive Linguistic Study of the Use of Irish in the Gaeltacht*. Dublin: Stationery Office. Available at: www.pobail.ie/en/IrishLanguage/Strategy/ Comprehensive%20Linguistic%20Study%20of%20the%20Use%20of%20Irish% 20in%20the%20Gaeltacht.pdf. (last accessed 1 November 2010)

Ó Giollagáin, C., Mac Donnacha, S., Ní Chualáin, F., Ni Shéaghdha, A. and M. O'Brien. 2007b. *Staidéar Cuimsitheach Teangeolaíoch ar Úsáid na Gaeilge sa Ghaeltacht: Tuarascáil Chríochnaitheach*. Dublin: Stationery Office. Available at: www.pobail.ie/ie/AnGhaeilge/Straiteis/Staid%C3%A9ar%20Cuimsitheach%20T eangeola%C3%ADoch%20ar%20%C3%9As%C3%A1id%20na%20Gaeilge%20s a%20Ghaeltacht.pdf (last accessed 1 November 2010).

Ó hIfearnáin, T. 2006. *Beartas Teanga*. Dublin: Coiscéim.

Ó hIfearnáin, T. 2007. 'Raising Children to be Bilingual in the Gaeltacht: Language Preference and Practice. *International Journal of Bilingual Education and Bilingualism* 10.4: 510–28.

Ó Ifearnáin, T. 2008. 'Endangering Language Vitality through Institutional Development: Authority, Ideology, and Official Standard Irish in the Gaeltacht'. In eds. King, K.A., Schilling-Estes, N., Fogle, L., Lou, J.J., and B. Soukup. *Sustaining Linguistic Diversity: Endangered and Minority Languages and Language Varieties*. Washington, DC: Georgetown University Press, 113–28.

Ó Riagáin, P. 2008. 'Irish-language Policy 1922–2007: Balancing Maintenance and Revival'. In: eds.Nic Phaidin, C. and S. Ó Cearnaigh. *A New View of the Irish Language*. Dublin: Cois Life, 55–65.

Spolsky, B. 2004. *Language Policy*. Cambridge: Cambridge University Press.

Spolsky, B. 2009. *Language Management*. Cambridge: Cambridge University Press.

Walsh, J. 2011. *Contests and Contexts: the Irish language and Ireland's socio- economic development*. Oxford: Peter Lang.

Walsh, J. and W. McLeod. 2008. 'An overcoat wrapped around an invisible man? Language Legislation and Language Revitalisation in Ireland and Scotland'. *Language Policy* 7: 21–46.

Irish: A 20-Year Strategy or Just More Waffle?

Dónall Ó Riagáin

In December 2009, the Department for Community, Rural and Gaeltacht Affairs published its *20-Year Strategy for the Irish Language: Draft*. Its launch clashed with the publication of the Murphy Report on clerical sex abuse in the Dublin Archdiocese and the salacious nature of the Murphy Report overshadowed the launch of the language strategy to the extent that its appearance passed almost unnoticed in the mass media. Be that as it may, it is of very considerable importance and merits more critical attention than it has hitherto received.

The first thing that one needs to say is that any commitment to language planning is to be welcomed. Indeed, I would venture to say that a positive, well-prepared language policy can be more critical for the future of any language than language legislation. It is all the more regrettable then that the *Draft 20-Year Strategy for Irish* is seriously flawed.

Language Planning

Sociolinguists recognise three main elements in language planning. They are Acquisition Planning, Corpus Planning and Status Planning.

By *Acquisition Planning* it is meant how people acquire a language. The most obvious and most important element is intergenerational transmission. Are Irish-speaking parents speaking Irish to their children? The second is educational provision. Is the language taught to all children? Is it being taught effectively? Can adults access language classes? Is there easy access to Irish-medium schools? And thirdly, there is language environment. By that, I mean would people pick up at least some knowledge of the language from hearing it spoken in the street, in shops, offices, factories etc. Do they see it written e.g. on public signage, in official documents, in newspapers?

Corpus Planning relates to the language itself. Is there a standard written form of the language – one that is accepted by all, used by the authorities and taught in schools? Are there dictionaries and grammars? Is there a recognised procedure for developing new terminology?

Status Planning relates to the *de facto* status of the language and its use in the various domains of everyday living.

Since the independent Irish state undertook the revitalisation of the Irish language back in 1922, there has been marked progress in some respects but disappointing results in others. We have succeeded in creating a substantial pool of secondary bilinguals. The 2006 Census of Population in the Republic shows 1,657,000 persons (40.8% of the population over 3 years of age) claiming an ability to speak Irish. Unfortunately, the questions in the Northern Ireland Census are not the same but we can extrapolate certain key information and safely add 150,000 speakers from there. This suggests that there are now *c*. 1.8m. people on the island who have an active ability in Irish. Even if we make allowances for varying degrees of fluency, this is still a substantial figure and places Irish among the more numerically strong lesser used languages of Europe. For all its failings – and God knows there are many! – most of the credit for this must go to the education system.

Unfortunately, these figures present an incomplete picture. In the Republic, only 85,076[1] persons said that they spoke Irish on a daily basis *outside* of the education system.

[1] *Census 2006* .Volume 9: *Irish Language*. Table 32A.

Another 97,089 said they spoke Irish at least once a week and 581,574 said they spoke the language less frequently. The Census figures do not cover Northern Ireland nor do they reflect passive use of the language e.g. people listening to television and radio programmes in Irish.

What they clearly show, however, is that there is a enormous gap between ability and usage. This is all the more striking when one considers the very high levels of attitudinal support for Irish shown in survey after survey, especially in *The Irish Lanaguage and the Irish People. Report on the Attitudes towards Competence in and Use of the Irish Language 2007–2008* published in 2009.[2] 93.4% of those surveyed either wanted the language revived or at least preserved. Only 6.6% felt is should be abandoned and left to die.

The inescapable conclusion is that the greatest need for planning is the area of Status Planning, i.e. providing opportunities and incentives to actually *use* Irish. Or, to put it bluntly, convert the latent ability and goodwill into actual usage. And one of the specific objectives of the draft strategy is to grow the number of daily speakers of Irish from the current level of 85,076 to 250,000. I believe that this is a reasonable target and an achievable one. It also aims to increase the number of people who *can* speak Irish in the state to *c*. 2m from 1,657,000.

The problem is that the draft strategy is vague and unconvincing as to how the daily users of Irish might be increased. Indeed, the most substantial part of the document is devoted to acquisition planning, rather than status planning.

An Ghaeltacht

The draft Strategy states that, 'The Government accepts the broad thrust of the recommendations in the *Report on the Linguistic Study of the Use of Irish in the Gaeltach*[3] with regard to Gaeltacht status being based on linguistic criteria. This will be given statutory status through a new Gaeltacht Act. The legal definition will be broadly based on the criteria outlined in the Report with some fundamental modifications'.

The draft Strategy proposed a number of remedial measures to contain the unremitting decline of Irish in the officially designated Gaeltacht areas and to stabilise its role in these communities. While one would find little fault with most of the proposed measures, no evidence is produced to show that the erosion of the Gaeltacht (as presently understood), either geographically or sociolinguistically, can be arrested, not to mention reversed. The most one could hope for is some kind of reasonably successful 'fire-fighting operation'. This is because the authors' concept of Gaeltacht is based on territory rather than on people.

In Ó Riagáin (2011),[4] I argued that we should change our concept of 'Gaeltacht' from a geographical one – one of scattered semi-Irish speaking districts, mostly on the western seaboard – to one of an Irish-speaking community wherever that community

---

[2] Micheál Mac Gréil, S.J. and Fergal Rhatigan, *The Irish Lanaguage and the Irish People. Report on the Attitudes towards Competence in and Use of the Irish Language 2007–2008*. Survey and Research Unit. Departmnet of Sociology. National University of Ireland Maynooth. 2009.

[3] Ó Giollagáin, C., Mac Donnacha, S., Ní Shéaghdha, A. and F. Ní Chualáin. *Staidéar Teangeolaíoch ar Úsáid na Gaeilge sa Ghaeltacht / Comprehensive Linguistic Study of the Use of Irish in the Gaeltacht.* Dublin. The Department of Community, Rural and Gaeltacht Affairs. 2007. Available at: www.pobail.ie/ie/AnGhaeltacht/AnStaidearTeangeolaioch/file,8677,ie.pdf

[4] Dónall Ó Riagáin. 'The Concept of Gaeltacht: Time to Revisit?', In eds. Kirk, J.M. and D.P. Ó Baoill. *Sustaining Minority Language Communities: Northern Ireland, the Republic of Ireland, and Scotland.* Belfast: Cló Ollscoil na Banríona, 2011. pp. 89–95.

may reside. The independent Irish state rightly perceived the importance of the Gaeltacht (as currently understood) as a repository of oral Irish, unbroken in tradition and rich in idiom. For this reason and for general humanitarian reasons, it seemed only right to support the Gaeltacht socially and economically. But the people of the Gaeltacht understandably have no interest in living in what some people see, even in a skewed patronising way, as a kind of 'Red Indian reservation' for Gaeilgeoirí. The survival and resurgence of the traditional Gaeltacht will come only in the context of Irish developing as a living community language throughout the country. If the draft Strategy's objective of having Irish spoken by 250,000 people on a daily basis is met, we can then expect to see a resurgence of the traditional Gaeltacht. The Strategy states:

> The Government considers it appropriate that a new type of 'network Gaeltacht' be recognised in the new Act. This category will allow for targeted language planning initiatives to develop new language communities/networks outside the Gaeltacht. These will be predominantly in urban communities that have achieved a basic critical mass of community and State support for the Irish language, such as childcare facilities through Irish, Gaelscoileanna, second level education through Irish, Irish language youth clubs and other services, including mother and toddler groups, Irish language religious services, etc. Specific criteria to be developed for this category will relate to public attitudes, language ability, provision of Irish-medium education and the willingness to actively participate in Irish language initiatives.
> The Department of Community, Rural and Gaeltacht Affairs and the new Údarás na Gaeilge will provide supports for such language plans. Support will also be available from Oifigigh Ghaeilge employed by local authorities and other experts within existing bodies.

The Oireachtas Joint Committee, which considered the draft strategy, was even more positive:

> It is also essential that other Irish speaking communities outside the recognised Gaeltacht are encouraged, supported and developed. In this regard a formula for recognising 'Pocket Gaeltachts' should be agreed and a method for creating 'Pocket Gaeltachts' should be devised. These communities should be recognised in an appropriate manner.

In principle, all this is excellent but what is meant by 'support' in this instance is unclear. How this might be undertaken – and by whom? – remains disturbingly vague.

Education

Some of the best recommendations in the strategy are in the section on education e.g. the teaching of at least one subject, other than Irish, through irish. Time constraints prevent me from discussing them. However, I repeat the question posed by two commentators – (both from Ulster!) – Mairéad Ní Chinnéide, writing in COMHAR (January 2010) and Eoghan Ó Néill writing in Gaelscéal – does the Department of Education and Science accept these recommendations? I don't know, but I suspect not. And, if the Department doesn't, then they are no more than waffle.

Irish in the European Union

Irish became an official and working language of the European Union on 1 January 2007. However, the relevant Council Regulatio[6] provided for a five year derogation from the obligation to draft all acts in Irish and to publish them in that language in the *Official Journal of the European Union* (Article 2). This was because there was a shortage of trained translators and interpreters capable of carrying out the work.

The Strategy proposes that this derogation be ended by the end of the period of the strategy i.e. within 20 years. This is daft! Besides the fact that there is no guarantee that the derogation will be renewed, it is crazy in a time of recession not to train an adequate number of young graduates in Irish as translators and interpreters when there are well-paid jobs in EU institutions waiting to be filled. Are some of our politicians afraid that an enhanced use of Irish at European level might undermine their cosy monolingual Anglophone set-up?

Corpus Planning

In this section we are told that a number of measures are already in place to ensure that up-to-date dictionaries, both English-Irish and Irish-English, will be developed with provision for updating/revising them periodically and for deriving shorter dictionaries from them. Fine! But what about other languages? I use French from time to time and, when working from Irish, am dependent on Risteard de Hae's *Foclóir Gaedhilge agus Frainncise* published in 1952 with pre-standardised spelling and in the Gaelic script. Am I to be in the same boat in twenty years time? Compare this to Catalan where there are dictionaries to and from languages such as French, Spanish, German and Dutch.

But to be fair, the section on corpus planning at least provides us with a good laugh! It is proposed that the historical Irish Dictionary being compiled by the Royal Irish Academy be completed by 2037. Why 2037, I asked myself: why not 2036 or 2038? It is all the more intriguing when one reads Rosita Boland's interview with Dr. Úna Uí Bheirn, the editor of the dictionary, in the *Irish Times*[6] on 27 March 2010. Dr. Uí Bheirn said that, with present staffing levels, it would take another century to complete the dictionary. It was suggested to me that the 2037 date arises from a misreading of what Máirtín Ó Murchú wrote in his book, *Ag Dul ó Chion*.[7] Anyway, I am pretty sure that I won't be around to enjoy it!

EuroVoc is a multilingual, multidisciplinary thesaurus covering the activities of the EU, the European Parliament in particular. It is managed by the EU Publications Office. It covers 23 languages but Irish, although an official and working language, is not one of them! Irish is the only official language of the EU not covered. Even Maltese (and Malta has a population of only *c*. 280,000) is included. But not Irish! EuroVoc is not even mentioned in the draft Strategy.

Unanswered Questions

In July 2010, the Oireachtas Joint Committee On Tourism, Culture, Sport, Community, Equality and Gaeltacht Affairs issued its *Third Report: The 20-Year Strategy for the Irish Language 2010–2030*. Various organisations and individuals made submissions to the Joint Committee and these contributions may account for the surprisingly positive approach of the Report in some respects. However, far too many issues are left untouched and unanswered.

[6] Council Regulation (EC) No. 920/2005 of 13 June 2005.
[7] Máirtín Ó Murchú. *Ag Dul ó Chion*. Baile Átha Cliath: Coiscéim. 2002.

There are a number of intriguing questions hanging over the strategy document itself. The first and most basic one is what is its status. If the Minister signs off on the document what will this mean? Will it be the policy of his Department alone or will it be Government policy, including that of the Department of Education and Science?

The next question is who were the final authors. The document was seemingly prepared by a team of five persons – two from Dublin City University and three from abroad. There is a disturbing rumour that the document prepared by this team was a much stronger and more coherent one than the one we are considering today. According to this account, senior civil servants went through the original document and cut out anything they considered to be too ambitious or costly. Thus, we are left with the present truncated (or should I say 'castrated') version.

Will it be an all-party policy? If opinion polls mean anything then the present Fianna Fáil-Green Alliance government will not see the end of 2011. It will almost certainly be replaced by a Fine Gael-Labour coalition. Enda Kenny, the leader of Fine Gael, wants to end Irish as an essential subject for study in the senior cycle of post-primary schools. [This has been an old chestnut of his for many years]. Such a step would deal a body-blow to Irish and would leave the strategy with little value other than as waste paper. Language planning is a medium>long term process. All-party commitment is needed to ensure that, whatever government is in power, the policy will be fully and conscientiously implemented.

Other critical questions remain unanswered. Údarás na Gaeltachta is to become Údarás na Gaeilge, responsible for the promotion of Irish throughout the country. But Foras na Gaeilge is to remain. What then will be the respective roles of the Údarás and of Foras? Údarás na Gaeltachta is at present a democratically elected authority, chosen by the residents of the officially designated Gaeltacht areas. Who then will elect the members of Údarás na Gaeilge – or will democracy be discarded? All reasonable questions, I think! And all unanswered.

Funding the strategy is another issue left untouched. Prof. Colm McCarthy's famous (or infamous!) 'Snip' report proposes the abolition of the Department for Community, Equality and Gaeltacht Affairs and Údarás na Gaeltachta and the incorporation of their operations into other departments and state agencies, conveniently unspecified! He also proposes the abolition of An Chomhairle um Oideachas Gaeltachta agus Gaelscolaíochta (COGG), which has done Trojan work for Irish-medium education in recent years, and its return to the Department of Education and Science, which did practically nothing to support Irish-medium education in over half a century. An this in the name of *efficiency*!

And then there is the all-important issue of monitoring! I am old enough to remember the Government White Paper on Irish published in January 1965 following on the report of the Commission on the revival of Irish published the previous year. Many people were disappointed by the White Paper but felt that if what was in it were implemented at least some real progress would be made. But weak and all as it was, the greater part of its recommendations were never implemented! There is a lesson there to be learned.

I find the low-key response and docility of Irish language organisations disappointing and disheartening. They clearly do not want to be seen as being hard-line or 'fanatical' as some people might suggest. They might also be concerned that their annual government subventions could become endangered if they spoke out too strongly. Be that as it may, those of us who care for the Irish language and its future will bear part of the blame if we remain silent and this vague, incomplete, wish-washy, amateur strategy becomes government policy.

The Irish Language and the Irish people deserve better!

Léargas ar an gCoibhneas Comhaimseartha idir an Earnáil Dheonach / an tSochaí Shibhialta agus Institiúidí Stáit I bPoblacht na hÉireann

Helen Ó Murchú

Achoimre

Chuimsigh an siompósiam atá mar bhonn leis an bhfoilseachán seo go leor ábhar éagsúil. Ar an mbonn sin, táim chun tosú le tagairt do na téarmaí 'Gaeltacht' , 'dátheangachas' agus 'institiúidí'. Ní gá gurb ionann mo thuiscintse ar na coincheapa seo agus an tuiscint choiteann. Féachfad ansin go hachomair ar idirfheidhmiú institiúidí éagsúla trí mheán chórais pháirtíochta sa chóras polaitiúil liobrálach daonlathach, á léiriú trí roinnt samplaí ó Phoblacht na hÉireann. Críochnód le tagairt d'impleachtaí áirithe don Straitéis 20-Bliain sa Phoblacht.

Téarmaíocht: Gaeltacht

I gcás an téarma 'Gaeltacht', ní ionann ar fad mo thuiscintse air, áfach, agus an míniú searbhghrinn i bhfoirm cudromóide a thug Myles na Gopalleen (Brian Ó Nualláin), iarcholúnaí de chuid an *Irish Times* agus údar *An Béal Bocht*:

	Breac-Ghaeltacht = áit a labhartar Gaeilge agus Béarla	
	Breac-Ghalltacht = áit a labhartar Béarla agus Gaeilge	
Dá bhrí sin	Breac-Ghaeltacht = Breac-Ghalltacht	
Da bhrí sin	Gaeltacht = Galltacht.	

Tá loighic urghnách éigin ceilte sa sampla grinn seo, mar sin féin, nár mhiste a bheith feasach nó comhfhiosach uirthi.

Is gaire mo thuiscintse do dhearcadh an tsocheolaí Glyn Williams,[1] is é sin gan rud ró-nithiúil scartha óna cuid chainteoirí a dhéanamh den urlabhra, gan *'reification'* a dhéanamh uirthi ach chun críocha áirithe amháin. Is *daoine* a bhíonn i gceist le pobal teanga. Is *gníomh sóisialta* go príomha é teanga a labhairt. Is é an pobal teanga féin, ní saineolaithe aon eolaíochta, a shainíonn a dteanga féin. B'in fíric a raibh ar bhaill an fhorais úd, An Biúró Eorpach do Theangacha Neamhfhorleathana (nach maireann), le linn a ré, dul i ngleic léi ó thaobh aitheantais agus idirdhealú idir na coincheapa 'urlabhra', 'teanga' agus 'canúint'.

B'fhearr liomsa dá réir an tír ar fad, thuaidh agus theas, a chuimsiú laistigh den tuiscint seo a leanas ar *Ghaeltacht:*

1. pobail a bhfuil an Ghaeilge á labhairt acu mar theanga dhúchais thraidisiúnta (ach é sin ar leibhéil éagsúla tréine ag brath ar an bpobal);
2. pobail foghlaimeoirí a bhfuil an Ghaeilge sealbhaithe acu go leibhéal ard mar dhara teanga ach í á labhairt acu mar chéad teanga *roghnaithe* laistigh d'oiread chomhthéacsanna is is féidir, cuid de na comhthéacsanna sin 'nádúrtha' (sa teaghlach), cuid eile díobh cruthaithe d'aonghnó i réimsí eile mar thaca don phobal urlabhra (san oideachas, sna meáin, sa saol sóisialta, sa saol siamsaíochta agus gnó);

---

[1] Plé pearsanta.

3. pobail Bhéarla go príomha sa chuid eile den tír ar féidir a rá go
    mbaineann siad leis an iar-Ghaeltacht[2] sa chiall gurbh í an Ghaeilge an
    phríomhtheanga cheannasach sna ceantair sin chomh maith go dtí le
    déanaí i dtéarmaí na staire.

Ar ndóigh, beidh daoine aonair a bhaineann le catagóirí éagsúla ar fáil laistigh d'aicmí
eile.

Téarmaíocht: Dátheangachas

Ní tearc iad na sainmhínithe ar choincheap an dátheangachais, go háirithe an
dátheangachas pearsanta ag leibhéal an indibhide, an chainteora aonair. Tá comhaontú
nach beag idir saineolaithe ar na sainmhínithe seo. Ní amhlaidh ar fad, áfach, i gcás an
dátheangachais phobail. Is lú fós an chomhintinn a fhaightear maidir le polasaithe
teanga don phobal dátheangach ina bhfuil teanga dhúchais neamhfhorleathan an
phobail teanga faoi shíorbhrú ag teanga cheannasach an mhórlaigh.

   Ar an ábhar sin, agus ag admháil réaltacht theangach chomhaimseartha na
hÉireann mar atá cruthaithe i suirbhéanna agus i saothair chuimsitheacha taighde,
cloítear san alt seo le tuiscint cuibheasach simplí ar pholasaithe atá dírithe ar athruithe
chun feabhais sa réaltacht sin i gcás pobail na teanga neamhfhorleithne. Is é sin, gur
gléas a bheadh in aon pholasaithe a cheapfaí nó a d'fheidhmeofaí, gléas d'fhonn staid
na teanga neamhfhorleithne a thabhairt ar aon leibhéal le staid na mórtheanga, dá
mb'fhéidir. Ar ndóigh, níorbh ionann an cur chuige laistigh de na trí rannóg a rinneadh
thuas den chointeanóid is 'Gaeltacht' ann, i mo thuiscintse; bheadh idirdhealuithe le
déanamh idir cainteoirí (ar leibhéil éagsúla cumais agus úsáide) agus cainteoirí
póitéinsealacha. Ach pointe éigin cothromaíochta bheith sroichte, bheadh rogha
fhírinneach ag baill an phobail theanga.

   I dtaca leis seo, meabhraíonn Colin Williams[3] (1994) dúinn nach mbíonn an pobal
mionteanga i bhfeighil go hiomlán ar thodhchaí a dteanga féin in ainneoin gur leo í:

> … it is the people of Wales and the Welsh diaspora who own the
> language by using and cherishing it…although we may own Welsh, we
> do not entirely control either its use or its legitimacy. Wales is a
> dependent society…a reactive rather than a purposive country in
> essence. (1994: 118)

In ainneoin athruithe ó 1994 i staid na Breataine Bige, tá brí fós leis an dearbhú seo i
gcás na Breatnaise agus na Gaeilge. Tagrófar tuilleadh do shaothar Williams sa chuid
eile den alt seo.

Téarmaíocht: Institiúid

Maidir leis an téarma 'institiúid', glactar leis gur crot nó foirm nó múnla atá i gceist
d'fhonn eagar nó ord a chur i bhfeidhm ar rud éigin, bíodh smaoineamh nó idé-
eolaíocht nó seirbhís nó gníomhaíocht i gceist, nó iad sin go léir i dteannta a chéile. De

---

[2] Ó Murchú, H. 'Coimisiún na hiar-Ghaeltachta: An Chéad Tuarascáil' i Ó Cearúil, M. (Eag.) 2000. *Aimsir Óg 2000*, 199–226. Baile Átha Cliath: Coiscéim.

[3] Williams, C. 'Development, Dependency and Democratic Deficit'. I ed. Thomas, P.W. *Fifth International Conference on Minority Languages,* Clevedon: Multilingual Matters. 1994. 101–27.

ghnáth, bunaítear chuige sin eintiteas éigin: institiúid nó foras nó údarás (téarmaí in úsáid ag leibhéal an stáit de ghnáth) nó cumann nó eagraíocht ag leibhéal na sochaí. (Is fearr liomsa an téarma 'eagraíocht' ná 'eagras' nó 'cumann' ar bhonn atá go hiomlán suibiachtúil pearsanta – braithim níos mó den eagar, den ghluaiseacht agus den ghníomhaíocht sa bhfocal 'eagraíocht').

Sa chomhthéacs seo, ní dochar comhairle Williams[4] a mheabhrú. I gcás pobail teanga, dar leis, ní mór a bheith aireach fiú agus an Stát mar a bheadh 'ag géilleadh' d'éilimh an phobail sin, agus é sin ar dhá chúis thábhachtacha. Ar an gcéad ásc, i bhfianaise thábhacht agus thionchar uileghabhálach an mhaorlathais Stáit i gcoitinne, d'fhéadfadh iarmhairtí gan coinne leanúint as glacadh nó leathadh na mionteanga i réimsí ar leith trí struchtúir sheanbhunaithe nó trí struchtúir nua de chuid an Stáit.

> ... we should [not] interpret the modern state as a benign benefactor, even if some of the tension between the state and the community has been eased by the granting of significant concessions (*pace*, recognised rights) on the part of the state. There is a real danger that this could amount to no more than the expropriation of the language and its ideological/value-laden culture. ... as these state-funded and controlled agencies exert their penetrative influence of social and cultural control ... the language may survive, but the culture – which is the real source of authenticity and resistance – may die ... to be replaced by a culture which has lost its independence and hence, rationale, to express its own values, ideas and ambitions. (1994: 104)

Is í mórán an argóint chéanna a léiríonn Daniel Bourgeois[5] i dtaca le cúrsaí oideachais do phobal na nAcadach i gCeanada maidir leis an ról ba chóir a bheith ag an institiúid oideachais sa réigiún sin, an *Conseil Scolaire Francophone,* mar atá chomh maith san áiteamh atá á dhéanamh athuair go mbunófaí bord nó eintiteas ar leith chun féachaint i ndiaidh ilriachtanas an oideachais Lán-Ghaeilge agus Ghaeltachta.

Dá réir, ní mór don phobal a bheith i gceannas a mhéid is is féidir ar a chuid institiúidí féin; mura mbíonn, seans gurb amhlaidh a bheidh luachanna agus cultúr na mór-theanga á seachadadh trí mheán na teanga neamhfhorleithne.

Páirtíocht: Baol agus Bua

Is cúis imní an méid thuasluaite a deir Williams maidir leis na himpleachtaí a d'fhéadfadh a bheith mar thoradh ar an státmhaoiniú agus ar an rialú stáit i réimsí institiúidithe mar na meáin agus an t-oideachas do mhionlaigh teanga. Is mó is cúis imní, áfach, an anailís a dhéanann sé ar na coibhnis nua a tharlaíonn idir an Stát agus saoránaigh nuair a dhéantar institiúidiú ar an mionteanga trí ghníomhaireachtaí nó áisínteachtaí úra, mar a phléifear níos faide síos.

Luaitear an stát agus an tsochaí d'aonghnó. In aon chóras daonlathach nua-aimseartha, ní mór aird a thabhairt ar dhá ghné den daonlathas. Is iad sin an ghné 'ionadaíoch' agus an ghné 'rannpháirtíoch'. Sa stát daonlathach comhaimseartha, de ghnáth, má tharlaíonn go ngéilltear cumhacht áirithe ón mbarr anuas, déantar sin trí chomhshocruithe ar leith idir ionadaithe nó iarrachtaí eagraithe an phobail agus institiúidí an Stáit. Meastar gur i bhfoirm *páirtíochta nó páirtnéireachta* le chéile is fearr

---

[4] *Ibid.*

[5] Bourgeois, D. 2010. *I dTreo Lánbhainistíocht Scoileanna Fraincisee i dTimpeallacht Mhionlaigh.* Baile Átha Cliath: COGG, Leagan Gaeilge.

a oibríonn an Stát eagraithe (nó institiúidí an Stáit) agus an tsochaí eagraithe (nó eagraíochtaí deonacha) ar cheisteanna ginearálta a bhaineann le folláine an phobail i gcoitinne.[6]

Ar ndóigh, is féidir go mbeadh bríonna éagsúla le coincheap na páirtnéireachta:

- Páirtnéireacht a chiallaíonn socruithe idir an Stát agus eagraíocht dheonach éigin; maoineoidh an Stát an eagraíocht d'fhonn gné áirithe de pholasaí an Stáit a fheidhmiú thar ceann an Stáit. Is coibhneas maoinithe atá eatarthu. Bíonn d'argóint ann go ndéantar dá réir gníomhairí Stáit, seachas gníomhaithe deonacha pobail, d'fhostaithe na heagraíochta, agus é sin in ainneoin bord deonach a bheith i gceist agus deonaigh ag saothrú taobh le taobh leis na fostaithe go minic. Labhartar ar an ocsamórón is 'deonachas státmhaoinithe' ann agus ar 'mheon na ndeontas'. Ar ndóigh, tá míthuiscint áirithe ansin ar fheidhmiú an daonlathais.

- Páirtnéireacht fhoirmiúil idir an eagraíocht (nó na heagraíochtaí) agus an státmhaoinitheoir. Tá na samplaí tearc go leor.

- Páirtnéireacht idir eagraíochtaí deonacha, bídís státmhaoinithe nó a mhalairt. Ní mór iad na samplaí a fheictear den chineál seo páirtíochta. Is ceann deacair é le bainistiú. Caitear comhshocruithe a bhaint amach ag leibhéal rialúcháin, físe, gníomhaíochta, maoinithe, riaracháin, measúnachta, agus cuntasachta. Bíonn an baol ann go mbuafaidh an t-amhras ar an tuiscint, an tuairisciú ar thorthaí na comhmhuiníne, an eagla roimh tháthcheangal ar an bhfonn comhoibrithe. Is fearr a oibríonn sé nuair a éiríonn sé go horgánach nádúrtha as riachtanais comhlántacha na n-eagraíochtaí féin; nuair is iad na heagraíochtaí féin a thúsaíonn an próiseas; nuair a bhíonn bunphrionsabail leagtha síos ó thosach.

Is í an ghné is suntasaí de na cineálacha páirtnéireachtaí seo ná go léirítear ceist cumhachta iontu go léir. Is léir, áfach, gur treise an chumhacht atá ag an maoinitheoir i ngach cás. Más é an Stát an maoinitheoir, is coibhneas cumhachta i bhfad níos éagothroime a bhíonn i gceist agus is lúide an gá a fheictear le comhurraim don chomhpháirtnéir pobail. Cruthaítear coibhneas an spleáchais, spleáchas atá bunaithe ar chumhacht an airgid amháin agus ní ar chomhchumhacht na dtorthaí maithe, spleáchas ar féidir go gcothófaí drochthréithe dá dheasca i gceachtar páirtí agus a chabhraíonn le coincheap an daonlathais a chur as a riocht – agus é sin, íoróineach go leor, in ainm an daonlathais. Cuireadh síos air mar choibhneas nó chóras 'feodach' sa phaimfléad uaim a luadh thuas faoi nóta 6. Cuireann Williams (op. cit.) síos air sna téarmaí seo:

> Rule by quango and grant-in-aid may be purposeful and efficient … another quango, the Welsh Language Board…It is possible to argue that with this new definition of democracy, joint-venture partnership works very well in that it allows patronage to reward the initiatives of dynamic individuals. The keywords of *this* democratic culture are initiative, venture, partnership and flexible accommodation to the global-local nexus. (1994:124)

---

[6] Ó Murchú, H. 2003. *Limistéar na Sibhialtachta: Dúshlán agus Treo d'Eagraíochtaí na Gaeilge, An Aimsir Óg, Paimfléad 2*. Baile Átha Cliath: Coiscéim.

Tógann sé ceisteanna íogaire ansin faoin leagan amach seo ar chúrsaí:

> Is this a new version of democracy, or is it an absence of democracy?
> What are its implications for the management of Welsh cultural and
> educational institutions? (1994: 124)

Tá trí chuid leis an bhfreagra a sholáthraíonn sé agus é ag argóint go bunúsach dá chás ar son féinrialú don Bhreatain Bhig. Is argóintí ginearálta iad, áfach, is féidir a thagairt do chásanna eile chomh maith.

> ... a process of 'negotiated sovereignty'... the real centres of power
> [cuma cén leibhéal] frequently escape democratic scrutiny and control
> ... relative autonomy of Welsh culture ... it all depends on the quality
> of the appointees in 'quangoland'... But should personality rather than
> accountable structures rule our futures?... Communal well being in
> Wales depends upon citizen involvement, through responsive local
> government structures which reflect the particularism of each region.
> (1994: 125)

Ag coimeád fainicí Williams in aigne, féachfar anois ar shamplaí den réasúnaíocht a dhéanann an Stát sa Phoblacht i dtaca le comhshocruithe i bhfoirm páirtnéireachtaí pobail nó eile. B'in rud a léiríodh sa cháipéis *Creatlach Téarnaimh*,[7] a chuir an Rialtas ó dheas os comhair na bPáirtnéirí Sóisialta agus an meathlú eacnamaíoch ag bagairt. Maidir leis na héifeachtaí sochaíocha a raibh coinne leo ag éirí as ábhar na cáipéise sin bhí nathanna ar nós 'gualainn le gualainn' agus 'gluaiseacht phobail' agus 'comhdhlúthú pobail' le cloisint. Is ar an earnáil dheonach go príomha a bhíonn fíorú na nathanna sin ag brath – rud a chruthaíonn idir dhainséar, dhúshlán agus dheis.

Is féidir córas nó próiseas a bhunú, ar ndóigh, d'fhonn struchtúr a chur ar an gcomhpháirtíocht seo, a mbeidh an Stát mar pháirtnéir gníomhach amháin ann, mar a luadh. Ach, mar a tharlaíonn in aon fhiontar daonna, beidh buntáistí agus fadhbanna ag gabháil leis *sa bhreis* ar a bhfuil luaite thuas. Tá de bhaol ann:

- go gcaillfidh ceachtar taobh radharc ar an mbunaidhm agus ar thorthaí ina leith don spriocphobal;
- go rachaidh ceachtar taobh lasmuigh dá gceart-ról;
- go ndéanfaidh an taobh deonach dearmad ar na pobail, ar an mballraíocht, a bhfuiltear ionadaíoch orthu nó in ainm is a bheith ag labhairt thar a gceann agus ar a son;
- i ngan fhios dá réir, go ngabhfaidh an taobh deonach chuici féin dearcadh an rialtais nó na n-údarás nó na mór-theanga;
- go dtarlóidh marbhántacht instiúideach nó eagraíochtúil.

Leagtar amach buntáistí na comhpháirtíochta sa chuid dheireanach den aighneacht[8] a d'ullmhaigh an Roinn Airgeadais sa Phoblacht don Ghrúpa Speisialta (*Special Group on Public Service Numbers and Expenditure Programmes*) a bhunaigh an Rialtas d'fhonn ciorruithe substaintiúla a aimsiú ar an gcaiteachas poiblí. Ba é an Grúpa seo a d'fhoilsigh an tuarascáil uileghabhálach dhá imleabhar ar tugadh tuarascáil 'An Bhoird

---

[7] Rialtas na hÉireann 2008. *Creatlach Téarnaimh*.
[8] An Roinn Airgeadais 2009. *Crosscutting Issues: Local Delivery Mechanisms*.

Snip Nua' (2009) uirthi. B'fhéidir *raison d'être* na comhpháirtíochta a áireamh in aighneacht na Roinne Airgeadais agus tagairt á dhéanamh do chláracha áirithe tacaíochta pobail. In go leor réimsí polasaí de chuid an Stáit, is ea a dúradh san aighneacht sin, is cuid bhunúsach den straitéis roghnaithe *tacú leis an gcur chuige ón mbonn aníos*, rud a chiallaíonn tacaíocht d'eagraíochtaí atá neamhstatúideach agus neamhspleách. I measc rólanna agus spriocanna, luadh liosta spéisiúil:

- cothú na comhpháirtíochta pobail ar bhonn gníomhach;
- tacú leis an deonachas mar rud maith ann féin (saoránacht ghníomhach);
- cothú na féinmhuiníne agus na féiníomhá dearfaí;
- soláthar seirbhísí áitiúla riachtanacha;
- soláthar eolais, comhairle, oiliúna agus fostaíochta;
- cothú na fiontraíochta;
- measúnú ar riachtanais;
- meastóireacht ar iarratais ar státmhaoiniú ar thograí.

Tá chomh maith san aighneacht seo ón Roinn Airgeadais athdhearbhú ar *ábharthacht leanúnach an pholasaí bhunaidh* a chothaíonn na heagraíochtaí éagsúla pobail a bhí faoi chaibidil. Feictear go bhfuil barántúlacht i gcónaí le coincheap an tsoláthair nó an tseachadta *áitiúil* ar na cúiseanna seo:

- pobail áitiúla a bheith comhpháirteach in ullmhú nó i ndearadh agus i soláthar na réiteach sin atá oiriúnach dá bhfadhbanna logánta féin;
- forbairt an spioraid phobail agus cuimsiú sochaíoch mar chuid den phróiseas.

Ní amháin sin, ach admhaítear *nach* acmhainn do Ranna agus do Ghníomhaireachtaí Stáit atá *lárnach* feidhmiú le héifeachtacht agus le héifeachtúlacht ar an mbonn *áitiúil*; níl de chumas acu *ar an scála logánta* an tsainfhadhb a aimsiú agus an réiteach cuí a sholáthar; bheadh sé neamheacnamaíoch fiú, dar leis an aighneacht, na tréanacmhainní a bheadh de dhíth chuige sin a chur ar fáil thar na Ranna agus na Gníomhaireachtaí ábhartha d'fhonn toradh a bheadh éifeachtach a shroichint. Seo í an Roinn Airgeadais ag soláthar *raison d'être* ginearálta an-bhreá don earnáil dheonach. Is ceann é a bhfuil a mhacalla le cloisint i bhformhór tíortha daonlathacha an Iarthair.

In ainneoin seasamh ginearálta chomh dearfach a bheith á léiriú ag an Roinn Airgeadais, áfach, is ar leibhéal *an eagrúcháin, na bainistíochta agus an riaracháin*, ar an leibhéal *struchtúrtha*, a cháineann an aighneacht seo an earnáil mar atá. Lorgaítear athruithe chun éifeachtúlachta dá réir, ar an earnáil *agus ar an Stát*. Ar na laigí luaitear:

- forluí ag eagraíochtaí ar a chéile maidir le bunsprioc agus le feidhmiú;
- nach freagra ar struchtúr éifeachtach iliomad saineagraíochtaí cuibheasach beag – fiú agus sainfheidhm ag gach ceann díobh, fiú agus iad ag feidhmiú laistigh de cheantar réamhshainithe;
- nach freagra ar struchtúr éifeachtach ach oiread an idirghníomhaíocht neamhfhoirmeálta nó fiú an chomhroinnt ar acmhainní áirithe más gan pleanáil é;
- nach comhionann i gcónaí an tseirbhís atá ar fáil ó cheantar go chéile; ach go mbeadh caighdeánú seirbhísí níos costasaí fós mura roghnófaí an t-ainmní comónta ab ísle mar shlat tomhais, *rud nach ionmholta* mar a admhaítear.

Spéisiúil go leor, admhaítear san aighneacht easpa éifeachtúlachta le modhanna maoinithe an Stáit; deacracht le saintorthaí a aithint i leith na maoinitheoirí éagsúla; ualach breise ar an eagraíocht dheonach a bheith ag ullmhú aighneachtaí agus ag soláthar tuairiscí do shraith de mhaoinitheoirí. Admhaítear chomh maith nach bhfuil ar fáil forléargas cuimsitheach ar na hacmhainní a dheonaítear i gcóimheas leis na torthaí ba chóir a bhaint amach nó atá bainte amach, anailís a admhaítear nach furasta a bheachtú i gcásanna áirithe, cúrsaí leibhéal na comhpháirtíochta pobail, mar shampla, (nó cúrsaí teanga go deimhin). Déantar roinnt moltaí dá réir:

- cumaisc a dhéanamh d'eagraíochtaí a bhfuil cosúlachtaí feidhme acu;
- aon fhoinse amháin maoinithe a lonnú *go lárnach* in aon Roinn sainithe amháin;
- aon fhoinse amháin measúnaithe agus meastóireachta a aithint *ar bhonn áitiúil* do cheantair ar leith (an Chomhairle Contae nó ceann de na hEagraíochtaí Comhpháirtnéireachta sa chás áirithe faoi chaibidil);
- cuid den mhaoiniú a thairiscint ar bhonn comórtais (*cé go n-admhaítear nach bhfuil a leithéid de chur chuige ag teacht le neamhspleáchas agus le leanúnachas eagraíochtaí*).

Is argóintí iad seo a fheicfear arís thíos sa chur chuige nua a theastaíonn ón struchtúr thuaidh/theas, Foras na Gaeilge.

Éifeachtacht agus Éifeachtúlacht: Cleas na Téarmaíochta

Rinneadh iarracht san aighneacht oifigiúil, *Local Delivery Mechanisms*, a bheith cuibheasach cothrom do cheachtar taobh: taobh an Stáit agus taobh na hEarnála Deonaí Pobail. Luadh 'éifeachtacht' (*efficiency*) minic go leor. Ba nod nó leide nó cód an téarma sin ar 'costas-éifeacht' nach bhfuil ach coiscéim idir é agus 'costasghearradh'. Níor luadh 'éifeachtúlacht' (*effectiveness*) minic go leor. Ar ndóigh, bheadh athrú áirithe meoin de dhíth agus critéir úrnua d'fhonn torthaí éifeachtúlachta a mheas i réimsí áirithe gníomhaíochta a mbíonn na *torthaí neamh-inbhraite* (*intangible*) orthu níos tábhachtaí uaireanta ná na torthaí inbhraite (*tangible*); a mbíonn an *próiseas neamh-inbhraite* iontu chomh luachmhar leis an *toradh inbhraite* – fíric ar féidir fírinne bhreise fós a bheith ag baint léi i gcúrsaí teanga de. Is baolach gur beag aird a thugtar air seo, in ainneoin iarrachtaí ar aschuir cháilíochtúla a áireamh i réimsí ar leith chomh maith leis na haschuir chainníochtúla. Is é an bhunfhadhb ná teacht ar na critéir chuí ar an ní is éifeachtúlacht ann, má tá sin indéanta ar chor ar bith, de réir réimse gníomhaíochta. Mura bhfuil sé indéanta ar mhodh muiníneach áititheach seachas ar mhodh na tairngireachta, b'fhearr do mhaoinitheoirí agus d'ionadaithe an státchórais é sin a admháil go hionraic agus dearbhú, dá thoradh, go bhfuil breisluach leis na gníomhaíochtaí sóisialta seo, breisluach nach bhfeictear a thoradh go minic ach sa bhfadthodhchaí; nach ann do na critéir fós chun é sin a thomhas agus nach bhfuil ach bonn teoranta *cainníochtúil* dáiríre le pé úsáid a bhaintear as an téarma 'éifeachtúlacht'. B'fhearr sin ná mí-úsáid neamheol ghaiseach ar bhrí an téarma. B'fhearr fós dá dtabharfaí faoi shainiú ar na critéir éalaitheacha seo. Chuige seo, ba ghá don mhaoinitheoir agus don státchoras plé leis na gníomhairí pobail agus le húsáideoirí seirbhísí pobail. Ar ndóigh, eascraíonn na deacrachtaí seo as comhthéacs áirithe a phléifear níos mine thíos i dtéarmaí cumhachta agus athruithe.

I dtaca leis an bplé áirithe seo ar théarmaíocht, luaitear nithe spéisiúla eile – a léiríonn na deacrachtaí tuisceana – san aighneacht chéanna thuasluaite ón Roinn Airgeadais:

> ... in éagmais cruashonraí, níorbh acmhainn éifeachtúlacht a bheith ar na critéir mheasúnaithe in úsáid; chun tabhairt faoi mheasúnú dá leithéid, bheadh gá mar réamhchéim le hathruithe maoinithe agus bainistíochta.

Tá easpa éigin loighice anseo, dar liom. Ba dhóigh le duine nár ghá athruithe maoinithe agus bainistíochta chun na cruashonraí inmhianaithe a aimsiú ní mó ná go leanfadh aimsiú na gcruashonraí pé athruithe maoinithe agus bainistíochta a dhéanfaí. B'fhéidir tabhairt faoin taighde inmhianaithe i gceachtar den dá chás. Ní léir ach oiread gur de thoradh taighde a thángthas ar an tuiscint go raibh athruithe de dhíth, athruithe a éascódh aimsiú na gcruashonraí a léireodh éifeachtúlacht an fhiontair nó a mhalairt. Is mó de dhearbhú meoin chomh maith le bonn éigin a chur le polasaí áirithe a bheith á lorg atá sa dearbhú seo gan bunús cuí i gcáipéis na Roinne. Feicfear an cur chuige céanna arís i gcás eile thíos, cás Fhoras na Gaeilge.

Chun na fírinne a insint, ní furasta teacht ar chritéir d'fhonn breisluach gníomhaíochtaí sóisialta nó teanga a mheas. Ní ionann sin, áfach, agus gan iarracht a dhéanamh iad a dhearadh. Ní freagra ar an bhfadhb gan í a aithint, nó í a bhréagnú, nó leas a bhaint as an téarma 'éifeachtúlacht' go míchruinn mícheart, nó as an dá théarma 'éifeachtacht' agus 'éifeachtúlacht' faoi mar gurb ionann brí dóibh.

Chuige sin, lorg mé le déanaí slat tomhais éigin chun an 'breisluach' nó 'éifeachtúlacht' a thomhas in aschuir eagraíochtaí deonacha teanga. Tá iarrachtaí áirithe déanta ach casta le leanúint agus le cur i bhfeidhm. Freagra amháin a fuair mé ó eacnamaí clúiteach – go mbeadh an duais Nobel aige dá mbeadh freagra cruinn aige ar an gceist ach go bhfuil eacnamaithe áirithe ag tabhairt faoi anois. Seans go bhfuil sin amhlaidh, ar ndóigh, toisc go bhfuil teipthe go pointe ar na foirmlí breátha matamaiticiúla a bhí forbartha go dtí seo chun teilgean a dhéanamh ar fhorbairt agus ar mheath an gheilleagair, beag beann ar shíceolaíocht an duine (seachas mar thomhaltóir ar a leas féin amháin) agus ar fholláine shóisialta an phobail. Cé nach bhfuil freagra le fáil ann ach chomh beag ar an gceist maidir le 'breisluach', is spéisiúil an cur chuige ar cheist na hinmharthanachta coitinne atá ag Tim Jackson.[10] Luaitear eacnamaithe ós rud é gurb é a léamh siúd ar an saol sóisialta agus a bhfriotal siúd, friotal an mhargaidh, a rialaíonn an saol sóisialta chomh maith leis an saol státmhaoinithe faoi láthair.

Cumhacht agus Roinnt Cumhachta

Den chuid is mó, is do ghníomhaíocht eagraithe ón mbonn aníos, an toil phoiblí á léiriú trí bhrúghrúpaí agus trí ghluaiseacht ar son cearta áirithe, a ghéilleann taobh an stáit. Cruthaítear institiúidí agus gníomhaireachtaí leathstáit nua dá réir le hintinn freastal ar riachtanais an phobail teanga. Is ceann de bhuntéiseanna Williams (op. cit.) é go n-athraítear dá thoradh cineál an choibhnis idir saoránaigh agus an stát ar dhá bhealach atá an-bhunúsach. Is amhlaidh a chruthaítear go comhuaineach riachtanas na comhpháirtíochta eatarthu ach go gcruthaítear coibhneas an spleáchais chomh maith feasta i gcás saoránach nó institiúidí nó ionadaithe an phobail teanga.

---

[9] Grin, F. (ECMI) and Tom Moring (EBLUL), Research Project Leaders, 2002. *Final Report: Support for Minority Languages in Europe*. Brussels: European Commission.

[10] Jackson, T. 2009. *Prosperity without Growth: Economics for a Finite Planet*. London: Earthscan.

Níos bunúsaí ná sin, áfach, tá laghdaithe ar neamhspleáchas an phobail teanga agus na hionadaithe acu sa mhéid is gur cuid anois iad de choimpléacs nua gníomhaíochta agus luachanna. Is coimpléacs é seo atá faoi cheannas threoir an mhargaidh cuid mhór, faoi mar atá an Stát féin go hinmheánach agus go seachtrach; ag iarraidh cothromaíocht áirithe a choimeád idir é agus éifeachtaí an domhandaithe, lena gcuid sochar agus dochar araon. I bhfocla Glyn Williams, agus é á lua ag Colin Williams (1994: 104):

> ... the Welsh language and its culture have been threatened, less by a 'state', than by a *social totality* of a liberal, parliamentary democracy operating within the moral , political and ideological hegemony of an advanced capital society. Within that totality the 'state' has been as much of a response as an originator.

I gcás na Gaeilge, baineann an comhthéacs athraithe le hiarmhairtí institiúidiú na teanga mar chuid áirithe den státchóras. A mhéid a bheidh ag éirí le pobal na Gaeilge an lonnú agus an stádas oifigiúil sin a bhaint amach don teanga is ea is mó a lagaítear ar a ról chun cur i gcoinne an stáit. Ina ionad sin, tarlaíonn mar a bheadh comhthuiscintí nó páirtíocht áirithe maoinithe nó eile idir an Stát agus an pobal teanga (nó ionadaithe is eagraíochtaí an phobail sin). Is é an dúshlán anois *idirspleáchas torthúil* de chineál eigin a bhaint amach in ionad an spleáchais mharbhánta. Ní neamhspleáchas an freagra, fiú dá n-aimseodh an earnáil dheonach an maoiniú chuige sin. Mar tá freagracht na teanga agus an phobail teanga ar an dá pháirtí, ar an Stát agus ar an bpobal teanga gona n-institiúidí deonacha.

Baineann an comhthéacs agus an coibhneas athraithe chomh maith le friotal agus le héilimh fhealsúnacht an mhargaidh shóisialta mar a luadh thuas. Má tá an Ghaeilge súite isteach sa státchóras, is cuid anois í de chreatlach machnaimh eile ar fad. Ar chomhchéim le coda eile den státchóras céanna, tá sí anois freagrach do rialacha eile. Cuireann Williams síos orthu sna téarmaí seo:

> ... re-routing the relatively autonomous needs of Welsh culture into a more state-wide institutional design so as to account for and control expenditure and subsidy ... Rather than being seen as an absolute right, granted to deserving citizens who wish to exercise their culture as fully as possible, current and future reforms will be made in accordance with the trinitarian principles ... namely the improvement of efficiency, the greater targeting of resources, and the reduction of 'waste' whenever possible. (1994:118)

Mar sin, d'ionadaithe an phobail teanga, leanann strácáil nua an strácáil a rinneadh d'fhonn aitheantas sa státchóras a bhaint amach don teanga. Tá eiliminti de na héilimh nua lán-inghlactha agus do-sheachanta; bheadh glacadh in aon fhiontar le cuntasacht, le trédhearcacht, le torthaí fónta intomhaiste, le hiarrachtaí aon vástáil a sheachaint. In am an ghátair san eacnamaíocht, is é is dóichí go mbeadh ionadaithe an phobail teanga lán-ullamh mar dhea-shaoránaigh a bpáirt a imirt agus an phian a fhulaingt. Ach tá eiliminti eile neamh-inghlactha. Pléifear na heiliminti sin faoi Fhoras na Gaeilge thíos. Baineann siad le feidhmiú cumhachta, le páirtíocht chóir, le buncheisteanna Williams: Cé leis an teanga? Cé tá i dteideal cinntí a dhéanamh ar a todhchaí?

Próiseas na Páirtíochta: Roinnt Samplaí

Níor mhiste féachaint anois ar *roinnt samplaí de phróiseas na páirtíochta*, go háirithe ar phróisis atá dírithe ar athruithe chun feabhais a aimsiú, i dtéarmaí fhriotail agus éileamh an mhargaidh. Díreofar go príomha ar an Roinn Gnóthaí Pobail, Comhionannais agus Gaeltachta (mar a bhí) ó dheas, sa Phoblacht, maille leis an dá fhoras thuaidh/theas faoi chúram na Roinne sin.

Páirtíochtaí Pobail faoin Roinn Gnóthaí Pobail, Comhionannais agus Gaeltachta

Thug an aighneacht sin na Roinne Airgeadais cur síos áirithe ar an gcóras comhpháirtíochta mar atá i réimse áirithe Stáit, go háirithe páirtnéireachtaí logánta faoin gclár Eorpach LEADER atá á riaradh ag an Roinn (nua-ainmnithe) Gnóthaí Pobail, Comhionannais agus Gaeltachta (GNPC agus G). Tugadh chomh maith an réasúnaíocht i dtreo athraithe ar son éifeachta, sa chiall acusan den téarma – athruithe i gcur chuige an Stáit agus na hEarnála araon:

- sa 'chuíchóiriú' inmhianaithe a bhíothas a lorg, níor samhlaíodh aon laghdú sna feidhmeanna ná sa leibhéal gníomhaíochta a bhí ar bun ag na heagraíochtaí a bhí faoi chaibidil san aighneacht; dearcadh beagán simplí nuair is riachtanas bunaidh don chostas-éifeacht anailís agus taighde a dhéanamh d'fhonn cruthúnas éifeachta a sholáthar i dtéarmaí (a) go bhfuil bunaidhm an fhiontair á shroichint agus (b) go leanfaidh sin gan athrú fiú le costas laghdaithe;
- rinneadh tagairt chomh maith don 'phróiseas leanúnach comhtháthaithe' a bhí ar siúl faoin Roinn GNPCandG maidir leis na páirtnéireachtaí aitiúla agus na cláracha LEADER faoina cúram d'fhonn líon na n-eagraíochtaí a laghdú ó 96 go 60. Is fiú an tagairt don phróiseas a lua ina hiomláine: De réir dealraimh, faoi Mhárta 2009: 'This process [had] taken a number of years to deliver results which indicates that reducing numbers of local organisations is not a simple task'.

Comhairle mhaith! Tagrófar arís da leithéid faoi Fhoras na Gaeilge thíos. Mar sin féin, pé ní faoi mhíshástacht leis na torthaí deireanacha, chun a ceart a thabhairt don Roinn, is próiseas comhphlé go pointe áirithe a bhí anseo; próiseas a chuimsigh den chuid is mó, de réir dealraimh, an dá thaobh a bhí i gceist, oifigigh na Roinne agus ionadaithe na n-eagraíochtaí ar an talamh. Chomh maith leis sin, fágadh am don phróiseas plé agus cainte mar is léir. Ag caint ag Cruinniú Cinnbhliana 2010 den scátheagraíocht, *The Wheel*, luaigh an tAire go raibh sé oscailte d'aon mhúnla sásúil a bhainfeadh amach an bhunaidhm, nó an laghdú agus an cuíchóiriú inmhianaithe.

Fágadh as an gcuntas seo tagairt do chláracha sa Ghaeltacht.

Uiscebhealaí Éireann

Maidir le *próiseas an bhainistiú ar athruithe*, luaitear sampla Uiscebhealaí Éireann, foras thuaidh theas a bhfuil seacht gcinn d'uiscebhealaí faoina chúram, foras a thagann faoi choimirce na Roinne a bhfuil cúram na Gaeilge agus na Gaeltachta uirthi. D'ullmhaigh agus d'eisigh an foras seo foireann nua rialúchán maidir leis na huiscebhealaí sa dlínse ó dheas i mí Iúil 2010 agus thúsaigh *próiseas comhairliúcháin*. Déanfar amhlaidh don tuaisceart ar ball. Níor tharla go comhuaineach toisc reachtaíocht éagsúil a bheith i bhfeidhm ó thuaidh.

Baineann an chéad chéim den phróiseas comhairliúcháin leis na geallshealbhóirí. Is iad sin na heagraíochtaí éagsúla atá ionadaíoch orthu siúd a bhaineann leas as na huiscebhealaí. Tugadh 15 sheachtain dóibh chun an t-abhar a scrúdú, é a phlé leis na baill acu, agus teacht ar ais le freagra comhtháite. Bhí i gceist ag an bhforas áirithe seo anailís inmheánach a dhéanamh ar na freagraí ansin sula rachfaí ar aghaidh go dtí an dara céim den phróiseas comhairliúcháin, is é sin leis an bpobal trí mheán fógraíochta poiblí. Ní chuirfear na rialúcháin i bhfeidhm go mbeidh an próiseas seo thart.

Cuirtear an próiseas seo i gcomparáid thíos le sampla forais eile, Foras na Gaeilge.

Foras na Gaeilge agus An Earnáil Dheonach

Tugtar an dá shampla thuas mar chomhthéacs leis an mbealach a bhfuil cúrsaí i gcás an fhorais eile thuaidh/theas eile, Foras na Gaeilge, i dtaca leis an Earnáil Dheonach Ghaeilge.

Ní miste téarmaíocht a mhíniú mar thús. Cuimsíonn *Earnáil na Gaeilge* struchtúir reachtúla (ranna, foras, údarás), móide an earnáil dheonach Ghaeilge (le maoiniú agus gan maoiniú Stáit), móide na pobail éagsúla cainteoirí, chomh maith le haon ghníomhaíocht nó aon ghrúpa nó aon eagraíocht chultúrtha a bhíonn ag cur chun leas na teanga, ar bhonn leanúnach nó ócáideach. Mar sin, áirítear in Earnáil na Gaeilge idir mhaoinitheoir agus thairbhithe an mhaoinithe sin. Tá an téarma Earnáil *Dheonach* na Gaeilge féinmhínitheach.

Gan dul go mion isteach i scéal atá mionphléite sna meáin Ghaeilge le déanaí, thosaigh Foras na Gaeilge próiseas thiar i dtús 2007 d'fhonn (i) comhordú a dhéanamh idir tosaíochtaí maoinithe agus aidhmeanna straitéiseacha an Fhorais (san ord sin) le tosaíochtaí an 19 eagraíocht dheonach Gaeilge a bhí á mbunmhaoiniú acu (miontuairiscí, Aibreán 2007); (ii) athbhreithniú a dhéanamh ar na heagraíochtaí sin (miontuairiscí, Meitheamh 2007). Ar an 19 eagraíochtaí sin bhí 8 a raibh dualgas a maoinithe aistrithe ó Roinn na Gaeltachta chuig an Foras nua agus iad luaite go sonrach san Acht (1999) a bhunaigh an Foras. Ar an 11 eile, bhí eagraíochtaí áirithe a bhíodh á maoiniú faoi Bhord na Gaeilge, réamhtheachtaí an Fhorais, agus ionchas réasúnta acu go leanfadh an maoiniú sin, chomh maith le heagraíochtaí a tháinig níos déanaí isteach ach a raibh obair riachtanach ar bun acu. Le cur leis seo go léir, bhí sraith de scéimeanna neamhbhuana gearrthéarmacha á maoiniú ag an bhForas féin faoi chóras iomaíochta, cuid acu sna réimsí céanna leis an earnáil dheonach, nó an-ghar dóibh. Is ar bhonn iarratas bliantúil agus tuairisciú rialta a bhí an 19 ag feidhmiú, agus bunmhaoiniú feidhmithe ar fáil chomh maith le deontais ar thograí áirithe. Níor chuir an Foras in iúl riamh nach rabhthas sásta le torthaí an mhaoinithe mar a bhí á léiriú sna tuairiscí seo.

Tharla litreacha agus cruinnithe ag lorg athruithe idir feidhmeannas an Fhorais agus na heagraíochtaí idir 2007 agus 2010 chomh maith le ráitis (a bhí lom go maith toisc staid geilleagrach agus airgeadais na tíre) ó Aire na Gaeltachta san am. Bhí an bhunteachtaireacht chéanna le cloisint sna teagmhála go léir: cuíchóiriú, athstruchtúrú, múnlaí úra maoinithe, luach ar airgead, laghdú coiteann ar líon na n-eagraíochtaí, ar fhoireann, ar oifigí, ar chaiteachas; béim ar chomhoibriú agus ar chomhordú. I ngach cás, lorg an Foras tuairimí na n-eagras ach níor tharla comhchainteanna substaintiúla i dtreo réitigh, comhchainteanna den chineál a mbeifí ag súil leo agus cúrsaí mar a bhí.

Faoina thionchar seo go léir, d'eisigh an Chomhairle Aireachta Thuaidh Theas (CATT) dhá ráiteas chomhaontaithe, 02 Nollaig 2009 agus 26 Bealtaine 2010, mórán ar an téad chéanna: ag lorg ar dtús go ngearrfaí maoiniú anuas go dtí eagraíocht amháin thuaidh/theas nó go cnuasach beag eagraíochtaí agus ansin ag glacadh i bprionsabal le samhail nua mhaoinithe a chuir Foras na Gaeilge chun tosaigh, samhail a mínítear na príomhghnéithe inti níos faide síos.

Le linn an ama, bhí an Earnáil Dheonach ag teacht le chéile agus ag déanamh taighde, ar thóir réitigh dóibh féin agus don mhaoinitheoir. Glacadh leis an bhfírinne go raibh gá le hathruithe agus go raibh airgead gann. Mar sin féin, nádúrtha go leor, níor mhiste leis an Earnáil, mar a tharla i gcás na Roinne mar shampla, go bhfeicfí dóibh go raibh íobairtí á ndéanamh chomh maith ag an bhForas agus nach ar Chiste na hEarnála amháin a bheadh sceanairt le déanamh. Lorgaíodh comhthéacs níos iomláine dá gcuid saothair sa mhéid is nár léir na tosaíochtaí straitéiseacha don Ghaeilge a bhí laistiar de phleananna an Fhorais. Thar aon ní eile, theastaigh ón Earnáil go mbeadh ardán ceart acu chun a seasamh féin a mhíniú agus iarracht a dhéanamh seasamh an Fhorais a thuiscint ina iomláine. Lorgaíodh gléas a bhí luaite i gcáipéis shamhail an Fhorais féin, Coiste um Bhainistiú Athraithe, ach gan toradh go ceann i bhfad.

Le cuntas lom mar seo, ní holc an chuma atá ar an scéal. Is mór an difear, áfach, idir an modh oibre sa chás seo agus sna cinn eile thuasluaite a raibh mórán an toradh céanna á lorg, is e sin athrú suntasach sa *status quo*. Bhí cuma éagcothrom ar chúrsaí i gcoitinne sa chás seo:

- Foras aontaithe amháin agus smacht an sparáin chomh maith le smacht an eolais acu ar a raibh á bheartú acu féin i gcoinne 19 eagraíochtaí a bhí éagsúil ó chéile ar mhórán bealaí;
- dhá phróiseas a lean ar aghaidh go hiomlán neamhspleách ar a chéile; ní raibh aon eolas á roinnt leis na heagraíochtaí mar chomhthéacs leis na hathruithe a bhí á lorg, ní bhfuaireadar iomlán torthaí an tsuirbhé a chuir an Foras á dhéanamh orthu ná léargas ar aon fhorphlean straitéiseach a bheith ag an bhForas a mbeadh ról dóibh ann gan trácht ar thuairim éigin faoi smaointeoireacht an Fhorais – seachas athrá ar chuíchóiriú agus tagairtí do sprioc am gairid, gan trácht ar réamhradharc ar an samhail nua mhaoinithe ná deis plé uirthi roimh ré;
- b'ionann próiseas comhairliúcháin le geallshealbhóirí i gcás an Fhorais agus iarratais leanúnacha orthu an gnó a dhéanamh iad féin gan aon leide faoi cén fhreagairt a bheadh ag an bhForas ar na torthaí;
- athstruchtúrú i bhfollús a bheith á lorg agus é sin laistigh d'achar gairid ama agus faoi bhrú chomh dian go raibh ar eagraíochtaí áirithe fógra iomarcaíochta a eisiúint dá bhfoireann, 'cheal eolais nó treorach.

Theastaigh ón Earnáil Bhunmhaoinithe struchtúr comhphleanála nó próiseas oscailte comhairliúcháin mar thaca dóibh sa tasc ríchrua a iarradh orthu nó eolas de chineál a thabharfadh comhthéacs dóibh. Ina ionad sin, le cabhair comhlachta, rinne an Foras a phlean féin a ullmhú beag beann ar na geallshealbhóirí agus fuair aontú 'i bprionsabal' air ón gCATT. B'intuigthe an cur chuige é ar fhianaise an 'phlean' chéanna. Ní luafar ach roinnt ghnéithe de:

- athrú ó bhonn sa mhúnla maoinithe; deireadh le bunmhaoiniú d'aon tsaghas;
- maoiniú feasta ní ar bhonn eagraíochtúil ach ar bhonn iarratais ar 'phunann scéimeanna';
- scéimeanna oscailte do chách ar bhonn iomaíochta;
- iarratas go leasófaí an tAcht a chuireann dualgas (éigin) maoinithe ar an bhForas i leith 8 gcinn de na heagraíochtaí;

- gan idirdhealú cuí idir riachtanais na teanga sa dá dhlínse, thuaidh agus theas;
- maíomh as 'eifeachtúlacht' na samhla nua gan aon chruthú go raibh mí-éifeacht le casadh leis an earnáil bhunmhaoinithe nó cén bealach a mbeadh éifeacht ann feasta nó cérbh iad na critéir chun é sin a thomhas;
- ba léir an critéar aonair tábhachtach ó ráiteas a rinneadh faoin gcéatadán de bhuiséad an Fhorais a bhí á chaitheamh ar na heagraíochtaí.

Nuair a rinne Foras na Gaeilge an tsamhail nua acu a oscailt do chomhairliúchán phoiblí, bhí ar an Earnáil a chur in iúl gur ar éigean a leanadh na gnáthnósmhaireachtaí.

Fágtar as san alt seo díospóireacht ar cúis mhaith a bheith nó gan a bheith le cuspóir an athstruchtúraithe ann féin; is ar *oibriú an phróisis* a leanadh atá béim á chur anseo. Sna cásanna eile d'athstruchtúrú a luadh thuas:

- ghlac an maoinitheoir comhpháirt ghníomhach sa tasc crua athstruchtúraithe – tugadh cáipéisí a thug míniú ar an athrú do na geallshealbhóirí le plé;
- tharla chomhchomhairliúchán de chineál éigin;
- críochnaíodh le níos lú struchtúr agus foirne, b'fhéidir, agus le laghdú caiteachais Stáit, ach rinneadh an t-athstruchtúrú sin laistigh den bhfrámaíocht cheanann chéanna a bhí ann roimis; níor tharla athrú ó bhonn.

Is spéisiúil, is suntasach fiú, sa chomparáid seo ar na próisis éagsúla a lean gníomhaireachtaí Stáit, na difríochtaí eatarthu. Níos tábhachtaí, b'fhéidir, feictear i gcás na gníomhaireachta teanga sa bhliain 2009 mórán dá raibh tuartha in alt Williams a foilsíodh sa bhliain 1994, bunaithe ar chaint a tugadh sa bhliain 1993.[11]

Is den tábhacht é chomh maith go ndéanfar beachtú idir na téarmaí 'éifeachtacht' agus 'éifeachtúlacht' maidir lena mbaineann le torthaí na hoibre deonaí státmhaoinithe ar shraith de chúiseanna. Ní amháin chun doiléire dearbhuithe a déantar ró-mhinic a sheachaint ach chun freastal ar riachtanais fhriotal an mhargaidh ar mhodh proifisiúnta mar atá riachtanach sa saol atá suas. Seans go gcabhródh sé chomh maith chun léargas níos fuarchúisí a thabhairt ar an gcóras 'feodach' agus na míbhuntáistí a ghabhann leis. Thar aon ní eile, léireofaí níos cruinne na fíorthorthaí ar an saothar deonach agus ar an maoiniú Stáit.

An *Straitéis 20-Bliain don Ghaeilge* sa Phoblacht

Tá baint nach beag ag an ábhar seo go léir leis an *Straitéis 20-Bliain don Ghaeilge 2010–2030*[12] sa Phoblacht.

In ainneoin nach bhfuil an Straitéis glactha ina hiomláine fós ná réidh le feidhmiú, tá trom-impleachtaí le háireamh sna heachtraí seo laistigh d'Earnáil na Gaeilge a chuimsíonn taobh an Stáit agus taobh an Phobail. Tá siad araon lárnach do thodhchaí na Straitéise, ceachtar taobh de réir a nádúir agus a sainróil féin.

---

[11] Fifth International Conference on Minority Languages, University of Wales at Cardiff, 5–9 July, 1993.

[12] An Roinn Gnóthaí Tuaithe, Pobail agus Gaeltachta, Samhain 2009. *Straitéis 20-Bliain don Ghaeilge 2010–2030, Dréacht / 20-Year Strategy for the Irish Language 2010–2010, Draft.*

Ní miste a dhearbhú ar dtús gur maith ann é an Straitéis seo don teanga a fógraíodh ar dtús sa *Ráiteas Rialtais i leith na Gaeilge 2006*, i mí na Nollag 2006, agus é sin ar go leor cúiseanna:

- mar dhearbhú áirithe ar an toil pholaitiúil i leith na Gaeilge agus mar leanúnachas ar an *Ráiteas Rialtais* seo, fiú más dréacht fós é an Straitéis chéanna;
- mar léiriú ar chomhthoil nó *consensus* áirithe polaitiúil de thairbhe comhráiteas air a bheith tagtha ón gComhchoiste Oireachtais[13] *ad rem* i mí Iúil 2010;
- mar iarracht chomhtháite chuimsitheach ar ghnéithe agus ar réimsí uile na teanga a fhreastal in aon straitéis amháin.

Ar an taobh eile, in ainneoin tagairt éigin don earnáil dheonach, agus dhá thagairt shonracha d'Oireachtas na Gaeilge, ní shainítear ann ról na hearnála deonaí Gaeilge. Bhí na tagairtí sin i bhfad níos láidre sa réamhthuarascáil a chuir foireann Fiontar[14] ar fáil agus sa tuarascáil a d'eisigh an Comhchoiste. Ar ndóigh, bhí aighneachtaí láidre faighte ag an gComhchoiste ón Earnáil ina hiomláine sular eisíodh an tuarascáil sin. B'fhéidir go bhfuil de mhíniú leis an easnamh seo gur gníomhaireachtaí Stáit is mó ar cuireadh freagracht agus béim orthu mar is gnách i gcáipéis Stáit; níor beachtaíodh ach oiread, áfach, comhrólanna an Fhorais thuaidh/theas agus an Údaráis nua Gaeltachta agus Gaeilge a bhfuil feidhmiú na Straitéise leagtha mar chúram air.

Ar shlí, is cuma faoi thagairtí nó easnaimh. Mar Straitéis a bhfuil mar aidhm aici pobal 250,000 cainteoirí laethúla Gaeilge a fhorbairt le linn a saolré, is léir go mbeidh a leithéid ag brath cuid mhaith ar na gnéithe sóisialta d'úsáid na teanga agus ar shlógadh an phobail mar ghluaiseacht a lorgóidh agus a bhainfidh leas as seirbhísí Stáit trí mheán na Gaeilge. Is sna hilréimsí seo oibre atá taithí agus saineolas na hEarnála Deonaí. Tá sé soiléir go mbeidh feidhmiú na Straitéise ar an talamh ag brath cuid mhaith ar eagraíochtaí deonacha agus pobail na Gaeilge, le tacaíocht na ngníomhaireachtaí Stáit. Ba dheacair a cheapadh gurb as scéimeanna scaipthe a thiocfadh inmharthanacht gníomhaíochta nó gluaiseachta, ach as tréanshaothar leanúnach comhoibritheach, fírinne dhosheachanta. Caithfidh na heiliminti agus na struchtúir (mar a sainmhíníodh ó thús an ailt seo) éagsúla d'Earnáil na Gaeilge a bheith ag obair i bpáirt le chéile chuige sin, ag roinnt acmhainní agus saineolais ar son na Gaeilge, nó is boichtede an pobal – sa mhíniú uileghabhálach ar 'Ghaeltacht' a tugadh thuas, an Ghaeilge agus an Straitéis. Tá ré na n-impireachtaí thart. Nó an bhfuil?

---

[13] Tithe an Oireachtais, An Comhchoiste um Ghnóthaí Turasóireachta, Cultúir, Spóirt, Pobail, Comhionannais agus Gaeltachta, Iúil 2010. *An Tríú Tuarascáil: An Straitéis 20-Bliain don Ghaeilge 2010–2030 (Uimhir Pharlaiminte A10/1097)*.

[14] Fiontar, Ollscoil Chathair Bhaile Átha Cliath, Feabhra 2009. *Straitéis 20-Bliain don Ghaeilge, Arna Hullmhú don Roinn Gnóthaí Pobail, Tuaithe agus Gaeltachta*

Some Comments on the Current Forms of Relationship between the Voluntary Sector / Civil Society and Organs of the State in the Republic of Ireland

Helen Ó Murchú

Abstract

The symposium which gave rise to this publication offered several differing but related themes. This article, following the lines of my oral presentation at that symposium, begins with some reference to the terms 'Gaeltacht', 'bilingualism', and 'institution', since my understanding of these concepts need not necessarily be shared by all. A brief exposition follows of the interplay between different institutions through forms of state-funded collaboration or partnership in the liberal democratic political system. This process is illustrated through several examples from the Republic of Ireland. Finally, some implications arising for the *20-Year Draft Strategy for Irish* are given.

Terminology: Gaeltacht

My understanding of the term 'Gaeltacht' is not altogether that given below of the satiric equation of Myles na Gopaleen (Brian Ó Nualláin/Brian O'Nolan/Flann O'Brien), past columnist in the *Irish Times* (*Cruiskeen Lawn* 1939–1966) and author of such well known works as *The Third Policeman*, *At Swim-Two-Birds* and *An Béal Bocht*. Ó Nualláin was born in Strabane to an Irish-speaking family but spent his life in Dublin.

Breac-Ghaeltacht = an area where Irish and English are spoken
Breac-Ghalltacht = an area where English and Irish are spoken

Therefore Breac-Ghaeltacht = Breac-Ghalltacht
Therefore Gaeltacht = Galltacht

Despite the humour, it might be well, nevertheless, to be aware, or at least conscious, of the weird – even wild – logic which seems to be embedded in this particular definition.

My understanding of the term 'Gaeltacht' is, in fact, closer to that of the social scientist, Glyn Williams,[1] who cautions against reification of language in contexts which, in fact, may serve to divorce the language from its speakers. A language community is composed of speakers. Language use is essentially a social act. It is the community of speakers that define their language, not experts of any particular 'ology'. The European Bureau for Lesser Used Languages (now defunct) had constantly to deal with this truth in attempting to recognise, or to distinguish between, the concepts 'speech', 'language' and 'dialect'.

My preference is to provide as inclusive a definition as possible of 'Gaeltacht':
1. communities who speak Irish as their traditional native language (although levels of intensity may vary);
2. communities of learners who have acquired Irish to a high degree of competence as a second language but who now use Irish as their *chosen* first language in as many contexts of use as possible; some of these

---

[1] Personal discussion.

contexts may be 'natural' (in the home), others may exist as a support system across a range of domains (which may include education, media, aspects of social life such as entertainment or business);
3. English-dominant communities who may be described as part of the 'iar-Ghaeltacht'[2] (previous Gaeltacht) insofar as Irish was the dominant majority language in these areas until relatively recently in historical terms.

Individuals may, of course, be found in each of these three categories who would more correctly be classed as belonging in another.

Terminology: Bilingualism

Many definitions and classifications exist of the concept of bilingualism, particularly at the level of the individual speaker. Nevertheless, there is a high level of agreement at this level. This is not altogether the case at the level of societal bilingualism. Lower still, however, is the level of consensus on the form language policies and interventions should take in cases where the traditional native language of a community is under constant pervasive threat from the dominant majority language and the speakers are themselves, of necessity, more or less bilingual.

For all these reasons, and keeping in mind the contemporary linguistic reality of Ireland as borne out in surveys and in comprehensive studies, a relatively simple understanding of policy to improve the position of the minority language is proposed. Any such policy, whether in concept or in implementation, should constitute primarily a mechanism having the sole aim of bringing the minority language, initially at least, to the same institutional and societal level as the majority language. Clearly, the approach could not be precisely similar in the three categories of the continuum of 'Gaeltacht' delineated above. One distinction might be that between 'speakers' and 'potential speakers', at differing levels of both competence and use. In any event, no real linguistic choice exists for the language community until some position of equilibrium is reached between the minority and the majority languages.

On this aspect, Colin Williams[3] (1994) remarks that the language community, although they may actually 'own' the language, are not in fact masters of its fate.

> … it is the people of Wales and the Welsh diaspora who own the language by using and cherishing it…although we may own Welsh, we do not entirely control either its use or its legitimacy. Wales is a dependent society…a reactive rather than a purposive country in essence. (1994: 118)

Despite changes since 1994 in the case of Wales, this statement still has relevance for both the Irish and Welsh languages. Williams' work will be further quoted below.

Terminology: Institution

It is accepted that 'institution' is generally defined as a way of giving form or shape to some ideology, or service, or activity, by imposing order in a more or less physical

---

[2] Ó Murchú, H. 'Coimisiún na hiar-Ghaeltachta: An Chéad Tuarascáil'. In ed. Ó Cearúil, M. (Eag.) 2000. *Aimsir Óg 2000*, 199–226. Baile Átha Cliath: Coiscéim.
[3] Williams, C. 'Development, Dependency and Democratic Deficit'. In ed. Thomas, P.W. 1994. *Fifth International Conference on Minority Languages*, Clevedon: Multilingual Matters. 101–27.

manner. Generally, this means the establishment of an entity of some kind: an institute or authority or body – terms often used in relation to more official entities – or an organisation or society at the community level. On purely subjective criteria, I find the term 'organisation' to convey better the notions of order, movement and activity.

The advice of Williams[4] is pertinent in this regard. Prudence and caution must be exercised by the language community, even in cases where the state is apparently in concessionary mode, responding to the demand of the community. Firstly, given the pervasive influence and importance of the modern state in citizens' lives, unexpected consequences may follow the acceptance or extension of the minority language through either re-organised or new state structures in any given domain.

> … we should [not] interpret the modern state as a benign benefactor, even if some of the tension between the state and the community has been eased by the granting of significant concessions (*pace*, recognised rights) on the part of the state. There is a real danger that this could amount to no more than the expropriation of the language and its ideological/value-laden culture. … as these state-funded and controlled agencies exert their penetrative influence of social and cultural control … the language may survive, but the culture – which is the real source of authenticity and resistance – may die … to be replaced by a culture which has lost its independence and hence, rationale, to express its own values, ideas and ambitions. (1994: 104)

This is more or less the same argument as made by Daniel Bourgeois[5] in reference to education for the Acadian language community in Canada and the kind of role envisaged for the educational institution in their regions, the *Conseil Scolaire Francophone*. It also finds an echo in the claims being made anew for the establishment of a separate board or similar entity to take in charge the many needs of Irish-medium education and Gaeltacht education.

The basis of the argument may be simply put. Unless the language community plays a central role in the running of its own institutions a real danger exists that it may in fact be the values and the culture of the majority language that are transmitted through the minority language.

Partnership: Advantages and Disadvantages

The possible implications for language minorities, as stated by Williams, which could follow from state funding and state governance in institutionalised domains such as media and education are a matter of concern. Even more disturbing, however, is his analysis of the new relationships which may occur between state and citizens when the minority language is institutionalised through new bodies or agencies. This issue receives attention further on.

State and society are here chosen for express mention. In any modern democratic polity, two aspects of democracy are salient: the 'representative' and the 'participative'. If, in a contemporary democratic state, a decision is taken to cede a certain degree of power from the top down, this usually takes the form of some joint arrangement between, on the one hand, representatives or organised initiatives of the community

---

[4] *Ibid.*
[5] Bourgeois, D. 2010. *I dTreo Lánbhainistíocht Scoileanna Fraincisee i dTimpeallacht Mhionlaigh*. Baile Átha Cliath: COGG, Leagan Gaeilge.

and, on the other hand, institutions of the state. It is generally accepted that such joint arrangements are best formalised through *partnerships* between the state and organised civil society, particularly in dealing with general issues that have to do with the welfare and wellbeing of society.[6]

The concept of partnership may, of course, be formally expressed in different ways.

- Partnership based on specific arrangements between the state and a particular voluntary organisation: the state contracts to fund the organisation to carry out an aspect of state policy on the state's behalf. This is a funding-based relationship. Arguments have been made that such a partnership implies, or even actually means, a change in status for the employees of the voluntary organisation, from community activists to state agents, notwithstanding the presence of a voluntary board and voluntary workers. The oxymoronic 'state-funded voluntarism' or the derisive 'grant-aided mentality' is often mentioned in the same context. Such arguments appear to reside in a misunderstanding of how a modern democracy tends to function.
- Formal partnership between the state funder and an organisation, or several organisations, for the sole purpose of effecting state policy. Such examples are relatively rare.
- Partnership between voluntary organisations, whether state-funded or not. These also are fairly rare. They may also be difficult to manage. Compromise and joint arrangements must underlie all levels: governance, vision, activities, funding, administration, evaluation and accountability. Mutual suspicion may win out over mutual understanding, selective reporting methods over mutual confidence, fear of a take-over over the desire to co-operate. Such partnerships work best when they arise organically out of the complementary needs of the individual organisations; when the process is set in train by the organisations involved rather than through external actors; when a set of basic operating principles are adopted from the very beginning.

The most salient characteristic of all these examples of partnership is the issue of power they all display. Clearly, the balance of power will lie with the funder in all cases, whether that is overtly wielded or not. In cases where the state is the funding body, the power relationship is, of necessity, much more unevenly distributed. The possibilities for parity of respect for the input of the community joint partner are lessened, even when endlessly articulated. A relationship of dependency is fostered, a dependency which has its roots solely in the power of funding and not in the notion of the joint empowering which comes with the fruits of good work. Such dependency may even foster undesirable traits in both parties and contribute to a distortion of democracy, ironically enough in the name of democracy. I described this as a 'feudal relationship' in the pamphlet mentioned under note 6 above, the supplicant figuratively on bended knees before the lord of largesse. Williams (op. cit.) describes it thus:

> Rule by quango and grant-in-aid may be purposeful and efficient ... another quango, the Welsh Language Board. ... It is possible to argue

[6] Ó Murchú, H. 2003. *Limistéar na Sibhialtachta: Dúshlán agus Treo d'Eagraíochtaí na Gaeilge, An Aimsir Óg, Paimfléad 2.* Baile Átha Cliath: Coiscéim.

that with this new definition of democracy, joint-venture partnership works very well in that it allows patronage to reward the initiatives of dynamic individuals. The keywords of *this* democratic culture are initiative, venture, partnership and flexible accommodation to the global-local nexus. (1994:124)

He then poses some pertinent questions regarding this type of arrangement:

Is this a new version of democracy, or is it an absence of democracy? What are its implications for the management of Welsh cultural and educational institutions? (1994:124)

He supplies a three-part reply which basically bolsters his argument for self-government for Wales. Nevertheless, the general thrust of his response has wider applicability.

… a process of 'negotiated sovereignty'… the real centres of power |at whichever level| frequently escape democratic scrutiny and control…
… relative autonomy of Welsh culture … it all depends on the quality of the appointees in 'quangoland' … But should personality rather than accountable structures rule our futures?
… Communal wellbeing in Wales depends upon citizen involvement, through responsive local government structures which reflect the particularism of each region. (1994:125)

While keeping Williams' warning in mind, let us now examine some examples of the reasoning which apparently underlies any type of joint arrangements in the form of community or other partnerships in the Republic. One such example is seen in the official document, *Framework for Recovery* (*Creatlach Téarnaimh*),[7] put before the Social Partners as the economic recession threatened. The social effects which it was hoped this document might encourage were expressed in slogans such as 'shoulder to shoulder' or 'community movement' and 'community solidarity'. The realisation of social effects such as these generally depend on the voluntary sector – a fact which simultaneously embraces threat, challenge and opportunity.

It is, of course, possible to establish a system or a process in order to put structure on joint partnerships in which the state is one of the active partners. But, as is common in all human endeavour, such structures will have both advantages and problems in addition to those already outlined. The possible difficulties may be listed:

- either partner may lose sight of the founding aim and consequently of the desired outcomes for the target community;
- either partner may go beyond or outside their proper role;
- the voluntary side may tend not to have proper regard for, or even forget, the very community or membership which it is intended either to represent or whose concerns it is meant to articulate;
- as a consequence, the voluntary side may, albeit unconsciously, adopt the viewpoint of the state, or of the official side, or of the majority language representatives;
- institutional or organisational inertia may occur.

---

[7] Government of Ireland 2008. *Framework for Recovery / Creatlach Téarnaimh.*

The advantages of partnership are well articulated in the latter part of the submission[8] prepared by the Department of Finance (D/F) in the Republic for the *Special Group on Public Service Numbers and Expenditure Programmes* established by the Government to make substantial cuts in public expenditure. This Group subsequently published the comprehensive two-volume report popularly referred to as the report of 'The New Bord Snip' (2009). Indeed the *raison d'être* of, and for, the concept of partnership involving the state is described in the section of the department's submission referring to certain community support programmes. All of these groups/organisations were locally-based, independent, non-statutory, not-for-profit in nature; a significant majority of them were small with no more than two or three staff and having voluntary boards or management committees in place.

The departmental submission clearly states that:

> In many policy areas, supporting a bottom-up approach is a key part of the selected strategy and supporting this approach means supporting independent non-statutory organisations.

Under rôles and objectives an interesting list is given:

- building community engagement;
- supporting volunteering [which is synonomous with active citizenship];
- building the confidence and esteem of disadvantaged individuals;
- providing essential community services;
- providing information [advice, training and assistance to gaining employment are also listed];
- promoting Rural Enterprise;
- assessing [...] needs;
- assessing [...] applications. (D/F: 5)

This submission of the Department of Finance in addressing the *original rationale* for local delivery mechanisms includes the fact that some services, (e.g. laundry for the elderly or transport for the disabled), now available through local organisations, 'would be neither provided by the State nor by the market' (D/F: 7). Interestingly, the document goes on to discuss the *continuing relevance of the original policy,* stating that 'the concept of a local level delivery is still valid', (D/F: 7). The reasons for encouraging community organisations in such local delivery are given thus:

- the continued desirability of engaging local communities in designing and delivering bespoke solutions appropriate to their own localities;
- ensuring the development of community and promotion of social inclusion. (D/F:7)

It is further admitted that:

> Central Government Departments and Agencies cannot by their nature efficiently and effectively engage at a local level in identifying the source of problems and in designing and delivering appropriate solutions. The resource intensity required across the many responsible Departments and Agencies would be uneconomic if implemented on a sufficient scale so as to be effective. (D/F: 7–8)

---

[8] Department of Finance 2009. *Crosscutting Issues: Local Delivery Mechanisms.*

Such a declaration from the Department of Finance constitutes a compelling rationale for the continued existence and operation of the voluntary and community sector. It finds an echo in most western democracies. The European Community commends and funds this type of approach in the interests of both subsidiarity and citizenship.

Nevertheless, notwithstanding this positive stance from the Department of Finance, problems and inconsistencies within the sector are also discussed. These arise mainly at the structural level, both organisational and administrative/managerial. Change towards increased effectiveness is sought, both at sectoral *and* state levels. A catalogue of weaknesses is given. They include observations on overlap and rationalisation which may be grouped as in the list below:

- overlap of organisations in the areas of basic aims and operations;
- too many small organisations do not provide a coherent efficient structure; even if each small organisation has been established for a specific purpose or even if each functions within a specific region or area;
- informal collaboration or even joint sharing of certain resources does not necessarily constitute an efficient structure, particularly if not within a context of co-planning;
- while the standard of service may fluctuate from area to area, standardisation of services could well prove a costly exercise unless the lowest common denominator is chosen as benchmark, [a practice dismissed in the document as undesirable].

A further caveat is also entered:

> A bottom-up approach to addressing local needs may still be the desired approach but planning for local needs cannot be carried out by every type of local organisation or it will be both ineffective and expensive. (D/F: 18)

It is not clear whether parallel planning by individual organisations rather than the joined-up variety is the focus of criticism here. Neither is any proof given of the projected ineffectiveness and expense.

The state does not escape criticism either, in particular with regard to lack of effectiveness in methods of funding from multiple official sources. From the departmental view, this approach results in difficulty in assigning specific outcomes to any particular funding source as well as placing an additional burden on organisations which must prepare multiple applications and supply multiple reports to their various funders. For these reasons no comprehensive overview or comparison is considered possible of the connection between the resources granted and the proposed or required or even actual outcomes attained as a result. It is admitted, however, that such precise analysis is not always possible in all cases, for example quantifying the level of community involvement. This particular argument may also be applicable to the measurement of the linguistic outcomes of certain interventions at community level.

The various criticisms made in the document result in some fairly predictable recommendations:

- amalgamating organisations having broadly similar functions;
- concentrating a sole inclusive funding source in a single designated department;

- designating a single appraisal body for all applications for funding at local level;
- proposing a single inclusive county level organisation which might also monitor sub-county organisations in receipt of funding;
- offering some of the available funding on a competitive basis.

These are all issues which will again be seen below in the new approach being sought by the north/south language body, Foras na Gaeilge. The discussion on the issue of competitive funding in the Department of Finance document is quoted more fully as being pertinent to current arguments being made by the Irish language voluntary sector.

> A system whereby the outputs to be produced by local level organisations are put out to tender would seem to be a rational future route to follow. It would however be a significant shift to move directly to such a system from the current situation and there are reasons why it may not be ideal:
> - The *outputs* delivered by the local organisations considered here are *often difficult to define and measure*, e.g. building community engagement.
> - The ethos underpinning the support for many of the local level organisations is to support the *bottom-up approach* where the initiative comes from the community itself. *The independence and continuity of each organisation can be an important feature which would not be compatible with a competitive tendering process.* [Italics added] (D/F: 15)

Efficiency and Effectiveness: Tricky Terminology

The official departmental submission quoted above, *Cross Cutting Issues: Local Delivery Mechanisms*, gave a relatively balanced account of the twin partners in locally-based state-funded initiatives, the State and the Community and Voluntary Sector. The term 'efficiency' received no small mention. Given that the brief of the document was to locate possible reductions in state expenditure, this term, 'efficiency', may be taken as code for 'cost-efficiency', which nowadays is no more than a pebble's throw away from 'costcutting'.

The terms 'effectiveness', or 'cost-benefit' even, appear to receive less mention in official documentation in current straitened circumstances, particularly in language matters. Even worse, 'efficiency' and 'effectiveness' are often used interchangeably and confusingly to such an extent that the user sometimes appears to understand them as synonomous in meaning. In discussion of expenditure cuts or funding changes, the very notion of 'impact assessment', let alone its application, is generally conspicuous by its absence. Comparative scenarios of possible impacts on which to base future policy are rare indeed.

Of course, such an approach would, of necessity, demand a different mindset as well as a new set of criteria capable of evaluating the outcomes in those social activities in which the more *intangible* results are often of greater impact than the *tangible* results; and where the *intangible process* may prove as potent as the more *tangible output*. This approach is highly applicable to language action in the community although, unfortunately, too often disregarded. Some attempts have been made in certain related domains to measure *qualitative* as well as quantitative outputs. Overall, however, even for the Arts, research remains more quantitative in nature, as in the study conducted by the former National Economic and Social Forum, *In the Frame or Out of the Picture? A Statistical Analysis of Public Involvement in the Arts* (2008). The underlying problem lies in the absence of appropriate criteria by which to judge the rather elusive concept of 'effectiveness' across a range of social activity, if indeed such evaluation does not prove too abstract to be useful. If the *effectiveness of outcomes* cannot be evaluated in convincing and reliable ways, rather than – as too often occurs – in personal anecdotal and at times almost prophetic manner, that fact should be admitted. In a spirit of integrity, funders and official spokespersons could then state unequivocally that *added value* does attach to social activities; that this added value may often not manifest except in the longterm; that, since there is a dearth of the appropriate criteria by which to assess this added value, the notion of 'effectiveness' resides in quite limited and non-absolute qualitative criteria. This approach would be preferable to untutored misuse of the term 'effectiveness'. It has been suggested that use even of the term 'value' tends towards a more monetary interpretation; that 'worth' expresses the intention more clearly.

Even more preferable would be an attempt to define the elusive criteria by which effectiveness could more precisely be evaluated. One possible approach would have the funder and state apparatus engaging with community activists and the users of community services in an attempt to agree appropriate and mutually acceptable criteria and methods of measuring the outputs of those criteria. This approach, however, serves to highlight the related issues of the relative distribution of power in any partnership and the difficulties associated with change that have not been mutually teased out, issues which will be further treated below. In any situation, gaining access to power, or to those who wield power, is not equally feasible for all who seek it. On the other hand, if those who wield power do so largely or solely as mere disbursers of funding, the situation and its possible consequences become even more complex.

In relation to the interpretation of terminology by different partners, the departmental document contains some relevant statements which may demonstrate these problems of mutual (non)comprehension.

> This paper does not attempt to examine the outputs or effectiveness of these organisations. This would be a huge task given the range and numbers of organisations (870) involved and the disparate nature of their activities nor does it look at the effectiveness of these organisations as the hard data to evaluate that is simply not there, due at least in part to the way that the local organisations are structured and funded and the reporting mechanisms used...Proposals..focus on changing the way these organisations are funded and managed, reducing the costs and number of organisations without necessarily removing any function. If these proposed changes can be made then it will lead to a situation where the evaluation of effectiveness can be properly addressed. (D/F: 3)

On closer examination, this statement appears not to possess a coherent internal logic. One could argue on the one hand that changes in funding and management are not necessarily the required or indeed the only initial step towards attaining the required hard data nor, on the other hand, that successful attainment of this hard data will automatically follow changes in funding and management. In either of these two cases, one could set about the kind of research or survey that would provide the hard data on the basis of other factors, including the stated aims and subsequent client experiences of the services involved. Neither is it clear from the D/F statement that the actual proposal itself arose from any research basis. One is left to assume that this unresearched proposal constitutes more a demonstration of a particular mindset or a desire to further a particular policy intent. A similar approach will be seen below in another case, that of Foras na Gaeilge, the north/south language body.

However, to be fair, locating appropriate criteria with which to evaluate the added value, or worth, and real effectiveness of activities and policies in social or linguistic domains is no easy task. This, of course, is no excuse for not at least attempting to design such criteria. To ignore, or to deny, the existence of the problem is not a solution; neither is misuse of the term 'effectiveness' or indiscriminate use of both terms, 'efficiency' and 'effectiveness', allowing the use of one to glide effortlessly into the meaning of the other.

In the search for appropriate criteria which might serve to guide the deliberations of the Irish language voluntary sector, I recently sought out references to benchmarks for setting and measuring added value or effectiveness in the outputs and outcomes of voluntary agencies working in the fields of social development or of language promotion and maintenance. While some examples[9] do exist, they tend to be rather complex to apply. One well known economist, while joking that he would deserve the Nobel prize if he could provide a clear and simple solution, did say that some economists are now beginning to work in this area. This may well be due to the relative failure of the elegant mathematical formulae elaborated up to now to project growth and failure in the economy. Formulae, of their nature, tend to disregard the human element, (except as consumers intent on their own personal needs), and do not comprehensively include all aspects of the social wellbeing of the community. While his work does not contain a reply to the actual issue of satisfactorily defining "effectiveness" in certain contexts, Tim Jackson[10] does give an interesting view on the issue of social sustainability in general. Economists, and their viewpoints, require mention since it is largely their take on social life, and their jargon, the language of the market, which currently appear to dominate discussion of aspects of social life and the state-funded sector in particular. This is not a truth to be ignored but rather one to be systematically unpacked in order to reach agreement on common and applicable tenets on appropriate measurement of 'effectiveness' in differing fields of social endeavour.

Power and Sharing Power

In general terms, the state in a democracy may at times concede to concerted demand from the bottom-up, to the public will as manifested through pressure groups or social movements seeking certain rights. In the case of a language community, institutions or semi-state agencies may be created as a result to cater to the needs of speakers. It is Williams' (op. cit.) thesis that this new situation changes the relationship between state and citizen in two vital ways, simultaneously creating the *need for partnership* but also *a relationship of dependency* for the representatives of the language community. In addition, the independence of the language community is further compromised as they move into a new complex of values and action. This new complex is largely directed by the exigencies of the market, as is the state itself, both internally and externally, as

---

[9] Grin, F. (ECMI) and Tom Moring (EBLUL), Research Project Leaders, 2002. *Final Report: Support for Minority Languages in Europe*. Brussels: European Commission.
[10] Jackson, T. 2009. *Prosperity without Growth: Economics for a Finite Planet*. London: Earthscan.

it attempts to maintain a degree of equilibrium between itself and the effects of globalisation, both good and otherwise. Colin Williams (1994: 104) quotes Glyn Williams to telling effect:

> ... the Welsh language and its culture have been threatened, less by a 'state', than by a *social totality* of a liberal, parliamentary democracy operating within the moral, political and ideological hegemony of an advanced capital society. Within that totality the 'state' has been as much of a response as an originator.

In the case of the Irish language, the changed context cited by Williams (1994) is a consequence of the institutionalisation of the language as a defined part of the state apparatus. Paradoxically, the more the Irish movement succeeds in gaining an official place for the language, the more its role to oppose the state weakens. Instead, certain partnerships or understandings come into being between the state and organised elements of the community. In this new situation, the challenge is to reach some *fruitful inter-dependency* rather than the inert dependency of which Williams warns. The answer does not lie in *independence* either, even if the voluntary sector had access to the financial means to be so. Responsibility for the wellbeing of both the language and the language community lies with both parties, on the state with its institutions and on the community with its different sectors.

As already noted, both the changed context and relationship are also marked by the ideology and jargon of the market. Having been drawn into the state apparatus, Irish is now embroiled in a new framework and mentality. As is the case with other sections of the same state apparatus, the language must now answer to rules of another kind. Williams puts it thus:

> ... re-routing the relatively autonomous needs of Welsh culture into a more state-wide institutional design so as to account for and control expenditure and subsidy...Rather than being seen as an absolute right, granted to deserving citizens who wish to exercise their culture as fully as possible, current and future reforms will be made in accordance with the trinitarian principles...namely the improvement of efficiency, the greater targeting of resources, and the reduction of 'waste' whenever possible. (1994: 118)

It would appear then that, for language activists and the language community, a whole new struggle begins on the heels of the struggle which succeeded in finding a place for Irish within the state apparatus. Some elements of the new demands are entirely acceptable and unavoidable. In any venture, particularly in state-funded ventures, there is no denying the value and necessity for accountability, transparency, sound measurable outputs and no waste of resources. These should not be a feature of straitened circumstances only. Losing sight of either efficiency or effectiveness is never acceptable. In times of recession, there is no reason to believe that the voluntary sector, as proponents of active citizenship, would not play their part and suffer any necessary pain. If these are acceptable elements of a changed situation and of new arrangements between state and language community, there exist also some more unacceptable elements. These will be discussed further below in a section dealing with Foras na Gaeilge. They are concerned with the exercise of power, with real partnership, with the basic questions posed by Williams: Who owns language? Who determines [its future]? (1994: 106)

The Process of Partnership: Some Examples

Some contemporary examples of the *process of partnership* are now briefly examined, in particular those processes which are directed towards changes considered for the better and of a type which are couched in the jargon and demands of the market. The primary focus of discussion is the Department of Community, Equality and Gaeltacht Affairs in the Republic together with the two north/south bodies which come under the aegis of that department. The discussion is based on information in the public domain, on websites and in other media, in Irish and in English.

Community Partnerships under the Department of Community, Equality and Gaeltacht Affairs

The D/F document previously quoted described one system of joint partnership in one area of state policy. This is the system of local partnerships largely funded by the EU LEADER Programme which is administered by the (newly named) Department of Community, Equality and Gaeltacht Affairs (D/CEandGA). The document also gives the reasoning for the desired changes in this area (largely to effect savings) but couched in terms of ensuring better outcomes, both in the case of the state and of the community and voluntary sector.

> Proposals ... focus on changing the way these organisations are funded and managed, reducing the costs and number of organisations without necessarily removing any function. If these proposed changes can be made it will lead to a situation where the evaluation of effectiveness can be properly addressed. (D/F: 3)

As already discussed above, the type of logic connecting the two parts of this statement on rationalisation is not entirely clear. In the context of 'cost-efficiency' alone, some level of preliminary analysis and research would be required to demonstrate that (a) the basic aim of the enterprise is being accomplished and (b) that that will continue without any change, even if costcutting and rationalisation are applied.

Reference was also made to the ongoing 'cohesion process' (D/F: 6) led by the D/CEandGA in an attempt to rationalise the community partnerships sector by reducing the number of organisations from 96 to 60. Interestingly, by March 2009:

> This process |had| taken a number of years to deliver results which indicates that reducing numbers of local organisations is not a simple task. (D/F: 6)

This advice could apply also in the case of Foras na Gaeilge and the Irish voluntary sector as outlined below. Leaving aside the more vexed question of partnerships in the Gaeltacht, and the undoubted dissatisfaction with the intent of the entire process, it would appear, however, that the *actual process itself* did involve to some extent the participation of both parties, officials of the relevant department and representatives of the local groups. The task to be accomplished was clearly outlined. Given the reference above to 'a number of years', it would also appear that time for discussion was given to the process. Speaking on the process at the annual general meeting 2010 of the umbrella organisation, *The Wheel*, the relevant Minister stated that:

My Department has clearly signalled that the integration strategy is not a 'one size fits all' approach. Where alternatives prove effective, we are more than happy to accept them.

He also stated that his Department was:

> ... open to ... other models ... as long as the proposed alternatives can achieve integrated and cost effective service delivery ... [but that it was] ... not possible to maintain the status quo..any alternative model has to show ... less structures ... potential for integrated delivery ... for introducing efficiencies ... and will reduce [administrative] burden.

Waterways Ireland

Waterways Ireland deserves mention as a good example of the *process of managing change* with relevant stakeholders. Waterways Ireland is one of the six north/south bodies established though the *Statutory Instrument 1999 No. 859, The North/South Co-operation (Implementation Bodies) (Northern Ireland) Order 1999* in the aftermath of what came to be known as the *Good Friday Agreement*. As in the case of another of these bodies, Foras na Gaeilge, it comes under the aegis of the D/CEandGA. Waterways Ireland is responsible for seven waterways. In July 2010, the body issued new regulations which it had prepared in relation to waterways in the Republic. (Since the legislative context is different in Northern Ireland, it is intended to issue separate regulation later for that jurisdiction). A process of consultation on the proposed changes with interested parties in the south then began.

The initial step of this process consisted of consultation with stakeholders, that is the various organisations which represent users of the waterways. Having been given the draft new regulations, these were allowed a period of 15 weeks to scrutinise the content, to discuss it with their membership, and to come back with their observations, preferably in integrated format. Waterways Ireland would then analyse the replies before embarking on the second step of consulting with the public through public advertisements. The regulations would not come into force until this process was complete. Comparison is interesting between this process and that conducted in fairly similar circumstances by Foras na Gaeilge.

Foras na Gaeilge and the Core-funded Voluntary Sector

Foras na Gaeilge also comes under the aegis of the same department as Waterways Ireland, D/CEandGA. In common with all six north/south bodies, FNG is also responsible to the North South Ministerial Council (NSMC) as this excerpt from the NSMC website explains.

Language Body
The Council meets in the LANGUAGE SECTOR in order to take decisions on policies and action to be implemented by the North/South Language Body with its two agencies – Foras na Gaeilge and Tha Boord O Ulstér-Scotch.

The Language Body is a single Body reporting to the NSMC, but composed of two separate and largely autonomous agencies: the Irish Language Agency, Foras na Gaeilge, and the Ulster-Scots Agency (Tha Boord o Ulstér-Scotch).

Foras na Gaeilge, which took over the functions of Bord na Gaeilge, has responsibility for the promotion of the Irish Language on an all-island basis. Tha Boord o Ulstèr-Scotch has responsibility for the promotion of greater awareness in the use of Ullans and of Ulster-Scots cultural issues, both within Northern Ireland and throughout the island.

It is assumed that 'in order to take decisions on policies and action to be implemented', the NSMC is presented with documentation and advice on which to base their decisions. It is further assumed that this advice is provided by civil servants of the two relevant ministries, north and south, and primarily by the language bodies involved.

In the interests of clarity, some preliminary explanation of terminology in frequent use are given. *Earnáil na Gaeilge* or the Irish Language Sector is generally taken to comprise all *statutory* agencies (departments and certain structures within departments, Foras na Gaeilge, Údarás na Gaeltachta) as well as the *Voluntary and Community Sector* (including cultural agencies) and also the various *speaker communities*. In other words, all agencies, communities or individuals or projects which play a role in language matters, whether statutory or voluntary, funded or non-funded, national or community-based, temporary or permanent.

Earnáil na Gaeilge then includes both funders and beneficiaries. The term Irish Language *Voluntary* Sector is self-explanatory although reference earlier in this paper to 'state agents' should be kept in mind. The *Irish Language Voluntary Core-funded Sector* refers to those organisations which receive operational funding from FNG.

The two examples of process already described are to some extent in contrast with the process conducted by the other north/south body, Foras na Gaeilge, in its dealings with the language organisations which it funds. It is not intended to rehearse here matters that have received no little coverage of late in the Irish-medium media. Instead, a brief account follows of the steps in a *process* relating to the voluntary organisations funded by it which was begun in early 2007 by FNG. A possible first step is seen in two references which appear in the minutes of FNG board meetings of April and June 2007 as published on the agency's website:

- the need for co-ordination of the funding priorities and strategic aims of FNG [in that order] with the priorities of the 19 organisations which FNG core-funded;
- the need for a review of the 19 organisations. [Translated from Irish]

Among those 19 organisations, there are 8 (one in Northern Ireland) which are specified in a schedule of the British-Irish *Statutory Instrument 1999 No. 859, The North/South Co-operation (Implementation Bodies) (Northern Ireland) Order 1999* when responsibility for their funding was transferred from the relevant Department to the new north/south body. The other 11 organisations comprise a certain number which had been funded by Bord na Gaeilge in the Republic, the precursor of the Foras. These would have a reasonable expectation that their funding would continue. Some of the remaining organisations had come into being later; all were engaged in different aspects of language promotion; some were functioning in Northern Ireland solely, others had an all-Ireland remit. All 19 organisations functioned on the basis of annual standard applications for funding to FNG followed up by regular reports. FNG at no point made it known to organisations that there was dissatisfaction with the results or outcomes of their funding which was twofold: core operational funding and funding for specific projects. Parallel with the activities of the 19 core-funded organisations, FNG was itself operating on a competitive basis a series of community and other schemes of fixed duration, all advertised publicly.

Between 2007 and 2010, letters and meetings between the executive of FNG and the 19 organisations took place – all centred on the need for radical change. Given the economic and fiscal context of the period, the (then) Minister with responsibility for the language in the Republic also issued some very direct warnings. All these contacts contained the same refrains. On the one hand were heard rationalisation, restructuring, new models of funding, value for money, reduction in the number of organisations, in staff numbers, in offices, in expenditure. On the other hand, emphasis on co-operation and co-ordination. Unfortunately, none of these aspirations or warnings was accompanied by an appropriate context in which *mutual deliberation* could take place. In all cases, FNG sought the views of the Core-funded Voluntary Sector but apparently no substantial *joint talks* took place between funder and funded that might have led to some resolution – as might have been expected in such a situation. The organisations participated in a review of them commissioned by FNG. They were not apparently privy to the entire report that ensued although selected sections were later released.

As part of this fairly complex matter, the NSMC, meeting in sectoral format on language, issued several joint communiqués, published on the Council website. The first, from 3 December 2009, gave very clear form to what was being expected of the 19 funded voluntary organisations:

10. The Council welcomed the Foras na Gaeilge review of its core-funded organisations. Ministers agreed that core-funding of the Irish language voluntary sector by Foras na Gaeilge be reconfigured on the basis that Foras na Gaeilge will set high level strategic priorities. Applications for funding will be invited from the voluntary sector, within these strategic priorities, for one or a limited number of organisations with a representational, information dissemination, resource and support provision and advocacy role for the sector as a whole; and at local area level, groups that take an integrated approach to promotion of the Irish language, including working in community, family, educational and youth settings. This reconfiguration is to ensure a more effective, streamlined and cost effective approach to funding of the sector.

This was followed on 26 May 2010 by new funding proposals for the core-funded sector presented by FNG.

7. The Council noted proposals that future funding to the Irish language sector would be provided on the basis of a number of discrete schemes. They agreed in principle that these proposals are within the parameters of the NSMC decision of December 2009. Ministers decided that officials from the sponsor Departments should now work with Foras na Gaeilge to agree by end-June 2010 the detail of these proposals and a timescale for their implementation. In the context of such agreement being reached by end-June, Ministers agreed that interim funding may be provided by Foras na Gaeilge to existing funded organisations to end-December 2010. The question of further interim funding after end-2010 will be considered at the next NSMC meeting in Language format in the light of the progress made in the interim on implementation. Foras na Gaeilge consulted with the sector in the course of undertaking the review and there will be continued consultation during the course of the implementation process.

Basically, two demands were being made:

- 'reconfiguration' from 19 organisations to merely one or several; this 'reconfiguration' to be accomplished by the organisations themselves on the basis of strategic priorities set by FNG;
- funding to be just as radically 'reconfigured' from core plus project funding to funding on the basis of 'discrete schemes' – these will be further considered below.

In addition, 'consultation', from the voluntary sector viewpoint, had acquired new meaning as will be discussed.

During this entire period, the response of the core-funded sector in the search for a solution both for itself and FNG included:

- active participation in the review commissioned by FNG;
- a series of meetings of the 19 organisations together with external speakers to consider the implications of what was being asked of them;
- independent research on almost the entire voluntary sector (up to 40 organisations across the spectrum of activity); this research was funded by FNG;
- the creation of a Forum of the 19 core-funded organisations;
- the appointment of several independent facilitators to guide discussion.

It was accepted that change is always a necessary part of development and that money was becoming more scarce. Naturally enough, however, the sector questioned whether all the parties involved were willing to make the same sacrifices as were being demanded of the sector and whether the axe was to fall solely on the voluntary sector funding mechanism. In the interests of working profitably together, the sector sought a more complete context since it was not easy to decipher the strategic priorities which underpinned the plans of FNG. Above all, the sector sought an appropriate mechanism which might enable the sector to explain its stance and also attempt to understand the stance being taken by FNG and so reach some level of consensus on the way forward in the interests of the Irish language. Such a mechanism had in fact received mention in the document on a new model of funding which FNG had presented to the NSMC in December 2009, entitled a Committee to manage change. A form of this was finally granted in October 2010. In the context of managing change in an organisation, it is noted that the NI Department for Employment and Learning is subsidising a new organisational development programme being run by the Northern Ireland agency for voluntary activity (*eNEWS*. NICVA: November 2010) with this very aim.

In a brief account such as this not all the nuances can be pursued. However, it is fairly clear that the *modus operandi, the process*, in this particular case does not resemble those outlined earlier although the basic aim was similar in all cases, that is, significant change in the *status quo*. Even more telling is the fact that an appropriate process was even more necessary in the case of FNG, given the scale of change sought. In the event, inequality between the parties was very evident on several fronts:

- the protagonists were very different in nature: on the one hand a single body which had not only control over the purse strings but also control over knowledge and information of their eventual plans which were not shared with the sector; on the other hand 19 very disparate organisations;

- two parallel processes which proceeded independently despite the efforts of the sector: no information was supplied as a plausible context for the immense changes being sought, apart from references to cost-efficiency; the complete results of the independent review of the sector commissioned by FNG were not shared with the Sector; neither was there evidence of a strategic superplan by FNG within which the future role of the Sector might be clarified; no indications were given as to the thinking of the funder apart from references to the need for rationalisation within a brief time period; the essential elements of the documents accepted by the NSMC did not come about as a result of consultation and co-planning between funder and funded;
- in this instance the consultation process with stakeholders seemed to consist of requests that they perform the 'reconfiguration' task themselves without any indication as to how the funder might view the results;
- restructuring in a vacuum was sought within a restricted time period and under pressure with regard to lack of knowledge on funding which meant several organisations had no option but to issue redundancy notice to staff in the absence of clear direction.

In such circumstances, the sector sought some form of joint planning structure or a more open form of consultation which might enable them to carry out the very difficult task they were given. Even some overall contextual framework would have been helpful. In the event, FNG prepared its own plan for the sector, with the assistance of external consultants, and without input into the planning from the stakeholders. This was the funding plan for the future accepted 'in principle' by the NSMC in May 2010.

The main elements of this *Samhail Nua Mhaoinithe* (New Funding Model) appeared to be based on two existing models: firstly, the fixed term schemes or projects of FNG itself; secondly, a proposal in a report[11] of a Commission to examine the role of Irish language voluntary organisations, established by the (then) Department of Arts, Culture and the Gaeltacht which had recommended, *inter alia* that:

> The funding system for voluntary organisations should be project-based, with definite targets which would be properly costed. An Chomhairle Ghaeilge [a new structure also recommended] would assess and fund projects. (Treo 2000: 19)

The new model for funding put forward by FNG recommended:

- an end to core funding of any kind;
- future funding on the basis of a group of 'schemes' devised by FNG (although input was later sought into the type of schemes and criteria), not on an organisational basis;
- these schemes to be open to all comers on a competitive basis.

An amendment to the 1999 Act which placed some responsibility on FNG for 8 of the core funded organisations was also sought.

---

[11] *Treo 2000*. Government of Ireland: 1997.

Among the several criticisms made of the New Model were the apparent lack of distinction between the very different factors pertaining to Irish in the two jurisdictions, north and south, as well as constant reference to the 'effectiveness' predicted to arise from the New Model. This despite the fact that no lack of effectiveness had been imputed to the Sector previously, nor any indication as to what constituted future effectiveness, nor to the criteria with which to measure it. Clearly, the more important criterion appeared to lie in a reference by FNG to the high percentage of the FNG total budget being expended on the core funded organisations. When FNG eventually began public consultation on the New Model, the period allocated was extremely brief.

This article does not discuss the pros and cons of the actual or possible *objectives* of the restructuring required of the sector nor of the new model of funding. The focus has been rather on the *operation of processes* within what may be loosely described as partnerships between state and the voluntary sector towards similar desired ends. In the first two examples of restructuring of a kind given above:

- the funder took an active part in the difficult task required of the funded or supplied documentation on the changes being sought to stakeholders for discussion and feedback;
- some form of *joint discussion* took place;
- the process may have ended with less structures, less staff, and less expenditure in one case, but the actual restructuring took place more or less within the existing framework – no radical change happened.

Comparison between the processes of engagement from state agencies throws up interesting, not to say noticeable, differences between them. Indeed, the essence of Williams' prediction in his article of 1994 (based on a lecture given the year before, in 1993)[12] may be seen in the issues of 2007–2010. For many reasons, it appears more than ever crucial to reach more precise definition of the concepts of 'efficiency' and 'effectiveness' in the field of state-aided voluntary endeavour. This, not only to avoid the ambiguity of many public statements, but to give appropriate attention, in a professional manner, to the demands of the jargon of the market mentality which pervade all state-funded enterprise nowadays. Such definition might also assist in providing a more discerning view of the disadvantages of a 'feudal' system. More importantly, it might more clearly distinguish the real outcomes of voluntary effort and state funding.

The most recent meeting of the NSMC (3 November 2010) provided the latest information on the implementation of the FNG approach:

FORAS NA GAEILGE REVIEW OF CORE FUNDED BODIES

11. The Council noted the current position in regard to the review of the core-funded organisations undertaken by Foras na Gaeilge. Ministers noted proposals in regard to the *enhanced implementation arrangements, including the appointment of a project manager and establishment of a steering committee and an advisory committee.* They agreed that, in the context of satisfactory progress on implementation being achieved, interim funding may continue to be provided by Foras na Gaeilge to existing funded organisations to end May 2011 and progress will be reported at the next NSMC Language meeting. [Italics added]

---

[12] Fifth International Conference on Minority Languages, University of Wales at Cardiff, 5–9 July, 1993.

The same communiqué also noted the following:

CORPORATE PLAN 2011–13

6. Ministers noted progress on the development of the Ulster-Scots Agency and Foras na Gaeilge Corporate Plans for 2011–2013, including the *emerging strategic objectives, priorities and efficiency proposals*. Both Ministers recognise the challenges presented by the current economic climate and have agreed to work together to implement the measures agreed between both Ministers of Finance in the context of their respective budgetary processes.

ANNUAL REPORTS AND ACCOUNTS

7. The Council noted that the Language Body's 2006 [consolidated] Accounts were laid in the Northern Ireland Assembly and Oireachtas on 24 September 2010 and that Audit fieldwork has been completed in respect of the Annual Reports and Accounts for 2007, 2008 and 2009 and that consolidation will follow as soon as possible.

FORAS NA GAEILGE STAFFING AND DECENTRALISATION

12. Ministers noted recent developments in recruitment, including nine appointments (five in Gaoth Dobhair and four in Dublin) and five offers of posts (four in Gaoth Dobhair and one in Dublin). The Council noted the current position in regard to the new English-Irish Dictionary Project, following approval of additional contract staff for Foras na Gaeilge with the cost to be met by reallocation of funding within approved budgets.

The references to 'enhanced implementation arrangements' and to 'emerging strategic priorities' proved no doubt of interest to the voluntary sector, as well as 'developments in recruiting' within FNG. More important for the sector, however, was probably the 'interim funding' to be provided for several more months while the New Model works itself out. What may follow that process could have repercussions wider than either FNG or the voluntary sector envisaged.

The 20-Year Strategy for Irish in the Republic

The events and developments described have fairly direct implications for the *20-Year Strategy*[13] for Irish in the Republic. Despite the fact that the final form of the Strategy has yet to be accepted by Government and implementation agreed, the events described above within the Irish Language Sector, which comprises both state and community, hold quite serious implications. Both sides are central to the working out of the Strategy, each in accordance with its own distinctive role.

The significance of this Strategy – first signalled in the *Government Statement on the Irish Language* of December 2006 – may be found in several factors:

---

[13] An Roinn Gnóthaí Tuaithe, Pobail agus Gaeltachta, Samhain 2009. *Straitéis 20-Bliain don Ghaeilge 2010–2030, Dréacht / 20-Year Strategy for the Irish Language 2010–2010, Draft.*

- as continuation of the aims of this 2006 Statement and as a declaration of political will with regard to Irish;
- as a demonstration of a certain degree of political cross-party consensus on Irish arising out of the report issued by the relevant Joint Committee of the Oireachtas in July 2010;[14]
- as an attempt to provide a comprehensive joined-up approach in a single Stategy across the various aspects and domains of language policy.

On the other hand, there were lacunae in the Strategy as originally published. Despite a passing reference to the voluntary Sector, and some specific references to the annual festival, Oireachtas na Gaeilge, no distinctive role for the voluntary sector appears. Indeed, a much stronger role was envisaged in both the preliminary report for the department prepared by the Fiontar[14] team and in the Oireachtas Committee report. It must be remembered that strong representations on several issues were made to the Joint Committee in advance of their report being published, the more important of which were incorporated in the report. Another possible explanation for the omission of the voluntary sector may lie in the fact that the emphasis in the Strategy is more on the responsibilities of State departments as is customary in such policy documents. However, neither is clarity given to the respective rôles of the north/south FNG and of the proposed new Údarás given responsibility for the functioning of the Strategy.

From one perspective, both references and lacunae are irrelevant. Since the ultimate aim of the Strategy during its lifespan is the development of a critical mass of 250,000 daily speakers of Irish, clearly the realisation of that aim will depend to no small degree on the social aspects of language use as well as on the mobilisation of the community as a movement which will demand and make full use of state services through the medium of Irish. These are precisely the areas in which the voluntary sector has knowledge, experience and expertise. Consequently, the operational aspects of the Strategy will then depend to no small extent both on the voluntary sector and on the different subsections of the Irish language community, with appropriate support from state agencies. The desired sustainability of either language action or movement will hardly flourish through temporary short-lived schemes, however worthy, but rather through sustained and continuous work on the ground. The unassailable truth lies in partnership towards the common desired end. The different elements and structures of the Irish Language Sector, as set out at the beginning of this article, have no option but to work together, sharing resources and knowledge on behalf of the future of the language, or the community – as inclusively interpreted earlier – the Irish language and the Strategy will all be the poorer for it. The age of empire is over? Or is it?

---

[14] Tithe an Oireachtais, An Comhchoiste um Ghnóthaí Turasóireachta, Cultúir, Spóirt, Pobail, Comhionannais agus Gaeltachta, Iúil 2010. *An Tríú Tuarascáil: An Straitéis 20-Bliain don Ghaeilge 2010–2030 (Uimhir Pharlaiminte A10/1097).*

[15] Fiontar, Ollscoil Chathair Bhaile Átha Cliath, Feabhra 2009. *Straitéis 20-Bliain don Ghaeilge, arna hullmhú don Roinn Gnóthaí Pobail, Tuaithe agus Gaeltachta.*

Forbairt Straitéise don Ghaeilge: Cur Chuige Comhbheartaithe á Thógáil

Janet Muller

Ó *Chomhaontú Aoine an Chéasta* 1998 (CAC), tá pobal na Gaeilge ag féachaint le dul chun cinn cinntitheach a dhéanamh i gcomhthéacs an chaidrimh a d'athraigh idir an dá chuid den oileán agus an dá rialtas a shocraíonn beartas don teanga sa dá dhlínse. Dhá bhliain déag anonn, is tráthúil an cás láithreach i dtaca le forbairt straitéise don teanga Ghaeilge a mheas leis an tslí is fearr chun tosaigh don teanga a dhearbhú.

Más é CAC an bonn atá faoi chur chuige láithreach an tuaiscirt d'fhorbairt teanga, is tábhachtach a lua, ainneoin go rianaíonn an cháipéis dualgais áirithe i leith na Gaeilge, go leagann sí gach ceann acu seo sa chomhthéacs go síneoidh rialtas na Breataine an *Chairt Eorpach um Theangacha Réigiúnacha nó Mionlaigh* (CETRM). Ní leagann an Comhaontú aon dualgais shainiúla i leith na Gaeilge ar rialtas Phoblacht na hÉireann. Ar ndóigh, éilíonn cuid de thorthaí an Chomhaontaithe páirteachas agus aontú an dá rialtas, go háirithe i dtaca le rochtain thrasteorann an bhealach teilifíse Gaeilge TG4 (nach bhfaigheann cistiú rialtais ach ón taobh Éireannach amháin), agus bunú an chomhlachta thrasteorann, An Foras Teanga, a chistíonn an dá rialtas faoi fhoirmle chionmhar aontaithe. Soláthraíonn rialtas na Breataine 25% de bhuiséad foriomlán na Gaeilge[1] agus cistiú 75% d'Albainis Uladh,[2] i gcomparáid le 75% don Ghaeilge ó rialtas an deiscirt agus 25% d'Albainis Uladh.

Tá An Foras Teanga, atá comhdhéanta de dhá chomh-mhír, Foras na Gaeilge agus Foras Albainis Uladh, faoi chomhstiúir Roinn Cultúir, Ealaíon agus Fóillíochta an tuaiscirt agus Roinn Gnóthaí Pobail, Tuaithe agus Gaeltachta an deiscirt (a athainmníodhmar Roinn Gnóthaí Pobail, Comhionannais agus Gaeltachta i 2010).

Ón tús mar sin de, bhí deis shuntasach ag Foras na Gaeilge, más fíor na coinníollacha a leagadh amach ina reachtaíocht bhunaidh, le beartas éifeachtach, comhlántach teanga a fhorbairt sa dá dhlínse. Ach, ós eol ról cinntitheach dhá Roinn éagsúla rialtais, is léir go mbeadh treoir an dá Aire ríthábhachtach i ndearbhú rath an Fhorais. Éamon Ó Cuív, Aire Gnóthaí Pobail, Tuaithe agus Gaeltachta an deiscirt de chuid Fhianna Fáil, a bhí i mbun na Roinne ó 6 Meitheamh 2002 – 23 Márta 2010, i ndiaidh é a bheith ina Aire Stáit le freagracht as gnóthaí Gaeltachta ó 1997. Tionchar úrnua ar fad a d'imir an bhaint leanúnach a bhí aige i múnlú chur chuige na Gaeilge sa deisceart thar thréimhse thrí bliana déag.[3] In 2010, tháinig a chomhghleacaí i bhFianna Fáil, Pat Carey, i gcomharbacht ar Ó Cuív sa Roinn athainmnithe Gnóthaí Pobail, Comhionannais agus Gaeltachta.

---

[1] Taispeánann Daonáireamh 2001 de na 167,460 duine sa tuaisceart a deir go bhfuil eolas ar an Ghaeilge acu, go liostaíonn breis agus 75,000 acu scileanna i léitheoireacht, i scríbhneoireacht, i dtuiscint agus i labhairt na Gaeilge. Ag Caitlicigh is dóchúla eolas ar an Ghaeilge a bheith acu (22.2%) ná ag Protastúnaigh (1.2%). Sna haoisghrúpaí níos óige atá na daoine ar dócha eolas ar an Ghaeilge a bheith acu (12–15 bliain, 23,8%; 16–24 bliain, 16%). Tá 80 Gaelscoil sa Tuaisceart agus tuairim is ar 300 sa Deisceart.

[2] Níl figiúirí Daonáirimh ann faoi dhaoine a bhfuil eolas ar Albainis Uladh acu, thuaidh ná theas. Ach, tá úsáid déanta ag Roinn Cultúir, Ealaíon agus Fóillíochta an tuaiscirt de Shuirbhé Life and Times (1999) mar tháscaire beag samplach. Ceistíodh 2,200 duine. Léirigh na torthaí gur thug 2% díobh seo le fios go raibh eolas ar Albainis Uladh acu. Ag eachtarshuí as an fhigiúr seo, áitíonn RCEF gurbh fhéidir go bhfuil 30,000 duine sa tuaisceart a bhfuil eolas ar Albainis Uladh acu. Den chéatadán i Suirbhé Life and Times, ba dhóchúla labhairt Albainis Uladh a bheith ag Protastúnaigh (2%) ná ag Caitlicigh (1%). Ba dhóchúla gur ag daoine os cionn 65 a bheadh eolas ar Albainis Uladh.

[3] Briseadh ar thréimhse Uí Chuív i nGnóthaí Gaeilge agus Gaeltachta idir 2001–2 nuair a chaith sé tréimhse ghairid ina Aire Stáit do Thalmhaíocht agus Bhia.

Sa tuaisceart, ó CAC, comhroinntear cúraimí aireachta mar a ordaíodh in CAC, le feidhmiú mheicníocht D'Hondt. Foirmle matamaitice atá anseo a léiríonn neart thacaíocht fhoriomlán páirtí, bunaithe ar a chion de na vótaí i ndáil leis na suíocháin a baineadh. Ag tús an chéad Tionóil ghearrthréimhse (2000–2),[4] níor iarr Sinn Féin (SF) ná Páirtí Sóisialach agus Daonlathach an Lucht Oibre (SDLP) an Roinn Cultúir, Ealaíon agus Fóillíochta, a bhí croífhreagrach as gnóthaí teanga. D'ainmnigh an Páirtí Aontachtach Oifigiúil ina dhiaidh sin í. Níos moille anonn d'fhógair an tAire Michael McGimpsey[5] gur 'Aire *aontachtach* Cultúir' a bhí ann agus gur fheidhmigh sé crosadh ar fhorbairt na Gaeilge le linn a thionachta. Óna luathlaethanta anall ba léir, agus ceangal corróg ar an dá Roinn thuaidh agus theas trí Fhoras na Gaeilge, gur cainéal é an comhlacht trasteorann féin a sheolfadh an cur chuige rialtas aontachtach/Briotanach ó dheas chomh héasca is a sheolfadh sé an tionchar deisceartach ó thuaidh. Má bhí an tAire theas míshásta agus macasamhail aontachtach sa tuaisceart aige, cuireadh míshásamh áirithe in iúl fosta le linn agóidí teanga sa tuaisceart i 2002, nuair a rinne rialtas an deiscirt ciorruithe aontaobhacha 1.5 milliún euro i mbuiséad Fhoras na Gaeilge.[6] B'ábhar díomá ag a lán é gur thug an taobh Éireannach, gan fhios dar leat, réasúnaíocht ar son ciorruithe rialtas na Breataine ar chistiú Gaeilge chomh luath sin i ndiaidh gealltanais a bhaint a saothraíodh go crua. Ba ghasta a lean rialtas na Breataine sampla na hÉireann agus ghearr a gcion féin de bhuiséad na Gaeilge.

Sa tréimhse díreach roimh athbhhunú na bhforas cineachta i 2007, chláraigh pobal na Gaeilge tacaíocht mhillteanach ar son Acht cuimsitheach, ceartbhunaithe Gaeilge a thabhairt isteach. Ó tugadh gealltanas gan éideimhne i gComhaontú Chill Rìmhinn go dtabharfaí an tAcht isteach, agus ó cruinníodh tacaíocht ollmhór d'athruithe i stádas agus i gcoinníollacha na Teanga sa tuaisceart, mhothaigh a lán sa phobal díomá ghéar nuair a lig na páirtithe náisiúnacha uathu, arís, an cúram Cultúir, Ealaíon agus Fóillíochta. Trí dheis a fuair Sinn Féin, an páirtí is mó de na páirtithe náisiúnacha, an Aireacht a roghnú, agus fuair an SDLP deis amháin. Sa deireadh, áfach, ba é Cultúir, Ealaíon agus Fóillíocht an Aireacht dheireanach a leithdháileadh, gabhadh i ndeireadh na dála í ag Páirtí Aontachtach Daonlathach (DUP) Ian Paisley, a raibh agus a bhfuil tuairisc phoiblí ar a naimhdeas gangaideach do chur chun cinn forásach na teanga Gaeilge.[7]

Ó CAC, níor tugadh iarracht ar bith oifigiúil leanúnach le beartas uile-Éireann don Ghaeilge a fhorbairt, ainneoin méid áirithe roscaireachta. Theip ar Fhoras na Gaeilge ina chuid iarrachtaí go sea, agus is ceist é an bhfuil straitéis mhionsonraithe inmheánach dó féin fiú ag an chomhlacht. Má bhí leoga aon amhras i measc lucht polaitiúil faoi chumas Fhoras na Gaeilge lena dhualgas a chomhlíonadh, bhí, áfach, roghanna eile a d'fhéadfaí a leanúint. I mí Iúil 2004, chruthaigh an tAire deisceartach Éamon Ó Cuív aonán eile, Fóram na Gaeilge, taobh amuigh de shainchúram CAC le

---

[4] Sna cúig bliana ó 2002–7 nuair a bhí an Tionól ar fionraí, bhí Rialtóirí Díreacha Briotanacha i mbun chur chuige 'cúraim agus cothabhála' i ngnóthaí uile roinne an Tionóil.

[5] BBC Raidió Uladh, 25 Deireadh Fómhair 2006, McGimpsey, Michael, Idirbheartaí Sinsearach UUP, CTR Béal Feirste theas agus iar-Aire Cultúir, Ealaíon agus Fóillíochta i dTionól TÉ 1999 –2002, athchraoladh ar chlár Gaeilge Raidió Uladh, *Blas*.

[6] D'fhógair rialtas na hÉireann ciorrú aontaobhach 1.5 milliún euro i mí na Samhna 2002, a spreag agóidí sa Tuaisceart ag grúpaí Gaeilge a mheas é a bheith ina ionsaí ar sholáthair CAC a saothraíodh go crua.

[7] I bhForógra an DUP do Thoghchán an Tionóil Feabhra 2007 bhí tiomantas le cur in éadan Acht na Gaeilge, agus bileoga do na meáin ag síorionsaí na Gaeilge agus an phobail. Féach mar shampla, *The Irish News*, 24 Deireadh Fómhair 2006, Roy Garland, 'Changing Times Signals the End for the Rhetoric'; *The News Letter*, 14 Samhain 2006, 'Scepticism over Government Offer on Ulster Scots'; *The News Letter*, 17 Samhain 2006, 'The Trojan Threat of the Irish Language Act'; *The News Letter*, 20 Nollaig 2006, 'Allister Broadside Attack on Irish Language Bill Document'.

hionadaíocht uile-Éireann, ach á roghnú ag páirtithe polaitiúla seachas ag an phobal féin. Ach, cé go ndearna an Fóram plé áirithe ar mholtaí straitéiseacha, níor forbraíodh riamh iad. Nuair a thosaigh Ó Cuív tar éis sin a dhréachtú Phlean 20-Bliain don teanga Ghaeilge, shuigh sé an fhreagracht as taobh istigh dá Roinn féin, a theorannaigh a scóip go dearfa don deisceart amháin. Ainneoin cuirí le cruinnithe comhairliúcháin ar an Phlean a thabhairt ó thuaidh, dhiúltaigh Ó Cuív.[8] Ar a fhoilsiú, d'admhaigh an tAire gur ar an deisceart amháin a bhí a phlean 'náisiúnta' dírithe agus nach raibh sé de chumhacht ag aire deisceartach beartas a shocrú sa Tuaisceart.[9] Dhiúltaigh sé cuireadh ón eagras neamh-rialtasach (ENR) Gaeilge POBAL,[10] labhairt le pobal na Gaeilge sa tuaisceart ar a dhréachtphlean, agus dhiúltaigh fosta státseirbhíseach sinsearach a chur le labhairt ina áit. San am céanna, mar a bheadh sé ag leagan béim ar thréigean an chur chuige uile-Éireann, d'fhógair Ó Cuív go raibh rún aige comhlacht úr, Údarás na Gaeilge, a chruthú le sainchúram 26 chontae amháin, agus thug le tuiscint, ba chosúil, go seolfaí cistiú rialtas na hÉireann d'Foras na Gaeilge isteach san aonán úr. Cháin cuid de thacadóirí Gaeilge an deiscirt an moladh mar gheall ar a impleachtaí d'fhorbairt cheantair Ghaeltachta.[11] Is intuigthe go gcuirfeadh cuid de na daoine sa deisceart fáilte chiúin roimh shaoradh bheartas na Gaeilge ar naimhdeas dochrach sa Roinn Thuaisceartach agus ar theip bhraite an chomhlachta thrasteorann féin. Ach, d'aithin cuid de thráchtairí an Deiscirt na himpleachtaí don teanga sa Tuaisceart.[12] Is cosúil gur choisc a dtuairimí, mar aon le haibhsiú dhearcadh an tuaiscirt ag ENRanna Gaeilge sa dlínse,[13] an dísciú substáinteach ar bhuiséad foriomlán an Fhorais i bhfabhar Údarás na Gaeilge, ainneoin go bhfuil éifeacht an chúlú reatha agus achumrú an chistiú atá ar fáil tríd an Fhoras ag eochairghrúpaí ag leanúint leo.

I mí na Samha 2010, ghlac an tOireachtas leis an Phlean 20-Bliain, faoi chruth leasaithe beagán, agus fógraíodh go gcuirfí an reachtaíocht ar aghaidh a theastaigh le hÚdarás na Gaeilge a bhunú. Ach, chóir a bheith comhuaineach leis seo, d'fhulaing geilleagar an deiscirt cliseadh tubaisteach, as ar tháinig idirghabháil ón Chiste Airgeadaíochta Idirnáisiúnta (CAI), ón Choimisiún Eorpach, agus leoga, ó rialtas na Breataine. Tá na meáin ar maos i nuacht faoi iasachtaí suas le £80 billiún agus brú i gcomhair luath-thoghcháin sa deisceart i 2011. Más amhlaidh an cás, beidh brú gan fasach ar an chaiteachas poiblí agus ar fheidhmiú beartais thar réimse leathan limistéar, san áireamh gan amhras, an beartas teanga.

Dréachtphlean 20-Bliain don Ghaeilge ó Dheas: Arbh Fhéidir é a Chur i Gcrích ó Thuaidh?

Fiú gan na buarthaí reatha eacnamaíocha, deir téacs féin an Dréachtphleana 20-Bliain arís agus arís eile gur seo plean don 'stát', ní hionann agus d'oileán na hÉireann. Dar leis an dréachtphlean, 'Is é an bonn atá faoin Straitéis 20-Bliain seo ná an stádas atá ag an teanga sa Bhunreacht', tagraíonn leath. 5 d'Airteagal 8 an Bhunreachta trí bhéim a leagan ar an ráiteas gur 'Stát dátheangach í Éire', tá an Straitéis bunaithe ar ráiteas

---

8 Níor cuireadh an Plean faoi réir chomhairliú poiblí taobh amuigh de Phoblacht na hÉireann.

9 *Nuacht 24*, 15 Bealtaine 2009, le hEoghan Ó Neill, 'Soiscéal Éamoin'.

10 Is í an t-údar Príomhfheidhmeannach POBAL.

11 *The Irish Times*, 21 Eanáir 2010, Harry McGee, Comhfhreagraí Polaitiúil, 'Call to Keep Údarás na Gaeltachta'.

12 Sliocht as an bhlag *igaeilge*, 16 Samhain 2009, '... is cinnte go gcaithfear a chinntiú nach bhfuil leithscéal á thabhairt d'Aontachtaithe atá nimhneach in éadan na Gaeilge, leithéidí Nelson McCausland, Aire Cultúir an tuaiscirt, cúlú ó dhualgaisí an stáitín ó thuaidh i leith na Gaeilge.'

13 Litir chuig Ó Cuív ó Chomhchoiste Ghrúpaí Bunmhaoinithe an tuaiscirt, 12 Samhain 2009.

2006 rialtas na hÉireann, a bhain leis na 26 contae amháin, agus, chomh maith leis an Bhunreacht, braitheann sí ar reachtaíocht mar *Acht na dTeangacha Oifigiúla 2003* de chuid an deiscirt, *Acht Oideachais 1998* an deiscirt, *Acht Pleanála agus Forbartha 2000* an deiscirt agus *Acht Craoltóireachta 2001* (a uasdátaíodh i 2009). Níl feidhm ag cuid ar bith den reachtaíocht seo sa tuaisceart, agus is buncheist í seo.

De 13 cuspóir atá luaite ag tús na cáipéise, is mórábhar amhrais é arbh fhéidir níos mó ná a leath a leathnú go dtí an Tuaisceart (mar shampla, baineann Cuspóirí 1-5 d'áit Bhunreachtúil agus reachtach na Gaeilge agus leis na ceantair Ghaeltachta nach n-aithnítear faoi reachtaíocht ach sa deisceart amháin.) Tá cuspóirí a bhaineann le teagasc na Gaeilge i scoileanna Béarla nasctha le reachtaíocht oideachais nach bhfuil feidhm aici sa tuaisceart, áit nach mbíonn an teanga á teagasc in am ar bith i scoileanna Protastúnacha (rialaithe), agus nach mbíonn sí ar fáil i gcónaí i scoileanna Caitliceacha (faoi Chothabháil) ach an oiread. Cé go mbraithfeadh Gaeilgeoirí gur beart dearfach é ábhar éigeantach a dhéanamh den Ghaeilge i ngach scoil Bhéarla, is éadócha go mór go gcuirfí i bhfeidhm sa tuaisceart é gan reachtaíocht a thacódh leis.

D'fhéadfadh cuspóirí a bhaineann le Gaeloideachas a bheith tairbhiúil, ach níl aon tagairt sa Dréachtphlean do chomhoibriú uile-Éireann tríd an dá Roinn Oideachais ar cheisteanna oideachais TG. Tá ceisteanna substaintiúla go fóill ann, mar sin de, faoi na meicníochtaí a theastódh agus faoin dóigh a dtiocfadh soláthar agus beartas thuaidh agus theas a chomhordú. Fá láthair, tá difríochtaí suntasacha beartais thuaidh agus theas ann fán dóigh le hoideachas TG a chur chun cinn, ar leibhéal iar-bhunscoile go háirithe.

Is féidir go mbeidh sochair iarmhartacha ag Cuspóirí 8 (Foras na Gaeilge), 9 (TG4, Raidió na Gaeltachta), 10 (An tAontas Eorpach) ar bhonn uile-Éireann. Baineann Cuspóirí 8 agus 9 le comhaontuithe idir-rialtais atá ann cheana féin agus ní comhartha iad d'aon tiomantas úr nó tionscnamh mionsonraithe leis an chomhoibriú a leathnú nó a fhorbairt. Ní thagraíonn Cuspóir 9 don Chiste Craoltóireachta Gaeilge (CCG) sa tuaisceart, agus mar sin de, is deacair a mheas an mbeadh éifeacht dhearfach, dhiúltach nó éifeacht ar bith ag na moltaí ar an CCG.

Suíonn Cuspóir 11 freagracht as an Phlean ar Roinn Gnóthaí Pobail, Tuaithe agus Gaeltachta an deiscirt gan aon tagairt do mheicníochtaí seolta ar bhonn uile-Éireann. Dá gcuirfí codanna den Phlean in áit sa tuaisceart, cé a mhaoirseodh iad? RCEF? Oifig an Chéad-Aire is an Leas-Chéad Aire (OCALCA)? Más amhlaidh, conas a thiocfar ar chomhaontú? Mura ndéanfaí maoirseacht oifigiúil orthu ar leibhéal rialtais, is ar bhonn deonach a bheadh aon fheidhmiú sa Tuaisceart.

Baineann Cuspóir 12 leis an Gharda Síochána agus is éadócha é a bheith ábhartha ar bhonn uile-Éireann.

Déanann Cuspóir 13 ráiteas fán earnáil dheonach Ghaeilge, ag tagairt is dócha do ghrúpaí sa deisceart. Tá ról agus caidreamh na hearnála deonaí leis an stát difriúil go stairiúil agus i bhfírinne thuaidh agus theas, agus oibríonn eagrais faoi choinníollacha difriúla reachtacha, beartais agus sóisialta. Tá atheagrú molta earnáil dheonach na Gaeilge á thiomáint ag an dréachtphlean seo, ach mura dtig an Plean féin a lánfheidhmiú ar bhonn uile-Éireann, caithfear struchtúir dheonacha sa tuaisceart a chosaint.

In achoimriú na gcéimeanna i dtreo fheidhmiú na Straitéise thar 20-bliain, is sonrach nár socraíodh spriocanna ar bith i dtaca le feidhmiú nó leathnú na Straitéise sa tuaisceart. Tá na spriocanna de ghnáth measartha doiléir, rud a mhéadaíonn an deacracht faoina fháil amach cad a dhéanfar, cá huair agus cé aige.

I mBliain 1 luaitear teagmháil idir spriocanna agus ábhar, acmhainniú agus struchtúir. Deir sé, 'Iarrfar pleananna oibríochta ó na gníomhaireachtaí poiblí forfheidhmiúcháin ar fad agus gheofar iad.' Ardaíonn sé seo arís an cheist an bhfuil gníomhaireachtaí feidhmithe ar bith sa tuaisceart, ó nár luadh aon chuid, agus maíonn an fhoclaíocht go bhfuil gá le leibhéal éigin dlíthiúil i sóláthar pleananna. Níl aon oibleagáid den chineál sin i mbeartas nó reachtaíocht reatha sa tuaisceart. Fiú dá n-aontófaí reachtaíocht úr, chuimsitheach láithreach don tuaisceart, ní thiocfadh an t-amchlár seo a fhreastal ar bhonn uile-Éireann.

Tá ráite go bhfuil 'trí fho-chéim' i mBlianta 4–15 ach arís tá an tréimhse fada (11 bliain) agus na mionsonraí gann. Luaitear 'measúnuithe rollála' agus 'feachtais' le manaí dearfacha a chur chun cinn agus a chothú. Déarfaí go mb'fhéidir gur seo réimse ina ndíreofaí aird go háirithe ar shainchúinsí an tuaiscirt, ach níl aon tagairt do riachtanais chur chuige uile-Éireann ar an cheist seo.

Tréimhse don neartú iad Blianta 16–20 de réir na Straitéise, agus do 'phríomhshruthú' na mbeart uilig. Ach, gan na meicníochtaí cearta agus an reachtaíocht cheart in áit sa tuaisceart, beidh príomhshruthú i gcónaí an-deacair. Ní thugann na spriocanna céimnithe, áfach, aon chomhartha den dóigh a ndéanfaí na hathruithe is gá sa tuaisceart le príomhshruthú ar bhonn uile-Éireann a cheadú. Mura ndéanfaí an príomhshruthú ach sa deisceart amháin, cad é chomh *príomhshrutha* is a bheadh sé?

Tugann an Dréachtphlean le fios go bhfuil acmhainniú ríthábhachtach agus go dtiocfaidh an t-acmhainniú seo ón Roinn Gnóthaí Pobail, Tuaithe agus Gaeltachta. Léiriú soiléir é seo gur ón rialtas sa deisceart a thiocfas an cistiú. Is éigean a shoiléiriú cé aca bhéidh nó nach mbeidh na hacmhainní imfhálaithe ag Teach Laighean (nó an Roinn) le feidhmiú an Phlean a cheadú ar bhonn uile-Éireann (.i. le grúpaí sa Tuaisceart a chistiú le hobair a dhéanamh nuair is ábhartha, ar aon dul le gníomhartha an Phlean) nó cé acu aontaíodh nó nár aontaíodh bearta le cistiú a cheadú trí Fhoras na Gaeilge do thionscnaimh den chineál sin sa tuaisceart. Más amhlaidh, an mbeidh an cistiú seo imfhálaithe i mbuiséad an Fhorais, agus ó nach bhfuil an Plean seo fréamhaithe i ndála agus i riachtanais iomlán na hÉireann, cén tionchar a d'oibreodh sé seo ar thograí riachtanacha do na 26 contae nach n-aithnítear faoi láthair sa Straitéis? Dár ndóigh, ní féidir a thomhas go fóill cad é an tionchar a imreoidh tubáiste eacnamaíoch an deiscirt ar acmhainniú an Phlean.

Baineann sainchuspóirí an Phlean uilig le heolas déimeagrafach agus spriocanna a leagadh amach do na 26 contae amháin. Go teoiriciúil, thiocfadh go mbeadh feidhm ar bhonn uile-Éireann ag an phointe urchair deiridh, líon na ndaoine a úsáideann seirbhísí Stáit trí Ghaeilge a mhéadú. Ach, sa tuaisceart, tá deacracht sa mhéid is nach bhfuil reachtaíocht áitiúil infheidhmithe ann a cheadódh soláthar seirbhísí suntasacha tríd an Ghaeilge. Ní léir go bhfuil athrú na staide sin lárnach sa Dréachtphlean féin, ó nár leagadh amach spriocanna ar bith faoi chúinsí an tuaiscirt, nár luadh acmhainní ar bith ná nár achoimríodh aon chur chuige.

Ar leath 6 tá ráite go bhfuil mar bhuntaca faoin Déachtphlean Ráiteas Rialtais an Deiscirt ar an Teanga Ghaeilge 2006, a bhfuil a shainchúram go hiomlán teoranta do na 26 chontae; agus ar thaighde a rinne Fiontar DCU agus Micheál Mac Gréil. Ní scrúdaíonn ceachtar de na staidéir seo dálaí na teanga ar bhonn uile-Éireann. Ní thagraíonn an staidreamh agus an measúnú uilig ach do na 26 chontae. Ní thugtar aghaidh ar an easpa reachtaíochta ná ar an saintionchar déimeagrafach mar gheall ar gan an Ghaeilge a bheith á teagasc i mbunús scoileanna Protastúnacha an tuaiscirt, nó iontu uilig, agus mar sin de, cé go dtiocfar méid áirithe dul chun cinn a dhéanamh ar líon na gcainteoirí ar bhonn uile-Éireann, níl creat nó reachtaíocht taca sa tuaisceart, agus ní thiocfadh tuilleadh forbartha ar an obair láithreach a dhéanamh ach ar bhonn ad hoc taobh amuigh de na 26 chontae.

Tá meicníocht mhaoirseachta an Phlean go daingean ar fad sna 26 chontae, trí oifig an Taoisigh, trí ghrúpa na n-oifigeach sinsearach agus tríd an Roinn Gnóthaí Pobail, Tuaithe agus Gaeltachta.

Deir an Dréachtphlean gur ar Údarás na Gaeilge (ÚnaG) a bheas, 'freagracht maidir le cúrsaí teanga ar fud an Stáit'. 'Gníomhaireacht nua náisiúnta' a thugtar air, bunaithe faoi reachtaíocht úr, rud a fhágann gur éadócha go mór go bhfeidhmeofaí ar bhonn uile-Éireann é. Beidh ról Fhoras na Gaeilge go fóill ina 'phríomhghné den struchtúr tacaíochta don teanga'. Ach, ní chuirtear síos ar mhionsonraí an ghaoil agus na ndualgas idir an comhlacht úr, Údarás na Gaeilge, agus an comhlacht uile-Éireann, agus is ábhar imní é go mb'fhéidir go dtarlódh dúbailt agus ionırall sna róil. Más é ról ÚnaG an Plcan a acmhainniú, cad eile sna 26 contae a thig a chistiú tríd? An bhfuil sé tuartha go mbeidh cistiú ann do ghníomhaíochtaí Gaeilge sna 26 contae NACH mbaineann leis an Phlean? Mura bhfuil, cad chuige a gcisteofaí cuid de na gníomhaíochtaí ag Foras agus cuid eile ag Údarás agus cad iad a impleachtaí seo ar bhonn uile-Éireann?

Ar leath. 8, tá ráite go mbeidh 'deathionchar ag Plean an Rialtais ar lucht labhartha na Gaeilge i dTuaisceart Éireann'. Maíonn sé seo nach gcuirfear an Plean féin i bhfeidhm sa tuaisceart. Ní thugtar aon eolas ar cad é a bheadh sna tionchair thairbhiúla, cad é mar a bhainfí amach iad agus cad iad na meicníochtaí lena ndéanfaí seo. Ó nach bhfuil an Plean bunaithe ar dhála an tuaiscirt, is doiligh a fheiceáil conas a thig a rá go mbeidh sé tairbhiúil ach sa chiall is ginearálta. I bhfírinne, d'fhéadfaí a áitiú fosta go leagann an limistéar liath a thimpeallaíonn feidhmiú agus tionchair tuilleadh míbhuntáistí ar phobal na Gaeilge sa Tuaisceart, ós rud é gur imeallaíodh a ndála agus a riachtanais sa bhuntaighde straitéiseach.

Ní dhéantar tagairtí don tuaisceart ach trí Fhoras na Gaeilge, *Acht na Gaeilge* agus 'feabhsú, cosaint agus forbairt na Gaeilge i dTuaisceart Éireann.' Is gealltanais iad sin uilig atá ann cheana féin. Is suimiúil a thabhairt faoi deara gur úsáideadh an fhoclaíocht 'feabhsú, cosaint agus forbairt na Gaeilge' in *Acht 2006 Chill Rìmhinn* i leith straitéis don Ghaeilge a bheadh le gabháil ag an Tionól. Ní luaitear seo mar straitéis, ná ní dhéantar soiléiriú ar an ghaol, más ann dó, idir cáipéis an Dréachtphleana 20-Bliain agus cháipéis ionchais an Tionóil. An bhfuil a leithéid ann? Mura bhfuil, nach n-ardaíonn sé sin tuilleadh ceisteanna faoina bhfuil i ndán don fheidhmiú ar bhonn uile-Éireann?

Tagraíonn leath 34 d'atheagrú radacach earnáil dheonach na Gaeilge le seirbhís 'chliabhán go seanaois' bunaithe ar an Dréachtphlean seo a sholáthar. Cibé buanna atá sa chur chuige seo sa deisceart, áit a dtig an Plean a fheidhmiú go hoifigiúil, tá amhras suntasach faoina shochar sa tuaisceart. Ós fíor é nach féidir straitéis rialtais na hÉireann a fheidhmiú go hoifigiúil i limistéar atá go fóill faoi dhlínse na Breataine, agus ag glacadh le fócas an taighde agus an tsaineolais ar a bhfuil an Plean bunaithe a bheith ar an deisceart amháin agus go bhfuil cuid mhór de mholtaí an Phlean ag brath ar bhonn reachtach nach ann dó ar chor ar bith sa tuaisceart, is cosúil go bhfuil argóintí láidre in éadan leathnú atheagrú an chistithe go dtí an tuaisceart. Agus leoga ní mholann an Dréachtphlean gur mar sin ba chóir an cás a bheith.

Ina áit sin, tagann athchumrú an mhaoinithe ó chinneadh de chuid an Chomhairle Aireachta thuaidh theas i mí na Nollag 2009 nuair a d'aontaigh an tAire deisceartach Ó Cuív agus an tAire tuaisceartach McCausland nár chóir go gcisteodh Foras na Gaeilge obair ar bith ach tograí áitiúla nó ceann nó líon teoranta d'eagraíochtaí abhcóideachta.

Tá áitithe ag na 19 eagras bunchistithe Gaeilge, thuaidh agus theas, nár chóir go mbeadh earnáil an tuaiscirt faoi réir atheagrú, nuair nach bhfuil straitéis dhearfach státurraithe sa tuaisceart d'fhorbairt na teanga. Cé go n-aithnítear go dtig le straitéis den chineál sin tógáil ar shineirgí le moltaí 20-bliain an deiscirt le cur chuige níos iomláine uile-Éireann a aimsiú, is deacair a fheiceáil conas a thig seo a dhéanamh mura bhfaighidh an bonneagar Gaeilge sa tuaisceart, atá measartha úr agus tearcfhorbartha, cosaint, cur chun cinn agus daingniú. Tá naimhdeas suntasach sna páirtithe Aontachtacha don Ghaeilge agus go háirithe d'eagrais ardphróifíle agus éifeachtacha. Is é an dualgas atá roimh pháirtithe Náisiúnacha a aithint go n-éileoidh cruthú chur chuige uile-Éireann atá éifeachtach seachas a bheith meabhlach, tacaíocht oiriúnach do shaineolas agus do thaithí ENRanna ag obair sa dá dhlínse agus solúbthacht níos mó i socruithe cistithe Fhoras na Gaeilge ná atá a lorg faoi láthair.

Pleanáil Straitéiseach sa Tuaisceart

Cé gur fíor go leagann clár phlean 20-bliain an Deiscirt béim ar a dhearcadh 26 chontae, os a choinne sin aibhsíonn a fhoilsiú fosta an dalladh beartaithe polaitiúil agus an folús beartais teanga sa tuaisceart. Mothaíonn a lán de lucht labhartha Gaeilge an tuaiscirt go bhfuil siad gafa idir dhá thine Bhealtaine. Fad atá cúrsaí an tuaiscirt imeallaithe i bPlean 20-Bliain an deiscirt, tá an bonneagar teanga Gaeilge ó thuaidh faoi bhagairt ag comhchealga thart timpeall ar an chlár theas. San fhadtréimhse, is eagal le Gaeilgeoirí a bheith faoi ghlas i gcur chuige beartais atá míshásúil, ad hoc agus deonach i dtaca le riachtanais fhorbartha sa tuaisceart. San idirlinn, cé go bhfuil dualgas soiléir reachtúil ar Thionól Thuaisceart na hÉireann straitéis a ghabháil do mhéadú na Gaeilge, is cosúil é a bheith in abar i maorlathas agus i mbun polaitíochta seictí.

Tá gealltanas tugtha ag rialtas na Breataine i gComhaontú Chill Rìmhinn 2006 reachtaíocht don teanga Ghaeilge a achtú. Mar atá taifeadta in áit eile,[14] ní léirítear an gealltanas seo in *Acht Chill Rìmhinn 2006* agus tá sé go fóill le comhlíonadh. Chumhdaigh an tAcht, áfach, gealltanas difriúil teanga ón Chomhaontú, á rá, 'Gabhfaidh an Coiste Feidhmiúcháin straitéis a leagfaidh amach conas atá rún aige forbairt na teanga Gaeilge a mhéadú agus a chosaint.'[15] Tá an dualgas seo á neartú ag moladh i dtuarascáil Aibreán 2007 Choiste Saineolaithe Chomhairle na hEorpa (COMEX) ar fheidhmiú an *Chairt Eorpach um Theangacha Réigiúnacha nó Mionlaigh*, ionstraim idirnáisiúnta a daingníodh i 2001. Ar mheasúnú thorthaí COMEX, iarrann Coiste na nAirí ar rialtas na Breataine, ar bhonn práinne, 'beartas cuimsitheach teanga Gaeilge a fhorbairt, ina mbeadh bearta a dhéanfadh freastal ar an éileamh méadaitheach ar oideachas trí mheán na Gaeilge.'[16]

Ainneoin an dá threoir cheangailteacha seo, sa tréimhse 3 bliana ó athbhunú na bhforas cineachta i mí Bealtaine 2007, níor fhoilsigh an Roinn Cultúir, Ealaíon agus Fóillíochta, a bhfuil cúram comhlíonta an dualgais uirthi, oiread agus aon cháipéis amháin faoina straitéis do chur chun cinn na Gaeilge. I mí Aibreáin 2008, d'eagraigh an ENR POBAL comhdháil mhór le cainteoirí eolacha ar chruthú beartais ón Bhreatain Bheag agus ó Albain,[17] chomh maith le Leas-Chathaoirleach COMEX an ama sin, Sigve Gramstad, a thug gearrchuntas ar a thuairimí faoi chomhdhéanamh an bheartais chuimsithigh a theastaigh. Comhordaíodh agus taifeadadh tuairimí agus moltaí an phobail. Aire Cultúir an ama sin, Edwin Poots a d'oscail an chomhdháil, á rá nach dtabharfadh sé isteach an tAcht Gaeilge a gealladh ach ina áit sin go

---

[14] Muller, J. *Language and Conflict in Northern Ireland and Canada: A Silent War*, Houndmills: Palgrave Macmillan. 2010.

[15] Tagraíonn fophointe eile sa pharagraf céanna do straitéis 'le teanga, oidhreacht agus cultúr Albainis Uladh a mhéadú agus a fhorbairt.' Acht Chill Rìmhinn TÉ 2006.

[16] COMEX Strasbourg 14 Márta 2007, RecChL(2007)2.

[17] PF Bhord na Breatnaise, Meirion Prys Jones; Iarcheannaire Chomunn Na Gàidhlig, Dòmhnall Màrtainn.

ndréachtódh sé straitéis, 'le buntaca an Chairt Eorpach um Theangacha Réigiúnacha nó Mionlaigh.'[18] Níor thionscnaigh a Roinn iarracht ar bith eile le dul i gcomhairle le pobal na Gaeilge ar an cheist.

I gcomharbacht ar Poots tháinig Gregory Campbell, a labhair le coiste scrúdain Chultúir, Ealaíon agus Fóillíochta ag an Tionól i mí na Nollag 2008. Agus é ag tabhairt ghearrchuntais ar a mholadh le haon straitéis amháin a tháirgeadh don Ghaeilge agus d'Albainis Uladh, dúirt an tAire,

> Chuir mé in iúl go cruinn ar roinnt ócáidí go bhfeictear dom an éagothroime thraidisiúnta idir chistiú don teanga Ghaeilge agus d'Albainis Uladh a bheith go huile is go hiomlán neamhbhuanaithe. Tá sí dochosanta, agus neamhbhuanaithe, agus ní rachaidh mé ina bun – ní dhéanfaidh mé é. Tá sin ráite go cruinn agam.'[19]

Cé gur dhearbhaigh sé a rún dréachtpháipéar a cur faoi bhráid an Fheidhmeannais a leagfadh amach prionsabail ardleibhéil go luath i 2009, níor nocht a leithéid de pháipéar. I mí Meithimh 2009, in ionad Campbell tháinig a chomhghleacaí páirtí, Nelson McCausland, a mhínigh i ráiteas Aireachta a chur chuige do bheartas teanga mar a leanas,

> Féachfaidh mé le haghaidh a thabhairt ar na héagothroimí faoi láthair idir Albainis Uladh agus Gaeilge agus beidh mé ag iarraidh comhurraim agus comhchistiú a bhaint amach dóibh beirt. Sílim go ndearna muid dul chun cinn suntasach go dtí seo. Mar shampla, idir 2005 agus 2008, chóir a bheith gur dhúbail leithdháiltí ar chistiú ón Roinn Cultúir, Ealaíon agus Fóillíochta d'Albainis Uladh, agus mhéadaigh cistiú don Ghaeilge faoi bheagán os cionn 6%. Tá dul chun cinn á dhéanamh.[20]

I mí Aibreáin 2010, i ndiaidh chuairt ar an láthair ag baill de COMEX, d'fhoilsigh Comhairle na hEorpa an 3ú tuarascáil ar fheidhmiú CETRM. I dtaca leis an straitéis, áitíonn COMEX,

> Leagann Acht Chomhaontú Chill Rìmhinn 2006 dualgas reachtach ar Fheidhmeannas TÉ straitéis a ghabháil leis an teanga Ghaeilge a mhéadú agus a chosaint. Níor gabhadh aon straitéis go sea. Ach, tá rún ag an Aire Cultúir, Ealaíon agus Fóillíochta (RCEF) straitéis amháin dár teideal 'Straitéis do Theangacha Réigiúnacha Dúchais nó Mionlaigh', a thabhairt chun tosaigh atá beartaithe a bheith ina haon straitéis don Ghaeilge agus d'Albainis Uladh. Tá imní ar Choiste na Saineolaithe go bhféachfaidh an straitéis i dtreo chothrom idir an dá theanga a bhaint amach agus mar sin, nach ndéanfaidh sí freastal ar riachtanais chainteoirí Gaeilge ná Albainis Uladh agus go gcuirfidh sí cúl ar fhorbairt an dá theanga.[21]

---

[18] *Ag forbairt polasaí cuimsitheach agus straitéise le cur chun cinn na Gaeilge a fheabhsú agus a chosaint i dTuaisceart Éireann*, Tuairisc ar an Chomhdháil, 7 Márta 2008, POBAL.

[19] Coiste Cultúir, Ealaíon agus Fóillíochta Tionól TÉ, Tuairisc Oifigiúil (Hansard), Straitéis Teanga, 4 Nollaig 2008, l. 9.

[20] Tionól TÉ, Nelson McCausland, Aire Cultúir, Ealaíon agus Fóillíochta, Ráiteas Aireachta ar Fhormáid Earnála Teanga CATT, 15ú Meán Fómhair 2009.

[21] COMEX Strasbourg 14 Márta 2007, leath. 13, parag. 57.

Ar 8 Samhain 2010, níor bhain díospóireacht fhada racánach a spreag ceist scríofa Tionóil ar cheist *Acht na Gaeilge* agus na straitéise, aon eolas úr ar an mhéid a bheas sa dréacht atá le fada ag teacht, ná fiú aon dáta foilsithe nó comhairlithe. Thug an comhalta Tionóil de chuid Shinn Féin, Billy Leonard ar an díospóireacht, 'liosta dalltaí, moilleanna agus oirbhearta stadta,' agus lean air, 'is é bunsmaoineamh na hargóna faoi chearta daonna nach mbaineann sé leis an tromlachas a bheith ag tabhairt cead ar a gcearta do dhaoine.'[22]

Is léir gur ábhar mórfhrustrachais é an mhoill fhada ar tháirgeadh straitéise Tionóil don Ghaeilge. Ach, thug Airí Cultúir i ndiaidh a chéile le fios dúinn fiú dá bhfoilseofaí an straitéis, nach suífí i gcomhthéacs sochtheangeolaíoch í faoin chóras reatha ná nach mbeadh sí bunaithe i riachtanais phobal na Gaeilge ná na teanga féin. Mar a thuar an COMEX, tá cur chuige na Roinne bunoscionn le pleanáil dhearfach teanga. Is léir go dteastaíonn slí eile le creat forbarthach a bhunú don Ghaeilge sa tuaisceart, creat atá fréamhaithe sa riachtanas agus a dtig leis comhoibriú le Plean 20-Bliain an deiscirt.

Ag deireadh 2009, agus an ENR POBAL ag tógáil a chuid oibre leanúnach ar an cheist, bhunaigh sé meitheal oibre le hionadaithe ó Ollscoil na Banríona, Béal Feirste, ó Ollscoil Uladh agus ó Choláiste Ollscoile Naomh Muire, le beartas cuimsitheach agus creat straitéiseach don teanga Ghaeilge a dhréachtú. Ag seimineár poiblí i mí Meithimh 2010, phléigh pobal na Gaeilge, polaiteoirí agus státseirbhísigh Dréachtphlean 20-Bliain an deiscirt; Straitéis Teanga TÉ nár foilsíodh a amharcann ar theangacha san oideachas; torthaí an COMEX agus na hachair tosaíochta i gcomhair forbartha, agus san áireamh reachtaíocht, oideachas, na meáin, seirbhísí poiblí agus bonneagar deonach na Gaeilge. Cé go bhfuair an tAire cuireadh, ní thiocfadh leis a bheith ann. Tá an Grúpa Oibre ag leanúint dá tionscnamh straitéiseach.

---

[22] *Tionól TÉ, Tuairisc Oifigiúil (Hansard)*, 8 Samhain 2010.

Irish Language Strategy Development: Building a Concerted Approach

Janet Muller

Since the 1998 *Good Friday Agreement* (GFA), the Irish language community has been attempting to make definitive progress in the context of an altered relationship between the two parts of the island and the two governments which make policy for the language in the two jurisdictions. Twelve years on, it is timely to assess the current situation in relation to Irish language strategy development in order to determine the best way forward for the language.

If the GFA is the basis for current northern approaches to language development, it is important to note that whilst the document outlines certain duties in relation to the Irish language, it places all of these in the context of the signing by the British government of the *European Charter for Regional or Minority Languages* (ECRML). The Agreement does not place any specific duties on the government of the Republic of Ireland in respect of Irish. Of course, some of the outworkings of the Agreement require the participation and agreement of both governments, in particular in relation to cross-border access to the Irish language television channel TG4 (which receives government funding solely from the Irish side), and to the establishment of a cross-border body, An Foras Teanga (The Language Board), funded under an agreed proportional formula by both governments. The British government provides 25% of the overall budget for Irish[1] and 75% funding for Ulster Scots,[2] compared with 75% for Irish from the southern government and 25% for Ulster Scots.

An Foras Teanga, made up of two consistutent parts, Foras Na Gaeilge (the Irish Language Board) and the Ulster Scots Agency is under the joint direction of the North's Department of Culture, Arts and Leisure and the South's Department of Community, Rural and Gaeltacht Affairs (renamed in 2010 as Community, Equality and Gaeltacht Affairs).

From the beginning therefore, Foras na Gaeilge, according to the conditions laid out in its founding legislation had a significant opportunity to develop effective, complementary language policy in the two jurisdictions. However, given the decisive role of two different government Departments, it is clear that the political direction of the two Ministers would be key in determining its success. Éamon Ó Cuív, the South's Fianna Fáil Minister for Community, Rural and Gaeltacht Affairs controlled the Department from 6 June 2002 – 23 March 2010, having previously been Minister of State with responsibility for Gaeltacht affairs from 1997. His almost continuous involvement in shaping Irish language approaches in the South over a period of some

---

[1] The *2001 Census* shows that of 167,460 people in the north with knowledge of Irish, over 75,000 list skills in reading, writing, understanding and speaking Irish. Catholics are more likely to have knowledge of Irish (22.2 %) than protestants (1.2 %). Those most likely to have knowledge of Irish are found in the younger age groups, (12–15 years, 23,8%; 16–24 yrs, 16%). There are 80 Irish-medium schools in the North, and some 300 in the south.

[2] There are no Census figures regarding people with knowledge of Ulster Scots, North or South. However, the North's Department of Culture, Arts and Leisure has used the Life and Times Survey (1999) as a small sample indicator. 2,200 people were questioned. Results indicated that of these, 2 % indicated knowledge of Ulster Scots. Extrapolating from this figure, DCAL contend that there may be 30,000 people in the north with knowledge of Ulster Scots. Of the percentage in the Life and Times Survey, Protestants were more likely (2%) to speak Ulster Scots than Catholics (1%). People over 65 were most likely to have knowledge of Ulster Scots.

thirteen years[3] represents an unprecedented influence. In 2010, Ó Cuív was succeeded as Minister in the renamed Department of Community, Equality and Gaeltacht Affairs, by his Fianna Fáil colleague, Pat Carey.

In the North, since the GFA, ministerial portfolios are shared out as stipulated in the GFA, using the D'Hondt mechanism. This is a mathematical formula which reflects the strength of a party's total support, based on its share of votes in relation to seats won. At the start of the short-lived first Assembly (2000–2),[4] neither Sinn Féin (SF) nor the Social Democratic and Labour Party (SDLP) sought the Ministry for Culture, Arts and Leisure, with core responsibility for language matters. It was subsequently nominated by the Official Unionist Party. Minister Michael McGimpsey[5] was to declare later that he had been 'a *unionist* Minister for Culture' and had exercised a veto over the development of the Irish language throughout his tenure. From its earliest days, it was obvious that, with the two Departments North and South joined at the hip through Foras na Gaeilge, the cross border body itself was a conduit equally capable of carrying unionist/British government approaches southwards as it was of carrying southern influence northwards. If the southern Minister was dissatisfied at finding himself with a unionist counterpart in the North, a certain disillusion was also expressed during Irish language protests in the North in 2002, when the southern government made unilateral cuts of 1.5 million euros to the budget of Foras na Gaeilge.[6] The seemingly unwitting provision by the Irish side of a rationale for British government cuts to Irish language funding so soon after the winning of hard-fought commitments disappointed many. The British government quickly followed the Irish example and cut their contribution to the Irish language budget.

In the period immediately prior to the re-establishment of the devolved institutions in 2007, the Irish speaking community registered overwhelming support for the introduction of a comprehensive, rights-based *Irish Language Act*. Having been given an unequivocal commitment in the *Northern Ireland (St Andrews Agreement) Act 2006* would be introduced, and having mobilised massive support for change in the status and circumstances of the language in the North, many in the community felt keen disappointment when both nationalist parties once more bypassed the portfolio for Culture, Arts and Leisure. Sinn Féin, the larger of the two nationalist parties had three opportunities to select the Ministry, and the SDLP had one opportunity. In the end, however, Culture, Arts and Leisure was the last Ministry allocated, claimed finally by Ian Paisley's Democratic Unionist Party (DUP), whose harsh opposition to developmental progress for the Irish language was, and is, a matter of public record.[7]

Since the GFA, there have been no sustained official attempts to develop an all-Ireland policy for the Irish language, in spite of a certain amount of rhetoric. Foras na

---

[3] Ó Cuív's period in Irish language and Gaeltacht Affairs was interrupted between 2001–2 when he served a brief period as Minister of State for Agriculture and Food.

[4] In the five years from 2002–7, during which the Assembly was under suspension, British direct rulers presided over a 'care and maintenance' approach to all Assembly departmental affairs.

[5] BBC Radio Ulster, 25 October 2006, McGimpsey, Michael, Senior UUP Negotiator, South Belfast MLA and former Minister for Culture, Arts and Leisure in the NI Assembly 1999–2002, re-broadcast on Radio Ulster Irish language programme, *Blas*.

[6] The Irish government announced a unilateral cut of 1.5 million euros in November 2002, sparking protests in the North by Irish language groups who saw it as an attack on hard-won GFA provisions.

[7] The DUP manifesto for the February 2007 Assembly elections continued a commitment to oppose the *Irish Language Act*, and media briefings consistently attacked the language and community. See for example, *The Irish News*, 24 October 2006, Roy Garland, 'Changing Times Signals the End for the Rhetoric'; *The News Letter*, 14 November 2006, 'Scepticism over Government Offer on Ulster Scots'; *The News Letter*, 17 November 2006, 'The Trojan Threat of the Irish Language Act'; *The News Letter*, 20 December 2006, 'Allister Broadside Attack on Irish language Bill Document'.

Gaeilge has failed in its attempts to date, and there is some debate as to whether the body even has a detailed internal strategy for itself. If there was indeed doubt in political circles as to the capacity of Foras na Gaeilge to fulfil its role, there were however other options that could have been pursued. In July 2004, southern Minister Éamon Ó Cuív created a separate entity, *Fóram Na Gaeilge* (The Irish language Forum), outside the remit of the GFA and with all-Ireland representation, albeit selected by political parties rather than the community itself. However, although the Fóram had some discussion on strategic proposals, they were never developed. When Ó Cuív subsequently began drafting a 20-Year Strategy for the Irish language, he located responsibility for it within his own Department, thus categorically limiting its scope to the South only. In spite of invitations to bring consultation meetings on the Strategy into the North, Ó Cuív declined.[8] On publication, the Minister acknowledged that his 'national' plan was for the South alone and that it was not in the power of a southern minister to determine policy in the North.[9] He turned down an invitation from the Irish language NGO POBAL,[10] to address the Irish speaking community in the North on his draft plan, declining also to send a senior servant to speak in his stead. At the same time, as if to further underline the turning away from all-Ireland approaches, Ó Cuív publicised his intention to create a new body, Údarás na Gaeilge, with a 26 county brief only, and gave what appeared to be strong indications that Irish government funding for Foras na Gaeilge would be channeled into the new entity. Some southern Irish language advocates criticized the proposal because of its implications for development on Gaeltacht areas.[11] It is understandable that some in the South might quietly welcome the freeing up of Irish language policy from retrograde hostility in the northern Department and the perceived failings of the cross-border body itself. However, some southern-based commentators have nonetheless identified the implications for the language in the North.[12] Their commentary, along with the highlighting of the northern perspective by Irish language NGOs in the jurisdiction,[13] seems to have averted the threatened substantial drain on the overall Foras budget in favour of Údarás na Gaeilge (ÚnaG), although the effects of current recession and the reconfiguring of funding available through Foras to key groups is ongoing.

In November 2010, the 20-Year Strategy, in somewhat amended form, was accepted by the Oireachtas and the announcement made that legislation required to establish Údarás na Gaeilge will be progressed. However, almost simultaneous with this, the southern economy has suffered a catastrophic crash, leading to intervention from the International Monetary Fund (IMF), the European Commission, and indeed the British Government. Loans of some £80 billion and pressure for an early election in the South in 2011 dominate the media. If this is the case, there will be unprecedented pressure on public expenditure and policy implementation across a wide range of areas, including without doubt, in language policy.

---

[8] The Plan has not been subject to public consultation outside of the Republic of Ireland.

[9] *Nuacht 24*, 15 May 2009, by Eoghan Ó Neill, 'Soiscéal Éamoin'.

[10] The author is CEO of POBAL.

[11] *The Irish Times*, 21 January 2010, Harry McGee, Political Correspondant, 'Call to Keep Údarás na Gaeltachta'.

[12] Extract from the igaeilge blog, 16 November 2009, '... is cinnte go gcaithfear a chinntiú nach bhfuil leithscéal á thabhairt d'Aondachtaithe atá nimhneach in éadan na Gaeilge, leithéidí Nelson McCausland, Aire Cultúr an tuaiscirt, cúlú ó dhualgaisí an staitín ó thuaidh i leith na Gaeilge.' '... certainly it must be ensured that Unionists hostile to the Irish language, such as Nelson McCausland, the North's Minister for Culture, are being given no excuse to retreat from the duties of the northern statelet in relation to Irish.' (Author's translation)

[13] Letter to Ó Cuív from Chomhchoiste Ghrúpaí Bunmhaoinithe an tuaiscirt, 12 November 2009.

The 20-Year Draft Strategy in the South: Could it be Implemented in the North?

Even without current economic concerns, the text of the south's 20-Year Draft Strategy for the Irish language repeatedly states that this is a plan for the 'state' as opposed to the island of Ireland. The Draft Strategy is, it states, 'built on the foundation of the Constitutional status of the Irish language' (p. 5); it refers to Article 8 of the Constitution to underline the statement that 'Ireland is a bilingual state'; it is based on the Irish government's statement of 2006, which was confined to the 26 counties alone; and as well as the Constitution, it depends on legislation such as the south's *Official Languages Act 2003*, the south's *Education Act 1998*, the south's *Planning and Development Act 2000* and the *Broadcasting Act 2001* (updated 2009). None of this legislation applies to the North, and this is a fundamental issue.

Of 13 objectives outlined at the start of the document, there are major question marks as to how more than half could possibly be extended to the North (for instance, Objectives 1-5 relate to the Constitutional and legislative position of Irish and the Gaeltacht areas recognised under legislation in the south only). Objectives relating to teaching of Irish in English medium schools are similarly tied to education legislation not applicable in the North, where the language does not figure at all in teaching in Protestant (contolled) schools, and is often unavailable also in Catholic (maintained) schools. Whilst Irish speakers may see making Irish a compulsory subject in all English-medium schools as positive, it appears extremely unlikely to be implemented in the North at present without legislation to support it.

Objectives in relation to Irish-Medium education could be beneficial, but there is no reference in the 20-Year Strategy to all-Ireland collaboration through the two Education Departments on IM education issues. There remain therefore substantial questions about the mechanisms that will be required and the way in which provision and policy North and South for IME might be co-ordinated. At present, there are significant policy differences North and South on how to progress IM education, particularly at post-primary level.

Objectives 8 (Foras na Gaeilge), 9 (TG4, Raidió na Gaeltachta), 10 (The European Union) of the Strategy may have knock-on benefits on an all-Ireland basis. The objectives 8 and 9 relate to existing inter-governmental agreements and do not represent any new commitment or detailed initiative to extend or develop collaboration. Objective 9 makes no reference to the Irish Language Broadcasting Fund (ILBF) in the North, so it is difficult to assess whether or not the proposals will have a positive, negative or no effect at all on the ILBF.

Objective 11 locates responsibility for the Strategy in the South's Department of Community, Rural, and Gaeltacht Affairs with no reference to roll-out mechanisms on an all-Ireland basis. If parts of the 20-Year Strategy were to be put in place in the North, who would oversee it? DCAL? The Office of the First Minister and Deputy First Minister (OFMDFM)? If so, how will agreement be reached? If it is not overseen officially at government level, any implementation will simply be on a voluntary basis in the North.

Objective 12 relates to the Garda Síochána and is therefore unlikely to be relevant on an all-Ireland basis.

Objective 13 makes a statement regarding the Irish language voluntary sector, presumably referring to groups in the South. The voluntary sector's role and relationship with the state is historically and actually different North and South, and organisations work in different legislative, policy and social circumstances. Proposed re-organisation of the Irish language voluntary sector is driven by the 20-Year Strategy, yet if the Strategy itself cannot be fully implemented on an all-Ireland basis, the rationale for re-organisation is clearly in question.

In outlining the phases towards implementation of the Strategy over 20 years, it is noticeable that no targets are established in relation to the implementation or expansion of the Strategy in the North. The targets are generally quite vague, which increases the difficulty in knowing what will be done, when and by whom.

Year 1 speaks of communication of goals and contents, resourcing and structures. The Draft Strategy states: 'Operational plans will be requested and received from all implementing public agencies.' This raises again the question of whether there are any implementing agencies in the North, since none are mentioned, and the wording suggests that there is some level of legal requirement in the matter of providing plans. No such obligation exists in current policy or legislation in the North. Even if new, comprehensive legislation were agreed immediately for the North, this timetable could not be met on an all-Ireland basis.

Years 2–3 refers to putting into 'place long term measures', but only then refers to qualified teachers and 'other specialists' and to 'materials for language education and literacy.'

Years 4–15 are said to have 'three sub-phases' but again the period is lengthy (11 years) and the detail scarce. It mentions 'rolling evaluation' and 'campaigns' for promotion and fostering positive attitudes. It would seem that this might be an area in which the specific circumstances of the North might have been given particular attention, but no reference is made to the requirements of an all-Ireland approach on this.

Years 16–20 will be a period of consolidation according to the Strategy, and of 'mainstreaming of all measures.' However, without the appropriate mechanisms and legislation in place in the North, mainstreaming will remain extremely difficult. The phased targets however give no indication of how the necessary changes in the North will be made to enable mainstreaming on an all-Ireland basis. If mainstreaming is done only in the South, how *mainstream* is it?

The Draft Strategy points out that resourcing is crucial and states that this will come from the Department of Community, Rural, and Gaeltacht Affairs. This clearly indicates that funding will come from the government in the South. It is necessary to clarify whether or not resources will be ringfenced by Leinster House (or the Department) to enable the implementation of the Strategy on an all-Ireland basis (ie to fund groups in the North to carry out work where relevant in line with the actions of the Strategy) or whether measures have been agreed to allow funding through Foras na Gaeilge for such initiatives in the North. If so, will this funding be ring-fenced within Foras's budget? Since the 20-Year Strategy is not grounded in the circumstances or needs of the whole of the Ireland, how would this impact on necessary projects not currently identified within the Strategy for the 26 counties? Of course, at this stage, the full impact of the South's economic calamity on resourcing of the Strategy cannot be determined.

The Specific Objectives of the Draft Strategy all relate to demographic information and targets set for the 26 counties alone. The final bullet point, to 'increase the number of people that use State services' could theoretically apply on an all-Ireland basis. However, in the North, there is a difficulty in that no locally enforceable legislation exists to enable the provision of significant services through Irish. It is not apparent that changing this situation is central to the Strategy itself, since no targets in relation to the circumstances of the North are set, no resources mentioned and no approaches outlined.

It is stated on page 6 that the Draft Strategy is underpinned by the South's governmental 2006 Statement on the Irish language, whose remit is confined entirely to the 26 counties; and on research carried out by DCU Fiontar and by Micheál Mac Gréil. Neither of these studies examines the circumstances of the language on an all-Ireland basis. All statistics and evaluation refer only to the 26 counties. The lack of legislation and the specific demographic impact of the exclusion of teaching Irish from most, if not all, Protestant schools in the North are not addressed, and therefore, whilst some general advances could be made on the numbers of speakers on an all-Ireland basis, there is no supporting framework or legislation in the North, and further development of current work could only be done on an ad hoc basis outside the 26 counties.

The oversight mechanism for the Strategy is firmly and exclusively in the 26 counties, through the office of the Taoiseach, the senior officials' groups and the Department of Community, Rural and Gaeltacht Affairs.

The Strategy states that Údarás na Gaeilge will have 'responsibility for language matters throughout the state'. It is referred to as 'a new national agency', established by new legislation which will make its official operation on an all-Ireland basis highly unlikely. The role of Foras na Gaeilge is to remain 'a key element'. However, the detail of the relationship and duties between the new body, Údarás na Gaeilge and the all-Ireland body are not described, and there is a concern at potential duplication and confusion in roles. If it is the role of ÚnaG to resource the Strategy, what else can be funded through them in the 26 counties? Is it foreseen that there will be funding for Irish language activities NOT connected with the Strategy in the 26 counties? If not, why would some activities be funded by Foras and others by Údarás and what are the implications of this on an all-Ireland basis?

On p. 8, it is stated that the Strategy 'will have a beneficial impact on speakers in the North'. This implies that the Strategy itself will not be implemented in the North. No information is given as to what any beneficial impacts might be, how they could be achieved and measured or by what mechanisms this would be done. Since it is not based on the circumstances of the North, it is hard to see what the justification is for saying it will be beneficial except in the most general sense. In fact, it might also be argued that the grey area around implementation and impacts on an all-Ireland basis further disadvantages the language community in the North, since their circumstances and needs are marginalised within the strategic research basis.

The only references to the North are through Foras na Gaeilge, the *Irish Language Act* and the 'enhancement, protection and development of Irish'. All of these represent existing commitments. It is interesting to note that the wording, 'enhancement, protection and development' are those used in the *Northern Ireland (St Andrews Agreement) Act 2006* relating to a strategy for the Irish language to be adopted by the Assembly. No reference to this as a strategy is made, nor is there any clarification on the relationship, if any, between the 20-Year Strategy document and the expected Assembly document. Is there one? If not, does this not raise further question marks around the future of implementation on an all-Ireland basis?

Page 34 refers to a radical re-organisation of the Irish language voluntary sector in order to provide a 'cradle to old age' service based on this strategy. Whatever the merits of this approach in the South, where the Strategy can be officially implemented, there is considerable doubt as to its benefit in the North. Given the reality that an Irish government strategy cannot be implemented officially in territory remaining under the British jurisdiction, the exclusively southern focus of the research and expertise upon which the Strategy is based and the fact that much of the Strategy's proposals are dependent upon a legislative basis that simply does not exist in the North, there would appear to be sound arguments against extending the re-organisation of funding to the North. Nor indeed does the Draft Strategy propose that this should be the case.

Instead, the reconfiguring of funding emanates from a decision in December 2009 of the North South Ministerial Council when southern Minister Ó Cuív and northern Minister McCausland agreed that the only work that Foras na Gaeilge should fund would be either localised projects or one or a limited number of all-Ireland advocacy groups.

All 19 core-funded Irish language organisations, North and South, have argued that in the absence of a positive state-sponsored strategy in the North for the development of the language, the northern sector should not be subject to re-organisation. Whilst there is recognition that such a strategy can build on synergies with the south's 20-year proposals to secure a more holistic all-Ireland approach, it is difficult to see how this can be done unless the relatively new and underdeveloped Irish language infrastructure in the North is protected, promoted and strengthened. Unionist parties have considerable hostilty to the Irish language and in particular to high profile and effective organisations. The challenge for nationalist parties is to recognise that the creation of an effective all-Ireland approach, rather than an illusory one, will require appropriate support for the expertise and experience of NGOs working in the different circumstances of the two jurisdictions and greater flexibility in Foras na Gaeilge's funding arrangements than is currently being sought.

Strategic Planning in the North

Whilst the contents of the South's 20-year Strategy underlines its 26 county focus, its publication also highlights, by contrast the deliberate political obfuscation and the language policy vacuum in the North. Many Irish speakers in the North feel they are caught between a rock and a hard place. Whilst northern affairs are marginalised in the southern 20-Year Strategy, machinations around it currently threaten to undermine the independence of the northern Irish language infrastructure. In the longer term, Irish speakers risk being locked into an inadequate, ad hoc and voluntary policy approach to the specific developmental needs in the North. Meanwhile, although there is a clear statutory duty on the Northern Ireland Assembly to adopt a strategy for the enhancement of the Irish language, it appears mired in bureaucracy and sectarian politicking.

The *Northern Ireland (St Andrews Agreement) Act 2006* contains a commitment by the British government to enact Irish language legislation. As documented elsewhere,[14] this promise was not detailed in the *Northern Ireland (St Andrews Agreement) Act 2006* and has yet to be fulfilled. The Act did however enshrine a different language commitment from the Agreement, stating that, 'The Executive Committee shall adopt a strategy setting out how it proposes to enhance and protect the development of the Irish language.'[15] The committee's duty is reinforced by the recommendation in the April 2007 report of the Council of Europe Committee of Experts (COMEX) on the application of the *European Charter for Regional or Minority Languages*, an international

---

[14] Muller, J. *Language and Conflict in Northern Ireland and Canada: A Silent War*, Houndmills: Palgrave Macmillan. 2010.

[15] A further sub point of the same paragraph refers to a strategy, 'to enhance and develop the Ulster Scots language, heritage and culture.' *Northern Ireland (St Andrews Agreement) Act 2006*.

instrument ratified in 2001. Concluding on the findings of the COMEX, the Committee of Ministers calls on the British government, as a matter of priority, to 'Develop a comprehensive Irish language policy, including measures to meet the increasing demand for Irish-medium education.'[16]

In spite of these two binding instructions, in the 3-year period since the re-establishment of the devolved institutions in May 2007, the Department of Culture, Arts and Leisure, charged with fulfilment of the duty, has not made public a single document in respect of its strategy for the enhancement of Irish. In April 2008, the Irish language NGO POBAL organised a major conference with expert speakers on policy formulation from Wales and Scotland,[17] as well as the then Vice-Chairperson of the COMEX, Sigve Gramstad, who outlined his views on what the comprehensive policy required might comprise. Community views and proposals were collated and recorded. The then Culture Minister, Edwin Poots opened the conference, stating that instead of introducing the promised *Irish Language Act*, he would draft a strategy 'underpinned by the *European Charter for Regional or Minority Languages*.[18] His Department initiated no further attempts to consult with the Irish speaking community on the issue.

Poots was later succeeded by Gregory Campbell, who addressed the Culture, Arts and Leisure scrutiny committee at the Assembly in December 2008. Outlining his proposal to produce a single strategy for Irish and Ulster Scots, the Minister stated,

> I have made it clear on a number of occasions that I regard the traditional disparity between funding for the Irish language and for Ulster Scots as totally and utterly unsustainable. It is untenable, unjustifiable and unsustainable, and I will not preside over it – I will not do it. I have made that clear.'[19]

In spite of stating his intention to place before the Executive a draft paper setting out high-level principles early in 2009, no such paper appeared. In June 2009, Campbell was replaced by party colleague, Nelson McCausland, who in a Ministerial statement described his approach to language policy in the following manner,

> I will seek to address the current imbalances between Ulster Scots and Irish and strive to achieve parity of esteem and parity of funding for both. I think that we have made significant progress to date. For example, between 2005 and 2008, funding allocations from the Department of Culture, Arts and Leisure to Ulster Scots almost doubled, and funding for Irish increased by just over 6%. Progress is being made.[20]

---

[16] COMEX Strasbourg 14 March 2007, RecChL(2007)2.

[17] CEO of the Welsh Language Board, Merion Prys Jones; Former head of Comunn Na Gàidhlig, Dòmhnall Màrtainn.

[18] *Developing a Comprehensive Policy and a Strategy to Enhance and Protect the Development of the Irish Language in the North of Ireland*, Report on the conference, 7 March 2008, POBAL

[19] NI Assembly, Committee for Culture, Arts and Leisure, Official Report (Hansard), Language Strategy, 4 December 2008, p. 9

[20] NI Assembly, Nelson McCausland, Minister for Culture, Arts and Leisure, Ministerial Statement on NSMC Language Sectoral Format, 15 September 2009.

In April 2010, following an on-the-spot visit by members of the COMEX, the Council of Europe published the 3rd report on the application of the ECRML. In relation to the strategy, COMEX contend:

> The *Northern Ireland (St Andrews Agreement) Act 2006* places a statutory duty on the NI Executive to adopt a strategy to enhance and protect the Irish language. So far no strategy has been adopted. However, the Minister for Culture, Arts and Leisure (DCAL) intends to bring forward one strategy, entitled, 'A Strategy for Indigenous or Regional Minority Languages' which is intended to be a single strategy for Irish and Ulster Scots. The Committee of Experts is concerned that the strategy will strive towards parity between the two languages and therefore not serve the needs of either the Irish speakers or the Ulster Scots speakers and will hold back the development of both languages.[21]

On 8 November 2010, a lengthy and turbulent debate produced by a written Assembly question on the issues of the *Irish Language Act* and the strategy, elicited no new information on the content of the long awaited draft, nor indeed any proposed date for publication or consulation. Sinn Féin Assembly member, Billy Leonard characterised the debate, as 'a list of obfuscations, delays and stalling tactics,' and continued, 'the whole idea of the human rights argument is that it is not about majoritarianism giving permission to people on their rights.'[22]

The lengthy delay in producing an Assembly strategy for the Irish language is clearly a matter of great frustration. However, successive Culture Ministers have made it clear that in the current dispensation, even if the strategy is published, it will not be set in a sociolinguistic context, nor based in the needs of the Irish speaking community nor of the language itself. As the COMEX has warned, the approach of the Department is simply at odds with positive language planning. Clearly, a different path is needed to establish a developmental framework for the Irish language in the North, a framework that is grounded in need and capable of working in harmony with the southern 20-Year Strategy.

At the end of 2009, the NGO POBAL, building its ongoing work on the issue, established a Working Group with representatives of the Queen's University Belfast, the University of Ulster and St Mary's University College, in order to draft a comprehensive policy and strategic framework for the Irish language (see Ó Baoill in this volume). At a public seminar in June 2010, the Irish speaking community, politicians and civil servants discussed the south's 20-Year Strategy; the unpublished Northern Ireland Languages Strategy which looks at languages in education; the findings of the COMEX and the priority areas for development, including legislation, education, the media, public services and the Irish language voluntary infrastructure. Although the Minister was invited, he was unable to attend. The Working Group is continuing its strategic initiative.

---

[21] COMEX Strasbourg 14 March 2007, p. 13, par. 57.
[22] *NI Assembly Official Record (Hansard)*, 8 November 2010.

Straitéis don Ghaeilge i dTuaisceart Éireann

Dónall P. Ó Baoill

Is é is aidhm le hullmhú Straitéise don Ghaeilge i dTuaisceart Éireann go ceann 20-bliain creatlach beartais a chur le chéile i gcomhthéacs *Chomhaontú Chill Rimhinn / Cairt na hEorpa do Theangacha Réigiúnacha nó Mionlaigh / Straitéis na dTeangacha (RO) / Straitéis do Theangacha Réigiúnacha nó Mionlaigh (RCEF) / Dréachtphlean 20-Bliain* de chuid Rialtas na hÉireann. Lena chois sin cuirfear íomhá dhearfach den Ghaeilge chun cinn.

Is mian linn ár seasamh féin a ghlacadh ar an scéal mar go bhfuil cúinsí ar leith ag baint le cás na Gaeilge i dTÉ cé go bhfuil gné uile oileánda ag baint leis. D'eascair straitéis an Deiscirt as bunreacht na tíre agus as beartas de chuid an rialtais féin. Tá Gaeltacht acu sa Deisceart agus an Ghaeilge fite go forleathan sa chóras oideachais rud nach bhfuil fíor faoi TÉ. Caithfear cearta an chainteora a chur i gcomhthéacs a bhfuil ag tarlú i dTÉ – sa Tionól, san AE agus i Westminster. Is léir gur fiú cloí lena bhfuil cheana i nDoiciméad Polasaí POBAL (2008) maidir leis na réimsí seo a leanas (a) Oideachas, (b) Na Meáin, (c) An Timpeallacht, Oidhreacht agus na hEalaíona, (d) Na Cúirteanna, (e) An tSeirbhís Phoiblí agus (f) Oideachas Sláinte

Is iad seo a leanas Téarmaí Tagartha na hoibre:

(i)   Straitéis Chumarsáide a chothú agus a chruthú
(ii) Comhordú a dhéanamh ar na gnéithe seo – taighde – ag tarraingt le chéile fráma oibre don straitéis – eolas a chur ar fáil ar bhealaí cuí do na páirtithe leasmhara – cáipéisí a dhréachtú – comhairle a thabhairt agus faisnéis a ghlacadh
(iii) Comhairle a chothú le saineolaithe cuí – ionchur an phobail a shlógadh
(iv) Tuairimí na saineolaithe ar chur i bhfeidhm na Cairte Eorpaí do Theangacha Réigiúnacha nó Mionlaigh a scrúdú agus a phoibliú
(v)   Íomhá dhearfa don Ghaeilge a chur chun cinn agus beartais chríochnúla a thabhairt chun cinn leis an méid sin a dhéanamh

Tá géarghá na bealaí is éifeachtaí leis na cuspóirí a chur chun cinn a aimsiú agus a thabhairt chun solais. Seo roinnt smaointe ar cheart iad bheith mar ábhar machnaimh againn:

(a) *Líon beag beartas* a phiocadh agus cloí leo, seachas liosta fada
(b) *Na beartais is fearr* a bhfuil ag éirí leo a roghnú agus iad a láidriú mar shampla: Oideachas, Na Meáin, Poist Aistriúcháin
(c) Gluaiseacht chomhordaithe a chothú *dírithe ar spriocanna cinnte* agus *taighde eolgaiseach nuálach a dhéanamh* le húsáid mar thacaíocht le hargóintí le ranna stáit, le polaiteoirí agus le daoine eile
(d) Díriú ar *chur chun cinn ceantracha* ina bhfuil abhantracha láidre, infhásta agus infhorbartha. Gaeilgeoirí agus fiontair a bhaineann léi ag stiúradh na forbartha

(e) **Comcheangal a dhéanamh leis na páirtithe leasmhara** sa rialtas, sa tSeirbhís Phoiblí, sa Státseirbhís, sna Meáin srl. le comhordú gníomhaiochta a thabhairt i gcrích

(f) **Feasacht an phobail a mhéadú agus a mhúnlú** ar bhealaí éagsúla atá go fóill le hoibriú amach ina n-iomláine

(g)**Smaointeoireacht úr nuálach a spreagadh,** a mheallfadh an pobal coiteann sa bhaile agus pobal na Gaeilge thar lear – an diaspóra mar a thugtar orthu

(h) Dul i **bhfheidhm ar earnáil an 3ú agus an 4ú leibhéil oideachais** beartais taighde ar **leibhéal idirnáisiúnta** ar ghnéithe éagsúla den **dátheangachas agus den ilteangachas** a chur sa tsiúl go leanúnach

(i) Cuid de **na bearnaí móra cultúrtha, oidhreachta agus idé-eolaíochta** sa phobal a líonadh

An Irish Language Strategy for Northern Ireland

Dónall P. Ó Baoill

The preparation of a 20-Year Irish Language Strategy for Northern Ireland proposes to agree an outline policy for the Irish language in the context of the *Northern Ireland (St Andrews Agreement) Act 2006 / The European Charter for Regional or Minority Languages / the Language Strategy being prepared by the Department of Education / the Strategy for Regional and Minority Languages / the 20-Year Draft Strategy for Irish* published at the end of 2009 by the Irish Government. Furthermore, it is our intention to present, promote and cultivate a positive image of the Irish language in society.

Considering the particular circumstances which apply to the Irish language and its use in NI, we propose to develop a strategy that take these circumstances into account, while at the same time taking into consideration the All-Ireland dimension pertaining to the language. The southern strategy arises from the constitutional position of Irish and has emerged from policies initiated by the government itself. The Gaeltacht dimension and the central role of Irish within all sectors of the educational system in the Republic of Ireland do not apply to NI. The rights of Irish speakers must be placed in context and relate specifically to what is happening within NI – in the Assembly, in the EU and in Westminster. Previous work indicates the benefits of adhering to what has been already outlined in POBAL's Policy Document (2008) which addresses a range of domains of usage such (a) Education, (b) the Media (c) Environment, Heritage and the Arts, (d) the Courts, (e) The Public Service and (f) Health Education.

The Terms of Reference can be summarised as follows:

    (i) To create and cultivate a Communication Strategy
    (ii) To co-ordinate the following – research initiatives – a framework for the strategy – informing interested parties through a series of suitable communicative strategies – the drafting of relevant documents – providing advice and gathering information
    (iii) To co-operate with relevant experts and to mobilize public opinion
    (iv) To examine and publicise expert opinion on the implementation of the European Charter for Regional or Minority Languages
    (v) To promote a positive image for the Irish language and propose definitive policies to enhance this image

It is imperative that the most efficient methods to promote and achieve our objectives be identified. The following are matters that need to be considered in light of our proposals:

    (a) To select and adhere to a ***finite number of definitive policies***
    (b) To select and strengthen those policies which have had a ***better success rate*** e.g. Education, The Media, Translation Work etc
    (c) To cultivate a co-ordinated movement directed at ***definite outcomes and to instigate innovative and informative research*** as a back up for discussion with state bodies, politicians, policy makers, language planners and any other interested parties

(d) To focus on the promotion of **strong Irish language communities** with promising hinterlands capable of strong growth and development. All developmental and innovative projects should be directed by Irish speakers with the right expertise within such communities

(e) To **create communicative networks with interested parties** within Government, the Public Service, the Civil Service, the Media etc. in order to co-ordinate activities and bring them to a satisfactory conclusion

(f) To **increase and modify public awareness and opinion** in different ways through methods still to be decided

(g) To inspire **new and innovative ways of thinking** in order to attract the attention of the general public at home and Irish diaspora abroad

(h) To **impact on 3rd and 4th level educational bodies** and to impress upon them the urgency and need for research policies and strategies to address linguistic issues **at international level** with particular relevance to aspects of **bilingualism and multilingualism** in society

(i) To fill some of the most glaring **gaps relating to cultural, heritage and ideological thinking** among the public at large

A Lid for Every Pot: The 20-Year Strategy and Northern Ireland

Aodán Mac Póilin

The *20-Year Strategy for the Irish Language: 2010–2030*, first issued in draft form on 26th November 2009, was approved by the Irish Government on 30th November 2010. While, as government policy, it applies only to the Republic of Ireland, since the publication of the draft *Strategy* there has been a lively and sometimes heated debate on its relevance to Northern Ireland.

I am going to approach this issue through a series of questions. I have also suggested a number of responses to these questions, some of them tentative and some of them rather more robustly assertive, but more often than not the responses take the form of new questions. I make no apology for this. Asking the right questions is the key to finding the right answers, and anyone who manages to read this paper will find that my central criticism of the *20-Year Strategy* is that in at least one critical area it has failed to ask the right questions.

Question 1: Can a declining language be revitalised through legislation?

It has been done. By 1780, what is now the Czech Republic had long been incorporated into the Austro-Hungarian Empire and the Czech language in had been for centuries in retreat before German, which was the dominant language in the large urban centres and rural areas bordering Germany and Austria, as well as being the language of central administration. There are remarkable parallels, at the end of the eighteenth century, between the situation of Czech and that of Irish. However, the fate of the two languages over the next two centuries was to diverge equally remarkably. The Czech language became the primary focus of Czech cultural nationalism, coinciding with a massive movement of rural Czech-speakers to the German-speaking cities following the emancipation of the serfs, where they eventually took over the administrative centres. Finally, after a brief period of legislative equality between Czech and German, Czech became the official language of the state (I'm over-simplifying a bit here). Result: Czech is the primary language of 96 percent of the citizens of the Czech Republic.

French in Quebec was being eroded by English when, in 1974, it was established by the *Official Language Act* as the only official language of the Province. This measure and a further series of legislative enactments first stopped and then reversed the decline of the language. Result: 80 percent of the population of Quebec is Francophone, and a goodly proportion of the rest is bilingual. A similar, if not so draconian process is going on in Catalonia, where public use of Catalan had been banned under the dictatorship of Franco – its use was forbidden in schools until 1970. Beginning in 1978, and culminating in the *Language Act* of 1983, which established Catalan and Castilian as official languages, a series of supportive legislative measures were introduced. This process has both stopped and reversed the decline in the use of Catalan.

Question 2: Have these examples any relevance for the 20-Year Strategy?

The three examples outlined above are of successful top-down language revitalisation brought about by legislation. Can they be used as models for state-sponsored language revitalisation in other circumstances? More specifically, can they be used as models for language revitalisation in the Republic of Ireland? I would argue that they cannot.

And for a very good reason. In all three cases – before state intervention – although Czech or French or Catalan may have been in retreat, each was still the language of the majority in its own society. In all three cases the legislation, which effectively discriminated against or at least disadvantaged monoglot speakers of the formerly dominant language, also reflected the popular will of the majority of the population.

When the southern state, in a gesture of Platonic aspiration, designated Irish as its national and then its first official language, it was far too late to revitalise the language simply by legislative will. What was needed was a language strategy that reflected the socio-linguistic realities of Irish society, the main reality being that the population of the southern state in the 1920s and 1930s was made up overwhelmingly of monoglot English-speakers, and that most of the state's Irish-speakers were also competent in English. Unfortunately, in the first half of the twentieth century, the necessary analytical tools and academic disciplines needed to inform a language revitalisation process in these circumstances had not even been considered, never mind developed. It was assumed that, by simply reversing one of the processes which influenced the decline of Irish, the education system (and, as an added incentive, by privileging Irish-speakers within state employment) the linguistic dynamic for the whole society would also be reversed. Fundamentally, it was assumed that widespread knowledge of the language would be followed by widespread use. The revival project foundered on the rocks of an education system that could not – and should not have been expected to – deliver the desired socio-linguistic outcomes. Teaching a language in schools does not of itself facilitate language shift within a society any more than calling a language the first national language could, of itself, make it the language of the population.[1]

The strength of the *20-Year Strategy* is that it envisages a coordinated, Government-led, multi-agency language planning throughout the state. Its success or failure will depend, more or less entirely, on just how effectively the Irish Government is in (a) creating, or facilitating, an adequate support infrastructure for language revitalisation, and (b) persuading a quarter of a million of its citizens to integrate the use of Irish into their daily lives. As a strategy, given that it is rooted, in part, in socio-linguistic reality, it may be better than what went before. Whether or not the *Strategy* proves to be a success remains to be seen, and it's failure to find any purchase in economic reality (it has never been properly costed) could prove to be a fatal flaw. There are, however, other weaknesses, which will be discussed below.

Question 3: What is the purpose of a language strategy?

I'm talking here about fragile languages which, unlike the Czech, French and Catalan examples above, are spoken by minorities within their societies. It seems to me that there are three possible answers. The purpose of a language strategy is either (a) to maintain established language communities, or (b) to grow established language communities, or (c) to create new language communities. Or it is all three of these things.

However, every single one of these actions involves a significantly different approach. In the Irish context, a language strategy which focuses on the maintenance of Irish in the historic Gaeltacht will involve a set of complexities that is significantly different to the complexities of a strategy that aims to underpin the revivalist movement in a large city that already has established networks of active Irish-speakers. This is

---

[1] The first language status of Irish is not without its uses, but that status has little or no potential for reviving the language. For more than a generation, its primary function has been to enable Irish language activists to challenge the Irish Government's tendency to marginalise the language further and further from the centre of national life.

different again to a strategy aimed at developing a new language community in a small town or rural setting which hasn't had an active Irish language community for hundreds of years. And even these broad categories are not sufficient: it will be necessary to develop a series of strategies focused on local circumstances and local communities. For example, within a Gaeltacht strategy, and within a single county, you will need a different strategy to underpin language maintenance in, say, Rannafast and Glencolmcille. The reason is quite simple: these two communities are, linguistically, in significantly different situations. What is needed in one is not yet needed in the other; what will work in one will not work in the other.

This is one of the problems I have with the *20-Year Strategy*. It is less a strategy for the Irish language than strategy (policy may be a better word) for the government of the Republic of Ireland that may or may not lead to the multiplicity of local strategies which may or may not lead to the maintenance of the language in the historic Gaeltacht, and to the development of significant, self-sustaining language communities outside the Gaeltacht.

Question 4: So what is a language community?

In this paper, so far, I have used the term 'language community' fairly loosely. The main purpose of this paper is to look at language revival rather than language maintenance issues, so I will not address the important issue of maintaining the historic Gaeltacht. Rather, I will be concentrating on issues that belong to the revival end of the language revitalisation spectrum, specifically those relating to the development of new language communities. In this context, is will be useful to explore what the term 'language community' may mean.

Joshua Fishman's definition of a language community is as good as any and better than some, as well as having the advantage of being fairly succinct. For Fishman, a language community is 'a socially integrated population of active speakers (or users)' of a particular language. This seems to me to be a valid definition, but it turns out to be extremely difficult to apply that definition to the majority of revivalist Irish language communities. If we restrict our definition of the Irish language community to those who actively use the language to any significant degree, and at the same time comprise an identifiable socially integrated population, do we have Irish language communities anywhere outside the Gaeltacht?

There is another, related problem. When you talk about a language community, are you implying that this is the only language the community speaks? The answer, by and large, is yes if it is a major language, and even more yes if the language in question has a Germanic root and a largely Romance vocabulary, is spoken by several hundreds of millions of people as their first language in some of the richest countries on the globe, and as a second language by even more hundreds or possibly thousands of millions of people. The answer, if it is a fragile minority language in daily contact with a more powerful language, is almost certainly no.

To translate that into rather more practical terms, in Ireland we have one dominant language community, using a tremendously rich, prestigious, vibrant, inescapable language, English, that is spoken by close to one hundred percent of the population. A minority of that that language community – a subset, if you like – can also speak another language, Irish, and a minority of these actually do so on a daily basis. Let me put that another way: except – possibly – in some Gaeltacht areas, what we call the Irish language community is actually no more and no less than a bilingual subset of an overwhelmingly monolingual English language community. It is this English-speaking community that comprises Fishman's 'socially integrated population of active speakers'. For the most part, what we call the Irish language community is, arguably, no such thing.

One of the strengths of the *20-Year Strategy* is that, albeit in a rather confused and backhanded way, it acknowledges that, while between them the language movement and the state have had a remarkable success in creating a comparatively large number of fluent speakers of Irish as a second language, they have failed, abysmally, to create from these individuals 'socially integrated populations of active speakers (or users)' of Irish. In other words, they have failed to create meaningful Irish language communities. In saying this – in this context, anyway – I am not necessarily criticising either the language movement or the state for their failure. I am saying it to record an incontrovertible fact that needs to be kept permanently in mind, and as an introduction to what follows.

Question 5: Why is it that, in Ireland, use of Irish so very rarely follows knowledge?

This issue – which could probably be defined as a branch of the emerging discipline of psycho-linguistics – is not specific to either of the two jurisdictions.

Lack of opportunity is one factor. To its credit, the *20-Year Strategy* has acknowledged this and tried to tackle it. However, it is also clear that the provision of opportunities to speak Irish, while essential, will not solve the problem. It will not solve the problem because there is another dynamic at work, and this dynamic can be observed by anybody with eyes to see and ears to hear. If we look at one example. Outside the Gaeltacht, west Belfast is probably the area in Ireland that has the best developed Irish language social infrastructure in the whole of Ireland. West Belfast has a remarkable concentration of Irish speakers and language organisations in a single defined area, as well as two centres for informal socialisation and a well-established urban neo-Gaeltacht. As a result, a fluent Irish speaker living in west Belfast has no lack of opportunity to use the language. However, that person will have to make a decision to avail of the opportunities on offer, and this is where the limitations of opportunity can be seen. Of all the thousands of people living in west Belfast who have been through Irish-medium immersion education since it was established in 1978, of the other thousands who learned Irish to a high level in English-medium schools or at night classes, of the hundreds, or possibly thousands, who learned Irish to a high level in jail, how many could be described as people who belong to a socially integrated population of active Irish-speakers?

Before responding to that question, I should emphasise at this point that I am not talking here about ceremonial use of the language, or the odd concert, or social occasion in a pub, or watching programmes on TG4, or listening to Irish language programmes on the BBC, or reading the odd book, or getting involved in an Irish language cluster on Facebook. All these activities are important to the people who do them, and they can contribute to maintaining a simulacrum of a community, the kind of thing people talk about when they speak of the pigeon-racing community, or the stamp-collecting community, or any group of people who cluster around an absorbing hobby. However, in terms of a socially integrated population of Irish-speakers, these activities are peripheral and tangential and secondary.

To get back to the question, how many of the Irish-speakers in west Belfast could be described as people who belong to a socially integrated population of active Irish-speakers? One answer is that the number of socially active Irish-speakers is impressively higher than it was thirty years ago but is still surprisingly low. And if this small group (which comprises the nearest we have to a socially integrated population of active Irish-speakers) is to develop into a sustainable Irish language community, it has to become a community that provides intergenerational transmission within the family. This raises another question: how many of the socially active Irish-speakers in west Belfast will pass on to the crucial stage of bringing up the next generation as Irish-speakers? The answer is even fewer.

The big question that remains unanswered in the *20-Year Strategy* – mainly because it was never asked – is why Irish society has failed to create socially integrated populations of active Irish-speakers. The *Strategy*, unfortunately, has not addressed two complex, but vital, questions. Why, in the first place, are there so many people who are fluent in Irish and have opportunities to use it regularly, but who do not avail of these opportunities in any socially meaningful way. And, secondly, how do you create the social dynamics that will persuade these people to become active Irish-speakers who could be identified as members of a socially integrated language community. Again, these issues, in which ideology meets social engineering in an almost totally unexplored area of socio-linguistic dynamics, does not appear to have a central place in the thinking behind the *Strategy*.

Question 7: Should the 20-Year Strategy be applied to Northern Ireland?

The rather unexceptional conclusions of the foregoing discussion are that (a) successful language revitalisation strategies do not always transfer from one society to another, and (b) the *20-Year Strategy* has a number of significant weaknesses. To this we could add that the *20-Year Strategy* has so far proved itself to be neither a success nor a failure within the jurisdiction for which it was designed. It would appear to be logical to assume that, as the circumstances of Northern Ireland are significantly different to those of the Republic of Ireland, a distinct language revitalisation strategy for Northern Ireland would have to be developed from first principles.

Unfortunately, this obvious conclusion has not been drawn. We will have to back-pedal a bit to follow the train of thought which led to an entirely different conclusion. It was decided, and noted in the draft document, that the new priorities of the *20-Year Strategy* required a re-alignment of the core-funded voluntary sector, a logical enough conclusion as far as the southern state is concerned. This proposal coincided with a wish to rationalise – i.e., spend less money on the sector and bring it closer under the control of central government, a desire that became even more urgent in the wake of the economic crisis enveloping the Republic at the time. Such a coincidence is never a good thing: there is always the danger that the priority of creating a more appropriate support infrastructure may become confused with the priority of saving money.

However, there was a further complication in this case, in that the 19 organisations in the core-funded voluntary sector were funded through Foras na Gaeilge, an all-island body. This itself need not have posed a major problem. Many of the organisations based in the Republic already worked on an all-island basis and could have continued to do so. Of the seven organisations based in Northern Ireland, all but one worked primarily or exclusively within the Northern Ireland context. Although few in number, and with limited funding, these organisations represent almost the entire support infrastructure for the Irish language in Northern Ireland, except in the areas of education and broadcasting (two of them play a critical and irreplaceable role within the Irish-medium education sector). They therefore have a particular importance for the language movement in the north.

In this context, the most desirable outcome would have been to (a) reorganise the southern-based organisations, while providing safeguards to ensure that the specific circumstances of Northern Ireland were taken into account, and (b) leave any reorganisation of the sector in Northern Ireland until an appropriate language strategy had been developed.

At this point another, political, factor inserted itself into the mix. Foras na Gaeilge, as an all-island body, is directed by and accountable to the North-South Ministerial Council (NSMC), in which the main players are, in the south, the Department of the Gaeltacht[2] and the Department of Culture, Arts and Leisure (DCAL) in the north. In matters relating to the Irish language, DCAL tends to play the role of a sleeping partner, or, as one critic put it, a nodding dog. At a NSMC meeting on 2nd December 2009 the DCAL Minister agreed to a proposal from the southern Minister that the entire Irish language core-funded sector be amalgamated into 'one or a limited number of organisations'. No analysis had been undertaken by DCAL officials of the implications of this for either the Irish language or the Irish language voluntary sector in Northern Ireland. It is also worth noting that the *Strategy*, the contents of which had been kept a closely-guarded secret, was published on 26th November 2009, a Thursday. The NSMC decision was taken the following Wednesday.

This radical proposal, which also proposed a spectacularly unrealistic short time-scale for its implementation (less than seven months) aroused opposition from within the entire core-funded sector, which responded on 12th February 2010 with a position paper entitled *I dTreo na Físe*, a rather twee title which translates as 'Towards the Vision'. The report was agreed by all 19 organisations in both jurisdictions. Among its recommendations was a section dealing with Northern Ireland, in which the sector argued that there were many political, legal, educational, social and infrastructural differences between the two jurisdictions, that the infrastructure in the north was both recent and comparatively weak, that the planning context in the north was non-existent, and that no research comparable to that which had informed the *Strategy* had been carried out. The organisations proposed that, until some of these limitations had been rectified, the northern-based organisations should be left out of the restructuring process (the text and translation of this portion of the report can be found in the Appendix to this paper).

This proposal was greeted with considerable hostility by Foras na Gaeilge and the Department of the Gaeltacht (DCAL maintained its state of slumber deep and unknowing). Board members dismissed it as 'useless'. Senior officials from both institutions accused people who made these arguments of partitionism (a particularly emotive term when directed at nationalists). To some, myself among them, it appeared that, by introducing a political argument into a socio-linguistic debate, these individuals were prepared to sacrifice the Irish language core-funded sector in Northern Ireland on the altar of nationalist dogma.

This entire issue revolves on whether or not the differences in the circumstances of Northern Ireland are sufficient to warrant significant differences in the support infrastructure for the language. On one side of this debate is the voluntary sector, which maintains that, while certain functions are best carried out on an all-island basis, others should be conducted on a separate jurisdictional basis. See the Appendix to this paper for an example of the detailed arguments for this case made by ULTACH Trust.

---

[2] As the Dublin Government is allowed only a restricted number of Government departments by the Constitution, this is always a sub-set of another Department, and changes its official title with every change in Government: Department of the Taoiseach and the Gaeltacht; Department of Arts, Heritage, Gaeltacht and the Islands; Department of Community, Equality and Gaeltacht Affairs.

It has been more difficult to ascertain the intellectual basis behind the alternative position, that which informed the decision by the North-South Ministerial Council of December 2nd 2009, and the following decision of 26th May 2010 (the May decision proposed a rather strained modification of the December decision, again on an all-island basis, and was itself based on a proposal from Foras na Gaeilge). It has proved impossible to obtain a rationale for their decisions from either Government department, and the defence of the principles of reorganising the sector exclusively on an all-island basis has been left to Foras na Gaeilge. As far as can be ascertained, the Foras arguments have not been committed to writing, or if they have they have not been made available to the public. As a result, we have to rely on statements made by people who appeared to be representing the view of the Foras.

One argument has been that Foras is an all-island body and is therefore obliged to reorganise the sector on an all-island basis. This argument need not detain us no longer than it takes to note that the Foras also has a statutory obligation to take differences between the circumstances of the two jurisdictions into account. A second thread of argument is that it is the same language north and south. Such a line of reasoning may work in the schoolyard, but is hardly the stuff of adult debate. The fact that French is spoken in both Quebec and Louisiana does not mean that the strategy for revitalising French in Quebec can be transferred, in whole or in part, to Louisiana. How much, if any, of the *Strategy* can transfer to Northern Ireland is, surely, a matter to be debated. Another argument has been that Foras is simply carrying out the will of the North-South Ministerial Council. This is persuasive until it is remembered that both NSMC decisions were, in fact, based on proposals from Foras, in one case as one of four options, and in the second as Foras na Gaeilge's sole recommendation.

The argument that appears to have most traction, however, is that the differences between north and south are of no great consequence. For this, as for the others, I have to fall back on anecdotal evidence, as there appears to be no other evidence available. I was recently, as a member of an advisory committee on the reorganisation of the sector, involved in a discussion with two Board members of Foras na Gaeilge on this issue. The Board members were, as it happened, also members of the Foras's Development Sub-Committee, and one of them was its Chair. This is a particularly important committee, as it was the Development Sub-Committee which brought to the Board those proposals which were later adopted by the NSMC. It could then be assumed that the two individuals on the advisory committee reflected the collective attitude of the Foras itself.

Representatives from the core-funded sector presented the case outlined in the Appendix. One Sub-committee member noted, correctly, that there were differences in language promotion throughout the island, and then, less correctly, that differences between north and south were no more significant than differences between a city and a rural area in the south. It is quite true that there are broad similarities between community-based language promotion north and south, provided that language promotion in the north is confined to nationalist communities. However, the northern organisations had not opposed all-island activities *per se*, but had emphasised organisational and infrastructural differences, particularly those which impacted on the interface between language movement and the state apparatus, as well as the issue of a unionist majority population largely hostile or indifferent to the language.

The response of the other sub-committee member was so revealing that I wrote his words down verbatim. He said: 'Is ionann na daoine a bhfuil suim acu sa Ghaeilge, thuaidh agus theas' which translates as 'Those who are interested in Irish are the same, north and south'. There is a series of breathtaking assumptions behind this remark.

Firstly it discounts the possibility that a language strategy may be directed at those who are hostile or indifferent to the language as well as at those who are interested in it. In this, the remark largely follows the priorities of the *20-Year Strategy* for the southern state, which focuses almost exclusively on those who already speak Irish, and are therefore already likely to be supportive of it. There is also a possibly unconscious assumption that only nationalists in Northern Ireland are or could be interested in the language (there are no southern-based Irish-speaking unionists, although a handful do exist in the north). The most glaring omission in the remark is, however, in its failure to address the contested nature of society in Northern Ireland, and the controversial place of the Irish language in the cultural politics of that society. What is most alarming in the attitude behind the remark is that it was not based on ignorance, as the sub-committee member had been in a position to read all the submissions made on this issue to Foras na Gaeilge. In some ways, his remark has confirmed the worst fears of the northern organisations, that the language movement in Northern Ireland will become no more than a bolt-on to the *20-Year Strategy*, and that those who control the limited resources for the promotion of Irish will not take due cognisance of the particular circumstances of the north.

In conclusion, to respond to the question of whether the *20-Year Strategy* should be applied to Northern Ireland, I believe that it would be extremely unwise to rush to apply any of it to the north. If you want a successful language strategy for Northern Ireland, what you do is first rigorously analyse, and then – through an equally rigorous debate – develop a strategy, or a series of strategies, to meet the circumstances of that society. What you do not do, and should not do, is impose a watered down version of a strategy – an untested strategy – that was established for an entirely different situation.

Appendix

ULTACH Trust

Differences between the situation of Irish in Northern Ireland and the Republic of Ireland

November 2010

Background

Foras na Gaeilge has two complementary functions. It is an all-island organisation which promotes the Irish language on an all-island basis. Foras also has a statutory duty to 'have regard to the positions of the language in the two jurisdictions'. In other words, it must take into account the fact that the circumstances in which the language exists is different in the two jurisdictions.

It is obvious that a balance needs to be struck between these two functions, and it is on this issue of balance that we have concerns. The evidence available to us indicates that Foras has failed to strike the required balance, or even to perceive the need to take both considerations into account.

One piece of evidence can be found in the *New Funding Model for the Core-Funded Organizations*, a document commissioned by Foras na Gaeilge from the consultants

Mazars and forwarded to the North South Ministerial Council in May 2010 as a formal recommendation. This document was the basis of the NSMC decision of 26th May 2010. This document was made available to the core-funded organisations on 9th July and to the broader public on 6th September 2010. Page 2 of the document outlines the terms of reference given to Mazars by Foras na Gaeilge:

- To propose a funding model for Foras na Gaeilge that takes into account;
- The NSMC decision [of 2nd December 2009];
- All-island considerations;
- The legal responsibilities of Foras na Gaeilge.

The emphasis here on 'all-island considerations' indicates that, rather than seeking a balance between all-island and jurisdictional considerations, Foras was concerned to privilege the first of these. This is consistent with all the dealings between Foras na Gaeilge and the core-funded sector since the NSMC decision of 2nd December 2009 (proposing an amalgamation of the 19 core-funded bodies into one or a limited number of organisations). In response to the December decision, the core-funded organisations argued strongly that the distinctive circumstances of Northern Ireland should be taken into account in any reorganisation of the core-funded sector. However, Foras insisted that the proposed amalgamation of core-funded organisations be carried out on an all-island basis. It appears that Foras (and the Department of the Gaeltacht) expect organisations applying under the new funding model agreed on 26th May 2010 (which proposed the abolishing of the core-funded sector entirely) to operate on an all-island basis.

Foras na Gaeilge may argue that the requirement to take into account 'the legal responsibilities of Foras na Gaeilge' includes that of having regard to the positions of the language in the two jurisdictions. This is debatable. As the NSMC decision and all-island considerations are themselves among 'the legal responsibilities' of the Foras, there was no need to single them out as issues requiring particular attention unless they were to be given priority. Significantly, there is no discussion at all in the document of the complex issue of Foras na Gaeilge's responsibility to 'have regard to the positions of the language in the two jurisdictions'. Indeed, the only additional legal responsibility discussed involves a different issue entirely – that of the eight organisations for which Foras na Gaeilge is obliged under the legislation to provide core-funding.

On 20th May 2010, shortly before the NSMC decision, the Chief Executive of Foras na Gaeilge gave evidence to the Culture, Arts and Leisure Committee on the issue of the new funding model for the Irish language voluntary sector. He was asked by the Committee if the obligation to take account of the different circumstances of the two jurisdictions would have any impact on the proposed new funding model. Unfortunately, the recording of that session is no longer available, but the Chief Executive's reply was on the following lines: 'language development is language development. People are people'. This may not capture the exact wording, but it is a fair reflection of the thrust of his reply, which was that the different circumstances were not significant enough to require a review of Foras na Gaeilge's approach to the new funding model.

This document is a response to the lack of recognition by Foras na Gaeilge and the sponsor departments of this important issue. It concentrates on those areas where there is a clear or marked difference between the circumstances of the two jurisdictions, and teases out some of the implications for language promotion of those differences.

ULTACH Trust believes that the issue of balance between all-island and jurisdictional considerations is a complex one. Elements of language development strategies for minority languages are universal, while others relating to the development of the Irish language are common to both parts of the island. But there are also significant differences in the context in which the language is developed in the two jurisdictions – political, legal, educational, social and infrastructural and these can require significantly different strategies.

In some circumstances, there is no doubt that the language can best be promoted on an all-island basis. In other circumstances, a case can be made for a structure involving all-island Irish language organisations which tailor certain language promotion activities to suit the different circumstances of both parts of the island. Foras na Gaeilge appears to take the position that an all-island organisational approach is suitable to all circumstances, while we would argue that certain functions can be most effectively carried out by organisations which have specialist knowledge, expertise and experience in one or other of the two jurisdictions.

There are strong reasons to take particular care to ensure that the unique circumstances of Northern Ireland are fully taken into account. The core-funded voluntary sector in NI is of recent origin, is comparatively undeveloped, and is much smaller than that of the south. Although there is a great deal of instinctive support for the language movement in the north from language activists in the south of Ireland, the actual level of awareness of the challenges facing the movement – particularly that detailed knowledge which comes from experience and full familiarity with the society – is quite low. Many language activists in the Republic of Ireland do not appear to be fully informed of the differences that exist between the two jurisdictions, nor of the implications of those differences. Over the next two decades, language development in the Republic will be dominated by a government-led language strategy: In fact, the Draft Strategy has argued that the voluntary sector must be reconfigured to take account of the Strategy. There will, of course, be no such comprehensive, government-led initiative in Northern Ireland in the foreseeable future. For all these reasons, there is a distinct risk that, unless adequate structural safeguards are put in place, the voluntary sector in Northern Ireland will become no more than a bolt-on, or afterthought, to that of the south.

These arguments are not based on the self-interest of the northern-based organisations nor do they imply a political position on the constitutional issue. They are based on a clear and objective assessment of a range of political, social, infrastructural and socio-linguistic realities, and on the implications for policy making of those realities.

There is a clear need for informed debate on the complex issue of how to strike a balance between the development of Irish on an all-island basis and on a jurisdictional basis, and another debate on how that balance should be reflected in organisational structures. Yet we have not had that debate with Foras na Gaeilge or with the sponsor departments. Meanwhile, the Foras and the departments continue to make and develop policies.

According to the Communiqué from the latest NSMC meeting (3rd November 2010), Foras is already well advanced in developing its detailed recommendations to the sponsor departments on the new funding model. We do not know what these draft recommendations contain. However, as the evidence clearly shows that to date insufficient weight has being given to the particular circumstances of Northern Ireland, and as Foras na Gaeilge has not engaged in meaningful debate with the sector to date, it is not unreasonable to infer that the recommendations being developed by the Foras will again fail to take these issues into account, or provide an in-depth analysis of the implications of its twin jurisdictional remit.

We have noted elsewhere that Foras na Gaeilge has made a number of proposals to the North South Ministerial Council without following guidelines from either jurisdiction on due process with regard to transparency, consultation with stakeholders, and apparently without undertaking any of the impact and risk assessments required by law and best practice. The sponsor departments do not appear to have carried out their oversight functions to ensure that the Foras complies with due process. Nor, it appears, have they carried out their own risk and impact assessments. In its turn, the North South Ministerial Council appears to have made decisions without seeking or weighing evidence, particularly that evidence which relates to Northern Ireland.

The role of DCAL in this matter is a cause for particular concern. DCAL has a statutory responsibility to 'enhance and protect the development of the Irish language' in Northern Ireland. Consequently, the department should have scrutinised the recommendations before NSMC on 2nd December 2009 and 26th May 2010 with their impact on Northern Ireland in mind. Thorough impact and risk assessments should have been conducted to ensure that the Foras' approach would not have a disproportionately negative effect on the Irish language voluntary sector.

While the entire process to date has been deeply flawed, it is not yet over. Foras has provided the sponsor departments with draft recommendations relating to the new funding model which were considered at the NSMC meeting of 3rd November 2010. These will presumably be scrutinised. Presumably also DCAL will also take into account the strong and principled opposition to the direction in which Foras na Gaeilge intends to take the voluntary sector. We believe that it is incumbent on DCAL, even at this late stage, to conduct thorough impact and risk assessments on the recommendations to ensure that the Foras' approach is fit for purpose and will, indeed, 'enhance and protect the development of the Irish language' in Northern Ireland.

In the following pages we have summarised some of the main points of difference between the two jurisdictions.

1. Perspective of the Irish language voluntary sector

On pages 11–12 of the document *I dTreo na Físe*, submitted to Foras na Gaeilge in February 2010 by all 19 organisations core-funded by the Foras, the core-funded organisations unanimously agreed the following statement:

Original	Translation
4. 4. 2 Cás Thuaisceart na hÉireann	4. 4. 2 The situation in Northern Ireland
Tá cúinsí na Gaeilge ó thuaidh difriúil ó chúinsí na teanga ó dheas agus tá difríochtaí suntasacha san infrastruchtúr teanga. Níl maoiniú stáit d'earnáil dheonach na Gaeilge ar fáil ach le tamall gairid ó thuaidh, áit a dtéann an comhthéacs polaitiúil agus sóisialta i bhfeidhm ar an gcaidreamh idir eagraíochtaí Gaeilge agus an stát. Is gá na heagrais Ghaeilge a chosaint agus a chaomhnú ar mhaithe le cur leis an méid atá bainte amach acu go dtí seo.	The situation of the Irish language in the north and the south are different, and there are marked differences in the language infrastructure. State funding for the voluntary sector has only recently been available in the north, where the political and social context affects the relationship between Irish language organisations and the state. It is imperative that Irish language organisations be protected and maintained in order to build on their achievements to date.

Tá folúntas maidir le bearta comhaontaithe idir an stát agus na heagrais Ghaeilge / lucht labhartha na teanga i dTuaisceart na hÉireann faoi láthair. Níl dréachtpholasaí ná straitéis maidir le forbairt agus feabhsú na Gaeilge ann. Níl cinnteacht ann maidir le cén próiseas nó cén beart riachtanach a bheidh curtha in áit le comh- straitéis a ullmhú agus a aontú leis na páirtithe leasmhara.

Cé go bhfuil taighde fiúntach déanta, níl staidéar cuimsitheach, iomlánaithe maidir le tosca sainiúla na Gaeilge agus riachtanais ar leith an phobail ó thuaidh curtha i gcrích. Tá anailís chuimsitheach ar chomhthéacs polaitiúil, sóisialta agus teangeolaíochta na Gaeilge sa tuaisceart de dhíth. Chomh maith leis seo, caithfidh forbairt polasaí don teanga ó thuaidh a bheith bunaithe ar ionchur ó shaineolaithe i bpleanáil teanga agus ar an idirphlé agus ar an gcomhairliúchán leis na heagrais Ghaeilge agus le lucht labhartha na Gaeilge. In éagmais a leithéide, níor chóir tabhairt faoi atheagrú infrastruchtúr na Gaeilge ó thuaidh.

At present, there is a vacuum regarding agreed actions between the state and Irish language organisations/speakers in Northern Ireland. There is neither a draft policy nor a strategy to develop and enhance the language. It is not clear what process or what necessary actions will be employed to develop a joint strategy and agree it with stakeholders.

Although valuable research has been carried out, no comprehensive, detailed research has been undertaken in relation to the particular circumstances of Irish in the north or the particular needs of the northern [Irish language] community. A comprehensive analysis of the political, social and sociolinguistic context of Irish in the north is required. In addition, the development of language policy in the north should be based on the input of experts in language planning and in consultation and partnership with Irish language organisations and the Irish language community. In the absence of such measures, the restructuring of Irish language organisations in the north should not take place.

2. Constitutional Status

Republic of Ireland	Northern Ireland
The Irish language was designated as the National Language in the 1922 Constitution of the Irish Free State and as the First Official Language of the state in the 1937 Constitution. There is an implicit constitutional imperative on the southern state to promote the Irish l	The Irish language has no constitutional status in Northern Ireland.

3. Legal Status

Republic of Ireland	Northern Ireland
In addition to the constitutional status of the Irish language in the Republic, and the legal implications of that status within the state, there is a large body of primary legislation which supports the language, including: The Ministers and Secretaries	The only statutory support afforded the Irish language in the north is contained within the limited commitments made in the Good Friday and St. Andrews Agreements, both of which have the force of an international treaty. From these has

(Amendment) Act (1956), which established the official Gaeltacht areas, the Údarás na Gaeltachta Act (1979), The Official Languages Act (2004), The British-Irish Agreement Act (1999), which is the RoI form of The North-South Co-operation (Implementation Bodies) (Northern Ireland) Order (1999), The Placenames (Irish Forms) Act 1973, and numerous other legislative and statutory instruments, which make significant references to and legislative provision for the Irish language.

The Government of the Republic of Ireland declined to sign the European Charter for Regional and Minority Languages on the basis that it could undermine the status of Irish in the state.

come two pieces of legislation: The North-South Co-operation (Implementation Bodies) (Northern Ireland) Order (1999), which established the Cross-Border Language Body, and an item in the Education (Northern Ireland) Order 1988 which led to the establishment of Comhairle na Gaelscolaíochta (The Council for Irish-medium education) and Iontaobhas na Gaelscolaíochta (The Trust for Irish-medium education). Legislation remains on the statute books which prohibits the use of Irish in the courts.

Irish is provided certain additional protection under the European Charter for Regional and Minority Languages.

4. The Official Languages Act, the Language Commissioner, Administrative Authorities and Public Bodies

Republic of Ireland

Every public body named under The Official Languages Act (2004) has a statutory duty to comply with Regulations made by the Minister with responsibility for Gaeltacht Affairs under section 9(1) of the Act. Under the Regulations, every public body named under the Act has a duty to prepare a language scheme when requested to do so by the Minister for Community, Equality and Gaeltacht Affairs and to implement that statutory scheme.

The scheme describes the services which the public body proposes to provide: (a) in Irish only, (b) in English only, or (c) bilingually. The public body must also specify the steps which it intends to take to provide the stated services in Irish or bilingually.

Implementation of the language schemes is overseen by the Language Commissioner, an independent figure established by statute to oversee the implementation of the Languages Act.

Northern Ireland

Northern Ireland does not have a language act or a language commissioner, and there is no equivalent to the legislative measures – or their accompanying legislative sanctions – which exist in the Republic.

In Northern Ireland, Government departments, and their associated bodies, facilitate customers who wish to conduct their business in Irish either orally or in writing. A telephone voicemail facility has been set up for members of the public who wish to conduct business in Irish.

5. Courts

Republic of Ireland	Northern Ireland
Either of the two official languages may be used in any court; in any pleading in any court or in any document issuing from any court. The court has a duty to ensure that any person may be heard in the official language of his or her choosing.	All proceedings in the courts, including any documentation relating to those proceedings, must be in English. The requirement that court proceedings be conducted in English was imposed by the Administration of Justice (Language) Act (Ireland) 1737, which is still in force. All similar acts were repealed elsewhere in the UK by the end of the nineteenth century.

6. State Policy towards the Irish language

Republic of Ireland	Northern Ireland
Since the foundation of the southern state, the revival of Irish has been identified as a fundamental state objective. This guiding principle has informed a wide range of legislation and public policies, education, broadcasting, publishing, public signage and many other areas within the state system.	For the first fifty years of the northern state, Irish did not enjoy any public presence except through the activities of voluntary organisations and, on an official level, in the education system. Provision within the education system was, in the main, a weak reflection of provision that had been established before partition. Since the 1980s there have been some advances in the position of the language within state policy.

7. Administrative Culture

Much of the work of the voluntary sector involves advocacy with the public sector. Although the administrative systems of both jurisdictions are rooted historically in the nineteenth century British administration, and while they both subscribe to the same principles of accountability, the systems have diverged significantly since partition.

The Republic of Northern Ireland is a sovereign state; Northern Ireland is a devolved region of the United Kingdom. Certain relevant powers, such as those relating to broadcasting, are reserved by the Westminster Government. In Northern Ireland, lobbying on areas such as Irish language broadcasting involve both the local and central administrations and local and UK-wide statutory organisations such as the BBC and Ofcom. Major decisions are made on a UK-wide basis, and lobbying often involves considerable knowledge of comparable provision for Welsh and Scottish Gaelic.

There are significant structural differences in areas such as funding mechanisms, and in the makeup of local administration and education structures. For example, there is no equivalent in the Republic of the north's Education and Library Boards, and management structures of individual schools are only recently beginning to converge.

There are also significant differences in decision-making mechanisms, both internal and external, and, in each jurisdiction, administrative and organisational cultures are influenced by a plethora of unwritten assumptions, conventions and explicit regulations. As least as important as these is the fact that the relationships between public servants and politicians on the one hand and the public on the other, not to mention interdepartmental relationships, tend to be different on either side of the border. As a result, the skill-sets needed by individuals and organisations to influence decision-making processes and policy outcomes are very different in the two jurisdictions.

8. Language Maintenance Policies

Republic of Ireland	Northern Ireland
The southern state is committed to maintaining the language in the historic Gaeltacht areas. These areas are designated in law, and a semi-state development body, Údarás na Gaeltachta was established in 1980 to strengthen the Gaeltacht. A branch of Government (originally a distinct Department) was set up in 1956 to facilitate Gaeltacht development and language promotion outside the Gaeltacht. The southern state has both a language maintenance role and a language revival role (see 5 below).	No historic Gaeltachts survive in Northern Ireland. The state neglected those areas in Northern Ireland in which there were still native speakers of Irish in the early years of the state.

9. Language Revival Policies

Republic of Ireland	Northern Ireland
For almost ninety years, efforts have been made by the government of the southern state to develop and implement a range of language maintenance and language revival strategies. The state takes the lead role in these strategies. Currently, a Twenty Year Strategy for the Irish Language is being developed. This is based on a considerable body of research and on a report compiled by an international panel of experts in language planning, commissioned by central government, and was three years in the making. Through the 20-Year Strategy the state intends to implement a comprehensive, coordinated, state-led multi-institutional strategy backed by the full resources of the state. Under its founding legislation, Foras na Gaeilge's role will be to implement state strategy.	The northern state has never had a state-sponsored language revival strategy. Although a minority language policy (for Irish, Ulster Scots and Sign Languages) is being discussed, no strategy has yet been agreed. It is clear, given the fact that Irish is a contested issue, that such a policy will not be a comprehensive one, that it will not have the full backing of the state, and that it will not be driven forward as a governmental priority. Little research has been carried out on issues relating to language planning in Northern Ireland. We are not aware of any sustained input from language planning experts in the initial stages of the development of Northern Ireland's minority language policy.

10. Infrastructural Support: Public sector

Republic of Ireland	Northern Ireland
Infrastructural support for the Irish language is well established in the south.	Infrastructural support is in its early stages in Northern Ireland, is limited,

This infrastructure covers wide areas of activity within the public sector both at central government and local authority level, and involves dedicated semi-state and public bodies, as well as a wide range of legislation and policies across the state apparatus. Recent activity by the Language Commissioner has strengthened this infrastructural support, and the 20-Year Strategy, when adopted, will strengthen it further.

patchy, often inconsistent, and deals with a narrow range of activities. The main sources of public sector infrastructural support are from the Department of Education and Foras na Gaeilge. There have been some recent developments in provision through broadcasting and the arts. Some local authorities (with supplementary support from Foras na Gaeilge) provide a measure of infrastructural support.

11. Infrastructural Support: Core-Funded Voluntary Sector

Republic of Ireland	Northern Ireland
Infrastructural support for the Irish language voluntary sector is well established in the south, where most of the core-funded organisations have their headquarters (some of them have an all-Ireland remit). These organisations received 81.7% of Foras funding – €6½ million.	There is a very small core-funded voluntary sector based in NI. (currently receiving circa £1¼ million – 18.3% of Foras na Gaeilge's expenditure on core-funded organisations).

12. Infrastructural Support: Private Sector

Republic of Ireland	Northern Ireland
A number of private businesses in the Republic of Ireland (e.g. television production companies, publishers, translation services, lawyers, consultants) provide services to the Irish language market and some conduct their business in whole or in part through the medium of Irish. Support has been made available to private businesses located in the Gaeltacht areas.	A small number of businesses provide services such as translation and television programmes in Irish. This is far less well developed than in the Republic. Few of the television companies which provide programmes in Irish for public service broadcasters conduct their business through the medium of Irish.

13. Public Opinion

Republic of Ireland	Northern Ireland
There is wide consensus in the southern state that the Irish language is a thing of value. The majority of people in the Republic are nationalists, most of whom agree that Irish is a national language. Most of the southern public are positively disposed to the Irish language, at some level. What opposition does exist tends to be less towards the language itself than towards some manifestations of the language in the public sphere.	The Irish language is a deeply contentious issue in Northern Ireland. Nationalists are in a minority and not all nationalists support the language. Within the unionist community there are large numbers who are either hostile to, or suspicious of, the Irish language, and there is a widespread view, sometimes articulated by unionist politicians, that the language is itself subversive of the state.

14. The Views of the Political Parties

Republic of Ireland	Northern Ireland
Every political party in the south supports the Irish language.	In the north, nationalist and unionist parties are deeply divided on the Irish language issue. While individual unionist politicians with specific statutory obligations may find themselves responsible for promoting the language, they are often less than wholehearted in carrying out their obligations, and the policies of their parties tend to be negative. More than 50% of northern politicians oppose the Irish language.

15. Competing Minority Languages

Republic of Ireland	Northern Ireland
No political party, community organisation or major pressure group in the south argues that state funding for Irish is at the expense of another indigenous language.	In Northern Ireland, parties which are hostile or indifferent to Irish support Ulster Scots. Many unionist politicians, including the Minister for Culture, Arts and Leisure, suggest that Ulster Scots is at a disadvantage because of Irish.

16. Irish in the Education System

Republic of Ireland	Northern Ireland
Irish is a compulsory subject in primary and secondary schools in the south for most children of statutory school age. Most children are exposed to Irish in the curriculum for thirteen years. Degree courses, full and part-time, are available through the medium of Irish, in subjects other than the Irish language, in two universities in the Republic of Ireland.	Apart from the Irish-medium schools sector, Irish is barely taught at primary level in Northern Ireland. Irish is taught to a certain degree at secondary level, mostly in the Catholic sector. A small proportion of the school population will study the language for seven years, but most of those who study Irish do so for five years or less. No degree courses in subjects other than Irish are made available.

17. Knowledge of the Language

Republic of Ireland	Northern Ireland
In the 2002 Census in the Republic of Ireland, 1,570,000 people (43.85% of the population) claimed a knowledge of Irish. Most of the remaining 46.15% have been taught Irish at school.	According to the 2001 Census, 167,000 of people in the north claim knowledge of the Irish language. That is 10.4% of the population. Most of the remaining 89.6% have not been exposed to any Irish at school.

18. Broadcasting

Republic of Ireland

Broadcasting responsibilities in RoI lie with the Dublin Government.

Public service broadcasters have made programming in Irish available in the southern state since the 1920s. Under its Charter as a public service broadcaster, RTÉ is obliged to recognize the bilingual nature of Irish society. The Republic of Ireland has a dedicated Irish language public service radio station, RnaG, and a dedicated Irish language public service television station, TG4. Commercial broadcasters and community broadcasters are obliged to provide some programming in Irish as well as English.

The Broadcasting Corporation of Ireland sets aside part of its funding for Irish language broadcasting.

There is one Irish language community radio station, Ráidió na Life, which receives support from Foras na Gaeilge.

Northern Ireland

Broadcasting in NI is not devolved and is the responsibility of the Westminster Government.

There was no public service broadcasting in Irish in Northern Ireland for sixty years. A limited amount of Irish language radio programming (15 minutes per week) was initiated by the BBC in 1981. The BBC now broadcasts 150 hours of radio in Irish per annum. Television broadcasting in Northern Ireland began in 1991 with a 40-minute programme. The BBC now broadcasts 40 hours of Irish language television per annum, including repeats. It also produces some on-line material in Irish.

Annual UK Government and BBC spend on Irish language broadcasting (excluding online) is under £4 million. This compares with £146 million for Welsh and £26 million for Scottish Gaelic.

An Irish Language Broadcasting Fund of £3 million per annum was established in 2004.

One Irish language community radio station, Ráidió Fáilte, receives support from Foras na Gaeilge.

19. Placenames Research

Republic of Ireland

The Placenames Branch, once a part of the Ordnance Survey, is now in the Department of the Gaeltacht. It has produced an interactive database (www.logainm.ie) which the public can access. It also produces resources for schools. It provides the official Irish language version of placenames and is widely used by both the public and private sector.

Northern Ireland

Funding for the Northern Ireland Placenames Project, hosted by Queens University since the 1980s, was not renewed in the summer of 2010. Project Staff are redundant and the Project has closed.

The southern placenames database covers some of the placenames in Northern Ireland.

Bilingualism: Conceptual Difficulties and Practical Challenges

Robert Dunbar

Bilingualism is a word which is widely used but often misunderstood. As a native of Canada, I am particularly attuned to this by virtue of the strong opinions that the word can still provoke, especially amongst certain Anglophone Canadians. In the wake of the introduction of the first Canadian *Official Languages Act* in 1969, one would frequently hear that 'French is being forced down our throats'. At least some Canadians seemed to believe that the federal government was seeking to make every Anglophone Canadian a French-speaker. As we shall see in the final section of this paper, this is not and was never the purpose of official bilingualism, although as we shall also see, in the second last section of the paper, Canadian education policies generally seek to promote the widespread acquisition of at least some French amongst non-French speakers and of at least some English amongst non-English speakers.

In this paper, I shall explore the concept of bilingualism from three different perspectives: bilingualism as a personal phenomenon, as a societal one, and as an institutional one. I will attempt to show that there are a range of ambiguities associated with the concept of bilingualism when it is viewed from each of these perspectives, and that these are particularly important in relation to language policy and planning for minoritised languages. Indeed, bilingualism in each sense – personal, societal and institutional – is associated with a series of challenges for minoritised languages, and I shall be making specific reference to the case of Scottish Gaelic to illustrate these. I shall also make repeated reference to Canada: in addition to being a 'bilingual' country, it is also an important model of official bilingualism, and one that has had a considerable impact on other states.

In considering the question of bilingualism in the context of policy and planning for minoritised languages, it is useful to consider the three conditions which François Grin has identified as being necessary to ensure that such a language is used. The first is the *capacity* to use a language: members of a community cannot hope to use a language if they do not know the language. The second is the *opportunity* to use the language: without the ability to use a language in a variety of settings, people who have the capacity to do so will be unable to. The third condition is the *desire* to use the language: speakers will only actually use it if they want to do so.[1]

Personal bilingualism is primarily a question of capacity: to what extent does an individual know two languages. Societal bilingualism is also to some extent a question of capacity: to what extent do members of a society know two languages. However, societal bilingualism also raises the question of opportunity: if not all members of a society know the two languages, the opportunity of those who do know them to use one of those languages (or, indeed, people who only know only that language) will necessarily be limited to those circumstances in which others with whom a bilingual individual (or an individual who knows only the one language) is communicating also know that language. As we shall see, societies (and communities within societies) are seldom perfectly bilingual in the sense that all their members know the same two languages, and usually one of these languages will be in a relatively more powerful position in the society (or community), and this will have important consequences for the long-term vitality of the other language.

---

[1] François Grin. *Language Policy Evaluation and the European Charter for Regional or Minority Languages*. Basingstoke: Palgrave Macmillan, 2003. pp. 43–4.

Institutional bilingualism is likewise to some extent a question of capacity: to what extent is a particular institution able to use two languages. However, institutional bilingualism also raises the question of opportunity: if not all employees and officers of an institution know the two languages, the likelihood that the institution as a whole will use both languages in all its interactions will be limited. As we shall see, policies to promote institutional bilingualism seek to address this question of opportunity by increasing the institution's capacity to use both languages. Furthermore, policies to promote institutional bilingualism often have the explicit or implicit aim of increasing the desire to use one of the two languages which benefit from such policies – often, the one which is the weaker. Frequently, the socially weaker language suffers from lower prestige than the more widely spoken language, and because it is not spoken as widely and therefore not previously used as frequently within institutions, the instrumental reasons for maintaining the language amongst its speakers or for speakers of the other language to learn it are weak. Institutional bilingualism addresses both the prestige of the language (by, for example, increasing its visibility and audibility) and its instrumental value, as delivering bilingualism requires the recruitment of staff with the necessary language skills, and support for and encouragement of their use of the language.

Personal Bilingualism

Personal bilingualism is a particularly complex and difficult concept, because there is no clear consensus amongst linguists as to precisely what level of proficiency in two languages is necessary in order for an individual to be considered a bilingual. Older approaches focused on whether an individual possessed a 'native-like control' of two languages. Such approaches are now generally rejected, partly because the concept of the native speaker is itself ambiguous and problematic.[2] In the report on the linguistic profile of Canada produced by the Government of Canada in the context of the 2006 Canadian Census, bilingualism was defined as 'the ability *to conduct a conversation* in both official languages'.[3] Even this, however, raises difficulties: there is, for example, a significant difference in the language skills required to conduct a relatively short conversation on relatively simple subject matter and those required for much more sustained and complex conversations, particularly ones of a technical nature. Scholarly attention is now focused not simply on questions of competence, but on the ways in which people use their two languages in different contexts (so-called 'functional bilingualism').[4] It is reasonably clear, though, that 'balanced bilingualism' – strongly similar, and high, levels of competence in two languages – is not the norm amongst people who do have some command and who make use of two languages, and that the two languages tend to be used to different extents in different social situations.[5] This tends to be particularly true of speakers of minoritised languages, such as Gaelic.

---

[2] Alan Davies. *The Native Speaker: Myth and Reality*. Clevedon: Multilingual Matters, 2003.

[3] Jean-Pierre Corbeil and Christine Blaser. *The Evolving Linguistic Portrait, 2006 Census*. Ottawa: Ministry of Industry, 2007. at p. 30; available at: www12.statcan.ca/census-recensement/2006/as-sa/97-555/pdf/97-555-XIE2006001-eng.pdf.

[4] There is now a massive literature on bilingualism; for a very good and comprehensive introduction, see, for example, Colin Baker. *Foundations of Bilingual Education and Bilingualism*. Fifth Edition. Clevedon: Multilingual Matters, 2011; and Carol Myers-Scotton. *Multiple Voices: An Introduction to Bilingualism*. Oxford: Blackwell, 2006.

[5] A functional separation of language use, with one language used in certain social contexts and another in'others, is known as 'diglossia': see, for example, Charles Ferguson. 'Diglossia'. *Word* 15, 1959. pp. 325–340; Joshua Fishman, 'Bilingualism with and without Diglossia; Diglossia with and without Bilingualism'. *Journal of Social Issues* 23.2, 1967. pp. 29–38.

At present, we do not have a great deal of data or research on language abilities of Gaelic speakers, either in Gaelic or in English. Aside, perhaps, from very small children who are being raised through the medium of Gaelic, all Gaelic speakers are bilingual in Gaelic and English (and, of course, some are multilingual, having a command of other languages besides Gaelic and English). However, what this means in terms of actual language ability, to say nothing of language use, is complex. In spite of our lack of information, it seems relatively clear that, not only is the bilingualism of virtually all Gaelic speakers, both L1s and L2s, unbalanced, but also it is unbalanced in different ways for different individuals, depending on the domain about which we are speaking, and on whether we are considering spoken or written Gaelic. Gaelic-English bilingualism could also be said to be incomplete for many, as it is clear that a considerable number of people with some competence in spoken Gaelic have limited literacy skills, while others have some literacy skills but extremely limited competence in (and even comprehension of) spoken Gaelic.

For example, it would appear that there are a large number of 'passive bilinguals': according to the *2001 Census*, there were 26,722 people aged 3 or over who claimed to understand, but not be able to speak, read or write Gaelic.[6] We do not know enough about this category of respondents, but at least some will be people who grew up in a Gaelic-speaking family or community, but who did not acquire full communicative fluency in spoken Gaelic. Obviously, this implies that English will be the dominant language in virtually all domains in which members of this group participate.

It is also clear that there is a significant number of Gaelic speakers with no or very limited literacy skills: according to the *2001 Census*, there were 18,181 people who claimed to be able to speak Gaelic but who could neither read nor write it, and a further 7,834 who could speak and read it but could not write it. As most L2s will have acquired literacy skills in Gaelic – both L2s who acquire their Gaelic in school and in various forms of adult education will acquire literacy skills in Gaelic as part of their instruction – it can be assumed that the overwhelming majority of people in this category are L1s, and the reason for their lack of literacy skills in Gaelic is likely attributable to the fact that many L1 Gaelic speakers did not benefit Gaelic-medium education or even instruction in Gaelic as a subject in the school curriculum. It is also almost certainly the case that this group of Gaelic-speakers will be literate in English – the same educational system which excluded Gaelic from their educational experience will have equipped them with literacy in English – with the result that in any domain in which literacy is necessary, English will be their dominant language. The fact that in 2001 almost 45 percent of Gaelic speakers had limited literacy skills is a major challenge for language planners, and will certainly have a significant impact, for example, on the uptake of any increased opportunities to use Gaelic in written form. By the same token, there were 4,744 people who could read, but could not speak or write Gaelic. These are almost certainly learners of the language, but their limited range of language skills implies English dominance in almost all domains; indeed, even as regards reading ability, it is highly unlikely their levels of competence would be as high as in English.

Amongst L1s, in addition to significant literacy problems which have just been noted, it would appear – although, once again, we do not have sufficient research on this, either – that a significant number – indeed, perhaps most – are English dominant in many domains, particularly H (or higher) domains, such as those relating to more

[6] All census data from General Register Office for Scotland, *Cunntas-sluaigh na h-Alba 2001: Aithisg Ghàidhlig / Scotland's Census 2001: Gaelic Report*. Edinburgh: General Register Office for Scotland, 2005. available at: www.gro-scotland.gov.uk/census/censushm/scotcen2/reports-and-data/scotcen-gaelic.

formal uses of the sort often associated with official contexts, as well as in certain types of employments, including the professions, various clerical 'white collar' occupations, as well as many skilled trades. This, too, is partly a function of the exclusion of Gaelic from many such domains. It is also due to the general exclusion of Gaelic from the school curriculum, the ongoing virtual impossibility of education through the medium of Gaelic at the secondary school level, and the complete absence of Gaelic-medium at the tertiary level, aside from its use as a medium of instruction on honours courses in Gaelic Studies in the Celtic Departments in Scottish Universities and on these and other degree courses offered by Sabhal Mòr Ostaig. An example here is the Christian ministry. The Highland Churches have often been referred to as the bedrock of the language community in 'heartland' areas and, until fairly recently, religious services, especially of Presbyterian denominations such as the Free Church, and clerical pastoral care generally have tended to be relatively strong domains in which Gaelic has had a significant presence. However, an on-line survey which I recently conducted on the training programmes of all major Christian denominations in Scotland revealed that instruction in seminaries and training institutions appeared to be solely through the medium of English. There do not appear to be any courses in Gaelic itself, either for learners or for L1s, nor any courses designed to increase Gaelic literacy. There are also apparently no courses in pastoral care through the medium of Gaelic, as well as instruction in sermonising in Gaelic. In even this important domain, then, it would be unsurprising to find that many Gaelic clergy, including L1s, are English-dominant.

We do not have much research on the language abilities or actual patterns of language use amongst young Gaelic speakers, particularly young L1s, although it is likely that similar patterns to those revealed amongst young Irish speakers in the Gaeltacht in the 2007 *Comprehensive Linguistic Study of the Use of Irish in the Gaeltacht*[7] would be evident, including limited use of Gaelic by young L1 Gaelic speakers amongst themselves, and language behaviour that is generally English dominant. Indeed, it is likely that amongst L1s, even in the 'heartlands' – those areas in which Gaelic is spoken by a majority of the local population – these patterns would be even more pronounced. Generally, smaller percentages of children are, based on the *2001 Census*, being brought up in Gaelic 'heartland' areas as Gaelic speakers,[8] Gaelic-medium Education (GME) is effectively limited to primary school for the overwhelming majority of students in the Western Isles, and even at primary, only about a third are enrolled in GME, whereas in the Irish Gaeltacht, Irish-medium at primary and secondary tends to be the norm. The reality is that young L1 Gaelic speakers will be English dominant for most purposes and for significant numbers and percentages, Gaelic has ceased being the language used with greatest facility and frequency in intimate domains.

Although we also lack data on the linguistic backgrounds of students in GME, it is very likely that a majority of them are from non-Gaelic speaking households; they will have little Gaelic before entry into Gaelic pre- or primary school, and therefore Gaelic is for them an L2, acquired largely at school. We have little detailed data on the

---

[7] Conchúr Ó Giollagáin, Seosamh Mac Donncha, Finola Ní Chualáin, Aoife Ní Shéaghdha, Mary O'Brien *Staidéar Cuimsitheach Teangeolaíoch ar Úsáid na Gaeilge sa Ghaeltacht: Príomhthátal agus Moltaí*. Baile Átha Cliath: Oifig an tSoláthair, 2007.

[8] Amongst 3–4 year olds, the strongest district in 'heartland' areas – districts in which Gaelic was spoken by a majority of the population as a whole – was Ness, on the Isle of Lewis, where only 44.4 percent spoke Gaelic; the weakest of these districts was Trotternish, at the north end of the Isle of Skye, where only 26.4 percent of 3–4 year olds spoke Gaelic. In Sleat, the district on the Isle of Skye in which Sabhal Mòr Ostaig is located, 53.4 percent of 3–4 year olds spoke Gaelic in 2001 – the sole district in which a majority of 3–4 year olds spoke the language – but only a minority of the population as a whole spoke Gaelic in that district.

linguistic attainment of such students,[9] their Gaelic language use outside of the school,[10] including amongst themselves, and their competence in and use of Gaelic in the longer term. In assessing the potential of GME to produce Gaelic speakers, the Canadian experience of French immersion for non-French speaking students is instructive, as it has existed since 1965. Research has indicated that French immersion can produce students who perform as well as L1 French speakers on tests of reading and listening comprehension, but that they typically do not show native-like proficiency in speaking and writing skills.[11] There are, however, several important differences between GME as it is currently practised and French immersion in Canada, and that because of the present structure of GME, several barriers exist to the achievement of high levels of fluency and, with it, the likelihood of significant Gaelic use outside of the classroom or over the longer term. One such barrier is the form that GME has taken to date: GME predominantly occurs in Gaelic-medium 'units' – classes in which Gaelic is the medium of instruction located in schools that are otherwise English-speaking.[12] The result is a much less intensive Gaelic experience than in a Gaelic-medium school, as outside of the immediate classroom, the school population is linguistically mixed, with the inevitable result that English, the common language and, as noted, the L1 of the majority of children in GME, becomes the default language. Another very significant barrier is the lack of continuity in GME from primary to secondary level. Aside from classes in the Gaelic language itself, the possibility of instruction through the medium of Gaelic at secondary level is extremely limited.[13] As a result, the immersion experience for almost all children in GME ends at the end of primary school. Such barriers conspire to ensure that many of the GME students who are not already Gaelic speakers when entering primary school (again, they are likely in the majority) will have a relatively limited competence, both in terms of language suitable to many H domains (which forms of language are often developed and enriched at secondary and post-secondary levels), but also in terms of language that is appropriate to and essential for many L domains (as, for many, Gaelic remains a 'school language', rather than one learned in

[9] See, however, Martina Müller. 'Language Use, Language Attitudes and Gaelic Writing Ability among Secondary Pupils in the Isle of Skye'. In ed. Wilson McLeod. *Revitalising Gaelic in Scotland: Policy, Planning and Public Discourse*. Edinburgh: Dunedin Academic Press, 2006. pp. 119–38.

[10] See, however, and for example, Morag M. MacNeil and Bob Stradling. *Emergent Identities and Bilingual Education: The Teenage Years*. Sleat, Isle of Skye: Lèirsinn Research Centre, 2000; and Morag M. MacNeil and Bob Stradling *Home and Community: Their Role in Enhancing the Gaelic Language Competencies of Children in Gaelic-medium Education*, Sleat, Isle of Skye: Lèirsinn Research Centre, 2000; and Elizabeth Cochran. 'Language Use and Attitudes among Adolescents in Gaelic-medium Education', unpublished M.Phil. thesis, University of Edinburgh, 2008.

[11] See, for example, Canadian Council on Learning (2007), *Lessons in Learning: French Immersion Education in Canada*, available at: www.ccl-cca.ca/pdfs/LessonsInLearning/May-17-07-French-immersion.pdf; www.ccl-cca.ca/pdfs/LessonsInLearning/May-17-07-French-immersion.pdf. For a good and accessible discussion of French immersion education in Canada, see Graham Fraser (2006), *Sorry, I Don't Speak French: Confronting the Canadian Crisis that Won't Go Away*, Toronto: McClelland and Stewart, especially chapter 8. See also the University of Michigan website 'French Immersion in Canada'. Available at: sitemaker.umich.edu/356.hess/home.

[12] At present, there are only two wholly Gaelic schools, in Glasgow and in Inverness; by contrast, there are 58 Gaelic units.

[13] Only one school offers significant provision at secondary level, Sgoil Ghàidhlig Ghlaschu (SGG), the Glasgow Gaelic School. In 2008–09, there were only 397 students at secondary level in Scotland taking a course other than Gaelic itself through the medium of Gaelic. In that school year, such courses were offered at only 19 secondary schools, and almost two thirds were accounted for by only two schools: 104 at SGG, and 85 at Portree High School, on the Isle of Skye. Relatively few students continue past Secondary 2: 297 of the 397 in Gaelic-medium classes were in S1 and S2. Source for enrolment data: 'Number of Pupils in Gaelic Medium Education and in Gaelic Classes in Secondary Schools, 2008-09', prepared for Bòrd na Gàidhlig by Prof. Boyd Robertson, Sabhal Mòr Ostaig.

and therefore appropriate to such domains). Although little research exists, it is highly likely that for most GME students, at least for those for whom Gaelic is an L2, competence will progressively be lost due to incomplete acquisition and lack of reinforcement outside of the school context.[14] The implications for long-term use patterns – certainly, for language reproduction but also for participation in any community of speakers – are negative and therefore extremely significant. Once again, to the extent that bilingualism is achieved, it may be transitory and is likely unbalanced, with English dominant for virtually all purposes, for most students in GME.

Finally, although significant work has been done on adult learners of Gaelic,[15] we still do not know enough about actual levels of Gaelic competence (or actual patterns of Gaelic use) amongst those who have achieved fluency. Indeed, although it is likely that such L2s make up a relatively small proportion of those who returned themselves as Gaelic speakers in the *2001 Census*, we do not know precisely how many adult learners have achieved fluency.[16] Undoubtedly, many L2s have attained quite high levels of fluency, in both written and spoken Gaelic, and also often have a strong command of the more technical vocabulary, where such exists, that would be appropriate for certain H domains. However, for virtually all of these L2s, English (or, in some cases, some other L1, often together with English) would remain the dominant language, in terms of competence (if not, always, in terms of personal preference), in virtually all domains. Also, given the nature of adult language acquisition, many L2s have a limited knowledge of registers and even vocabulary appropriate to intimate or informal L domains – formal university level courses, night school classes, and self-instructional material have tended not to focus on such forms, although this may change with newer forms of adult instruction, such as Ulpan courses (which are now being supported by Bòrd na Gàidhlig) and other methodologies such as Total Immersion Plus (TIP) (which has informed the development of the 'Gàidhlig aig Baile' programmes which are now being employed in Nova Scotia). Given the fundamental importance which has been placed on intergenerational transmission in the home in the literature on maintenance and revitalisation of minoritised languages,[17] the development of facility in such domains is absolutely critical.

From the foregoing, I think that it is reasonably safe to claim that most Gaelic speakers, whether L1 or L2, are not balanced bilinguals, and are in fact English dominant in most, and for many L1s as well as effectively all L2s, in *all* domains. This is a very serious situation, because there would appear to be a link between language *dominance* and language *preference*: while there are a range of factors, including attitudinal and ideological ones, which affect preference, competence, both actual and self-perceived, plays a role in the language which is chosen in any particular domain. This has obvious, and significant implications for actual patterns of language use, and consequently for initiatives in use and status planning. Thus, enriching the competences

---

[14] Doctoral research being done at the University of Edinburgh by Stuart Dunmore, as part of the Soillse project, is expected to provide the first significant evidence in respect of these questions, as he is tracing, amongst other matters, the linguistic trajectory of students enrolled in GME from 1985, when GME began in two schools, one in Glasgow and one in Inverness, to 1998. Evidence from Canada, where French-immersion education for English speaking students has existed for well over forty years now, and where it is possible for students to receive such education to the end of secondary school, tends to show that French language competence is highly variable, and that levels of competence and use tend to drop off after graduation.

[15] See, in particular, Alasdair MacCaluim, *Reversing Language Shift: The Social Identity and Role of Scottish Gaelic Learners*. Belfast: Cló Ollscoil na Banríona, 2007.

[16] This, of course, assumes that some reliable measure of fluency.

[17] See, for example, Joshua A. Fishman. *Reversing Language Shift: Theoretical and Empirical Foundations of Assistance to Threatened Languages*, (Clevedon: Multilingual Matters, 1991), still the single most influential

of different sorts of Gaelic speakers is a very serious challenge for language planners. To a significant degree, this is a question of acquisition planning. There are very major gaps and weaknesses in provision for virtually all categories of speakers discussed above. Thusfar, initiatives have focused largely on school education, with some significant initiatives at pre-school level and also some support for adult learners. More, however, needs to be done to enhance transmission in the home, and much needs to be done to support the enrichment of the language skills of virtually all categories of speakers, particularly literacy skills. However, we must also recognise that competence is not fostered only by formal educational initiatives. Much acquisition takes place through use, and therefore an expansion in domains in which Gaelic is used is also essential. Gaelic media certainly has an important role to play, particularly in terms of diffusion of terminology and expansion and enrichment of registers.

Societal Bilingualism

As in the context of the individual, the concept of bilingualism is vague when applied societally. Here, a consideration of Canada is instructive. Canada is often referred to as a bilingual country, but this needs to be qualified. If by bilingualism in a societal sense, we mean the presence of two languages within the population, then Canada is certainly a bilingual society: according to the 2006 Canadian census, 57.8 percent of the Canadian population were Anglophones (as defined for the purposes of the census, people with English as their mother tongue) and 22.1 percent were Francophones (people with French as their mother tongue). Indeed, Canada could be said to be a multilingual country, as 20.1 percent of the population were Allophones (that is, people for whom a language other than English or French was their mother tongue).[18] If, though, by bilingualism in a societal sense, we mean a society in which all or at least the overwhelming majority of the population are personally bilingual, Canada is certainly not a bilingual society: according to the 2006 Canadian census, while 42.4 percent of Francophones claimed to be bilingual in French and English, only 9.4 percent of Anglophones claimed to be bilingual in those two languages, and only 12.1 percent of Allophones claimed to be bilingual in them (and therefore, in effect, trilingual).[19] In total, slightly less than 20 percent of the Canadian population is bilingual. However, societies which are bilingual in the sense that virtually all of their members are personally bilingual are extremely rare.

While the *Gaelic Language (Scotland) Act 2005* recognises, in a fashion, that Gaelic is an official language of Scotland,[20] Scotland is certainly not a 'bilingual' society in the second sense used here; indeed, given that less than two percent of the population have any competence in Gaelic at all, it is only very weakly and contingently 'bilingual', in the sense that two languages are present, the first sense described here. In spite of the claims of the local council, Comhairle nan Eilean Siar, that it is a 'bilingual community',[21] even the so-called Gaelic heartland of the Western Isles cannot be

---

[18] Corbeil and Blaser (2007), *supra*.

[19] Corbeil and Blaser (2007), *supra*. The percentages vary widely between provinces, though: in 2006, 68.9 percent of Anglophones and 50.2 percent of Allophones in Quebec, the one predominantly Francophone province, claimed to be bilingual in English and French, whereas in the rest of Canada, 7.4 percent of Anglophones and 5.6 percent of Allophones claimed to be bilingual, while in Quebec, 35.8 percent of Francophones claimed to be bilingual but in the rest of Canada, 83.6 percent claimed to be bilingual.

[20] Section 1(3).

[21] See, for example, the Council's *Gaelic Language Plan*, created under the *Gaelic Language (Scotland) Act 2005*, at para. 1.8 (e), p. 6: Comhairle nan Eilean Siar, *Plana Gàidhlig 2007–2012 / Gaelic Language Plan 2007–2012*. Available at: www.cne-siar.gov.uk/sgioba/documents/languageplan/plan_e.pdf.

referred to as societally 'bilingual' in the second sense of the term: in the *2001 Census*, only 61 percent of the population aged three or over spoke Gaelic,[22] and given that there are essentially no monolingual Gaelic speakers left, it can be assumed that virtually all of the population speak English.

In such circumstances, patterns of diglossia amongst speakers of the minoritised language tend over time to be unstable. Where there is a language which is common to all in a community, and where there is likely to be significant social interaction between members of the community, that language tends to be the 'default' language, the one in which those interactions will take place. Where there are also inequalities of status, as usually exist in circumstances such as these, and the common language is the socially dominant one, the non-dominant language tends to be used over time in fewer and fewer domains. Although more work needs to be done on actual patterns of language use in the Western Isles, this is precisely what seems to be occurring there.

Some societies do have the explicit aim of creating a bilingual society in the 'strong' sense of being one in which all or virtually all of their members are personally bilingual, and seek to accomplish this result through the education system. Wales is one example. As a result of the *Education Reform Act 1988*, Welsh is now one of four core subjects in the Welsh school curriculum that all pupils in Wales between the ages of 5 and 16 must take;[23] one of the aims of this provision was to ensure that '*all* children should by the time they complete their compulsory schooling at sixteen ... have acquired a substantial degree of fluency in Welsh'.[24] Whether this goal can be accomplished through the teaching of Welsh as a subject is another matter, and as the Canadian experience suggests, and that of Ireland, where Irish has been a required subject in the Irish school curriculum since the 1920s,[25] without resulting in widespread bilingualism,[26] the answer is likely to be negative. The goal of creating a bilingual Wales, in the sense of a society in which all people can speak both Welsh and English, has nevertheless been repeated in important policy documents of the Welsh Assembly Government.[27] The Government of Catalonia has the same goal of achieving societal bilingualism in Catalan and Castilian Spanish in the 'strong' sense referred to here, although it does so through the pursuit of a more vigorous education policy in which effectively all primary and secondary pupils in the Autonomous Community of Catalonia are required to be educated through the medium of Catalan (rather than receive instruction in Catalan as a subject in the school curriculum), and in which Catalan is now the main language of instruction at the tertiary level as well.

Whether the achievement of societal bilingualism in the 'strong' sense described

---

[22] 71.56 percent claimed some competence in Gaelic (including the ability to understand, but not speak, read or write it).

[23] 1988, *c.* 40, sections 3(1)(b) and 3(2)(c).

[24] Welsh Office, *Welsh for Ages 5–16: Proposals of the Secretary of State for Wales*, Cardiff, 1989.

[25] See, for example, Gearóid Ó Tuathaigh. 'The State and the Irish Language: an Historical Perspective'. In eds. C. Nic Pháidín and S. Ó Cearnaigh. *A New View of the Irish Language*. Dublin: Cois Life, 2008. 26–42, at p. 29.

[26] In the 2006 Irish census, for example, 1,656,790, or 41.9 percent of the population, claimed to be Irish speakers, but much smaller numbers and percentages actually use Irish on a regular basis, and it is clear that a very significant proportion of those who claim to be Irish speakers have a very limited command of the language, see Helen Ó Murchú (2008), *More Facts About Irish*, (Baile Átha Cliath: Coiste na hÉireann den Bhiúró Eorpach do Theangacha Neamhfhorleathana Teoranta), pp. 45–9, 69, 70–9. For a discussion of the relatively poor levels of Irish attained by students taking Irish as a subject, see John Harris. 'Irish in the Education System', in eds. C. Nic Pháidín and S. Ó Cearnaigh, *ibid.*, 2008. pp. 178–90.

[27] See, for example, Welsh Assembly Government (2003), *Iaith Pawb: A National Action Plan for a Bilingual Wales*. Cardiff: Welsh Assembly Government.

above is, by itself, sufficient to ensure the creation of conditions which favour stable diglossia is, however, unclear. Some, such as the Canadian political scientist Jean Laponce,[28] raise questions about whether such stability is ever possible, as in any given territory, one language or another will be socially dominant, with negative consequences for the maintenance of the other. This scepticism has certainly driven Quebec language policy, which is not aimed at promoting either bilingualism or any form of stable diglossia, but the social dominance of French, as a means of securing it against strong anglicising forces which would, it is assumed, absent such a policy, weaken the language over time. It is because of such scepticism that Quebec language planners and politicians sometimes seem to perceived as indifferent to the fate of Francophone minorities outside Quebec: it is not that they are unconcerned about the fate of such communities, but that they appear to doubt, given the strongly anglicising forces in English-dominant provinces, and the limited policy tools available to address these forces – a topic to which we shall return in the last section, below – that such communities can maintain themselves over the longer term.

While, as we shall see, official bilingualism in Canada does not have the explicit goal of making all Canadians bilingual, policy-makers at both the federal and provincial levels have sought to promote the widespread acquisition of at least some French amongst non-French speakers and some English amongst non-English speakers. In English-speaking provinces, for example, some period of French language instruction is compulsory for all students in all provinces for at least part their period of primary and secondary education; similarly, in Quebec, English is a compulsory subject.[29] However, given the limited ability of such instruction to produce functional bilinguals, the implicit language policy cannot be said to be aimed at creating a society in which all can communicate effectively in two languages.

Scotland does not have the goal, either explicitly or implicitly, of creating a bilingual society in the strong sense of the word. At a national level, neither the Scottish Government, the main Bòrd na Gàidhlig, national Gaelic language planning body for Scotland, nor any other relevant body has a policy, either explicit or implicit, of promoting societal English-Gaelic bilingualism; given then tiny numbers of students in GME or who take Gaelic as a subject at secondary school, and the very limited number of education authorities in which any instruction at all in Gaelic is available, the achievement of such a policy would be a massive task requiring huge political will and sizeable expenditure. Strikingly, though, it does not appear that governments, and in particular relevant local authorities such as Comhairle nan Eilean Siar, or, indeed, Bòrd na Gàidhlig, have the goal of promoting societal bilingualism in the 'strong' sense in those areas in which Gaelic is still widely spoken. The creation of a truly bilingual community in the Western Isles, for example, would require as a starting point the setting of a goal of promoting bilingualism amongst all English monolinguals living in that community. There is, however, no explicit statement, for example, in its Gaelic Language Plan created under the auspices of the *Gaelic Language (Scotland) Act 2005*, that this is the policy of Comhairle nan Eilean Siar, and Bòrd na Gàidhlig has not, for

---

[28] See, for example, Jean Laponce, *Languages and Their Territories*, Toronto: University of Toronto Press, 1987.

[29] Generally, the teaching of French as a subject in the curriculum – referred to in Canada as 'core French' – begins in Grade 4 (i.e. Primary 4) and continues until Grade 9 (i.e. Secondary 3), at which point it becomes an optional course for the final three years of secondary school (it is not, however, compulsory before the final three in every province, although it is most). In total, about 90 percent of the total Anglophone school population is enrolled in core French. See Michael Byram, ed. *Routledge Encyclopedia of Language Teaching and Learning*. London: Routledge, 2000. pp. 94–6.

[30] Bòrd na Gàidhlig (2007), *Guidance on the Development of Gaelic Language Plans*. Inverness: Bòrd na Gàidhlig. available at: www.gaidhlig.org.uk/Downloads/Language-Plans/ Stiuireadh%20Phlanaichean%202007%20Beurla.pdf.

example, in its National Gaelic Language Plan, 2007–2012, articulated such a policy. In its guidance on the preparation of statutory Gaelic Language Plans,[30] Bòrd na Gàidhlig does articulate the goal of a qualified institutional bilingualism in the Western Isles, and this shall be discussed further in the final section of this paper. Both the Comhairle's Gaelic Language Plan and Bòrd na Gàidhlig's *National Gaelic Language Plan*[31] and other important Bòrd policy documents such as *Ginealach Ùr na Gàidhlig*[32] support increased acquisition of Gaelic, particularly through the school system, but also through adult learning programmes such as Ulpan courses. However, to ensure the sort of 'strong' societal bilingualism referred to here would, as a minimum, require an education policy of making GME effectively the only option at pre-school, primary and secondary levels in the Western Isles (as we see in Catalonia); at present, only somewhat more than a third of primary school pupils in the Western Isles are in GME, and a very tiny percentage do any subjects, other than Gaelic itself, through the medium of Gaelic, and neither the Comhairle nor Bòrd na Gàidhlig (nor the Scottish Government) have articulated a policy that would radically alter this reality, to say nothing of a policy of making GME the norm.

Institutional Bilingualism

> A bilingual country is not one where all the inhabitants necessarily have to speak two languages; rather it is a country where the principal public and private institutions must provide services in two languages to the citizens, the vast majority of whom may well be unilingual.[33]

This quote, taken from the final report of the Canadian Royal Commission on Bilingualism and Biculturalism, which set the stage for Canada's first *Official Languages Act* of 1969, captures very effectively the nature and the goals of institutional bilingualism, at least as it was and continues to be understood in Canada. As is clear from this quote, the goal of Canadian official bilingualism policy was not the promotion of societal bilingualism in the 'strong' sense, explored in the immediately preceding section of this paper. Rather, its overarching goal was, and remains, to ensure that French speakers and English speakers will be able to receive services from the federal government and all other federal public institutions as well as a small number of federally-regulated industries, in the language of their choice, wherever in Canada they live. This is the so-called 'personality' principle.[34] Even this goal is qualified in practice, as neither the Canadian *Constitution* of 1982 nor the most recent version of the *Official Languages Act* actually guarantee that all services in every government office anywhere in the country will be delivered bilingually; rather, it guarantees that such services will be available from the federal Parliament itself and from the head offices of all federal government departments and other federal government institutions to which the legislation applies, and that in local offices, such services may be available, depending on local demand.[35]

The Canadian federal policy is one of institutional bilingualism because it is

---

[31] Bòrd na Gàidhlig. *The National Plan for Gaelic 2007–2012*. Inverness: Bòrd na Gàidhlig, 2007.

[32] Bòrd na Gàidhlig. *Ginealach Ùr na Gàidhlig: An Action Plan to Increase the Number of Gaelic Speakers*, Inverness: Bòrd na Gàidhlig, 2010. Available at: www.gaidhlig.org.uk/Downloads/Ginealach-Ur-na-Gaidhlig-English–2011.pdf.

[33] Report *of the Royal Commission on Bilingualism and Biculturalism*, Book I, *The Official Languages*. Ottawa: Queen's Printer, 1967. p. xxviii, at paragraph 29.

[34] See, for example, Will Kymlicka and Alan Patten. *Language Rights and Political Theory*, Oxford: Oxford University Press, 2003. pp. 1–50. 'Introduction'.

[35] Part IV, Official Languages Act 1988, R.S.C. 1985, c. 31 (4th Supp.).

addressed in the first instance at the way in which institutions – in this case, a variety of federal institutions – operate linguistically. However, it is a fairly limited form of institutional bilingualism, because in addition to the qualified nature of the personality principle which is expresses, it is also sectoral: it applies only to the federal Parliament, federal government departments, Crown corporations, and a small number of federally-regulated enterprises. It does not seek to regulate the linguistic behaviour of other institutions, notably provincial governments and the bodies for which they have legislative authority (because of the restrictions imposed on the reach of the federal government by the Canadian constitution),[36] and, especially, because it generally does not attempt to regulate the linguistic behaviour of private and voluntary sector institutions.

Significantly, as the Canadian example shows – as was made clear in the quote with which this final section of the paper began – institutional bilingualism does not require societal bilingualism. Indeed, it does not even require that all employees of the institutions to which the regime applies are bilingual, although in practice many, but by no means all, federal civil servants and other employees of institutions to which the official bilingual regime applies are bilingual.[37] However, when official bilingualism was first introduced, the federal bureaucracy was disproportionately Anglophone, and the institutionalisation of official bilingualism has required the recruitment of significant numbers of bilingual staff and, indeed, the linguistic training of a large number of existing Anglophone staff. Thus, bilingual skills are valuable, and it is at least partly for this reason that provincial education policies seek to ensure that schools provide at least some significant instruction in French to English-speaking pupils and in English to French-speaking pupils.

The Canadian approach to institutional bilingualism differs in important ways from that of other jurisdictions. Take, as an example, the Autonomous Community of Catalonia, where the goal of the language policy is the 'normalisation' of the Catalan language, by which is meant making possible the living of one's life through the medium of Catalan. This goal may require societal bilingualism, or something very close to it, but it also clearly involves the development of institutional bilingualism in all public, private and voluntary sector institutions, for it would be difficult for a Catalan speaker to conduct all aspects of his or her daily life through the medium of Catalan if the institutions with which he or she deals were not capable of providing services in that language. Thus, both the *2006 Statute of Autonomy* of Catalonia[38] – essentially, the constitution of the autonomous community – and the *1998 Act on Language Policy*[39] create a regime under which individuals have the right to use either Catalan or Castilian Spanish in dealing with public institutions[40] and in the receipt of public services.[41] In this, the regime is similar to Canada's one of official bilingualism,

---

[36] The sole exceptions being in respect of education – a provincial matter – where the 1982 Constitution, in the Canadian *Charter of Rights and Freedoms*, contains a right to minority language education for French-speakers in English dominant provinces and for English-speakers in the French-dominant province of Quebec.

[37] Bilingual skills are generally required of managerial staff of federal institutions in the national capital region, and in the more senior reaches of the civil service, though some departments have a better track record than others in achieving this.

[38] *Organic Act 6/2006*, (of 19 July, 2006).

[39] Act No. 1, of 7th January 1998, on linguistic policy (DOGC Nº. 2553, of 9th January 1998).

[40] Under Article 6(2) of the *2006 Statute of Autonomy*, Catalan, together with Castilian Spanish, is the official language of Catalonia.

[41] Article 33 of the *2006 Statute of Autonomy* provides that each individual has the right to be served orally or in writing in the official language, Catalan or Castilian Spanish, of his or her choice.

although the personality principle is not qualified in any way, as it is in Canada, by reference to sufficiency of demand in local areas outside the capital in order to be guaranteed the right to service in both languages. However, the Catalan regime goes beyond the Canadian federal bilingual regime by also specifying a right to receive services from private and voluntary sector enterprises in Catalan or Castilian Spanish, as the citizen chooses,[42] and by requiring, for example, all signage and advertising to be in Catalan, although other languages, including Castilian Spanish, can also appear.[43] In order to satisfy the requirements of this regime, bilingualism in Catalan and Castilian Spanish must be widespread, for it would be difficult for private and voluntary sector enterprises, to say nothing of the state sector, to satisfy these rights without competence in the two languages being widespread. It is partly for this reason that education in Catalonia is through the medium of Catalan alone (Catalan being widely but not universally spoken, and having been marginalised in Catalan society and therefore effectively minoritised over a long period of time before the creation of autonomy pursuant to the Spanish constitution of 1978).

A final aspect of the nature of institutional bilingualism in Canada which should be noted is that, in addition to creating rights to services in the language of choice, French or English, the regime regulates language use within the federal institutions to which it applies, as it provides that French and English are the languages of work in such institutions and that all employees of such institutions have the right to use the language of choice, French or English,[44] although these guarantees are relaxed in respect of offices of such institutions outside of the national capital region.[45] The Catalan regime specifies that Catalan is the official language of the autonomous community, implying that it will be the usual language of internal communication in all public institutions of the community, but guarantees that Castilian Spanish can also be used.[46]

With regard to Scottish Gaelic, the *Gaelic Language (Scotland) Act 2005* creates no rights to use Gaelic at all, either in dealing with public institutions (or within the workplace in such institutions) or in dealing with the private or voluntary sectors. It also makes no reference to bilingualism as either a concept or a policy goal. The main mechanism for extending opportunities to use Gaelic is that of Gaelic language plans, which the Act empowers Bòrd na Gàidhlig to require public authorities to prepare. The Act makes no provision for the regulation of the private or voluntary sectors, and in this sense, the Scottish regime resembles the Canadian one in taking a 'sectoral' approach. This, however, is a more common approach than that taken in Catalonia, as very few jurisdictions seek to regulate so extensively language use by institutions outside the public sector. In preparing their Gaelic language plans, public authorities must have regard to a number of matters, including the extent to which the public which the public authority serves uses Gaelic and the potential for developing the use of Gaelic in relation to those public services; they must also have regard to any guidance issued by Bòrd na Gàidhlig.[47] In 2007, the Bòrd issued such guidance. The guidance makes no specific reference to bilingualism as a concept, and does not explicitly require the

---

[42] Article 34 of the *2006 Statute of Autonomy* provides that each individual, as a user of consumer of goods, products and services, has the right to be served orally or in writing in the official language of his or her choice, Catalan or Castilian Spanish.

[43] See Articles 35 and 36 of the 2006 Statute of Autonomy.

[44] Section 34, *Official Languages Act 1988.*

[45] Section 35 *et seq., Official Languages Act 1988.*

[46] Article 6(2), *2006 Statute of Autonomy.*

[47] Section 3(5), *Gaelic Language (Scotland) Act 2005.*

introduction of a policy of institutional bilingualism of the sort being considered here. However, with regard to core commitments of such plans in respect of identity (i.e. corporate identity and signage), communications with the public, publications, and staffing, the guidance recognises that '[i]n recognition of the varying levels of Gaelic provision that may be achievable in different areas of the country, we have sought to provide different levels of commitment within each internal process or service delivery area', and notes that the Bòrd has 'identified four broad categories of expected Gaelic language provision'. The guidance then provides that:

> for public authorities that operate in areas where persons who understand, speak, read or write Gaelic form a majority of the population, the expectation is that the public authority will work towards, within a reasonable timescale and having regard to its particular circumstances, creating the conditions in which Gaelic can be used across all of its services to the public, and in which any employee who wants to use Gaelic in the execution of their duties can do so. These authorities should endeavour to identify a comprehensive range of commitments to include in their Gaelic Language Plan, most of which may be of a relatively high level, to ensure Gaelic is given a high profile and to provide a variety of means by which Gaelic speakers will be encouraged and enabled to interact with the authority through the medium of Gaelic.[48]

While hedged with conditions, the guidance appears to contain at least an implicit expression of a policy of institutional bilingualism in public authorities to which this level of expectation applies. For example, it refers to creating the conditions 'in which Gaelic can be used across *all of its services to the public*', and also makes reference to allowing '*any* employee who wants to use Gaelic in the execution of their duties' to do so. The question that remains to be answered is the extent to which Gaelic language plans which are actually prepared by public authorities to which this level of commitment would apply and approved by Bòrd na Gàidhlig actually implement this principle. The conditional language in the passage quoted above is probably necessary, because no public authority in Scotland is, at present, close to being able to implement a policy of full institutional bilingualism; this would require a significant expansion in the Gaelic capacity of any public authority in Scotland, including those located in the 'heartlands'. Clearly, close consideration will need to be given by Bòrd na Gàidhlig of the barriers which exist to the full implementation of the guidance, and strategies for addressing those barriers will need to be developed as a matter of some urgency.

---

[48] Bòrd na Gàidhlig. *Guidance on the Development of Gaelic Language Plans*. Inverness: Bòrd na Gàidhlig, 2007. p. 20.

The *Barail agus Comas Cànain* Survey of Community Language Use, Ability and Attitudes: Some General Observations regarding Future Gaelic Language Policy Planning in Scotland

Gillian Munro

Background

In 2009, Bòrd na Gàidhlig, the public agency in Scotland charged with the coordination of language planning for Gaelic in Scotland, commissioned a research project called *Barail agus Comas Cànain* ['Language Attitudes and Abilities']. The research contract was awarded to a team of researchers based at Sabhal Mòr Ostaig.[1] The research report was submitted to Bòrd na Gàidhlig, for consideration by its committees, in the Autumn of 2010. The report has gone through due process and, in Spring 2011, its findings have now been accepted.

The research brief for *Barail agus Comas Cànain* was deemed by the research team to contain three relatively discreet research elements, each of which was led by one of the three main researchers:

- the development and piloting of a language audit tool that could be administered by employers, with employees, to assess workforce Gaelic language use, workers' self-assessed Gaelic language skills, and their Gaelic language training requirements;
- the development of a Gaelic language fluency assessment scale;
- and an assessment of Gaelic language attitudes and abilities in a community where 'facility in Gaelic is dominant'.

I presented some early findings from the community study of Scottish Gaelic language attitudes and abilities at the Tenth Language and Politics Symposium in Queen's University

Belfast, and had hoped to discuss the findings in more depth in this chapter. However, the findings for the community study of Scottish Gaelic language attitudes and abilities have raised some important questions about Scottish Gaelic language revitalisation policy in Scotland: Bòrd na Gàidhlig is currently discussing the findings with other agencies and with the community studied, and will then decide how these conversations, together with the research report, may impact on future Bòrd na Gàidhlig language revitalisation policy and strategy in Scotland. For these reasons, I will not discuss the detailed research findings of the *Barail agus Comas Cànain* community study, but will reflect more generally on the report findings and will refer also to important work done by other academics. I do this in order to make some recommendations for the next *National Plan for Gaelic*, which will succeed the current *National Plan for Gaelic, 2007–12*.[2]

---

[1] The original team comprised of three researchers: Iain Mac an Tàilleir (SMO), Dr Gillian Munro (SMO), and Dr Marsaili MacLeod (Scottish Agricultural College). Dr Mike Cormack (SMO) was the project adviser throughout, and Lèirsinn research staff members Brian MacDonald and Maria Russell were involved in questionnaire data input and analysis. Dr MacLeod left the project in 2010; and Dr Timothy C. Armstrong then joined the project in 2010 as one of the three principal researchers.

[2] www.bord-na-gaidhlig.org.uk/National-Plan/National%20Plan%20for%20Gaelic.pdf.

Positionality

Following the example of John Walsh in this volume, I should state my own positionality in relation to my writing and research. I learnt my Gaelic in the Western Isles and in Skye in the 1980s and have spent most of my work life since researching and teaching in, and about, Scottish Gaelic and community. As a Gaelic learner, with no cultural background in the Gaelic-speaking parts of Scotland today, I have a strong attachment and belief in the existence of community, in all its myriad forms. I have been especially interested in the dynamics of social and linguistic change and power negotiation affecting 'traditional' Scots- and Gaelic-speaking communities (e.g. Munro 2000a, Rothach 2006). I have this interest despite – some might say perhaps because of - me being new to the Gaelic language community. I am, I hope, aware of some of the complex dynamics of power and of negotiation of community membership in the knitting together of old and newer forms of community or 'networks of interest' around Scottish Gaelic (Munro, 2000b).

I myself was brought up with a strong sense of 'traditional' community, based on human geographical proximity, kinship and close social and economic ties, in a North-East fishing town. I speak a dialect of Scots that had no social prestige beyond its community of users, and I have a keen sense of how this feels. I have also lived long enough to see that 'traditional' community which I grew up in be largely reconstituted through socio-economic and population change, and this is having a long-term, profound influence on our Scots dialect. During the preparation of my PhD, I researched my community background in North-East Scotland through an anthropological lens, and I have since continued pursuing my interest in minority language and community through my involvement, most recently, in the community study of language abilities and attitudes for the *Barail agus Comas Cànain* project. What I write below is therefore strongly influenced by personal and academic experience.

In the text that follows, I make reference to the *Barail agus Comas Cànain* community research to suggest three core areas which require clarity in the next iteration of a *National Plan for Gaelic*: clarity about the size, nature and context of the community to be served; clarity in the understanding and marketing of the idea of bilingualism; and lastly, clarity of purpose within the Gaelic language speaking community, which I suggest urgently needs the development of a network of community language planning bodies and local community language plans, along the lines of the *Mentrau Iaith* in Wales.

What do We Know about the Scottish Gaelic Language Community?

Census figures gathered each decade in Scotland show a relentless drop in numbers of Scottish Gaelic speakers. Even in the 'Gaelic heartlands' of the Western Isles, the attrition is inexorable (see Mac an Tàilleir, 2010). It is probably safe to bet that Census 2011 figures will show further attrition nationally and in the heartlands – even if there will be bits of good news, such as a rise in numbers of speakers in the towns and cities of Scotland. Since 2001, language revitalisation agencies have had to base their knowledge of where Gaelic speakers are on the increasingly out of date census results; the *Barail agus Comas Cànain* research team came across this problem in trying to identify in 2009 a 'Gaelic dominant community' using census material that was eight years old; eventually, we decided to rely on local knowledge.

The level of detailed information collected in the Census is very limited. It is impossible to interrogate the Gaelic data for levels of ability, and actual Gaelic language use is not tracked, making it impossible to know how, and even if, those who self-report to have Gaelic are actually using Gaelic during those ten years. These features make the Census results of limited ideological or practical use in language policy formation. Scottish Gaelic requires a better statistical and qualitative knowledge base on which to plan the language's future, a knowledge base which tracks not just numbers of speakers, but abilities, use and attitudes through thorough research (see Dunbar, 2010) and reporting activities. Regular updating and mapping of numbers, abilities, and usage of Gaelic (and English) would allow for more accurately targeted programmes of intervention to boost language use and improve attitudes to it. Two options Bòrd na Gàidhlig might consider are: organising a more frequent census nationally/ conducting a national Gaelic census once every five years; or systematically collecting detailed local information about abilities, attitudes and language use as part of community or area language plans.

It is widely expected that the results of the *2011 Census* will show that there are more Gaelic speakers recorded as living outside rather than inside the traditional Gaelic-speaking areas of Scotland. This single fact raises a number of questions about how Bòrd na Gàidhlig will plan to support and increase Gaelic usage in non-traditional areas across non-traditional forms of networked or 'symbolic community' (Cohen, 1985). Therefore, I suggest that more research and mapping work needs to be done to understand how non-traditional language networks operate, so that plans to support them are effective. Research could be undertaken to investigate, for example, how parents, in seeking to raise a child to be fluent in Gaelic, use different forms of support network to create a language community for themselves and their children.

The *Barail agus Comas Cànain* research concurred with a point previously made by Mac an Tàilleir (2010): Gaelic is now a minority language in the Western Isles, because everyone speaks English but not everyone speaks Gaelic, and because respondents reported poor levels of usage of Gaelic in community public locations. As in Ireland, the situation of Gaelic in Skye and the Western Isles, and in other parts of a 'Gaelic heartland', is that of 'linguistic fragmentation' (Mac Giolla Chriost, 2006: 240). I would suggest that communities, language and community planners, researchers and the Scottish government must fully accept this fact, and must gain a better understanding of the nature of Scottish Gaelic communities/networks, in order to engage more effectively with language communities and networks.

Because Gaelic is now a minority language, it operates in networks of speakers which are not synonymous any more with geographical and physical community (see Macdonald 1997 on the difficulty with defining community). Also, abilities as well as usage patterns vary, further fragmenting the picture of use in networks. Analysis of Gaelic transmission between parents and children, in *Barail agus Comas Cànain*, has backed up McLeod's (2002) indication of the likelihood that inter-generational transmission has all but ceased in traditional Gaelic communities. This *Barail agus Comas Cànain* finding can probably be extrapolated and applied to the Gaelic heartland areas generally, to suggest that Gaelic is not being reproduced among younger age groups as a 'natural' language community in the heartlands. Traditional Gaelic communities will now require sensitive, well targeted language interventions, in order to create the much higher levels of Gaelic intergenerational transmission required to make the language sustainable.

What the above suggests is that the ideological basis for traditional Gaelic communities and of language revitalisation policy and strategies is undergoing a profound shift. The writers of the forthcoming *National Plan for Gaelic* can no longer assume that there is a stable, 'natural', self-replicating, traditional Gaelic language community that forms a stable basis of common cultural content associated with speaking Gaelic. This does not mean that the children of native Gaelic speakers, or the 'traditional' significations of Gaelic – the imputed cultural content and thus ideological premise of Gaelic language revitalisation – are no longer relevant or powerful. The debate about why Gaelic matters, and why people want future generations to speak Gaelic, can still draw on concepts of tradition, inheritance and cultural value. But if the language is to survive, that debate must include new definitions of the Gaelic language community.

The linguistic content of Gaelic in traditional communities is also undergoing a profound shift, particularly amongst the younger generations of speakers; this raises questions of what Gaelic is, how it will change, and how best all varieties of speech can be supported. Valuable insights into some of the important linguistic and cultural identity issues, to be faced in a new National Plan for Gaelic, are to be found in the work of several academics. MacCaluim (2006) has pointed out that huge numbers of learners must reach fluency each year to replace loss of fluent speakers through age-related death, but this is not happening. McEwen-Fujita (2010) has raised the issue of the difficulties facing Gaelic learners in being successfully integrated into networks of native speakers in traditional Gaelic communities. Timothy Armstrong, a *Soillse* research fellow at Sabhal Mòr Ostaig, is currently researching the experiences of 'heritage' learners in trying to learn or relearn Gaelic and in re/-integrating into Gaelic language networks. The future research results of this will no doubt give some clearer indication of the re-/integration challenges for heritage, and for other, learners, and for the host language community. The future *National Plan for Gaelic* would benefit from consideration of these research findings.

Meg Bateman (2010) gives voice in her work to the concerns of young native speakers about their own Gaelic, when they come into contact with traditional Gaelic grammar rules. Another valuable piece of research is currently underway by *Soillse* PhD student Julia Landgraf (based at Sabhal Mòr Ostaig), who is asking Gaelic-medium Education children in various urban and island schools about their ideas of what Gaelic is and why it matters. Her research, through use of quotes, demonstrates the range of language skills present in children who will be adults in just over a decade. Landgraf's and Bateman's research indicate that the new *National Plan for Gaelic* may help to give us a clearer picture of how future Gaelic speakers see and relate themselves to the language, what their sense is of the personal, social, local and national value of speaking Gaelic, and what their personal challenges are in being part of the future of Gaelic. Thus the new *National Plan for Gaelic* might well consider the research findings above in order to clarify: what Gaelic is and will become; who speaks and will speak it; and where Gaelic will be spoken in the next five to ten years. Dunbar (2010) gives a cogent exposition about why future Gaelic policy would benefit from being based on research evidence.

Bilingualism

While knowing your Gaelic community is one prerequisite for having an effective language policy and strategies of implementation, clarity about what use is being proposed for the language is also critical. Bilingualism in English and Gaelic – equal fluency in both – is surely the desired goal and outcome. Many of the authors in this volume show that meanings of bilingualism can be underspecified, and that this can result in misunderstanding of language goals by all parties, and in 'mismatches' of expectation between different parties (see Walsh, Armstrong, etc., in this volume; Ó hIfearnáin 2010). What fluency in a minority language means is hard to specify, when set against a background of significant, rapid linguistic change happening amongst almost all speakers of different abilities and backgrounds. However, it is important to try to consider definitions of appropriate bilingual practice, and of minority language fluency markers, in the new iteration of the *National Plan for Gaelic*.

While definitions of what is being aimed for – fluent bilingualism – are important, equally important is the marketing of the fact that major and minority languages do not co-exist on a level playing field: use of a minority language must be planned for, protected and monitored. The public message has to be clear that the odds are stacked against the minority language in all spheres of daily life, including the public but also the private spheres. Any attempt at achieving equal fluency, or bilingualism, has to be supported by clear specification of where it is intended that Gaelic is to be the normal language of daily interaction, and this has to be backed up by advice, examples and encouragement, and by a mechanism for reviewing progress against stated targets.

Certain perceptions may have to be publicly discussed, and even challenged, before obstacles to bilingual practice can be removed. McEwen-Fujita (2010) refers to native speakers' behaviour of speaking English when one or more non-natives are present. She suggests that this behaviour may be akin to an 'ethic of politeness', after Trosset's (1986) work in Wales, or can be likened to an 'etiquette of accommodation', after Woolard's (1989) work on Catalan (all quoted in McEwen-Fujita, 2010: 46). The *Barail agus Comas Cànain* research showed that some people in the community expressed regret about the lack of opportunity to speak Gaelic in public settings. What the solutions to situations like these are would have to be openly discussed. A similar anxiety about changing established patterns of language use with friends and family emerged in the *Barail agus Comas Cànain* research also, while at the same time the interviewees regretted and wished to see an improvement in the use of Gaelic locally. This is another area of private and public tension that would have to be debated. Bòrd na Gàidhlig could take a leading role in having these discussions, stimulated by a *National Plan for Gaelic* policy of supporting bilingualism but of clarifying the use of Gaelic in public space and encouraging stronger use of Gaelic in private spheres.

To date, bilingualism has been discussed as a policy aim and language outcome in relation particularly to Gaelic-medium Education. The *Barail agus Comas Cànain* research comments that the uptake of Gaelic-medium Education (GME) in the study area has been steady but not really growing in recent years, and now more than half of the children in the study area local school are in English-medium Education. McLeod (2002) comments that there has not been the will in local education policy to ensure that all children are fluent in Gaelic upon completion of primary school, and that there has not been a genuine policy of bilingualism (*ibid.*: 284). This is despite the situation in which the vast majority of adult respondents hoped that future generations will speak Gaelic. The role of GME is clearly crucial to language survival in this community: the Gaelic-speaking children reported to be using Gaelic, even to a limited extent, beyond the school classroom in any community context, including the family home, were almost exclusively only those in GME classes. This begs the question of whether the current policies regarding the promotion and uptake of GME in the

Western Isles are strong enough to confront the cessation of inter-generational transmission and the decline in use of Gaelic in virtually all domains of life in the Western Isles.

In the *Barail agus Comas Cànain* research, there was some indication that parents rely on GME to bring their children to fluency in Gaelic – making it a comparable situation to that in Ireland (Mac Giolla Chriost, 2006). Simultaneously, there appeared to be surprise in the community that GME was not, on its own, producing fully fluent Gaelic speakers. This suggests that, although Bòrd na Gàidhlig has cautioned against this (2007: 11), there may be widespread community and parental expectations that GME alone will give children fluency in Gaelic. The 2010 Bòrd na Gàidhlig document *Ginealach Ùr na Gàidhlig* ['The New Gaelic Generation'] does, however, identify specific projects and aims that would support a clarification of what GME aims to do in terms of a child's Gaelic fluency levels and suggests that using Gaelic in the home is essential to strengthen what can be achieved in the GME classroom. This part of the work proposed in *Ginealach Ùr na Gàidhlig* remains to be implemented.

Community Language Plans

Perhaps the most startling aspect for me of the *Barail agus Comas Cànain* research was the reaction of residents who were consulted about Gaelic use, ability and attitudes in their area. They expressed genuine surprise and pleasure that a public agency would canvass their opinions in such detail about Gaelic. Response rates to the three bulky questionnaires, where participation in the study was voluntary, were exceptionally high (99%, 82% and 66%). I came to the conclusion that the discussion of why Gaelic continues to atrophy has not been held directly, and in a comprehensive way, between agents of the state and the language community members.

Although the *National Plan for Gaelic 2007–12* identifies 'community' as an area for development, and although it also mentions the Mentrau Iaith models of community development, there remains, to date, no widespread community or even regional language development structure that draws in local residents to plan their own priorities for local linguistic developments. It is true that BnG and CnaG have set up a successful but small number of *Iomairt* project areas, which have involved establishing a local development officer and a local committee to oversee development priorities. But the Iomairt areas, I would argue, are huge, and so development officers necessarily have to focus on only one or two development priorities. Local language planning requires a much more comprehensive, detailed assessment of need. A comprehensive local language plan needs sufficient human, intellectual and financial input to implement and carry out its language planning work. We need a new and expanded model of *Iomairt*, which draws much more directly and heavily on *Mentrau Iaith* examples of local and regional planning bodies and resource centres.

I believe that, following Mac Giolla Chriost (2006) writing about Irish in Ireland and following the recommendations of the *Western Isles Language Plan* (2006) – if reversing language shift efforts are to be successful in relation to Gaelic in Scotland's traditional Gaelic-speaking communities, micro-level language planning is a priority for both the agents of the state and for the communities, or networks, of Gaelic speakers. Through this nexus, critical areas of language planning can be debated and clarified, such as agreeing what we mean and aspire to in promoting bilingualism; and the importance and role of inter-generational transmission in the home in reversing language shift in Gaelic communities.

I suggest that micro-level language plans need to be based on the premises which Dauenhauer and Dauenhauer describe for community-based language revitalisation efforts, in their article 'Technical, Emotional, and Ideological Issues in Reversing Language Shift: Examples from Southeast Alaska' (1998). They state that there needs to be 'widespread, intense conviction that this is the right thing to do' (p. 96); the community must be aware that they have to do it for themselves; and 'the foundation of language reversal is the family and community link' (p. 97). Their work provides good guidelines for a programme of local language plans. Without creating a stronger, more sustainable local micro-economy in villages and local areas which is attuned and supportive to minority language usage, Gaelic speakers will continue to decline in Gaelic usage statistics and in human number in the traditional language communities.

Nahir's work (1998) is also useful, in that it identifies some important factors in effecting language revitalisation, the most important of which, for Scottish Gaelic, are probably political and economic forces, which help explain the contraction of Scottish Gaelic and which influence the chances of survival of Scottish Gaelic in the future. Schiffman (2006) provides a useful analysis of the main issues to be addressed, in order that a language policy does not fail during implementation. Perhaps most helpfully of all, the operation and success of the *Mentrau Iaith*, described so clearly by Colin H. Williams (2000) demonstrates the value of engagement directly between the community of speakers and the agencies who seek to support them.

In Conclusion

I am grateful to Bòrd na Gàidhlig, and to the editors of this volume, for their patience in the negotiations of the contents of this paper. As academics and policy makers, we are all committed to finding answers as to how to revitalise our minority languages. In this chapter, I have proposed some basic ideas of areas where I think we might, in the future *National Plan for Gaelic*, benefit from greater clarity, particularly in relation to our group membership, our common purpose, and our channels of dialogue.

References

Armstrong, T.C. 2011. 'Bilingualism, Restoration and Language Norms'. In Kirk and Ó Baoill. 2011. 170–7.
Bateman, M. 2010. 'Gàidhlig Ùr'. In eds. Munro, G. and I. Mac an Tàilleir. 87–98.
Barail agus Comas Cànain: Aithisg rannsachaidh airson Bòrd na Gàidhlig. 2010. Unpublished Report.
Bòrd na Gàidhlig. 2007. *Plana Nàiseanta na Gàidhlig 2007–2012 / The National Plan for Gaelic 2007–2012.* Inverness: Bòrd na Gàidhlig.
Bòrd na Gàidhlig. 2010. *Ginealach Ùr na Gàidhlig: An Action Plan to Increase the Number of Gaelic Speakers.* Inverness: Bòrd na Gàidhlig.
Cohen, A.P. 1985. *The Symbolic Construction of Community.* London: Routledge.
Comhairle nan Eilean Siar. 1996. *Bilingual Policy.* Stornoway: Western Isles Council.
Comhairle nan Eilean Siar. 2007. *Plana Gàidhlig 2007–2012 / Gaelic Language Plan 2007–2012.* Stornoway: Comhairle nan Eilean Siar. [Available at: www.cne-siar.gov.uk/sgioba/documents/languageplan/plan_g.pdf]

Dauenhauer, N.M. and R. Dauenhauer. 1998. 'Technical, Emotional, and Ideological Issues in Reversing Language Shift: Examples from Southeast Alaska'. In eds. Grenoble L.A. and L.J. Whaley. *Endangered Languages, Current Issues and Future Prospects*. Cambridge: Cambridge University Press. 57–98.

Dunbar, R. 2010. 'A Research Strategy to Support Gaelic Language Policy in Scotland', In eds. Munro, G. and I. Mac an Tàilleir. 139–60.

Euromosaic Project: *Language Use Survey*. 1994.

Jones, K. and D. Morris. 2005. 'Welsh Language Socialization within the Family'. [Available at: www.npld.eu/Documents/ Welsh%20Language%20Socialisation%20in%20the%20Family.pdf]

Kirk, J.M. and D.P. Ó Baoill eds. 2011. *Strategies for Minority Languages: Northern Ireland, the Republic of Ireland, and Scotland*. Belfast Studies in Language, Culture and Politics 22. Belfast: Cló Ollscoil na Banríona. [the present volume]

MacCaluim, A. 2006. 'Air Iomall an Iomaill? Luchd-ionnsachaidh na Gàidhlig ann an Ath-thilleadh Gluasad Cànain'. In ed. McLeod, W. 185–97.

Macdonald, S. 1997 *Reimagining Culture. Histories, Identities and Gaelic Renaissance*. Oxford: Berg.

McEwen-Fujita, E. 2010. 'Ideology, Affect, and Socialization in Language Shift and Revitalization: The Experience of Adults Learning Gaelic in the Western Isles of Scotland'. *Language in Society* 39: 27–64.

Mac Giolla Chriost, D. 2006. 'Micro-level Language Planning in Ireland'. *Current Issues in Language Planning* 7.2/3: 230–50.

MacLeod, D.J. 2003. 'An Historical Overview'. In eds. Nicolson, M. and MacIver, M. 1–14.

McLeod, W. 2002. 'Gaelic Scotland: A 'Renaissance without Planning'. In *Hizkuntza Biziberritzeko Saoiak / Experiencias de Inversión del Cambio Lingüístico / Récupération de la Perte Linguistique / Reversing Language Shift*. Vitoria-Gasteiz: Servicio Central de Publicaciones del Gobierno Vasco. 279–95. [available from www.euskara.euskadi.net/r59-738/eu/contenidos/informacion/argitalpenak/eu_6092/adjuntos/EREMU.PDF]

McLeod, W. ed. 2006. *Revitalising Gaelic in Scotland: Policy, Planning and Public Discourse*. Edinburgh: Dunedin Academic Press.

McLeod, W. 'Gaelic Medium Education in the International Context'. In eds. Nicolson, M. and M. MacIver. 15-34.

Mac an Tàilleir, I. 2010 'A' Ghàidhlig anns a' Chunntas-shluaigh'. In eds. Munro, G. and I. Mac an Tàilleir. 19–34.

Munro, G. 2000a. *How do Individuals Relate to their Local Communities through Work and Family Life? Some Fieldwork Evidence*. University of Aberdeen: Arkleton Institute for Rural Development Research.

Munro, G. 2000b. *The Highland Problem': State and Community in Local Development*. University of Aberdeen: Arkleton Institute for Rural Development Research.

Munro, G. and K. Hart. 2000. *'The Highland Problem': State and Community in Local Development*. University of Aberdeen: Arkleton Institute for Rural Development Research.

Munro, G. 2004. 'Cò leis an dùthaich? Ceistean Cànain, Cultair agus Cruth na Tìre an Latha An-diugh air Ghaidhealtachd' ['To whom belongs the land? Questions of Language, Culture and Landscape Today in the Highlands of Scotland']. In eds. McLeod, W. and M. Ní Annracháin. *Cruth na Tìre*. Dublin: Cois Ceum. 266–303.

Munro, G. and I. Mac an Tàilleir. 2010. *Coimhnearsnachd na Gàidhlig an-Diugh / Gaelic Communities Today*. Edinburgh: Dunedin Academic Press.

Nahir, M.S. 1998. 'Micro-Language Planning and the Revival of Hebrew: A Schematic Framework'. *Language and Society* 27.3: 335-57.

Nicolson, M. and M. MacIver. 2003. *Policy and Practice in Education*. Edinburgh: Dunedin Academic Press.

Ó hIfearnáin, T. 2010. 'Institutionalising Language Policy: Mismatches in Community and National Goals', In eds. Munro, G. and I. Mac an Tàilleir. 35–48.

Pròiseact Plana Cànain nan Eilean Siar: Rannsachadh agus Toraidhean Ìre 1 dhen Phròiseact, Aithisg Dheireannach. 2004. [www.liguae-celticae.org/dateien/planaire1.pdf]

Rothach, G. 2006. 'Gàidhlig aig an Oir'. In ed. McLeod, W. 221–37.

Schiffman, H.F. 2006 'When Language Policies Fail: The Problem of Implementation'. (Powerpoint presentation given in Stockholm, September). Available at: www.docstoc.com/docs/38829632/When-Language-Policies-Fail-The-Problem-of-Implementation.

Trosset, C.S. 1986. 'The Social Identity of Welsh Learners'. *Language in Society* 15: 165–92.

Walsh, J. 2006. 'Language and Socio-economic Development. Towards a Theoretical Framework'. *Language Problems and Language Planning* 30:2:127–48.

Walsh, J. 2011b. 'Bilingualism, Ideology and the 20-Year Strategy for Irish'. In eds. Kirk and Ó Baoill. 2011b. 55–69.

Williams, C.H. 2000. 'Community Empowerment through Language Planning Intervention'. In ed. Williams, C.H. *Language Revitalisation. Policy and Planning in Wales*. Cardiff: University of Wales Press. 221–46.

Woodard, K.A. 1989. *Double Talk: Bilingualism and the Politics of Ethnicity in Catalonia*. Stanford, CA: Stanford University Press.

Bilingualism, Restoration and Language Norms

Timothy Currie Armstrong

What does bilingualism mean when we use it as a policy goal? If an organisation or polity declares itself bilingual or subscribes to a policy of bilingualism, what sort of language use should we expect as a result of that policy? 'Bilingual' and 'bilingualism' are terms that strain under the semantic burden of a wide range of meanings as they are used to describe both individuals and groups in a number of different contexts, from sociolinguistics to applied linguistics, anthropology, child development, education, language policy and planning, as well as in popular and political discourses on language use and ability (see Dunbar in this volume). And bilingualism is also frequently named as an objective in language policy and planning documents. Certainly, bilingualism in one form or another is a common policy goal at all levels in Ireland and Scotland, but we could ask, given this uncertainty and multiplicity of meanings, is it always clear what specific norms of language use are being advanced when an organisation or polity adopts a policy of bilingualism?

Language norms are one element of language ideology (Kroskrity 2004; Woolard and Schieffelin 1994), and as a link between language ability and use, language ideology plays a key role in the success of language revitalisation. In my research, I have been studying language ideology in small groups, and particularly, language norms in the context of language revitalisation movements. I am interested in the question of how new minority language norms are established in the course of language revitalisation. This is an important question, I might even argue, the most important question, when it comes to the practicalities of revitalising a language at the micro level. How do we establish new norms of minority-language use in key sites, domains or situations, in businesses, in communities, in schools, and so on?

My interest in this question grew out of my time spent at Sabhal Mòr Ostaig, the Gaelic college on the Isle of Skye, first as a student, and more recently, as a lecturer and researcher. Sabhal Mòr Ostaig is a fascinating place and we are trying to do something truly unique at the College, or rather, we are trying to do two different unique things. First, we are trying to build an entirely Gaelic-speaking academic community for students and staff at the College. All of our full-time courses are taught in Gaelic, but also, we are trying to encourage our students and staff to use Gaelic as the common language socially outside of class as well. And second, we are one of the few businesses in Scotland that endeavours to work entirely through the medium of Gaelic.

These two policy goals are quite ambitious, and we do not always succeed, but we do often come close, and we spend a lot of time and money planning and implementing language policy designed ever to strengthen the use of Gaelic at the College. I have been involved in that planning and implementation process for several years now, and in the course of my involvement, I have noted that we run up against this central question again and again: how can we establish Gaelic as the normal language in our small, new Gaelic community? And by 'normal' here, I mean that the norm of language use at the College would be to speak Gaelic. How do we establish and strengthen norms of Gaelic use amongst speakers of different abilities, backgrounds and confidence, speakers who come to the College with various different language ideologies they have acquired in different socialisation sites, in traditional communities or as learners or as urban Gaelic activists, all with different expectations of diglossic patterns and appropriate use of English and Gaelic together? How do we establish a new language ideology at the College against the always-encroaching and powerful Anglophone ideology that is hegemonic in Britain?

This is not only an important and difficult question for Sabhal Mòr Ostaig, but it is the sort of question that confronts anyone who seeks to restrengthen a threatened language. To revitalise a language, we have to establish a new ideology about the value and use of that language, but I don't believe that we have a clear picture yet of how this process works. Much of my research interest centres on this question, and I have conducted most of this research in Ireland, looking at the circulation of language ideology in new Irish-language communities, in Gaeltachtaí nua, both in the Republic of Ireland and in Northern Ireland, and specifically, investigating how these communities work to establish norms of Irish-language use, and how they debate, agree on and defend these norms over time.

In this paper, I will discuss just one of these communities, Carntogher, near Maghera in Northern Ireland. I chose Carntogher, in part, because I would like to recommend this initiative as an example of good practice in language development at the community level. I believe that the Carntogher Gaeltacht project represents a model of language revitalisation that would be of interest to other small towns and rural areas in Ireland and Scotland that are working to revitalise Irish or Scottish Gaelic in their own communities. But I also chose Carntogher because their stated goal includes the notion of creating a bilingual community, and this project will provide us with a good jump off point for discussing bilingualism as a policy goal in general and what that goal might imply concerning language norms at the micro level.

Carntogher refers to the rural areas to the north and west of Maghera, with the little village of Tirkane as its focus. Maghera is a medium-sized market town on the A6, about an hour by car from Belfast. The Carntogher initiative is being organised by the Carntogher Community Association (Coiste Forbartha Charn Tóchair), a vanguard of successful community activists that live in and around Maghera. Their goal is to re-establish their community as a Gaeltacht within fifty years or two generations, and they define what they mean by a Gaeltacht as a community that is bilingual but that functions predominantly through the medium of the Irish Language, as we read here in their primary objective,

> Within two generations or 50 years to develop a bilingual community where the Irish-language becomes the accepted medium of communication of the majority of the community. (Coiste Forbartha Charn Tóchair agus Glór na nGael, Carn Tóchair 2008: 11)

This is an ambitious goal, and at first glance we would be tempted to dismiss the Gaeltacht project as un-doable. In Ireland, in the 20th century, here have been many more examples of neo-Gaeltacht initiatives that have failed than have succeeded. Nonetheless, after meeting the activists involved, and studying their project, I would suggest that we should take this project seriously. This Gaeltacht revival is not being proposed by a lone individual or a new group, but by an established group of experienced community development activists that can boast that they have already successfully completed a long and impressive list of community and language development projects. But it is certainly an ambitious goal, and a large part of their task is selling their community on the notion of reviving the Gaeltacht. In the course of my research, I observed the activists spending much time and effort on promoting their project and involved in what Joshua Fishman would call ideological clarification in their community. (Fishman 2001a: 451–8; discussed in Dauenhauer and Dauenhauer 1998, King 2000) In interviews with language activists in the community, I investigated this ideological process.

The definition of a Gaeltacht offered by the Community Association is relatively specific, and it is backed up by an extensive strategy document published by the Community Association that details their vision of a bilingual community. (Coiste Forbartha Charn Tóchair agus Glór na nGael, Carn Tóchair 2008) It is clear from the policy goal we read above, when the Community Association proposes that 'the Irish-language becomes the accepted medium of communication of the majority of the community,' that they are proposing a new language norm, that Irish will be the normal language of communication in the community, although the community will still be, in some sense, bilingual.

However, the Irish-revival movement in Carntogher is bottom-up and grass-roots to a large degree, and not all Irish language activists in the area are closely connected to the Carntogher Community Association. I conducted interviews with Irish-language activists in the Carntogher area in 2007 and 2008, and in these interviews, I noted that activists at different degrees of remove from the Community Association understood the notion of a bilingual community as a policy goal in different ways.

These following interviewees are all Irish-language activists who were not closely connected to the Community Association. The first interviewee is somewhat pessimistic about the chances that the Gaeltacht initiative will succeed, and expresses this by drawing a distinction between an Irish-speaking area and a bilingual community,

> Well in terms of this becoming an Irish-speaking area again, would you be saying like if people would be turning this area into the majority of people speaking Irish for example, I think that's very, very long term. I would be surprised to see that happen within 50 years. [...] I think at best you can make it bilingual and so when it comes to this area, you know, maybe bilingual is more realistic.

Although it is not exactly clear from this extract how he understands the word bilingual, the interviewee is clear that he understands that bilingual is different from Irish-speaking, and implies somehow less Irish use. If this interviewee believes that the Community Association may be aiming too high, the next interviewee believes that the Community Association is not aiming high enough, but uses a similar distinction between Irish-speaking and bilingual to express her aspirations for the language,

> Well, I will be pushing to have a completely Irish-speaking area within 50 years instead of a bilingual area.

I was intrigued by these different understandings of the word bilingual, and where possible, I asked interviewees to elaborate. The following interviewee is describing how she understands the goal of the Gaeltacht project,

> TCA: What do you think [the Community Association's] general goal is for the language?

> Interviewee: Their goal is to have Irish as... that we will be bilingual, not that we will be an Irish-speaking community, I think they would

say that's not realistic, but that we will be bilingual. I think that's what they're aiming for.

TCA: Do you think that they have a specific idea of what bilingual means? Are they shooting for a certain percentage of the population or do they want to see Irish spoken in certain areas of life? What do you think they mean by bilingual?

Interviewee: I think that they mean that they would like to see it generally that people would be as comfortable speaking Irish as English and that they would be able to use it in all aspects.

In my second question, I suggest a couple ways that bilingualism might be understood, demographically or in terms of language use, but the interviewee rejects both these definitions, and instead explains that she understands the goal of bilingualism as speakers generally being comfortable in both languages, and also perhaps, as the opportunity to choose to use either Irish or English in all aspects of life in the Carntogher area. I will come back to this notion of free choice below, but for now, it is enough to see again that the interviewee understands that a bilingual community and an Irish-speaking community are two different things, and that this understanding is different from how the Community Association understands the goal of a bilingual community as a Gaeltacht.

The confusion here is clearly with the word bilingual and the concept of social bilingualism. Gaelic/English bilingualism is not only a policy goal advanced in this small community, but in one form or another, it is also a frequently cited policy goal in Scotland and Ireland at all levels: in families, businesses, schools and universities, voluntary organisations and governmental bodies both local and national. In the case of the strategy document under special consideration in this volume, the 20 Year Strategy for the Irish Language, the words bilingual and bilingualism appear frequently throughout the document. In the prospectus for the conference that proceeded the papers in this volume, I detect some unease with bilingualism as a policy goal, a sense, perhaps, that bilingualism is underspecified and could make for weak policy as a result. The relevant section of the prospectus reads,

Repeatedly, throughout the Strategy draft, the notion of **bilingualism** is raised, but is it a policy for bilingualism which lies behind the Strategy, and if so what is that Policy? In the context of the Strategy, what does it mean to be bilingual? If a truly bilingual Ireland is to be achieved, what are the key elements needed to bring it about? The Strategy may be a springboard for bilingualism, but it isn't a mission statement as there are many implications not spelled out, and many weak links. (emphasis in the original)

My research in Carntogher would confirm that bilingualism as a policy goal is problematic and that social bilingualism is understood in a range of sometimes contradictory ways. In the course of my research, I witnessed the activists on the Carntogher Community Association doing an admirable job of clarifying their goals and promoting their project to their community. However, we can see from the data I presented here that there is still some confusion, and that not all Irish-language activists in the community understand bilingualism in the same way as it is understood in the strategy documents published by the Community Association. I would say that the Community Association are doing the right thing and clarifying what they mean by bilingual with reference to specific norms of language use. And hopefully, over time, as they continue working on ideological clarification in their community, this linkage between bilingualism and specific norms of Irish use will become generally clearer to all.

The problem is that unless this linkage is made, bilingualism is underspecified and is a poor policy goal in this respect. I would suggest that it may be time to reassess bilingualism as a policy goal in Ireland and in Scotland at all levels. Bilingualism is often understood as a choice between two languages in a given situation, or in society as a whole. Citizens are imagined as linguistic consumers who can choose to live their lives in Gaelic or English, or a mix of both. This neo-liberal notion of free choice may sit more comfortably next to ideologies of civic nationalism, but it fails to describe how languages are actually used in a multilingual and multiglossic society. (Petrovic 2005, McEwan-Fujita 2005) In actual practice, language use is rarely a matter of free choice alone. (Clayton 2008) The choices we make about the languages we use are tightly structured by powerful linguistic norms. As a dominant ideology, the Anglophone ideology of English use in Britain and Ireland has been naturalised, de-historicised and de-politicised to the extent that it is largely invisible to social actors from day to day, but it nonetheless compels us to use English in most situations. Unless there are some situations or sites where Irish use and Scottish Gaelic use are made the accepted norms, the languages will not be spoken.

As an illustration of the role of norms in language revitalisation, consider two successes of the Scottish Gaelic Revival: BBC Radio nan Gàidheal (Cormack 2004) and Gaelic-medium primary education (NicNeacail and MacÌomhair 2007, O'Hanlon 2010). These two projects are both successful by at least two different measures. They have a teleologic value in that they provide important services in Gaelic, namely, broadcasting in Gaelic and educating children in Gaelic. But they also have an intrinsic value in that they open up new sites of Gaelic use and this further strengthens Gaelic as a normalised spoken language in everyday life. In other words, by this intrinsic measure, they are successful insofar as they establish new Gaelic language norms. Of course, in both cases, there is an element of choice involved. Where the service is available, listeners can choose to tune into Radio nan Gàidheal or not, and where a Gaelic unit is available, parents can choose to have their children educated in Gaelic or not. And further, depending on qualifications and employment opportunities, teachers and radio presenters may have a choice to work in the Gaelic sector or not. But when it comes to the sites of language use themselves, there is no choice. In both cases, a new Gaelic language norm has been established and is daily defended. Undoubtedly, most presenters on Radio nan Gàidheal agree with the Gaelic language ideology of the station and willingly speak Gaelic on air, but nonetheless, their use of Gaelic in that specific situation is not subject to their own personal choice. If a Radio nan Gàidheal presenter chose to broadcast in English, she would be told to return to speaking Gaelic on air or find a new job. So too, if a teacher of a Gaelic-medium class chose to speak primarily in English to his students, he would eventually be told to return to teaching in Gaelic or find a post teaching an English-medium class. Teleologic value is typically a measure of the value of the explicit purpose of a project, and therefore it is not surprising that when we evaluate revival and revitalisation projects, we tend to pay greater attention to the projects' teleologic value than the projects' intrinsic value in establishing new norms. However, I suspect that if we were to closely examine different successful language revival and revitalisation projects from around the world, we would find that many or even most of these projects are successful *because* they establish new language norms in strategic sites or situations.

In this paper I am focusing on the question of norms and social bilingualism, but social bilingualism also implies some degree of individual bilingualism, and just as a bilingual policy can be ambiguous concerning expectations of language use, it can also be ambiguous concerning expectations of language ability. If an organisation or a polity subscribes to a policy of bilingualism, who will be expected to know which languages and to what degree? Is it always clear, and if it is not clear, what is happening behind that unclarity? Will everyone be expected to acquire both languages, or as is often the case, will ability in only one language, the dominant language, be required of all members, and what then does this say about the relative status of the threatened language and the relative power of its speakers? In popular and political discourse, a bilingual policy may be understood as a commitment to treat both languages equally and all speakers fairly, but this can be a further point of confusion. If in practice a bilingual policy implicitly sanctions unidirectional bilingualism (Fishman 2001b: 9) and therefore sanctions the continuing privilege of monolingual speakers of the dominant language, then the two languages will not have equal status. In this way, the potential unclarity of bilingualism as a policy goal can mask unequal power and privilege based on language.

I would suggest that, in place of bilingualism, or perhaps, in addition to bilingualism, it may be time to reconsider an older policy goal, and that is restoration. In the Irish context, restoration and bilingualism are often understood as opposing meta-policies, (cf. Ó Croidheáin 2006: 131–263; Ó Laoire 2005: 258–278), but in practice, each contains the other. For example, even if Irish was restored as the normal language in most domains in the Republic of Ireland, the Republic would certainly remain to some extent a bilingual, or indeed, a multilingual society. Johann Gottfried von Herder's (2002) conception of the nation as a single culture with a single language is deeply embedded in the ideology of nationalism in Europe (Blommaert and Verschueren 1998, Dorian 1998), but we now understand that the truly monolingual polity is a rare anomaly and that language contact and social multilingualism are overwhelmingly the rule (Aikhenvald 2002). And at the same time, as I am arguing here, any meaningful definition of sustainable social bilingualism implies the restoration of Irish as the normal means of communication in some domains, situations or sites.

I would argue that restoration may be a useful policy goal, both in Ireland and in Scotland, because it foregrounds the question, where? Where will Irish be restored? Where will Scottish Gaelic be restored? And where will English remain the dominant language? The danger with bilingualism is that it is so underspecified, it elides the question of where specifically minority languages will be used. If we are going to restore the use of Irish or Scottish Gaelic, we should ask, where, when, in what specific sites or situations will Irish or Scottish Gaelic be used as the normal means of communication? In a multilingual society and in the context of multiple contested language ideologies, the question of what norms of language use will apply in what situations can be sensitive and politically difficult, and we might be tempted to postpone the debate with deliberately vague policy goals. But while this question might be postponed, if the debate on norms and goals is put off indefinitely, the dominant, naturalised, default language ideology will inevitably prevail.

Effective language planning is about attending to actual language use above all else: asking at each stage of the planning process how a given strategy, initiative or development will lead to real use of the language. Restoration as a policy goal is valuable because it emphasises norms of language use and encourages us to ask in concrete detail where and how norms of minority language use will be established and defended.

Acknowledgments

This paper is based on research undertaken in the pursuit of a PhD and I would like to thank my advisors, Iain Mac an Tàilleir, Dr. Meg Bateman and Dr. John Walsh, as well as my examiners, Dr. Gillian Rothach and Professor Roibeard Ó Maolalaigh, for their assistance and advice. I would also like to thank Niall Ó Catháin and Liz NicIllEathain who commented on a draft of this paper. This research was made possible by a generous grant from the trustees of Sabhal Mòr Ostaig.

References

Aikhenvald, A. Y. 2002. 'Traditional Multilingualism and Language Endangerment'. In eds. D. and M. Bradley. *Language Endangerment and Language Maintenance*. London: Routledge Curzon. 24–33.

Blommaert, J. and Verschueren, J. 1998. 'The Role of Language in European Nationalist Ideologies'. In eds. B. B. Schieffelin, K. A. Woolard and P. V. Kroskrity. *Language Ideologies, Practice and Theory*. Oxford: Oxford University Press. 189–210.

Clayton, S. 2008. 'The Problem of 'Choice' and the Construction of the Demand for English in Cambodia'. *Language Policy* 7.2: 143–64.

Coiste Forbartha Charn Tóchair agus Glór na nGael, Carn Tóchair. 2008. *An Bealach Chun Tosaigh; Straitéis don Ghaeilge i gCarn Tóchair agus i Machaire Rátha*. www.ancarn.org/projects/language-development/strateis–22.pdf, retrieved: 29-9-2010

Cormack, M. 2004. 'Gaelic in the Media'. *Scottish Affairs* 46: 23–43.

Dauenhauer, N. M. and Dauenhauer, R. 1998. 'Technical, Emotional, and Ideological Issues in Reversing Language Shift: Examples from Southeast Alaska'. In eds. L. A. Grenoble and L. J. Whaley. *Endangered Languages, Current Issues and Future Prospect*. Cambridge: Cambridge University Press. 57–98.

Dorian, N. C. 1998. 'Western Language Ideologies and Small-language Prospects'. In eds. L. A. Grenoble and L. J. Whaley. *Endangered Languages, Current Issues and Future Prospect*. Cambridge: Cambridge University Press. 3–21.

Fishman, J.A. 2001a. 'From Theory to Practice (and Vice Versa): Review, Reconsideration and Reiteration'. In ed. J. A. Fishman. *Can Threatened Languages Be Saved?* Clevedon: Multilingual Matters. 451–83.

Fishman, J. A. 2001b. 'Why is it so Hard to Save a Threatened Language?' In ed. J. A. Fishman. *Can Threatened Languages Be Saved?* Clevedon: Multilingual Matters Ltd. 1–22

Herder, J.G. 2002. *Philosophical Writings*. Cambridge: Cambridge University Press.

King, K.A. 2000. 'Language Ideologies and Heritage Language Education'. *International Journal of Bilingual Education and Bilingualism* 3.3: 167–84.

Kroskrity, P.V. 2004. 'Language Ideologies'. In ed. A. Durant. *A Companion to Linguistic Anthropology*. Oxford: Oxford University Press. 496–517.

McEwan-Fujita, E. 2005. 'Neoliberalism and minority-language planning in the Highlands and Islands of Scotland'. *The International Journal of the Sociology of Language* 171: 155–71.

NicNeacail, M. and Maclomhair, M.M. eds. 2007. *Foghlam tro Mheadhan na Gàidhlig.* Edinburgh: Dunedin Academic Press.

Ó Croidheáin, C. 2006. *Language from Below, The Irish Language Ideology and Power in 20th Century Ireland.* Oxford: Peter Lang.

O'Hanlon, F. 2010. 'Gaelic-medium Primary Education in Scotland: Towards a New Taxonomy?' In eds. G. Munro and I. Mac an Tàilleir. *Coimhearsnachd na Gàidhlig an-Diugh / Gaelic Communities Today.* Edinburgh: Dunedin Academic Press. 99–116

Ó Laoire, M. 2005. 'The Language Planning Situation in Ireland'. *Current Issues in Language Planning* 6.3: 251–314.

Petrovic, J. E. 2005. 'The Conservative Restoration and Neoliberal Defenses of Bilingual Education'. *Language Policy* 4: 395–416.

Woolard, K. A. and Schieffelin, B. B. 1994. 'Language Ideology'. *Annual Review of Anthropology* 23: 55–82

Observations on Bilingualism in Digital Media

Dòmhnall Caimbeul and Eilean Green

Introduction

This paper reflects upon the need for the Gaelic language to avail itself of 'new media' in order to grow and survive. The main premise of the discussion is how the Gaelic speaking population is and should be beginning to use new digital media, or rather how it should experiment with it. Firstly, this paper will look at why BBC ALBA as a Gaelic channel, not a bilingual channel, has a strong bilingual offering to its audiences. Secondly, the paper will explore how the Gaelic language is dealing with the arrival of a phenomenon that is becoming at least as important as television, that is, new media.

BBC ALBA: A National Television Offering

For Gaelic to survive and grow in the twenty-first century, the champions of the language will have to adopt radical and brave strategies. BBC ALBA, launched on 19 September 2008, is only available on the digital satellite platform and still awaits the decision of the BBC Trust on whether or not universal carriage into all television-viewing households in Scotland will be achieved any time soon. The Gaelic channel, a long held aspiration for many Gaelic speakers, has been established but it has taken some fifty years to do so since television first entered our households; and even now it only has partial coverage in a world of fragmented digital media provision.

A recent Ofcom report confirmed that in Scotland we watch an average of 4.2 hours of television per day[1]. For many, Television is their most common and constant influence: it can stand in for mother, father, teacher and often babysitter, and for others it is their companion throughout the day. Now this friend of ours can finally speak Gaelic. A challenge for BBC ALBA is that it competes with almost 500 other channels, almost all of which are English language. One of the characteristics of broadcasting, much like publishing, is that it is the communication of the few to the many. Regulators and legislators impose obligations and conditions, while the audience makes demands for entertainment, information, education, and increasingly for innovation and inspiration. Ultimately it is the audience that counts – if viewers desert the channel, the channel will fall. Television is an expensive business and this places responsibility on the handful of people who commission and schedule the channel. This small team must meet the aspirations of the audience whilst also satisfying the social, economic, linguistic and corporate demands of communities, stakeholders, regulators and others.

For channels such as BBC ALBA, however, the normal challenges of television are supplemented by the demands of broadcasting in a minority language. An indigenous language channel's approach to bilingualism depends on the mission of the channel and whether the channel aspires to speak only to the language community or whether its programming is for speakers and non-speakers alike. The Inuit Broadcasting Corporation and Maori Television, for example, have quite different approaches to television. The following features on the Inuit Broadcasting Corporation website:

---

[1] Ofcom Communications Market Report, Scotland: 19.08.2010

> At IBC, we use the technology of television to make programming that matters to Inuit – programming in our own language of Inuktitut.[2]

Maori Television however, claims:

> We consider that it is a critically important requirement to ensure that Maori Television is deemed to be delivering a high quality and inclusive indigenous television service for all New Zealanders.[3]

The distinction between the two approaches is manifest and undoubtedly comes from the differing needs of the two languages and cultures. Inuit television would appear to be a service about the language community, by the language community, for the language community and Maori Television is an offering by the language community, for the language community, and for all New Zealanders. Closer to home, TG4 and BBC ALBA are nearer to the Maori model – a national television offering. In fact BBC ALBA is tasked with reaching 10 percent of Scottish viewers when less than 2 percent actually speak Gaelic. This therefore drives out a very practical approach to bilingualism – subtitled documentaries, sports and music are key attractions for non-speakers. Sports coverage is visually rich; music transcends language; and documentaries are carefully chosen to have themes that will appeal to wide Scottish audiences and are fully subtitled in English. However BBC ALBA is not a bilingual channel; it is a Gaelic channel that aims to be accessible to non-speakers at certain times through a practical approach to bilingualism.

Embracing Non-broadcast Digital Media to Increase the Richness of Language

In the age of digital media, indigenous languages are once again facing significant challenges from the emerging technology. Those under the age of 15, the so-called 'digital natives', hold Facebook and the iPod to be as necessary to their lives as food and drink. We ought to ask ourselves, will we use the new technology and all it offers to help save our language or will we watch from the sidelines as the new digital media world unfolds around us? With digital technology, connectivity, devices and brands so prominent in the lives of our young people, it is critical to seize the moment; indeed, what part will Gaelic play in this new digital reality and how quickly can we intervene so as to make digital media our friend and advocate?

In the sixth century BC, The military strategist Sun Tzu reputedly wrote in *The Art of War* that:

> Strategy without tactics is the slowest route to victory.
> Tactics without strategy is the noise before defeat.

A strategy is needed if Gaelic and digital media are to have common purpose. Does anyone know what this strategy should be, who should design it or who will implement it? Once we have the strategy, what will be our tactics to deliver it? Furthermore Joel Barker, in his motivational film entitled *The Power of Vision*,[4] stated that:

---

[2] www.inuitbroadcasting.ca/mandate_e.htm

[3] Jim Mather, CEO Maori Television, Personal Communication of 9 June 2009.

[4] Barker, J. 1990. *The Power of Vision* www.media-partners.com/motivation/
the_power_of_vision_by_joel_barker.htm.

> Vision without action is a dream. Action without vision is simply passing
> the time. Action with Vision is making a positive difference.

If Gaelic is to grasp digital media as an enabler of new communities and a facilitator of communication and creativity, we must sometime soon express a shared vision based on a shared understanding of what makes new media so different from old media. We must grasp the fact that there has been a paradigm shift, that old models of top-down intervention and strategy are unlikely to work, and that in all probability the realisation of the vision will depend on opportunism and personal drive at grass-roots level.

The difficulty with digital media is that brands evolve at speed and are not controlled by regulated or political entities. Communications are channelled through powerful global brands – applications such as YouTube, Bebo, Facebook, Twitter, Myspace or devices such as the iPod and iPad – the longevity of which is almost impossible to predict. Already some brands are showing signs of fatigue, and soon we will have moved on to watching Google TV on our television sets, and even to surfing YouTube or Facebook with our families on Saturday nights to watch our friends wedding or holiday videos, or connecting with them on Skype to discuss the programme we are watching. The way we consume our media is changing fast and a Gaelic digital media strategy is needed to move with the trend.

The real paradigm shift is in content-creation. Distribution channels and brands will come and go, but content is king and content will remain king. We no longer need a television commissioner to take decisions – we are all potential commissioners of our own content. We are able to publish our videos, photos, or philosophical musings on a variety of distribution channels to global audiences and we can do so at little or no cost. Media is no longer only about the communication of the few to the many – it is now also about the communication of the many to each other. One difficulty inherent in the use of technology for minority language maintenance is the fact that the web, software, and hardware tend to operate using the English language. Although language-groups in the EU already positively avail themselves of the internet and IT, minority languages are disadvantaged in that technology such as: word-processors, internet browsers, IT manuals, etc, are not available in their languages. There is a niche in the market for investment in these sorts of language resources (Thomas, King, and Jones: 2000). The dominance of English is even a cause for concern for some European state languages, let alone minority languages such as Welsh and Gaelic.

Al Gore, former Vice President to Bill Clinton, once recited a story of the eight-year-old son of the Kyrgyzstan president who told his father:

> I have to learn English.

President Askar Akayev wanted to know why his son, living in a central Asian country, wanted to learn English. His son replied:

> Because, father, the computer speaks English.[5]

Although technology has the potential to hinder the development of minority languages, its' cultural neutrality can be tailored to create new avenues of success for minorities. For example, some minority languages have already integrated themselves into the much standardised world of social media networks. Ó Riagáin *et al.* (2008: 33)

---

[5] Anecdote recited by Al Gore, cited in Erickson, J. 'Cyberspeak: The Death of Diversity. Will the English-Dominated Internet Spell the End of Other Tongues?' 2010 [Available at: cgi.cnn.com/ASIANOW/asiaweek/98/0703/feat_7_millenium.html].

assert that 'informal, interpersonal contexts' have been so important in promoting minority language usage by young people in Ireland, Wales, Catalonia and the Basque region – Scottish Gaelic therefore has a lot to gain from more exposure on these sites. The very fact that the social networking site (SNS), Facebook, is available in 'Pirate English' but not Gaelic demonstrates how much progress is yet to be made for Gaelic on the internet and in social media.

It is important that Gaelic does not simply become the language of the school grounds and that it is expanded out into the social media networks of the young and old. If Gaelic is to prosper, young people in particular need to acknowledge it as their own language and not just as a subject they study in school. New media and the internet are increasingly suitable mediums with which to support and develop Gaelic among the younger generations. In the UK, 49 per cent of children aged 8–17 who use the internet have set up their own profile on a SNS. The likelihood of setting up a profile is highest among 16–24 year olds (54 per cent) (Ofcom, 2008). Gaelic needs to be ever-present in social media; tapping into online and authentic social networks is essential for developing language practice.

What can we Learn about Bilingualism in New Media just from Observation?

Twitter has 75 million users. Apparently 41 percent of its content is *'pointless babble'* and 38 percent is conversation. Very little of this is in Scots Gaelic. *Bbcnaidheachdan*, the Gaelic news broadcaster on twitter, has 144 followers, while Stephen Fry has 1.8 million followers! Of the 144 followers, well over 20 are organisations. Given that the BBC's tweets are wholly in Gaelic and therefore require a Gaelic speaking audience, it is surprising that only a handful of the followers themselves actually tweet in Gaelic, most preferring English. *Gaelicsinger*, on the other hand, has 1,234 followers – tweeting regular bilingual tweets that teach Gaelic words and phrases.

In July 2010, Facebook had 500 million active users – this is equivalent to one in fourteen of the world's population. One of those is Derek 'Pluto' Moireach who has an account to promote his very popular Gaelic radio programme, *Siubhal gu Seachd le Pluto*. Given that one needs to be somewhat fluent in Gaelic to follow this radio programme, it is interesting to note that Pluto adopts a wholly bilingual approach to promoting the programme on Facebook; however ensuing prompts from Pluto, the discussions can veer to Gaelic or English, or be wholly bilingual. There is no rule in play and it is not possible to say with certainty what is driving language choice. It is as if we, as Gaelic speakers, are dipping our toe in the waters, so to speak, and trying to make up our mind what identity our online selves should present.

> [T]he fact remains that the Internet, at this point, is overwhelmingly dominated by a handful of languages ... even if some web sites arise which employ a local language, **speakers of the local language will make greater use of the Internet in a non-local language.**' [Bold added] (Grenoble and Whaley, 2006: 10)

Not a lot of research has been carried out with regard to the presence of Gaelic on social media networks. The most relevant and recent work on this was carried out in Wales by Daniel Cunliffe, Delyth Morris and Cynog Prys (2010: 13), who found that the internet was fundamental to the lives of the majority of the research participants in Wales. All focus group participants had broadband internet access in their houses and some had mobile phones or personal media players (e.g. iPod Touch) with internet access. The internet was the principal source of entertainment in the home for many of the participants who used the internet for social networking, gaming, homework, shopping, and viewing television programs. The researchers also found that their Facebook community was a close reflection of their real world community. However Facebook offered easier access to a wider community and the focus group participants used the SNSs (mainly Facebook) to keep in touch with friends from different towns, and their extended family that lived outside of their local community. Interestingly, a key research finding was that individuals tend to speak just one language with another individual and do not change according to the form of communication. The language use of those included in this study was the same on SNSs as the language use in their daily lives. There were a further two notable points: Facebook users writing in Welsh were likely to 'code-switch', often using English words and sentences in Welsh messages; secondly, status updates, which are a form of mass communication to all Facebook friends, tended to be in English. Reasons given included the desire to be inclusive.

The work conducted by Honeycutt and Cunliffe (2010) shows that the Welsh language has been normalised to some extent within Facebook. It emerged that 45 percent of the personal profiles which featured Welsh, featured only Welsh. Conversely, 29 per cent of Welsh speakers were not using Welsh on their profiles at all (Hodges, 2006, 2009 cited in Cunliffe, Morris and Prys, 2010). Studies on the use of Welsh in texts and emails revealed that young people in the South East of Wales, who have been educated through the medium of Welsh, are not predisposed to speaking Welsh with each other. However these same young people use Welsh to a great extent when texting and emailing each other (Hodges, 2006, 2009, cited in Cunliffe, Morris and Prys, 2010). The reverse was true in the Gaeltacht in Ireland where Fleming and Debski (2007, cited in Cunliffe, Morris and Prys, 2010) found that while young, fluent Irish speakers spoke Irish with their friends in person, they considered English to be the language of 'networked communications'.

The reality is that new media, such as SNSs, offer new avenues for minority languages such as Welsh and Gaelic especially with regard to the younger population with whom the future of the language depends. The more a minority language is integrated into social media; the better off it will be as a result. According to *Digital Inspiration: A Strategy for Scotland's Digital Media Industry*:[6] 'One of the abiding truths of all societies is that if you don't innovate you evaporate.' As David Crystal puts it: 'an endangered language will progress if its speakers can make use of electronic technology'. (2000: 141) The belief that digital media can enhance the riches of language and can offer new opportunities to minority language communities is shared by many. There is so much potential for Gaelic in the media. Minority language media at the grassroots level can voice out local stories; create a community of minority language speakers online; and make a language more accessible to second-language learners. New media will help to bond Gaelic communities that are geographically dispersed. MG ALBA Board Member, Ken MacKinnon, suggests that the key to language prosperity is to use the media to our advantage:

> If there is to be no effective strategy to retain living Gaelic communities,
> is it reasonable to ask what would replace them as the principal means

---

[6] The Scottish Digital Media Industry Advisory Group. *Digital Inspiration: A Strategy for Scotland's Digital Media Industry.* [available at: www.digitalinspiration.org.uk/Digital-Inspiration.pdf, last accessed September 2010].

of ensuring language reproduction? Could a virtual Gaelic community located somewhere in cyberspace ensure a future for the language? (MacKinnon 2006)

Although the media is no replacement for passing on a language through the family and community, it cannot be ignored. Using Gaelic in social/communication media will help to normalise the language and raise the profile of the Gaelic language as a living language, and at next to no financial cost. The media are crucial for communicating and sharing cultures, and producing cultural resources that will be available online and worldwide for years to come (Cormack, 2004: 2).

To conclude, we should ask ourselves what Sun Tzu would be saying if he had a Facebook page. This military strategist would look at the map of Scotland and the distribution of Gaelic speakers and, amongst other things, advise a *strategy* to create new communities of electronically networked individuals who are prepared to champion Gaelic at a grassroots level together. The *tactics* should be to offer incentives to stimulate Gaelic new media creation, to use television to create celebrities and role models and to create the conditions for Gaelic digital media 'super users' to emerge. An example of such development already underway is the MG ALBA FilmG project which in its first two years created conditions for over 50 new user-generated short films in Gaelic and in 2010 attracted 71 such films, more than one short film per 1000 speakers!

Whatever Sun Tzu would advise, the parting thought is that the champions of Gaelic should plan and act now and not rely on a 'wait and see' approach to digital media. The stakes are too high and the opportunity is now. A top-down approach driven by regulation and policy will not work. Instead those in a position to make policy and investment decisions should ensure that Gaelic speakers and learners become super-literate in digital media and have many different opportunities for digital media participation with fellow speakers and learners in whatever way, shape or form they choose and using whichever brands and channels that are currently in vogue. We should embrace the digital-only future with the aim of reviving our language communities and for this to succeed our speakers and learners need to be active creators of, as well as consumers of media.

References

Cormack, M. 2004. 'Gaelic in the Media'. *Scottish Affairs* 46.
[available at: www.scottishaffairs.org/backiss/pdfs/sa46/SA46_Cormack.pdf]
Crystal, D. 2002. *Language Death*. Cambridge: Cambridge: Cambridge University Press.
Cunliffe, D., Morris, D. and C. Prys, C. 2010. 'Investigating the Differential use of Welsh in Young Speakers' Social Networks: A Comparison of Communication in Face-to-face Settings, in Electronic Texts and on Social Networking Sites'. Unpublished Paper.
Fleming A. and R. Debski. 2007. 'The Use of Irish in Networked Communications: A Study of Schoolchildren in Different Language Settings'. *Journal of Multilingual and Multicultural Development*. 28.2: 85–101.
Grenoble L.A. and L.J. Whaley. 2006. *Saving Languages: An Introduction to Language Revitalization*. Cambridge University Press.

Hodges, Rh. 2006. *Cymoedd y De: Defnydd o'r Gymraeg ar ôl Cyfnod Ysgol? Astudiaeth o Bobl Ifanc yng Nghwm Rhymni* / The South Wales Valleys: The Use of Welsh after Leaving School: A Study of Young People in the Rhymni Valley. Unpublished MA Thesis, Bangor: University of Wales.

Hodges, Rh. 2009. 'Welsh Language Use Among Young People in the Rhymney Valley'. *Contemporary Wales* 22: 16–35.

Honeycutt, C. and D. Cunliffe. 2010. 'The use of the Welsh Language on Facebook: An Initial Investigation' *Information, Communication and Society* 13.2. 226–48.

King, T.N. and G. Jones. 2000. *Linguistic Diversity on the Internet: Assessment of the Contribution of Machine Translation*, European Parliament: Stoa Publications.

MacKinnon, K. 2006. 'Migration, Family and Education in Gaelic Policy Perspective'. Presentation to the Language-Planning and Policy Seminar: Migration and Gaelic Community Dilution, University of Edinburgh, 8 March 2006. [Available at: www.sgrud.org.uk/anfy/celtic/mig_family_edu/mig_fam_edu.htm last accessed September 2010]

Ó Riagáin, P; Williams, G; and F. Xavier Vila i Moreno, F. 2008. *Young People and Minority Languages: Language Use outside the Classroom*. Dublin: Trinity College Centre for Language and Communication Studies.

Thomas, N., King A. and E.H. Gruffydd Jones. 2000. *Linguistic Diversity on the Internet: Assessment of the Contribution of Machine Translation*. Study commissioned by the European Parliament. STOA Publications.

'From Politics to Practice': A' Cruthachadh Plana Gàidhlig do Phàrlamaid na h-Alba

Alasdair MacCaluim

Ro-ràdh

Bheir an taisbeanadh seo sùil air cruthachadh plana Gàidhlig reachdail Pàrlamaid na h-Alba, a' coimhead air a' phròiseas, air na dùbhlanan agus air na cothroman a bha an lùib seo. Tòisichidh sinn le bhith a' toirt sùil air an fhrèam reachdail airson planadh cànain airson na Gàidhlig ann an Alba.

Achd na Gàidhlig (Alba) 2005

Ghabh Pàrlamaid na h-Alba ri Achd na Gàidhlig le taic thar-phàrtaidh anns a' Ghiblean 2005. B' e adhbhar na h-Achd a bhith a' brosnachadh na Gàidhlig ann am beatha phoblach na h-Alba agus a bhith a' brosnachadh cleachdadh na cànain anns an dachaigh, anns a' choimhearsnachd, ann am foghlam agus san àite obrach. Tha an Achd:

- A' stèidheachadh buidheann Ghàidhlig reachdail, Bòrd na Gàidhlig, gus a' Ghàidhlig a bhrosnachadh.
- Ag iarraidh air a' Bhòrd 'Plana Nàiseanta na Gàidhlig' a dheasachadh a bhrosnaicheas cleachdadh is tuigse na Gàidhlig, foghlam Gàidhlig agus cultar na Gàidhlig. Tha na prìomhachasan is amasan airson leasachadh na cànain air an cur an cèill sa phlana seo.
- A' toirt cumhachd don Bhòrd toirt air buidhnean poblach planaichean Gàidhlig a dheasachadh, a' nochdadh mar a chleachdas iad Gàidhlig agus mar a bheir iad cothrom a cleachdadh.

A rèir na h-Achd, feumar na dleastanasan aig Bòrd na Gàidhlig, a' gabhail a-steach am Plana Nàiseanta, a bhith air an cur an gnìomh *'with a view to securing the status of the Gaelic language as an official language of Scotland commanding equal respect to the English language'*.

Bha Buidheann Chorporra Pàrlamaid na h-Alba (*The Scottish Parliamentary Corporate Body* – SPCB) air aon de na ciad sia buidhnean poblach air an do dh' iarr Bòrd na Gàidhlig plana Gàidhlig a chruthachadh.

Gàidhlig ann am Pàrlamaid na h-Alba

Bha an SPCB toilichte gun deach iarraidh air Plana Gàidhlig a stèidheachadh, chan e a-mhàin a chionn 's gun deach an Achd aontachadh anns a' Phàrlamaid ach cuideachd a chionn 's gun robh a' Phàrlamaid a' dèanamh tòrr airson na Gàidhlig mar-thà. Bha seo a' gabhail a-steach còir sgrìobhadh don Phàrlamaid anns a' Ghàidhlig, a bhith a' foillseachadh roghainn farsaing de dh'fhoillsichidhean anns a' Ghàidhlig, a bhith a' toirt seachad seirbheisean foghlaim sa Phàrlamaid agus sa choimhearsnachd agus a bhith a' fastadh oifigear Gàidhlig.

Thug am plana tòrr chothroman dhuinn. Ged a tha a' Phàrlamaid a' dèanamh tòrr airson na Gàidhlig mar-thà, thug am plana cothrom dhuinn. Mar tè de na buidhnean poblach a bha a' cleachdadh na Gàidhlig as motha, thug e cothrom dhuinn ar deagh chleachdadh a nochdadh do bhuidhnean eile agus a bhith a' seatainn dè ghabhadh dèanamh ann am planaichean Gàidhlig nàiseanta.

Thug am plana cothrom dhuinn sùil a thoirt air a' Ghàidhlig tron bhuidhinn air fad agus a bhith ag àbhaisteachadh na Gàidhlig anns na pròiseasan againn far a bheil sin iomchaidh. Chunnacas an t-àbhaisteachadh seo an gnìomh ann am pròiseas sgrìobhaidh a' phlana oir chaidh seo a dhèanamh le buidheann-ghnìomha le luchd-obrach às a h-uile prìomh sgioba anns a' Phàrlamaid – gus am beachdan fhaighinn, gus dèanamh cinnteach gun robh an taic ri amasan a' phlana bhon chiad dol a-mach agus gus dèanamh cinnteach gun toireadh am plana buaidh air a' Phàrlamaid air fad.

A bharrachd air na cothroman, bha dùbhlanan ann cuideachd. A chionn 's gun robh sinn air aon de na ciad buidhnean a bha a' deasachadh plana Gàidhlig, bha sinn ann am pròiseas ionnsachaidh, mar a bha Bòrd na Gàidhlig fhèin! Cha robh teamplaid no eisimpleir ann airson plana a b' urrainn dhuinn leantainn agus cha deach an stiùireadh reachdail air deasachadh planaichean Gàidhlig a chrìochnachadh gus an robh ar plana aig ìre gu math adhartach.

Bha a' Phàrlamaid ann an suidheachadh air leth a chionn 's gur sinne a' chiad bhuidheann nàiseanta a chruthaich plana Gàidhlig. Bha na buidhnean eile a dh'ullaich Plana Gàidhlig aig an aon àm uile nan ùghdarrasan ionadail no nam buidhnean poblach air a' Ghàidhealtachd.

Cha robh e furasta a bhith a' co-dhùnadh dè an ìre de sholarachadh a bhiodh iomchaidh airson buidheann phoblach nàiseanta. Anns a' phlana, bha againn ri aontachadh gu bheil sinn 'airson am prionnsabal a chur an gnìomh gu bheil Gàidhlig agus Beurla airidh air spèis cho-ionnan'. Anns an reachdas fhèin, chaidh an abairt 'co-ionnanachd spèise' (no *equal respect*) a chleachdadh gus cur ri inbhe na Gàidhlig ach a bhith ag aithneachadh aig an aon àm gun robh diofar shuidheachaidhean aig a' chànain ann an diofar sgìrean ann an Alba agus gus diofar ìrean de sholarachadh a cheadachadh ann an diofar àiteachan is shuidheachaidhean. Bha an t-sùbailteachd seo feumail ach bha e a' ciallachadh gun robh e gu math doirbh a bhith cho cinnteach ri cinnteach dè dìreach a bha 'co-ionnanachd spèise' a' ciallachadh a chionn 's nach deach a shònrachadh is a mhìneachadh gu h-iomlan is gu soilleir. Bha e doirbh gu sònraichte a bhith cinnteach na bha 'co-ionnanachd spèise' a' ciallachadh aig an ìre nàiseanta. Agus cha robh mòran idir anns an stiùireadh reachdail aig Bòrd na Gàidhlig air na bhathar a' sùileachadh bho bhuidhnean nàiseanta nas motha.

Tha an stiùireadh aig Bòrd na Gàidhlig air planaichean Gàidhlig ag innse dhuinn gu bheil 'spèis cho-ionann' a' ciallachadh gum bu chòir dhuinn a bhith 'cho taiceil agus cho coibhneil 's a ghabhas ri leasachadh na Gàidhlig' no *supportive and generous to Gaelic development* agus gum bu chòir do phlanaichean a bhith air an deasachadh 'le sùil ri cleachdadh na Gàidhlig a dhèanamh cho furasta 's a ghabhas a rèir an t-suidheachaidh aice fhèin' no *with a view to facilitating the use of Gaelic to the greatest extent that is appropriate to its individual circumstances'*. Dh'obraich sinn gu dlùth leis a' Bhòrd air ceist na co-ionnanachd spèise.

Bha Bòrd na Gàidhlig fada den bheachd gun robh ceuman samhlachail gus inbhe na Gàidhlig a thoirt am follais barrachd leithid soidhnichean dà-chànanach air leth fhèin cudromach airson buidhne nàiseanta mar an SPCB. Airson solarachadh sheirbheisean, chaidh a ghabhail ris gun robh eadar-dhealachadh ann eadar buidheann phoblach Ghàidhealach agus an SPCB mar bhuidhinn nàiseanta stèidhichte an Dùn

Èideann agus mar sin, dh'fhaodte nach fheumar an aon ìre no roghainn de sheirbheisean Gàidhlig a thoirt seachad. Ged a b' urrainn dhuinn na seirbheisean againn airson na dùthcha air fad a thoirt seachad gu dà-chànanach – leithid ar làrach-lìn is foillseachaidhean – bha sinn a' faireachdainn mar eisimpleir nach robh e practaigeach dèanamh cinnteach gum biodh daoine le Gàidhlig anns an ionad-fhàilte no air an *switchboard* a chionn 's gum biodh ìre cleachdaidh nan seirbheisean seo ìosal agus nach biodh seo na dheagh chleachdadh de na goireasan a bh' againn. A dh'aindeoin seo, ge-tà, tha sinn a' toirt seachad roghainn fharsaing de sheirbheisean Gàidhlig mar a chithear a dh'aithghearr.

B' e an dùbhlan mu dheireadh dhuinn an t-eadar-dhealachadh eadar an SPCB agus Pàrlamaid na h-Alba fhèin. Tha na dreuchdan reachdail aig Pàrlamaid na h-Alba eadar-dhealaichte bho na dreuchdan rianachd aig an SPCB. Is e an SPCB a' bhuidheann air an deach iarraidh plana Gàidhlig a dheasachadh agus bha an t-eadar-dhealachadh seo doirbh don phoball tuigsinn, gu h-àraidh a chionn 's gu bheil cleachdadh na Gàidhlig ann an gnothaichean oifigeil na Pàrlamaid cudromach gu samhlachail do thòrr dhaoine.

Tha solarachadh ann airson cleachdadh na Gàidhlig, gun teagamh, ach tha seo taobh a-muigh raon-ùghdarrais an SPCB agus thathar a' dèiligeadh ri seo tro Ghnàth-riaghailtean [*standing orders*] na Pàrlamaid agus mar sin, dh'fheumadh atharrachadh sam bith tighinn tron Phàrlamaid fhèin agus chan ann tron phlana Ghàidhlig againn.

Na th' ann am Plana Gàidhlig Buidheann Chorporra Pàrlamaid na h-Alba (SPCB)

B' iad seo na prìomh gheallaidhean ùra anns a' phlana Gàidhlig againn:

- A' toirt a-steach ìomhaigh chorporra dhà-chànanach
- A' cur suas barrachd shoidhnichean dà-chànanach anns a' Phàrlamaid (tha na soidhnichean poblach agus na soidhnichean treòrachaidh uile a-nis dà-chànanach)
- A' toirt a-steach roghainn de dh'fhoirmean Gàidhlig
- A' toirt a-steach barrachd chothroman goireasan eadar-theangachadh mar-aon a chleachdadh aig coinneamhan poblach.
- A' cur ris na foillseachaidhean a tha rim faighinn anns a' Ghàidhlig – tha na foillseachaidhean fiosrachaidh is foghlaim uile a-nis rim faighinn sa Ghàidhlig.
- A' leasachadh duilleagan Gàidhlig Pàrlamaid na h-Alba (a' gabhail a-staigh URL Gàidhlig ùr)
- A' cur air dòigh trèanadh mothachaidh Gàidhlig (*Gaelic Awareness Training*) airson luchd-obrach a bhios ag obair leis a' phoball.
- Ag atharrachadh pròiseasan fastaidh gus feart a thoirt air a' Ghàidhlig
- A' dèanamh cinnteach gum bi a' Ghàidhlig mar phàirt de phròiseas poileasaidh is measaidh na Pàrlamaid.

Togaidh seo air an t-solarachadh a th' againn mar-thà a tha a' gabhail a-steach:

- A' cur fàilte air litrichean/post-d/fianais/athchuingean anns a' Ghàidhlig
- Cothrom a thoirt don phoball fios a chur don SPCB tro oifigear Gàidhlig an SPCB
- Seirbheis foghlam Gàidhlig taobh a-staigh is taobh a-muigh togalach na Pàrlamaid

- Cothrom aig luchd-obrach an SPCB Gàidhlig ionnsachadh.
- Tro na ceuman seo, cuiridh sinn ri faicsinneachd na Gàidhlig agus ri mothachadh air a' Ghàidhlig agus cuiridh sinn ris na cothroman a th' aig a' phoball, aig Buill Pàrlamaid na h-Alba agus aig luchd-obrach an SPCB air seirbheisean tron chànain.

Chaidh ar plana fhoillseachadh san t-Samhain 2008 le ar n-Oifigear-riaghlaidh, Ailig MacFheargais BPA, mar phàirt den chiad latha Gàidhlig againn. Bha an latha seo a' gabhail a-steach leasanan Gàidhlig agus tursan saor is an-asgaidh airson luchd-obrach, a' phobaill agus airson nam ball; agus seiminear poileasaidh airson buidhnean poblach. Bha seo na latha trang airson na Gàidhlig anns a' Phàrlamaid oir chaidh deasbad pàrlamaideach a chumail air an aon latha mun chànain agus chaidh an cuairt dheireannach den deasbad bhliadhnail eadar sgoiltean Gàidhlig a chumail cuideachd. Chùm sinn an darna latha Gàidhlig againn san t-Samhain 2010.

Tha sinn a' cur a' phlana an gnìomh an-dràsta agus tha sinn air taic-airgid fhaighinn bhon Bhòrd airson tòrr de na pròiseactan againn. Tha an trèanadh mothachaidh Gàidhlig, a tha a' toirt cothrom don luchd-obrach ionnsachadh mu shuidheachadh na Gàidhlig san àm a dh'fhalbh agus san latha an-diugh, air a bhith an dà chuid mòr-chòrdte agus feumail. Tha seo air tuigsinn a bhrosnachadh a thaobh na Gàidhlig agus tha e cuideachd air dèanamh cinnteach gum bi daoine nas bàidheile ris na poileasaidhean Gàidhlig againn.

Thèid am plana a sgrùdadh le buidheann air an taobh a-staigh a bhios an urra ri bhith a' sgrùdadh agus ag ùrachadh a' phlana agus airson a bhith a' cur aithisgean measaidh don Bhòrd. Chaidh a' chiad aithisg a chur don Bhòrd na bu thràithe am-bliadhna. Bidh dleastanas air a' bhuidhinn seo cuideachd a bhith a' deasachadh an ath phlana Ghàidhlig, a thoisicheas ann an 2013. Tha Bòrd na Gàidhlig an dùil gun cuir na buidhnean poblach ris an ìre de sholarachadh airson na Gàidhlig anns gach plana a nì iad.

Is e fear de na prìomh dhùbhlanan anns a' phlana seo – agus airson an ath phlana – a bhith a' cur ris an ìre cleachdaidh de sheirbheisean anns a' phlana. Chan eil luchd-labhairt na Gàidhlig cleachdte ri cothrom a bhith aca Gàidhlig a chleachdadh ann a bhith a' dèiligeadh ri buidhnean poblach agus mar sin, tha an ìre cleachdaidh gu math ìosal mar as àbhaist. Mar as trice, chaidh an fheadhainn aig a bheil fìor dheagh Ghàidhlig bho thùs tro mheadhan na Beurla agus mar sin, tha iad nas cofhurtaile a bhith a' cleachdadh na Beurla is iad a' dèiligeadh le buidhnean poblach ged a tha iad cho fileanta ri fileanta anns a' Ghàidhlig. Air an làimh eile, ged a tha barrachd den luchd-labhairt òga oideachadh tro mheadhan na Gàidhlig, mar as trice, tha iad air Gàidhlig ionnsachadh mar dàrna cànain agus tha iad mar as trice nas fileanta is nas cofhurtaile anns a' Bheurla. Gus an ìre cleachdaidh àrdachadh agus gus dèanamh cinnteach gu bheil an luchd-obrach againn mothachail air a' phlana, tha sinn air plana conaltraidh Gàidhlig a dheasachadh. Am measg rudan eile, tha seo a' gabhail a-steach:

- Targaidean a chruthachadh airson na h-ìre cleachdaidh de sheirbheisean foghlaim
- A' cruthachadh liosta-sgaoilidh nas fhèarr airson foillseachaidhean Gàidhlig agus fios mun Phàrlamaid
- A' toirt seachad seirbheisean a tha ag amas gu sònraichte air luchd-ionnsachaidh leithid duilleagan-lìn agus leabhranan ann an Gàidhlig shìmplidh.

- A' cur air dòigh duilleagan-lìn anns a' Bheurla airson daoine aig nach eil Gàidhlig ach aig a bheil ùidh anns a' chànain agus anns a' Phàrlamaid.

Tha an dòigh-obrach againn air aithneachadh gu bheil trì diofar buidhnean ann a tha cudromach ann am planaichean Gàidhlig agus ann an leasachadh na Gàidhlig. A bharrachd air na daoine a tha fileanta air an deach iomradh a thoirt mar-thà, feumar cuimhneachadh gu bheil na mìltean de luchd-ionnsachaidh inbheach ann. Tha luchd-ionnsachaidh inbheach air aon de na buidhnean as misneachaile ann an saoghal na Gàidhlig agus tha na mìltean mòra aca ann. Tha solarachadh leithid foillseachaidhean ann an Gàidhlig shìmplidh a' toirt cothrom do luchd-ionnsachaidh pàirt a ghabhail anns a' Phàrlamaid agus an cuid Gàidhlig a thoirt air adhart aig an aon àm.

Gu math tric, bithear a' dèanamh dearmad air buidheann air leth cudromach anns an deasbad air leasachadh na Gàidhlig – am poball aig nach eil Gàidhlig. Tha ceuman a tha ag amas air a' bhuidhinn seo air leth cudromach. Tha sinne a-nis ag obair air barrachd foillseachaidhean dà-chànaineach, cinn Ghàidhlig ann am foillseachaidhean Beurla agus, nas cudromaiche, soidhnichean Gàidhlig agus dhà-chànaineach air leth cudromach. Tha seo a' ciallachadh gum faic gach duine a thig don Phàrlamaid, a sgrìobhas thugainn no a chì ar làrach-lìn no ar foillseachaidhean beagan Gàidhlig. Tha seo air leth cudromach oir a rèir an t-seann-fhacail, 'an rud nach fhaic sùil, cha ghluais e cridhe'.

Tha faicsinneachd na cànain deatamach ann a bhith a' togail mothachadh, agus ùidh anns a' Ghàidhlig agus ann a bhith a' cruthachadh spèis cho-ionnan don chànain gun luaidh air a' bhuaidh air an ìre cleachdaidh airson clasaichean Gàidhlig agus airson foghlam tro mheadhan na Gàidhlig. Tha am plana Gàidhlig againn a' cur ri seo rud beag. Tha an fhaicsinneachd agus an spèis cho-ionainn seo cudromach cuideachd ann a bhith a' brosnachadh dhaoine aig a bheil Gàidhlig bho thùs a bhith nas misneachaile mun chànain aca fhèin agus a bhith a' cleachdadh seirbheisean Gàidhlig.

Tha deasachadh Plana Gàidhlig na Pàrlamaid air a bhith na phròiseas ionnsachaidh dhuinn agus airson buidhnean poblach eile a tha a' cur phlanaichean ri chèile. Tha sinn air a bhith soirbheachail ann a bhith a' toirt ìomhaigh na Gàidhlig am follais barrachd taobh a-staigh agus taobh a-muigh na Pàrlamaid agus tha sinn dòchasach gun tèid an t-iarrtas air seirbheisean tron Ghàidhlig am meud mar thoradh air ar plana.

'From Politics to Practice': Creating the Scottish Parliament's Gaelic Language Plan

Alasdair MacCaluim

Introduction

This presentation will look at the development of the Scottish Parliament's statutory Gaelic Language Plan, covering the process, the challenges and the opportunities involved in this. We will start by looking at the statutory framework for Gaelic language planning in Scotland.

The Gaelic Language (Scotland) Act 2005

The Gaelic Language (Scotland) Act was passed by the Scottish Parliament cross-party support in April 2005. The purpose of the Act is to promote the use of Gaelic in Scottish public life and to encourage the increased use of Gaelic in the home, community, place of learning and workplace.

The Gaelic Act:

- Establishes a statutory Gaelic body Bòrd na Gàidhlig to promote the Gaelic language.
- Requires the Bòrd to develop a National Plan for Gaelic to promote the use and understanding of Gaelic, Gaelic education and Gaelic culture. This plan sets out the priorities and targets for Gaelic development.
- Gives the Bòrd the authority to issue a statutory notice to devolved public bodies requiring them to draw up Gaelic plans setting out how they will use and enable the use of Gaelic.

The functions of Bòrd na Gàidhlig, including the national plan, are to be undertaken 'with a view to securing the status of the Gaelic language as an official language of Scotland commanding equal respect to the English language'. The Scottish Parliamentary Corporate Body (SPCB) was amongst the first six public bodies to be asked to draw up a Gaelic Language Plan.

Gaelic in the Scottish Parliament

The SPCB was happy to be asked to draw up a Gaelic Language Plan as not only had the Parliament passed the act but already made a great deal of provision for the language. This included the right to write to the Parliament in Gaelic, the production of a variety of Gaelic publications and webpages, the provision of education and outreach services and employing a Gaelic language officer.

The plan offered us many opportunities. While the Parliament already made much provision for Gaelic, the plan gave us an opportunity to codify and review current provision. As one of the public bodies making the most use of Gaelic, it gave us the opportunity to demonstrate our good practice to others and to show what could be achieved in national Gaelic language plans.

The plan enabled the Parliament to look at Gaelic across the whole organisation and to mainstream Gaelic issues in our processes where appropriate. This was reflected in the development of the plan, which was undertaken by a working group of staff drawn from key teams in the Parliament in order to draw on their expertise and ensure early buy-in to ideas as well as joined-up thinking and a corporate approach.

In addition to opportunities, there were also some challenges. As one of the first bodies to draw up a Gaelic plan we were in a learning process – as were Bòrd na Gàidhlig themselves! There was no template or example for a plan that we could follow and the statutory guidance on drawing up Gaelic plans wasn't completed until our plan was at an advanced stage.

The Scottish Parliament was unique in being the first national organisation to submit its plan. Other bodies drawing up plans at this time were either local authorities or bodies serving the Highlands.

Deciding the appropriate provision for a national public body presented some challenges. In our plan, we had to commit to 'seek to give effect to the principle that the Gaelic and English languages should be accorded equal respect'. In the legislation itself, the term 'equal respect' was adopted in order to enhance the status of Gaelic while at the same time recognising the very different position of Gaelic in different parts of Scotland and allowing different levels of provision in different areas according to circumstances. This flexibility was welcome but means that the term was difficult to pin down as it has not been fully and clearly defined. Additionally, there was little in Bòrd na Gàidhlig's statutory guidance on statutory Gaelic plans on what was expected from national groups.

Bòrd guidance on Gaelic plans states that 'equal respect' involves being 'supportive and generous to Gaelic development' and that plans should be prepared 'with a view to facilitating the use of Gaelic to the greatest extent that is appropriate to its individual circumstances'. We liaised closely with the Bòrd on the issue of equal respect.

Bòrd na Gàidhlig were clear that symbolic measures to raise the profile of Gaelic such as bilingual signage were extremely important for a national body like the SPCB. For service delivery, it was accepted that, as a national body based in Edinburgh, the SPCB differed from Highland public bodies and did not necessarily have to provide the same level or range of services. While services serving the whole country – such as our website and publications – could be delivered bilingually, we felt it could not be justified, for example, to make sure that reception staff or switchboard staff were Gaelic speakers as the use of these services would be low and wouldn't make best use of the available resource for Gaelic development. Having said that, however, we do offer a very wide range of services as will be discussed shortly.

A final challenge for us was the distinction between the SPCB and the Scottish Parliament. The legislative and other functions of the Scottish Parliament are distinct from the administrative functions of the SPCB. The SPCB was the group asked to develop a Gaelic plan, and this difference was difficult for the public to understand, particularly given that the use of Gaelic in parliamentary business is symbolically important to many.

There is, of course, provision for the use of Gaelic in Parliamentary business but this was outwith the competency of the SPCB plan and is covered instead through the Parliament's Standing Orders.

Contents of SPCB Gaelic Language Plan

Our main new commitments in the Gaelic plan were as follows:
- Introducing a bilingual corporate identity
- Expanding Gaelic signage in the Parliament (all public and directional signage is now bilingual)

- Introducing a range of forms in Gaelic
- Increasing provision for simultaneous translation facilities for public meetings
- Expanding the range of public information publications available in Gaelic
- Improving the Scottish Parliament's web pages (including the introduction of a Gaelic url)
- Introducing Gaelic awareness training for front of house staff
- Revising recruitment procedures to take Gaelic into account
- Ensuring that Gaelic is considered in the policy making and monitoring process.

These build on our existing provision which also includes

- Welcoming written correspondence in Gaelic
- Enabling the public to contact the SPCB in Gaelic through the Parliament's Gaelic Development Officer
- A Gaelic education and outreach service
- The availability of Gaelic learning opportunities for SPCB staff.

Through these measures, the SPCB will raise awareness of Gaelic, its visibility and will increase the opportunities for members of the public, Members of the Scottish Parliament and SPCB staff to access SPCB services through Gaelic.

Our plan was launched in November 2008 by our Presiding Officer, Alex Fergusson, MSP as part of a Gaelic Language Day featuring free Gaelic lessons and tours for staff, Members and the public and a Gaelic policy seminar for public bodies. This was a busy day for Gaelic in the Parliament as on the same day a parliamentary debate was held on the subject of the language and the annual inter-school Gaelic debating competition took place. Our second Gaelic Language Day was held in November 2010.

We are currently implementing the plan and have benefited from financial support from the Bòrd for several of our initiatives. One of these initiatives which has proved particularly useful and popular is Gaelic Awareness training which enables staff to learn about the history and present situation of Gaelic. This has helped to encourage understanding of Gaelic issues and buy-in to our Gaelic policies.

The plan will be monitored by an internal group which will be responsible for reviewing and updating the plan and for submitting monitoring reports to the Bòrd. The first such report was submitted earlier this year. This group will also have responsibility for drawing up the next Gaelic Plan which will commence in 2013. It is expected by Bòrd na Gàidhlig that public bodies will incrementally increase Gaelic provision in each successive plan.

One of our key challenges for this plan – and for our next – is to increase uptake of the services offered in the plan. Gaelic speakers are not accustomed to being able to use their language in dealing with public authorities so typically uptake of Gaelic services is low. Older speakers with a high level of fluency in Gaelic tend to have been educated through English and be more comfortable using English for dealing with public bodies. Conversely, while younger speakers have often been educated through the medium of Gaelic, they are normally still more fluent and comfortable using English. To address the issue of uptake and to ensure that internal awareness about the plan is maximised, have created a Gaelic Communications Plan. Amongst other things, this includes:

- creating targets for uptake of education and outreach services
- creating an improved distribution list for Gaelic publications and information such as weekly summaries of business
- providing services aimed directly at Gaelic learners such as web pages in simple Gaelic
- Setting up web pages in English about Gaelic in the Scottish Parliament for non-Gaelic speakers who are interested in the language and the Parliament.

Our approach has recognised that Gaelic plans and Gaelic development in general involves three different groups. In addition to the fluent speakers just referred to, the many thousands of adult learners must also be remembered. Adult learners who are not yet fluent are one of the most motivated groups in the Gaelic scene and number many thousands. Making provision such as special 'easy read' publications in simple Gaelic enables learners to engage with the Parliament while also improving their Gaelic.

The group most often forgotten in discussing Gaelic development is the general non-Gaelic speaking public. Measures aimed at this group such as bilingual publications, inclusion of Gaelic headings in English publications and, most importantly, our bilingual signage and corporate identity are crucial. All visitors to the Scottish Parliament see some Gaelic as do all those corresponding with the Parliament or using our website or reading our leaflets. As the Gaelic proverb goes: *an rud nach fhaic sùil, cha ghluais e cridhe* ('the thing which the eye doesn't see can't move the heart'). Visibility of Gaelic is crucial in raising public awareness and interest in Gaelic and in creating equal respect for the language not to mention uptake of Gaelic classes and Gaelic-medium education. The Scottish Parliament's Gaelic plan contributes to this in a small way. This visibility and equal respect is also important in encouraging native speakers to value their language and to use Gaelic services.

Drawing up the Scottish Parliament's Gaelic Plan has been a useful learning process for ourselves and for other public bodies drawing up plans. We have been successful in raising the profile of Gaelic both internally and externally and we are optimistic that uptake of Gaelic-medium services will increase as a result of our plan.

Implementing the Gaelic Plan Using Translation Software at the University of the Highlands and Islands

Ruairidh Mackay

The University of the Highlands and Islands (UHI) came into existence properly in 2011. Previously it was known as the UHI Millennium Institute. The UHI is the only Higher Education organisation based in the Highlands and Islands of Scotland that provides access to University-level education via a unique educational partnership of colleges and research institutes. There are 13 establishments or Academic Partners which are geographically widespread throughout the north of Scotland and as a result, are very individual, drawing on their location and the various cultures within it (see Appendix Map). As these Academic Partners are autonomous in their own rights, UHI was created solely to undertake executive and professional duties, and to coordinate and support UHI network functions. It is for these purposes that UHI also has a core staff body responsible for the delivery of services such as curriculum and staff development, learning and information services, promotion of research, etc and this body is referred to as Executive Office. It is through these unique partnerships that make UHI a prime example of how to develop a bilingual approach within a multi-partnered organisation.

Whilst the UHI Gaelic Plan focuses on the development of Gaelic within higher education learning opportunities and research throughout the entire partnership, it also aims to expand on the provision of Gaelic medium materials, information and services delivered by the UHI corporate body, but not by the Academic Partners. This is due to the constitutional structure of UHI and, more importantly, the independence of the UHI partner organisations. As some of the partners are located in areas where the Gaelic culture was never part of the local area, it may not be possible to develop a bilingual institute to the same extent, but that there may be still a Gaelic presence, whether through the courses delivered, (as UHI is at the forefront of distance learning and is very active in Video Conferencing delivery throughout the partnership), or through increased promotion material of the Gaelic community, outlining Gaelic classes on offer. Many of these Academic Partners will also be undertaking the development of their own Gaelic language plans over the next few years, which will allow them to decide on the future for Gaelic within their own recognised community.

Indeed, from discussions during the symposium, it was interesting to hear how some organisations, who have developed a Gaelic plan are putting it into action. It was obvious that there are wide variations on how they are putting the plans into practice, as examples were shown of those who have had the plan for a number of years, but are still not displaying a bilingual logo (see further McLeod, in this volume) or any sign of Gaelic within their website. On the other hand, it was encouraging to hear that a delegate, who was present at this symposium, had contacted Scotrail about the lack of Gaelic signage at the railway stations around Greater Glasgow, and his local station promptly erected a bilingual sign version of the station name.

The implementation of the UHI Plan, therefore, will have an immediate effect on making aspects of the Executive Office bi-lingual, but it is the added developments such as increasing the use of technology to improve consistency with Gaelic terminology that will hopefully assist this and in turn, will be re-used to benefit those involved in

Gaelic throughout the Academic partners. The savings on time and money can be passed on through the network by re-using previously translated material. Equally, the experiences learnt with developing the UHI Gaelic plan will also help with language plan creation within the Academic Partners, and bring further cohesive benefits throughout the network.

I therefore intend to discuss the impact that corpus development will have on the strategic plans for Gaelic within UHI Millennium Institute and how the implementation of the UHI Gaelic Language Plan will assist with furthering the creation of a bi-lingual Higher Educational organisation and indeed how both can be developed together.

The concept for a corpus arose during the research phase of one of the UHI Gaelic projects, which was to establish the use of translation memory software within the organisation. This type of software had not been widely used with Scottish Gaelic and the project was created to explore its effectiveness on the translation process, primarily within the UHI network and secondly, with a view to developing a service for external Gaelic organisations. From discussion and the trialling of the software with Gaelic department staff, who are based throughout the network, it became clear early on that as well as the time savings to be made by using TMS, other important advantages, such as improvements with terminology consistency also became apparent. To this end, and in collaboration with those Academic Partners, that deliver Gaelic programmes of study, great inroads have been made in creating terminology lists applicable to the UHI network, but that could also be of future benefit to the wider Educational community.

Initially, we have developed terminology lists in areas such as Job Titles, Department Names and Academic Institute Names. These lists will form the basis for a UHI termbase, which when used in conjunction with the memory software, will ensure their consistent and accurate usage, throughout the UHI Gaelic network. However, it is our intention that these lists will not reside solely within the software, but will also be useful for the wider non-Gaelic UHI network, and also as a guide for other Educational Institutes, with the development of their Gaelic plans in the near future. The importance of community, as mentioned yesterday, is paramount to ensuring that the widespread network are all able to contribute to this development.

Our aim has always been to develop these lists as part of an on-going process, and in collaboration with partnership institutes, therefore when a new English title or name is used; the need for a Gaelic translation will also be required. To develop this, the process requires a central body to maintain the content of these lists, and indeed, through the use of the software, it is possible to moderate the new entries and ensure that only agreed terms then become visible to all, thus ensuring a continuous Quality Assurance process is in place.

It is intended that the adoption of these terms will come from a collaborative agreement, initially by those involved with Gaelic developments across the UHI network, and secondly, with input from a dedicated terminology group; An Seotal. Their panel, which consists of a researcher who investigates the terms requested, is also made up of a number of terminology experts who meet to discuss new terms and ensure that it meets current standards in terms of orthography etc. It was deemed important that the UHI terms should not be agreed by only those within the UHI network, but instead be discussed and approved by an authority on terminology lists. This then gives the terms national approval, rather than simply the organisation's approval. It is hoped that this new partnership between UHI and An Seotal will also continue as the service develops, and indeed that An Seotal also builds on its reputation in the wider Gaelic world by developing further terminology with other organisations.

One of the core commitments, from the Gaelic plan, outlined to the Academic Partners, was regarding UHI's identity, in particular, the focus on signage in and around the organisation. Although Executive Office has a large number of bilingual signs displayed at present, it is expected that this amount will increase in order to create a stronger, more visible bilingual appearance, and to further demonstrate UHI's commitment to the Gaelic language. It is also vital that we incorporate these phrases and guidance into our translation memory databases, so that they can be made available for use by others in the future, both through using the software and via updated terminology lists. Indeed, achieving University title will allow for rebranding, and the creation of a bilingual logo, as opposed to two separate Gaelic and English logos, as it is at present. The first proofs of the new logo have been created and are out to consultation with the Academic partners, where it is hoped that they will also adopt a similar style of logo to make the UHI 'brand' more identifiable throughout the network. (See McLeod, in this volume)

The terminology lists will ensure that a consistent approach is continued throughout those institutes developing Gaelic plans, and that this will hopefully reduce instances of multiple translations for the same English sign appearing, around the partnership. The risk is that a visitor arriving in the various institutes could be met with different Gaelic translations for the same sign, which as well as causing some confusion to Gaelic speakers, could also limit the ability for non-Gaelic speakers to recognise familiar Gaelic terms. With a consistent approach, non Gaelic speakers would become accustomed to seeing them and understand what they mean. A delegate mentioned the use of bilingual signage for education purposes and indeed, ensuring the usage of these phrases will undoubtedly assist with visitor's awareness of Gaelic, to any of the locations across the UHI partnership, by consistently using the same phrases.

In terms of the visual appearance of an organisation, there is no outlet more powerful than its website. It is envisaged that developing a bilingual website will be a main focus, for the Academic Partners to review within their future language plans. For many, the website is the first port of call for prospective students, searching for information and advice on what is on offer. UHI currently offer a web service, based on their own website, which academic partners can choose to adopt and which also has the advantage of already being available in both languages. This means that the partners can acquire the UHI web templates and that they would then only need to develop the content to be added. Again, with a Gaelic version already available throughout the UHI website, we can ensure strong continuity throughout other partnership websites by the use of agreed terms and phrases for web-links.

This should also hopefully lead to further continuity for students when navigating the various websites, belonging to the different Academic Partners. With an increase in online services, such as enrolments and course information, the opportunity to display this information in both Gaelic and English, will be a valuable asset to any institute wishing to improve their bilingual profile. As a website aims to reduce the need to speak to the institutes directly, the more the user can do on-line would be a definite advantage. These terms and phrases would also be added to the databases for ensuring any new changes and alterations are quickly made available to all. Further down the line, by using the stored translations, it should also be possible to deliver a single bi-lingual website as well, which will enhance the usability of the website, and to demonstrate its equal status, within the organisation.

Increasing the level of Gaelic throughout the UHI network is also being further developed with producing more bilingual communication material. According to the UHI Gaelic Plan:

> The preparation of Gaelic versions of forms, applications and similar documents, can also assist in expanding the range of Gaelic terminology and the awareness of the Gaelic speaking public of such terminology, thus helping the development of the language itself.

Whilst UHI have been actively producing bilingual material for a number of years, it is hoped that this will lead to an increase in bilingual material produced throughout the UHI partnership. Making the contents of bilingual news releases and e-mail bulletins available to other Gaelic departments will encourage the sharing of resources and also establish the flow of terminology which has been outlined before.

Much of the information contained within the UHI prospectus relates to Gaelic courses delivered at some of the Academic Partners, and sharing this information between organisations has been very useful in terms of consistency. Indeed the more bilingual material that can get sent out to the general public, the more opportunity there is to demonstrate our commitment to the language and increase our profile within the Gaelic world.

To this end, UHI also recently launched what is believed to be the first national television advertisement, broadcast in Gaelic. As part of the advertising campaign to attract more students to study with UHI, a Gaelic advert and an English advert were broadcast independently on Channel 4 and Channel 5 over the summer months of 2010. The Gaelic version, in particular, reinforced the message that the language is a vital part of UHI's present and future development. It also showed that UHI is becoming increasingly known as an academic institute that can encompass those from all walks of life, wherever they live and bring them together. This inclusiveness has a particular bearing on the location of our students, who are able to participate due to the collaborative approach of the Academic partners and Learning Centres at the heart of UHI.

With regards to the other Gaelic projects currently on-going at UHI, which aim to meet the needs of the core-commitments outlined in the Gaelic plan; there has been a lot of work carried out on increasing the amount of online Gaelic modules for students. This will lead to a wider subject choice being available, and also increase the opportunity to attract a larger student base, as these modules could effectively be studied anywhere nationally. The wide variety of courses are designed to attract fluent adult learners, whose circumstances may dictate that they cannot attend face to face classes, and by making them online, will give the students a greater deal of flexibility to achieve them.

It is also UHI's intention to develop Gaelic modules that can be included within non-Gaelic courses, which the student can elect to take. Taking these modules will still count towards his/her course attainment, but, as a wider benefit, it may also encourage the student to take up further Gaelic modules, throughout their learning career. This of course could reap great benefits on the Gaelic courses uptake, as the modules could then interest students to possibly enrol on a Gaelic-medium course, at a later date. The accessibility of these modules then ensures that they reach a wider target audience than simply those within the Gaelic stream at present.

Some of these modules also benefit from being available in both Gaelic and English and as a result of which, the intention is that the content of them can reside within the software databases. The subject specific terminology that would be developed through their creation could also lead to the development of a terminology list, which would ensure that any further modules created on that subject, will be adhering to the appropriate terms. This will be of particular relevance to the writers, who are possibly working independently on their module, but are still developing it as part of a specific subject module batch.

Another core commitment of the Gaelic plan is Staffing, and a Human Resources and Staff Development strand of the Gaelic projects was also created. This project focuses partly on the delivery of courses on Gaelic awareness and Gaelic Learning classes, throughout the UHI network, and demonstrates how non-teaching staff, employed by UHI and the Academic Partners, are also contributing to the development of a bilingual organisation. Through courses run by UHI, at the various Academic Partner locations, many front-line staff have taken up the opportunity to attend the Gaelic Awareness courses, and some have even gone on to attend Gaelic classes, to further their Gaelic learning. This development has perhaps a greater impact on the front-of-house staff, which provides the first impression for visitors, and it would be an important language plan target if the staff were able to welcome visitors, either in person, or on the phone, with a bilingual greeting. Bearing in mind, some of the points raised in the previous discussions, regarding tokenism, it is not intended to introduce this simply as a one-off, but instead, to develop it within those staff who are willing to extend their own personal Gaelic development. The intention is that these staff will then become more fluent and proficient in the language, and will become a normal part of their daily life.

The HR project could also benefit from the use of terminology development; simple bilingual phrase cards could be created to help with those learning Gaelic, and could be kept close to hand, again in particular for the front of house staff on Reception. The terminology lists would also assist staff, when dealing with callers who wish to speak to specific personnel; the job title and department list would be very useful for ensuring a continually consistent approach to using those terms, within the network. This list could become a useful terminology tool for learners and fluent speakers alike.

The use of Corpus development within the UHI network is therefore, diverse and wide ranging; it is vital however, that when developing a bilingual organisation that care is taken to promote Gaelic in such a way that makes it accessible for all, without causing any issues. Developing Gaelic material and information to maintain a Gaelic pathway for those students already enrolled on Gaelic courses is vital to ensuring that we keep those students here. In particular, with students from the Gaelic college Sabhal Mòr Ostaig and Colaisde a Chaisteil, if they plan to progress onto the UHI degree courses, it is important that they view UHI as a continuation with Gaelic or the next step on from these Gaelic colleges. There has always been a strong pull from the big cities for many students from the North of Scotland, and keeping existing students whilst attracting new students to UHI must be a key priority. The hope is, in the future, to be able to offer as wide a range of courses as possible to those wishing to continue with Gaelic studies.

For those students, throughout the UHI network, who are enrolled on non-Gaelic courses; raising the profile of Gaelic via the increased availability of bilingual material and information will certainly lead to an increased awareness of the language within the student population. This may be the limit of its impact for some, but it is hoped that with others, it will lead to an interest in pursuing Gaelic modules, Gaelic Classes and an increase in the uptake of Gaelic courses.

The impact that corpus development can have on staff is also wide ranging. With Gaelic department staff and through the continued use of the translation memory software, it is anticipated that the sharing of resources will bring about a more consistent approach to Gaelic and its delivery throughout the various organisations. The terminology lists are vital in ensuring that there is a unified approach to the delivery of Gaelic throughout the network and any inconsistencies that can lead to confusion and a reduced understanding are removed.

However, non-Gaelic speaking staff can also benefit from introductory lessons into Gaelic, which will inform them as to the status and, more importantly the relevance, of Gaelic within the UHI network. Making use of terminology lists will be a useful tool for them to refer to for assistance with promoting a bilingual UHI and to help further their own Gaelic development. Whilst there may be limited benefits for the terminology lists to be available in hard copy, there is more benefit to have them on-line or at least in some appropriate electronic form. It is hoped that the content of these terminology lists could be developed into an online resource, accessible by staff and students and also by the wider outside world. This searchable database could be kept as a web page within the UHI web-site and allow instant access to the term contained within the software.

Primarily the advantage of this is again, continuing to maintain the consistent usage of these terms within UHI, but also to act as a reference tool for those who are learning Gaelic. Although no discussions have taken place at present, it would also be an additional bonus to have other external terminology lists added to the search tool, to allow a wider spread of terms. These terms would be available to all via the web, but would also be contained within the translation memory software and thus ensure their consistent use with all internal translation work. `

It was interesting to hear the valuable points that were raised yesterday regarding community and the difficulties in developing the number of Gaelic speakers due to the location of a community. I feel that a community or network, such as the UHI partnership, brings many challenges in English and Gaelic, and that there is a need to turn to technology to bring staff and students together as one community.

Whether this can work in reality is an unknown, but the hope is that through the development of Gaelic plans by the Academic Partners, the level of Gaelic, both spoken and written, will increase, as will the awareness and ensure that students and staff throughout the partnership have a sense of belonging to the Gaelic UHI community.

To sum up then, the outcome of all of this is to ensure that Gaelic is seen as a major element at the heart of UHI and that measures are being taken to ensure there is an increase in the visibility and awareness of the language, primarily within Executive Office, but also to extend this to those academic partners that wish to develop their own bilingual image. The UHI Gaelic plan aims to address all of the priority areas outlined within it, but with the assistance of new technology, it is hoped that this process can be made easier. The work being carried out with corpus development will be accessible to all those who wish to use it, throughout the entire UHI network, and the experiences UHI encounter whilst implementing the Gaelic plan will assist the partners, with their own Gaelic plans, to be part of a cohesive institute that embraces Gaelic.

Appendix: The 13 Institutions of the University of the Highlands and Islands

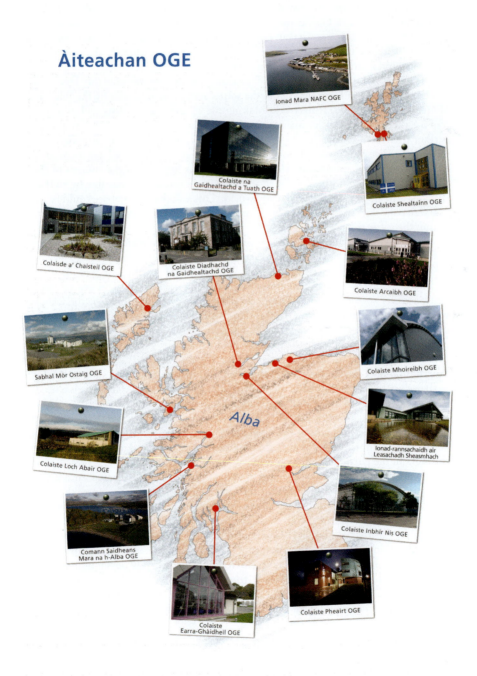

Àiteachan OGE

Ionad Mara NAFC OGE

Colaiste na Gaidhealtachd a Tuath OGE

Colaiste Shealtainn OGE

Colaisde a' Chaisteil OGE

Colaiste Diadhachd na Gaidhealtachd OGE

Colaiste Arcaibh OGE

Sabhal Mòr Ostaig OGE

Colaiste Mhoireibh OGE

Alba

Ionad-rannsachaidh air Leasachadh Sheasmhach

Colaiste Loch Abair OGE

Comann Saidheans Mara na h-Alba OGE

Colaiste Inbhir Nis OGE

Colaiste Earra-Ghàidheil OGE

Colaiste Pheairt OGE

Gaelic Language Plans and the Issue of Bilingual Logos

Wilson McLeod

This paper considers a potentially significant change in the 'linguistic landscape' of Scotland, as prestigious and prominent public bodies come to include Gaelic in their corporate logos as part of their statutory Gaelic Language Plans. For much of the twentieth century, Gaelic was effectively invisible in public spaces in Scotland, even in Gaelic-speaking areas. The use of Gaelic in a public body's logo is, both literally and metaphorically, a symbolic recognition of the importance of the language. There can be a risk of tokenism in such measures, however, if the organisation in question is doing little else to promote the language. Conversely, the different approaches adopted so far demonstrates that some bodies are more willing to accommodate the symbolic use of Gaelic, while others show more resistance (cf. May 2000).

The *Gaelic Language (Scotland) Act 2005* and Gaelic Language Plans

Under the *Gaelic Language (Scotland) Act 2005* (2005 asp 7), public authorities in Scotland may be required to produce formal Gaelic language plans. Such plans must 'set out the measures to be taken by the relevant public authority in relation to the use of the Gaelic language in connection with the exercise of the authority's functions', with 'functions' defined to include both 'functions relating to its internal processes, and ... the provision by the authority of any services to the public' (section 4(a), 10(4)). It is contemplated that plans will vary according to, among other things, 'the extent to which the persons in relation to whom the authority's functions are exercisable use the Gaelic language' and 'the potential for developing the use of the Gaelic language in connection with the exercise of those functions' (section 5(b) and (c)).

As of April 2011, fifteen public authorities had published Gaelic language plans:

Argyll & Bute Council
Caledonian Maritime Assets Ltd
Comhairle nan Eilean Siar
Crofters Commission
Glasgow City Council
Highlands and Islands Enterprise
Highland Council
Her Majesty's Inspectorate of Education
Learning and Teaching Scotland
Scottish Funding Council
The Scottish Government
Scottish Natural Heritage
Scottish Parliamentary Corporate Body
Scottish Qualifications Authority
UHI Millennium Institute (now the University of the Highlands and Islands)

A further 27 authorities are currently preparing their plans, with some of these now at an advanced stage.

Bòrd na Gàidhlig, the statutory body responsible for the approval and implementation of these plans, has published detailed guidance on their purpose and content (2007). Among other things, the guidance identifies 'four core areas that it wishes public authorities to address when preparing their plans': identity, communications, publications and staffing (2007: 19). The Bòrd explains the importance of identity as follows: 'The presence of Gaelic in the corporate identity of a public authority can greatly enhance the visibility of the language, and makes an important statement by a public authority about how Gaelic is valued and how it will be given recognition' (2007: 22).

This article focuses on one important aspect of the issue of identity: the corporate logo used by the authority. Both public bodies and private companies see their logo as a vitally important mechanism for advertising the purpose and ethos of the organisation, and are willing to spend large sums of money on their design. For example, £400,000 was spent on the logo for the 2012 Olympics, and Pepsi spent $1 million designing a new logo in 2008 (*The Guardian* 2007; Logomentor 2008).

In light of their diverse functions, different public authorities use their corporate logo in different ways: a public authority like Glasgow City Council presents itself in a much wider range of contexts and to a much wider range of people than the Scottish Funding Council, the specialist body responsible for funding universities and colleges in Scotland. The *Scottish Parliamentary Corporate Body's Gaelic Plan* gives a particularly detailed list of the specific places where its new bilingual logo is to appear. In addition to all internal and external signs, both permanent and temporary, these include:

> uniforms, pre-printed stationery (letterheads, envelopes, compliments slips, business cards, acknowledgement cards); shop stock; ... electronic templates, including for official publications ... , sundry items (tickets, lanyards for holding passes, events branding on podium, DVD art work). (Scottish Parliament 2007: 17–18)

The diversity of contexts and places where a corporate logo may appear is particularly important in relation to those bodies that have adopted parallel English and Gaelic versions of their logo, rather than a single bilingual version. For such authorities there is a possibility that the English version will serve as the default version, with the Gaelic version only appearing in specifically 'Gaelic' contexts. In such circumstances the great majority of people coming into contact with the authority may not actually see the Gaelic version, and its symbolic value will therefore be greatly attenuated. In one example of this unhelpful practice, the organisers of the 2014 Commonwealth Games in Glasgow (not a public authority within the scope of the *Gaelic Language Act*) have developed a Gaelic version of the Games logo but specify that 'its use is strictly governed by audience' and that it 'should only be reproduced where Gaelic language is being used'. (Glasgow 2014: 11)

Gaelic and the Linguistic Landscape

The study of linguistic landscape has become an increasingly important sub-field in language policy studies. Following the pioneering work of Landry and Bourhis (1997), the academic literature in this area has grown significantly in recent years (e.g. Shohamy & Gorter 2008; Shohamy, Ben-Rafael & Barni 2010). Following Landry and Bourhis, linguistic landscape 'refers to the visibility and salience of languages on public and commercial signs in a given territory or region', including 'the language of public road signs, advertising billboards, street names, place names, commercial shop signs, and public signs on government buildings' (1997: 23, 25).

The use of Gaelic in the logos of Scottish public authorities is thus only one small element in the wider linguistic landscape of Scotland, which remains overwhelmingly English. Nevertheless, the increased use of Gaelic by public bodies is not the only factor leading to a greater presence for Gaelic in this landscape, as the Scottish National Party government elected in 1997 has brought in a number of measures to expand the use of Gaelic on signs at entry points such as airports and border crossings and on the national railway network. Ó hIfearnáin explains the importance of such measures and the policy challenges to which they give rise:

> The presence of Gaelic on television and in the education system, on road signs and on the websites of government agencies is not simply a passive reflection of the current state of popular opinion towards the language. It is a key element of policy, participating in and giving legitimacy to particular linguistic practices. ... The institutionalisation of Gaelic in the public domain may lead to more confidence in the community of speakers, in turn leading to more usage and transmission to the youth and learners, but unless the development of this area of public policy is managed ... the linguistic landscape may simply come to reflect the position that Gaelic already has in the lives of the vast majority of the population (Ó hIfearnáin 2010: 37–8).

Significantly, these measures in relation to signage (especially at train stations in greater Glasgow) have prompted negative comment in the 'quality' press (e.g. Jack 2010; Sorooshian 2010). For the mid-market *Daily Express*, arguably the newspaper currently most hostile to Gaelic, such measures amount to an attempt to create a 'Gaelic Brigadoon':

> Gradually, parts of the country that have not heard a Gaelic voice in centuries are being dressed up with Gaelic place names. There is an obsession within government education circles to teach nursery school children the language, whether their parents want this or not.
>
> As Scotland becomes more internationally minded due to improved communications, travel and exposure to other cultures, too many in the establishment seem to be trying to force a kind of Gaelic Brigadoon upon us. If people want to learn the Gaelic language and study its culture, let them, but it is time for what's known, in English, as a reality check (*Daily Express* 2010).

Corporate Logos and Gaelic Language Plans

The public bodies that have adopted Gaelic language plans to date have taken quite divergent approaches to the issue of corporate identity generally and corporate logos specifically. It is somewhat difficult to arrange these typologically but the following broad strategies may be discerned:

1.   A monolingual Gaelic logo
2a.   A bilingual logo that gives equal prominence to English and Gaelic.
2b.   A bilingual logo that gives greater prominence to English than to Gaelic.
3.   Parallel English and Gaelic logos
4.   A monolingual English logo

To date, the only authority to adopt a monolingual Gaelic logo is Comhairle nan Eilean Siar (Western Isles Council). This practice is a direct consequence of the decision, pursuant to the *Local Government (Gaelic Names) (Scotland) Act 1997*, to adopt a Gaelic name for the council with no English equivalent.

However, the strongly Gaelic identity suggested by the logo is somewhat misleading: Comhairle nan Eilean Siar is far from a monolingual Gaelic organisation, and indeed its current *Gaelic Language Plan* (Comhairle nan Eilean Siar 2008) is surprisingly weak given the strength of Gaelic in the Western Isles.

2a is the practice adopted by Highland Council, Scottish Natural Heritage, the Scottish Parliament and University of the Highlands and Islands (UHI). All these authorities use a bilingual logo for all purposes, although a strict interpretation might relegate them to type 2b, given that the English text is placed above the Gaelic. Highland Council and UHI give the Gaelic text a rather more prominent colour, however, and for UHI there is a match between the colour of the Gaelic text and the accompanying sea and mountain image. In the case of Scottish Natural Heritage, the

organisation had previously used three logos (one English, one Gaelic and one bilingual) and in its plan has undertaken to 'move towards the use of the bilingual version ... as the norm across all areas of [its] operation' (Scottish Natural Heritage 2010: 23). An unusual move by SNH is its rotating website strapline, which alternates between the English and Gaelic versions of the logo every three seconds.

Also in this category is Historic Scotland, which was remarkably proactive in this area, adopting a new Gaelic name and new bilingual logo (and erecting bilingual signs at its Edinburgh headquarters) even before putting its draft Gaelic language plan out to consultation. Here, one might quibble that English has greater prominence given that in both English and Gaelic one reads from left to right.

Learning and Teaching Scotland
Ionnsachadh agus Teagasg Alba

Scottish Funding Council
Promoting further and higher education

Comhairle Maoineachaidh na h-Alba
A' brosnachadh foghlam adhartach agus àrd ìre

There are different permutations on type 2b. Both Highlands and Islands Enterprise and Caledonian Maritime Assets Ltd (which owns Caledonian MacBrayne ferries) use both the English and Gaelic versions of their names, but give great prominence to the abbreviated English forms HIE and CMAL.

The Crofters Commission and Learning and Teaching Scotland use both names but use a larger font for the English name. The font for 'Crofters Commission' is bolder too, while the LTS logo includes the English name twice, once within a monolingual emblem.

The Scottish Funding Council and Scottish Government can be said to have taken approach 3, although their strategies differ. SFC have two logos, one English and one Gaelic, but its plan is unusually ambiguous in relation to the use of these logos:

> The Council's corporate identity includes our symbol and the English and Gaelic versions of our name and strapline ... We will extend the application of the Gaelic-only version of our logo (as used on business cards) for external use ... At the same time we will develop further our guidelines on logo usage. (Scottish Funding Council 2009: 12)

The implication here would seem to be that the English-only version will be retained for certain purposes, perhaps many purposes, and that no bilingual version is planned. As of April 2011, the website strapline was English-only, and several SFC publications issued following the adoption of the plan have used only the English logo.

The Government, meanwhile, has both a monolingual logo and a bilingual one (which, as with type 2b, gives greater prominence to English by printing the Gaelic name in a much smaller font).

The Government's Gaelic Plan makes the following statements in relation to the use of these logos:

> We will make use of the bilingual version of the Scottish Government logo as the norm across all areas of our operations. ... Our bilingual logo has recently been developed however we will look to include Gaelic under the terms of 'equal respect' when any rebranding exercise is undertaken. (Scottish Government 2010: 27)

There are several difficulties in this statement. The phrase 'will make use of' instead of the simple 'will use' seems slippery and the 'bilingual' version of the logo gives strong prominence to English in any event. The reasons for failing to develop a bilingual logo in connection with the 'recent' redesign are not made clear; this was actually done in late 2007, more than two years after the enactment of the *Gaelic Language Act*, following the Scottish National Party's victory in the election of 2007 and its renaming of the Scottish 'Executive' as the Scottish 'Government'. Finally, there is no indication as to when a 'rebranding exercise' might take place.

Finally, Argyll & Bute Council, Glasgow City Council and, arguably, the Scottish Qualifications Authority have taken approach 4. Argyll and Bute's plan, adopted in June 2008, states that 'the Council, with support from Bòrd na Gàidhlig, will investigate and evaluate designs for a bilingual logo in order to provide options for consideration

by the full Council before the end of 2009' (Argyll and Bute Council 2008: 64). As of April 2011, however, there was no sign of a bilingual logo on the Council's website. Producing a bilingual logo is not remotely difficult in terms of graphic design; it would seem that political will is lacking here. Glasgow's plan states that the Council 'will develop corporate guidelines for the use of the Gaelic language *in conjunction with* the corporate logo' (Glasgow City Council 2010: 43 – emphasis added). This provision would appear to contemplate that the logo itself would not become bilingual, or incorporate any Gaelic element at all. As of 2011, the logo on the council's website remained English only.

Although SQA's plan states that the authority will 'devise a new bilingual letterhead to be used in all sites', it makes clear that 'SQA's logo will continue to be displayed in its current format' (SQA 2011: 14). This logo is based on the English name of the organisation (rather than the Gaelic *Ùghdarras Theisteanas na h-Alba*) and includes the letter Q, which is not used in the Gaelic alphabet. The organisation did consider seriously the possibility of using UTA but there was a possibility of confusion given that there are several other organisations using these initials (Waters 2011).

Conclusion

The diversity of current practice in relation to public bodies' logos is striking. It is significant that several important national bodies such as Historic Scotland, Scottish Natural Heritage and the Scottish Parliament have been willing to adopt a fully bilingual logo, while local authorities such as Argyll & Bute and Glasgow have been more resistant. Arguably, Bòrd na Gàidhlig might have done more to push public bodies further in the direction of bilingualism; it is difficult to construct a principled argument against this, given the basic purpose of the *Gaelic Language Act* to 'secur[e] the status of Gaelic as an official language of Scotland commanding equal respect with the English language'.

One principled argument, albeit not one that a public body would probably like to articulate, is that a bilingual logo without a genuine commitment to bilingual operation is tokenistic and constitutes mere 'appeasement' (Cox 1998). Yet the best response must surely be to press for improved bilingualisation of the organisation, rather than proposing a symbolic ratification of existing monolingualism.

Acknowledgement

The logo of the Scottish Parliament is copyright SPCB and is reproduced with kind permission of the SPCB. Copyright of each other logo reproduced in this article is held by the respective public body. The author and publishers gratefully acknowledge their kind permission to use them here.

References

Argyll and Bute Council. 2008. *Plana Gàidhlig 2008/09–2011/12. Gaelic Language Plan 2008/09–2011/12*. Lochgilphead: Argyll & Bute Council.

Bòrd na Gàidhlig, 2007. *Stiùireadh air Deasachadh Phlanaichean Gàidhlig / Guidance on the Development of Gaelic Language Plans*. Inverness: Bòrd na Gàidhlig.

Comhairle nan Eilean Siar. 2008. *Plana Gàidhlig 2007–2012 / Gaelic Language Plan 2007–2012*. Stornoway: Comhairle nan Eilean Siar.

Cox, R.A.V. 1998. 'Tokenism in Gaelic: The Language of Appeasement'. *Scottish Language* 17: 70–81.

Daily Express. 2010. 'Don't force Gaelic on us' (leader). 31 August.

Glasgow City Council. 2010. *Gaelic Language Plan 2009 to 2012*. Glasgow: Glasgow City Council.

Glasgow 2014. 2010. 'Media Brand Guidelines'. Available at: www.glasgow2014.com/assets/1a9e6db9-c167-4cb1-bdfe-9ea3b0a76064.pdf [last accessed 21 April 2011].

Gorter, D. ed. 2006. *Linguistic Landscape: A New Approach to Multilingualism*. Clevedon: Multilingual Matters.

The Guardian. 2007. 'Jowell Defends Olympic Logo as Inspectors Arrive', 12 June.

Jack, I. 2010. 'Saving a Language is one Thing, but I'm Saddened by Scotland Going Gaelic'. *The Guardian*, 11 December.

Landry, R. and R.Y. Bourhis. 1997. 'Linguistic Landscape and Ethnolinguistic Vitality: An Empirical Study'. *Journal of Language and Social Psychology* 16:1: 23–49.

Logomentor. 2008. 'Pepsi Logo – New – Design and History'. Available at: logomentor.com/pepsi-logo-new [last accessed 21 April 2011].

May, S. 2000. 'Accommodating and Resisting Minority Language Policy: The Case of Wales'. *International Journal of Bilingual Education and Bilingualism*, 3:2: 101–28.

Ó hIfearnáin, T. 2010. 'Institutionalising Language Policy: Mismatches in Community and National Goals'. In eds. Munro, G. and I. Mac an Tàilleir. *Coimhearsnachdan Gàidhlig An-diugh / Gaelic Communities Today*, Edinburgh: Dunedin Academic Press. 35–47.

Scottish Funding Council. 2009. *Plana Gàidhlig / Gaelic Language Plan*. Edinburgh: Scottish Funding Council.

The Scottish Government. 2010. *Plana Gàidhlig / Gaelic Language Plan*. Edinburgh: The Scottish Government.

Scottish Natural Heritage. 2010. *Plana Gàidhlig / Gaelic Language Plan*. Inverness: Scottish Natural Heritage.

The Scottish Parliament. 2008. *Plana Gàidhlig Buidheann Chorporra Pàrlamaid na h-Alba 2008–2013 / Scottish Parliamentary Corporate Body Gaelic Language Plan 2008–2013*. Edinburgh: The Scottish Parliament.

Scottish Qualifications Authority. 2011. *Plana Cànan na Gàidhlig / Gaelic Language Plan*. Glasgow: Scottish Qualifications Authority

Shohamy, E. and D. Gorter. eds. 2008. *Linguistic Landscape: Expanding the Scenery*. London: Routledge.

Shohamy, E., Eliezer, B.R. and M. Barni. eds. 2010. *Linguistic Landscape in the City*. Bristol: Multilingual Matters.

Sorooshian, R. 2010. 'Leave Endangered Languages to Die in Peace'. *Sunday Herald*, 19 September.

Waters, M. 2011. Email from Marilyn Waters, SQA, to the author, 10 May.

Growing a New Generation of Gaelic Speakers: An Action Plan in Response to a Ministerial Initiative

Kenneth MacKinnon

At the 'Voices of the West' Conference (at Eden Court, Inverness on 20th June 2009), the Minister with Responsibility for Gaelic, Mike Russell announced a new policy priority for Gaelic development authorities, namely of increasing the number of Gaelic speakers, stating that he did not wish to see the numbers of Gaelic speakers continue to decrease on his watch.

This was a bold initiative, but nevertheless essentially welcome in various ways. This paper reviews the opportunities for achieving this objective.

Numbers of Gaelic speakers were last assessed at the *2001 Census*, and the next is due on 27th March 2011. If total numbers are to show an increase on the 2001 figure of 58,969 there is limited time and few specific opportunities to do so.

Gaelic speakers cannot be conjured out of thin air, and their numbers cannot be increased by waving a magic wand, earnestly wishing them to do so, or passing resolutions. The sources are specific, and comprise as follows:

1. Newly-born children of Gaelic speaking parents being brought up as Gaelic speakers themselves;
2. Children acquiring effective Gaelic abilities through preschool and playgroup experience;
3. Children consolidating this through effective primary school experience;
4. Children continuing to do so at secondary school;
5. Adults learning Gaelic e.g. at evening classes, Ulpanim, etc.;
6. Persons only able to read and / or write Gaelic developing speaking ability;
7. Persons only able to understand spoken Gaelic developing the confidence to speak it;
8. Persons who have abandoned Gaelic in later life re-acquiring confidence and ability;
9. Migrant Gaelic-speakers who have left Scotland returning to it.

It is difficult to think of other effective sources of speakers. This paper reviews the circumstances of each of the above situations and assesses practicalities:

1. Gaelic Upbringing

In 2001, there were 1,753 households all of whose 3,771 adults (18+) were Gaelic-speaking, and 2,100 or 71.8% of their children (3–18) spoke Gaelic. In these otherwise entirely Gaelic-speaking families, we need to know why, in over a quarter of the cases, the parents abandoned Gaelic as the language of upbringing. In the Western Isles, the chief remaining stronghold of the language, the situation was only a little better: 942 households, all of whose 2,058 adults spoke Gaelic, with 1,247 or 79.5% of their children speaking Gaelic.

More households were of mixed linguistic character. There were 5,719 households where 6,058 adults spoke Gaelic, and 1,892 children (or 21.6% of the total) were being brought up to speak it. In the Western Isles, the corresponding figures were 825 households, with 942 Gaelic-speaking adults and 530 or 38.5% of the children.

The 1,663 Lone Parent households where all 2,833 adults present spoke Gaelic were bringing up 644 or 38.2% of their children in Gaelic. In the Western Isles, 638 such households with 1,251 Gaelic-speaking adults were bringing up 201 or 56.1% of their children in Gaelic. In the 1,586 Lone Parent households where 1,695 adults spoke Gaelic, 70 or 17.2% of their children were being brought up in Gaelic. In the Western Isles, the corresponding figures were 204 households, with 243 Gaelic-speaking adults and 15 or 39.4% of their children speaking Gaelic.

These cases of households with Gaelic-speaking parents and children represent a little over a quarter of all households with Gaelic speakers in Scotland and about a third of all such cases in the Western Isles. It is worthy of note that families which are otherwise strongly Gaelic show such weaknesses in bringing up children in the language. So far no research has focused on this, and we do not know the reasons why.

The families with no Gaelic-speaking adults do, however, produce some Gaelic-speaking children and this is undoubtedly strongly assisted by Gaelic-medium education and pre-school experience. In Scotland as a whole, such children totalled 3,648, of whom 366 were the Western Isles. This underlines the importance and contribution of Gaelic-medium education to the viability of the Gaelic language group – especially outwith the Western Isles. (Source: GROS 2005, RGS 2001)

2. Acquisition of Gaelic through Preschool and Playgroup Experience.

In the school year 2009–10, 858 children were in Gaelic-medium education authority nursery schooling in 58 units. In the voluntary sector, the principal organisation promoting, supporting and co-ordinating preschool Gaelic groups is TAIC (a word which means 'support' and is the new name adopted last year for the former CNSA (Comhairle nan Sgoiltean Araich / Council of Nursery Schools). It is the principal organisation for Gaelic pre-school groups. It reports numbers of children in Gaelic-medium voluntary sector preschool groups for June 2009 as 573 under 3 years, 316 4–5 years, and 889 in total, attending 67 groups nationally. (Communication to Bòrd na Gàidhlig dated 18th March 2010)

This sector has at times come closest to providing the numbers corresponding to mean annual net loss of Gaelic speakers. However the numbers do not readily transfer into Gaelic-medium primary schooling.

3. Acquisition of Gaelic through Primary Schooling

In the school year just completed (2009–10) there were 2,256 children in 60 Gaelic-medium primary units and schools. There has been some small and steady increase in these numbers in recent years. It is probably fair to say that the chief problem in expanding this sector has been the supply and availability of qualified Gaelic-medium teachers.

Numbers in preschool are very far from transferring completely into GM primary entry. There were 864 pupils in Gaelic-medium council nurseries in 2008–9, and 390 in Gaelic-medium Primary 1 classes in 2009–10. Numbers in GM primary education are likewise failing to transfer completely or even mainly into GM secondary provision. There were 295 pupils in GM Primary 7 classes in 2008–9, and 183 in GM Secondary

1 classes, albeit with 271 in Fluent Speakers' classes and 1,026 in Learners', (Sources: Strathclyde 2009, Bòrd na Gàidhlig 2010.)

4. Provision of Gaelic-medium Secondary Education.

In the school year just completed (2009–10) there were 390 secondary aged-children being educated through the medium of Gaelic at some 14 schools. In addition to this there were also 1,028 pupils in fluent speakers' classes in 38 schools, and 2,824 in learners' classes in 33 schools. Few of these latter pupils are likely to achieve fluency – any more than pupils taking school French.

To overcome demographic loss of speakers between 1991–2001, GME + fluent speakers provision needed at least 733 pupils in each preschool, primary and secondary school year. This would require the present Gaelic-medium provision to be expanded by several multiples of its present size, and this cannot be done by 2011.

5. Adult Education.

The *2001 Census* (Table UV12) identified 7,014 persons able to read and / or write but not to speak Gaelic. GROS Census Division regards these as a measure of 'Gaelic learners'. The traditional means for Gaelic to be acquired by adults has been the weekly evening class. Whilst useful this has not been particularly effective in promoting fluency. Recent developments, such as the Ulpan method, and 'TIP' (total immersion), which have been adapted from models in Israel, Wales and Canada, are proving more effective. Other means have included weekend courses and summer schools.

Adult education can make a significant but small contribution to reversing language shift (but cf. MacCaluim 2007).

6. Readers and Writers but not Speakers of Gaelic

Nevertheless the 7,014 persons in 2001 able to read and/or write Gaelic but not to speak it represent one of the most immediate opportunities to expand the number of actual speakers. How to bring this about will not be at all easy. People only reading or writing Gaelic are probably limited to these abilities through specific difficulties in developing them into full speaking confidence and understanding ability. Again the research necessary to understand this has just never been done.

7. Understanders of Spoken Gaelic.

At the time of the *2001 Census* there were 27,219 persons able to understand spoken Gaelic but not able to speak, read or write it. These brought the total of all persons with Gaelic abilities to 93,282. For the most part these 'understanders only' probably represent 'semi-speakers', i.e. persons brought up in a Gaelic environment but who lack the confidence to regard themselves as fully fluent. They represent the greatest and most immediate challenge to expanding the number of 'Gaelic-speakers'. With the development of Gaelic media, increasing everyday exposure to broadcast Gaelic may give them added confidence. Specific targeting e.g. through a dedicated radio and television series to boost Gaelic oracy may help to bring this about.

However the present availability of BBC Alba on satellite and Freesat platforms only, means that less than half of Scotland's population can receive it (probably around

23% of all television sets.). Whilst bandwidth on Freeview has been found for STV+1, regulation should ensure that BBC Alba becomes readily available also on Freeview and cable provisions.

8. Abandonment and recovery of Gaelic.

Migration removes people from the Gaelic-speaking communities and Gaelic-speaking families and takes them elsewhere. By 2001 11.6% of Scotland's population had thus been on the move annually. By 2001 over 11.1% of Gaelic speakers were similarly mobile.

In a non-Gaelic environment an isolated speaker rapidly loses the everyday experience of using the language. This is where the development of Gaelic media becomes so important in language retention.

It is no surprise that many Gaelic speakers in such circumstances fail to tick the box on a census questionnaire after some years away from a Gaelic environment. An estimate of anticipated numbers prior to the 1991 census revealed that some thousands of such individuals by then middle-aged and living in the lowlands who had ticked the box at earlier censuses no longer did so, having lived for years away from the Gaidhealtachd.

Such cases of language abandonment can only be recovered by powerful and renewed involvement in a Gaelic environment. The development of Gaelic media may similarly enable such language recovery to take place.

9. Returners

In 2001, of Scotland's 58,969 Gaelic speakers, some 6,568 or 11.1% had changed their address within the previous year. Of these some 604 or just under 1% of Gaelic-speakers had migrated back to Scotland. Country of birth tables indicate that 8.3% of Scotland's resident Gaelic population had been born outwith Scotland. (Census 2001 Table S206.) There is an unknown number of Gaelic speakers who are usually resident outwith Scotland and these represent a pool of potential Gaelic-speaking population who might return at some time for work or retirement. If 'Homecoming' persuades them to do so, some modest increase of Gaelic speakers might possibly result.

Structure of the Gaelic population and its implications

The assessment of this problem is illustrated in the accompanying population profiles. **Figure 1** illustrates the age profiles of Scotland's Gaelic and non-Gaelic populations. These demonstrate very clearly the very different characteristics of the Gaelic population compared with the non-Gaelic population. Both of them evidence a 'demographic deficit', but the Gaelic-speaker profile is the more 'top-heavy', indicating an ageing population profile. However, probably chiefly as a result of GME policies there is a 'bulge' in the 5–14 age-group. This is not entirely being carried forward and upward into the 15–29 age-groups. Thus this contributes little to the viability and vitality of the Gaelic-speaker age-profile. For this to occur, some 33.3% of the Gaelic population would need to be aged under 25. In fact only 13,258 or 22.4 % of Gaelic-speakers were under 25 in 2001.

There is a conspicuous difference in the age-profiles for younger Gaelic speakers between the populations of education authority areas which have Gaelic-medium units and those which do not. This situation is illustrated in **Figure 2**. The incidence of Gaelic speakers among young people is very greatly attenuated in the areas without Gaelic-medium education, clearly indicative of what the situation would be like in all areas without GME.

Reproduction of the language-group has diminished very specifically in the family. However the 'bulge' in the age-cohorts of full-time educational attendance indicates that Gaelic-medium education as at present functioning makes a measurable effect towards Gaelic language-group viability, but not yet at the level of reversing language shift. This is not carried through beyond the 10–14 age-group owing to weakness at the secondary level. Analysis of the actual age-groups of successive education sectors makes this point even more strongly.

In the case of the Western Isles in 2001 (**Figure 3**) only 25.7% of the primary school roll was in Gaelic-medium education and far fewer of secondary age. Only some 44.5% of the 5–11 primary age-group then spoke Gaelic, and some 57.1% of the statutory secondary age-group 12–15, which is in itself a measure of the rapidity of language shift.

The diminishing number of children speaking Gaelic was producing an insufficient proportion of population under 25 years to overcome language loss. The proportion of the total Gaelic speaking language group in the Western Isles aged under 25 years was 19.4%, which fell far short of the 33.3% minimum for potential viability. However the non-Gaelic population registered a thoroughly viable 39.2% aged under 25, indicating that it was rapidly growing, and the Gaelic population continuing rapidly to shrink. The non-Gaelic population presented a noticeably pyramidal shape indicating viable growth. We would have to go back a century to see a similar pattern in the Scottish population as a whole. This does however provide a target profile in the age-groups of youth for GM provision to aim for.

In Wales reversing language shift is being successfully addressed with robust policies in education, media, and society. If the current Gaelic situation in Scotland is similarly to be resolved, effective and long-term measures will also be necessary. The effects of education and other policies have had substantial effects upon the population structure of Welsh speakers compared with non-Welsh speakers. (See **Figure 4**.) This situation stands in some contrast with that in the Western Isles (**Figure 5**) where on a smaller scale something of the sort might have been a possibility. Although daunting, such a change can be brought about.

The current Welsh language situation (illustrated above in **Figure 4**) shows a quite remarkable proportion of Welsh speakers aged under 25, and evidenced a thoroughly viable proportion under 25 of 44.2%. This can be compared with the non-Welsh speaking population of Wales, where the proportion of non-Welsh-speakers under 25 was 27.8% – technically not fully reproducing itself. In Wales reversing language shift is being successfully addressed with robust policies in education, media, and society. If the current Gaelic situation in Scotland is similarly to be resolved, effective and long-term measures will also be necessary.

The population profiles for Gaelic speakers in the principal Gaelic-area education authority areas show the effects of Gaelic-medium education even more plainly. (See **Figures 6, 7 and 8**.) Although there are conspicuous 'bulges' of Gaelic speakers in the age-groups of school attendance, these are not followed through. Moreover, none of this is however yet at a level which can effectively reverse language shift.

The other (Lowland) areas with Gaelic-medium education likewise evidence this 5–14 years 'bulge' of young Gaelic speakers, which nevertheless reduces in subsequent

Figure 1: Population Pyramid: Non - Gaelic - and Gaelic - speakers Census 2001 Scotland.
Source: GROS special tabulations 30.05.08; 15.07.09.

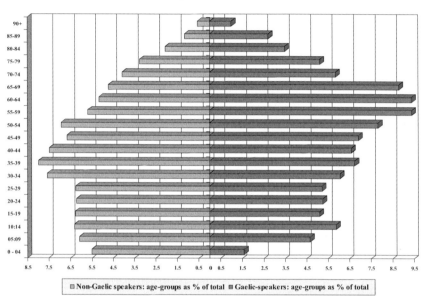

Figure 2: Population Pyramid: Gaelic-speakers in Council Areas with and without GME 2001
Source: GROS special tabulations 30.05.08.

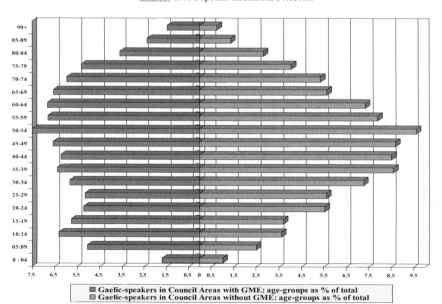

Figure 3: Population Pyramid: Non - Gaelic - and Gaelic - speakers Eileanan Siar (Western Is.) 2001.
Source: GROS special tabulations 30.05.08.

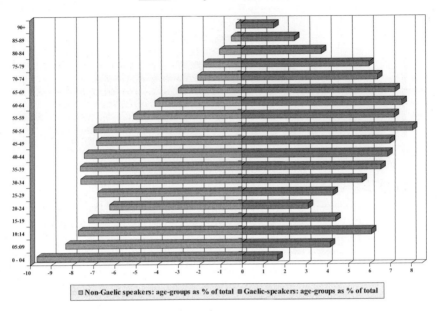

Figure 4: Population Pyramid: Non - Welsh - and Welsh - speakers Census 2001 Wales.
Source: Welsh Language Board, special tabulation Table CO946.

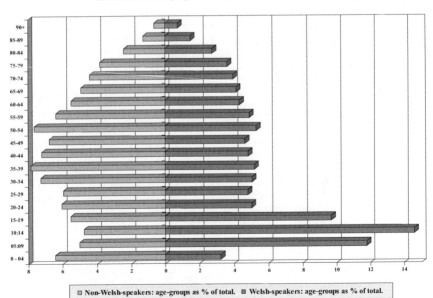

Figure 5: Population Pyramid: Non - Gaelic - and Gaelic - speakers Eileanan Siar (Western Is.) 2001.
<u>Source:</u> GROS special tabulations 30.05.08.

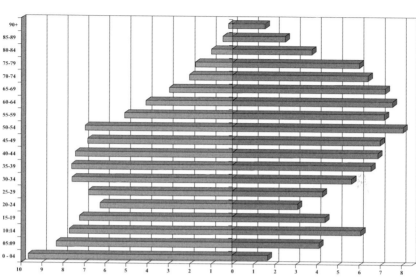

Figure 6: Population Pyramid: Gaelic - speakers Eileanan Siar (Western Isles) 2001.
<u>Source:</u> GROS special tabulations 30.05.08.

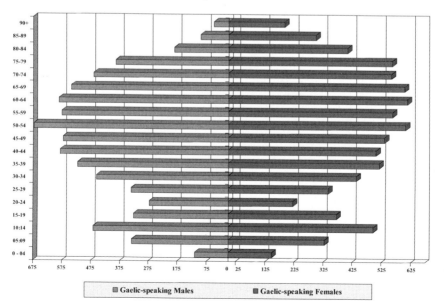

Figure 7: Population Pyramid: Gaelic - speakers Highland Council Area 2001.
Source: GROS special tabulations 30.05.08.

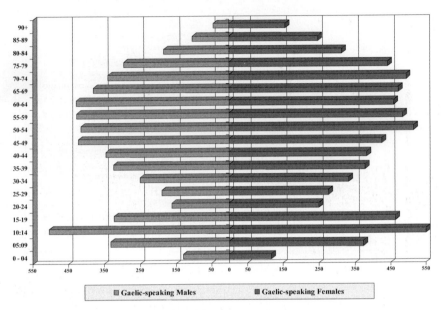

Figure 8: Population Pyramid: Gaelic - speakers Argyll & Bute Council Area 2001.
Source: GROS special tabulations 30.05.08.

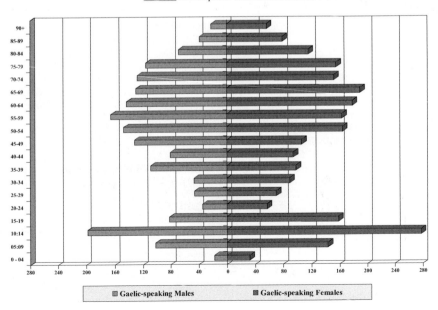

years and in most cases fails to produce overall reversal of language shift. However the areas without Gaelic-medium education show very clearly what the overall situation would be like without it: a very sharply attenuating profile whose subsequent ageing is very likely mitigated only by retirement of Gaelic-speakers to their original home areas.

Strategies for Growth

The above nine categories represent the chief sources for increasing the numbers of actual speakers of Gaelic. In order to turn that potential into reality, specific and effective strategies will need to be adopted in each of these particular circumstances. Such policies have clear resource implications.

The circumstances of each of these situations will need to be understood – and that calls for research. Effective policy cannot be created blind. Hit or miss ad hoc policies are not assured of any success. Over the past year, Bòrd na Gàidhlig has commissioned research into such areas as attitudes and abilities re Gaelic in the community, adult learners, technologies in support of corpus, assessment of Gaelic projects, contextual support for young people, placenames, lexicography, Gaelic-medium education, and Gaelic electronic gaming. Other current research includes further analysis of the *Western Isles Language Plan*[2] (2004–5).

Bòrd na Gàidhlig initiated a *National Gaelic Plan 2007–12*[2] and an associated *Gaelic Education Strategy*[3] in 2007. This represents the most concerted means to date for developing measures which can address language shift in the Gaelic community.

As the direct result of the ministerial challenge in June 2009, and using the analysis undertaken for this paper, Bòrd na Gàidhlig developed a targeted strategy over autumn 2009 to early spring 2010 aimed at increasing actual numbers of Gaelic speakers. This plan *Ginealach Ùr na Gàidhlig / An Action Plan to Increase the Number of Gaelic Speakers*[4] was published on 13 April 2010 and comprises the priorities of the Bòrd from April 2010 to March 2012. It supports the present *National Plan 2007–12*,[5] and will establish the groundwork for the *Second National Plan 2012–17*.

The plan identifies five Priority Action Areas:

1. Support for parents;
2. Promotion of Gaelic acquisition;
3. Adult learning;
4. 0–5 years education;
5. 5–18 years education.

Emphasis is made on initiatives within the family, developing new technologies in support of Gaelic, and new means of acquisition such as total immersion, Ulpanim, Gaelic social and learning centres, online and broadcast resources, as well as strengthening existing initiatives in education.

In his Sabhal Mòr Ostaig lecture,[6] in December 2009, Michael Russell called for

---

[1] www.cne-siar.gov.uk/sgioba/documents/languageplan/plan_g.pdf.

[2] Available at: ww.bord-na-gaidhlig.org.uk/National-Plan/National%20Plan%20for%20Gaelic.pdf.

[2] www.sfc.ac.uk/nmsruntime/saveasdialog.aspx?IID=1264&sID.

[3] Available at: ww.gaidhlig.org.uk/Downloads/Ginealach-Ur-na-Gaidhlig-English-2011.pdf.

[5] see footnote 2.

[6] available on video at ww.smo.uhi.ac.uk/A-Cholaiste/Naidheachdan/M-Russell_en.php.

fresh ideas: some new thoughts; some direct, targeted action; some urgency; and some results. He asked Bòrd na Gàidhlig to address three specific requests:

1. Identify £600k from within existing budgets to channel towards additional language acquisition projects;
2. Examine the delivery mechanisms we have in place and find more effective ways of using current funding to increase speakers;
3. Find ways of supporting councils to increase the numbers of Gaelic speakers through work in schools.

The Gaelic language is undoubtedly undergoing a major transformation today, probably even more radical than its five or so previous transformations – as the language of an incursive colonising settle¬ment; as the language of the early Scottish state; as the language of an autonomous Highlands/Hebrides; as a language-group transforming from feudalism to clan system; and as the language of the crofting community (MacKinnon 1991). The question is whether or not the language will be capable of a further transformation, and become involved in the formation of new realities and have a new and continuing place in Scottish society.

David Crystal (2000: 141–2) observes that 'an endangered language will progress if its speakers can make use of electronic technology … The internet in particular offers endangered languages … a fresh set of opportunities whose potential has hardly begun to be explored.' Gaelic has indeed begun to exploit the new technology. I would go further than Crystal and say that the new technology enables new cyber communities to be established and the language to be embed¬ded in new activities in addition to the traditional local communities and the new urban social networks. Minority-language groups such as Gaelic need to embrace the new technology or die.

References

Bòrd na Gàidhlig. 2010. *Number of Pupils in Gaelic-medium Education 2009–2010*. Inverness.
Crystal, D. 2000. *Language Death*. Cambridge: Cambridge: University Press.
Registrar General for Scotland. 2008. Source: GRO(S) *Census 2001. Scotland: Special Tabulation 13.08.08*. Gaelic in Households.Edinburgh: Census Customer Services
General Register Office for Scotland. *Census 2001. Scotland*. Table S143.Gaelic in Households; S206 Sex and Age and Whether Born in Scotland by Knowledge of Gaelic; UV12 Knowledge of Gaelic.
MacKinnon, K. 1991. *Gaelic a Past and Future Prospect*, Edinburgh: Saltire Society.
Registrar General for Scotland. 2005. *Census 2001. Scotland Gaelic Report*. Edinburgh: General Register Office for Scotland, Table 26: Dependent children 3+ speaking Gaelic in Gaelic speaking households
University of Strathclyde Education. 2009. Pupil Numbers in Gaelic Education 2008–09.

The Human Factor: Community Language Workers and National Strategies

Michelle Macleod

Introduction

National language strategies rely on various groups and individuals to implement them. Often these individuals work in challenging conditions removed from the strategists yet their work is vital to the success of any language plan. With this in mind it is essential that language *animateurs* or strategy enablers are supported and valued. This paper discusses some findings from recent fieldwork carried out with workers in this sector and illustrates issues which need to be addressed to support these individuals to give the national strategies every chance of succeeding.

Background

Language planning literature and research gives us some insight into the importance of developing and maintaining what are essentially good human resource strategies in order to maximise the output of any language plan and strategy (Mac Donnacha 2000, Kaplan and Baldauf 1997): the difficulty of effective management in this area is alluded to, if not of central concern. There is certainly a paucity of research in issues relating to language development *animateurs*; this is in spite of the heavy reliance placed upon small groups and individuals in communities to ensure the success of various strategies. In Scotland the *The National Plan for Gaelic* has the establishment of community initiatives as one of its key projects:

> Bòrd na Gàidhlig, together with key partners, will investigate and then establish local development initiatives to increase the use of Gaelic in communities, having particular regard to the example of the Welsh *Mentrau Iaith*. (Bòrd na Gàidhlig 2007 p. 23)

It is anticipated that this action will strengthen the use of Gaelic in the community, which is one of the Bòrd's priority areas for action.

The strategy does not go further in demonstrating how it will create these local initiatives, although we know that Comunn na Gàidhlig (CnaG) have been contracted to develop such a network of language initiatives (*Iomairtean Cànain*); neither does the *National Plan* indicate what support mechanisms will be put in place for these, or existing community initiatives or workers. Of course, it is not necessarily the place of a national language plan to discuss the minutiae of implementation; but the strategists should take care to consider support and training methods for individuals involved in this sector somewhere, as they do, for example, in relation to the Gaelic journalism sector, which the *National Plan* does discuss in terms of human resource management and development (2007: 25). Training needs have also been recognised for other Gaelic employment sectors: for example the arts sector recognises the need for professional development (*A National Gaelic Arts Strategy 2009–2012*) and current trends in supporting Gaelic teachers are very positive (e.g. Bòrd na Gàidhlig 2007: 62); these should be taken as paradigms for developing support mechanisms in the community sector.

However, to understand fully how best to support community language workers in order that they may fulfil their part of any national / macro language policy, there needs to be a better understanding of what they do, why they do it, how they feel about it and how successful they are at their jobs. A survey of this nature is potentially intimidating to an employee, yet a full representation of their work practices is essential.

Grin, in addressing the cost-effectiveness of various projects and establishing a framework for economic analysis, noted that in general 'evaluation instruments' were 'largely missing' in language planning (1999: 1). Kaplan and Baldauf (1997) have noted that with regard to on-the-ground activity, effective measurement of language planning and language development initiatives is particularly difficult and has not been effectively addressed. One of the main reasons for this is the difficulty in assessing well-intentioned language *animateurs* in the community: there is the risk that critical assessment of these efforts (often by volunteers or low-paid staff) may lose the good will of the individuals (which is vital for language development) or possibly even turn away these *animateurs*.

Several aspects of this occupation require that research in this area is carried out sensitively and respectfully; based on the results of the survey (discussed below) and from mainstream literature on community development work, the factors which make this sector challenging include:

- people work in isolation or in small groups: it tends to be isolating and isolated
- work is often project-based commonly resulting in employees on short-term contracts and work being very outcome-focussed (known as the 'casualization' process [Henderson and Glen, 2006: 284])
- the work is in full view of the community
- inconsistency in the personnel; the mainstream literature suggests that personnel change rapidly in community work (Henderson and Glen, 2006)

With regard to the last point, above, the numbers from the fieldwork (discussed below) do not, at least superficially, tend to support this with five people out of twenty having worked in their positions for more than nine years, and six out of twenty working for between four and eight years, thus indicating a lot of experience. However, there is correlation between the experience of main-stream community workers and a number of comments from individuals in the Gaelic community sector which state quite explicitly that there is a failure to progress in the sector professionally which leads to people leaving.

Before looking in detail at the results of the survey, it is pertinent to consider one other challenge in this sector: and this is to do with the difficult relationship between 'funder' and 'recipient', especially where the funder is the strategist and the recipient is a strategy-enabler. In a study of the voluntary language sector movement in Ireland, this 'difficult' relationship has already been described:

> Tá ról an-deacair acu [Foras na Gaeilge] chomh maith, dar leo toisc go mbíonn muid go léir ag troid, agus mar sin de, faoi chúrsaí áirithe. Tá ról an-deacair acu mar níl   fhios acu an mbaineann siad leis an stát nó an mbainean siad linne, muinntir na Gaeilge, agus níl sé sin oibrithe amach acu agus níl fhios agam an féidir leo é a oibriú amach. Ach is buncheist í, an bhfuil siad linn nó inár gcoinne?

> They [Foras na Gaeilge] have a very difficult role as well because we are all fighting and so on about certain issues. They have a very difficult role because they don't know if they are connected to the State or to us, Irish language people, and they haven't worked it out and I don't know if they can work it out. But the fundamental question is, are they with us or against us? (Donoghue 2004: 36)

Clearly it would be hard to make a case that Foras na Gaeilge are in fact against the language activists, but the perception noted is important and is similar to some views expressed in recent fieldwork in this sector in Scotland.

To date, most research carried out in this sector and examining the work practices of these *animateurs* / enablers has been commissioned studies of a specific group(s) on behalf of a stakeholder often with some kind of management capacity, i.e. as a result of internal systems review or on behalf of the funder; Kaplan and Baldauf note that when evaluations have been carried out, that these are often 'for restricted audiences and have not therefore been published' (1997: 90). We find several examples of publicly available studies in Wales, including surveys of, for example, the *Urdd* (the Welsh youth movement), *Twf* (the early intervention organisation promoting and supporting bilingualism in the family) and the *mentrau iaith* (both independent *mentrau* and as a group). A major report into the activity of the *mentrau iaith*, which was carried out in 2000, nine years after the first one started, was exceptionally positive about the commitment and enthusiasm shown by *mentrau* employees, but it did point out quite strongly that there was a lack of training and professional experience in relation to language planning amongst the employees. It also stated that management structures needed to improve as did pay and conditions; particular mention was made of the need to provide relevant training; although this might sound negative, the assessment of the mentrau was on the whole very positive (Jones and Ioan 2000). In Scotland Bòrd na Gàidhlig commissioned some evaluation of its funded projects in 2009 and Fèisean nan Gàidheal (2005) commissioned a piece of research into their activities. With regard to independent research, there has been one small piece of research carried out on a CnaG project (Gaelic in the Community) and the writer, McEwan-Fujita commented on the inappropriateness of the Scheme's internal assessment procedures, noting that the 'measurable outcomes' were too closely aligned to socio-economic practice and 'could work against the goals of minority language-planning' (McEwan-Fujita 2005: 167). It is in this arena that my present research is positioned: it is a challenging work environment; there is suggestion of a difficult relationship between funder and contractor; there is little history of independent research into community-based language development activity and there is already an indication from similar work environments that there are weaknesses in human resource management. My research is based upon a survey, about which I will now report.

The Survey

The survey, which I conducted in Summer 2010, was largely modelled on human resources questionnaires and guided by the principals adopted in the survey of community development workers in England in 2009 (see, Sender, Carlisle, Hatamian and Bowles 2010); it was conducted via post/email amongst individuals who work at community level in different locations and doing different roles: although all are clearly community language *animateurs*. These individuals were identified to me through contacts with organisations, advice from people who have or had been involved in this sector or from personal knowledge. The Chief Executives from both Comunn na Gàidhlig and Fèisean nan Gàidheal willingly distributed the questionnaire amongst relevant employees and other national and local organisations also participated: 25 responses were received representing views from seven organisations. Twenty responses have been used to inform my discussion as five replies came from volunteers or self-employed language activists. All bar one of these organisations follows the structure of being a company limited by guarantee with charitable status and again all bar one relies heavily on grant funding from a combination of sources. The one exception in this group is a Local Authority and, although they do not fall into the same structural organisation patterns as the others, it was clear from correspondence with the two employees that many, if not all, of the issues which affected the other respondents also affected them. All of the respondents chose to participate in the survey and no-one was required to do so; thus it is a self-selecting group and might not necessarily be representative of all of this sector.

Much of the analysis below gives some indication of what enablers and implementers of national strategies have to say about the developing situation in the language planning sector, where stakeholders are guided largely by one strategy (as opposed to mainly working independently of one another in the past). The results of this fieldwork study with community language workers gives some insight into the capacity and disposition of this group of key individuals, on whom the success of part of the strategy rests. Particular components of the research pertaining to training, communication practices, working conditions, support systems and assessment procedures are of most relevance to this issue of interaction between the coal-face workers and the strategists.

Training

More than two thirds of the respondents had a degree (or post-graduate degree) in some or other subject and nearly half had received some kind of training in their work. Training could involve anything from child protection, to dealing with money, committee management, first aid etc. None had received any training in language planning, language development and only one was a qualified community education worker; compare this figure to the findings of the Community Development Foundation in England which found that 46 per cent of paid practitioners had a qualification relevant to community development (Sender, Carlisle, Hatamian and Bowles 2010: 51). In spite of this, the majority of people thought that they had the appropriate knowledge and training to undertake their job, even though two out of five of them did not receive any type of induction training. Two Chief Executives of the larger organisations who have employees in different communities indicated in correspondence that they feel it would be beneficial to their employees to receive training in some area aligned to language planning and development. Indeed when the employees had the opportunity to chose from a list provided what type of training they would like 18 out of 20 said that they would like to receive examples of good practice in minority language development; 13 out of 20 said that they would like training in language planning theory and community development. This point was made clearly by one respondent who said:

> Training in community work is essential if workers are not to burn out
> with exhaustion and feelings of being ineffectual . Firing young Gaelic

speakers into communities with no training or professional support does not help communities and just results in the young person becoming dissatisfied, dispirited and eventually leaving.

The *animateurs* also identified other areas that they would like to receive training in, including: managing an organisation, facility management, events management, fundraising etc. Two of the respondents quite clearly made the link between training and developing and maintaining the expertise in this sector: one pointing out that there seemed to be a failure to support staff to progress thus not allowing future leaders to come through (as witnessed in the difficulty recently in filling senior jobs in the Gaelic development sector).

> A clearer sense of career structures; opportunities for lateral and vertical movement within the sector; a stronger sense of cohesion within the context of planning; and a stronger sense that people understand and appreciate the difficulty of working in development. In the absence of these things, people who gain some experience tend to take it elsewhere rather than using it for the enhancement of their current organisation or the other elements of the Gaelic development sector, which leads to a lack of capable people at a variety of ranks.

Communication

With regard to communication, most of the informants said that they use Gaelic in their day-to-day work. Amongst colleagues, most maintain that there is good communication and that they have the opportunity to participate in planning and in the internal governance of their organisation and to pass opinion when appropriate; this is a very healthy sign for the individual groups concerned: providing a sense of ownership and belonging. However, more than half thought that there was not good communication within the Gaelic development sector as a whole. This topic drew quite a lot of comments from the respondents, indicating strength of opinion on this: those who did make comment felt that Bòrd na Gàidhlig did not understand the work they were doing and one other commented on the need for improved channels for sharing good practice:

> Bhiodh e math cuideachd nan cuireadh na daoine a bhios ag aontachadh phlanaichean 's eile, gu sònraichte aig Bòrd na Gàidhlig, fiu 's beagan eòlas air dè cho math 's a tha iad a' freagairt air coimhearsnachdan.
> (*It would be good also if the people who agree the plans etc, especially at Bòrd na Gàidhlig, would get to know, even a little, how these suit the communities.*)

> Those with the purse strings actually understanding what we do and why.

> Communication is a major problem, as indicated above. There is no real network for sharing information; Bòrd na Gàidhlig don't seem to know who is actively working for the language (even when they have given them funding !); many people seem happy to work inside their own wee box but, because funding will always be tight, we need to share every

good idea and working practice we can; there is a very small 'talent pool' so we need to help young people to develop skills.

Còmhradh onorach agus aonta fhaighinn air dè dha rì-ribh a tha sinn a' dol a dhèanamh gun a bhith ag atharrachadh phlanaichean a h-uile mìos.
(*Honest conversation to get agreement on what exactly we are going to do with changing plans every month*)

Working conditions

With regard to working conditions: obviously these need to be satisfactory in order for a person to function to his or her best ability in order to get the best results. It is obvious from the survey that most of these individuals do a lot of travelling for their work and that many of them work a lot outside of the workplace. Although the majority say that they have colleagues, a majority also say that in general they work alone. So, this is a picture of an isolated and possibly stressful work-pattern.

With regard to management structures, the majority work to a management committee and the majority of people do have access to a supervisor with expertise. Most agree that they have the necessary equipment to allow them to carry out their work.

One place where there is a clear weakness is in relation to job status. Two thirds were unhappy with the lack of job security and a little more than that agreed that there was no career structure or promotion pathway. It is hard to build a career or promotion structure into short-term project work, which is a common structure in this sector; clearly these factors, even in permanent positions, can lead to demotivation. Obviously a demotivated workforce is not conducive to an active one. One informant made the following comment:

> Community work is very much driven by the individual's own motivation so keeping the batteries charged is very important. The factors which demotivate are job insecurity, low pay, and lack of recognition.

Again, it is interesting to compare this situation with that of 'mainstream' community development workers. From a UK-wide survey carried out between 2001 and 2003, Henderson and Glen noted:

> 'Casualization' is the word used in the survey report to describe the occupational sector in community development work. Short-term contracts, with many workers having to spend significant amounts of time fundraising for their own posts, are clear manifestations of the situation. (2006: 284)

However Sender *et al.* noted from the 2009 survey that the situation seemed to have improved with the majority of paid respondents employed on a permanent contract (68 percent); they highlighted the importance of this with a quote from a respondent: 'Staff have permanent contracts which promotes long-term trust and development.' (Sender *et al.* 2010: 35)

Support Systems / Assessment

Within the various groups, it is apparent that two thirds are appraised on their work and they are happy with this: significantly there is a third who do not have access to appraisal systems. A little more than half of the group were of the opinion that too much is expected of them in their work and that there are not enough people to do the work. To put this into context: a number of Comunn na Gàidhlig's new *Iomairtean Cànain* development officers have responsibilities for large or dispersed communities: for example Lochaber, north-west Lewis, Glasgow. This belief that the sector was understaffed came out not only through the questions, but also in comments left by individuals. This information is significant as it shows us again that these employees are likely to be in stressful work environments. Connected to this, more than half of the respondents maintain that they do not have enough time to carry out their duties.

> Cha robh daoine gu leòr ann gus seirbhis fìor phroifiseanta a thoirt seachad.
> (*There weren't enough people to give a truly professional service.*)

Linked to appraisal and esteem, the majority were of the opinion that their work was appreciated by the local community; however, the proportion was not so high with regard to how they felt they were valued by national language planners with two out of five of the opinion that their work was not valued by national strategists. This emphasises again that there seems to be a problem between the strategy implementers and the strategy writers. It is unlikely that it is just a communication problem as the majority of the respondents said that they understood their role in the national language strategy. What it does indicate however is that there is lack of confidence in this sector: in fact two out of five reported that there was not good confidence in their organisations.

Conclusion

The survey has shown that this is a thoroughly committed workforce and that there is a lot of experience amongst this group. There is an indication, however, that morale is sometimes low due to stressful work patterns and that there is a communication failure between strategists and implementers. The conclusion that has to be made from this research is that it is time to view this somewhat disjointed group as a sector in its own right: to bring them together, albeit on a theoretical or virtual network of some kind, to put in place appropriate training and communication procedures that allow the sharing of best practice and a collegiate sense of partnership that involves not only the different groups, but also the strategists.

References

Bòrd na Gàidhlig 2007. *Plana Nàiseanta na Gàidhlig 2007–2012 / The National Plan for Gaelic 2007–2012*, Inverness: Bòrd na Gàidhlig.

Cobarrubias, J. and J.A. Fishman. eds. 1983. *Progress in Language Planning: International Perspectives*, Berlin: Walter de Gruyter.

Donoghue, F. 2004. *Consistence and Persistence: Roles, Relationships and Resources of Irish Language Voluntary Organisations*, Dublin: Comhdháil Náisiúnta na Gaeilge and The Centre for Nonprofit Management.

Edwards, V. and L.P. Newcombe. 2005. 'When School is Not Enough: New Initiatives in Intergenerational Language Transmission in Wales'. *The International Journal of Bilingual Education and Bilingualism* 8.4: 289–312.

Gaelic Arts Strategic Development Forum. 2009. *The National Gaelic Arts Strategy 2009–2012.*

Grenoble L.A. and L.J. Whaley. 2006. *Saving Languages: An Introduction to Language Revitalization.* Cambridge University Press.

Grin, F. and F. Vaillancourt 1999. *The Cost-effectiveness Evaluation of Minority Language Policies: Case Studies on Wales, Ireland and the Basque Country.* Flensburg: European Centre for Minority Issues.

Henderson, P, and A. Glen. 2006. 'From Recognition to Support: Community Development Workers in the United Kingdom'. *Community Development Journal,* 41.3: 277–92.

Jones, K. and G. Ioan. 2000. *Venturing Onwards: Review of the Mentrau Iaith,* Castell Newydd: Cwmni Iaith Cyf.

Kaplan, R.B. and R.B. Baldauf, Jr. 1997. *Language Planning from Practice to Theory,* Clevedon: Multilingual Matters.

Lewis, G. and A. Richards. 2004. *A Review to Measure the Effectiveness and Efficiency of Urdd Bobaith Cymru's National Activities Network.* Report Presented to the Welsh Language Board, March.

Mac Donnacha, J. 2000. 'An Integrated Planning Model'. *Language Problems and Language Planning* 24: 11–35.

Macleod, M. 2007. 'Measuring Gaelic Language Planning'. *Scots Language* 26: 61–78'

McEwan-Fujita, E. 2005. 'Neo-liberalism and Minority Language Planning in the Highlands and Islands of Scotland'. *International Journal of the Sociology of Language* 171: 155–71.

Sender, H., Carlisle, B., Hatamian A. and M. Bowles. 2010. *Report on Survey of Community Development Practitioners and Managers.* London: Community Development Foundation.

Broad S. and J. France. 2005. *25 Bliadhna de na Fèisean / 25 years of the Fèisean. The Participants' Story: Attitudinal research on the Fèis Movement in Scotland,* Glasgow: RSAMD National Centre for Research in the Performing Arts.

Welsh Language Board. 2006. *Voluntary Sector Strategy.*

Williams, C. and J. Evans 1997. *The Community Research Project.* Cardiff: The University of Wales, Cardiff and The Welsh Language Board.

Williams, C. 2000. *Language Revitalization Policy and Planning in Wales.* Cardiff: University of Wales Press.

Plans, Plans, Plans

Brian Ó hEadhra

When I was a teenager growing up in Dublin I had two ambitions (let's call them plans); one was to be a lead singer in a band and the other was to work for the Irish language (is that so strange?). I recorded my first album with the band Anam in Stiúideo a Seacht at the back of Bórd na Gaeilge in Merrion Square, Dublin in 1993. The band used to walk through the building to get to the studio and I used to be in awe of the various office workers striving every day to save our language and culture. Believe it or not, they were heroes in my mind. Who knows, some of you may be sitting in the audience today! The fact is that I realised early on that to get ahead in life you needed to have ambition, achievable targets and some sort of plan to reach each target set. I believe this applies across the board, whether it is a matter of when during the week you are going to mow the lawn to long term planning for a national arts strategy. Some plans you write down, others you just store in your mind to act upon when necessary.

What I aim to do in this presentation is to discuss planning at three levels. The first is Personal Plans; how you want to live your life and how you want to bring up your children (if you have any). The second is Local or Community Plans; what committees you sit on and how you interact with your friends, neighbours, colleagues. Third is the most challenging, which are National Plans; these are plans which you have a small part to play and aims to progress the nation as a whole. I am going to draw on my personal experiences and keep it focused on the Scottish Gaelic language. In a way, this is just a snap shot of my life and I hope it will come across a positive reflection on how we can work together to make our language and culture a normal part of everyday life in Scotland.

Personal Plans

I started learning Scottish Gaelic in 1999. My wife and I were just married and we were fortunate to get a scholarship to attend Sabhal Mòr Ostaig for a year's course in Gaelic. I had been living in the central belt of Scotland since 1997 and although I was interested in Irish Gaelic I never seemed to be able to break into the whole Scottish Gaelic world. It seemed like a club which you almost needed a password to get into. Is it still like this? Anyway, the plan was to study Gaelic in Skye for a year and then see where things took us. Since learning Gaelic in 1999/2000 I have never been out of, or in want of work. By learning Gaelic I soon became immersed in this rich and diverse culture. I knew it existed, as it does in Ireland, but when I lived in Edinburgh, I can tell you, it seemed like a million miles away.

Having left Sabhal Mòr Ostaig I became the first manager of the new Gaelic Arts and Culture Centre, Taigh Dhonnchaidh, in Ness, in the north of the Isle of Lewis, Outer Hebrides. Myself and my wife were warmly welcomed to this rural community and we were involved in planning many projects such as language, music, song and dance workshops, concerts and festivals. My Gaelic was coming on leaps and bounds and I planned at this point that I would aim to use the language in all levels of my life; personal and at work. Since then I have worked in the Gaelic language in the public and private sector as: a Gaelic Development Officer with Comunn Na Gàidhlig,

Artistic Director of the Blas festival, Ùlpan tutor of Gaelic, Professional Musician/singer, Manager of Nòs Ùr song competition for Cetlic and Scots languages, among other things.

We moved to Inverness in 2001 and although it was very different to Ness where Gaelic is an everyday language, I managed to find plenty of Gaelic speakers to mingle with and also plenty of work as I mentioned above. My personal plan to learn Gaelic and immerse myself in the Scottish Gaelic culture was going great guns.

Now Fiona and I are lucky to have two lovely daughters, Órla (5) and Róise (3) NicChoinnich Ní Eadhra (did you notice the Irish and Scottish Gaelic thing going on there?). I had to make a serious decision when Órla was born as to what language I would speak with her. English is my first language and the one in which I know all the terminology, songs, terms of affection in, etc. But I had plans for my children to be fluent Gaelic speakers, not like me who had to spend years struggling to learn Irish and then years learning Scottish Gaelic. So, I bit the bullet and decided to never ever speak to my children in English. Even when I get angry with them I stick to my language plan, and I'll tell you, that's tricky.

The children go to the local Gaelic school – Bunsgoil Ghàidhlig Inbhir Nis. Parents had been campaigning for this school for 20 years and we were fortunate that we it opened when our children were ready for school and also that we lived close by. Unlike my experiences as a child, the children at the bunsgoil love going there and are very comfortable with their bilingualism. Saying that, I have to admit that they often use English in their everyday speech. There is so much English spoken around them by their peers, television, adults, it is impossible to win. I am confident however that they will grow up to be confident and fluent Gaelic speakers. Like me, having Gaelic will, no doubt, offer them far greater job opportunities; especially if they stay in Scotland.

Local and Community Plans

I've already mentioned that parents in Inverness spent two decades fighting for a Gaelic school. Soon after moving to Inverness I saw that there was a need for a group to campaign for the rights of Gaelic language speakers in the area. Monolingual signs were common place and, at the time, there seemed to be little regard for the needs and wishes for Gaelic speakers and families by the authorities. Myself and a friend, David Boag, started Fòram Gàidhlig Inbhir Nis which aimed to be *Guth nan Gàidheal*, the voice of the Gaelic community. We got together a committee, charitable status, set up a website (www.inbhirnis.org), and started a number of campaigns to encourage the community, media and authorities to take the needs of the Gaelic speakers in the community seriously. Things have moved on greatly over the past 10 years but there are still major hurdles to overcome.

Fòram Gàidhlig Inbhir Nis are currently managing a huge undertaking in trying to establish a major Gaelic language centre beside the Bunsgoil. This building is the first of its kind in Scotland and will have three elements to it. Firstly it will have a Gaelic medium wrap-around childcare centre ages 0-5 and after-school activities. The second part of the building will be office space for all the main Gaelic language organisations based in Inverness, including Bòrd na Gàidhlig, Comunn Na Gàidhlig, Clì Gàidhlig, Fèisean nan Gàidheal and An Comunn Gàidhealach. Finally, we will have an arts and cultural space to encourage events, talks and learning activity, all through the medium of Gaelic. This is an extremely ambitious project which will, we hope, create a strong Gaelic language environment (campus) encompassing the new Gaelic centre, the bunsgoil and the Royal Inverness Academy (IRA), all of which are in the same area. I must say that we take great encouragement from the successes of projects such as An Cultúrlann in Belfast and Áras Chrónain in Dublin.

As chair of the local Gaelic language parents association called Comunn nam Pàrant-Inbhir Nis, I and the committee campaign for Gaelic medium education (GME) across the city and surrounding area. There are huge difficulties in keeping children in GME in secondary school and it is also difficult to find teachers for all the subjects required. Ultimately we see the need for at least one or two other Gaelic medium primary schools in the city, a standalone Gaelic secondary school and many more preschool groups supported across the region.

There are many more community activities promoting the Gaelic language and culture in Inverness. I have only mentioned some of the activities I am currently involved in. There is a huge amount of goodwill and voluntary time put into planning and initiating Gaelic language activity on a local level. This sector needs support from the funders and language planners and should never be taken for granted. I also believe the time is ripe for increased communication and co-operation between Gaelic speakers and communities across Ireland, Scotland and the Isle of Man. Send me an email!

National Plans

In April 2010, I became the first Gaelic Arts and Culture Officer working for both Bòrd na Gàidhlig and the newly created Alba Chruthachail/Creative Scotland, which was a merger between the Scottish Arts Council and Scottish Screen. So, in effect, I have two line-managers, two business cards, two email addresses, two different sets of colleagues. One of my key roles in this post is to bring Gaelic Arts and Culture to a wider audience and create links between the Bòrd and Alba Chruthachail as well as other national and local bodies.

Of course, as you would expect, the plans I work to are much bigger in size, budget, and scope than what I have already mentioned. In my work I have to be informed about what national plans impact on the Gaelic arts and culture. As Bòrd na Gàidhlig and Alba Chruthachail are my employers I make sure to firstly adhere to and support their own different plans. As you would expect, Bòrd na Gàidhlig is interested in primarily growing the numbers of Gaelic speakers and opportunities for people to use Gaelic. In the Bòrd's work plan, *An Ginealach Ùr na Gàidhlig*, there is a keen focus on young Gaelic speakers. If we don't, for example, keep the teenagers interested in speaking the language then it is unlikely they will, in time, send their own children to Gaelic medium education or use Gaelic in the home.

Creative Scotland aims to *invest in talented people and exciting ideas, develop the creative industries and champion everything that's good about Scottish creativity*. I'm sure most of you will agree that the arts play a key role in getting people interested in language and culture as well as keeping them engaged throughout their life. A considerable amount of Bòrd na Gàidhlig's budget is used in supporting various Gaelic arts bodies and projects.

I primarily work to a document called the National Gaelic Arts Strategy (NGAS). This ambitious plan runs from 2008–12 and helps me and others to focus on how we can develop and promote the various Gaelic arts across the nation. The main thing which I have learned over the time I have been working as Gaelic Arts and Culture Officer is that no matter what a plan says communication between bodies and individuals is the most important thing. For any plan to remain relevant it also needs to be flexible. Society, politics and the economy are changing at a rapid pace and it is up to public servants (like me) to keep tweaking our work plans to keep up with what the public and practitioners expect of us.

Plans, strategies, reports don't necessarily have to be huge weighty tomes which are inaccessible to the average reader. One might argue that too many public servants have, in the past, spent too much time talking about, researching and writing plans rather than actually getting down to delivering practical and effective projects and activities within the community. In this current economic climate everything is under scrutiny, and rightly so. When I meet with arts groups, local authorities and public bodies I constantly ask them how are they co-operating with others; how do their plans fit in with others; how are their plans going to encourage people to learn or speak Gaelic?

Our indigenous languages are under constant threat. We all have a part to play, no matter how big or small, in helping to keep them alive. I'll finish by asking you a short question: What's *your* plan?

The Culture of Gaelic in Ireland and Scotland: *An Saol Gaelach agus An Saoghal Gaidhealach*

Gordon McCoy

This is a personal and anecdotal attempt, with tongue somewhat in cheek, to compare the Scottish and Irish Gaelic scenes[1], based upon my own experiences as a learner of both languages. For Irish speakers, Gàidhlig is a way of trying something new; Scotland is an alternative Gaelic universe. I am looking at Scotland through Irish eyes, and can only guess at the view from the other side.

A simultaneous sense of recognition and bewilderment begins when an Irish speaker first encounters written Gàidhlig. This seems at times to the Irish to be like a conservative version of their own language; the orthography is quite traditional, even baroque, to Irish eyes. Some words are poetic, even romantic, with resonances of Irish literature. For example, the Gàidhlig word *uaine* ('green') appears in Irish poetry; *glas* is the everyday word for 'green' in Ireland. Yet Gàidhlig throws up some obstacles for the Irish learner. There are numerous false friends; words that sound the same but have different meanings. Here are some:

Gàidhlig word (Irish spelling in brackets, if different)	Scottish meaning	Irish meaning
bruidhinn (*bruíon*)	talk	quarrel
dealan (*dealán*)	electricity	sunny spell between showers
dealbh	picture	statue
dìon (*díon*)	defence	roof
dòigheil (*dóighiúil*)	fine	pretty
gasta	nice	quick
neach	person	apparition
oileanach (*oileánach*)	student	islander

Thus when I first read about primary school children making *dealbhan* at school, I wondered why sculpture was on the curriculum. The common Gàidhlig greeting *A bheil thu gu dòigheil?* ('Are you fine?') sounds a bit like a romantic proposition in Irish – it is heard as *An bhfuil tú go dóighiúil?* ('Are you pretty?'). I know one Irish speaker who was driven crazy by the semantic similarities and gave up, and a Scot who pronounced Gàidhlig like Irish after attending a course in Donegal; it took him a couple of weeks to shake the habit. People who try to learn both languages speak in awe of those who can switch from one language to another in the blink of an eye. Yet stalwarts of Ulster Irish are pleased that features of their dialect which are treated as parochial by southern Irish speakers are considered to be standard Gàidhlig.

Irish speakers have their explanation for the similarity of the Gaelic languages. The Annals of Tigernach refer to an invasion of Scotland by the Irish around the year 500

---

[1] I will refer to Scottish Gaelic as 'Gàidhlig' and use the term 'Gaelic' to refer to the cultures of the languages, or features shared by both languages.

CE, when Fergus Mór mac Eirc 'came with the people of Dál Riata, and took part of Britain, and died there' (cited in Koch 2006: 740). This event heralded the birth of the Scottish nation, for the Gaels pushed north and east, overcoming the Britons and Picts who occupied the rest of the country.

I first encountered Gàidhlig on a university course called 'Irish dialects'. But the Irish origins of Gàidhlig are disputed by some. There is no hard archaeological evidence that Irish Gaels invaded Scotland in great numbers. Recently some Scottish historians have claimed that Gaelic settlement in Argyll precedes the Dalriadan invasion by many centuries.

The most famous exponent of this theory is the archaeologist Ewan Campbell, who has deconstructed the Dalriadan migration. According to Campbell, Argyll was Gàidhlig-speaking from at least the Iron Age and it was here that the kingdom of Dál Riata was formed. During the early medieval period this kingdom extended its influence in Antrim, and later Irish writers, using a process of reverse engineering, claimed that the Irish Dál Riata was the progenitor of the Scottish Dál Riata rather than vice versa. The Scottish Dalriadans thought they came from Ireland because they could understand Irish speech (and not the Scottish Picts), or perhaps they even invented the origin myth to claim sovereignty over the Irish Dál Riata (Campbell 1999: 14–15).

Campbell's theory has sown seeds of Dalriadan doubt in Scotland. I read the following in an exhibition in Skye:

> According to Gaelic tradition, the Scots first came there from the north of Ireland in about 500AD. They won their lands from the Picts and named their kingdom Dàl Riata after their home in Ulster ... the archaeology points to a continuity of population in this part of Scotland and no invasion ...

Irish historians dispute Campbell's theory, citing complex evidence of ring forts, ogham inscriptions, and crannogs which proves the flow from Ireland to Scotland, rather than the reverse (Ascherson 2002: 63). Campbell has amassed counter-crannog chronologies, citing evidence of duns and crannogs which were used in Scotland from the early Iron Age, 'so they cannot have been introduced from Ireland by Fergus' (Campbell 1999: 13).

As we grope our way out of the diverse mists of time, we find that contemporary Gaelic Scotland and Ireland differ in terms of politics and religion. Such issues are often concerned with whom people like to contrast themselves. Anglophobic Irish speakers often expect the Scots to be nationalist and anti-English, like themselves. When the Scots tell the Irish of the Clearances, they please the Anglophobes, for the Clearances were a sort of expulsion by the 'English' by proxy, courtesy of the clan chiefs. Scots can, like the Irish, blame the English for the travails of Gàidhlig. Yet today there are far more English people speaking Gàidhlig than Irish, which is not unsurprising perhaps, given that there are far more English people living in Scotland than Ireland. But the existence of so many English speakers of Gàidhlig challenges recent media hype about Scottish Anglophobia. When they cast a cold eye east as well as south, Scottish Gaels find good cause to blame their fellow countrymen for the decline of the language.

The politics of language are certainly more complicated in Scotland than in Ireland. By no means are all Gàidhlig speakers supporters of the Scottish National Party, and the Liberal Democrats had a lot of support in the Highlands. Brian Wilson, the former

Labour MP and a stalwart of Gàidhlig, is a cultural nationalist who opposed Scottish devolution. Those accustomed to the nationalist/unionist split on the Irish language in Northern Ireland can only wonder at the support of the Scottish Conservatives for Gàidhlig.

Furthermore, Gàidhlig is not perceived as being a national language by many Lowlanders. On a visit to the Scottish Parliament I had a friendly chat with a member of staff about the strange lack of mobile phone reception, and we wondered if this was by accident or design. I then lifted a leaflet about the parliament in Gàidhlig, but he stopped me, saying, 'Not that one – it's in a foreign language!' before handing me a leaflet in English. This was despite the fact that Gàidhlig signage was quite common at the Parliament. Official status for Gàidhlig seems to have quite a journey ahead.

Certainly Gàidhlig names are novel to many Scots. A girl called Eilidh was non-plussed to have her name pronounced on a public address system as 'eyelid'. In 2003 the General Register Office for Scotland refused to accept the attempt of Austin Boyle to register his daughter as Aoife Nic Bhaoille as it was a name in 'a foreign language'. Boyle complained that an official 'said using Gaelic would be like registering a name in Sanskrit' (*Press and Journal* 31 May 2003). The decision was overturned when the Scottish Executive intervened. Such official obstructionism is impossible to imagine in the Republic of Ireland and a post-conflict Northern Ireland which is struggling to become politically correct. Yet even in the Republic of Ireland, being called Sadhbh and Caoimhe or even Fionnuala can lead to 'a lifetime of frustration' as 'the Irish struggle with Irish names' (Ward 2008).

The gap between the Irish Republic's Gaelic ideal and Anglicised reality requires a degree of doublethink unimaginable in Scotland. Irish is the first official language and every school child is required to learn it, but only 1.5 percent of staff in the Department of Education can provide a service through the language (*Gaelscéal* 4 Feabhra 2011). A recent report found that 9.1 percent of the Irish-born population claimed to be fluent in Irish and 93.4 percent supported efforts to preserve or revive Irish; only 6.6 percent wanted to discard it (Mac Gréil 2009: 110). So Irish has a lot of public support, but at the same time the vast majority wish to speak only English and hope others would actually bother to preserve the language. Few politicians in the Dáil would dare to put on headphones for a simultaneous translation during speeches in Irish, thereby admitting they cannot speak the first official language.[2] I met one southern activist who will only speak to police officers in Irish, yet an insistence by a defendant on holding a court case in Irish is considered noteworthy enough to get a mention in the *Irish Times*. Language activists complain that the Government and its agencies are compelled to facilitate Irish speakers, but do so begrudgingly. The first official language is a 'necessary fiction', as one language enthusiast put it to me for, if the government started to unravel the exalted status of Irish, the whole edifice will collapse.

Thus I was quite surprised to learn that in Scotland Gàidhlig is associated by many with only the Highlands and Islands – the Gaidhealtachd. Irish is also spoken as a community language in its own western Gaeltacht, but has more of a national image. For many activists in Ireland, speaking Irish expresses their national identity and they expect the same of the Scottish Gaels. In 2009 I helped out when a Gàidhlig psalm-singing group from Lewis visited Belfast. A Scottish flag was placed on stage by the organisers. When question time came a member of the audience asked the psalm

---

[2] In February 2011, TG4 broadcast a debate in Irish between the leaders of the three main political parties in the Republic, Fianna Fáil, Fine Gael, and the Workers' Party. This was described as 'oíche stairiúil don Ghaeilge' ('an historic night for the Irish language') by the Irish language newspaper *Gaelscéal* (*Gaelscéal* 18 Feabhra 2011).

singers if they sang in Gàidhlig to express their separation from England. The spokesman of the group was taken aback by the question. When he gathered himself, he replied that psalm singing in Gàidhlig was an expression of their religious beliefs, and they spoke Gàidhlig because they came from Lewis.

The incident revealed a similar feature of both Gaelic Ireland and Scotland. I have noticed that learners in both countries often express their motivations in terms of nationalist beliefs, whereas native speakers do not really invest their language with a lot of nationalist ideology. They speak Gàidhlig and Irish because they were raised to do so, and the languages can embody local community identities, rather than national ones.

The British aspects of the Scottish Gael can lead to some surprises for the enquiring Irish. Scottish Highlanders are very proud of their sacrifices during the World Wars and proudly wear their British Legion poppies, regardless of the nationalist feelings of some. British Legion halls have cèilidhs, Highland war monuments are inscribed in Gàidhlig, and highly-esteemed Gaels can be awarded OBEs. I still experience a sense of disbelief when I hear members of the British armed forces speaking Gàidhlig on BBC Alba. This embrace of 'perfidious Albion' is anathema to the average Irish speaker. On my first visit to Skye in 1994 I was even surprised by a picture of a policeman in a Gàidhlig children's book, so long was I accustomed to the anti-RUC stance of the Irish language media.

In 2002 I attended a Gàidhlig class in Belfast. The basis for the lesson was the weekly *Litir do luchd-ionnsachaidh* ('Letter for learners') by Ruairidh MacIlleathain (Roddy Maclean). The *letter* is a rich source of Gaelic culture, as well as language, and historical pieces carry echoes of the Scottish tradition of the 'lad o' pairts', who despite his humble origins does well in life. Quite often this up-and-coming Gael had done well by serving in the Imperial army. I remember reading in *Letter 195* about two officers, Colonel Baillie and Sir Hector Munro, who are said to have written to one another in Gàidhlig while campaigning against Tippu Sultan, the ruler of Mysore, a kingdom in India. This was an interesting cultural mismatch; as the class I attended was in the Cultúrlann, on the Falls Road, I assume the sympathies of my classmates lay with Tippu Sultan rather than the British officers, Gàidhlig-speaking or otherwise. The 'great man' in the Irish language tradition is more likely to be a rebel than a peer of the realm. My favourite song in Irish, *Amhrán Pheadair Bhreathnach,* is about an outlaw who flees to an island to escape unknown pursuers.

As for doing well in life, Irish language folklore records the various woes which drove people to emigrate, but seems to record little of what happened to the emigrants, good or otherwise. The Irish language has no colony elsewhere but Gàidhlig has Gaelic Canada, which preserved musical and dance traditions and mainland dialects which are dwindling in the mother country. For example, Canada escaped the Balmorilisation of the song tradition, which entails singing in a manner befitting a Victorian drawing room, often to the accompaniment of a piano. This singing style is unusual to the Irish, whose music remains closer to its rural roots. Neither do Irish learners of Gàidhlig expect to meet so many Canadian speakers of the language.

In terms of religion, the Irish language scene is more homogenous. The vast majority of Irish speakers are Catholic and anyone else is a curiosity[3]. In Scotland things

---

[3] I recall an interesting conversation which took place during a programme in the series 'Comhrá', broadcast by TG4 in 2009. Máirtín Tom Sheáinín was interviewing Seosamh Watson, who was raised as a Protestant and is now a member of the Baha'i faith. Máirtín commented that Conamara people would know little about Protestants and then went on to ask Seosamh if Protestants believed in God and the Virgin Mary. Seosamh replied in the affirmative, without raising an eyebrow.

are more diverse, with most Gàidhlig speakers being Presbyterian, but there are Catholic Gàidhlig-speaking communities in the southern islands of Barra and South Uist, and Episcopalian Gàidhlig speakers on the mainland. What is unusual for Irish speakers is the influence of Highland Presbyterianism on Gàidhlig. Sunday is *Latha na Sàbaid* ('the Sabbath day') in the Presbyterian islands and *Di-dòmhnaich* in the Catholic ones; the latter is closer to the Irish *Dé Domhnaigh*.

I recall an incident, related to me by a third party, which happened when a new employee arrived at Sabhal Mòr Ostaig. The newcomer discovered that another employee owned a book that he had wanted to read, so he asked if he could borrow it, or take the book – '*an leabhar a ghabhail*', as he put it. The owner of the book told him to call to the house later. When the newcomer arrived, he was presented with the Bible and expected to read aloud from it; that is what '*an leabhar a ghabhail*' meant.[4]

The Biblical approach to Gàidhlig turns up in some unusual places, or unusual for the Irish, at any rate. The frontispiece to my copy of *Colloquial Scottish Gaelic* carries a quotation from *Revelation,* Chapter 7, '*às gach uile thrèibh, agus theangaidh, agus shluagh, agus chinneach …*' which translates as, 'of all nations, and kindreds, and people, and tongues ...' (Spadaro and Graham 2001). An Irish learner of Gàidhlig recalled to me how at university his professor was always opening the Bible to explain some aspect of the language.

The Bible in Irish is not at the heart of the Irish literary tradition, although there are many prayers and devotions. To greet someone in Irish one usually blesses them into the bargain; the commonest greeting among learners is *Dia duit* 'God be with you' and the response is *Dia is Muire duit* 'God and Mary be with you'. Leaving aside the Mariolatry, this is an unusual practice for Protestants, unaccustomed as they are to casual blessings. Catholic thought permeates the Irish language. To express something of primary importance in an idiomatic fashion, one talks about *an chloch is mó ar mo phaidrín* 'the biggest bead on my rosary'. Ironically, Scottish Presbyterians who have a good acquaintance with the Classical Gàidhlig of their Bible find that it helps them to understand modern Irish. For example, the Biblical *feuch* conveys to the Scots a sense of other-worldliness encompassed by the term 'behold!', whereas to the Irish *féach* is the everyday command 'look' (see Meek 1990).

Scots like to remind the Northern Irish that their culture is not sectarian; both Scottish Catholics and Protestants speak Gàidhlig. Compared to the appalling situation in Northern Ireland, where Irish can at times be little more than a Catholic shibboleth, Scotland is a model of ecumenism. Certainly Gàidhlig in Scotland is much less contentious than Irish in Northern Ireland. I was surprised on a visit to Edinburgh to see Gàidhlig speakers spontaneously burst into song in a city centre bar; there are few bars in central Belfast where Irish could be sung. One Scot told me of an incident which happened on a ferry from Scotland to Northern Ireland. He was part of a group of Gàidhlig speakers on a trip to Donegal to learn Irish. The Scots decided to sing together in Gàidhlig. Their session was brought to an abrupt end when a ferry employee told them, 'Stop that!' and when asked why, insisted, 'People won't like it!' This was the first time they had experienced such a reaction. Unbeknownst to them they had entered a grimmer Gaelic world, although Scotland was still within sight.

Underneath the non-sectarian surface of the Gàidhlig world lie occasional rumblings. Bill Innes, the biographer of Dòmhnall Mac an t-Saoir (Donald MacIntyre) of South Uist, believes that Mac an t-Saoir's poetry, as well as the work of Dòmhnall

---

[4] A Presbyterian minister in Belfast was unsurprised by this story, since in the past the only books in many Presbyterian homes were the Bible and a dictionary.

Mac na Ceàrdaich (Donald Sinclair) of Barra, was neglected partly because their use of Catholic imagery ruffled Calvinist feathers. A Scottish learner told me of his shock when his Gàidhlig teacher referred to a Catholic as a *Papanach* 'Papist'; she had no idea that the term could be controversial. On the other hand, a Catholic Gàidhlig speaker once told me, 'We kept the faith,' implying that Protestants had changed or lost theirs. When talking about the Reformation, Irish speakers prefer the term *an t-athrú creidimh* ('the change of religion') to the more complementary *an leasú creidimh* ('the reform of religion').

In Ireland there is an advanced learners' culture. Irish is a compulsory subject in the Republic's curriculum, so by default every school child is an Irish learner. In fact native speakers can feel quite outnumbered in some circumstances, and seem more at home in certain domains, such as the Oireachtas, the annual Irish language festival. Native speakers sometimes worry that they are not experts at Irish grammar and cannot write 'official Irish', and thus they cannot look for a job involving the language. The western Gaeltacht sometimes feels neglected by Irish language policies formulated in the east.

In Scotland the focus is more on the native speaker (who may nevertheless struggle with the neologisms of 'BBC Gàidhlig'). I recall my surprise at a half-hour interview on television with a young man in Lewis who was talking about his commitment to staying in the community and keeping Gàidhlig alive. When asked by the interviewer what he thought of learners, he told her that he had no time for them. The interviewer laughed as she appeared to share this frustration with bothersome learners. Alasdair Mac Caluim's account of learners in Scotland (2007) contains many accounts of the refusal of native speakers to talk to learners in Gàidhlig.

This dismissal of learners by native speakers would never be voiced publicly in Ireland where there too many learners to be annoyed, and the Gaelic economy needs them. Some parts of the Gaeltacht are quite dependent on the income from Irish language summer colleges, attended by 28,000 students every year. Learners hold too many purse strings in Ireland, but the native speakers rule the roost in Gaelic Scotland. Even so, I am told the TV interview was watched with discomfort by many Gàidhlig speakers, and that the young Lewis man was told off by his mother for insulting learners!

Learners were certainly a novelty to some native speakers in Scotland. One Gàidhlig learner had a conversation with an elderly lady on a bus from Benbecula to South Uist. He spoke to her in Gàidhlig, only to be answered in English. The entire thirty-minute conversation was conducted in this fashion. Some Gàidhlig learners told me native speakers enquired why on earth they bothered; did they have any family connections with the Highlands, or did they have a Highland surname? The Irish Gaeltacht has always been more acquainted with learners through the Irish summer colleges. Native speakers of Irish have always been accustomed to *Gaeilge na leabhar*, the formal and stilted book Irish of the learner, whereas the Scottish native speakers have not been as exposed to learners. Although native speakers of Gàidhlig are becoming more accustomed to learners, they express incredulity at the accents of Glasgow Gàidhlig, just as native speakers in Ireland sometimes strain to understand Belfast and Dublin Irish.

One attraction of Gàidhlig lies in its evocation of the beautiful landscapes of the western isles and mountains. An example is the custom of giving romantic names to the islands; Skye is *Eilean a' Cheò* ('The Island of Mist') and Lewis is *Eilean an Fhraoich* ('The Island of Heather'). BBC Alba is very much Gàidhealtachd-centred; it is the channel of lofty mountains, sparkling rivers, the deer in the mist. There are rock shows and reality shows such as cooking challenges, but the Highlands still have a strong pull on Gàidhlig television. If BBC Alba is a true window on Gaelic Scotland, then fishing, hill-walking and mountain-climbing seem to be more popular with Gàidhlig speakers than with Irish language enthusiasts. Ruairidh MacIlleathain's weekly *Litir do luchd-ionnsachaidh* ('Letter for learners') confirms this predilection, for the notable Gaels he writes of were often fond of hill walking. Love of the great outdoors is more a part of the Scottish psyche than the Irish one, which is unsurprising perhaps, given that the Highland landscape is far more dramatic than its Irish equivalent. Until very recently, hill-walkers in the Donegal Gaeltacht were looked upon with incredulity by locals, who only climbed hills to look for sheep.

The Gàidhealtachd focus is revealed in other ways in Scotland. To find out what is happening on the Gàidhlig scene in Glasgow one may buy the *West Highland Free Press,* which is published in Skye, but carries notices for Gàidhlig events in the cities. On the other hand, an interesting shift of emphasis is revealed in the columns of the *Andersonstown News*, which carried many articles on Donegal Irish speakers in the early 1980s, revealing the traditional Belfast preoccupation with the Gaeltacht. By the 1990s articles about the Irish language focused on the revival in Belfast. An editorial of the Irish language newspaper *Gaelscéal* even declared that the death of Irish in Donegal would have little influence on the Irish language in Belfast (*Gaelscéal* 17 Meán Fómhair 2010). While I was on a compulsory university trip to an Irish language college in Rann na Feirste in Donegal, other students joked that the university would keep a close eye on our attendance. This was because on a previous year a lecturer had met two students in a Belfast street when they were supposed to be in Donegal. Having rarely left Belfast, they were so traumatised by the rural lifestyle that they returned early.

Thus the Irish language scene is much less Gaeltacht-centric. A lecturer of Irish in Dublin once commented at a conference that his students would understand no native speakers in the Gaeltacht, as they were accustomed to speaking an Anglicised Irish with Dublin accents. In terms of ethos, TG4 is less Gaeltacht-focused than BBC Alba. There is a tension between preserving Gaeltacht traditions, such as *sean-nós* singing and respectful interviews with the old people of Conamara, and the postmodern material produced by the young urbanites, such as travel programmes in urban Irish (or 'dodgy' Irish to the purists). The young are keener to slay the sacred cows in Ireland, and they are a powerful influence in TG4.

What is a Gael, if you're learning Gaelic? In Ireland the Gael is spontaneous and informal, and even the Irish language itself is believed to be informal. In Irish-medium schools children are told to address their teachers by their forenames, as Irish does not readily employ address terms for 'Miss' and 'Mr'. Irish-speaking learners of Gàidhlig struggle with formal plural pronouns (as with the French *tu* and *vous*) on Gàidhlig courses, although they go on to discover that many young speakers have discarded them.

In the Irish language world an invitation to attend an event at nine o'clock means 'nine for half nine' and not bothering to reply to the RSVP. In my experience the Scots are more punctual and nine o'clock carries the implication 'nine sharp'. This is certainly true in Sabhal Mòr Ostaig, which I attended on two occasions with Irish learners of Gàidhlig. We sauntered into the class in dribs and drabs in the morning as the teacher wondered how many would turn up. There is something to be said for the punctilious Scots; Irish language events can fray at the edges due to Celtic 'spontaneity' and 'informality'. The timetable for the 'organised' weekend trip to the Gaeltacht can dissolve in beer.

Scottish formality can lay traps for the unwary Irish. At Sabhal Mòr Ostaig we were invited to the obligatory end-of-course cèilidh. We were not sure what to expect at a Scottish cèilidh – some dancing perhaps? The occasion took a rather intimidating form; a Scot would sing on stage and then the Irish were asked to contribute. Fear and panic gripped the Irish, as we had few songs between us, and I desperately tried to scrabble down the verses of my one imperfectly-learned song. As performance anxiety mounted, the Irish resorted to Dutch courage, stereotypically drinking copious amount of alcohol. A low point was reached when an elderly Irishman drunkenly staggered onto the stage with a learners' song book, and proceeded to leaf through it slowly to find something he could recognise. The day was saved by a semi-professional Irish singer who breezed in and matched the Scots song for song. This was a very near miss in this slowly-unfolding cultural car crash. At the second cèilidh I attended a college employee watched our discomfort from the wings, and later he told me that he considered the event to be too 'formal'.

In 1998 I helped to organise a conference on Irish and Gàidhlig. One of the Irish delegates remarked that the Scots were easy to distinguish, as they were more likely to wear suits than the Irish. The suit is *de rigueur* for the male member of the 'Gaelic Mafia', the leaders of the revival in Scotland who come from a Highland background, usually Lewis, and who are well-acquainted with one another. Harris tweed has been long-abandoned by the Gaelic Mafia. The Scottish Gaels are aware that their language was not traditionally appreciated by the powers-that-be in Edinburgh and consequently run their revival like a business with illustrative indices, flow diagrams and spend projections. The Scots inhabit the system. In the 1980s the Scots used a right-wing economic think-tank, the Institute of Economic Affairs, to persuade Margaret Thatcher to fund Gàidhlig television. Playing the game worked well, and Mrs Thatcher provided an initial grant for £8.5 million, making her one of the leading and unlikely benefactors of Gàidhlig.

In complete contrast to the suited-and-booted Scot, the Irish speaker is self-consciously informal. This was conveyed in the traditional dress sense of the language activist. The male of the species was not entirely of this world; a beard, an Aran jumper, perhaps a safari suit surviving beyond the seventies, with sandals and an out-of-place fisherman's cap. Some hang on to their Irish tweed jackets, but the suit is more common these days, although an ill-matched shirt and tie may be used to express the Irish discomfort with formality. In the Black North, the Irish speaker's dress sense may convey working-class street cred in the form of subdued darker tones. Combat jackets may still be worn to convey a sense of youthful militant rebellion, despite the soaring salary and expanding waistline of the middle-aged wearer, as well as the discrete relocation to the wealthy suburbs from the council estate. South of the border TG4 has replaced Aran jumpers with gravity-defying haircuts, slim-fit shirts, and man bags. The pale and shy convent schoolgirl, pulling her cardigan over her hands, has been transformed into the radiant TG4 babe, causing a few to wonder aloud if Irish speakers have better genes.

The business approach of the Gàidhlig revival means that it costs a lot to learn the language. The best self-taught course, *Speaking our Language,* was very expensive, and most learners occupy the upper income brackets. The southern Irish scene also has a middle-class ethos, but the revival in Northern Ireland has a distinct working-class flavour, and the term 'middle-class' seems to be a label of abuse, regardless of the income of the abuser. Unlike Scotland, there has been a traditional voluntarism on the Irish language scene. In the early 1990s I attended a summer college in Ros Goill,

County Donegal. Learners paid £35 and stayed as long as they wished. The teachers taught for free, and most of the money went towards a céilí in the local hotel. Irish voluntarism declined as more funding was made available for Irish language projects and expectations were raised. The teachers in the Ros Goill college are now paid, which has increased the fees, but the voluntarist ethos lingers elsewhere. In Northern Ireland, one never took money for teaching Irish in the old days, and some teachers are still old-fashioned.

Irish speakers have long lamented the amateurism and ad-hockery of their scene (although it is perhaps more welcoming for being so). The Scottish business approach to Gàidhlig has an emphasis on professionalism; also the Scots are always networking and looking for new allies. In 2002 I attended a Comunn na Gàidhlig conference at which the key speaker's address was in English. This was because he was not a Gàidhlig speaker, but an important figure in the local educational authority who was favourable to the language. So he was wooed by being invited to speak. Favourable noises made by government officials are reproduced by the language movement to gently encourage them to do more. The openness of Gaelic Scotland is also reflected in recent innovations in Gàidhlig song, influenced by current trends in electronic and world music. By contrast, Irish Gaelic music is still bogged down in Celtic mist.

In Ireland there is more of an all-encompassing Gaelic approach that is more exclusive in nature. A conference held by an Irish language activist organisation would tend to be in Irish. Simultaneous translation through headphones would represent the height of inclusivity. There is much less wooing and more finger-wagging, a reminding of the 'Others', the authorities, of their responsibilities towards Irish. In the Republic of Ireland there is a sense of more having been achieved in the past and of present-day retreat. The appointment in 2010 of a Fine Gael spokesman on the Gaeltacht who did not speak Irish was greeted with incredulity by the language movement and protest letters to the press. In August of the same year place-names in Irish briefly disappeared from the digital destinations of Irish buses. Suspicious Irish speakers were reassured by Bus Éireann that this was 'a slight and minor technical issue' (www.gaelport.com/sonrai-nuachta?NewsItemID=4819, accessed 19 August 2010).

An example of the difference between the two countries is the controversy about road signs in Gàidhlig in Scotland. There seems to be a widely-held belief in Scotland that road signs in two languages will lead to driver confusion and more accidents. I read with interest a report on how the Scottish Government Transport minister signed a letter which claimed that the cognitive ability of drivers was reduced by 41 percent when confronted with bilingual signs (*West Highland Free Press* 3 April 2009). While there is some concern with the rate of road accidents in the Republic of Ireland, no-one is suggesting that the mandatory bilingualism of road signs is a cause. In both countries enthusiasts share despair at the bad spelling of road signs in Gaelic, and the newspaper *Foinse* even ran a competition to find the worst road sign in Irish. Badly-spelt signs represent another official retreat for Irish speakers, and embody the long uphill struggle for the Scots.

I was quite surprised in my *Colloquial Scottish Gaelic* course by one little vignette. A girl comes home from school crying because a fellow pupil has called her, among other things, *pròseil* or 'proud' (Spadaro and Graham 2001: 185). Upon enquiring, I was told that the Highland Gael is modest and unassuming and does not want to be *mullach a' bhaile* or 'the talk of the town.' Róisín Elsafty, a singer from County Galway, has noticed a difference, '*Bhí na hAlbanaigh an-socair, ciúin agus múinte. Tá siad difriúil linn.*' ('The Scots were very calm, quiet and polite. They're different from us.') (*Irish*

Times 22 September 1999). Alan Campbell noted the problem with being a campaigner for Gàidhlig, 'It's not natural for the Gael to be impolite or inappreciative ...' (Hutchinson 2005: 181).

Campbell's comment would amuse language activists in Northern Ireland accustomed to strident campaigning coupled with a traditional hostility to the authorities. Moreover, on both sides of the Irish border, more Gaels are noisier and self-confident – the Alpha Gaels. I remember an employee at Sabhal Mòr Ostaig telling me about a visit of Irish language teachers from Northern Ireland, 'They're very strong in their culture,' she said, cautiously expressing a difference. Yet the 'in-your-face' approach of the Irish Alpha Gael may send the Scot running for cover at times. Gàidhlig speakers tend to be lower-key. The downside of Scottish modesty is too much self-effacement. The Irish Alpha Gaels are confident in the success of the revival, and their own considerable contribution to that revival. Confidence is a step away from arrogance, and Alpha Gaels can be too fond of lecturing, even hectoring, others. At times they evince an unwillingness to listen, or even improve their own Irish.

Confidence in Gaelic revivalism divides Ireland and Scotland. Many Scots worry about the success of the Gàidhlig revival and the Irish wonder if this is realism or an attack of Calvinist fatalism. Certainly there are plenty of 'experts' who are willing to promote this discourse of doom, pronouncing Gàidhlig 'dead' as the language had less than 60, 000 speakers in the *2001 Census* (McEwan-Fujita 2006). I once heard a Gàidhlig speaker talk about the young lead actor in the television series *Gruth is Uachdar;* his Gàidhlig was flawless, his accent wonderful. It was almost as if the concept of a young native speaker was a contradiction in terms. This view is both chilling and ominous for Irish language enthusiasts.

In Ireland there is a concern that many Gaeltacht children are switching to English and there is a commonly-held view that their spoken Irish is becoming impoverished or *níos tanaí* ('thinner'). There is less talk about the language actually dying altogether, with one notable exception; a major study on the future of the Gaeltacht warns that given current trends the Irish language will not be the main family and community language in its traditional heartland within 15 to 20 years (Ó Giollagáin and Mac Donnacha et al 2007).

Scots can be more whimsical when talking about the Gaelic world than the Irish; the use of the term 'Gaeldom' seems quaint to Irish ears. The reverse is true about academia. In terms of their approach to intellectual life, Irish speakers are more celebratory and self-congratulatory than the Scots. The Irish tend to be emollient, and devastating intellectual critiques are less common, except perhaps when the passage of time (particularly death) emboldens the writer. I have read many shrewd assessments of the early years of the Gaelic League, but have encountered little of a similar mettle regarding the contemporary revival. Yet the contributions to *Rannsachadh na Gàidhlig*, the biennial conference on Gàidhlig research, are remarkable for their criticism of certain features of Gàidhlig life. I will never forget a detailed and critical analysis of the Mod, for example[5].

Scottish academics are more ready to outline the flaws in the revival, and even say, with a focus on little more than Gàidhlig-medium education and television, that the 'Gàidhlig emperor has no clothes'. In Ireland the academic Irish speaker is likely to be critical of the attitude of the wavering authorities to Irish, but is more muted on the failures of revivalists. I can, for example, imagine a damning indictment of TG4 by an

---

[5] Such views are not welcomed by all, especially some language activists who see little point in making a bad situation worse. One said to me after various presentations, 'They're vandalising Gàidhlig ... He doesn't even speak Gàidhlig ... Ask him if he speaks it!'

economist, but not by an Irish-speaking sociologist. Irish academics seem to be more afraid of being denounced for betrayal. This is particularly true in Northern Ireland, where to state publically that there is something at fault in the language revival is perceived as 'washing dirty linen in public' and playing into the hands of the enemies of Irish, the unionists and civil servants, who look for weaknesses in the Gaelic/nationalist armour. Fear of finding fault in the Gaelic scene is understandable, for in small circles people are afraid of criticising each other, as they will be bumping into each other time and time again. The Gàidhlig scene is smaller than its Irish equivalent, but the Scottish academic knife is keener.

The Gaelic world differs because of the development of nationalism in both countries; cultural nationalism is much stronger in Ireland, whereas Scottish nationalism is premised on institutional distinctiveness. Thus Irish speakers can present themselves as bearers of the sacred flame of nationalism, and some even delude themselves into believing that they should be paid to speak the language. Gàidhlig speakers need to convince many of their fellow countrymen that their language is of national importance at all, and have no nationalist laurels to rest upon.

Some differences are difficult to explain. Nonetheless, the distinctiveness of the Gàidhlig world recalls my experiences of Protestant culture in Northern Ireland: the low-key, less ebullient approach; the weighing of words before giving them breath; respect for and expectation of a degree of formality; the love of punctuality and precision; and an inability at times to tell the difference between thinking and worrying.

One must be aware of powerful regional differences *within* Ireland and Scotland. By no means are all Scottish Gaels cautious and all Irish Gaels carefree; for example, the advent of TG4 has led to a contractual broadcasting industry in Irish within which budgets and turnarounds are tight. Episcopalian, Catholic, and Presbyterian Gàidhlig speakers can have different approaches to the same issue, and some are more formal than others. The Irish speakers of Donegal are often as modest as those in the Scottish Highlands; few can be described as Alpha Gaels. The formation of Guth na Gaeltachta in Donegal, to campaign for Gaeltacht rights in official policy, is the first instance of a language pressure group of national importance to be based in that county. Some of the differences between Scottish and Irish Gaelic culture are being eroded by time. Secularism is a growing influence in both countries, impacting upon religious beliefs and practices, although fossilized religious phrases are remarkably resilient. Yet enough differences remain between Ireland and Scotland to confound any attempt to define and prescribe a singular 'Gaelic' world-view and way of life.

References

Ascherson, N. 2003. *Stone Voices: The Search for Scotland.* London: Granta Publications.

Campbell, E. 19199. *Saints and Sea-kings: The First Kingdom of the Scots.* Edinburgh: Canongate Books.

Hutchinson, R. 2005. *A Waxing Moon: The Modern Gaelic Revival.* Edinburgh: Mainstream Publishing Company.

Koch, J.T. ed. 2006. *Celtic Culture: A Historical Encyclopaedia.* Vol II. Santa Barbara and Oxford: ABC-CLIO.

MacCaluim, A. 2007. *Reversing Language Shift: The Social Identity and Role of Scottish Gaelic Learners.* Belfast: Cló Ollscoil na Banríona.

Mac Gréil, M. 2009. *The Irish Language and the Irish People: Report on the Attitudes towards, Competence in and Use of the Irish Language in the Republic of Ireland in 2007- 08.* Maynooth: Department of Sociology National University of Ireland Maynooth.

McEwan-Fujita, E. 2006. 'Gaelic Doomed as Speakers Die?: The Public Discourse of Gaelic Language Death in Scotland'. In ed. McLeod. W. *Revitalising Gaelic in Scotland: Policy, Planning and Public Discourse*. Edinburgh: Dunedian Academic Press. 279–93.

Meek, D.E. 1990. 'Language and Style in the Scottish Gaelic Bible (1767 – 1807)'. *Scottish Language* 9: 1–16.

Ó Giollagáin, C., Mac Donnacha S., Ní Chualáin, F., Ní Seaghdha, A., and M. O'Brien, M. 2007. *Comprehensive Linguistic Study of the use of Irish in the Gaeltacht: Principal Findings and Recommendations. A Research Report prepared for the Department of Community, Rural and Gaeltacht Affairs*. Dublin: Stationery Office.

Spadaro, K. and K. Graham. 2001. *Colloquial Scottish Gaelic: The Complete Course for Beginners*. Routledge: London and New York.

Ward, F. 2008. 'How the Irish Struggle with Irish Names'. *The Irish Times* 1 November.

The Ministerial Working Group on the Scots Language

Christine Robinson

The **Ministerial Working Group on the Scots Language** was set up in the wake of a memorable conference in Stirling, on the 9 February 2009. This conference was convened to discuss the results of the Scottish Government's audit on the Scots language. The Culture Minister at that time, Linda Fabiani, announced that the Scottish Government was pledged to adopt a policy of actively encouraging Scots. One of the first manifestations of their commitment was the formation of the Working Group announced later that year by her successor, Michael Russell, at the Voices of the West II conference in Inverness. He said: 'Formation of the Scots Language Working Group is the next step in exploring ambitions and aspirations for Scots, but most importantly what practical steps can be taken to raise awareness of the language and promote its use in a range of settings'. The Report was finally submitted to Fiona Hyslop MSP, the incumbent Minister for Culture and External Affairs, on 30 September 2010 and published on 30 November 2010. The Government published its response on 18 March 2011.

The group was asked to report on the status of Scots in national life and to offer recommendations to the Scottish Government to assist them in developing a strategy to carry out their stated policy of encouraging and developing the language. The remit was to be bold and ambitious but to bear in mind the financial realities.

Together, the members of the group covered a wide spectrum of Scots Language interests. As chair, **J. Derrick McClure**, recently retired from the University of Aberdeen, brought a lifetime of native-speaker knowledge and academic research to the table. **Professor John Corbett**, then of the University of Glasgow, has broad interests in literature, language and education. **Billy Kay**, writer and broadcaster had a special role to play in the Group's deliberations on media and the author **Janet Paisley**, who regularly writes for the broadcast media, is also highly experienced in this area. Authors **James Robertson** and **Matthew Fitt** have been very active in education through their acclaimed Itchy-coo publications for children (see www.itchy-coo.com/) and also through direct work with teachers and in the classroom. Matthew Fitt had considerable influence in the inclusion of Scots in the *Curriculum for Excellence*. **Rab Wilson**, poet and activist extended the geographical spread in the south west, while **Sandy Stronach** represented Doric grassroots. **Laureen Johnston** from Shetland ensured that Insular Scots, and Shetland Dialect in particular, was well represented and brought firsthand knowledge of the excellent work being done in her community by *Shetland ForWirds*. **Alastair Allan** was present as a long time supporter of Scots and member of the Scottish Parliament. **Michael Hance**, in his role as director of the Scots Language Centre has a particular interest in the politics of language planning and in the representation of Scots on the Internet. His work with the General Register Office for Scotland (GROS) on the Scots question in the 2011 Census provided essential insights. **Christine Robinson**, the present writer, attended primarily as Director of Scottish Language Dictionaries, a scholarly and well-maintained historical dictionary being central to any language planning strategy. She also offered her teaching experience at the University of

---

[1] Russell's remarks are to be found at www.scotland.gov.uk/News/Releases/2009/10/29151643; the Report of the Ministerial Working Group on the Scots Language at www.scotland.gov.uk/Publications/2010/11/25121454/0; the Government's Response at www.scotland.gov.uk/Resource/Doc/346190/0115217.pdf.

Edinburgh and the University of the Highlands and Island Millennium Institute, involvement with the Scots Language Society as Preses and with the Association for Scottish Literary Studies as chair of the Language Committee. **Douglas Ansdell** and **Janet MacMillan** of the Scottish Government were in attendance. Their perspective was particularly valuable in helping the group to channel enthusiasm into recommendations for realistic and achievable courses of action. Janet MacMillan provided a helpful and efficient the secretariat.

As might be expected from such a diverse assemblage of people, there were many points of view and some lively exchanges, but the degree of consensus was truly remarkable. In spite of coming at various questions from different angles, members were broadly in agreement and established general basic principles early in the discussions. The status of Scots as one of the three indigenous languages of Scotland, deserving of official recognition and support was a basic tenet of the Group's deliberations and it was agreed that, while there have been major improvements in recent years, much still remains to be done. This Government has indicated its wish to fulfill the terms of the *European Charter for Regional or Minority Languages*[2] in a well considered manner and, in this context, the need for a national Scots language policy was manifestly recognised in the setting up of this working group.

Areas where the need for change was mostly urgent were identified at the first meeting as Education, Broadcasting, Publishing, Creative Writing, International Contacts, Public Relations and Public Awareness and Dialects. Members of the Working Group presented discussion papers on these and related topics for debate and discussion at meetings and a summary of these discussions appear in the final report. A summary of the meetings is provided in Appendix I. What follows in this paper is my own interpretation of the papers and my memory of the discussion, assisted by reference to the minutes. When this paper was originally presented in Belfast in September 2010, the Report had not yet reached its final draft and it was only possible to give an outline of the Group's approach to the task and the kind of factors that were considered. With the publication of the report at the end of November 2010 (see footnote 1), it is now possible to include the major recommendations. The Minister, Fiona Hyslop has since replied; her response was published on 18 March 2011.[3] I shall summarise discussion and recommendations on each of the main topics in turn, and make reference to the Minister's responses to the key recommendations. These were generally extremely encouraging in tone and, while Fiona Hyslop perceived many of the recommendations as falling under the remit of Creative Scotland, her answer to others were such as to allow us to anticipate positive sentiments being translated into practical measures should an SNP minister be in office after the elections in May 2011, as will be indeed the case.

General

The key recommendation was that:

> the Scottish Government should develop a national Scots Language policy with reference to the *European Charter for Regional or Minority Languages*; and this should be enshrined in an Act of Parliament.

---

[2] *European Charter for Regional or Minority Languages*. 1992. Strasbourg: Council of Europe. conventions.coe.int/Treaty/EN/Treaties/Html/148.htm.

[3] The Response from the Scottish Government, published on 18 March 2011, is at www.scotland.gov.uk/Publications/2011/03/18094509/1.

This elicited the response that:

> The Scottish Government will take the opportunity of the next cycle of the Council of Europe *Charter for Regional and Minority Languages*, commencing in 2011, to develop a policy on Scots. This will consider all aspects necessary to strengthen the use and status of the Scots Language.

Education

The discussion on education was initiated by a paper by John Corbett and another by Matthew Fitt and Laureen Johnson.

John Corbett made reference to the *Audit of Current Scots Language Provision in Scotland*[4] published in 2009 and challenged its findings in relation to Higher education. The position of Scottish Literature and Scots Language in Scottish universities is precarious and becoming ever more marginalised. Research in Scottish Literature is further devalued by the UK research ranking criteria. If Scottish Literature and Language are perceived as 'national' research areas, he claimed that there is a disincentive to research and publish in these areas in the UK. Given the lively interest in these subjects internationally, this is a strange state of affairs, and there is at this time a great opportunity to capitalise on this international interest through exchange programmes and other encouragement for teaching Scottish Literature, Language and Culture courses in North America and elsewhere, with ancillary benefits for tourism and publishing. He drew attention to some of the major AHRC-funded projects, Glasgow University's *Scottish Corpus of Texts and Speech* (SCOTS)[5] and the *Corpus of Modern Scottish Writing 1700–1945* (CMSW)[6] and raised the problem, widely appreciated in academic circles, that project funding is all very well, but it is for a limited period and such projects require ongoing maintenance if they are to retain their undoubted usefulness to the academic and wider community.

The paper by Laureen Johnston and Matthew Fitt focused on the need for additional support for teachers in the form of a network of Scots co-ordinators and clearer guidance from HMIE. They also identified specific requirements such as a picture dictionary and additional web-based resources. They made a plea for the increased recognition of dialects. This was a matter which was of major concern to many in the Group. Laureen Johnston spoke to the Shetland perspective. Groundbreaking work has been done there in nursery education with the production of the *Ditty Box*, a very attractive set of resources for young children, and this has now been extended into the early years of primary.

The Group endorsed their views. In particular, respect for Scots and its use in nursery provision is of great importance. This is the child's first encounter with the education system. If it is a 'foreign language' experience, at worst the child starts with a negative experience of education from which he or she may never recover. The more linguistically able and aware child will, like so many of us, be left with the impression that Scots is not 'good' enough for school and that our own natural speech is inferior. *Curriculum for Excellence*[7] aspires to producing 'confident' pupils, and it will not do this

---

[4] *Audit of Current Scots Language Provision in Scotland* (2009) Edinburgh. Available at: www.scotland.gov.uk/Publications/2009/01/23133726/3.
[5] *Scottish Corpus of Text and Speech.* 2004. Glasgow. www.scottishcorpus.ac.uk.
[6] *Corpus of Modern Scottish Writing.* 2010. Glasgow. www.scottishcorpus.ac.uk/cmsw/
[7] *Curriculum for Excellence.* 2009. www.ltscotland.org.uk/understandingthecurriculum/ whatiscurriculumforexcellence

if they are afraid to open their mouths for fear of speaking in a proscribed manner. It is at this stage that the groundwork for bilingualism in Scots and English, and the perception of both as high status languages must be laid down. The main recommendation states:

> In light of the announcement that Learning and Teaching Scotland (LTS) and Her Majesty's Inspectorate of Education (HMIE) are to re-organise as Scottish Education Quality and Improvement Agency (SEQIA), there is now an historic opportunity for the Scottish Government to create a dedicated permanent Scots Language / Scottish Literature Bureau within the new organisation to meet the growing demand from Scotland's teachers for high-quality training, information and resources.

Fiona Hyslop replied:

> Both HMIE and LTS have an important role to play in the use of the Scots language in the classroom. We will seek to ensure that this continues and that the new agency builds on the work undertaken previously by HMIE and LTS. The Minister for Education and Lifelong Learning has tasked LTS with producing a new online resource, *Studying Scotland*, which will provide practitioners with free access to high quality material for all the Scottish elements of the curriculum. The resource will seek to place Scots on an equal footing with the other Scottish elements of the curriculum. [...] The first phase of the work will consist of a re-branding and web-redesign exercise of the existing resources. The second phase will be part of the work plan for 2011/12 and will be taken forward by LTS and the new education agency. This will include taking into consideration expert advice on the various strands which would make up *Studying Scotland*. They will also take into consideration the recommendations on Scots and Scottish literature in the English Excellence Group report. [...] The creation of the new agency is also an opportunity to refresh and broaden our vision of Scots and consider its potential to drive other agendas, for example, the role of Scots in social inclusion.

The Group also recommended the setting up of a network of Scots Co-ordinators. This was a proposal which met with an enthusiastic response from Fiona Hyslop, who said:

> At this stage, I am particularly interested in making progress on establishing the network of co-ordinators which could really drive promotion of the language at a local level. I have seen at first-hand the positive impact Falkirk schools are seeing following an increase in use of Scots in the classroom. The proposed network would allow sharing of experiences and encourage an increase in the use of Scots in the classroom.

Other recommendations included the establishment of Chairs in Scottish Literature and Language in all Scottish Universities and appropriate teacher training and the development of online resources.

Broadcasting

Billy Kay summarised of the sporadic and inadequate use of Scots in Broadcasting. He made creative suggestions for the kind of programmes that we would all enjoy and rejoice to hear or see. Among his many suggestions were cartoons and children's shows dubbed with a Scots voice-over, rugby and football commentaries in Scots and chat shows in Scots. He called for more Scots drama and regular weather forecasts in Scots from different dialect areas, so we can tune our ears into the variety of dialects. Another of his suggestions concerned natural history programmes in Scots emphasising the Scots names e.g. for birds, plants, place names, etc. The opportunities presented by these local names is something that Scottish Language Dictionaries has been trying to promote in schools through the Scuilwab, and this cross-curricular approach, combining environmental studies and language is absolutely in the spirit of Curriculum for Excellence. His recommendations, which were warmly received by the group covered inter alia the need for recognition of Scots in the media, greater coverage which also reflects dialectal diversity, positive discrimination in favour of Scots. Perhaps we have something to learn from Northern Ireland here. Janet Paisley also produced a thoroughly researched paper with quite alarming statistics showing the degree to which Scots has in the past been under-represented. The recommendations which were put to the group arising from these papers dealt with broadcasting and programming at a very detailed level and together the group summarised and condensed Kay and Paisley's recommendations to provide an effective strategy for change. (One heartening development is the appointment of Jeff Zycinski as Head of Radio at BBC Scotland. His approach to Scot is enthusiastic and forward-looking. In a recent conversation, following a training session on Scots which he requested for BBC staff, he expressed his view that people from all over Scotland could and should, through broadcasting, become familiar with a variety of dialects.) The Minister undertook to contact these relevant bodies to make them aware of the recommendations. In addition, she stated:

> All relevant media organisations will be invited to consider that a knowledge of spoken Scots should be regarded as an important qualification, within the context of wider employment requirements.

Publishing

Publishing discussions centred around a paper by James Robertson. He examined Scottish writing in its historical context. Again, the inter-related nature of our key topics was demonstrated in the discussion of Scots publishing for young people in the context of the decline in Scottish publishing generally. Scots materials have all to often been produced by dedicated individuals or small groups. He outlined the aims and achievements of Itchy-coo, which, I might add, in spite of Lottery and Scottish Arts Council (SAC) funding, now expired, falls into the category of inspired individuals with slim purses. The Working Group was convinced that there is a market and a need for publishing in Scots and agree that there is a need to incentivise publishers. The Gaelic model of Comhairle nan Leabhraichean (the Gaelic Books Council) was invoked and the role of a similar body for Scots publishing was examined. SAC has always been as supportive of Scots writing as their resources would permit, although their recent withdrawal of funding for Lallans in its present form was lamented, and it was hoped that the funding previous channelled into Scots literature could be continued by

Creative Scotland through an alternative route such as a Scots Book Council. The Minister emphasised the role of Creative Scotland

Creative Writing

Creative Writing was the subject of a detailed and strongly argued paper by Janet Paisley, itemising the many difficulties faced by authors and stressing the role of Creative Scotland. For example, she identified the need for financial support for writers, increased literacy in Scots at all levels and the need for Scottish bookshops to be independent in their purchasing from their Anglo-centric headquarters. She also covered drama, radio and television. In an eloquent closing summary, she wrote:

> Like Scottish Gaelic, Scots is a language which only Scotland has custody and care of. Having been dropped as the language of state and education following the Union of the Parliaments, it has suffered from neglect by state and education and is seriously eroded. Its survival as the spoken language of the majority of Scotland's people, and as a tool of literature, proves its necessity. But progress can only be made in a culture of growing literacy in the language. Without that, we lose connection with our literature, heritage, culture, history and geography, and become a nation suffering amnesia, not knowing who we are, or the journey we have made, lacking a sense of ourselves, and unable to walk confidently into the future as equals with other nations on the international stage.

International Contacts

Derrick McClure started discussion with a very upbeat paper. The long established international interest in the Scots language, and in Scottish literary and cultural studies in general, has increased in recent years, largely the result of active efforts by academics and others to raise the profile of Scottish studies and extend the network of international links. Among successful initiatives have been the Association for Scottish Literary Studies (ASLS) publications such as *Scottish Language*, *New Writing Scotland*, and the *Scottish Literary Review* which attract international contributions. The online magazine *The Bottle Imp* reaches a wide readership and the success of the ASLS participation in Modern Language Association Conferences in America has been phenomenal, growing from a little table of Scottish publications to a major presence that always creates a buzz among delegates. ASLS also has an International Committee, chaired by Suzanne Gilbert of Stirling University, which is active in building up a world-wide network of scholars with an interest in Scottish studies, including the Scots language. Another active organisation is the Forum for Research in the Languages of Scotland and Ulster (FRLSU), which hosts international conferences. Queen's University of Belfast's International Symposia on Language and Politics in Scotland and Ireland make a significant contribution, and Derrick McClure described the proceedings volumes as 'being published, with astonishing expediency, in the series *Belfast Studies in Language, Culture and Politics*'. The Scots Language Centre provides and promotes a lively international internet presence. Derrick McClure praised the role of individual scholars who through their own teaching, writing, network and attendance at conferences are making a significant contribution to the international profile of Scots. In that respect I would put forward as an example a recent publication of poetry by Liz Niven, following a tour in China. I would also add the role of the online Dictionary of the Scots Language, which is consulted by scholars from all over the world and which received overwhelming international support in its darkest hour before government funding was confirmed at the aforementioned Stirling conference. Scottish Language Dictionaries' work is the subject of postgraduate research from Japan to the Ukraine. Discussion took this topic beyond academic fields into tourism, the Homecoming, the Commonwealth Games and other possible opportunities for development, with VisitScotland's involvement. The minister embraced these proposals and replied:

> VisitScotland will work to enhance the cultural impact of the Scots language within the areas where it is relevant to reflect a sense of place. Examples of activity may include internal signage in Visitor Information Centres, development of commonly used phrases which could be distributed to visitors, captions on images etc. VisitScotland will use the model of its Gaelic Language Plan as the basis for such activities.

Raising Awareness

This huge topic was presented by Michael Hance. Most of the themes are all too familiar: the hostility of many newspapers and other media, the negative view taken by Scots speakers themselves, weakening inter-generational transmission, lack of visibility in public spaces etc. He provided a supplementary paper on the Scots Language question in the census for which the Scots Parliamentary Cross Party group have been lobbying since its inception. Michael Hance has been working with GROS on the wording of the question and has been doing his utmost to ensure that sufficient public information is disseminated to ensure that Scots speakers know that they are indeed Scots speakers. Currently, all too many will tell you that they do not speak Scots – they speak 'Dundee' or 'Wick' or 'Galashiels', and they do not identify these as dialects of Scots. The Scots Language Centre website is making valiant efforts to assist GROS in addressing this issue.

A visit to Muirkirk in Ayrshire at the invitation of Muirkirk Enterprise Group to observe the way in which the Lapraik Festival and other local initiatives support the Scots language while encouraging economic regeneration inspired the suggestion of 'establishing 'Scots Touns', 'dialect conservation areas' or 'sites of special linguistic interest' in areas with high concentrations of speakers should be investigated. A possible approach would be the awarding by a national body of the designation 'Scots toun' as an accolade for local work done to promote the Scots language. The Minister asked that the Scots Language Centre should move forward with this suggestion.

Dialect

This leads us into the paper presented by Laureen Johnson. In her words:

> The most important thing about a dialect is the life force still within it. A living spoken tongue is a priceless inheritance, and often commands a fierce loyalty. As many Scots/dialect speakers instinctively feel, a distinctive native speech is part of one's very identity. [...] The converse of that dialect pride is an unwillingness to admit to similarities to the

Scots of other areas, an insistence on seeing one's own tongue as too different to be part of a bigger picture. Perhaps there is simply not enough knowledge about the subject. Exposure to a wider range of Scots, e.g. through websites, recordings, radio and television, plays a vital part in helping us all to hear the 'family resemblances'.

She reminded us of the centrality of spoken Scots in all its variety and asserted

Any national initiative must take account of how it will play in strong dialect areas. The best way to proceed on a national level is not to dictate from the centre, but to act in consultation and co-operation with people on the ground. They are to be valued and supported in their own mother tongue and their differences seen to be understood and accepted.

Shetland ForWirds[8] provides some useful templates for wider implementation in other dialect areas.[1]

The minister reiterated her intention that:

the Scottish Government will consider the development of a policy with reference to the *Council of Europe's Charter on Regional and Minority Languages*. [...] We will take the opportunity of the Council of Europe Charter cycle commencing in 2011 to develop a policy on Scots and to bring this recommendation to the attention of local authorities.

Reports and submissions from other bodies and individuals as detailed in the report were submitted for consideration.

Pulling it together

Draft reports prepared by Derrick McClure were submitted to the Working Group and subjected to intense scrutiny. The second-last meeting was devoted to the prioritising and wording of recommendations. Some of these, such as the aspiration that 'The Scottish Government should develop a national Scots Language policy with reference to the *European Charter for Regional or Minority Languages*; and this should be enshrined in an Act of Parliament' are ambitious. Others, such as the encouragement of 'Scots Touns' are modest and achievable even in difficult times. It has been a very labour intensive operation. In particular, those who provided papers put a great deal of time and thought into their preparation. All members of the group were far from passive in their reading of these papers, actively identifying areas for clarification, highlighting areas of unanimity and, often, refining extensive discussions into key points. We are confident that the report is broadly representative of the views of the group and provides a practical and realistic set of recommendations to form the basis of a sound Scots language strategy.[1]

The Report has been welcomed by Fiona Hyslop, who initially responded:

Scots is a key part our heritage and culture. It is important that we look at ways of improving the status and use of Scots throughout Scotland. This report offers us practical recommendations on how we can make progress with this aim.

---

[8] *Shetland ForWirds* (2010) Kirkwall, www.shetlanddialect.org.uk

In the light of the published reponse, we are confident that these practical recommendations will be acted upon in the very near future.

Appendix I: Working Group Meetings

24 November 2009: Mike Russell, MSP, Minister for Culture, External Affairs and the Constitution

12 January 2010: Dave Francis, Chair of the Traditional Arts Working Group Catriona West, TNS-BMRB Researchers – Research on Public Attitudes to the Scots Language

24 February 2010: Business Structuring; Education; Broadcasting and the Media

7 April 2010: Report Template; Education; Broadcasting; Publishing; Creative Writing

19 May 2010: Presentation by Nat Edwards and Mary Hudson of the Robert Burns' Birthplace Museum; International Contacts; Census

22 June 2010: Dialects; Public Relations / Public Awareness / Advocacy; Legislation

18 August 2010: Recommendations; Draft Report

29 September 2010: Finalisation of Scots Language Working Group Repor

20 November 2010: Submission of Scots Language Working Group Repor

18 March 2011: Scots Language Working Group Report: Response from the Scottish Government

A Language Strategy for Scots?

Andy Eagle

> *Strategy n.* a plan of action designed to achieve a long-term or overall aim.
> (*Oxford English Dictionary*)

On 1 July 2001, the *European Charter for Regional or Minority Languages*[1] came into effect, whereby the United Kingdom government recognised that 'Scots and Ulster Scots meet the charter's definition of a regional or minority language for the purposes of Part II of the Charter'. Within the terms of the charter the United Kingdom government is obliged, among other things, to:

- Facilitate and/or encourage the use of Scots in speech and writing, in public and private life.
- Provide appropriate forms and means for the teaching and study of Scots at all appropriate stages.
- Provide facilities enabling non-speakers living where Scots is spoken to learn it if they so desire.

The above obligations imply the implementation of a language strategy.

Developing language strategies is not new in a European context. However, in the case of Scots, this has only recently become a serious possibility. As a consequence, many of those who may be involved in developing and implementing a language strategy for Scots will likely have limited knowledge and experience of such endeavours. Ultimately, developing and implementing a language strategy is a political exercise and as such is dependent on the resources that politicians are willing to allocate to it. In these budget-conscious times, what lessons can be learnt from corporate strategy planning in order to maximise the effective deployment of the resources that politicians are willing to allocate?

To survive in a competitive environment businesses engage in strategic planning, clearly defining realistic objectives founded on facts and empirical data rather than supposition, anecdotal evidence or unrealistic wish lists. Both the internal and external situation of the business or organisation has to be assessed in order to implement the strategy, progress needs to be evaluated and any necessary adjustments made in order to ensure that the strategy fulfils the objectives which have been set.

A simplified overview of the strategic planning process can be summarised as follows:

1. Objectives have to be clearly defined and measurable.
2. The environmental scan identifies available resources and analyses the environment in which the strategy is to be implemented, often by analysing the political, economical, social and technological (PEST analysis) factors. The internal factors are usually analysed in terms of strengths and weaknesses and external factors in terms of opportunities and threats (SWOT analysis).
3. Strategy formulation is usually based on the information from the environmental scan, where strengths are matched to the opportunities identified while addressing weaknesses and external threats.

---

[1] *European Charter for Regional or Minority Languages.* 1992. Strasbourg: Council of Europe. conventions.coe.int/Treaty/EN/Treaties/Html/148.htm.

4. Strategy implementation is often done by people other than those responsible for formulating the strategy. It is therefore essential to communicate the strategy and the reasoning behind it in order to ensure success.
5. Evaluation and control is carried out by monitoring the strategy, determining if the previously defined measurable parameters have been met and then making adjustments as necessary to ensure the desired outcome.

When determining and implementing the various aspects or elements of a strategy, what lessons can be learnt from commercial marketing in order to maximise the strategy's potential? Marketing implementation decisions often fall into four controllable categories referred to as the 'four Ps', also known as the 'marketing mix'. All elements of the 'marketing mix' need to be coordinated in order to ensure that they all contain the same 'message' and avoid confusion by sending. For example, is the objective of the language strategy of which the 'marketing mix' is a component to encourage and secure diglossia or bidialectalism, or a process of language planning? Are the elements of the strategy consistently promoting one or the other or sometimes appearing to promote one and sometimes appearing to promote the other?

A simplified overview of the 'four Ps' and examples of the kind of questions that may be asked in order to define the marketing mix for elements of a strategy for Scots may be summarised as follows:

Product
- What do Scots-speakers want? What needs are satisfied?
- How and where will it be consumed by Scots-speakers?

Price
- What is the value to Scots-speakers of what is made available?
- How much time and effort are Scots-speakers prepared to invest in what is made available?

Place
- Where do Scots-speakers expect to consume what is made available?

Promotion
- Where and when will Scots-speakers be made aware of what is available?
- What are the choices for promotional activity?

Once answers to the four Ps above have been found it is usual to look at each 'P' again using 'why' and 'what if' questions in order to challenge the 'marketing mix'. *Why* do Scots-speakers need what is made available? *What if* changes and adjustments are made to what is made available? How will that affect interest and uptake of what is on offer? Answers have to be based on sound knowledge and facts. What market research or facts still need to be gathered? Finally, the 'marketing mix' of what is offered has to be tested from the consumer's, in this case the Scots-speaker's, perspective:

1. Does it meet their needs? (**product**)
2. Will they find it where they expect it? (**place**)
3. Will they be prepared to invest time and effort in accessing it? (**price**)
4. And will the publicity reach them? (**promotion**)

What are the objectives of a language strategy for Scots?

1. Encouraging and securing diglossia or bidialectalism through dialect maintenance where standard English remains the 'H' variety and the Scots dialects the 'L' variety. A situation in which literacy in Scots would likely consist of little more than a knowledge of dialect writing, thus negating the need for any written standard or regularised literary form for use in domains occupied by the 'H' variety.

2. A process of language planning (cf. Haugen 1961) to facilitate bilingualism, either in a diglossic situation or in one where Scots may function as a ubiquitous alternative to Standard English with the attendant implications of a written standard (or at least a regularised orthography) but not necessarily a spoken standard.

How will a language strategy be influenced by popular perceptions of the status of Scots *vis-à-vis* language or dialect definitions? In developed literate western societies, the popular consciousness generally thinks of a language as having a standard written form and, perhaps also, a standardised spoken form which are taught in schools and used as a medium of instruction, with the standard form generally being used for public discourse in both print and electronic media. Closely related varieties lacking the above characteristics are generally considered dialects of the standard language which fulfils the functions described above. That position closely mirrors the *Ausbausprache – Abstandsprache – Dachsprache* framework described by Kloss (1967), also reflected in the findings of the 2010 'Public Attitudes Towards the Scots Language' study (see below). The study determined that 64 percent of the adults in the sample agreed that they do not think of Scots as a language. Interestingly, those who speak Scots most frequently are least likely to agree that Scots is not a language. However, overall support for the use of Scots in culture (arts, drama, music, etc.) and broadcasting was found to be high, and with regard to education a majority were in favour of encouraging children in Scotland to speak Scots.

Presumably an integral objective of a language strategy would be ensuring intergenerational mother-tongue transmission rather than merely good things or impressive symbolic splashes. (Fishman 1991: 12) Nevertheless, securing bidialectalism would tend to conform to the popular perception that the varieties of Scots are heteronomous to and thus dialects of, Standard English, where English functions as the *Dachsprache*. However, the terms of the charter[2] would imply planning for bilingualism in autonomous languages, something a sceptical public would be unlikely to accept. Such scepticism would tend to indicate that an attempt to establish Scots as a ubiquitous alternative to Standard English would be met with both derision and hostility. However, attitudes can be changed by government action, as has been shown by legislation and awareness campaigns, over a period of decades, directed against prejudice and discrimination based on race, ethnicity, gender and sexuality. Such measures have resulted in considerable changes in public attitudes regarding such issues.

Implementation of the obligations entered into under the *European Charter for Regional or Minority Languages* has generally come to be the responsibility of the two devolved jurisdictions, Scotland and Northern Ireland.

Since the implementation of the Charter, government policy towards Scots has been incoherent, poorly assembled and implemented in a half-hearted and contradictory manner, with little evidence that the issue of language policy for Scots has been or is being taken seriously. (Millar 2005: 76, 82) In the Scottish Executive's *National Cultural*

---

[2] General Provisions, Article 1: Definitions, a. 'it does not include [...] dialects of the official language(s) of the State'.

Strategy[3] published in 2000, Scots was little more than a footnote.

In 1997 the Labour-Liberal Democrat coalition which formed the then Scottish Executive published *A Strategy for Scotland's Languages: Draft version for Consultation*,[4] which stated little more than that 'the Scots language will be treated with respect and pride' and 'encouraging Scots language and literature in schools where appropriate.' There was no mention of how it was intended to ensure that Scots will be 'treated with respect and pride'; nor of what is considered appropriate or inappropriate use of Scots in a school environment. As such, the document fails as a strategy with respect to Scots. (Unger 2010: 104) The cosnsultation responses to the draft strategy were also made available.[5] Although not a strategy, the report certainly included what could be the objective of a strategy in that Scots should 'have an established, institutionalised and formally recognised place in all aspects of the national life, comparable to that enjoyed by Welsh in Wales and Scottish Gaelic in Scotland'. The recommendations then focused on the following fields: education, broadcasting, literature and the arts, international contacts, public awareness and dialects. A number of responses suggested that the document was indeed not a strategy, criticizing the contradictory nature of the proposals and lack of joined up thinking. The seriousness of any commitment to fulfilling the terms of the Charter with regards to Scots was also questioned, in particular the lack of a proposal to ensure an explicit mention of Scots in future curricula guidelines and the subsumption of Scots in the 'different languages of Scotland', which includes immigrant languages. Furthermore, the accuracy of the conclusion that 'Scots is not an endangered language' was also questioned as no supporting evidence was cited.

Shortly after publication of the draft strategy, elections resulted in a new SNP Executive, now rebranded as the 'Scottish Government'. Consequently a final version of *A Strategy for Scotland's Languages* never came to fruition. However, the then and current SNP Government has shown signs has shown signs of a willingness to take the issue of language policy for Scots more seriously and published an Audit of Current Scots Language Provision in Scotland in 2009.[6] The findings were presented at the Scots Language Conference, a report of which was published.[7] In 2010, a survey of public attitudes towards the Scots language was published.[8] In October 2009, a ministerial working group with the task of making recommendations on steps to promote the Scots language was established.[9]

The report of the ministerial working group was subsequently published in November 2010.[10]

Although not a strategy, the report certainly included what could be the objective of a strategy in that Scots should 'have an established, institutionalised and formally recognised place in all aspects of the national life, comparable to that enjoyed by Welsh in Wales and Scottish Gaelic in Scotland.' The recommendations then focused on the following fields: education, broadcasting, literature and the arts, international contacts, public awareness and dialects.

The issues of Scots-speakers' awareness of their own and other dialects, literacy in Scots and the place of Scots in schools, further education institutions, adult learning,

---

[3] www.scotland.gov.uk/nationalculturalstrategy/docs/cult-00.asp.

[4] www.scotland.gov.uk/Publications/2007/01/24130746/2.

[5] www.scotland.gov.uk/Publications/2007/06/29140150/0.

[6] www.scotland.gov.uk/Publications/2009/01/23133726/0.

[7] www.scotland.gov.uk/Publications/2009/06/08164441/9.

[8] www.scotland.gov.uk/Publications/2010/01/06105123/9.

[9] www.scotland.gov.uk/News/Releases/2009/10/29151643.

[10] www.scotland.gov.uk/Resource/Doc/332491/0108193.pdf.

museums etc., the creative arts and the media were a thread throughout the report. Suggestions made towards addressing those issues were; to include a permanent 'Scots Language/ Scottish Literature Bureau' within the new Scottish Education Quality and Improvement Agency (SEQIA), to establish a nationwide network of coordinators able to deliver Scots language training and advice on resources, and to ensure greater availability of free teaching resources and improved teacher training. It was also recommended that the existing Scots bodies be consolidated and strengthened in order to ensure a source of expertise and that publicly funded media and culture organisations be 'actively encouraged to develop specific Scots language policies.'

A further recommendation was the 'recognition of dialect diversity'. The summary of discussions described the 'existence of striking differences between local dialects' and that 'divergent though the dialects are, they are nonetheless forms of the same Scots language.' The report recognised the 'need to preserve the individual dialects and respect their distinctive identities, while at the same time developing the language as a whole, will require careful planning: in particular, the necessity of developing a standard form of Scots for official purposes must be presented so as to avoid any appearance of a threat to the dialects.' It is assumed that 'standard form' refers to institutionalised transactional writing, and the present author is not aware of anyone who advocates a spoken standard. People are free to indulge in creative and dialect writing as they please. Nevertheless, the differences between the (broad) Scots dialects are not as 'striking' as they may at first appear, all Scots dialects share the same underlying phonological system and much the same syntactical and morphological conventions. The different pronunciations of the same general Scots words are largely predictable, the differences are more often than not on the level of accent, particularly among the Central Scots dialects spoken south of the Tay. A number of words do, however, have only local or regional currency, in particular the insular dialects. An emphasis on divergence may run the risk of causing Scots-speakers to assume their dialect is specific to their locality and has little in common with the dialects spoken in elsewhere in Lowland Scotland. That may then unwittingly foster a feeling among Scots speakers that their dialect is marginal and of little relevance or use elsewhere in Lowland Scotland, thus encouraging the use of more (standard) English rather than the habitual use of more Scots. It would perhaps be more profitable to describe Scots as being comprised of a number of (closely) related spoken dialects accompanied by a literary tradition employing established and prestigious (pan-dialect) orthographic conventions,[11] thus emphasising languageness rather than dialectness.

In March 2011 the Scottish Government published its response to the Scots Language Working Group Report.[12] The response was wholly positive with most all of the recommendation being 'taken on board' and some already implemented. With the election of a majority SNP government in the May 2011 elections there is an increased likelihood of further recommendations being implemented. However, whether there will be an integrated policy or strategy geared towards ensuring long-term intergenerational mother tongue transmission, or a continuation of uncoordinated ad hoc measures remains to be seen.

A question on Scots was included in the *2011 Census*[13] asking whether respondents

---

[11] And the Scots tongue has an orthography of its own, lacking neither 'authority nor author.' (Stevenson 1905: 152) [...] Scots remains the one British dialect which may be represented today by a consistent (and traditional) orthography. (Scragg 1975: 37).

[12] www.scotland.gov.uk/Resource/Doc/346190/0115217.pdf.

[13] www.scotlandscensus.gov.uk/en/faq/209.htm.

[14] www.ayecan.com.

can understand, speak, read or write Scots. However, in answer to the question 'Do you use a language other than English at home?' Scots speakers will presumably have written Scots under 'other'. In order to address concerns about respondents' linguistic awareness, the website *Aye Can*, presenting examples of both spoken and written Scots, was set up to address the issue.[14]

Broadcasting is a reserved matter and as such outwith the remit of the devolved administrations. Of the six public purposes expressed in the 2007 BBC Trust Charter which defines the main objective of the organisation, one is representing the UK, its nations, regions and communities,[15] which includes a commitment to 'support the UK's indigenous languages where appropriate'. However, no elucidation is provided about what is considered appropriate.

The presence of Scots on television and radio is currently marginal and usually limited to comedy. The 2008 'Platform for Success' final report of the Scottish Government's Scottish Broadcasting Commission[16] does not mention Scots at all. Mention is made of 'Gaelic and other languages' in relation to community radio output and a proposal to expand programming in the English language on the new Gaelic-language television service BBC Alba (MG Alba).

Interest in Scots in Ulster was until fairly recently marginal but gained prominence from the 1980s, often being seen as a Unionist effort to match the growing popularity of Irish and influence of Irish language activists. In some quarters, the varieties of Scots spoken in Ulster being promoted as a sister language to Scots in Scotland – justified by such fanciful claims as that the relative positions of the two are analogous to those of Irish and Scottish Gaelic. (Robinson 2003: 112) However, the linguist James Milroy observed that the Scots varieties spoken in Antrim and North Derry are barely distinguishable from those of Ayrshire. (1982: 27)

In Northern Ireland, what was traditionally referred to as (*braid*) Scots or Scotch (Traynor 1953: 36, 244, Nic Craith 2002: 107) by native speakers has been rebranded as 'Ulster-Scots' – the hyphen emphasising its separate status (Kirk 2008: 217) – and was recognised as such in the 1998 *Belfast / Good Friday Agreement*.[17] In the agreement between the United Kingdom and Ireland establishing implementation bodies,[18] the term 'Ullans' was used, defined as the variety of the Scots language traditionally found in parts of Northern Ireland and Donegal. The Ulster-Scots Agency was established as part of the Language Body,[19] its legislative remit being 'the promotion of greater awareness and the use of Ullans [...] both within Northern Ireland and throughout the island'.

One immediate result of the Charter and the 'parity of esteem' expressed in the Good Friday Agreement was the appearance of numerous *Ulster-Scots* versions of official publications, most of which were symbolic rather than transactional in nature – being largely unintelligible to native speakers, often using mixed orthographies bearing little resemblance to that of the established literary tradition.

Proposals for an Ulster-Scots Academy had been circulating for a number of years,

[15] www.bbc.co.uk/bbctrust/assets/files/pdf/about/how_we_govern/purpose_remits/nations.pdf.

[16] www.scottishbroadcastingcommission.gov.uk/Resource/Doc/4/0000481.pdf.

[17] www.nio.gov.uk/agreement.pdf.

[18] www.nio.gov.uk/agreement_between_uk_government_and_irish_government_establishing_implementation_bodies.pdf.

[19] www.northsouthministerialcouncil.org/index/north-south-implementation-bodies/language_body.htm.

[20] www.dcalni.gov.uk/index/languages/public_consultation_on_proposals_for_an_ulster_scots_academy.pdf.

[21] www.dcalni.gov.uk/index/languages/usaig_-_consultation_-_full_responses__53_-2.doc

and in 2007 the Northern Ireland Department of Culture, Arts and Leisure published a public consultation document regarding proposals for such an Academy.[20] However, the reaction of academia in the responses[21] was generally critical. The Ulster-Scots Agency criticised the proposed Academy for intending to promote Ulster-Scots as a language distinct from Scots. If Scots in Ulster is to be promoted as a sister language to Scots in Scotland, in particular with a divergent orthography, any advantages gained by economies of scale would be seriously diminished.

Although explicit mention of Scots in Scotland is absent in documents referring to BBC objectives, Ulster Scots fares better receiving mention in the UK Department for Culture, Media and Sport's 2006 *A Public Service for all: The BBC in the Digital Age*.[22] The BBC Northern Ireland Management Review for 2009–10[23] mentions coverage of Ulster-Scots stories and events and a new Ulster-Scots website rather than programming in Scots. In February 2010 the United Kingdom Government announced a pledge of £5 million for an Ulster-Scots Broadcasting Fund, but indications are that most programming will be about aspects of Ulster-Scots culture rather than in Scots.

In August 2010, the Department of Culture, Arts and Leisure (DCAL) Research and Statistics Branch published a survey of 'Public Views on Ulster-Scots Culture, Heritage and Language in Northern Ireland'.[24] Some 57 percent of respondents, of which more than 70 percent were over 50, said they were aware of the 'Ulster-Scots language', but only 18 percent expressed any interest in learning more about 'the language' and only 22 percent of them thought that children should have the option to study 'the language' in school.

One of the objectives of the DCAL Business Plan[25] for 2010–11 is to protect and enhance indigenous minority languages in line with the *European Charter* and the *Northern Ireland (St Andrews Agreement) Act 2006*[26] by developing a Minority Languages Strategy and putting in place the conditions for the establishment of the Ulster-Scots Academy mentioned above. Although an informal and interim Ulster-Scots Academy Steering Grouop has existed for some time, a Ministerial Advisory Group on the Ulster-Scots Academy was formally established on 24 March 2011.[27]

A question on ability to understand, speak, read or write Ulster Scots was included in the *2011 Census*,[28] a formulation implying that Scots-speakers from Scotland could indicate speaking ability only if they were able to imitate a Northern Irish accent.

Those recent reports and surveys have certainly gone some way towards identifying the available resources and analysing the environment in which a language strategy for Scots would be implemented. However, what information the census may deliver for language planners remains to be seen. Nevertheless, the inclusion of a question on Scots language ability will at least raise awareness of Scots as an issue.

Although a situation exactly comparable to Scots is difficult to find elsewhere, language revitalisation and planning endeavours in Europe and further afield certainly provide insights into the issues likely to be confronted when developing a language strategy for Scots.

Language revitalisation endeavours in Catalonia, Friesland, Luxembourg and Norway involved, among other things, the establishing of normative orthographies

[22] www.official-documents.gov.uk/document/cm67/6763/6763.pdf

[23] www.bbc.co.uk/northernireland/audiencecouncil/docs/nations_mr_northern_ireland_0910final.pdf

[24] www.dcalni.gov.uk/ulster-scots_follow-up_report_-_secondary_analysis-2.pdf4

[25] www.dcalni.gov.uk/departmental_business_plan_2010-11_-_final_version_-_april-2.doc

[26] www.nio.gov.uk/st_andrews_agreement.pdf

[26] www.northernireland.gov.uk/news-dcal-240311-appointments-to-the?WT.mc_id=rss-news.

[27] northernireland.org.uk/appointments-to-the-ministerial-advisory-group-for-the-ulster-scots-academy.

[28] www.nisranew.nisra.gov.uk/census/pdf/proposals.pdf.

and the expansion of the use of previously marginalised languages into domains from which they were previously largely excluded.

Catalan provides insight into a situation where a politically autonomous or devolved 'region or nation' enacted a process of language normalisation. In Catalonia the policy of recent decades has been to institutionalise Catalan as a functional language in all of the most powerful domains of modern life and overcome the legacy of native-speaker illiteracy and inferiority inherited from the Franco years, when official policy was to displace Catalan in favour of the closely related Castilian Spanish. From the thirteenth to the sixteenth century Catalan was the language of a considerable Mediterranean empire. By the nineteenth century Spanish had made serious inroads into all formal domains, but upper middle-class vernacular use of Catalan survived even up to the twentieth century. Immediately following the Spanish civil war, Catalan was denied any public presence and all public use of Catalan banned. The language was declared a mere dialect and those who spoke it described as 'barking like dogs' or as 'non-Christian'.

Frisian illustrates a situation in which a dominant language, Dutch, is spoken alongside a lesser-used but closely related language, Frisian, still spoken as a mother-tongue by approximately 54 percent of the population. The Fryske Akademy[29] was founded in 1938 as a scientific centre for research and education concerning Frisia , its people and language. Frisian is also an ethno-cultural expression of Frisianness. Frisian is taught in public schools as a school subject and is often used when communicating with local service industries and local government. The provincial public broadcaster Omrop Fryslân transmits exclusively in Frisian during its daily 17 hours of radio and two hours of television. Some programmes are subtitled in Dutch, such as the documentaries Fryslân DOK, which are also broadcast on a national channel. Apart from that, Frisian is heard extremely rarely on national radio and television. In the courts, spoken Frisian is accepted, but documents in Frisian are only accepted as accompaniments to the official and obligatory Dutch ones. In the provincial assembly presentations can be made in either Frisian or Dutch without translation.

Luxembourgish, recognised as the national language of Luxembourg, is a High German variety, containing some French loans, and is thus closely related to Standard German. An official orthography was introduced in 1975, with further modifications made in 1999. Pre-school education is in Luxembourgish, primary education is in German and French, and secondary education is in French. Parliamentary debates are usually in Luxembourgish, though some French is also used. However, laws are drafted in French. When dealing with the authorities people are free to use French, German or Luxembourgish. Luxembourgish is also used in broadcasting.

The situation in **Norway** illustrates a longer-term language planning process which established a national language. From the sixteenth to the nineteenth centuries, Danish was the standard written language of Norway. During the twenieth century an ongoing process of developing a national language ensued, which resulted in the two official forms of *written* Norwegian – Bokmål (a Norwegianised variety of Danish) and Nynorsk (based on the traditional Norwegian dialects) – currently used. There is no officially sanctioned standard spoken Norwegian. The basis and rationale of the language planning process was and is dialect maintenance. Consequently, most Norwegians speak their own dialect in all circumstances.

Swiss German offers an example of a fairly stable diglossia between the use of an essentially extraterritorial written standard and autochthonous dialects for verbal communication. In Switzerland almost all writing is done in Standard German, albeit

---

[29] www.fryske-akademy.nl/fa.

a marginally differentiated Swiss variety thereof. However, it is normal for all people in German-speaking Switzerland to speak their own dialect in all social situations. At the end of the nineteenth century, indications were that Standard German was on the way to becoming the prestigious spoken form. However, during the early twentieth century a number of popularly supported *Mundartwellen* (dialect waves) swept German-speaking Switzerland. Those started in Bern with a renaissance of dialect literature and the use of dialect in the Canton parliament, spreading to Zürich by the 1930s, then soon becoming part of the *geistige Landesverteidigung* (intellectual defence of the country) against Nazi Germany. The ultimate outcome was a tradition of vigilance and respect for the dialects which, from the 1960s, saw the use of spoken dialect spread into almost all domains of everyday life. Nevertheless, the dialects are under pressure from the standard language in a process whereby dialect lexis is replaced by standard equivalents, dialect levelling is brought about by increased mobility and there is what is known as *Großratsdeutsch*, where Standard German vocabulary and syntax is expressed using a Swiss-German pronunciation rather than being translated into dialect.

Examples of the development of bidialectal education policies can be found in the **Caribbean** and the **United States**. There, until relatively recently, the norm for education policy was to enforce the superiority of the English spoken by the 'social elite' and, by extension, the superiority of that group itself, a consequence of which was to denigrate non-standard varieties of English and Creole, and devalue the speakers of such varieties themselves. Since at least the 1960s, more culturally responsible curricula have been developed where strategies for improving Standard English acquisition among non-standard speakers value and celebrate diversity in language (and other areas) as good for everybody. For example, in Trinidad and Tobago, official guidelines encourage bidialectism between local Standard English and Creole by including works of fiction in both Caribbean English and Creole in the curriculum, in particular ensuring that Creole is not limited to the functions of amusement. In the United States the recognition that African American Vernacular English is a linguistic system rather than simply 'bad English' had begun to shape approaches to improving Standard English proficiency amongst AAVE-speaking pupils. The so-called Oakland Ebonics Controversy illustrated how negative publicity can undermine the 'marketing' of an inclusive language policy by failing to bridge the chasm between popular ill-informed language beliefs and professional specialist expertise. The 'controversy' raged around misinterpretations, based on prejudice and ignorance, of proposals which recognised that Standard English proficiency amongst AAVE-speaking pupils could be improved by applying principles derived from bilingual or second language learning in a bidialectal situation. A common popular misconception, finding resonance in the media, equated the proposals with teaching pupils slang or drug culture.[30] The situation was mirrored in the United Kingdom, where a commentator in the *Daily Express* summarised the Teaching and Learning Scotland's website[31] content about Scots in Schools as an exercise in teaching pupils how to send mobile telephone text messages in slang.[32]

---

[30] *Daily News* (New York 26.12.1996) 'Don't Get Hooked On Ebonics'.
www.nydailynews.com/archives/opinions/1996/12/26/1996-12-26_don_t_get_hooked_on_ebonics.html
[31] www.ltscotland.org.uk/knowledgeoflanguage/scots/index.asp
[32] *Daily Express* (21.08.2010) 'Schools Teach Children How to Text in Slang'.
www.express.co.uk/posts/view/194590/Schools-Teach-children-how-to-text-in-slang

References

Corbett, J. 2003. 'Language Planning and Modern Scots'. In eds. Corbett, J., McClure J. D. and J. Stuart-Smith. *The Edinburgh Companion to Scots*. Edinburgh: Edinburgh University Press. 251–72.

Deumert, A. and Vandenbussche, W. eds. 2003. *Germanic Standardization Past to Present*. Amsterdam: John Benjamins.

Eagle, A. 2011. 'German-Speakin Swisserland: A Paitren for Dialect Uphaud?' In eds. Kirk, J.M. and D.P. Baoill. *Sustaining Minority Language Communities: Northern Ireland, the Republic of Ireland, and Scotland*. Belfast: Cló Ollscoil na Banríona. 259–65.

Falconer, G. 2005. 'Breaking Nature's Social Union: The Autonomy of Scots in Ulster'. In Kirk, J and Ó Baoill, D. eds. *Legislation, Literature and Sociolinguistics: Northern Ireland, the Republic of Ireland, and Scotland*. Belfast: Cló Ollscoil na Banríona. 48–59.

Fergusson, C. 1959. 'Diglossia' *Word* 15.2: 325–40.

Fishman, J. ed. 1974. *Advances in Language Planning*. The Hague: Mouton.

Fishman, J. A. 1991. *Reversing language Shift: Theoretical and Empirical Foundations of Assistance to Threatened Languages*. Clebedon: Multilingual Matters.

Gardner, J.R., Rachlin, R. and Allan Sweeny, H.W. eds. 1986. *Handbook of Strategic Planning*. New York: John Wiley and Sons.

Gorter, D. 2008. 'Developing a Policy for Teaching a Minority Language: The Case of Frisian'. *Current Issues in Language Planning* 9.4. 501–20.

Haugen, E. 1961. 'Language Planning in Modern Norway'. *Scandinavian Studies* 33: 68–81.

Haugen, E. 1966. *Language Conflict and Language Planning: The Case of Modern Norwegian*. Cambridge, MA: Harvard University Press.

Haugen, E. 1972. 'Dialect, Language, Nation'. In eds. Pride, J.D. and J. Holmes. *Sociolinguistics: Selected Readings*. Harmondsworth: Penguin. 97–111.

Horner, K. ed. 2009. *Luxembourg*. Special Issue of *Language Problems and Language Planning* 33.2.

Jahr, E.H. 2008. 'On the Reasons for Dialect Maintenance in Norway'. *Sociolinguistica*. Berlin. Walter de Gruyter. 157–70.

Kaplan, R.B. and Baldauf, R.B. 2005. *Language Planning and Policy in Europe*. Vol. 1. Clevedon: Multilingual Matters.

Kirk, J.M. 2008. 'Does the UK Have a Language Policy?' *Journal of Irish and Scottish Studies* 1.2: 205–22.

Kloss, H. 1967. '*Abstand* Languages and *Ausbau* Languages'. *Anthropological Linguistics* 9: 29–41.

Mac Póilin, A. 1999. 'Language, Identity and Politics in Northern Ireland'. *Ulster Folklife* 45: 108–31.

Máté, I. 1996. 'Scots Language. A Report on the Scots Language Research Carried out by the General Register Office for Scotland in 1996'. Edinburgh: General Register Office (Scotland).

McClure J.D., Aitken, A.J. and J.T. Low. 1980. *The Scots Language: Planning for Modern Usage*. Edinburgh: The Ramsay Head Press.

Millar, R. 2006. 'Burying Alive: Unfocussed Governmental Language Policy and Scots'. *Language Policy* 5.1: 63–86.

Milroy, J. 1982. 'Some Connections between Galloway and Ulster Speech'. *Scottish Language* 1: 23–9.

Nero, S.J. ed. 2006. *Dialects, Englishes, Creoles and Education*. Hillsdale, NJ: Lawrence Erlbaum Associates

Nic Craith M. 2002. *Plural Identities: Singular Narratives*. Oxford: Berghahn Books.

Niven, L. and Macleod, I. 2002. *The Scots Language in Education in Scotland*. Leeuwarden: Mercator-Education. [Available at: www1.fa.knaw.nl./mercator/regionale_dossiers/PDFs/scots_in_scotland.PDF]

Perreault, W.D., Cannon, J.P. and E.J. McCarthy. 2008. *Basic Marketing: A Marketing Strategy Planning Approach*. New York: Irwin/McGraw-Hill.

Robinson, P. 2003. 'The historical Presence of Ulster-Scots in Ireland'. In eds. Cronin M. and C. Ó Cuilleanáin. *The Languages of Ireland*. Dublin: Four Courts. 112–26.

Ris, R. 1979. 'Dialekte und Einheitssprache in der deutschen Schweiz'. *International Journal of the Sociology of Language* 21: 41–61.

Stell, G. 2006. 'Luxembourgish Standardization: Context, Ideology and Comparability with the Case of West Frisian'. Louvain-La-Neuve: Peeters.

Taylor, H.U. 1989. *Standard English, Black English and Bidialectism: A Controversy*. Frankfurt: Peter Lang.

Traynor, M. 1953. *The English Dialect of Donegal*. Dublin: Royal Irish Academy.

Trudgill P. 1975. *Accent, Dialect and the School*. London: Edward Arnold.

Trudgill P. 1979. 'Standard and Non-Standard Dialects of English in the United Kingdom: Problems and Policies'. *International Journal of the Sociology of Language* 21: 9–94.

Unger, J.W. 2009. 'Economic Discourses of Scots on Bourdieu's 'Linguistic Market''. In eds. Kirk, J.M. and D.P. Ó Baoill. *Language and Economic Development: Northern Ireland, the Republic of Ireland, and Scotland*. Belfast: Cló Ollscoil na Banríona. 204–10.

Unger, J.W. 2010. 'Legitimating inaction: Differing identity constructions of the Scots language'. *European Journal of Cultural Studies* 13: 99–117.

Wolfram, W. 1998. 'Controversy Language Ideology and Dialect: Understanding the Oakland Ebonics Controversy'. *Journal of English Linguistics* 26: 108–21.

Wright, S. ed. 1999. *Language, Democracy, and Devolution in Catalonia*. Multilingual Matters Ltd. Clevedon.

Ten Years of Language and Politics: Impact and Whither Now?

*John M. Kirk and Dónall P. Ó Baoill**

This paper reviews the ten years of Language and Politics symposia on the Gaeltacht and Scotstacht which have been heldat Queen's University Belfast from 2000–2010. It addresses the impact which the symposia have made and considers their possible futures.

Background

The inspiration for the symposia came directly from the *Belfast / Good Friday Agreement* of 1998 which propelled language centre-stage. But they also came about because, following Dónall Ó Baoill's appointment as Professor of Irish at Queen's in July 1998, we were eager to work together and cross the boundaries between our subjects in a genuinely inter-disciplinary way. Without either that ambition or the good rapport which we established, the symposia would not have happened.

The Agreement states:

> All participants recognize the importance of respect, understanding and tolerance in relation to linguistic diversity, including in Northern Ireland, the Irish language, Ulster-Scots and the languages of the various ethnic communities, all of which are part of the cultural wealth of the island of Ireland.

Whereas that statement was a dynamic declaration of recognition, it entailed of itself no further action. It was in the next paragraph, with reference to the aspirations of the *European Charter for Regional or Minority Languages*[1] that a commitment to action was stated:

> In the context of active consideration currently being given to the UK signing the Council of Europe Charter for Regional or Minority Languages, the British Government will in particular in relation to the Irish language, where appropriate and where people so desire it:
> - take resolute action to promote the language;
> - facilitate and encourage the use of the language in speech and writing in public and private life where there is appropriate demand;
> - seek to remove, where possible, restrictions which would discourage or work against the maintenance or development of the language;
> - make provision for liaising with the Irish language community, representing their views to public authorities and investigating complaints;
> - place a statutory duty on the Department of Education to encourage and facilitate Irish medium education in line with current provision for integrated education;

* We are most grateful to Gavin Falconer, Wilson McLeod, Colin Neilands and Dónall Ó Riagáin for comments on an earlier draft, and to all those who took part in the discussion on 21 September 2010 about the future of the project.

[1] *The European Charter for Regional or Minority Languages* is a European treaty (CETS 148) adopted in 1992 under the auspices of the Council of Europe to protect and promote historical regional and minority languages in Europe. It is to be found at conventions.coe.int/Treaty/EN/Treaties/html/148.htm.

- explore urgently with the relevant British authorities, and in cooperation with the Irish broadcasting authorities, the scope for achieving more widespread availability of Teilifís na Gaeilge in Northern Ireland;
- seek more effective ways to encourage and provide financial support for Irish language film and television production in Northern Ireland; and
- encourage the parties to secure agreement that this commitment will be sustained by a new Assembly in a way which takes account of the desires and sensitivities of the community.

Although these wordings are directly taken over from the European Charter, the Charter had not, by 1998, been signed by the UK Government. No doubt under the pressure of the *Belfast Agreement, 1998,* the UK Government finally signed the Charter on 17 March 2000 and ratified it to take effect from 1 July 2001.

Languages which are official within regions or provinces or federal units within a State (e.g. Catalan in Spain) but which are not classified as official languages of the State may not benefit from the Charter. Nor may dialects of State languages (such as Hiberno-English or Scottish English). On the other hand, the Republic of Ireland has not signed the Charter on behalf of the Irish language as a minority language for it is designated as a 'national' language. Although France signed the Charter, it has not ratified it on behalf of its other languages because of its Constitution in favour of French as the sole language of State.

The Charter provides a large number of different actions which national governments can take to protect and promote historical regional and minority languages. There are two levels of protection – all signatories must apply the lower level of protection (as specified in Part II of the Charter) to qualifying languages. Signatories may further declare that a qualifying language or languages will benefit from the higher level of protection (Part III). Part III lists a range of actions from which states must agree to undertake at least 35.

The UK Government ratified the Charter with regard to Scottish Gaelic and Scots in Scotland; Welsh in Wales; and Irish and, doubtlessly following the *Belfast Agreement*, what was referred to as 'Ulster-Scots' in Northern Ireland, although for us it is a dialect of Scots (cf. Kirk 1998, 2004, 2011).[2]

The Charter is an international convention and thus has status under international law (Dónall Ó Riagáin, personal communication). By ratifying it to bring it into force, the UK Government and its devolved institutions were committing themselves to courses of action with regard to the languages named, to producing reports on those action every three years, and to receiving feedback on those reports by the Council of Europe's Committee of Experts.[3] These commitments, according to Ó Riagáin (2001), are 'real and substantive' and, with regard to Scots as well as Irish, 'necessitate a dramatic shift in public perception of linguistic diversity in Northern Ireland'.

The first group of commitments – known as Part II provisions – are of a general nature and set out the broad areas of principle that underpin the thrust of the Charter. The second group – set out in Part III – are specific and appear under the following headings: 'education', 'judicial proceedings', 'administration', 'media', 'culture', 'economic issues', and 'trans-frontier links'.

---

[2] In 2002, Cornish was added for England. In 2003, Manx Gaelic was also added to the UK instrument of ratification.

[3] These reports may be found at conventions.coe.int/treaty/Commun/ChercheSig.asp?NT=148and CM=1and DF=and CL=ENG.

Dónall Ó Riagáin, one of the European Charter's authors, has expressed the view that, for minority languages and the development of a shared society in Northern Ireland, the Charter is 'a godsend'. 'It is not a concession to anyone. It is the application of European standards to all – standards of language rights, of human rights [...] an excellent basis for developing language policy.' (2001: 54)

As Tony Blair records in his autobiography *A Journey*, Ulster Scots (Ullans) became not only a very late inclusion in, but a deal-breaker for, the *Belfast / Good Friday Agreement* (2010: 173–4), so that the references to it alongside those to Irish could not be ignored.

Where Irish is referred to as 'the Irish language', there is no such designation around Ulster Scots, so how is its status to be interpreted? Is the 'language' designation of Irish to be conferred to Ulster Scots by co-textual association? Or is Ulster Scots a dialect, as linguists have been describing, or a variant of a sub-dialect as the *Scottish National Dictionary* has claimed? In *Statutory Instrument 1999 No. 859, The North/South Co-operation (Implementation Bodies) (Northern Ireland) Order 1999*, the status of Ulster Scots is defined as follows: 'Ullans [i.e. Ulster Scots] is to be understood as the variety of the Scots language traditionally found in parts of Northern Ireland and Donegal.' If the Scots found in Ulster is a dialect, variety or variant of Scots, why is the label 'Scots' not used? In due course, it emerged that activists were seeking to establish Scots in Ulster not so much as part of a dialect-based continuum with Scotland but as an apperceptionally-based but officially-backed counterbalance to Irish. As the *Belfast Agreement* had been so clearly influenced by the European Charter, and as the Charter does not deal with dialects (Article 1), Ulster Scots had to be classified as a language – a political rather than linguistic motivation.[4] Consequently, with the Charter's recognition of two 'minority or regional' languages in Northern Ireland, there emerged a further voice which cut across the provisions of the Charter and which called for equality between Irish and Ulster Scots in every respect, including funding, seeking to link the fate of each so that neither could benefit without the other.

And so, in the aftermath of the *Belfast / Good Friday Agreement*, it quickly became clear that political and linguistic opinion were not aligned. By 2000, we were struck by the need for a Forum for debate about both 'languages', where all sides and parties, linguists as well as politicians, implementers as well as practitioners, could participate. At the same time, it became clear that it would be pointless to discuss Irish and Ulster Scots in Northern Ireland without discussion of Irish and Ulster Scots in the Republic of Ireland (shared linguistic continua, separate jurisdictions), and Gaelic (separate language) and Scots (shared dialect) in Scotland (shared UK jurisdiction).

First Symposium

With these considerations in mind, **the first symposium** was organised for 12 August 2000, as a one-day event within *Dialect 2000*, a joint conference of the Forum for Research on the Languages of Scotland and Ulster (FRLSU), and the Irish Association for Applied Linguistics (IRAAL).[5] The primary theme for that day was 'discrimination', arising from the contention that provisions such as those in the European Charter were necessary because there was a feeling that speakers of those languages had been discriminated against. However, we widened the debate to include

---

[4] Ulster-Scots is included in the list of languages covered by the Charter. See languagecharter.eokik.hu/byLanguage.htm lists.

[5] The academic papers from *Dialect2000* are published as Kirk and Ó Baoill 2001a, with our long Introduction as Kirk and Ó Baoill 2001c.

gays,[6] speakers of immigrant languages,[7] and deaf speakers.[8] The then devolved Minister of Education, Seán Farren, gave an address.[9] The distinguished BBC NI broadcaster, Noel Thompson, chaired the entire proceedings, which were published in December 2000 as **Kirk and Ó Baoill 2000a**, with our long Introduction as Kirk and Ó Baoill 2000b.

Symposium Series

About that time, the then Arts and Humanities Board initiated a number of research centres, including one for Irish and Scottish Studies at the University of Aberdeen (RCISS), with Queen's University Belfast and Trinity College Dublin as junior partners. Because of its organisation of *Dialect 2000* with the Irish Association for Applied Linguistics (IRAAL), the FRLSU was invited by the centre's first director, Prof. Tom Devine, to contribute a series of symposia to the centre's work. The continuation of the languages and politics theme was an obvious choice, so that, in turn, on behalf of the FRLSU, we were invited to organise what became the next four symposia in 2001, 2002, 2003 and 2004. At the same time, for the purpose of wider dissemination, we became obliged to produce from each symposium an edited volume of proceedings (Kirk and Ó Baoill 2001, 2002, 2003, 2004.

Mindful that it was the European Charter which had inspired the provisions in the *Belfast / Good Friday Agreement*, we quickly decided that the programme for these seminars should not only deal with what we came to formulate as the Gaeltacht and Scotstacht,[10] covering Scotland and the Republic of Ireland as well as Northern Ireland, but also directly with the Charter's provisions and include as many non-academics and politicians as possible. At the same time, we decided to include presentations about other minority or regional languages, particularly in Europe, with which Irish and Ulster Scots might beneficially be compared.

The **second symposium**, in August 2001, thus addressed the issue of policy head-on. In addition, there were valuable comparisons with Frisian and with Norway and Switzerland. And papers or addresses were given by two MSPs (Mike Russell, MSP, who at the time was preparing a Private Member's Bill on Gaelic, and Irene McGugan, MSP, who had become the first chairperson of the Scottish Parliament's Cross-Party Group on the Scots Language), and by the Lord Laird of Artigarvan, by then the Chairman of the Board of the Ulster-Scots Agency. These papers are published as **Kirk and Ó Baoill 2001b**, with our long Introduction as Kirk and Ó Baoill 2001d. For a review, see Ó Riain [2002].

The **third symposium**, in September 2002, tackled the issue of Irish-medium and Gaelic-medium education. The question of Scots and education had a different orientation and was accompanied by a set of papers on issues of standardisation. Wider perspectives, particularly with regard to human rights, were raised in important keynote papers by the internationally renowned linguists Tove Skutnabb-Kangas and Robert Phillipson. And political papers were given by Irene McGugan, MSP, previously mentioned; the then Minister for Tourism, Culture and Leisure in the Scottish Executive; and the then Minister for Employment and Learning in the Northern Ireland Executive, Carmel Hanna, MLA. These papers are published as **Kirk and Ó**

---

[6] Mag Lochlainn 2000.
[7] Foley 2000, Watson 2000.
[8] McCullough 2000.
[9] Farren 2000.
[10] Our earliest use is in Kirk and Ó Baoill 2001b: 2.

Baoill 2002a, with our long Introduction as Kirk and Ó Baoill 2002c. For a review, see Bird 2004.

By then, we had covered four areas of the Charter's provision: 'status', 'discrimination', 'rights' and 'education'. The **fourth symposium**, in September 2003, tackled other areas of Part III provision: 'the media', 'cultural activities and facilities' and 'economic and social life'. We divided the papers into the following sections: 'broadcasting', 'the press', 'culture in the shape of the performing arts', and 'the economy'. International comparisons were made with Basque and Walloon. Éamon Ó Cuív, TD, Minister for Community, Rural and Gaeltacht Affairs, made an important after-dinner address on the Republic's views towards Irish in the light of the *Official Languages Act 2003*. One of the papers on language and the economy was given jointly by Esmond Birnie, MLA, and Steven King, then an adviser to David Trimble, First Minister.[11] These papers are published as **Kirk and Ó Baoill 2003a**, with our long Introduction as Kirk and Ó Baoill 2003b. For a review, see Simpson 2004 and Moriarty 2006.

The **fifth symposium**, in September 2005, concluded the survey of Part II provision by tackling the trans-frontier issue of Irish in the European Union, Irish by then having become an official language in the EU. It also tackled the impending Gaelic Bill in Scotland, the question of literary uses of Irish, Gaelic and Scots, and also the sociolinguistics of each language. Comparisons were also made with Maltese, which had provided the key to the recognition of Irish in the EU, and Kashubian. These papers are published as **Kirk and Ó Baoill 2005a**, with our long Introduction as Kirk and Ó Baoill 2005b.

During 2005, the AHRC RCISS became funded for a second period of five years from 2006–2010 (Phase II). This time, no doubt in reflection of the success of the first five symposia and accompanying publications, and the association of Queen's with the event, we became invited directly to organise a further five annual symposia and accompanying publications.

At the fourth symposium, in 2004, the session on language and economy proved so stimulating that we became urged to devote an entire symposium to the topic. This was the immediate choice of theme at the **sixth symposium** in September 2006. We had the good fortune that, for this purpose, François Grin devised a set of four paradigms which could link language with economic development and which each contributor addressed. As a result, we constructed a coherent set of position papers for Irish, Gaelic and Scots, some looking back to explain the present position, others looking forward to see how the matters could or should be developed. These papers were published as **Kirk and Ó Baoill 2009a**, with our Introduction as Kirk and Ó Baoill 2009b.

Following the sixth symposium, the *Northern Ireland (St Andrews Agreement) Act 2006* of December 2006 promised to bring forward heads of a Bill for a new *Irish Language Act* in Northern Ireland. Some Irish activists construed this as meaning that there would be an Irish Language Act. The British Government fulfilled the letter of the agreement by bringing forward heads for a Bill but the whole project was vetoed by the DUP. The Agreement also promised an Ulster-Scots Academy.

The **seventh symposium**, in November 2007, tackled the question of communities in which Irish, Gaelic and Scots were spoken, how they might be sustained, and what policies might ensure their sustainability. There was a central focus on the adequacy of

---

[11] Papers on many of the topics of this and the previous two symposia were also presented at a symposium on Language and Law in Northern Ireland, held at Stormont in February 2003, and published as Ó Riagáin 2003.

current arrangements and practices for minority languages in Ireland and Scotland, the importance of infrastructure, environment, society, employment, urban renewal, culture, the role of education, the vibrancy of the languages themselves, and whether minority language sustainability is a matter for a top-down or bottom-up approach. A further group of papers dealt with Scots, by applying similar questions, and a final set dealt with similar situations facing certain comparable minority languages elsewhere. These papers are published as **Kirk and Ó Baoill 2011a**, with our long Introduction as Kirk and Ó Baoill 2011c.

The **tenth symposium**, in September 2010, of which the present volume forms the edited proceedings, takes its cue from the publication of the draft *20-Year Strategy for the Irish Language*.[12] The symposium sought to consider what it means to be 'bilingual' in Ireland, what the role of policy and education to this end is supposed to be, and what wider concepts and experience need to be considered for implementing the 20-Year Strategy. Given the continuum of language but separation of jurisdiction, the symposium also focuses on the implications of the Strategy for Northern Ireland. A *Strategy for Indigenous or Regional Minority Languages* has long been promised by DCAL, but none so far has appeared. Finally, the symposium received a report on the first set of recommendations to the Scottish Government by the Ministerial Advisory Group on Scots. These papers are published as **Kirk and Ó Baoill 2011b**, with our long Introduction as Kirk and Ó Baoill 2011d.

By refering to our detailed Introductioons, we are mindful to oned reviewer's comment: '... anyone who finds it impossible to read [all these volumes] should, to make up the deficit, at least read the invaluable familiarising introductions provided in each volume by the editors ... .' (Macaulay 2002)

From these eight symposia, there have arisen eight core volumes of language and politics papers. Other papers by ourselves arising from the symposia are Kirk 2000a-b, 2004, 2005, 2008, 2010, 2011; and Ó Baoill 2001, 2002, 2004, 2005, 2006a-c, 2011a-b.

We should record that the **eighth symposium**, in November 2008, took on a different character and looked at the question of language and politics during the Age of Revolution which culminated in the Act of Union which took effect in 1801. Responses to the American Revolution and the French Revolution led to the creation of a huge body of poetry and songs in Irish, Gaelic, Scots, English and even Latin.[13] What emerges is that the responses to these historical events in each country in the different languages are varied and show different facets to radicalism in the face of loyalist oppression and backlash – hence the title of *United Islands?* From this symposium, and a sequel which was held in September 2009, two volumes of proceedings have been edited: **Kirk, Noble and Brown forthcoming, Kirk, Brown and Noble forthcoming.**

The **ninth symposium**, in October 2009, formed a thematic strand within the Sixth Irish-Scottish Academic Initiative Conference, entitled *Global Nations? Irish and Scottish Expansion since the 16th Century*, at the University of Aberdeen, where a range of language and politics papers as well as papers on language contact and borders were presented. As those papers were not published as a volume, the references are Connolly 2009, Dunbar 2009, Hickey, 2009, Kirk 2009, published as Kirk and Kallen 2011, Loester 2009, Millar 2009b, McCafferty 2009, McLeod 2009b, and Ó Riagáin 2009b.

Concurrent with these symposia during the first decade of the twenty-first century has been a number of key developments, which we now list:

---

[12] www.pobail.ie/ie/AnGhaeilge/.
[13] Of note here is the work of the Scottish radical, Rev. Alexander Geddes.

In the Republic of Ireland

For Irish

2002 *Official Languages (Equality) Bill, 2002.*

2003 *Official Languages Act 2003 / Acht na dTeangacha Oifigiúla 2003.*[14]

2003 Office of Irish Language Commissioner established.[15] Seán Ó Cuirreáin is appointed as first Commissioner.

2006 Rialtas na hÉireann / Government of Ireland, publication of *Ráiteas i Leith na Gaeilge 2006 / Statement on the Irish Language 2006.*[16]

2007, 1 January, Irish becomes an Official Language of the European Union.

2007 November. Publication of *Staidéar Teangeolaíoch ar Úsáid na Gaeilge sa Ghaeltacht / Comprehensive Linguistic Study of the Use of Irish in the Gaeltacht: Principal Findings and Recommendations.*[17]

2009 February. Publication of *20-Year Strategy for the Irish Language*, prepared for the Department of Community, Rural and Gaeltacht Affairs, by FIONTAR, Dublin City University.[18]

2010 April. Publication of *Dréacht-Straitéis 20-Bliain Don Ghaeilge 2010–2030 / Draft 20-Year Strategy for the Irish Language 2010–2030.*[19]

2010, December. Launch of the (final) *Straitéis 20-Bliain Don Ghaeilge 2010–2030 / 20-Year Strategy for the Irish Language 2010–2030.*[20]

In Northern Ireland

For Irish

1998 *Belfast Agreement* [the *Good Friday Agreement*].

1999 Establishment of the North/South Language Body (An Foras Teanga).

1999 Establishment of Foras na Gaeilge.

2001 Ratification of the *European Charter for Regional or Minority Languages (Chairt Eorpach um Theangacha Réigiúnacha nó Mionlaigh).*

2004 Announcement of Irish Language Broadcast Fund (Ciste Craoltóireachta na Gaeilge).

2008 Inter-departmental Charter Implementation Group.

2006 *Northern Ireland (St Andrews Agreement) Act*, interpreted by the Democratic Unionist Part as mandating a non-legislative strategy, and by the Irish-language community as mandating legislation.

A *Strategy for Indigenous or Regional Minority Languages* has long been announced by DCAL as forthcoming.

---

[14] The *Official Languages Act 2003 (Acht na dTeangacha Oifigiúla 2003*) sets out rules regarding use of the Irish language by public bodies, establishes the office of An Coimisinéir Teanga to monitor and enforce compliance by public bodies with the provisions of the *Official Languages Act* and makes provision for the designation of official Irish language versions of place-names and the removal of the official status of English place-names in the Gaeltacht. See Coisdelbha, in this volume.

[15] See www.coimisineir.ie/.

[16] For text, see www.pobail.ie/en/IrishLanguage/.

[17] A Research Report prepared for the for the Department of Community, Rural and Gaeltacht Affairs by Acadamh na hOllscolaíochta Gaeilge / National University of Ireland, Galway by Conchúr Ó Giollagáin and Seosamh Mac Donnacha, Fiona Ní Chualáin, Aoife Ní Shéaghdha and Mary O'Brien. For text, see www.pobail.ie/en/IrishLanguage/.

[18] This report was prepared by Peadar Ó Flatharta, Caoilfhionn Níc Pháidín, Colin Williams, François Grin, and Joseph Lo Bianco. For text, see www.pobail.ie/en/IrishLanguage/

[19] www.pobail.ie/en/IrishLanguage/Strategy/Strategy.pdf.

[20] www.pobail.ie/en/IrishLanguage/.

2011, May. Carál Ní Chuilín, new Minister for Culture, Arts and Leisure announces intention to revive the preparations for an *Irish Language Act*.

For Ulster Scots
1998 *Belfast Agreement* [the *Good Friday Agreement*].
1999 Establishment of the North/South Language Body (The Noarth/Sooth Leid Boadie).
1999 Establishment of the Ulster-Scots Agency (Tha Boord o Ulstèr-Scotch).
2001 Ratification of the *European Charter for Regional or Minority Languages (European Chairter fer Locail ir Minoritie Leids*).
2004 Announcement of Budget for an Ulster-Scots Academy.
2005–06 Ulster Scots Academy Implementation Group.
2006 Public Consultation on Ulster Scots Academy Implementation Group's proposals for an Ulster-Scots Academy.
2006 *Northern Ireland (St Andrews Agreement) Act*, which states: 'The Government firmly believes in the need to enhance and develop the Ulster-Scots language, heritage and culture and will support the incoming executive in taking this forward'.
2008 Inter-departmental Charter Implementation Group.
2009 Deloitte produce a Business Case for an Ulster-Scots Academy.
2011, March. Appointment of Chair and Members of Ministerial Advisory Group, Ulster-Scots Academy.
A *Strategy for Indigenous or Regional Minority Languages* has long been announced by DCAL as forthcoming.

In Scotland

For Gaelic[21]
1997 Publication of *Secure Status for Gaelic / Inbhe Thèarainte dhan Ghàidhlig* by Comunn na Gàidhlig.
1999 Presentation of *Draft Brief for a Gaelic Language Act / Dreach Iùil Airson Achd Gàidhlig* by Comunn na Gàidhlig.
2000 Publication of *Revitalising Gaelic: A National Asset* (The MacPherson Report)[22] which recommended that a Gaelic Development Agency should, *inter alia*, facilitate the process of achieving secure status for the language.
2002 Publication of *Cothrom Ùr don Ghàidhlig*, the Report by the Ministerial Advisory Group on Gaelic, chaired by Professor Donald Meek ('the Meek Report'), which set out further detail on the role and position of such a Development Agency and called for an Act.
2002 Private member's Bill on Gaelic (Michael Russell). This Bill aimed to require certain public bodies to publish, maintain and implement plans based on the principle that the Gaelic and English languages should be treated on a basis of equality as far as was appropriate in the circumstances and reasonably practicable.
2003, April, Establishment of Bòrd na Gàidhlig as an Executive Non-Departmental Public Body, which prepared the Gaelic Language Act.
2005 The *Gaelic Language (Scotland) Act 2005*. *Inter alia*, the Act established Bòrd na

---

[21] For a Gvernment narrative of these developments, see www.scotland.gov.uk/Topics/ArtsCultureSport /arts/gaelic/gaelic-english/17910/Gaelic-language-plan.
[22] For a critical appraisal by Alasdair MacCaluim and Wilson McLeod, see www.arts.ed.ac.uk/celtic/poileasaidh/ipcamacpherson2.pdf.

Gàidhlig as a national language planning body, requires the Bòrd to publish a National Gaelic Language Plan every five years and requires certain public authorities to prepare Gaelic Language Plans.[23]

2007 Bòrd na Gàidhlig publishes the first *National Gaelic Language Plan 2007–12.*

2008 Launch of the digital television service MG ALBA.

For Scots

2000 Scottish Executive *Creating our Future … Minding our Past: Scotland's National Cultural Strategy.*[24]

2004 Committee of Experts, First Monitoring Report on the European Charter.[25]

2007 Scottish Executive *A Strategy for the Scotland's Languages.* Draft version for consultation. Scottish Executive Education Department, Cultural Policy Division.[26]

2007 Committee of Experts, Second Monitoring Report on the European Charter.[27]

2008 Establishment of Scots Language Audit.

2009 February. Conference on the Scots Language, University of Stirling, at which the Audit Report was presented.

2009 Establishment of Ministerial Advisory Group on Scots, under the Chairmanship of J. Derrick McClure.

2010 Committee of Experts, Third Monitoring Report on the European Charter.[28]

2010. 30 November. Publication of Report of the Ministerial Advisory Group on Scots presented to the Scottish Government.[29]

2011. 18 March. Government Response to MAGOS Report published.

With regard to Irish and Gaelic, Scots and Ulster Scots, as these time lines indicate, in each of our jurisdictions, it has been a decade of activism and advocacy leading gradually but eventually to implementation, with differing political emphases in each jurisdiction. The pace of progress has inevitably been slow and uneven, with the reports by the ECRML Committee of Experts pointing to a considerable lack of progress particularly with regard to Scots and Ulster-Scots in need of addressing.

As these incremental milestones were ultimately reached, Language and Politics provided a forum for discussion and critical debate. Language and Politics was thus a child of its time, arising after the creation of the North/South Language Bodies, and also about the same time as Iomairt Cholm Cille, now simply known as Colmcille.[30] Many of those involved with the advocacy, advising, reporting and implementing have been the very people who have participated in the symposia. For them, critical reflection and appraisal which the symposia generated proved no only invaluable, there grew an

---

[23] For discussion of the Gaelic Plan for Glasgow, see Walsh and McLeod 2011.

[24] www.scotland.gov.uk/nationalculturalstrategy/docs/cult-00.asp.

[25] www.coe.int/t/dg4/education/minlang/Report/default_en.asp.

[26] www.scotland.gov.uk/Publications/2007/01/24130746/0. See also Scots Language Centre compilation of responses to *A Strategy for the Scotland's Languages.* Draft version. at www.scotslanguage.com/.

[27] see footnote 25.

[28] see footnote 25.

[29] For text of report, see www.scotland.gov.uk/Publications/2010/11/25121454/0; see also Robinson and Eagle, in this volume. For a report on the Group's work, see

[29] www.scotslanguage.com/articles/view/227830.

[30] According to its website, 'Colmcille is a partnership programme between Foras na Gaeilge and Bòrd na Gàidhlig, promoting the use of Irish Gaelic and Scottish Gaelic in Ireland and Scotland and between the two countries. Colmcille aims through its work to foster understanding of the diverse experience and culture of the Irish and Scottish Gaelic communities, and to encourage debate on common concerns in social, cultural and economic issues with a view to building self-confidence within the Gaelic language communities.' www.colmcille.net [accessed 7 April 2011].

inevitable and valuable symbiosis on both a North-South as well as East-West basis between their own groups and constituencies and the symposia, each influencing the other in incalculable ways, in an unstoppable cycle. The first decade of the new millennium has turned out to be a glotto-political journey for many, with the proceedings volumes documenting the way and providing documentation.

It has to be noted, however, with the exception of Colmcille, which cuts across all jurisdictions, no funding came directly to the symposia or their publications from any Scottish body, even although a sizeable component of our deliberations and papers was concerned with Gaelic and Scots. Academics and activists domiciled in Scotland regularly commented upon the fact that, to discuss the politics of Gaelic and Scots, they had to be invited to – and funded by – an event in Belfast.

Assessment

The success of these symposia was undoubtedly due to a cocktail of several ingredients. Firstly, within sociolinguistics, although many journals have carried relevant material for some time, such as the *International Journal for the Sociology of Language*, we have certainly helped with the development of 'Language and Politics' as a subject area or 'language policy and planning studies', to which some of the leading core textbooks now devote entire chapters,[31] and for which there are specialist textbooks,[32] and two journals.[33] However, our specific focus has been on the continua of the Gaeltacht, from the Butt of Lewis to the ring of Kerry, and what we came to call the Scotstacht, from Unst in Shetland to the Irish border counties Cavan, Donegal, and Monaghan.[34] Cutting across these continua are the political jurisdictions: the sovereign states of the Republic of Ireland and the United Kingdom of Great Britain and Northern Ireland and, within the latter, there are now devolved Executive/Government in Edinburgh and Belfast. In so doing, our orientation has been East/West as much as North/South, with Northern Ireland occupying a pivotal position between the two, being both British and Irish as well as neither, what Edna Longley has called a 'cultural corridor' or 'zone where Ireland and Britain permeate one another, with British and Irish identities open at either end' (1993: 340). For in each jurisdiction and within each devolved area, language policy has evolved separately, seemingly without co-ordination. Irish is treated very differently in the North from the South – and, whereas it is the same language, the *Official Languages Act 2003* and the 20-Year Strategy in the Republic do not apply to Northern Ireland, where an *Irish Language Act* was rejected by two of the five parties forming the 2007–11 power-sharing Administration through exercising a veto, despite a majority of consultation responses being in favour on two occasions. Arrangements for Scots in Edinburgh and Belfast have also pursued different directions, despite the UK Government's obligation to report by now three times on the European Charter, leading Kirk (2008) to conclude that the UK does not have a coherent language policy.

---

[31] e.g. Mesthrie et al. 2009; Meyerhoff 2006; Wardhaugh 2009.

[32] e.g. Kaplan and Baldauf 1997; Ricento 2005; Spolsky 2004, 2009.

[33] *Journal of Language Policy*, vol. 1–, 2002-, originally edited by Bernard Spolsky, published by Springer Verlag; *European Journal of Language Policy*, vol. 1–, 2009–, edited by Michael Kelly, published by Liverpool University Press. In *Language Policy*, of especial interest to the concerns our symposia are Walsh and McLeod 2007, a version of which was presented at the 2007 symposium, and Millar 2006.

[34] Within those continua, we were also interested in the various Travellers languages, particularly Gammon, or Irish Cant, a quite separate phenomenon from Scottish or Scots Cant. From a separate symposium, with supplementation, we edited a volume of papers **Kirk and Ó Baoill 2002b**, with our long Introduction as Kirk and Ó Baoill 2002d. The volume contains six candid descriptions and accounts of use and attitudes by Travellers themselves. The academic papers are interdisciplinary, dealing with linguistic phenomena as well as ethnic and cultural identity. For important reviews, see Bakker 2006, Matras 2006 and Salzmann 2007.

At each symposium, we have encouraged presentation in these languages, providing simultaneous translation facilities, quite a new experience for many.[35] We have edited and published in those languages.[36] Although our earlier Introductions were intended to summarise all articles and be of especial use for readers without Irish or Gaelic, we have provided full translations in later volumes.

The content of our symposia focussed centrally on language policy for the minority/regional languages in the three jurisdictions in question, taking our cue from the *European Charter for Regional or Minority Languages*. Through the symposia and their publications, we created a set of critical position papers on the Charter's domains for language use: education, law, administration and public authorities, the media, etc., as well as other areas. We identified connections and disconnections between languages, speakers, policies, and practices. We incorporated an international dimension which enabled valuable contextualisation and provided useful clarification and insights. We achieved a great mix of participation (see below). Through the exchange of academic insight and applied or vocational experience, we raised awareness of all aspects of the equation: especially declining linguistic diversity, the need and means for reversing such declines, and the sustainability, including economic sustainability, of languages and communities. There was a recurrent emphasis on education. For everyone who participated, we deepened the quality of discussion.

We were at all times conscious that parallel developments, some of them of an exciting and relevant nature, were happening in other European countries. We felt that we should exchange models of good practice, to see what we could learn from each other. Although the situation of Scots had already been compared with that of German-speaking Switzerland (Meier 1977) and Norway (e.g. McClure 1988, 1995, 1997, 2009; also Vikør 1993, 2001; Millar 2009) and of Frisian (Meier 1997, Görlach 1985), for each we invited fresh reviews (Fischer, 2001, McCafferty 2001, Görlach 2001). Likewise, Celtic connections have long been made with Basque, Galician and Austurias (Celtiberans and the seven the Celtic nation) so that we invited new reviews (Ruiz Vieytez, 2003, on the similarities and differences between Irish and Basque, and O'Rourke 2011 on the similarities and differences between Irish and Galician). All the same, mindful that both Scots and Irish were up against a 'large' language and were eager to draw comparisons with other languages 'eclipsed' (as D. Ó Riagáin 2003 puts it) by larger languages. Accordingly, we invited presentations about Estonia (Tender 2011), Tatarstan (Solnishkina 2011) and Ukraine (Pavlenko 2005, 2011), where the local languages were being eclipsed by Russian, Poland where Kashubian was being eclipsed by Polish (Wicherkiewicz 2005), and Belgium, where Walloon was being eclipsed by French (Fauconnier 2003; also Carruthers 2003). Finally, we were eager to hear about countries where multilingualism is the norm: Slovenia (Novak-Lukanovič 2009) and Hungary (Solymosi 2011). In a Preface to the first volume, Cormack (2000) comments briefly on languages in Kosovo. Finally, the acceptance of Irish as an official language of the EU was greatly advantaged by the recognition of Maltese, the subject of another paper (Zammit-Ciantar 2005).

To the symposia also came scholars who had researched the linguistic situation here. Cordula Bilger presented a PhD thesis on 'the language of the Troubles' to the University of Zürich (Bilger 2007), part of which was presented in 2002. Göran Wolf

---

[35] We are grateful to all those who have helped with translation, especially Philip Campbell, Malachy Duffin, and Dónall Mac Giolla Chóill for translations from Irish, Dolina MacLennan and Maolcholaim Scott for translations from Scottish Gaelic, and Máire Uí Bhaoill from French. We are indebted to TOBAR Productions, Tandragee, An Chultúrlann, POBAL and others, and Donegal County Council for the supply and use of translation equipment.

[36] Kirk and Ó Baoill 2002, for instance, has papers in Irish (Muller), Gaelic (Mac Ille Chiar), Scots (Macafee) and Ulster Scots (Parsley) as well as English.

(Technische Universität Dresden), whose paper on Northern Ireland sociolinguistics was presented at the 2007 symposium (Wolf 2011), ran a Hauptseminar in 2008–09 on Northern Ireland Language and Politics, which he will run again in 2011. We know our publications have been used as set texts at the University of Aberdeen and the National University of Ireland, Galway. No doubt, there will be many other uses of which we are unaware.

To make contributions to the symposia came above all scholars of world-class standing: John Edwards (Francis Xavier, NS), Jean-Luc Fauconnier (Brussels), Markku Filppula (Joensuu), Andreas Fischer (Zürich), Manfred Görlach (Köln, twice), François Grin (Geneva, twice), Stephen May (Waikato), Kevin McCafferty (Bergen), Dónall Ó Riagáin (formerly of EBLUL), Robert Phillipson (Copenhagen Business School), Eduardo Ruiz-Vieytez (Bilbao), Tove Skutnabb-Kangas (numerous affiliations), Nancy Stenson (Minnesota), Colin Williams (Cardiff), and Joe Zammit Ciantar (Valetta and Naples).[37]

In addition, we welcomed the following minority language experts: Tomasz Wicherkiewicz (Gdansk), Alexander Pavlenko (Taganrog, Russia, twice), Sonja Novak-Lukanovič (Ljubljana, Slovenia), Bernadette O'Rourke (Galician), Judit Solymosi (Budapest), Tõnu Tender (Turku, Estonia), and Marina Solnishkina (Kazan, Tatarstan).

To the rather different eighth symposium in 2008 we welcomed, in addition to numerous world-class UK and Ireland academics, Leith Davis (Simon Fraser, Vancouver), Iain McCalman (Sydney), Katie Trumpener (Yale), and Julia Wright (Dalhousie, Halifax).

As well as the world coming to the symposia, we have been beckoned by the world. During the ten years of the symposia, John Kirk gave invited talks in Berlin, Bonn, Chemnitz, Chisinau, Dresden, Freiburg, Potsdam and Tallinn; Dónall Ó Baoill gave invited talks in Halifax, NS and Vancouver, BC. A related volume of papers arising from a conference on minority languages in Europe held in Dublin, *Voces Diversae* (Ó Riagain 2006), was launched at the Irish Embassy to the EU in Brussels, at which John Kirk gave an address.

We have also been aware that policy issues were not topics to be left to academic researchers alone, but needed input from all sides: government ministers,[38] politicians,[39] civil servants[40] and all their advisers,[41] statutory and institutional practitioners,[42]

---

[37] We also thank Jo Lo Bianco Melbourne for his effort in trying to contribute by video link from Chile in September 2010.

[38] Government Ministers: Seán Farren, MLA 2000, Carmel Hanna, MLA 2002, Éamon Ó Cuív, TD, Mike Russell, MSP 2001 and Mike Watson, MSP 2002. Over the years, many who had been invited were not able to accept; for instance, to the 2010 symposium were invited Nelson McCausland, MLA, Pat Carey, TD, and again Michael Russell, MSP.

[39]Politicians: Ian Adamson, MLA 2005, Alasdair Allan, MSP 2000, Esmond Birnie, MLA 2003, Irene McGugan, MSP 2001, 2002, as a stalwart before election, Ian James Parsley 2000, 2001a, 2001b, 2002, 2005, and the Lord Laird of Artigarvan 2001.

[40] Civil servants: Patricia McAlister 2003, Stephen Peover 2002 and Edward Rooney 2001 from Northern Ireland; Brendán Mac Cormaic 2001, Seán Ó Cofaigh 2001, Bertie Ó hAinmhire 2001, and from the Republic of Ireland; various officials from DCAL and from the Scottish Executive have also attended.

[41] Edmund 2002.

[42] E.g. from Northern Ireland: Mark Adair 2000 and Mari FitzDuff 2000 from the Northern Ireland Community Relations Council, McCoy 2001, 2003, 2011 and Mac Póilin 2011 from ULTACH Trust, Muller 2002, 2011 from POBAL; from the Republic of Ireland: Ó Cearnaigh 2009, Ó Coisdealbha 2011a, 2011b from the Irish Language Commissioner's Office, Ó hAoláin 2009, 20011a, 2011b, 2011c from Údarás na Gaeltachta; Ó Murchú 2000, 2002, 2011 from Comhar ma Múinteoirí Gaeilge; and from Scotland: Campbell 2009 and MacIver 2011 from Bòrd na Gàidhlig, Mackay, R. 2011 from the University of the Highlands and Islands, West and MacLeòid 2009 from Highlands and Islands Enterprise.

linguists,[43] language consultants,[44] language historians,[45] lawyers,[46] educationalists,[47] anthropologists,[48] broadcasters,[49] journalists,[50] media consumers,[51] economists,[52] writers of all kinds,[53] actors, producers,[54] film-makers,[55] librarians,[56] activists,[57] as well as interested and informed individuals.

To the symposia also came broadcasters and media people eager for content and coverage. There was regular annual coverage on BBC Northern Ireland's Irish Language magazine programe *Blas* and on its Ulster-Scots magazine programme *Kist o' Wurds*. In the Republic of Ireland, the symposia have featured on TG4 and Raidió na Gaeltachta. In Scotland, there was coverage at times on the BBC's Gaelic Service, Craoladh nan Gàidheal, Radio nan Gàidheal and BBC Alba (now MG Alba).

A further strength of the symposia grew out of the regular involvement or participation of a core group of individuals, who willingly provided encouragement and advice as the series developed: John Corbett, Andy Eagle, Gavin Falconer, François Grin, Michael Hance, Dauvit Horsbroch, Derrick McClure, MBE, Gordon McCoy, Seosamh Mac Donnacha, Aodán Mac Póilin, Janet Muller, Róise Ní Bhaoill, Pádraig Ó hAoláin, Chris Spurr, Ian James Parsley, and especially to Kenneth MacKinnon, Wilson McLeod, Dónall Ó Riagáin, and John Walsh. We are hugely indebted to those individuals for their unstinting support over the years, and for all their help in making suggestions and guiding us in the right direction. We owe a very considerable amount to Dónall Ó Riagáin for generously making available his considerable expertise in language policy formulation and for introducing us to the many European minority language experts whom we came to invite. And much less would have been achieved without the support of the AHRC RCISS, for which core funding we are indebted to

---

[43] Armstrong 2011, Bilger 2002, Corbett 2002, Corbett and Anderson 2011, Corbett and Douglas 2003, Dolan 2002, Dunbar 2001, 2003, 2009, 2011, Eagle 2001, 2011a, 2011b, Falconer 2001, 2005, 2011, Gupta 2002, Hickey 2009, Kirk, 2000b, 2009, 2011; Kirk and Kallen 2011, Lamb 2005, Loester 2009, Macafee 2001, 2002, MacCaluim 2011, McClure 2002, Mac Ionnrachtaigh 2011, MacKinnon 2001, 2003, 2009, 2011, MacLeod, M. 2011, McLeod 2002, 2003, 2005, 2009a, 2009b, 2011, Millar 2009a, 2009b, 2011, Munro 2011, Ní Dhúda 2011, Ó Duíbhín 2003, Ó Giollagáin 2005, Ó Laighin 2005, Ó Riagáin, P. 2009, Phillipson 2002, Robinson 2011a, 2011b, Skutnabb-Kangas 2002, Smith 2005, Unger 2009, Walsh 2002, 2003, 2009, 2011, Walsh and McLeod 2007, 2011, Wolf 2009.

[44] Ó Riagáin, D. 2000, 2001, 2003, 2009a, 2009b, 2011a, 2011b.

[45] Andrews 2000, Connolly 2009, McCafferty 2009.[46] Hadden 2000.

[47] de Bhál 2002, Douglas 2002, Galloway 2011, Harris 2002, 2011, Mac Ille Chiar 2002, MacDonnacha 2011, MacIver, M. 2002, McKendry 2002, Mac Nia 2002, MacNeil 2011, Malcolm 2011, Munro 2011, Ní Fheargusa 2002, Nig Uidhir 2002, Niven 2002, Ó Baoill 2011, Ó Coinn 2002, Robertson 2002, Rohmer 2002.

[48] McCoy 2001, 2003, 2011.

[49] Caimbeul 2011, Cormack 2003. Cunningham 2003, Eirug 2003, Hegarty 2003, Kay 2011, McHardy 2003, Mac An Iomaire 2003, MacKay 2009, MacLennan 2003, MacNeill 2003, Ní Nuadhain 2003, Ó Ciardha 2003, Ó Cuaig 2003, Spurr 2003.

[50] Blain and Gifford 2003, Cormack 2003, Law, A. 2003, Mac Donald 2003, MacLeod 2009, Ó Pronntaigh 2003.

[51] Ó Clochartaigh 2003, Ó hEadhra 2011, Robinson 2003, Titley 2003.

[52] Bradley 2009, Birnie and King 2003, Chalmers 2003, 2009, Chalmers and Danson 2011, Grin 2003, 2009, Walsh 2003, 2009, Mac Donnacha 2003, MacLeod 2009, McLeod 2003, 2009, Ó Cearnaigh 2009, Williams 2009.

[53] Brown 2009, 2011, Findlay 2003, Herbison 2005, Paisley 2003, Purves 2003, Titley 2005, Whyte 2005.

[54] Grant 2003.

[55] O'Rawe 2003.

[56] Delargy 2001, 2011.

[57] Hance 2005, 2009 and Horsbroch 2000, 2001a, 2001b, 2002 from the Scots Language Centre; Law, J. 2003, 2011 from the Scots Language Society; Smith and Montgomery 2005 from the Ulster-Scots Language Society.

Tom Devine and Cairns Craig, and the Centre's Boards. We are also deeply indebted to our external funders, especially Foras na Gaeilge, Colmcille, and the Ulster-Scots Agency, and we are especially grateful to Deirdre Davitt and Maolcholaim Scott for their personal commitment to our work.

Whereas, for the AHRC RCISS, we became obliged to produce an annual volume, there was also a willingness to subvent these publications. Each volume produced by Cló Ollscoil na Banríona has been funded by Foras na Gaeilge. The Ulster-Scots Agency supported Kirk and Ó Baoill (2000, 2003, 2005). The Northern Ireland Community Relations Council supported Kirk and Ó Baoill (2000, 2001, 2002 and 2005). Colmcille supported Kirk and Ó Baoill (2009, 2011a, and 2011b). To each of these funders we are extremely grateful. We have always been delighted to acknowledge that the Northern Ireland Community Relations Council 'aims to promote a pluralist society characterised by equity, respect for diversity and interdependence.' We also wish to recognise that those funders were willing to support the publication of Irish, Gaelic, and different varieties of Scots in the same volume.

And so evolved the formula for these symposia to provide and provoke critical reflection and discussion in language policy pertaining to the Gaeltacht and Scotstacht.

Publication

As desired by the AHRC RCISS, we have produced an annual publication, thereby ensuring an after-life for the symposia and a more permanent contribution concerning language policy in the three jurisdictions. As already mentioned, we produced multi-lingual volumes, which, despite general support for linguistic diversity, are quite a rarity. The list of references below also serves as a comprehensive bibliography of the publications generated by the symposia.

We were able to use the volumes in our teaching. John Kirk has used them on his *Language, Culture and Politics* undergraduate module, in which the BSLCP volumes formed the basis for many final assignments, including some on languages other than English. Dónall Ó Baoill uses the texts on his MA course on the *Sociolinguistics of Irish*. We know that the books are set texts at the University of Aberdeen and the National University of Ireland, Galway, and no doubt elsewhere, too.

John Edwards (2006) concludes his review of vols. 1–12 of our *Belfast Studies in Language, Culture and Politic*s series, as follows:

> The books reviewed here present a large number of valuable perspectives on current linguistic conditions in the British Isles. Of special significance is the central focus on Northern Ireland, since material dealing with (southern) Irish language, culture, and politics has typically been more available; this focus is a reflection of contemporary trends within Britain, and, in a larger context, within the European Union. Overall, it is hard to think of a more immediate and up-to-date introduction to Scottish and Irish sociolinguistics and the sociology of language than that provided by this fine and expanding set of volumes. And, as with all significant discussions of particular contexts, the coverage here also offers insights whose value extends in much more general directions. On both counts, the series editors, John Kirk and Dónall Ó Baoill, deserve our thanks.

The BSLCP series has attracted other publications, each of which is germane to our concerns, especially Ó Riagáin (2003, 2005). There have been two monographs on Gaelic (Lamb 2008, which, in an appendix, includes an excellent grammar of contemporary Gaelic, reviewed by Ní Laoire 2008; and MacCaluim 2008, reviewed by MacKinnon 2008 and Dorian 2009); a monograph on Irish (Mac Corraidh 2007), a selection of essays on the translation of literary topics in and out of Irish (Dillon and Ní Fhríghil 2008), and a thesis about attitudes to all aspects of language across the Northern Ireland border (Zwickl 2002). Finally, Irish-Scottish studies more broadly feature in four volumes of research papers (Kirk and Ó Baoill 2001, Longley *et al*. 2003, Alexander *et al*. 2004, McClure 2004, and Alcobia-Murphy *et al*. 2005).

Outcomes

As the list above shows, we intentionally and successfully attracted to the symposia a very broad range of participants. For those engaged in the promotion of minority languages, we provided a suitable forum for cross-fertilisation. We encouraged communities to consider and reflect on their heritage in new and refreshed ways. We injected into the debate new information, models, insights, and case-studies. We believe we also helped non-academics to learn and adapt new skills. We encouraged and accommodated the use of the minority languages. Because of the dual-strand approach of symposia and publications, we further believe that we raised awareness and fostered an enhanced understanding of our diverse language heritages in Ireland and Scotland. We have examined the role of Government policies and legislation; we have provided academic leadership through bringing together and bridging the sectors; we have generated critical syntheses and made recommendations; and we have cast some reciprocal illumination on comparable linguistic situations in Europe.

We believe we have had both political and policy outcomes. We injected scientific right-mindedness and rigour into the debates both on Irish and Scots and gave support and confidence to many in the wider community willing to respect the views of academic research and science. In particular, both Ministers and civil servants from the Governments or Executives of each jurisdiction took part and presented papers or gave addresses, most of which were published (see above). We impacted on civil servants, officials, advisers and opinion-formers through our publications that Scots in Northern Ireland is *not* a language separate from Scots in Scotland. To the question about what Scots in Scotland is, we have offered numerous approaches and categorisations. We know that debates on an *Irish Language Act* for Northern Ireland have been influenced by our publications, and that we have influenced public policy, especially on linguistic diversity and multiculturalism in Northern Ireland more generally, even from before the *Belfast Agreement* of 1998.

A clear achievement was the creation of a volume of studies about economic development through language following Grin's four paradigms for doing so: 'the firm, market and management paradigm', 'the development paradigm', 'the language sector and multiplier paradigm', and 'the welfare paradigm'.

A further achievement has been the creation of a specialist network comprising language practitioners, policy-makers, educationalists, and many others, with academics and researchers. Within the network, we have created consultative relationships as well as a sustainable and mutually beneficial set of multi-participative partnerships.

Because we have deliberately targeted both the Gaeltacht and the Scotstacht as well as the pairs of languages within each jurisdiction, we have provided that 'cultural corridor' which has proven necessary for the debate in Northern Ireland between Irish and Ulster Scots (the dubious debate about equality and the need for Part III recognition for Ulster Scots). In so doing, we feel that we have strengthened the language policy sectors within UK and the Republic of Ireland. It was a need which we identified and have filled. At the 2010 symposium, several board members of Bòrd na Gàidhlig were present. During his tenure as CEO of Foras na Gaeilge, Seosamh Mac Donnacha attended every symposium. Members of each of our funders' boards have attended the symposia throughout the series.

We have also benefited the general public through the media attention we have attracted and through our support for policies which promote respect for language and its use.

Thus, we would contend, as a package of symposia and publications, which created a symbiosis for debate and discussion, Language and Politics has made impact. We have made contributions to knowledge, understanding, analysis, policy, planning, skills, and, ultimately, it was argued, to an enhancement in the quality of life. Furthermore, the content of the symposia and volumes suggests to us the verdict of a significant and original contribution to the improvement of Irish-Scottish relationships and the development of Irish and Scottish Studies. We set the bar high at the outset, and we believe we have lived up to these expectations.

Language and Politics has also been financially successful, attracting external investment of up to 2–3 times the initial AHRC RCISS investment, and similar amounts again for publications. In a nutshell, ten years of Language and Politics generated *c*. £250,000. We also believe that the chemistry and synergy between ourselves, linked to our imagination and desire to create something new, our hands-on-ness, and also our initiative and entrepreneurship, have all valuably contributed to its success. For the symposia and publications, we acknowledge with heartfelt gratitude once again the financial assistance which we have received.[58]

At an individual level, Dónall Ó Baoill has been a member of POBAL's research group which in 2009 delivered to the Department of Education a two-year research publication on *The Specialist Educational Needs of Bilingual (Irish/English) Children Attending All-Irish Schools in Northern Ireland*, funded by the Department of Education. Its recommendations will now become part of the Department of Education's future planning initiatives. In November 2000, Ó Baoill was appointed by the Minister for Education in Northern Ireland as one of six trustees of Iontaobhas na Gaelscolaíochta, which co-ordinates the work of the All-Irish Education Trust and provides support for Comhairle na Gaelscolaíochta (Council for All-Irish Medium Education). The function of the Trustee Board has been mainly of a financial nature, with a budget of £2.5 million pounds for the first three years. In 2005, he was appointed for appointed for a second five-year term. Since 2001, Ó Baoill has also acted as an adviser to DCAL's Language Diversity Section on matters relating to Irish Translation and Standardisation problems in Irish.

John Kirk was short-listed in 2003 for the UNESCO Linguapax Prize, which is awarded every year by the UNESCO Linguapax Institute in Barcelona.[59] In 2008, he formed a consortium of academics and language advisers which bid – and was short-listed – for the Scottish Government's Scots Language Audit. Since 2000, Kirk has

---

[58] We also acknowledge funding from the Northern Ireland Community Relations Council for funding towards the publication of several volumes of symposia proceedings.

[59] According to the Linguapax Institute in Barcelona, 'The prizes are awarded to linguists, researchers, professors and members of the civil society in acknowledgement of their outstanding work in the field of linguistic diversity and/or multilingual education ... or in improving the linguistic situation of a community or country.'

been a member of the Scottish Parliament's Cross-Party Group on the Scots Language. He was a founder member of the Forum for Research on the Languages of Scotland and Ulster in 1985 and has been its Treasurer since 2004. He was also a nominee to the Ministerial Advisory Group on Scots.

In all of these ways, we have enhanced the reputation of Queen's University Belfast by acting as a catalyst for debate on language policy.[60]

Whither Now?

After ten symposia and just as many volumes of proceedings, we feel that on Language and Politics we have certainly delivered. With some satisfaction, we could retire gracefully.

However, the business of language policy development is ongoing, with yet more work to be done. There comes to mind immediately the *20-Year Strategy for the Irish Language 2010–2030* in the Republic, the desire for an *Irish Language Act* and an Ulster-Scots Academy in the North, the need for Gaelic Plans on the part of public authorities in Scotland, and the Scottish Government's response to the report of the Ministerial Advisory Group on Scots and ensuant developments – all material enough for another symposium or several more. There will almost certainly be more Government initiatives in the coming years. We have created a network of about a hundred or so individuals active in the field who could readily be called upon for co-operation and support.

A strength of our success, we cannot stress too strongly, has been the availability and generosity of funding. Our role within the AHRC RCISS always ensured our core funding, which we were then able to offer as our contribution for external or matching funding. Without that initial funding, the securing of external funding would almost certainly have proven much more difficult.

However, it may be possible to turn the funding arrangement inside out. As our funders have backed us unflinchingly, there might be a case for those organisations to mount a series of symposia themselves, carrying all the administrative and financial arrangements, but subcontracting the programming and editing of proceedings to ourselves or others. That way, financial management would rest with the funders. We know that Foras na Gaeilge has undertaken a number of projects jointly with the Ulster-Scots Agency.

During the past ten years, there have two other exciting developments at university level: the expansion of Sabhal Mòr Ostaig and the creation of Acadamh na hOllscolaíochta Gaeilge within the National University of Ireland, Galway, which would appear to have very similar functions and objectives. The Mission Statement of Sabhal Mòr Ostaig reads:

> Sabhal Mòr Ostaig is committed to being a centre of excellence for the development and enhancement of the Gaelic language, culture and heritage, by providing quality educational, training and research opportunities through the medium of Scottish Gaelic; and by interacting innovatively with individuals, communities and businesses, to contribute to social, cultural and economic development.

---

[60] At the AILA Conference in Essen in August 2008, it was proposed that Queen's University Belfast might be a possible venue for Inaugural Conference of the International Society for Language Policy and Language Planning Advisers, intended to be a society of professional accreditation.

The Mission Statement of Acadamh na hOllscolaíochta Gaeilge reads:

> The mission of an tAcadamh is to promote and exhibit innovation among the Irish language community, within the Gaeltacht areas and outside those areas. This innovation will enhance the social, cultural, economic and language development of those communities and of people of Ireland in general. To bring this mission to fruition, the objective of an tAcadamh is to promote the sustainable development of university courses, research, services and university activities through the medium of Irish and their delivery and administration.

Both colleges offer a range of graduate and postgraduate degree programmes through the medium of Gaelic and Irish respectively. In so doing, they are promoting the use of Gaelic and Irish both among the college communities as well in the their catchment areas. Each college's activities are greatly enhanced by co-operative links within the wider Gaelic and Irish communities. An tAcadamh offers courses in Business Administration, Communications – Radio and Television Broadcasting, Translation Studies, Interpreting, Language Planning, Education, the Arts and Information Technology.

Sabhal Mòr Ostaig also plays a leading role in the promotion of the Gaelic arts and culture and hosts a programme of residencies for artists in music, literature and the visual arts. Each college provides opportunities and high-quality facilities for in-depth research in these areas, too. An tAcadamh's academic co-ordinator, Seosamh Mac Donnacha, a regular contributor to our symposia (cf. Mac Donnacha 2003, 2011a, 2011b) has a particular interest in pursuing research into organisational and strategic aspects of language planning. Sabhal Mòr Ostaig is home to a number of major creative and cultural research projects such as Tobar an Dualchais,[61] Faclair na Gàidhlig and the multimedia and design company Cànan, and a new £5.29 million partnership project called *Soillse*[62] ('Enlightenment') has been set up to support the Gaelic language and culture.

In his inaugural lecture, 'Theory, Research and Other Dirty Words in Language Policy and Planning', in December 2010, Soillse's Senior Research Professor, Rob Dunbar, argued that theory and research can aid Gaelic revitalisation and explored ways in which the work of specialists can be useful to Gaelic language campaigners.

In a press release at the time of his lecture, Dunbar comments, as follows:

> A common feature of minority language maintenance and revitalisation movements is the fundamental role that passionate activists have in them. Frequently, though, they have only a limited background in language planning theory or practice, and a lack of information to inform and to guide their development initiatives. Although specialists can provide insights and knowledge to these movements, the relationship between specialists and activists can at times be difficult,

---

[61] Its Scots title is *The Kist o Riches*, indicative of its sizeable Scots component. See www.tobarandualchais.co.uk.

[62] *Soillse* is headed by the University of the Highlands and Islands, especially its partner colleges Sabhal Mòr Ostaig on Skye and Lews Castle College on Lewis, and the universities of Aberdeen, Edinburgh and Glasgow. The four institutions are working with key agencies, including the national development agency Bòrd na Gàidhlig, to boost national and local efforts to reverse the decline of the Gaelic language, and to encourage the use of Gaelic in areas where it has not traditionally been spoken.

due to a variety of factors which could be summed up by the phrase 'culture clash'. In my lecture, the theoretical tools relevant to language policy and planning for minority languages such as Gaelic, the experience on which such tools are based, and the research needs and priorities which such tools help us to define, will be considered. Can theory and research inform and support policy-making and practice in ways that allow us to avoid the 'culture clash'?

A major success of our Language and Politics symposia was the bridging of that very relationship between specialists, activists and practitioners.

It strikes us that Acadamh na hOllscolaíochta Gaeilge and Sabhal Mòr Ostaig would form a natural partnership for the purpose of continuing the appraisal of language policy development in these islands. Queen's University Belfast would make an obvious third partner. Whether such a Phase II of Language and Politics concerned itself solely with the Irish-Gaelic continuum or whether the Scots continuum should continue in parallel still needs further discussion.

Within the UK, of course, further partnerships could be added – notably with Welsh and Cornish, and yet remain within the UK's responsibilities under the European Charter. Given its recognition by the European Charter, Manx, too, might be considered.

Any such tie-ups need not exclude the exploration of European partnerships. Our symposia (as well as others such as *Voces Diversae*) have shown the value of such comparisons, and various European models have been applicable to the local situations – e.g. Strubell's Supply and Demand Catherine-Wheel Model for Language Planning (Strubell 1999, quoted in McLeod 2009: 153–4) or Grin's four Language and Economic Development paradigms (Grin 2009). The EU Commission for Education, Culture, Multilingualism and Youth has many funds.[63] Currently, the Union has 23 official languages and over 60 indigenous regional and minority languages – some of which have local official status, such as Sami, Sorbian, Sardinian and Basque.

The website on 'EU Languages and Language Policy' states that 'EU language policies aim to protect linguistic diversity and promote knowledge of languages – for reasons of cultural identity and social integration, but also because multilingual citizens are better placed to take advantage of the educational, professional and economic opportunities created by an integrated Europe. The goal is a Europe where everyone can speak at least two other languages in addition to their own mother tongue.'

Within its programme on Multilingualism, the Commission has issued a number of key policy documents in the last few years. These 'language policy milestones' mark key stages in the formulation of current multilingualism policy.[64] The most recent is the *Strategic Framework for Co-operation on Education and Training* (2009), in which there is a call for further Commission action to promote language learning, e.g. for adults as part of vocational training, and to help migrants learning the language of the host country. In 2008, there appeared the EU *Strategy for Multilingualism* (2008) which sets out what the EU should be doing to promote language learning and protect linguistic diversity. Also in 2008, there appeared *Multilingualism: An Asset for Europe and a Shared Commitment* (2008), which assesses what needs to be done to turn linguistic diversity into an asset for solidarity and prosperity, and an *Inventory of EU Actions in the Field of Multilingualism*, which is a full report on action to promote languages in all fields. In

---

[63] For an overview of funding possibilities, see ec.europa.eu/education/languages/eu-programmes/index_en.htm.

[64] For an overview, see ec.europa.eu/education/languages/eu-language-policy/index_en.htm.

2007, there took place an online consultation on multilingualism, which later made available both the results and the discussion that followed. Finally, in 2005, a *New Framework Strategy for Multilingualism* appeared as the first strategy of its kind but has now been superseded by the 2008 strategy. Thus, there is already in place a considerable amount of European thinking about language planning and language strategies for a Phase II to connect with and build on.

In the EU, 2010 was the target date for many initiatives. New initiatives have since been set for 2020, under a strategic framework for European co-operation in education and training entitled 'Education and Training 2020 – Diverse Systems, Shared Goals'. This framework is intended to build on progress made under the previous Education and Training work programme and has set four strategic objectives: making lifelong learning and mobility a reality; improving the quality and efficiency of education and training; promoting equity, social cohesion and active citizenship; enhancing creativity and innovation, including entrepreneurship, at all levels of education and training. These would certainly lend themselves as objectives for a Phase II project.[65]

A further possibility for future Language and Politics symposia might be more theoretical – to set up a project critical reflection upon the merits and demerits of language policies in a broad range of situations, with a view to establishing afresh the top-down criteria for the components of a first-rate policy. A start may have been made by the EU as well as by recent textbooks which are concerned with policies on a world-wide basis. That, too, might well form a theme for a further symposium or two.

However, there is a final, not inconsiderable point which we have already mentioned and wish to end on. These symposia and publications arose from a voluntary collaboration between a Celticist and a Scotticist who happened to be in the same place at the same time, who found each other eager to push back the boundaries of their respective disciplines, and who found that their different sets of skills and expertise, the interpersonal chemistry of their rather different personalities, and their willingness to be flexible and adaptable, all enabled them to work extraordinarily well together. Such productive inter-disciplinary links are rare, but it would be a not insignificant factor if others were to build on our foundations. As we have repeatedly acknowledged, we Language and Politics was a genuine partnership, which we simply could not have undertaken without each other.

---

[65] ec.europa.eu/education/languages/eu-language-policy/doc120_en.htm.

References

Adair, M. 2000. 'Boundaries, Diversity and Inter-culturalism : The Case of Ulster-Scots'. In eds. Kirk and Ó Baoill, 2000. 143–7.

Adamson, I. 2005. 'The Ullans Academy'. In eds. Kirk and Ó Baoill. 2005. 65–8.

Alcobia-Murphy, S., Archbold, J., Gibney, J. and C. Jones, eds. 2005. *Beyond the Anchoring Grounds: More Cross-currents in Irish and Scottish Studies.* Belfast Studies in Language, Culture and Politics 14. Belfast: Cló Ollscoil na Banríona.

Alexander, N., Murphy S. and A. Oakman, eds. 2004. *To the Other Shore: Cross-Currents in Irish and Scottish Studies.* Belfast Studies in Language, Culture and Politics 12. Belfast: Cló Ollscoil na Banríona.

Allan, A.J. 2000. 'Language and Politics: A Perspective from Scotland'. In eds. Kirk and Ó Baoill. 2000. 127–31.

Andrews, L.S. 2000. 'Northern Nationalists and the Politics of the Irish Language: The Historical Background'. In eds. Kirk and Ó Baoill. 2000. 45–63.

Armstrong, T.C. 'Bilingualism, Restoration and Language Norms'. In eds. Kirk and Ó Baoill. 2011b. 172–9.

Bakker, P. 2006. Review of [Kirk and Ó Baoill 2002b]. *Language in Society* 35: 429–32.

Bilger, C. 2002. 'War Zone Language: Language and the Conflict in Northern Ireland'. In eds. Kirk and Ó Baoill. 2002. 318–26.

Bird, B. 2004. Review of [Kirk and Ó Baoill 2002a]. *Scottish Language* 23: 118–20.

Birnie, E. and S. King. 2003. 'Not such a big deal? The Economy–Language Interaction'. In eds. Kirk and Ó Baoill. 2003. 224–8.

Blain, N. and A. Gifford. 2003. 'Scottish political Identity Construction in the Media; Learning and Teaching Questions around the Theme of Inclusiveness'. In eds. Kirk and Ó Baoill. 2003. 119–30.

Blair, T. 2010. *A Journey.* London: Hutchinson.

Bradley, F. 2009. 'Regional Innovation Environments in the Knowledge Society: Identifying a Place for Irish'. In eds. Kirk and Ó Baoill. 2009. 81–91.

Brown, I. 2009. 'Drama and Literature in Scots as an Economic Generator'. In eds. Kirk and Ó Baoill. 2009. 196–203.

Brown, I. 2011. 'Drama as a Means for Uphaudin Leid Communities'. In eds. Kirk and Ó Baoill. 2011a. 243–8.

Caimbeul, D. and E. Green. 2011. 'Observations on Bilingualism in Digital Media'. In eds. Kirk and Ó Baoill. 2011b. 180–6.

Campbell, A. 2009. 'Making Gaelic Work for Scotland'. In eds. Kirk and Ó Baoill. 2009. 111–6.

Carruthers, J. 2003. 'The Walloon-Scots Comparison: Are There Further Parallels with Other *Langues d'Oïl?*' In eds. Kirk and Ó Baoill. 2003. 303–8.

Chalmers, D. 2003. 'The Economic Impact of Gaelic Arts and Culture: A Response to François Grin'. In eds. Kirk and Ó Baoill. 2003. 245–9.

Chalmers, D. 2009. 'Mapping Language, Arts, Culture and Community: Continuity and Change'. In eds. Kirk and Ó Baoill. 2009. 130–3.

Chalmers, D. and M. Danson. 2011. 'The Economic Impact of Gaelic Arts and Culture in Glasgow'. In eds. Kirk and Ó Baoill. 2011a. 176–87.

Connolly, P. 2009. 'The Divergent Development of the *After*-Perfect in Irish and Scottish Gaelic'. Paper given at Ninth Language and Politics Symposium, Aberdeen.

Corbett, J. 2002. 'The Language Component in the 'Higher-Still' Examinations in 'English': Confessions of an Item-Writer for a Token Exam'. In eds. Kirk and Ó Baoill. 2002. 203–11.

Corbett, J. and W. Anderson. 2011. 'Using it or Losing it? Scots and Younger Speakers'. In eds. Kirk and Ó Baoill. 2011a. 225–37.

Corbett, J. and F. Douglas. 2003. 'Scots in the Public Sphere'. In eds. Kirk and Ó Baoill. 2003. 198–210.

Cormack, M. 2003a. 'Programming for Gaelic Digital Television: Problems and Possibilities'. In eds. Kirk and Ó Baoill. 2003. 83–7.

Cormack, M. 2003b. 'The Case for a Weekly Gaelic Newspaper in Scotland'. In eds. Kirk and Ó Baoill. 2003. 95–9.

Cormack, R.J. 2000. 'Preface: Kosovo in the Spring'. In eds. Kirk and Ó Baoill. 2000. 1–2.

Cunningham, M. 2003. 'BBC Radio Scotland and Scots'. In eds. Kirk and Ó Baoill. 2003. 88–9.

De Bhál, P. 'Teaching through the Target Language: Preparation of Teachers'. In eds. Kirk and Ó Baoill. 2002. 61–4.

Delargy, M. 2001. 'Linguistic Diversity Education Project'. In eds. Kirk and Ó Baoill. 2001. 61–6.

Delargy, M. 2011. 'Buíon dar Slua thar Toinn do Ráinig Chugainn' / 'Some have Come from a Land beyond the Wave'. In eds. Kirk and Ó Baoill. 2011a. 65–8.

Dillon, C. and R. Ní Fhríghil, eds. 2008. *Aistriú Éireann*. Belfast Studies in Language, Culture and Politics 21. Belfast: Cló Ollscoil na Banríona.

Dolan, T.P. 2002. 'Language Policy in the Republic of Ireland'. In eds. Kirk and Ó Baoill. 2002. 144–56.

Dorian, N.C. 2009. Review of [MacCaluim 2007]. *Journal of Sociolinguistics*, 13: 266–9.

Douglas, S. 2002. 'Unblocking the Right Nostril'. In eds. Kirk and Ó Baoill. 2002. 192–7.

Douglas, S. 2003. 'The Scots Leid in the Performing Airts the Day'. In eds. Kirk and Ó Baoill. 2003. 194–7.

Dunbar, R. 2001. 'Minority Language Rights Regimes: an Analytical Framework, Scotland, and Emerging European Norms'. In eds. Kirk and Ó Baoill. 2001. 231–54.

Dunbar, R. 2003. 'Gaelic-medium Broadcasting: Reflections on the Legal framework from a Sociolinguistic Perspective'. In eds. Kirk and Ó Baoill. 2003. 73–82.

Dunbar, R. 2009. 'Two Nations Warring in the Bosom of a Single State? Reflections on the Linguistic (and Cultural) Highland Line'. Paper given at Ninth Language and Politics Symposium, Aberdeen.

Dunbar, R. 2011. 'Bilingualism: Conceptual Difficulties and Practical Challenges'. In eds. Kirk and Ó Baoill. 2011b. 150–62.

Eagle, A. 2001. 'Wha Ye Writin For?' In eds. Kirk and Ó Baoill. 2001. 169–78.

Eagle, A. 2011a. 'German-Speakin Swisserland: A Paitren for Dialect Uphaud'. In eds. Kirk and Ó Baoill. 2011a. 259–65.

Eagle, A. 2011b. 'A Language Strategy for Scots?' In eds. Kirk and Ó Baoill. 2011b. 256–66.

Edmund, J. 2002. 'Ulster-Scots Language and Culture'. In eds. Kirk and Ó Baoill. 2002. 175–82.

Edwards, J. 2006. 'Contemporary Scottish and Irish Studies in Language and Society'. Review Article of *Belfast Studies in Language, Culture and Politics*, vols. 1–12. *Language in Society* 35: 419–27.

Eirug, A. 2003. 'Towards the BBC's Minority Language Policy'. In eds. Kirk and Ó Baoill. 2003. 33–5.

Falconer, G. 2001. 'The Scots Leid in the New Poleitical Institutions'. In eds. Kirk and Ó Baoill. 2001. 135–58.

Falconer, G. 2005. 'Breaking Nature's Social Union: The Autonomy of Scots in Ulster'. In eds. Kirk and Ó Baoill. 2005. 48–59.

Falconer, G. 2007. *Scots: Decline, Revival, Divergence*. Unpublished PhD Thesis, Queen's University Belfast.

Falconer, G. 2011. 'Hiberno-Central as an Unroofed Dialect of Scots'. In eds. Kirk and Ó Baoill. 2011a. 249–58.

Farren, S. 2000. 'Institutional Infrastructure Post-Good Friday Agreement: The New Institutions and Devolved Government'. In eds. Kirk and Ó Baoill. 2000. 121–5.

Fauconnier, J.-L. 2003. 'Les Langues Moins Répandues l'Exemple du Wallon et du Scots'. In eds. Kirk and Ó Baoill. 2003. 294–300.

Findlay, B. 2003. 'Modern Scots Drama and Language Planning: A Context and Caution'. In eds. Kirk and Ó Baoill. 2003. 165–174.

Fischer, A. 2001. 'Language and Politics in Switzerland'. In eds. Kirk and Ó Baoill. 2001. 105–22.

FitzDuff, M. 2000. 'Language and Politics in a Global Perspective'. In eds. Kirk and Ó Baoill. 2000. 75–80.

Foley, N. 2000. 'Language, Discrimination and the Good Friday Agreement: The Case of Ethnic Minority Languages'. In eds. Kirk and Ó Baoill. 2000. 101–5.

Galloway, J. 2011. 'Language Shift and Cultural Change in the Gàidhealtachd: What Prospect for the Cultural Identity?' In eds. Kirk and Ó Baoill. 2011a. 36–43.

Görlach, M. 1985. 'Scots and Low German: The Social History of Two Minority Languages'. In ed. Görlach, M. *Focus on Scotland*. Amsterdam: John Benjamins. 19–36.

Görlach, M. 2000. 'Ulster-Scots: A Language?' In eds. Kirk and Ó Baoill. 2000. 13–31.

Görlach, M. 2001. 'Frisian and Low German: Minority Languages in Hiding'. In eds. Kirk and Ó Baoill. 2001. 67–88.

Grant, D. 2003. 'Language, Culture and Politics: A Theatrical Perspective'. In eds. Kirk and Ó Baoill. 2003. 138–42.

Grin, F. 2003. 'From Antagonism to Convergence: Economics and Linguistic Diversity'. In eds. Kirk and Ó Baoill. 2003. 213–23.

Grin, F. 2009. 'Promoting Language through the Economy: Competing Paradigms'. In eds. Kirk and Ó Baoill. 2009. 1–12.

Gupta, A.F. 2002. 'Privileging Indigeneity'. In eds. Kirk and Ó Baoill. 2002. 290–9.

Hadden, T. 2000. 'Should a Bill of Rights for Northern Ireland Protect Language Rights?. In eds. Kirk and Ó Baoill. 2000. 111–20.

Hance, M. 2005. 'The Development of Scots Language Policy in Scotland since Devolution'. In eds. Kirk and Ó Baoill. 2005. 71–6.

Hance, M. 2009. 'Scots and the Economy'. In eds. Kirk and Ó Baoill. 2009. 183–5.

Hanna, C. 2002. 'Symposium Address'. In eds. Kirk and Ó Baoill. 2002. 20–2.

Harris, J. 2002. 'Research, Innovation and Policy Change: Lessons from the ITÉ Evaluation of the Irish Programme at Primary Level'. In eds. Kirk and Ó Baoill. 2002. 82–99.

Harris. J. 2011. 'Minority Languages, Community and Identity in Ireland and Scotland'. In eds. Kirk and Ó Baoill. 2011a. 11–21.

Hegarty, K. 2003. 'BBC Northern Ireland and Irish'. In eds. Kirk and Ó Baoill. 2003. 36–9.

Herbison, I. 2005. 'The Revival of Scots in Ulster: Why Literary History Matters'. In eds. Kirk and Ó Baoill. 2005. 77–85.

Hickey, R. 2009. 'Linguistic Borders in Ireland'. Paper given at Ninth Language and Politics Symposium, Aberdeen.

Horsbroch, D. 2000. 'Mair as a Sheuch Atween Scotland an Ulster: Twa Policie for the Scots Leid?' In eds. Kirk and Ó Baoill. 2000. 133–41.

Horsbroch, D. 2001a. 'A Twalmonth an a wee Tait Forder'. In eds. Kirk and Ó Baoill. 2001. 123–34.

Horsbroch, D. 2001b. 'A Hairst for a Bit Screive: Writin Historie in Scots'. In eds. Kirk and Ó Baoill. 2001. 187–94.

Horsbroch, D. 2002. 'The Executive o Scotland's Language Apairtheid'. In eds. Kirk and Ó Baoill. 2002. 157–64.

Kaplan, R.B. and R. Baldauf. 1997. *Language Planning: From Practice to Theory*. Clevedon: Multilingual Matters.

Kay. B. 2011. 'Lowsin Time, Yokin Time: The Scots Leid in Twa Thoosan an Seiven'. In eds. Kirk and Ó Baoill. 2011a. 206–11.

Kirk, J.M. 2000a. 'The New Written Scots Dialect in Present-day Northern Ireland'. In ed. Ljung M. *Linguistic Structure and Variation: A Festschrift for Gunnel Melchers*. Stockholm Studies in English XCII. Stockholm: Almqvist and Wiksell International. 121–38.

Kirk, J.M. 2000b. 'Two Ullans Texts'. In eds. Kirk and Ó Baoill. 2000. 33–44.

Kirk, J.M. 2004. 'Archipelagic Glotto-Politics: The Scotstacht'. In ed. Tristram, H.L.C. *The Celtic Englishes III*. Heidelberg: Carl Winter. 339–56.

Kirk, J.M. 2005. 'Language Symbolism and Nation Building: Northern Ireland, Estonia and Moldova'. In ed. Coretchi, A. *From Misunderstanding towards Openness and Collaboration in Multicultural Societies*. Chisinau: Pontos, published for the East-East Program: Partnership Beyond Borders of the Soros Foundation Moldova. 73–100.

Kirk, J.M. 2008. 'Does the UK Have a Language Policy?' *Journal of Irish and Scottish Studies* 1.2: 205–22.

Kirk, J.M. 2009. 'Political Border as Language Border in the North and South of Ireland'. Paper given at Ninth Language and Politics Symposium, Aberdeen.

Kirk, J.M. 2010. 'Devolution and Language'. Paper presented to the Irish-Scottish Forum, The Scottish Parliament, November 2010.

Kirk, J.M. 2011. 'Scotland and Northern Ireland as Scots-speaking Communities'. In eds. Kirk and Ó Baoill. 2011a. 193–205.

Kirk, J.M. and J.L. Kallen. 2011. 'The Cultural Context of ICE-Ireland'. In ed. Hickey, R. *Researching the Languages of Ireland*. Uppsala: Uppsala University Press.

Kirk, J.M. and D.P. Ó Baoill, eds. 2000a. *Language and Politics: Northern Ireland, the Republic of Ireland, and Scotland*. Belfast Studies in Language, Culture and Politics 1. Belfast: Cló Ollscoil na Banríona.

Kirk, J.M. and D.P. Ó Baoill. 2000b. 'Introduction: Language, Politics and English'. In Kirk and Ó Baoill. 2000a. 3–12.

Kirk, J.M. and D.P. Ó Baoill, eds. 2001a. *Language Links: The Languages of Scotland and Ireland*. Belfast Studies in Language, Culture and Politics 2. Belfast: Cló Ollscoil na Banríona.

Kirk, J.M. and D.P. Ó Baoill, eds. 2001b. *Linguistic Politics: Language Policies for Northern Ireland, the Republic of Ireland, and Scotland*. Belfast Studies in Language, Culture and Politics 3. Belfast: Cló Ollscoil na Banríona.

Kirk, J.M. and D.P. Ó Baoill. 2001d. 'Introduction: Language Links'. In Kirk and Ó Baoill. 2001a. xiii–xix.

Kirk, J.M. and D.P. Ó Baoill. 2001d. 'Introduction: Linguistic Politics in the Gaeltacht and Scotstacht'. In Kirk and Ó Baoill. 2001b. 1–21.

Kirk, J.M. and D.P. Ó Baoill, eds. 2002a. *Language Planning and Education: Linguistic Issues in Northern Ireland, the Republic of Ireland, and Scotland*. Belfast Studies in Language, Culture and Politics 6. Belfast: Cló Ollscoil na Banríona.

Kirk, J.M. and D.P. Ó Baoill, eds. 2002b. *Travellers and their Language*. Belfast Studies in Language, Culture and Politics 4. Belfast: Cló Ollscoil na Banríona.

Kirk, J.M. and D.P. Ó Baoill. 2002c. 'Introduction: Language Planning and Education: Linguistic Issues in Northern Ireland, the Republic of Ireland, and Scotland. In Kirk and Ó Baoill. 2002a. 1–19.

Kirk, J.M. and D.P. Ó Baoill. 2002d. 'Introduction: Travellers and their Language. In Kirk and Ó Baoill. 2002b. 1–8.

Kirk, J.M. and D.P. Ó Baoill, eds. 2003a. *Towards Our Goals in Broadcasting, the Press, the Performing Arts and the Economy: Minority Languages in Northern Ireland, the Republic of Ireland, and Scotland*. Belfast Studies in Language, Culture and Politics 10. Belfast: Cló Ollscoil na Banríona.

Kirk, J.M. and D.P. Ó Baoill, eds. 2003b. 'Towards Our Goals in Broadcasting, the Press, the Performing Arts and the Economy: Minority Languages in Northern Ireland, the Republic of Ireland, and Scotland'. In Kirk and Ó Baoill. 2003a. 1–28.

Kirk, J.M. and D.P. Ó Baoill, eds. 2005a. *Legislation, Literature and Sociolinguistics: Northern Ireland, the Republic of Ireland, and Scotland*. Belfast Studies in Language, Culture and Politics 13. Belfast: Cló Ollscoil na Banríona.

Kirk, J.M. and D.P. Ó Baoill. 2005b. 'Introduction: Legislation, Literature and Sociolinguistics: Northern Ireland, the Republic of Ireland, and Scotland'. In Kirk and Ó Baoill. 2005a. 1–15.

Kirk, J.M. and D.P. Ó Baoill, eds. 2009a. *Language and Economic Development: Northern Ireland, the Republic of Ireland, and Scotland*. Belfast Studies in Language, Culture and Politics 19. Belfast: Cló Ollscoil na Banríona.

Kirk, J.M. and D.P. Ó Baoill. 2009b. 'Language and Economic Development: Northern Ireland, the Republic of Ireland, and Scotland'. In Kirk and Ó Baoill. 2009a. xii–xiv.

Kirk, J.M. and D.P. Ó Baoill, eds. 2011a. *Sustaining Minority Language Communities: Northern Ireland, the Republic of Ireland, and Scotland*. Belfast Studies in Language, Culture and Politics 20. Belfast: Cló Ollscoil na Banríona.

Kirk, J.M. and D.P. Ó Baoill, eds. 2011b. *Strategies for Minority Languages: Northern Ireland, the Republic of Ireland, and Scotland*. Belfast Studies in Language, Culture and Politics 22. Belfast: Cló Ollscoil na Banríona.

Kirk, J.M. and D.P. Ó Baoill. 2011c. 'Introduction'. In Kirk and Ó Baoill. 2011a. 1–8.

Kirk, J.M. and D.P. Ó Baoill. 2011d. 'Réamhrá/Introduction: Strategies for Minority Languages'. In Kirk and Ó Baoill. 2011b. 1–10.

Kirk, J.M. and D.P. Ó Baoill. 2011e. 'Ten Years of Language and Politics: Impact and Whither Now?'. In In Kirk and Ó Baoill. 2011b. 267–99.

Kirk, J.M., Brown, M. and A. Noble eds. forthcoming. *The Cultures of Radicalism in Britain and Ireland*. [in the series *Political Poetry and Song in the Age of Revolution*]. London: Pickering and Chatto.

Kirk, J.M., Noble. A. and M. Brown eds. forthcoming. *The Languages of Resistance*. [in the series *Political Poetry and Song in the Age of Revolution*]. London: Pickering and Chatto.

Laird of Artigarvan, J. Lord. 2001. 'Language Policy and Tha Boord o Ulstèr-Scotch'. In eds. Kirk and Ó Baoill. 2001. 37–42.

Lamb, W. 2005. 'The Sociolinguistics of Contemporary Scottish Gaelic'. In eds. Kirk and Ó Baoill. 2005. 126–37.

Lamb, W. 2007. *Scottish Gaelic Speech and Writing: Register Variation in an Endangered Language*. Belfast Studies in Language, Culture and Politics 16. Belfast: Cló Ollscoil na Banríona.

Law, A. 2003. 'Language and the Press in Scotland'. In eds. Kirk and Ó Baoill. 2003. 105–18.

Law, J. 2003. 'Scrievin anent Scots: A Psychopathological Study o a Puckle Scots Journalism'. In eds. Kirk and Ó Baoill. 2003. 131–7.

Law, J. 2011. 'The Scots Commonty'. In eds. Kirk and Ó Baoill. 2011a. 212–7.

Loester, B. 2009. 'Scotland and Bavaria as Linguistic Communities'. Paper given at Ninth Language and Politics Symposium, Aberdeen.

Longley, E., Hughes, E. and D. O'Rawe, eds. 2003. *Ireland (Ulster) Scotland: Concepts, Contexts, Comparisons*. Belfast Studies in Language, Culture and Politics 7. Belfast: Cló Ollscoil na Banríona.

Macafee, C. 2001. 'Scots: Hauf Empty or Hauf Fu?' In eds. Kirk and Ó Baoill. 2001. 159–68.

Macafee, C. 2002. ''Auld Plain Scottis' and Pre-emptive Staunardisation o Inglis'. In eds. Kirk and Ó Baoill. 2002. 165–174.

McAlister, P. 2003. 'The Department of Culture, Arts and Leisure's Language Diversity and Broadcasting Policy'. In eds. Kirk and Ó Baoill. 2003. 29–32.

Mac An Iomaire, T. 2003. 'Irish Language Broadcasting', In eds. Kirk and Ó Baoill. 2003. 49–52.

McCafferty, K. 2001. 'Norway: Consensus and Diversity', In eds. Kirk and Ó Baoill. 2001. 89–104.

McCafferty, P. 2009. 'Language Shift on Headstones in the Donegal Gaeltacht, A.D. 1830–2000'. Paper given at Ninth Language and Politics Symposium, Aberdeen.

MacCaluim, A. 2007. *Reversing Language Shift: The Role and Social Identity of Scottish Gaelic Learners*. Belfast Studies in Language, Culture and Politics 17. Belfast: Cló Ollscoil na Banríona.

MacCaluim, A. 2011a. ''From Politics to Practice': A' Cruthachadh Plana Gàidhlig do Phàrlamaid na h-Alba'. In eds. Kirk and Ó Baoill. 2011b. 187–91.

MacCaluim, A. 2011b. ''From Politics to Practice': A' Cruthachadh Plana Gàidhlig do Phàrlamaid na h-Alba'. In eds. Kirk and Ó Baoill. 2011b. 192–5.

Macaulay, D. 2002. Review of *Belfast Studies in Language, Culture and Politics*, vols. 1–3. *Scottish Language* 21: 73–7.

McClure, J.D. 1988. *Why Scots Matters*. Edinburgh: The Saltire Society.

McClure, J.D. 1995. *Scots and its Literature*. Varieties of English around the World, G14. Amsterdam: John Benjamins.

McClure, J.D. 1997. *Why Scots Matters*. Second Edition. Edinburgh: The Saltire Society.

McClure, J.D. 2002. 'Developing Scots: How Far Have We still To Go?' In eds. Kirk and Ó Baoill. 2003. 186–91.

McClure, J.D. ed. 2004. *Doonsin' Emerauds: New Scrieves anent Scots an Gaelic*. Belfast Studies in Language, Culture and Politics 11. Belfast: Cló Ollscoil na Banríona.

McClure, J.D. 2009. *Why Scots Matters*. Third Edition. Edinburgh: The Saltire Society.

Mac Cormaic, B. 2001. 'An Struchtúr tacaíochta atá le bunú faoi Alt 31 den Acht Oideachais 1998: An Chomhairle um Oideachas Gaeltachta agus lánGhaeilge'. In eds. Kirk and Ó Baoill. 2001. 227–30.

McCoy, G. 2001. 'From Cause to Quango? The Peace Process and the Transformation of the Irish Language Movement'. In eds. Kirk and Ó Baoill. 2001. 205–18.

McCoy, G. 2003. '*Ros na Rún*: Alternative Gaelic Universe'. In eds. Kirk and Ó Baoill. 2003. 155–64.

McCoy, 2011. 'The Culture of Gaelic in Ireland and Scotland: An Saol Gaelach agus An Saoghal Gaidhealach'. In Kirk and Ó Baoill. 2011b. 235–45.

Mac Corraidh, S. 2008. An thóir an dea-chleachtais: *The Quest for Best Practice in Irish-medium Primary Schools in Belfast*. Belfast Studies in Language, Culture and Politics 18. Belfast: Cló Ollscoil na Banríona.

McCullough, B. 2000. 'Language, Discrimination and the Good Friday Agreement: The Case of Sign'. In eds. Kirk and Ó Baoill. 2000. 91–5.

Mac Donald, C. 2003. 'The Symbolic Value of Gàidhlig in the Scottish Sunday Newspapers'. In eds. Kirk and Ó Baoill. 2003. 100–4.

Mac Donnacha, J. 2011. 'The Role of the University in Sustaining Linguistic Minorities: An Irish Case Study'. In eds. Kirk and Ó Baoill. 2011a. 53–64.

Mac Donnacha, S. 2003. 'Is acmhainn luachmhar eacnamaíochta í an Ghaeilge do Phobal na hÉireann ar fad'. In eds. Kirk and Ó Baoill. 2003. 234–7.

Mac Donnacha, S. 2011. 'The Role of Capacity Building in the Implementation of the 20-Year Strategy for the Irish Language'. In eds. Kirk and Ó Baoill. 2011b. 11–20.

McGugan, I. 2001. 'Scots in the Twenty-first Century'. In eds. Kirk and Ó Baoill. 2001. 29–36.

McGugan, I. 2002. 'More Progress for Scots in the Twenty-first Century'. In eds. Kirk and Ó Baoill. 2002. 23–6.

McHardy, S. 2003. 'Broadcasting and Scots'. In eds. Kirk and Ó Baoill. 2003. 90–2.

Mac Ille Chiar, I. 2002. 'Na toir breith gus nach toirear breuth ort: Tuilleadh 's a' choir measaidh ann am Foghlam na h-Alba'. In eds. Kirk and Ó Baoill. 2002. 111–23.

Mac Ionnrachtaigh, F. 2011. 'Ón Bhun Aníos: Resisting and Regenerating through Language in the North of Ireland'. In eds. Kirk and Ó Baoill. 2011a. 132–55.

MacIver, M. 2003. 'Structures for Gaelic-medium Education'. In eds. Kirk and Ó Baoill. 2002. 56–60.

MacIver, M. 2011. 'Sustaining Minority Languages'. In eds. Kirk and Ó Baoill. 2011a. 188–91.

MacKay, J.A. 2009. 'Gaelic-medium Broadcasting and the Economy'. In eds. Kirk and Ó Baoill. 2009. 175–82.

MacKay, R. 2011. 'Gaelic Plans at the University of the Highlands and Islands'. In eds. Kirk and Ó Baoill. 2011b. 196–202.

McKendry, E. 2002. 'Irish and Curriculum Review in Northern Ireland'. In eds. Kirk and Ó Baoill. 2002. 136–45.

MacKinnon, K. 2001. '*Fàs no Bàs* (Prosper or Perish): Prospects of Survival for Scottish Gaelic'. In eds. Kirk and Ó Baoill. 2001. 231–54.

MacKinnon, K. 2003. 'Celtic Languages in the 2001 Census: How Population Censuses Bury Celtic Speakers'. In eds. Kirk and Ó Baoill. 2003. 250–61.

MacKinnon, K. 2008. Review of [MacCaluim 2007]. *Scottish Language* 27: 111–4.

MacKinnon, K. 2009. 'Celtic Languages in a Migration Society: Economy, Population Structure and Language Maintenance'. In eds. Kirk and Ó Baoill. 2009. 166–74.

MacKinnon, K. 2011. 'Growing a new Generation of Gaelic Speakers: An Action Plan in Response to a Ministerial Initiative'. In eds. Kirk and Ó Baoill. 2011b. 210–20.

MacLennan, I. 2003. 'BBC Craoladh nan Gàidheal: Co sinn?' In eds. Kirk and Ó Baoill. 2003. 67–72.

MacLeod, M[arsaili]. 2009. 'Gaelic Language Skills in the Workplace'. In eds. Kirk and Ó Baoill. 2009. 134–52.

MacLeod, M[ichelle]. 2011. 'The Human Factor: Community Language Workers and National Strategies'. In eds. Kirk and Ó Baoill. 2011b. 221–8.

McLeod, W. 2002. 'Alba: Luchd an Aona-Chànanais agus Buaidh na Cairt Eòrpaich'. In eds. Kirk and Ó Baoill. 2002. 284–9.

McLeod, W. 2003. 'Gàidhlig agus an Eaconamidh: Nàdar nan Deasbadan ann an Alba An-Diugh'. In eds. Kirk and Ó Baoill. 2003. 238–44.

McLeod, W. 2005. 'Bile na Gàidhlig: Cothroman is Cunnartan'. In eds. Kirk and Ó Baoill. 2005. 36–45.

McLeod, W. 2009a. 'Expanding the Gaelic Employment Sector: Strategies and Challenges'. In eds. Kirk and Ó Baoill. 2009. 153–65.

McLeod, W. 2009b. 'Language Legislation in Scotland and Ireland: Challenges of Implementation'. Paper given at Ninth Language and Politics Symposium, Aberdeen.

McLeod, W. 2011. 'Gaelic Language Plans and the Issue of Bilingual Logos'. In eds. Kirk and Ó Baoill. 2011b. 203–11.

Mag Lochlainn, P.A. 2000. 'Language, Discrimination and the Good Friday Agreement: The Case of Gays'. In eds. Kirk and Ó Baoill. 2000. 107–10.

MacNeil, C.A. 2003. 'The State of Gaelic Broadcasting in Scotland: Critical Issues and Audience Concerns'. In eds. Kirk and Ó Baoill. 2003. 60–6.

MacNeil, M. and D.P. Ó Baoill. 2011. 'Research Development and the Implementation of Am Bradán Feasa Programme: Early Thinking of the Potential within a Social Issues / Applied Language Work-Stream'. In eds. Kirk and Ó Baoill. 2011a. 29–35.

Mac Nia, S. 'Irish-medium Assessment and Examinations'. In eds. Kirk and Ó Baoill. 2002. 100–10.

Mac Póilin, A. 2011. 'A Lid for Every Pot: The 20-Year Strategy and Northern Ireland'. In eds. Kirk and Ó Baoill. 2011b. 132–49.

Malcolm, I. 2011. 'Young Protestants and Sustaining Irish in the Protestant Community'. In eds. Kirk and Ó Baoill. 2011a. 44–52.

Matras, Y. 2006. Review of [Kirk and Ó Baoill 2002b]. *Romani Studies* 15: 191–200.

Meier, H.H. 1977. 'Scots is Not Alone: The Swiss and Low German Analogues', In eds. Aitken, A.J., McDiarmid, M.P. and D.D. Thomson. *Bards and Makars*. Glasgow: Glasgow University Press. 201–13.

Meyerhoff, M. 2006. *Introducing Sociolinguistics*. London: Routledge.

Mesthrie, R., Swann, J., Deumart, A. and W.L. Leap. 2009. *Introducing Sociolinguistics*. Second Edition. Edinburgh: Edinburgh University Press.

Millar, R. 2006. 'Burying Alive? Unfocussed Governmental Language Policy and Scots'. *Language Policy* 5.1: 53–86.

Millar, R.McC. 2009a. 'Dislocation: Is it Presently Possible to Envisage an Economically-based Language Policy for Scots in Scotland?' In eds. Kirk and Ó Baoill. 2009. 186–95.

Millar, R.McC. 2009b. 'The Politics of Scots and its European Analogues'. Paper given at Ninth Language and Politics Symposium, Aberdeen.

Millar, R.McC. 2011. 'Linguistic Democracy?' In eds. Kirk and Ó Baoill. 2011a. 218–24.

Moriarty, M. 2006. Review of [Kirk and Ó Baoill 2003a]. *Journal of Sociolinguistics* 10: 270–2.

Muller, J. 2003. 'An bhFreastalaíonn Cuid III den Chairt Eorpach ar Réalaíochtaí agus Oideachais Mheán Eile?' In eds. Kirk and Ó Baoill. 2002. 131–5.

Muller, J. 2011a. 'Forbairt Straitéise don Ghaeilge: Cur Chuige Comhbheartaithe á Thógáil'. In eds. Kirk and Ó Baoill. 2011b. 110–18.

Muller, J. 2011b. 'Irish Language Strategy Development: Building a Concerted Approach'. In eds. Kirk and Ó Baoill. 2011b. 119–127.

Munro, G. 2011. 'The *Barail agus Comas Cànain* Survey of Community Language Use, Ability and Attitudes: Some General Observations regarding Future Gaelic Language Policy Planning in Scotland'. In eds. Kirk and Ó Baoill. 2011b. 163–71.

Ní Dhúda, L. 2011a. 'Pobal Gaeltachta an Bhreacbhaile: Cás-staidéar Sochtheangeolaíoch agus Eitneagrafaíoch sa Bheartas Teanga'. In eds. Kirk and Ó Baoill. 2011a. 96–113.

Ní Dhúda, L. 2011b. 'The Breacbhaile Gaeltacht Community: A Sociolinguistic and Ethnographic Case Study in Language Policy'. In eds. Kirk and Ó Baoill. 2011a. 114–31.

Ní Fheargusa, J. 'Struchtúir Éagsúla an Ghaeloideachais'. In eds. Kirk and Ó Baoill. 2002. 52–5.

Ni Laoire, S. 2008. Review of [Lamb 2007]. *Scottish Language* 27: 115–8.

Ní Nuadhain, M. 2003. 'Irish Language Broadcasting'. In eds. Kirk and Ó Baoill. 2003. 53–7.

Nic Craith, M. 2001. 'Concepts, Rights and Languages'. Review of [Kirk and Ó Baoill 2000a]. *The Irish Review* 28: 147–51.

Nig Uidhir, G. 2002. 'Initial Teacher Training for Irish-medium Schools'. In eds. Kirk and Ó Baoill. 2002. 65–75.

Niven, L. 2002. 'Nae Chiels: Scots Language in Scotland'. In eds. Kirk and Ó Baoill. 2002. 198–202.

Novak-Lukanovič, S. 2009. 'Economic Aspects of Language: The Case of Slovenia'. In eds. Kirk and Ó Baoill. 2009. 37–53.

Ó Baoill, D.P. 2001. 'Language Planning and the Sociolinguistics of Register'. In eds. Dickson, D., Duffy, S. Cathakson, D, Ó hÁinle C. and I. Campbell Ross. *Ireland and Scotland: Nation, Region, Identity*. Dublin. 32–8.

Ó Baoill, D.P. 2002. 'Curaclam, Pleanáil, Sochtheangeolaíocht agus Réimeanna Teanga'. In *Curaclam na Gaeilge*. LCCXXX11, Maigh Nuad: An Sagart. 7–18.

Ó Baoill, D.P. 2004. 'The Changing Face of the Irish Language'. Invited plenary lecture presented at the International Conference on the Languages of Ireland, hosted by the Canadian Association for Irish Studies, Halifax, NS.

Ó Baoill, D.P. 2005. 'Language Planning and Implementation in Gaeltacht Areas and the Future of Irish'. Paper presented at Éigse Uladh (International Symposium on Bilingualism and Language Planning).

Ó Baoill, D.P. 2006a. 'Minority Language Revival and Revitalization – Lessons and Pitfalls: The Case of Ireland'. First Guest Lecture as Lansdowne Visiting Professor at the University of Victoria, BC.

Ó Baoill, D.P. 2006b 'Language Standardization and the Role of Dialect'. Second Guest Lecture as Lansdowne Visiting Professor at the University of Victoria, BC.

Ó Baoill, D.P. 2006c 'Language Planning Issues and the Practical Application of Language Policies'. Third Guest Lecture as Lansdowne Visiting Professor at the University of Victoria, BC.

Ó Baoill, D.P. 2011a. 'Cultural, Social, Linguistic and Environmental Issues in Minority Language Development and Maintenance'. In eds. Kirk and Ó Baoill. 2011a. 22–8.

Ó Baoill, D.P. 2011a. 'Straitéis don Ghaeilge i dTuaisceart Éireann'. In eds. Kirk and Ó Baoill. 2011b. 128–9.

Ó Baoill, D.P. 2011b. 'An Irish Language Strategy for Northern Ireland'. In eds. Kirk and Ó Baoill. 2011b. 130–1.

Ó Cearnaigh, S. 2009. 'Forbairt Eacnamúil agus Cúrsaí Teanga in Éirinn: Fíricí agus Fáthanna'. In eds. Kirk and Ó Baoill. 54–60.

Ó Ciardha, P. 2003. 'Celtic Language Broadcasting'. In eds. Kirk and Ó Baoill. 2003. 58–9.

Ó Cofaigh, S. 2001. 'An Ghaeilge: Reachtaíocht'. In eds. Kirk and Ó Baoill. 2001. 219–24.

Ó Coinn, S. 2002. 'Struchtúir na Gaelscolaíochta I dTuaisceart Éireann'. In eds. Kirk and Ó Baoill. 2002. 52–5.

Ó Coisdealbha, C. 2011a. 'Cur i Bhfeidhm / Géilliúlacht: Ceachtanna Foghlamtha ó Iniúchadh Scéimeanna Teanga'. In eds. Kirk and Ó Baoill. 2011b. 34–38.

Ó Coisdealbha, C. 2011b. 'Ensuring Implementation/Compliance: Lessons Learned from Auditing Language Schemes'. In eds. Kirk and Ó Baoill. 2011b. 39–42.

Ó Cuaig, S. 'Súil Eile', In eds. Kirk and Ó Baoill. 2003. 47–8.

Ó Clochartaigh, T. 'Spiorad'. In eds. Kirk and Ó Baoill. 2003. 150–4.

Ó Duibhin. C. 2003. 'A Comment on the Presentation of the Results of the Irish Language Question in the 2001 Census of Northern Ireland'. In eds. Kirk and Ó Baoill. 2003. 262–4.

Ó Giollagáin, C. 2005. 'The Sociolinguistics of Contemporary Irish'. In eds. Kirk and Ó Baoill. 2005. 138–62.

Ó hAinmhire, B. 'Coimisiún na Gaeltachta agus an Gaeltacht'. In eds. Kirk and Ó Baoill. 2001. 225–6.

Ó hAoláin, P. 2009. 'Economic Development through Language: The Gaeltacht Experience'. In eds. Kirk and Ó Baoill. 2009. 61–9.

Ó hAoláin, P. 2011a. 'Sustaining Minority Language Communities: Yin and Yang Juncture for Irish!' In eds. Kirk and Ó Baoill. 2011a. 81–8.

Ó hAoláin, P. 2011b. 'Straitéis 20-Bliain na Gaeilge: Promhadh ár gCreidimh'. In eds. Kirk and Ó Baoill. 2011b. 21–6.

Ó hAoláin, P. 2011c. 'The 20 Year Irish Language Strategy: Testing the Faith of Irish Speakers'. In eds. Kirk and Ó Baoill. 2011b. 27–33.

Ó hEadhra, B. 2011. 'Plans, Plans, Plans'. In eds. Kirk and Ó Baoill. 2011b. 231–4.

Ó Laighin, P.B. 2005. 'Stádas na Gaeilge i Réim Theangacha an Aontais Eorpaigh'. In eds. Kirk and Ó Baoill. 2005. 1–15.

Ó Murchú, H. 2000. 'Language, Discrimination and the Good Friday Agreement: The Case of Irish'. In eds. Kirk and Ó Baoill. 2000. 81–8.

Ó Murchú, H. 2002. 'A Response from Ireland'. In eds. Kirk and Ó Baoill. 2002. 279–83.

Ó Murchú, H. 2011a. 'Léargas ar an gCoibhneas Comhaimseartha idir an Earnáil Dheonach / an tSochaí Shibhialta agus Institiúidí Stáit I bPoblacht na hÉireann'. In eds. Kirk and Ó Baoill. 2011b. 76–89.

Ó Murchú, H. 2011b. 'Some Comments on the Current Forms of Relationship between the Voluntary Sector / Civil Society and Organs of the State in the Republic of Ireland'. In eds. Kirk and Ó Baoill. 2011b. 90–109.

Ó Pronntaigh, C. 2003. '*Lá*: A Daily Newspaper in Irish'. In eds. Kirk and Ó Baoill. 2003. 93–4.

O'Rawe, D. 2003. 'Language and the Irish Cinema Question'. In eds. Kirk and Ó Baoill. 2003. 143–7.

Ó Riagáin, D. 2000. 'Language Rights as Human Rights in Europe and in Northern Ireland'. In eds. Kirk and Ó Baoill. 2000. 65–73.

Ó Riagáin, D. 2001. 'Language Rights / Human Rights in Northern Ireland and the Role of the *European Charter for Regional or Minority Languages*'. In eds. Kirk and Ó Baoill. 2001. 43–54.

Ó Riagáin, D. 2003. 'Walloon and Scots: A Response to Jean-Luc Fauconnier'. In eds. Kirk and Ó Baoill. 2003. 301–2.

Ó Riagáin, D. 2009a. 'An Ghaeilge agus an Saol Eacnamaíoch – Athmhachnamh'. In eds. Kirk and Ó Baoill. 2009. 103–10.

Ó Riagáin, D. 2009b. 'Some Green Shots: A Glance at some Recent Positive Developments for Linguistic Diversity'. Paper given at Ninth Language and Politics Symposium, Aberdeen.

Ó Riagáin, D. 2011a. 'The Concept of Gaeltacht: Time to Revisit?' In eds. Kirk and Ó Baoill. 2011a. 89–95.

Ó Riagáin, D. 2011b. 'Irish: A 20 Year Strategy or Just More Waffle? In eds. Kirk and Ó Baoill. 2011b. 71–75.

Ó Riagáin, D. 2003. *Language and Law in Northern Ireland*. Belfast Studies in Language, Culture and Politics 9. Belfast: Cló Ollscoil na Banríona.

Ó Riagáin, D. 2006. *Voces Diversae: Minority Language Education in Europe*. Belfast Studies in Language, Culture and Politics 15. Belfast: Cló Ollscoil na Banríona.

Ó Riagáin, P. 2009. 'Global and Local in Gaeltacht Areas: Corca Dhuibhne 1960–1986'. In eds. Kirk and Ó Baoill. 2009. 92–102.

Ó Riain, S. [2002]. Review of [Kirk and Ó Baoill 2001b]. www.seanoriain.eu/English.htm

O'Rourke, B. 2011. 'Sustaining Minority Language Communities: The Case of Galician'. In eds. Kirk and Ó Baoill. 2011a. 266–80.

Paisley, J. 2003. '*Whit wey fur no?* Scots and the Scripted Media: Theatre, Radio, TV, Film'. In eds. Kirk and Ó Baoill. 2003. 179–83.

Parsley, I.J. 2000, 'Language, Discrimination and the Good Friday Agreement: The Case of Ulster-Scots'. In eds. Kirk and Ó Baoill. 2000. 89–90.

Parsley, I.J. 2001. 'Ulster-Scots: Politicisation or Survival?' In eds. Kirk and Ó Baoill. 2001. 177–80.

Parsley, I.J. 2002. 'Twa Ulster Scotses: Authentic versus Synthetic'. In eds. Kirk and Ó Baoill. 2003. 183–5.

Parsley, I.J. 2003. 'Wad the Ulster-Scots Tongue Richtlie be Gan Foreairt?'. In eds. Kirk and Ó Baoill. 2003. 211–2.

Parsley, I.J. 2005. 'The Ulster Scots: A New Wey Foreairt'. In eds. Kirk and Ó Baoill. 2005. 69–70.

Pavlenko, A. 2005. 'An Eastern Slavonic Perspective on Scots'. In eds. Kirk and Ó Baoill. 2005. 173–8.

Pavlenko, A. 2011. 'Sustaining Minority Language Communities: The Case of Ukrainian in Southern Russia'. In eds. Kirk and Ó Baoill. 2011a. 300–6.

Peover, S. 2001. 'Encouragement and Facilitation: A New Paradigm for Minority Language Education'. In eds. Kirk and Ó Baoill. 2001. 195–204.

Peover, S. 2002. 'The Current State of Irish-medium Education in Northern Ireland'. In eds. Kirk and Ó Baoill. 2002. 124–30.

Phillipson, R. 2002. 'English for Emerging or Submerging Multiple European Identities?' In eds. Kirk and Ó Baoill. 2002. 267–78.

Purves, D. 2003. 'Scots and Identity'. In eds. Kirk and Ó Baoill. 2003. 175–8.

Ricento, T. 2005. *An Introduction to Language Policy: Theory and Method*. Oxford: Wiley-Blackwell.

Robertson, A.G.B. 2002. 'Teacher Training in Gaelic in Scotland'. In eds. Kirk and Ó Baoill. 2002. 76–81.

Robinson, C. 2003. 'Scots in Soaps'. In eds. Kirk and Ó Baoill. 2003. 184–93.

Robinson, C. 2011a. 'The Role of Dictionaries in Sustaining a Language Community'. In eds. Kirk and Ó Baoill. 2011a. 238–42.

Robinson, C. 2011b. 'The Ministerial Working Group on the Scots Language'. In eds. Kirk and Ó Baoill. 2011b. 247–55.

Rohmer, L. 'Specialist Study of Language within the English Higher Curriculum: Approaches to Practice'. In eds. Kirk and Ó Baoill. 2002. 212–20.

Rooney, E. 2001. 'Language Policy Implementation: A DCAL Civil Servant's Perspective'. In eds. Kirk and Ó Baoill. 2001. 55–60.

Ruiz Vieytez, E.J. 2003. 'Basque and Language Rights'. In eds. Kirk and Ó Baoill. 2003. 265–93.

Russell, M. 2001. 'Language and Politics in Scotland'. In eds. Kirk and Ó Baoill. 2001. 23–8.

Salzmann, Z. 2007. Review of [Kirk and Ó Baoill 2002b]. *Language* 83: 220–1.

Simpson, J.M.Y. 2004. Review of [Kirk and Ó Baoill 2003a]. *Scottish Language* 23: 120–2.

Skutnabb-Kangas, T. 2002. 'Irelands, Scotland, Education and Linguistic Human Rights: Some International Comparisons'. In eds. Kirk and Ó Baoill. 2002. 221–66.

Smith, J. 2005. 'The Sociolinguiustics of Contemporary Scots'. In eds. Kirk and Ó Baoill. 2005. 112–25.

Smyth, A. and M. Montgomery. 2005. 'The Ulster-Scots Academy'. In eds. Kirk and Ó Baoill. 2005. 60–4.

Solnishkina, M. 2011. 'Sustaining Minority Language Communities: The Case of Tatarstan'. In eds. Kirk and Ó Baoill. 2011a. 292–9.

Solymosi, J. 2011. 'Sustaining Minority Language Communities: The Case of Hungary'. In eds. Kirk and Ó Baoill. 2011a. 281–5.

Spolsky, B. 2004. *Language Policy*. Cambridge: Cambridge University Press.

Spolsky, B. 2009. *Language Management*. Cambridge: Cambridge University Press. 2010.

Spurr, C. 2003. 'The BBC Northern Ireland Ulster-Scots Unit'. In eds. Kirk and Ó Baoill. 2003. 40–6.

Strubell, M. 1999. 'Polítiques Lingüístiques i Canvi Sociolingüístic a Europa'. In *Polítiques Lingüístiques a Països Plurilingües*. Barcelona: Departament de Cultura de la Generalitat de Catalunya. 9–26.

Tender, T. 2011. 'Sustaining Minority Language Communities: The Case of Estonian.' In eds. Kirk and Ó Baoill. 2011a. 286–91.

Titley, A. 2003. 'The Coming of the Radio'. In eds. Kirk and Ó Baoill. 2003. 148–9.

Titley, A. 2005. 'Irish Literature and its Expression'. In eds. Kirk and Ó Baoill. 2005 103–11.

Unger, J.W. 2009. 'Economic Discourses of Scots on Bourdieu's 'Linguistic Market'', In eds. Kirk and Ó Baoill. 2009. 204–10.

Vikør, Lars S. 1993. *The Nordic languages. Their Status and Interrelations.* Oslo: Novus Press.

Vikør, Lars S. 2001. *The Nordic languages. Their Status and Interrelations.* Second Edition Oslo: Novus Press.

Walsh, J. 2002. 'Language, Culture and Development: The Gaeltacht Commission 1926 and 2002'. In eds. Kirk and Ó Baoill. 2002. 300–17.

Walsh, J. 2003. 'Teanga, Cultúr agus Forbairt I gCás na hÉireann: i dTreo Cur Chuige Nua'. In eds. Kirk and Ó Baoill. 2003. 229–33.

Walsh, J. 2009. 'Ireland's Socio-economic Development and the Irish Language: Theoretical and Empirical Perspectives'. In eds. Kirk and Ó Baoill. 2009. 70–81.

Walsh, J. 2011a. 'Dátheangachas, Idé-eolaíocht agus an *Straitéis 20-Bliain don Ghaeilge*'. In eds. Kirk and Ó Baoill. 2011b. 43–56.

Walsh, J. 2011b. 'Bilingualism, Ideology and the 20-Year Strategy for Irish'. In eds. Kirk and Ó Baoill. 2011b. 57–70.

Walsh, J. and W. McLeod. 2007. 'An Overcoat Wrapped around an Invisible Man? Language Legislation and Language Revitalisation in Ireland and Scotland'. *Language Policy* 7.1: 21–46.

Walsh, J. and W. McLeod. 2011. 'The Implementation of Language Legislation in Dublin and Glasgow'. In eds. Kirk and Ó Baoill. 2011a. 156–75.

Wardhaugh, R. 2009. *An Introduction to Sociolinguistics*. Sixth Edition. Oxford: Wiley-Blackwell.

Watson, A.M.-W. 2000. 'Language, Discrimination and the Good Friday Agreement: The Case of Chinese'. In eds. Kirk and Ó Baoill. 2000. 97–9.

Watson, M. 2002. 'Towards a Language Policy for Scotland'. In eds. Kirk and Ó Baoill. 2002. 27–42.

Watt, J. and A. MacLeòid. 2009. 'Gaelic and Development in the Highlands and Islands of Scotland'. In eds. Kirk and Ó Baoill. 2009. 117–29.

Whyte, C. 2005. 'MacLean and Modernism: 'Remembered Histories''. In eds. Kirk and Ó Baoill. 2005. 86–102.

Wicherkiewicz, T. 2005. 'Kashubian as a Regional Language'. In eds. Kirk and Ó Baoill. 2005. 163–72.

Williams, G. 2009. 'Language and Economic Development'. In eds. Kirk and Ó Baoill. 2009. 13–36.

Wolf, G. 2011. 'On Some Implications of Sociolinguistic Labels'. In eds. Kirk and Ó Baoill. 2011a. 69–80.

Zammit-Ciantar, J. 2005. 'The Making of the Maltese Language'. In eds. Kirk and Ó Baoill. 2005. 179–94.